THE SOCIAL ECOLOGY OF RELIGION

In Usukuma, Tanzania, in 1962, several women were killed by mobs of male villagers on the grounds that they were witches. Personal misfortunes are attributed to witchcraft and spirit diviners are approached to ascertain the witch's identity. Once the witch has been found, a special cry is used to alert others to her presence. When sufficient men have gathered, they strip off her clothes, chase her to the edge of the village with freshly cut sticks, and beat her severely, sometimes to death.

THE SOCIAL ECOLOGY OF RELIGION

*

VERNON REYNOLDS
RALPH TANNER

New York Oxford
OXFORD UNIVERSITY PRESS
1995

Oxford University Press

Oxford New York
Athens Auckland Bangkok Bombay
Calcutta Cape Town Dar es Salaam Delhi
Florence Hong Kong Istanbul Karachi
Kuala Lumpur Madras Madrid Melbourne
Mexico City Nairobi Paris Singapore
Taipei Tokyo Toronto

and associated companies in
Berlin Ibadan

An earlier edition of this book was published by Longman
Publishers in 1983 as *The Biology of Religion*

Published by Oxford University Press, Inc.
200 Madison Avenue, New York, New York 10016

Library of Congress Cataloging-in-Publication Data
Reynolds, Vernon.
The social ecology of religion / Vernon Reynolds, Ralph Tanner.
p. cm.
Rev. and updated ed. of: The biology of religion, 1983.
Includes bibliographical references and index.
ISBN 0-19-506973-0 — ISBN 0-19-506974-9 (pbk.)
1. Experience (Religion) 2. Life cycle, Human—Religious aspects.
3. Sociobiology—Religious aspects. 4. Religions. I. Tanner, R.
E. S. (Ralph E. S.), 1921- . II. Reynolds, Vernon. Biology of
religion. III. Title.
BL53.R484 1995
306.6—dc20 94-12183

2 4 6 8 9 7 5 3 1

Printed in the United States of America
on acid-free paper

To Amoret and Frankie

ACKNOWLEDGMENTS

In this new version of our previous book, we remain grateful to all those whose help was acknowledged therein: to Mr. B. A. L. Cranstone, Prof. S. Fukushima, Prof. C. Geertz, Prof. E. Hulmes, Prof. G. A. Harrison, Dr. R. Raychaudhuri, Dr. and Mrs. H. Kawakatsu, Prof. M. Cullen, Mr. D. Dickins and Dr. W. I. Stevenson and others at Longman who put all their energy into producing a splendid publication. In preparing the new version, we have been helped by Ms. C. Read, Dr. R. Davis-Floyd, and a number of anonymous reviewers. For further development of our ideas on religion we are grateful to Prof. E. L. Jones, Dr. D. Coleman, Mr. P. Stewart, Prof. E. Schlicht, Dr. J. Crook, and Dr. J. Odling-Smee. For help with library research we thank Sue Wilkinson and Alastair Smith. Word processing was admirably done by Mrs. V. de Newtown and Mrs. J. Thomas.

The figures were drawn by Penelope Dell, and we record with sadness her death before this new version of the book could appear. The text figures and tables were redrawn from works mentioned in the source notes for each. We are grateful for permission to reprint them. We are also grateful to the following for permission to reproduce copyrighted material:

Academic Press Inc for extracts from "Religion & Health" by K. Vaux *Preventive Medicine* (1976); George Allen & Unwin Ltd for an extract by C. D. Darlington from *Evolution of Man & Society* (1969); American Public Health Association for our fig 2.1 from pp. 1101–64 *Am. J. Public Health* (1962); Armand Colin Editeur for our table 4.4 (Lachiver & Dupaquier 1969); Cambridge University Press for our fig 4.2 (Laslett 1977), & our figs 8.4 & 8.5 (Flandrin 1979); Indian Journal of Medical Research for our table 12.2 (Singh et al 1962); National Council on Family Relations for our table 4.5 (Ukaegbu 1977); Oxford University Press for our fig 13.3 by D. C. Gajdusek *Tropical Neurology* ed. J. D. Spillane (1973); Pergamon Press Inc for our table 11.1 (Maddison & Viola 1968), & our table 14.1 (Comstock et al 1972).

CONTENTS

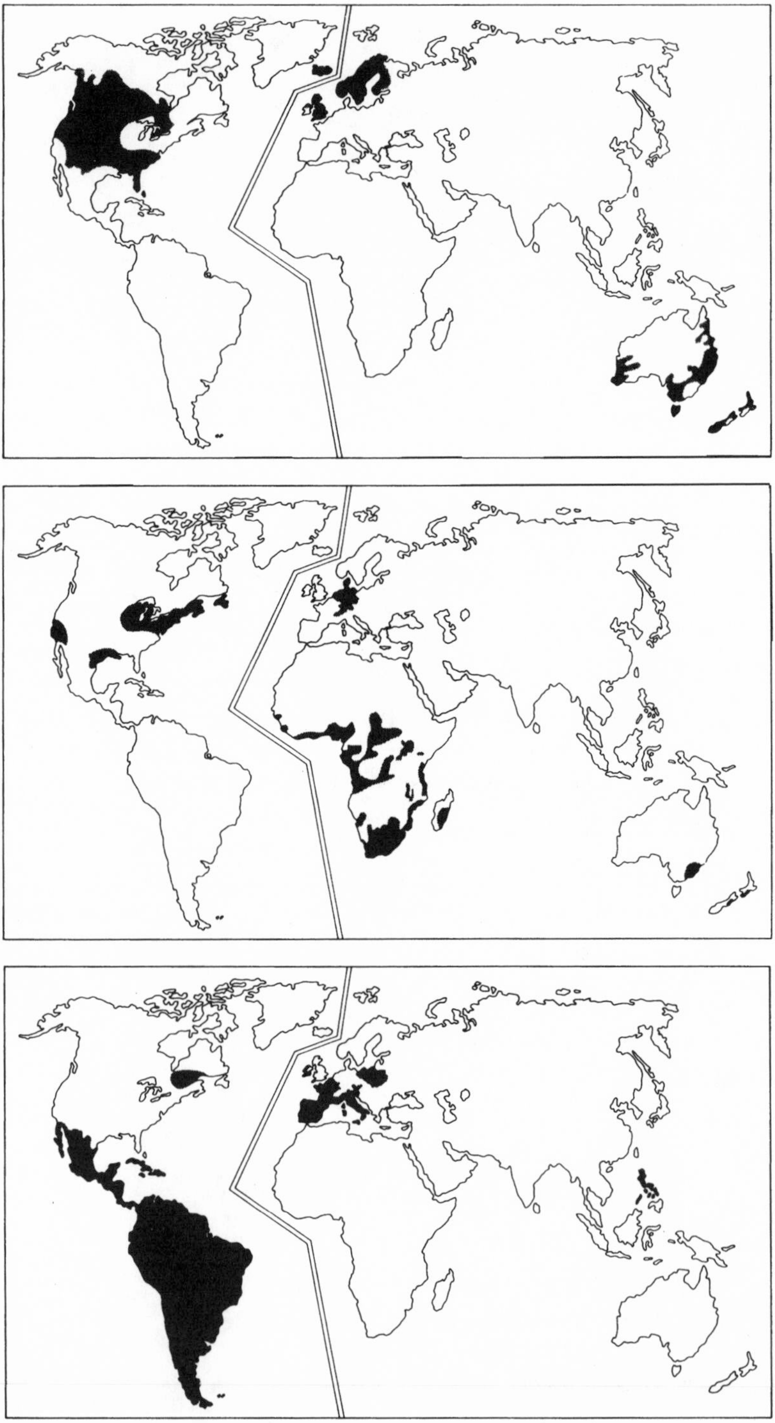

Distribution of the major world religions—Christianity: Protestant (*top*); Christianity: mixed Protestant and Roman Catholic (*middle*); Christianity: Roman Catholic (*bottom*)

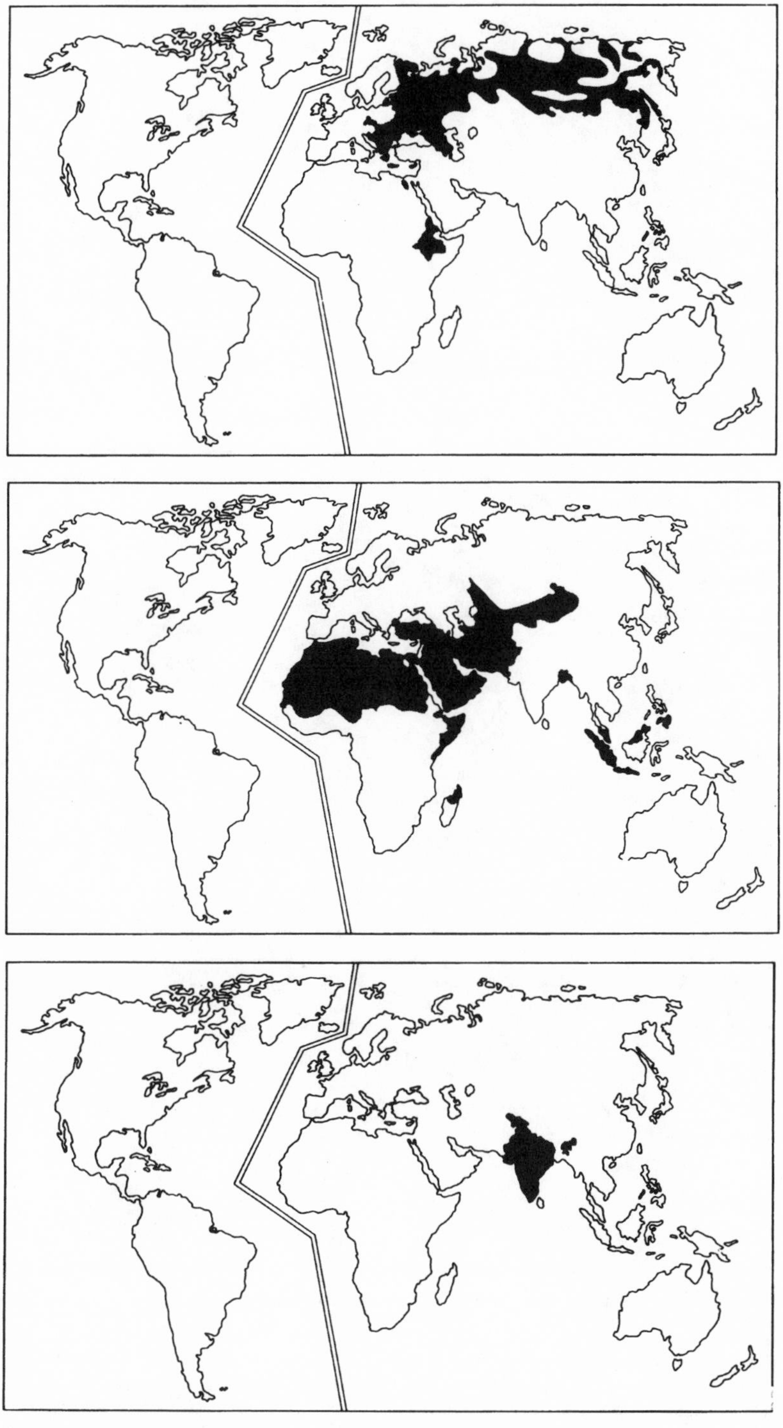

Christianity: Orthodox (*top*); Islam (*middle*); Hinduism (*bottom*)

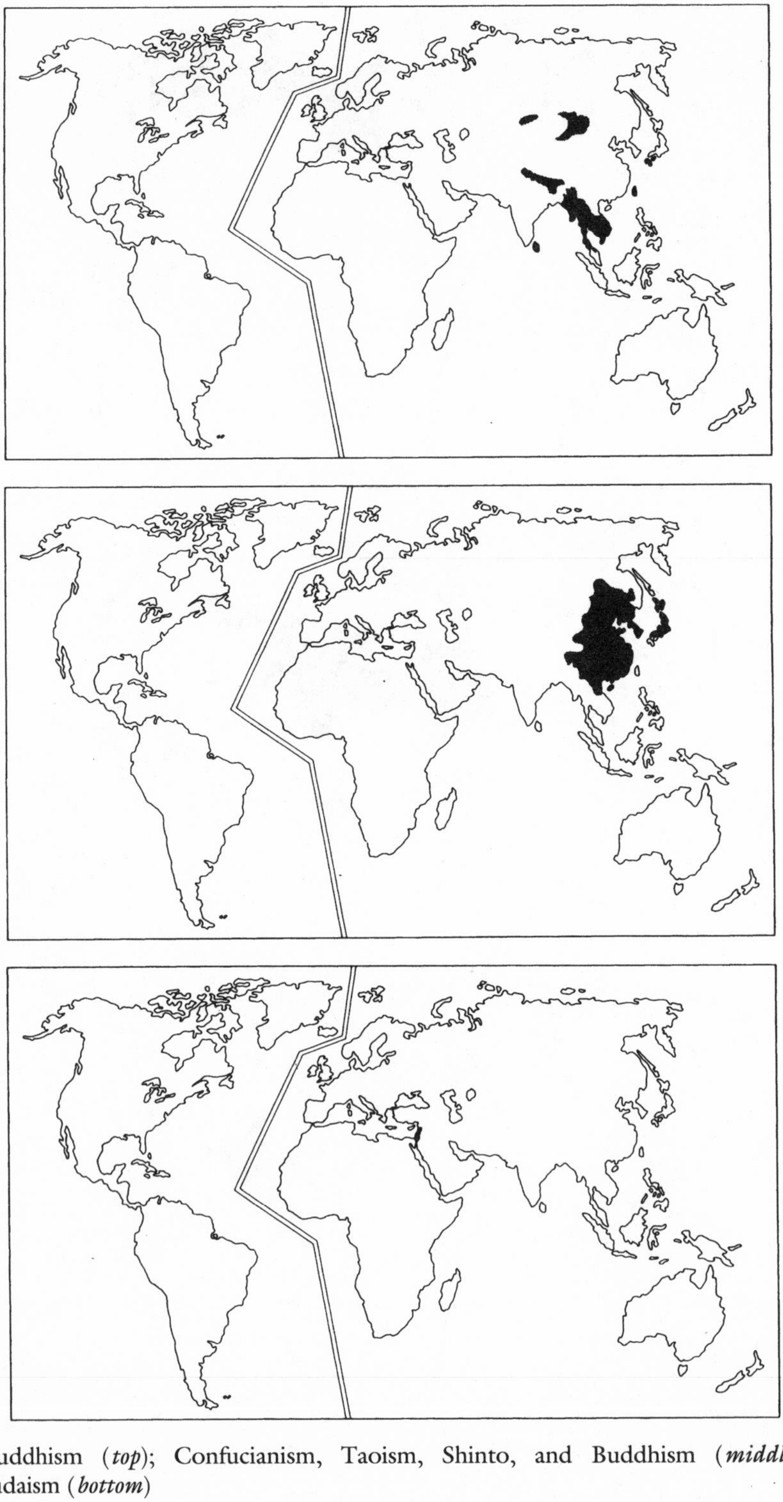

Buddhism (*top*); Confucianism, Taoism, Shinto, and Buddhism (*middle*); Judaism (*bottom*)

PART I

Introduction

1

Why Religions?

Against expectations, religion has, in the 1990s, become a topic of everyday conversation and concern. Whether or not the war in the Gulf was about oil or colonialism or something else, it was dubbed by one of the protagonists a jihad, or holy war. "Is this your civilization?" asked one of the survivors of the bombing of a Baghdad bunker in which hundreds of civilians were killed, when confronted by a Western TV journalist. He might as well have asked, "Is this your religion?" Even though the Islamic nations of the Middle East and elsewhere were divided about the Iraqi invasion of Kuwait or the Israeli occupation of the West Bank of the River Jordan, there is little doubt that anti-Christian and anti-Jewish sentiments were revived among the Islamic people of the Middle East as a result of the bombing of civilians in Iraq, and old wounds were reopened. In the former Yugoslavia, too, "ethnic cleansing" has taken place not only on national and linguistic grounds but also along religious lines, again primarily between Christians and Muslims.

Why religions? Why do religions go on? What makes them persist? Cannot modern secular states look after themselves? Are they too weak? Why do modern governments look to God, to Allah, for support? Why do Indians join fundamentalist Hindu parties in which naked ascetics share the platform with politicians?

The modern state insists on a birth certificate: it wants to know who has been born. It insists on a marriage certificate: it wants to know who marries whom. It insists on a death certificate: it wants to know who can be struck off the books. With all this knowledge, why does it also turn to God? One of the reasons is historical. The state was not always distinct from the church; at one time not so very long ago religious institutions

1.1. Kotsu Anzen, Kaiun Takuyoke Goshugo, from Kinkajuji Fudoson (a Buddhist Temple in Kyoto). This type of lucky charm is found in Shinto contexts in Japan. It is often stuck on the windscreen of cars and taxis as a guard against accidents.

had political and economic power in England, Scotland, and Wales. They still do in the Middle East, where Islam and the state are indivisible. Are we, then, just seeing the past lingering on into the present? No. There is more to life, it seems, than the secular state can encompass. People want religion and faith; many of them could barely imagine life without these things.

The place of religion in the modern world is as fascinating as it is difficult to account for. On the one hand, people the world over are modernizing, either rushing or crawling toward the Western style of living if they possibly can. In Asia Westernization has proceeded apace. In Africa it has yet to happen in many areas, but the desire is there. Yet even where Western ideas have caught hold with a vengeance, as in Japan, religions have maintained their existence, even multiplied and spread. What are they doing? We shall explore this matter in detail, expecting to find religions right at the heart of the everyday lives of ordinary people.

Reader, you may or may not be "religious." That is a matter with which we shall not be concerned in this book. To be religious is to believe in some supernatural power, something that may or may not make itself manifest, once or twice in a lifetime, or every minute of every day. We may call it God; think of it as a vaguely apprehended essence, as in the Bhagavad Gita of the Hindus; or have very precise, well-defined ideas about it, perhaps derived from the Old and New Testaments or the Koran. To be religious is to be a certain kind of person, one who subjects his or her thoughts and actions to critical appraisal in terms of a set of ideal values, who feels beholden, observed, unalone. This can be a comforting feeling in times of crisis and a worrisome one in times of moral uncertainty.

To be religious or irreligious is a choice available to people in the Western world, something that some people think about a lot and others not at all. We know whether we are religious or not. We may, from time to time, feel that we ought to be more religious than we are, or we may be strongly atheistic. This is very much a Western phenomenon. Most people the world over are in some sense of the word religious; they readily accept (or at least do not deny) the existence of things supernatural, hold superstitions, accept some aspects of astrological prediction, or believe in good and bad luck. Some Westerners prefer to call themselves agnostic and would not accept the label of atheist. To be an atheist is to claim knowledge about the nature of the universe that one can scarcely justify at a time when astronomers and physicists themselves are constantly writing about God and the Creation. The atheist says, "I know better than that; I know there is nothing but matter in the world." This, if anything, is a statement of faith. It is safer and intellectually humbler to be an agnostic.

One reason why many of us in the West are atheists or agnostics is that we have personally experienced the failure of our religion or its ministers to meet our needs or answer our questions at times of crisis. This is due, in part, to the rapid rate of change in modern Western society. One of the interesting features of the major religions, to which we shall return from time to time, is their relative conservatism, their apparent slow pace of change, the difficulty they have in adjusting to the world (to which, in the end, they do adjust). Old religions are full of anachronisms and irrelevancies in a fast-changing world. Why, we shall ask, are they relatively slow to change? Why, for example, can there still be a lively theological debate about the Virgin Birth in Great Britain in the 1990s? On the face of it, it seems absurd. Among mammals (of which *Homo sapiens* is one) virgins cannot give birth because female mammals do not produce sperm, without which fertilization of the egg cannot occur, and so the process leading to a new individual cannot get started. Yet bishops and archbishops argue about this. Why? The answer has to do with the question not of virgins but of *faith*. Similarly, orthodox Moslems believe that the Koran is the word of Allah. To accept the Virgin Birth, or to believe that Allah dictated the Koran, is an example of accepting articles of faith within the Christian and Islamic traditions. Faith is important in two ways. First, it is important to the organized church because it ensures the survival of institutional structures and the adherence of their followers. Here we can develop theories of religious organizations acting competitively in the free market to win over faithful adherents, rather like firms vying for customers in the economic sphere. Second, it is important to the adherents because of the calming and psychologically satisfying feeling it imparts to some, or the practical course of action it imparts to others, in an insecure world.

Anthropology promotes a relativist stance in such matters. Humans have evolved from animals and have created cultures. Different cultures have various ways of approaching the same questions. The panoply of religions found in individual countries and cultures of the world is a colorful and impressive display of symbolism. Quite apart from the question of whether or not God exists, religions have provided the context for some of the most beautiful music ever composed, the noblest works of art and architecture, and the most colorful dances, rites, and rituals. Here, in these joyful and anxious expressions, we see the human spirit reaching out to acknowledge, to give thanks, to worship, to praise, to honor a deity.

At other times, when he or she is angered by human evil, the deity may need to be appeased. In Africa, in subsistence economies, people accept the possibility that the deity may bring drought; in ancient Greece Sophoclean drama implied that the gods brought sickness to the Thebans as a consequence of Oedipus' incest; in medieval England the plague was attributed by theologians and commoners alike to the sins of all, and princes in particular. In all these cases, it is necessary for people to make sacrifices to appease the angry god or gods. The process of sacrifice is also intelligible as a mechanism by which worried, perplexed, or frightened people grapple with immense natural forces such as earthquakes and floods. Religious wars are also a form of response: If the threat is social rather than natural, holy wars occur. From preaching love and peace, religions like Christianity and Islam start preaching the virtues of death in a just cause, the moral obligation to defend the faith, to kill the enemies of God. In today's world the West is viewed as "satanic" by some Middle Eastern Moslem fundamentalists. What lies behind the ideological conflict? Some would say it reflects political competition for the most valuable resource in the world—oil—which lies buried below the Islamic countries of the Middle East yet is essential to the continued functioning of the Christian West. If true, this would be an example of religions articulating practical, secular, materialist concerns. One of the main objects of this book is to demonstrate over and over how religions do just this.

Religion and the Physical World

It should not be thought that by the physical world we mean only the soil, the air, the elements, houses, food, and other such aspects of the universe. Far from it. Life itself is physical and material. Whether or not we believe that God instills a breath of life in each living thing, or that we humans (and animals too, as the Northwest Coast Indians of North America and the Eskimos believed) have souls, there can be no doubt that people and animals are physical beings. They are made of bones, fat, water, protein, and so on. They have weight. They are subject to gravity. In other words, we have bodies. Now it might be thought that this "body" aspect of humanity is the aspect of least interest to religions. Surely, they are more interested in spiritual qualities than physical ones? Is it not precisely this fact that marks religion off from, say, medicine or biology?

Our answer is negative. Religions, the world over, are concerned with human physical existence, human bodies, what they may and may not do, when they may and may not do it, how they should be conceived, born, fed, cleaned, dressed, and buried.* Religions want to get involved with our sexual behavior and with menstruation, which is the subject of religious taboos on both women, who often have to hide away, and men, who may not have sex with them at this time without risking pollution.

Humanity is one, and all of us have much the same preoccupations—with the welfare of our parents and children, with keeping healthy, with forming friendships and managing enmities, with love and sex, with status and esteem, with getting food, a place to live, a bit of leisuretime to relax and have fun. Religions have things to say about how we should accomplish all these things, as we shall see in the course of this book.

There is also that other preoccupation we have already mentioned, with answering the deeper questions, about who we are and where we

* A few examples: Catholic theologians ruled for many years that for the woman to be above the man in sexual intercourse was against the order of nature as the semen would not be retained in her vagina. Classical Hinduism ruled that giving birth was ritually unclean so that it tended to take place outside the home in a disposable hut with the mother attended by outcaste women. Seventh Day Adventists do not allow their followers to eat certain foods, Moslems wash themselves before their daily prayers, Amish and orthodox Jews dress in distinctive ways, and the Bontoc-Igorot of the Philippines exhume their dead and keep their bones on shelves under their homes.

come from and where we are going. These are the questions religions specialize in and it is in regard to these deeper questions that religions claim to have *exclusive* and *particular* access to the truth. "Jesus saves," proclaimed from a billboard, is not a relative statement. It implies that the way to salvation is through Jesus and not through any other route. If we seek to be saved, then we have to decide whether to give our souls to Jesus or to turn away unsaved. Most people in modern Western cities turn away; they regard the whole thing as some kind of spiritual con game, operated by a sect or a church trying to increase its membership, and indeed there is an element of truth in this perception. Yet despite the impact of Westernization, spirituality survives, not always in an orthodox form but often, as in the United States and Japan, in the form of a plethora of small sects or even cults that meet or even live together to emphasize the spiritual side of life. And in some parts of the modern Western world Christianity is on the increase; for example, the Mormon form of Christianity emanating from Salt Lake City in Utah is spreading rapidly and promises to be the mainstream form of Christianity in the United States. Nevertheless, it is especially in the West, with its techno-scientific culture, its all-pervasive commercial consumerism, that the values of Christianity have been disregarded and downgraded. They don't allow you to earn enough money; indeed they threaten to turn you into a pauper if you take the gospel of Christ too literally and seriously question materialist assumptions. There is, however, a constant interaction between religious ideas and those of secular society, and this interaction requires much further study. Commercialism and orthodox religions have always coexisted among the mass of the populations of, for instance, India or Peru, Thailand or Kuwait. Secularism and profane values may at times war with, but can also come to terms with, religious values. Atheism does not inevitably triumph: Communism bid fair to eliminate religion from the world; it failed, and the old orthodox religions of Eastern Europe and Russia resurged in the late 1980s and early 1990s, as soon as the stranglehold exerted on them by Communist states was relaxed.

This book isn't about any one religion, nor is it proselytizing. We do not want any reader to convert to some new kind of religion we are here about to offer. Rather, we write about religion as an interesting subject. We look at "religions" in the plural rather than "religion" as an abstract concept. We ask the following questions: "What are religions doing in the world?" "What are they interested in?" "Why are religions still thriving, even resurging, in this secular, scientific age?" We acknowledge that there are answers in the mystical or spiritual sphere, but religions go further than that. It is rather too easy to reply, when asked about religion, that it is concerned with all the things that technology and science cannot deal with, man's spiritual and moral nature. That is true, but it is only part of the answer. Religions are also down to earth, and we believe it is this contact with the material world that explains the continued existence of religions in all countries, why they have survived and multiplied during history, and why they are a very real force in the world today.

Religious Experience

This is not a book about religious experience as such. Anthropologists such as Nadel[1] believed that the "thrill" associated with religious experience was one of the most important reasons for its powerful hold over people. Others have written movingly about the numinous, the ineffable or inexplicable. Alister Hardy[2] collected a very large number of accounts from ordinary people from all walks of life in Great Britain concerning mystical experiences they had themselves had (see the analysis by G. Ahern).[3] Often such experiences involved seeing a dazzling white light, and a dearly beloved, now deceased person who appears and speaks. Contact with the dead is the essence of some spiritualist movements. Speaking in tongues, or glossolalia (see Goodman),[4] and other phenomena such as automatic writing have attested to the fact that people can be moved in ways quite inexplicable to conventional science. For most religious people, religious experience is the central core of their belief; it may have a cleansing or purifying effect, and it provides for them the proof (if any were needed) of God's existence. Music has often been held to engender such feelings of sublime elation associated with religious experience. It has also been the case that in quite recent times large numbers of ordinary people have seen visions of the Virgin Mary; for example, she appeared to them over a period of several months at Medjugorje, a village in Yugoslavia, as described by Jackson.[5]

In recent times, neurophysiologists and neuropsychologists have shown changes in the levels of brain hormones, or endorphins, to be associated with such experiences. This has raised complex questions of the relation between religious experience and other out-of-body experiences such as those of the mentally ill and of people affected by drugs.

We can distinguish three states of mind associated with religious observances, in order of intensity: meditation, trance, and ecstasy. There is a considerable literature on each of these, and useful summaries of what is involved in each can be found in Lehmann and Myers' *Magic, Witchcraft and Religion.*[6] A variety of studies have shown that *meditation* can lead to changed behavior, restructuring of consciousness and of our understanding of the realities of the world around us. *Trance* goes beyond meditation in that it is a clearly defined and structured departure from the normal state of being in which the individual considers himself or herself to be, and is considered to others to be, involved in another world. *Ecstasy* is the state of mind of the person in trance.

Our brains, as part of our bodies, exist within a cultural context, and each culture has it own preconceptions about which brain states are normal and which are abnormal. Meditation, brought in to Western cultures from the Oriental religions, is incompatible with normal activities at the workplace but is becoming more popular as a way of relaxing and regaining a sense of proportion in our own culture. Western cultures put a premium on alert states of consciousness for people in most public contexts and frown upon states of delirium or ecstasy except in specially defined private circumstances. In other cultures, for instance among the Yanomami of Venezuela, such states were part of the normal life of adult men, induced by the use of drugs. Religious specialists, often called shamans, use drugs or intoxicants in a variety of cultures to achieve cures or contact with the spirit world. Among many African peoples, spirit possession enabled the person in trance to know what his ancestors were thinking.

Meditation is not a single, clearly defined state of mind. Sanskrit, the religious language of Hinduism, identifies more than twenty-two different states of consciousness, (see Schuman).[7] Meditation has been defined by Shapiro[8] as a family of techniques which have in common a conscious attempt to focus attention in a nonanalytical way and an attempt not to dwell on discursive ruminating thought. Attempts to study the neurophysiology of the meditative state by comparing it with that of resting controls have been criticized by Holmes;[9] in general it appears that different individuals show different neurophysiological patterns when meditating, and the whole experience is very personal and specific to the individual. However, there is evidence that both alpha and theta wave activity is changed by meditation and that these features are associated with subjectively felt serenity and happiness.

Some meditative sects use the method to obtain enlightenment, and indeed some Indian Sadhus have been shown to achieve a remarkably low metabolic rate and to go without movement, food, or drink for many days while meditating. The state of mind of people in such deep meditation remains a mystery, however. The rhythmic repetition of a verbal mantra is enjoined in some religious forms of meditation, for instance in Zen Buddhism, and this evidently has a rhythmic effect on neural functioning and achieves the calming function this provides.

All the literate religions have developed meditation as part of their methods for personal betterment. Manuals for meditation exist in them all, and well-known saints in both Christianity and Islam have practiced and publicized their own particular methods. For example, the Islamic method of Al-Ghazali gives great importance to personal cleanliness as a necessary prerequisite to successful meditation. This mirrors the Islamic emphasis on washing before prayer.

Trance has been defined by Shor[10] as "a state in which there is functional nonawareness of the structural frame of reference . . . which supports, interprets, and gives meaning to experience." In other words, the person in trance is in a structured situation, possibly devised especially for the purpose; he or she is unaware of this situation while in trance, but the people watching give his or her actions and words special meanings. Trance is also known to be infectious—one or more people watching a "possessed" person may become possessed themselves. The classic state of possession is seen in the Voodoo cults of Haiti, where this state of mind is linked to witchcraft and can lead to madness and even death. Witchcraft is also found in many parts of Africa at the present time and is associated with trance and possession of various kinds, involving demons and other occult beliefs.

In other contexts, trance may be much less associated with evil. Among the Navaho, individuals could make contact with spirits through trance, while among the now extinct Mandan Indians young men in bygone times practiced severe forms of self-mutilation and masochism in order to discover their tutelary spirits. Trancelike states are also found in Christianity, for example among the Shakers and early Quakers, and some Pentecostal and other fundamentalist movements at the present time; in all cases it is the entry of the spirit into the person that accompanies the trance. Trance connects with meditation in the form of "transcendental meditation," which is a form of self-hypnosis involving sensory deprivation. At the neurophysiological level there appear to be no distinctive correlates of trance.

Ecstasy is an abnormal state of consciousness in which the reaction of the mind to external stimuli is either inhibited or altered in character. The person so possessed may be impervious to messages from without and can sometimes feel no pain. Examples of the latter include bare-backed Catholic men carrying bundles of cacti on their shoulders during a Good Friday procession in Taxco, Mexico, or whipping themselves with thorn-studded ropes in Manila, Philippines (also on Good Friday), while showing signs of experiencing great happiness or rapture.

Ecstatic mental states can also be induced by drugs such as LSD, magic mushrooms, or certain cactus seeds after protracted fasting. Equally, the same state of mind can be elicited in teenagers at a pop concert, who are in a very real sense "worshiping" their idols. As with trance, the neurophysiology of ecstasy is very complex and varies from person to person and from one kind of ecstasy to another. The phenomenon of ecstatic religions is treated at length by Lewis.[11]

Complex Theologies

A very different area of study, but one every bit as complex as that of the neurological basis of religious experience, is the field of philosophical arguments about whether God exists or not, and how to go about the matter of proof. These are issues not so much of religion as of theology and philosophy. How do such theological issues relate to the life events of the "common man"? The answer is, In direct terms, not at all. Theology disembodies faith and it is not the province of theology to deal with the everyday emotional and physical happenings of ordinary people, which are our object of attention in this book.

This matter of complex theologies raises an important point, which needs to be borne in mind throughout the discussion of religion and the common man. This is that for the ordinary individual in any society, religion involves a very different and much simpler set of ideas than it does for the priests and other officials of the institutions associated with the religion. The ordinary person may be imbued with faith, may be firm in his or her religious convictions, may have a good working knowledge of the names of the gods or prophets or other religious dignitaries, but is likely to be largely unaware of the debates, positions, arguments, and sectarian disagreements that have characterized the theological history of the faith. From the time of the Gutenberg Bible there has developed an ever-widening gulf between those who study holy writ and those who try to live by religious principles. The points of dispute learned by the incumbents of high religious office in the course of their training may enable them to deal with arguments and disagreements that arise in the course of their ministry. But they are not taught as such to the faithful, who are, rather, given the "one true version." Practicing priests do not stand up in public and confound their congregations with opposing theological positions; indeed, they very often decry or at best ignore the views of opposing sects.

For the "ordinary" religious person (i.e., nonpriest, nontheologian) there are a faith, a set of beliefs, and a set of practices, some formal and some informal, such as a general attitude to the poor or the needy. At higher levels in the structure of what we may call the "church" or the "ministry" or the "temple" there are those in whose care are the religious texts, who study them and are aware of their complexities. In Roman Catholicism there are, for example, edicts and encyclicals carefully preserved, to which reference can be made in justifying a stand on, say, abortion or birth control. The careful Catholic scholar is aware that such edicts have, at different times, adopted different positions and that there is no unanimity in the church's history. For example, there were severe penalties for abortion before the twelfth century, providing for up to ten years fasting according to the age of the fetus (see Kelly).[12] The Pope's medical adviser, who in 1621 was a priest, stated that the ensoulment of the fetus took place at fertilization. There are repeated debates in the Vatican, and the Pope's statements of dogma are the result of such debates, in which he takes part. To the less educated public they are the words of God, which he transmits should they be listening or even feel it necessary to listen. Sermons have been described as being washed over by holy words. For such people there is neither time nor need for studying the edicts of earlier centuries, nor indeed of current controversies, since they are believers first.

Caution is thus needed in the approach to the role of religion in relation to the common man, the person in the street. The higher reaches of theology do not reach the people at all. Thus there is no possibility of taking theological arguments as indicative of the part played by religions in the world today. What religions do is bound up with the lives of ordinary people, with steering them through the phases of their existence, and not with arguments about with whom a married man spends eternity after resurrection or whether or not the Prophet Mohammed traveled from Arabia to Jerusalem in a single night.

Books such as *The Philosophy of Religion* by Mitchell[13] and *An Introduction to the Philosophy of Religion* by Davies[14] concern themselves with falsification, verification, free will; whether God exists, whether it is reasonable to debate this, whether faith needs to be based on verifiable assertions or falsifiable ones; and so on. Arguments in this field are based on logic: there is no sense of the social significance of religion or its functions for individual human beings living in the real world. Philosophers of religion are concerned with arguments, proof, reason, and belief. If we do not concern ourselves with these matters in the following pages, it is not because we regard them as irrelevant to the study of religion. They are highly relevant to the study of any religion. Our book, however, is not a philosophical one, nor are we philosophers. We leave those fundamental matters (which, philosophers agree, are unlikely ever to be resolved) to one side; we accept that many people believe in gods and spirits, and we work forward from there, to ask questions about what those beliefs are, how they affect people's thoughts and actions, and what their functions might be for individuals in the context of their social and physical existence.

Finally there are questions about the relation between religion and morality. Philosophers such as Helm[15] have debated whether morality arises out of religion or vice versa, and how rationality, humanism, and other secular bases for morality and ethics are related to the values embodied in religious belief and doctrine. Such questions are debated mainly in traditional terms, with reference to Christian culture and Western morality only, and have as a result only limited general applicability to a worldwide survey. For our purposes they tackle an interesting question in the modern, doubting world of the West. Mitchell's book is subtitled *The Dilemma of the Traditional Conscience,* which gives the clue as to how the author sees things. The problem at issue is how to comprehend a Christian approach to morality in an increasingly secular world, one in which moral judgments are increasingly being made on secular, non-Christian grounds.

This is indeed a problem for Christians, but it is not one for Moslems or the propitiators of ancestors living south of the Sahara. They may, of course, have equivalent problems, arising from the collapse of traditional life and the advent of Western secularization. We are interested in these matters, as the following pages will show. Religions, it appears to us, have to adapt to changing environments. In particular, what may be called "intensive growth" can change levels of real wealth in societies and lighten the struggle for existence for many people, one among several causes of the decline of religion in the West.

We see morality as prior, logically and evolutionarily, to religions. We derive morality from evolutionary processes operating on the reciprocal behavior of intelligent creatures living in social groups. In this we follow the ideas of Alexander.[16] There is thus no problem of priority; the matter is settled. Our position is that morality is "natural," and no doubt some philosophers will want to point out that this position is untenable in various ways. Nevertheless, it is buttressed by many sound arguments within biology, anthropology, and primatology into which moral philosophers have not yet extended their considerations.

One final note. Some people, when they hear the word *religion* today, point straight to the fact that religions have been the cause of wars throughout history, that we can no longer, in the modern world, risk the dangers of allowing religious fanaticism to cause rifts and wars and assassinations in the world. All too recently, Saddam Hussein, in an Iraq under siege, called for a jihad, an Islamic holy war, against the United States and its allies. And as we write, Moslem and Christian forces are fighting each other in what used to be Yugoslavia and in parts of the old Soviet Union. We acknowledge this side of religions. Religiously inspired armies can be terribly dangerous. The call by political and military leaders to their subjects to die a glorious death for their faith, as was repeatedly made by Iranian and Iraqi leaders in recent wars, is one of the strongest appeals they can make and is frequently heard in times of war. This indeed is the dark side of faith.

There are exceptions. Within Christianity certain pacificist sects, notably the Quakers, refuse to fight at times of war, whatever the circumstances and whoever the enemy may be. In Buddhism and Hinduism, passive resistance can be the religious response to attack, whatever the consequences. But in the main, religious institutions are closely linked with the political heart of their country and fall in line with political ambitions for conquest or political necessities in defense. War is a terrifying catastrophe, and hence the context in which religions play a large part. While deploring religious wars and the role of religions in war, we have to try to understand why things are so and not be dismissive. Just as religions concern themselves with birth, marriage, and death, so they also do with war. When religion supports expansionist aggression, it exposes its Achilles heel, and who can be blamed for rejecting it?

But let us not end this chapter on a negative note. Let us return to our question "Why religions?" What is it that takes people to their local church on Sundays, leads them to fold their hands in prayer and speak to an invisible, half-understood deity? Why do Japanese followers of Shinto hang little pieces of paper with prophecies on the branches of a sacred tree? Why do Moslems kneel on floor mats facing Mecca and bow their heads low five times a day? Why do Hindus ring a bell to call up one of the local gods, and leave offerings of rice and flowers at his or her temple? Why do African villagers sacrifice a goat to propitiate their ancestors who are thought to be angry?

We must never forget the sheer complexity of our chosen topic. The outer forms of religious actions, and their underlying meanings, are as diverse as they could be. We seek in vain for one underlying meaning to explain them all. Anthropologists are humbled by the complexity of this subject. As Max Weber wrote in his book *Ancient Judaism,*[17] "It would require more than a lifetime to acquire a true mastery of the literature." And he was writing of Judaism alone. In the present book we are not concerned with the literature or the official theology of the world's faiths, but rather with *what people do when they are acting in religious ways.*

Again, the distinguished anthropologist E. E. Evans-Pritchard[18] wrote, "Generalizations about 'religion' are discreditable. They are always too ambitious and take account of only a few of the facts. The anthropologist should . . . restrict himself to religions of a certain type . . . in favour of limited conclusions reached by inductive analysis of observed facts" (pp. 6–7). Nevertheless anthropologists such as Guy Swanson, in *The Birth of the Gods,*[19] after quoting both of the preceding warnings, pointed out that *science* proceeds both by careful descriptions of particular cases and by generalizations: "The movement of scientific knowledge requires both, and both should have the resources to play their equally indispensable parts" (p. viii). With this statement we are in agreement, and it forms the basis of the present work.

Swanson was concerned with the *origins* of religious beliefs, and his own generalizations followed a Durkheimian approach. This approach seeks to understand the origins of the forms of religious (or supernatural) experience in the forms and powers of society itself. Man is to society as a worshipper is to a god.

This is not our own approach, or the method of generalization to be found in the present work. Our approach is not concerned with the origins of religions so much as their *functions.* We relate and explain the force of religious ideas by reference to the needs of individuals in their everyday lives, not to society and its forms. If the Durkheimian approach can explain the *forms* religions take or the particular beliefs they emphasize, it does not seem to us to emphasize with sufficient force the real part played by religion in the lives of actual people. As a result of our investigations we have become convinced by the evidence worldwide that *the function of religions is to respond to human needs,* to help people at times of personal crisis (e.g., at funerals), or when they are undergoing a change of status (e.g., at weddings), or generally in relation to the everyday strains of normal life. Ours is thus a *functional* approach.

It is also, in the anthropological tradition, *comparative.* So many books and writings about religion in the Western literature concern themselves either with Christianity alone or with Christianity and

Judaism, as if that is where religion ended. For anthropologists this is quite impossible. The field worker who goes out to study a people in the heart of Africa or another part of the underdeveloped world finds immediately that the concepts of Christianity, or Judeo-Christianity, are either missing or greatly changed. There may be no churches, no priests, no concept of sin, no evidence of religious morality, no special time of day for "services," no actual "prayer," no universal god. Instead, parts of the landscape may be held sacred as in Australia, spells may be cast into the storm to calm the wind and the ocean as in the Trobriand Islands, crops may be unable to grow without prayers as in South America, and pregnancy may be, in part at least, the result of a spirit's entering a woman's belly (Australia again).

The comparative approach underlies the whole of this book. It does not explicitly compare one religion with another, or concentrate on its modern manifestations. It compares by juxtaposing the various ways different religions approach the same basic human situations. There is a great strength in this approach: All humans pass through essentially the same phases of the lifecycle. There is thus a common basis for comparison. We are born; we reach puberty; we encounter disappointment, disease, and death; and in due course we too die. Some of us remain single but most get married and have children, some get divorced, many are widowed. In short, there is a basic pattern to life everywhere and we have found that religions play their main roles in relation to this pattern.

The book is divided into three parts. In part I (chapters 1–3) we take a look at the more important ways that anthropologists have attempted to understand religions in the past, and why they have for a variety of reasons failed to come to grips with this complex subject. At first, Frazer, Tylor, and others believed that an evolutionary sequence could be discerned, from primitive magic to the complex religions of our own culture. Later, under the sociological influence of Durkheim, attention shifted to understanding religions and rituals as mechanisms for sanctifying and thus strengthening the secular institutions of society. A functional approach was adopted by Malinowski, who clearly described the part played by magic and ritual in the day to day lives of the Trobriand Islanders of the Pacific as they cultivated their gardens and interacted with the elements, above all the wind that made sea travel dangerous. But a thoroughgoing functional approach to religions in terms of the life cycle of ordinary people has had to await the present work. That is its central characteristic. Since Malinowski's there have been many works describing the religions of peoples the world over. The library shelves are full of such works, and we draw on many of them. But integrative works are rare, as Geertz[20] has pointed out, and he identifies the cause as the sheer complexity of the material, the difficulty of knowing where to begin. Geertz's own work, on Islam, highlights how even one and the same religion can be quite different in different parts of the world, and this leads him to the necessity of historical analysis in order to understand the reasons for different interpretations of the same religious beliefs. This we fully accept. Religious beliefs are nowhere the same today as they were as recently as a hundred years ago. Our own approach is more synchronic: we take as our baseline the life cycle of ordinary people; we see this as consisting of a number of transitions, the points marked by van Gennep's "rites of passage"; and we look at the ways they are managed by religions in all parts of the world, including developed as well as less developed countries. Indeed, it is part of our project to show that we are no exceptions to the general rules. The challenge our modern secular way of life presents to the world's old religions, questioning them at every point, is looked at in chapter 3, and we find that whether religions are ready to take on the challenge or not, their functions are so valuable that people cannot do without them.

In part II (chapters 4–11) we look at the life cycle itself, moving from conception and contraception, through infanticide and abortion; birth and childhood; adolescence; marriage (with a look at celibacy), divorce, and widowhood; through middle and old age to death itself. In every chapter we skip from culture to culture, but we do not make the mistake Frazer made early in this century in *The Golden Bough:* we are not butterfly collectors, commenting on the exotic wherever we find it. Just the contrary; our movement from country to country, from culture to culture, from one religion to another is held in check by the power of the life cycle analysis itself, which shows how each example is the way that one particular problem is dealt with in one particular place.

In part III (chapters 12–14) we examine religious functioning in relation to sickness and here we make a surprising discovery. For in their institutions for dealing with human problems religions do not always follow the strict rules of hygiene; sometimes they appear to have health issues in mind but at other times they do not. Thus we find religious practices enhancing as well as reducing the risk of disease. In a way this is not surprising, as mechanisms of spread of contagious diseases have only in recent years been discovered and many religious practices are centuries or even millennia old, and slow to change. Nothing stays still, however, and we can expect disease-enhancing rituals to disappear in due course.

Chapter 15 presents a summary of our general conclusions about the role of religions in the world today; it is probably true to say that religions are as vital to people as they ever have been, not only to individuals in other cultures but to us in our own, and appear to be set to continue down the ages. By the end of this book the reader should have a clearer idea of how religions everywhere interact with the lives of ordinary people, steering them along and helping them cope with life's vicissitudes. Each religion is doing what it can, where it can, to give meaning and structure to people's lives. That is the message of this book.

Notes

1. Nadel, S. F. (1954). *Nupe religion.* Routledge, London. Geertz, C. (1960). *The religion of Java.* Free Press, New York.

2. Hardy, A. (1983). *The spiritual nature of man.* Oxford University Press, London.

3. Ahern, G. (1990.) *The spiritual/religious experience in modern society.* Alister Hardy Research Centre, Oxford.

4. Goodman, F. D. (1972). *Speaking in tongues.* University of Chicago Press, Chicago.

5. Jackson, M. (1990). "An agnostic at Medjugorje." *Numinis,* 6, 1–4. Alister Hardy Research Centre, Oxford.

6. Lehmann, A. C., and Myers, J. E. (eds.). (1985). *Magic, witchcraft and religion.* Mayfield, Palo Alto, California.

7. Schuman, M. (1980). "The psychophysiological model of meditation and altered states of consciousness: A critical review," in J. M. Davidson and R. J. Davidson. *The psychobiology of consciousness.* Plenum Press, New York.

8. Shapiro, D. H. (1984). "Overview: Clinical and physiological comparison of meditation with other self-control strategies," in D. H. Shapiro et al. (eds.), *Meditation: class and contemporary perspectives.* Aldine de Gruyter, New York.

9. Holmes, D. S. (1987). "The influence of meditation versus rest on physiological arousal: A second examination," in M. A. West. (ed.). *The psychology of meditation.* Clarendon Press, Oxford.

10. Shor, R. E. (1959). "Hypnosis and the concept of the generalized reality-orientation." *American J Psychotherapy,* 13, 582–602.

11. Lewis, I. M. (1989). *Ecstatic religion.* Routledge, London.

12. Kelly, D. F. (1979). *The emergence of Roman Catholic medical ethics in North America: An historical methodological bibliographical study.* Edwin Mellen Press, New York, p. 20.

13. Mitchell, B. G. (1971). (ed). *The philosophy of religion: The dilemma of the traditional conscience.* Oxford University Press, Oxford.

14. Davies, B. (1993). *An introduction to the philosophy of religion* (2nd ed). Oxford University Press, Oxford.

15. Helm, P. (ed.). (1981). *Divine commands and morality.* Oxford University Press, Oxford.

16. Alexander, R. D. (1987). *The biology of moral systems.* Aldine de Gruyter, New York.

17. Weber, M. (1952). *Ancient Judiasm,* H. H. Gerth & D. Martindale. (trans.). Free Press, Glencoe, Illinois.

18. Evans-Pritchard, E. E. (1954). "Religion," in E. E. Evans-Pritchard et al. (eds.), *The institutions of primitive society.* Free Press, Glencoe, Illinois.

19. Swanson, G. E. (1960). *The birth of the Gods: The origin of primitive beliefs.* University of Michigan Press, Ann Arbor.

20. Geertz, C. (1975). *The interpretation of cultures.* Hutchinson, London.

2

Prior Approaches to the Study of Religion

As our title states, in this book we approach the study of religion through what can be called "social ecology." The social ecology of religion relates religious beliefs and practices to the social and physical environment of the people concerned. By the social environment we mean the people we live with and encounter in our everyday lives, and the complex ways we relate to them and they relate to us. The physical environment is the non-human world as it relates to us, from the air we breathe (about which we can do very little) to the diseases that attack us (about which we try to do a lot). Our analysis of religion concerns how real people, living in a social world, try to solve the problems of human existence. We do not so much mean philosophical or intellectual problems as everyday problems such as how to cope with our own feelings, with the selfishness of others, with the grief engendered by death, with misdemeanors, and with natural disasters. Many of these events are beyond our control, and in our study we show how humans the world over have recourse to religious ideas and practices in an attempt to cope.

How does this approach compare with, and differ from, earlier writings on religion? In one important respect there is a basic difference: We are not concerned with the origins of religions, we are concerned with their functions in the here and now as well as in recorded history. In this respect we differ from anthropologists of earlier generations, who nearly all tried to piece together the history or evolution of religions from the earliest times, often building their ideas on details of the religious beliefs and practices of so-called primitive peoples.

A convenient review of some early anthropological approaches to the study of religions is that of Evans-Pritchard,[1] who goes to some trouble

2.1. A rice-seedling planting-out ceremony (Mibu Ohana-Taue) directed at the deity Sanbai-Sama in modern Japan. This Shinto rite involves a flautist and a number of drummers who attend the first planting out by the women of the community.

to distinguish among a number of different theories of religion. The theories he distinguishes are in the main psychological and sociological, and they have one feature in common: they all try to explain the origins of religion. One kind of psychological theory of religion is what he calls "natural-sensory." Muller,[2] for example, held that religiosity arose from a "sense of the infinite," a sort of nature mythology. Spencer,[3] on the other hand, developed what can be called a "natural-rational" theory: that on the basis of fallacious reasoning primitive peoples came to believe that their ancestors became ghosts and/or gods. Tylor[4] developed the view of primitive animism—that objects and animals were falsely endowed by simple peoples with spirits and souls— while Frazer[5] formulated a three-stage theory, in which the evolution of human thought passed from magic through religion to science. Science and magic are, for Frazer, similar in that both of them hold that performing certain actions on the physical world leads to certain results; religion, by contrast, interposes an intermediary level between human actions and the physical world, namely the world of the gods.

Evans-Pritchard regarded all the preceding theories as intellectualist (i.e., the outcome of armchair theorizing) and said that they could be neither refuted nor sustained because in the final analysis "there is no evidence about how religious beliefs originated" (p. 29). They were also evolutionist, and whereas at the time of Tylor, Frazer, and Spencer the effort to trace the evolution of societies along similar lines to the evolution of animal life was in vogue, it ceased to be so as it became clear that it was a speculative and unscientific enterprise, at least in the way it was being conducted then.

Can anything be rescued from the psychological theories described? From the evolutionary orientation, nothing. But a moment's thought is enough to convince us that psychology is highly relevant to the explanation of religion. It is just a matter of turning away from a supposed past and looking at a very real present. Marrett[6] already described the psychological dimension of religion when he wrote about the emotional catharsis achieved by primitive peoples in the course of performing their magical substitute actions to achieve results (i.e., to make rain or calm the

2.2. Among the Sukuma of Tanzania, rainmakers carry out ceremonies at the end of the dry season in waterless streambeds. They sacrifice a black goat and throw "thunder" stones onto the ground.

sea). He wrote of "the consecration of life, the stimulation of the will to live and do," and here we must agree with him and to some extent follow this line in the present book: religion comes into human life to give it added force and the will to continue against the odds. Here we come closer to the view of Crawley[7] that religion is a product of fear, and the emphasis placed by Malinowski[8] on awe. Evans-Pritchard[9] regards such theories as "guesswork" (p. 43) but this seems to us to be rather harsh: unlike the earlier evolutionist theories, these latter psychological ones are based on emotions we all understand and share and relate to the here and now, and this seems to us to be unobjectionable.

The second class of theories examined by Evans-Pritchard are the sociological ones. Here the underlying argument is that religion is valuable in that it makes for social cohesion and continuity. The emphasis shifts away from the level of individual psychology toward social organization and structure. The authors Evans-Pritchard associates with variations on this position are Herbert Spencer, Robertson Smith, Henry Maine, Fustel de Coulanges, and, above all, Durkheim. All of them, including Durkheim, are castigated for the evolutionary nature of their arguments.

If we take Durkheim as the architect of sociological theory in general, here as applied to religion, and ask what exactly is the argument, the general lines are as follows: Religion arises out of the nature of society; religion is a social fact. It is not just what it appears to be to the people concerned. Thus a totemic animal worshiped by a clan in Australia is not just a sacred animal with certain powers, which must be honored or appeased or sacrificed to in certain ways. That is how the Aborigines view it (what we would call their "emic" perception of the situation). It is also the clan itself, mirrored in the sacred world. The totem exists to give the people a concrete symbolic representation of their social unit; it sanctifies the social unit, reifies it, gives it existence and permanence. Religions express the relationship between people and their own society and its institutions. Where there is a single king there is a single god, where there are many clans there are many totems, where lineages are important there are ancestor cults. The whole religious edifice has come into being to strengthen the forms of society itself.

Evans-Pritchard, while clearly impressed by Durkheim's insight, regards it as unacceptable as a theory of religions. "What about primitive peoples who have . . . lineages but no ancestor cult?" he asks (p. 75). He could also have pointed out that whereas totems are quite rare, clans are common. There are many exceptions, and in his view they disprove the sociological theory of religion. From our point of view in the present book, Durkheim's theory has little to offer. Whether religions reflect and strengthen the structures of society or not seems to us of less relevance than whether they offer benefits to individuals in their relationships with one another and in their approach to the world at large.

Having dismissed both the psychological and the sociological theories of religion, Evans-Pritchard ends his review rather lamely, with no theory of his own. He says there are no general answers, that religious facts have "to be accounted for in terms of the totality of the culture and society in which they are found" (p. 112). This seems to us very tame, and here we try to show that religions do have a firm basis in the social ecology of the peoples concerned. In throwing out psychology so thoroughly, he lost the baby with the bathwater, and in rejecting Durkheim but remaining essentially within the social anthropology camp he was left with nothing but "the totality of . . . culture and society" to help explain religion. His 1956 work on the religion of the Nuer of the southern Sudan follows through on his own self-imposed principles: it is a detailed description of the religious beliefs and practices of the Nuer of the southern Sudan, set in the context of this cattle-keeping people. Everything is described, and everything is explained in terms of Nuer culture, but the essential "bite" of religion itself is lost, and the relation between this one religion and others in other parts of the world, necessary for comparative study, becomes almost impossible to determine. Perhaps indeed the real dialectic in these studies is between the detailed case study and the generalizing synthesis. If so, that makes studies of religion akin to studies in other branches of science, for it is precisely this dialectic that leads to the refining of hypotheses and eventually to improved understanding.

A more recent author who to some extent shares our views on religion is Edward Norbeck.[10] In the second part of his book, on the role of religion, he expresses a clear sympathy for functionalist writers such as Malinowski. He writes much on ritual and its significance, for example the Chisungu ritual for girls at puberty among the Bemba of Zimbabwe, or the Indian Kota funeral rituals, which he interprets as expressions of status change, and also as the opportunity for the "assuaging of grief" (p. 164). He writes of "crisis rites" and of the social and individual functions of religion. Norbeck also describes the interactions between medicine and religion—beliefs in harmful intrusive spirits, in spirit possession, in shamans and other kinds of so-called witch doctors. We too have found in our analysis that religions are deeply concerned with disease and cure.

Norbeck also, like us, concerns himself with religious movements, which he sees as arising from disturbed social conditions which present individuals with crises. Messianic sects can and do arise in such conditions, as people come together to try to resolve their personal fears in concerted action. Norbeck notes the existence of salvation sects in the modern United States, often refuges for the poor and the dispossessed. Outside mainstream U.S. life he notes the messianic movements of some North American Indian tribes whose cultures have disintegrated, the proliferation of native churches with Christian and non-Christian elements intertwined in Africa, the cargo cult movements of Pacific islands, and the devilish practices of the dispossessed and disgruntled Mau Mau of Kenya. One could add the curious Alice Lokwena cult of modern northern Uganda, which taught that adherence to its rules would make men impervious to bullets, with disastrous results in the country's recent civil wars.

Like us, too, Norbeck does not draw an arbitrary line between so-called primitive religions and those of modern societies. Anthropologists perhaps feel they should do so, dividing sharply between the local, primitive religions and the global, or global-aspirant "universalist" ones. Certainly there are important differences between the religions of small-scale societies with shared norms and limited variation in possible life-styles, and religions that claim their universal truths are applicable to all humankind. The main difference is that, for a universalist religion to be relevant and thus successful, nothing can be assumed about the cultural ideas and practices of the people in different parts of the world to whom it addresses its messages. It therefore has to preach at a high level of abstraction, with messages of peace, goodwill, joy, sin, repentance, forgiving, love, blasphemy, and so on. That is not to say there is no detail; there is a mass of detail but it is theological; It is based on the interpretation of the historical doings of the great men and women of the faith, and their interpretation down the ages. In all the great universalist faiths, especially Christianity, Islam, Judaism, and Buddhism, there are written texts to which the cognoscenti of the religion address themselves in order to understand the faith and pass it on to the people. For the people themselves there is the theology as received from priests and ministers, but there is also a strong element of that same level of incorporation into religion as we find in small-scale "primitive" societies, that is, the preoccupation with life's crises, with birth and marriage and divorce and death; with illness, war, and natural disasters. In short, universalist faiths do not constitute a separate category from small-scale religions; they contain the same ingredients exactly at the local level, but at the wider level they add a further tier of abstractions.

Norbeck in his discussion of modern religions points out, following Talcott Parsons, that they are much concerned with morality, with ideals and goals about which people feel strongly. Christianity in particular can

2.3. Throughout Hindu India cows, because of their religious significance, roam freely in both town and countryside and are not prevented from eating human food displayed for sale in shops.

be very dogmatic; it is a serious religion which probes into the innermost part of our being, seeking out sinful thoughts and exhorting total dedication to its values. In this it has much in common with its ancestral faith Judaism, and with Islam, which came later. Buddhism and Hinduism are less dogmatic, more variegated in their forms and beliefs, and they are also less centralized, with no Mecca, no Jerusalem. The progress of science in Western cultures has clashed with Christianity, which has seen the confrontation as a serious battle for the minds of the people, offering its creation myth, for example, in opposition to the evolutionary story of the scientists, and thereby losing the confidence of most of the educated population. This was a mistake of the leaders of the faith. They should have conceded that Darwin was right more quickly. The problem that has arisen with the loss of confidence in the dominant faith in Western countries is that people have also lost what was good about their religion, its means for handling life's difficult situations.

In our book we show, by our comparative approach, in which we consider both small-scale and great religions, how they do, wherever they are incorporated into people's lives, engage with people in the most matter-of-fact ways, instructing them about their hygiene, their sexual behavior, how when and where to have children, how to manage the difficulties of adolescence, and so on, through the life cycle until death. This functional approach of ours goes back to Malinowski at least, but it is modern nonetheless, for we find ourselves able not only to consider modern situations all over the world, but also to take into account more modern theories of religion, which by and large eschew the false evolutionary scenarios of the old anthropologists and try to integrate the religious ideas of contemporary peoples with the emphases of their various cultures, thus moving from the general to the particular. We fully acknowledge the variety of themes and messages in the world's religions; we acknowledge that they are comprehensible only in their social and historical contexts, that they contain lags from previous eras and are often slow to respond, as for example Hinduism in rural India. Religions may be all-embracing or they may be quite peripheral to their (nominal) adherents. Generalizations about religion may indeed be hard to find. But we shall show that they share a common preoccupation with the interpretation of life's main situations and happenings to ordinary people. Like Norbeck, we would say that religion will go on in an increasingly secular and scientific world, because of "the emotional satisfaction it provides" (p. 279), or in our terms the functions it serves for ordinary people in the course of their lives.

Lastly, in this brief review, we arrive at Clifford Geertz and what may with justification be called the modern anthropological position with regard to religion. We can begin with his *Islam Observed,*[11] in which he compares Islam in North Africa and Indonesia on the basis of his fieldwork in Morocco and Java. But he has in mind to move from the particular to the general; that is, he is concerned to derive general principles from the study of this one religion in two almost totally different settings, "the antipodes of the Muslim world," as he calls them. The general question he sets himself, here as in his other work, is what, in the final analysis, "religion comes down to as a social, cultural and psychological phenomenon" (p. xii).

One interesting point about Geertz's analysis is the pervasiveness of not so much history as a historical dimension. In both the cultures he looks at, Islam is the product of a series of historical events, and in each case they are very different. It is these different predisposing historical circumstances that have shaped modern Islam in Morocco and Java. In Morocco he finds a religion of saint worship and moral severity, magical power and aggressive piety, close to the original source of the faith, while in Indonesia, carried there by traders, Islam became merged with the prior Buddhist–Hindu faiths of the people, and the result is a case of religious syncretism.

Geertz is not concerned only with the superficial similarities and differences, however. He wants to probe deeper, to the conceptions of life itself that inform the everyday thoughts and feelings of people. In this his approach is more thoroughgoing than those of his predecessors in anthropology and sets the tone for the anthropological studies of the particular situations that people find themselves in in today's world. He is aware of what he calls the "dazzling multiformity which is the hallmark of modern consciousness," brought about by the clashes of values: Western materialism versus Oriental mysticism, belief in science versus belief in gods, and so forth. Islam is affected by this multiformity in both Morocco and Java and responds in different ways because of the difference of cultures: in Morocco it responds by rigorism, in Java by flexibility. In his concern not just with the forms and functions of tribal religions but with the dilemmas and paradoxes of a great faith in diverse modern cultural settings Geertz tackles real issues that are sidestepped in much anthropological writing.

His fourth chapter is called "The Struggle for the Real." Here he is talking about the ways in which people come to understand the puzzling phenomena of life, but he is not just comparing one way with another; rather he is concerned with what is the nature of the process of conceiving of "reality." Thus he complains that Malinowski (with whose functional approach we have a certain amount of sympathy) was wrong in overemphasizing the practical, pragamatic side of cultural (including religious) practices; it is not just a matter of how people cope with the problems of life but how they *conceive* of life, which in turn sets the stage for how they cope with it. Here he is undoubtedly right; we cannot assume that we know what the problems of life are for people in other cultures. Nevertheless as the present work shows, a number of problems do exist for all people everywhere, namely the problems of childbirth, of death, of suffering, and so on, and therefore religions do have some sort of common ground. Geertz is more interested in the particular ways in which these common problems are formulated, however, than with their brute biological similarities, and in this we follow him, for even death is not death in some absolute sense but is either a passing into another stage of life, or a withdrawal to the ancestors, or a move to paradise, or a stage in a cycle, or a final dissolution, or a transmigration into another form, depending on religion. Geertz writes of the "dialectic between religion and common sense" and this is a recurrent theme in his work; he wants to analyze how religion goes beyond common sense and changes it so that reality is somehow redefined. He sees this as a shift in anthropology to try to understand the "systems of significance" of cultures, the way they use rituals in a semantic way, to give special enhanced meaning to everyday events. Here his project is the same as ours: We are also concerned with the transformations of everyday events by religions, how they incorporate convictions of the nature of reality, and how in this way they satisfy human need for psychological order. He writes of the "felt inadequacies of common sense . . . in the face of . . . experience," and finds that Islam "renders life less outrageous" than it would otherwise be.

In 1975 a set of essays by Geertz was published under the title *The Interpretation of Cultures.*[12] In one essay, "Religion as a Cultural System;" he elaborates some of the themes of *Islam Observed*. Again he stresses the importance of thinking in terms of "culture" when discussing religion; that is, a set of *meanings* rather than a structure of a set of baldly defined functions. It is the meanings of a culture which give rise to the particular form of social reality people accept as given, and these "givens" form the tradition of a culture, changing as we move from one to another as well as through time. It is important to understand that Geertz does not deny that religions perform functions or do things for people, but he is at pains to emphasize that religious ideas create worlds of meaning within which these functions are carried out.

What are the functions of religion in Geertz's view? He emphasizes that the human mind cannot tolerate chaos, and that religions attempt to cope with chaos in the world, with human bafflement, with situations that drive people to the limits of their endurance. Religions propose that life is comprehensible and that we can orient ourselves within it, come to terms with it, and learn thereby to cope with our lives. This is not quite the same as saying that religion gives people confidence and happiness, for "over its career religion has probably disturbed men as much as it has cheered them" (*Interpretation*, p. 103). It is not the avoidance of suffering that religion is about so much as how to suffer, how to endure, how to cope. This is very much the view we take in the present book. Religions formulate a new order for the world by means of symbols, and in this new order everything, including the most joyous and the most tragic experiences of life, finds its place.

But how is it, he asks, that religious formulations are believed? Why do people in all cultures accept this symbolic reinterpretation of reality in the face of the harsh realities of the world? The answer is the authority of the religious symbols, traditions, and rituals. Unlike common sense, religious explanations claim to be authoritative, and they act out their authoritative statements in rituals. Rituals of all kinds, be they sacrifices or church services, fuse the real and the imagined worlds through symbolic actions. It is the enactment of the rituals, given authority by the priest or senior person in charge, that leads to their acceptance and thereby the acceptance of the religious approach to the problems and paradoxes of everyday life and experience. We move in and out of the world of religious symbols. Generally we are in the everyday world where things go wrong and disasters happen. Then we move into the world of ritual for a time to achieve a reconciliation, then back out into the harsh light of day.

This movement between religious observance and ordinary existence leads straight into our own work. We shall show that all through life, people in all parts of the world, in great religions and small, move into religious activity at times of crisis and then move out again to get on with ordinary living. This book is about how people have come to incorporate a religious dimension into all the main doings of their lives, from birth to death. Everything about life is a puzzle. Conception is a puzzle and so religions concern themselves with fertility. Birth is painful and death in childbirth is common; religion is present at the time of birth. Puberty is a time of great difficulty; religions provide complex rites of passage to normalize what is going on. Marriage is joyous; religions sanctify the joy and give meaning to the event. Sickness is frightening; religions offer rituals to ward off evil and effect cure. Death is saddening; religions offer hope of renewal.

Notes

1. Evans-Pritchard, E. E. (1965). *Theories of primitive religion.* Clarendon Press, Oxford.

2. Muller, F. J. (1882). *Introduction to the science of religion.* Royal Institution, London.

3. Spencer, H. (1882). *The principles of sociology,* vol I. Appleton, New York.

4. Tylor, E. B. (1891). *Primitive culture* (3rd ed). 2 vols. John Murray, London.

5. Frazer, J. G. (1922). *The golden bough* (3rd ed). 2 vols. Macmillan, London.

6. Marret, R. R. (1914). *The threshold of religion* (2nd ed). Methuen, London.

7. Crawley, A. E. (1909). *The idea of the soul.* A. and C. Black, London.

8. Malinowski, B. (1925). "Magic, science and religion." In J. Needham. (ed.). *Science, religion and reality,* 19–84. Sheldon Press, London.

9. Evans-Pritchard, E. E. (1965). *Theories of primitive religion.* Clarendon Press, Oxford. Farooq, M., and Mallah, M. B. "Behavioural pattern of social and religious water-contact activities in Egypt-49 Bilharziasis project area." *Bulletin World Health Organisation,* 35, 377–87.

10. Norbeck, E. (1961). *Religion in primitive society.* Harper, New York.

11. Geertz, C. (1968). *Islam observed.* Yale University Press, New Haven, Connecticut.

12. Geertz, C. (1975). *The interpretation of cultures.* Hutchinson, London.

3

The Challenge of Modernity

Religions have always had practical concerns. Before the advent of our own species, Neanderthals had a cave bear cult to ward off these dangerous predators from their living sites. With the beginning of historical times, the first known writing consists of marks thought to represent the amount of grain in storage at a temple at Jericho, some ten thousand years ago in the Middle East. Ancient Vedic texts, from the birthplace of Indian civilization, include rules for the slaughtering of horses and how much should be given to the priests. The religion of ancient Egypt betrayed a preoccupation with the provision of food for the afterlife, at any rate for those rich enough to warrant embalming and a large tomb. There was also a religious preoccupation with ensuring the continuation of the annual Nile flood on which the entire society depended. The Old Testament book of Leviticus is deeply concerned with what may and may not be eaten, with personal hygiene, and with sexual behavior.

In the modern, consumerist world of the West one might therefore expect its religions (Christianity, Islam, and to a lesser extent Judaism) to be concerned with profit maximization. But there is a problem: Jesus turned the money-changers out of the temple; originally Christianity opposed the pursuit of profit and the values engendered by money. Islam rules against usury and so Islamic banks cannot give interest on deposits; in consequence they make clients shareholders. This did not apply to Jews, who therefore, until the modern era, were the prime dealers in money. Today only the remnants of this division continue, and it is considered quite acceptable for Christians and Moslems to engage wholeheartedly in the marketplace. How can that be?

The answer seems to be that at their beginnings, the world religions were all revolutionary; their founders—Buddha, Moses, Jesus, Muhammad—were visionaries, innovators, and radicals. But from the charismatic leaders of the early days, all the religions that have spread have become institutionalized, organized; have developed status hierarchies and forged links with secular agencies in the economic and political sectors of society. They have come close to government, for example by sanctifying the English kings, or have taken it over, as in the government of Iran by the ayatollahs. Once institutionalized, the nature of religion changes, from a radical freethinking of dissident citizens with charismatic leaders to more conservative dogmas in keeping with the demands of the economic and political realities of the social environment.

In this way radical new faiths become managed by political authorities in exchange for access to a degree of power. The bishops' palaces, cathedrals, and theological colleges of Christianity have replaced the revolutionary working class setting of the days of the Apostles, when the leaders of the faith were carpenters' sons and fishermen. Muhammad had no palace, but the palaces of Islam are legendary and its mosques among the most beautiful and costly of the world's buildings. The Taj Mahal itself is a building of inspired Islamic beauty built as an extravaganza by Akhbar for his favorite wife, with wealth amassed by conquest.

Conclusion: organized, institutionalized religion tends to fall in step with the secular world, to enjoy the fruits of power. But what about the common man? He gets no share in the power of the state or its religion except what he can achieve by his own efforts. How does the common man see religion in the modern world? What is his relationship to the priesthood, the clergy, the temple, the mosque? By and large, his contact with these people and buildings and the ideas they promote is strongest at particular life events, at birth and incorporation and marriage and death, and in the control of crises. Religions take an interest in the life process of their adherents. They try to control the way their adherents live their lives. It is a kind of deal: religions say, "Live your life according to the faith, and you will get benefits, some in this life, some in the next." It is this extraordinary "deal" that we write about in this book—the various forms it takes in different faiths. Even in the consumerist environment of the West, religion plays this part. Churches are by no means empty in Western Europe; indeed, there appears to be a religious revival going on in the U.S. Midwest. Baptisms, marriages, and funerals have not disappeared. In the affluent West we may not need much from religion, but many people still in large measure accept that it has a role to play in their main life events. American university students sometimes pray for the success of their basketball teams, and British football and rugby players can occasionally be seen to cross themselves as they run onto the field of play. For the rest, we feel we can manage without religious supports, preferring material ones.

The reverse is the case in many parts of the world. Not everyone has the range of materialist accoutrements available to us in the West, though in most of the world's cultures there is an eager desire to have more and more of them. This is not the place to digress into the attractions of consumerism, or the faults. We simply need to note that among people all over the world there is a desire to Westernize the interface between themselves and the natural environment. For the !Kung Bushmen of the Kalahari and Namibia until the midtwentieth century this desire was very limited. Their technology consisted of digging sticks, spears, gourds, clothes, some simple jewelry, fire-making equipment, and temporary shelters. For many rural Africans today, possessions are limited to a house, a hoe, some cooking pots, a bicycle, clothes, baskets, and gourds. Those who can afford it also have a tape recorder or radio, but such is the poverty that in many cases batteries are not obtained. In much of rural India, and a good many other countries, the situation is not far different. The contrast with the West is enormous. Yet, without patronizing, on such slender materialist means full lives are led. The problem for such people is that their lack of physical resources limits their ability to respond to disease or accident or disaster of any kind, except by means which we think to be ineffective in scientific terms. They are not, however, short of faith and hope and are well provided with traditional priests and traditional remedies. The quality of life of the world's poor is curiously undiminished by materialist deprivation, as visitors to poor countries are often surprised to discover.

Do consumerism and materialism diminish faith? At root, materialism is about being able to resist the hardships and difficulties and dangers of the physical world. The most important materialist possessions are those which enable a person to avoid hunger, thirst, disease, and injury and to maintain a comfortable edge on the fluctuations and occasional disasters of life. To take an example: in the late 1980s there were two urban earthquakes of almost identical force, one in northeastern Iran, the other in San Francisco. The former killed thousands as poorly built concrete houses crashed to the ground; the latter killed a handful, mainly on an unwisely built overpass. The difference was one of wealth: San Francisco was built and continues to be built by using a technology skilled in resisting earthquakes, as it is known to be on a fault; Iran is also known to be earthquake-prone, but the country's wealth has not been directed at improving and controlling its construction industry. In some societies, of which Iran is an example, poor people fall back on religious beliefs in the absence of material remedies for dealing with disasters. In Sicily there are monuments at the edges of lava flows from a recent eruption of Mount Etna which testify to the fact that it stopped just there thanks to the intervention of the Virgin Mary, responding to the prayers of nearby villagers.

Earthquakes provide a dramatic example of the difference in ability to respond, and kind of response, of different peoples to disasters. Lesser examples are found everywhere. If a Westerner has a bad accident or falls seriously ill, a telephone call to a nearby doctor has him or her hospitalized and undergoing emergency treatment within minutes. In a house in

3.1. Where volcanic eruptions occur religious rituals are often used in attempts to control the flow of lava.

a village in India, such a person has no means of instant communication with the medical authorities even if they are close by; a neighbor or relative has to walk or run ten or twenty miles to find a bus or a telephone, the telephone may not work, and so on; death may intervene before adequate Western-style treatment occurs. However, a local medicine man or priest is likely to be called in to apply locally available remedial treatment in a culturally acceptable ambience, and hopes are pinned on him. Religion thus comes to the fore in relation to disease, injury, or the possibility of death, where rapid hospital treatment is unavailable. Even where such medical care is available, sufferers and their families often follow parallel courses of traditional treatment from local sources with which they are familiar.

The previous remarks really amount to saying that religious beliefs have a greater opportunity to survive and thrive where Western technical modernity has not made much impact. They still have a job to do. But a moment's reflection shows that many beliefs are not "functional" in this sense. Orthodox Hindus abhor the flesh of the cow but eat pork; Moslems, living in the same part of northern India, often in the same villages as neighbors to Hindus, regard pig flesh as inedible but enjoy eating beef. Islam and Judaism concur on this matter of the pig taboo; Christianity and Hinduism have other taboos. Whether the cow, the pig, the horse, the dog, or the rat is seen as acceptable or taboo is a consequence of history, of what at a different time for special reasons became dogma in the written or unwritten traditions of the faith. Sometimes such taboos serve as social markers, distinguishing the faithful from the infidels, the washed from the unwashed. A church is a community of believers, what the sociologist Max Weber called a "Gemeinschaft," a group with a common sense of unity and purpose. From the point of view of the individual, when he has his children baptized, or, in the case of Jews, pays for his son to become a full member of his religion through the bar mitzvah ceremony, or teaches him the five times and the ways of prayer to Allah, he is not just perpetuating the faith in his family, but is perpetuating the religious community to which he belongs. This the priests want him to do, for their continued existence depends on it. Thus we can see a balance of benefits: the individual benefits from membership of his religious community and from being thought of as a right-thinking and trustworthy person, while the religious institution benefits from continuity.

It is against this background that the incorporation of religious ceremonies into the life events of ordinary individuals has to be understood. If religion is still a force in the world today (and who would deny it?), that is because the reciprocal rights and benefits still exist. This appears to be the case not only in the largely secular, consumerist society in which we live, but also elsewhere, all over the world, and as we shall see in the chapters of this book, religions are alive and well, often permeating to the heart of the lives of their adherents to a greater extent than we in the West would consider possible.

Material Progress and Religious Values

The idea of progress has taken a hammering in the twentieth century. Our Victorian ancestors were confident in it, but two world wars, a series of smaller-scale but very bloody conflicts, and the loss of empires by the European powers have had salutory effects. Today's world is marked by a good deal less of the ideology of white supremacy than the previous century was, and this is a kind of moral progress. However, there is an even more real sense in which we can talk about progress, namely in respect of health, and of material goods and products, the results of increasing technological sophistication. There have been real and indisputable advances in the field of medicine and in our knowledge of the properties of materials, in our capacity to create synthetic materials, and in our capacity to use these to manufacture tools and other objects that can and do make life easier for us. The intermediary concept is energy. By using technology to harness more and more energy for the common person, Western-style civilization, based on consumerism, has achieved a sort of urban–industrial triumph: a large percentage of the population can live without tilling the soil or engaging in any physical labor, day by day.

Here we come back to the great paradox for Christianity in modern times: traditionally it deplores an obsession with worldly goods, which is precisely what modern consumerist capitalism has as its primary article of faith. Christianity and other similar faiths thus find themselves obliged to adapt to the marketplace in the modern West. Their strength lies in the other things they still do, in baptisms and marriages and funerals, and in the ideas they stand for, the ideas of charity and love and hope and forgiveness, all of which have their place in life today as they always had, and which are not (with a few exceptions such as secular charities) part of the concerns of other organizations in society. Yet even in the process of advocating charity many religions have accumulated enormous quantities of corporate property. We see this in Christianity and Islam, but it has been so in other places at other times. A Chinese source in A.D. 1700 estimated that nearly 14 percent of all cultivated land was owned by religious bodies not related to clans according to Welch.[1]

We can see this as a dual process, of conflict of values on the one hand and increasing moral isolation on the other. Historically, at first churches get rich; later, with increasing general affluence, individuals get rich in their turn. First the church has a double standard, then the population and the clergy have to find ways of accommodating traditional teachings to modern circumstances. This process is not unique to Christianity but is a feature of all religions when the process of material development and modernization gets under way. It is when real incomes reach the level where large numbers of people start to become affluent that social fragmentation sets in, and religions increasingly find themselves forced to adapt to the strident, selfish mass philosophy emerging from materialism.

But not everyone is a beneficiary in the consumerist society. Our care of the aged and insane is worse than that found in nonindustrial societies; such people are defined as useless and shut away, a fate they would never suffer in, say, an African village where they have status because of their proximity to the ancestors. The poor of London sleep out in the cold; ordinary people in Africa or India would be amazed at this. Religious (and some secular) organizations do a lot of charitable work, including running hospitals. United States Methodists in 1960 ran 76 general hospitals;[2] Roman Catholics at that time administered 950 general hospitals with a bed capacity of 156,000.[3] But the extent of the problem of poverty and deprivation arising from social isolation in affluent societies is beyond the capacity of religious charities and has in consequence been taken over by the state.

The Demographic Transition

The greatest change that has come about in Western and, more recently, Asian societies since the time of the industrial revolution, fostered by the increase in material affluence, is the process known as the demographic transition, and it is this that has presented religious institutions with some of their major challenges and forced adjustments on reluctant, conservative faiths. The term *demographic transition* designates the changeover from large to small family size with the increase in material affluence of ordinary people. This change, with a few exceptions, has followed or is currently following a very similar pattern in all the countries in which Western-style affluence has emerged. We can, broadly, distinguish three stages.

The first stage predates the transition. In this stage people have low incomes, with little or no surplus wealth, and large families. There is a high rate of mortality of all kinds, especially child mortality. The pronatalist strategy is designed to produce some surviving children at the end of the parents' working lives, to look after them and to carry on the family's smallholding or trade into the next generation. At this stage it is largely impossible for families to increase their real wealth because there is no developed economy in which entrepreneurial skills can be set to work to generate capital; instead there are a peasant market system and an affluent upper class with inherited wealth derived largely from ownership of land.

The second stage arises when the stability of the first stage is shattered by the onset of the industrial revolution or its equivalent. With the ability of ordinary individuals to set up businesses of their own, in the context of a growing commercial free-enterprise economy, a percentage of the population can "make" money by using the labor of others, and the net effect of this (after a bad start marked by poverty, social dislocation, and the exploitation of the working poor by the entrepreneurial

3.2. Poor African families suffer from malnutrition during periods of food shortage with the result that the infant mortality rate is high.

nouveaux riches) is a general growth of real wealth, as *everyone* engaged in the commercial–industrial–service economy benefits from the energy, goods, and services provided by everyone else. During this phase, family size is still high, but the growth of medical resources such as mass immunization against fatal diseases, better housing, better sanitation, and improved personal hygiene leads to a reduction in the mortality rate and an increase in the size of the population. This is experienced by individuals as a rise in the cost of living, as more and more demands are made on the goods and services available.

This process heralds the third and final stage of the demographic transition. With the tendency of the cost of living to rise, real incomes stabilize or even decline, and people find themselves increasingly in competition with each other in the new world of higher standards. At this point marginal economies are practiced, and the first of these is a reduction in family size, brought about by two factors. First there is the security of knowing that even if only two or three children are born, health care will likely ensure their survival. This is in marked contrast with the situation where there is inadequate health care, in which having a small family would entail the risk of losing all the children in an epidemic of, say, smallpox or tuberculosis. Second, there follows the growth of a contraceptive culture and a contraceptive industry, involving radical changes of attitudes among millions of people. All this is a slow process, but it is characteristic of the third and final stage of the demographic transition and has occurred in much of the Westernized world.

From the perspective of religion, the third stage of the demographic transition entails the most difficult adjustment. In the first stage, in Europe, little villages and towns had their churches, attendance was high, and the local vicar or priest was a powerful and rich man, with high social status. In the second stage the church already found itself doing battle with the new zest for greedy self-improvement and comforting the poor and the dispossessed. The third stage finds the church adapting to modern conditions, seeking to maintain its authority and the status of its priests.* The widespread use of mechanical means of contraception comes directly into conflict with the doctrines of the Roman Catholic church, while all Christian churches to some extent deplore eroticism for its own sake, preferring to link up sexual intercourse with, on the one hand, the state of holy wedlock, and on the other the desire to have children.

We have painted a picture of a world that has become and is still becoming increasingly dedicated to materialist values, with consequences

* We describe here mainly the situation in the Christian West. In other parts of the world the process has been different. For instance, in Iran Islamic leaders were materially deprived by the shah and his Westernizing policies. Under such influences, the demographic transition might have gotten under way. However, there followed a wave of fundamentalism which was at least in part a claim by religious leaders (not the clergy as such) to regain status. This pattern is not applicable to Western politics, which has for centuries been divorced from the established church.

of all kinds, some good (freedom from disease and hunger), some not so good (poverty and neglect of the weak and old), and some that have good and bad aspects (the increase of abortion and reduction in family size). Within the various contexts, all over the world, of secular materialism, religions have had to adapt and reshape their messages. What is perhaps most interesting is the fact that religious faith does not disappear under the onslaught of materialism but maintains a surprising amount of energy and involvement with everyday life. In other words, religions adapt, and this is a dynamic process. It may be a slow one, and there are often lags between the demands of the prevailing social and physical environment and what religions are telling people to do. In this sense religions act as a conservative force, slowing down change in people's attitudes and behavior patterns. This may be no bad thing, for overrapid change can lead to a backlash if conditions revert to their former state. Thus a country that is modernizing too quickly may undergo a state of political instability and revert to poverty; we see this happening in African states all too often. In such cases, religions have a part to play in holding together the fabric of people's lives in what may be very difficult conditions with civil war and disease all around.

The social ecology of religions, that is, the relationship between religions and their social and physical environments, is a huge and fascinating topic. A totally new and enormously challenging approach to the answer was attempted by E. O. Wilson, the founder of sociobiology, who argued that all of human culture was the outcome of an interaction, during evolution, between the human genetic potential and the ecological pressures bearing on it. In chapter 8 he looked at religion, which he regarded as the supreme challenge to the sociobiological method of analysis, as indeed it surely is. Can religion, too, be explained in purely materialistic terms? Wilson certainly believed it could and set out to do so. Religions, he says, "evolve in directions that enhance the welfare of the practitioners" of those religions. He acknowledges that "even if there is a materialist basis of religious process . . . it will be difficult to decipher for two reasons": because religions are unique to human beings, thus depriving us of the comparative mammalian approach; and because the learning rules and genetic motivations underlying religions are hidden from the conscious minds of individual people.

Wilson's approach sees three levels of selection operating on religions during their evolution. There is the surface level, at which "ecclesiastical selection" takes place, when clerics and other practitioners make choices about the shape and forms of prayers, ceremonies, and so on. Second is the middle level, at which "ecological selection" takes place, where the environmental conditions of life select religious features as important while other aspects are neglected and disappear. Third is the deepest level, that of "genetic selection," at which the genes of those people who are able, willing, and motivated to act, think, and believe in religious ways are selected over those unable or unwilling to do so.

In many ways, our own approach in this and our previous work on this subject concentrates on the middle level, that of ecological selection. We would, however, want to call it "socioecological selection" because we are very concerned with the social environment in which people live, and how religions respond to this. In this book, we leave the surface level very much untouched, although it is undoubtedly true that changes in the surface forms of religions are occurring all the time. We also leave the genetic basis untouched, and here it is much less certain that such a level exists at all, although Wilson, and later Lumsden and Wilson,[4] were very concerned to explore this level and how it might operate.

In a central passage of his chapter on religion, Wilson writes of the ecological level: "We need to ask: What are the effects of each religious practice on the welfare of individuals and tribes? How did the practice originate in history and under what environmental circumstances?"[5] These are certainly questions close to our concerns in the present book. Whether or not we accept Wilson's argument that "sociobiology can account for the very origin of mythology by the principle of natural selection acting on the genetically evolving material structure of the human brain" (p. 192), there is no doubt at all that religious experience is a human universal and has enormous power to mold human minds and direct human actions.

Finally Wilson makes it clear that while sociobiology may be able to explain religions on the basis of scientific naturalism, religion itself will endure because of "the spiritual weakness of scientific naturalism." That is, religions, because of human nature itself, have power to move people to action, whereas scientific explanations lack this power.

Our own earlier version of the present book, *The Biology of Religion*,[6] was certainly concerned with the middle level of analysis of Wilson's work. We put forward a set of ideas about the relationship between environmental and demographic variables, on the one hand, and religious rules and beliefs, on the other. Our analysis led us to the conclusion that in environments where levels of disease and frequency of natural disasters were high, where poverty was great, expectation of life low, infant mortality rate high, and confidence in the future poor, then religious attitudes to childbearing were pro-natalist: that is, religions fostered the view that it was altogether a good thing for parents to have many children. We found this kind of religious attitude to be prevalent in many Moslem countries, in Hindu India, and in rural African societies. In such cases religions were, we argued, acting adaptively, because in promoting pronatalist ideas they were ensuring the survival into maturity of at least a few children who would then be able to support their parents and continue the family line down the generations.

Conversely, we showed that in environments where disease levels and frequency of natural disasters were lower, where affluence prevailed, expectation of life was high, infant mortality rate low, and people's confidence in the future strong, then religious attitudes to childbearing were anti-natalist: religions did not emphasize the production of large numbers of offspring by parents. This attitude we found to be characteristic of modern Westernized countries, whose primary religion is Christianity. Once again, we argued that this was adaptive because such ideas would tend to reduce family size and this would be in keeping with the high cost of rearing and educating even a small number of children.

We called pro-natalist religions "r+" and anti-natalist ones "r−" and showed how their attitudes made good sense in the particular social and economic circumstances where they occurred. In the present book we put much emphasis on the social side of the analysis. The treatment of sexuality by religions, which underlies their pro- or anti-natalist orientation, is shown to be not only a reflection of environmental pressures but a set of guidelines for people to help them determine how to plan their families. Indeed we described religions in our earlier book as "handbooks of parental investment," and this view is the one we have chosen to emphasize here, along with all the other ways in which religions provide guidelines for action. Perhaps the most fascinating contrast remains that between Christianity on the one hand and Islam or Hinduism on the other, the former being geared to the needs of individuals in the affluent Westernized countries, the latter to those of the poorer countries of the Middle East and much of Asia.

But as Geertz[7] has shown, Islam differs dramatically from North Africa to Indonesia, and Christianity does so from, say, North America to Africa or indeed to South America. What we see in reality are continuous gradations of belief, always more or less in tune with prevailing socioeconomic conditions. But there is no simple determinism. Religious customs have a life of their own; they can take off in any direction. Thus the great pilgrimages of Hindus or Moslems cannot be predicted from socioeconomic conditions; nor can the carrying of the Virgin Mary by devout Catholics on Holy Days, or the carrying of native gods in Bali, be predicted from the material circumstances of their lives.

There is thus a constant dynamic between religions and the physical circumstances in which they occur. Each—the set of religious ideas and the set of environmental forces—works on the other in an evolving way. When we see hungry children in Africa on our TV screens we may wonder why people do not have smaller families. The answer is that the cultures and religions of Africa promote large family size precisely because mortality rates are so high. This is a vicious circle which can be broken only by the modernization process referred to earlier, a process that has barely begun in some modern African countries. Our message about religions and the important part they play in organizing people's lives, and especially their reproductive strategies, has implications for aid agencies such as the World Bank or WHO and other organizations that are involved in family planning programs in less-developed countries. To ask a rural Ugandan family, for instance, to limit the number of its children without remedying the underlying social and ecological situation is to invite disaster for the family and to ensure failure of the family planning program. To repeat what we said in 1983: "Religions act as culturally phrased biological messages. They arise from the survival strategies of past group members and continue to advise at the present time. As such, a religion is a primary set of reproductive rules, a kind of parental investment handbook" (p. 294).

How do religions adapt to environmental circumstances? The answer we find most satisfactory is in terms of human needs. In any given situation people have a set of needs. The needs of people in the United States or Britain are quite different from those of people in sub-Saharan Africa. It is in terms of their needs that people seek solutions, and it is part of the functioning of their cultures, including their religions, to phrase these solutions in ways they understand clearly, to provide guidelines for action.

Religions and Human Needs

Our approach in this book is to ask, "What functions have religions performed during their history and what functions do they perform now?" The question of the "functions" of social institutions contains a hidden problem. The institutions and structures of the world's societies are patterns of thoughts and ideas expressed in action and are often unpredictable and difficult to translate into our own culture-specific concepts. If we take a concept such as "mana" which is used in the Pacific region, it has no immediate equivalent in English, and it is necessary to read the works of a social anthropologist such as Malinowski to gain some understanding of the term, which refers to the "power" or "spirit quality" pertaining to certain ritual objects, places, and people. The term *busebu,* used by the Sukuma of Tanzania, has a similar quality. Religious ideas and whole cosmologies built up out of such unfamiliar concepts can be only dimly apprehended by people like us from another culture. The problem is one of meaning. Anthropologists are largely the purveyors and interpreters of exotic meanings to those who are bound into the ideas of other cultures. They open windows to possibilities we should certainly not otherwise encounter.

But one can go too far in concluding that because the cultural worlds of different peoples are noninterchangeable, have different emphases, and see the world in different ways, these cultural worlds cannot be understood in terms of function. On the contrary, if we can wrest ourselves from the role of discoverer of cultural differences and ask the more mundane question, "What have these cultures got in common?," then we find a surprising extent of overlap. For example, all societies have kinship systems; all have rules of diet; all have rules pertaining to who may or may not have sexual and social intercourse with each other; all have modes of dress and adornment; all have rules of hygiene; all have patterns of greeting, rules for the entertainment of visitors, rules of reciprocity, marriage rules, and rules for the management of birth, sickness, and death; and all have some kind of worship of spirits, gods, or other kinds of belief in supernatural powers. In the words of Marvin Harris, "One of the fundamental assumptions of anthropology is that cultural differences and similarities cannot be explained if they are looked upon merely as isolated entities. . . . *The functional unity of cultural systems is a basic postulate underlying all of cultural anthropology.*"[8]

Why should this be so? Where we find all cultures sharing a concern with something, it seems likely they are responding to some kind of human need, and to respond to a need is to perform a function. Cultural responses may be quite matter-of-fact, or they may be quite exotic. In Africa, dress is sometimes reduced to a loincloth or even just a set of beads; contrast the heavily veiled yashmak of the women of Afghanistan. The beads say, "I am an attractive girl; look how nice I am"; the yashmak says, "I am an attractive woman, but it is taboo for you to look at me in public, so I am hidden behind these clothes." Likewise a badly dressed person is saying, "My appearance doesn't matter," and a person dressed in rags is saying, "I am a pauper." People may not actually be what their appearance "says" they are, but their dress makes some sort of statement about them, something that their fellows understand. Dress communicates. Its function is to inform other members of society about appropriate behavior. It fulfills this need, for we need to know how to respond to each other. It may also fulfill another need, namely keeping the body warm or dry. Needs are not mutually exclusive: many can be fulfilled at once, and Malinowski distinguished clearly between primary needs (food, shelter, and so on) and secondary needs expressed in traits and institutions practiced by members of societies but not vital to their biological demands.

Needs

Religions are found in every society and so it is sensible to ask, "Why do people appear to need religion?" We avoid experiential answers, which must in some shape or form include reference to interaction between humans and the supernatural. For example, a believer might say that God has manifested Himself to us, and as a result we (or at any rate believers) are now able to make contact with Him; our need for Him is a consequence of the fact that we are not truly whole without Him. This would be a Judeo-Christian answer, which might not appeal to a Buddhist, who might want to answer in terms of the human mind and its need for equilibrium attainable only by the extinction of desire. The question, asked of believers from different religions or different sects, would elicit different answers and different arguments, couched in terms and concepts derived from the theology of the religion of the person answering. We, by contrast, seek for secular answers, that is, answers derived from the nonreligious sector, from the processes of ordinary, materialist, biological life. We base our analysis on the functioning individual, the man and woman and child living a life of sleeping, waking, eating, drinking, falling sick, regaining health, arguing and having social difficulties, making amends, falling in love, falling out again, learning from family and friends and teachers, gaining sexual experience, getting married and perhaps divorced, having children and discovering the pleasures and fears they bring, getting old and decrepit, and finally expiring—a life cycle, in short, not far from that of our animal relatives, but marked off from theirs by the existence of the ceremonies and accoutrements of culture, and a much more sophisticated and complex set of social institutions in which life is necessarily lived. Our answer to the questions "Why religion?" and "Why do people need religion?" is that religions have evolved to provide legitimating or "safe" ways of dealing with those events in life that bring human beings into a state of danger or fear or anxiety or just an overwhelming feeling of pointlessness. The nodal points of life, what can be called "life crises," are the foci of religions. The priest, or medicine man, or prophet, or shaman moves in at such times, to a person in need of explanation, or comfort, or simply social recognition. We shall document this in great detail in the pages that follow.

According to Maslow,[9] needs exist in a hierarchy of prepotency, from lower (physiological, e.g., safety) to higher (social, e.g., self-esteem and self-actualization). Maslow considers self-actualization to be the highest level of need. However, the highest needs (goodness, wholeness) cannot be fulfilled until lower needs, including safety, love, belongingness, and esteem, are satisfied. Higher needs are, therefore, in Maslow's scheme, less urgent subjectively than lower ones. Nevertheless, they produce more desirable social and subjective results, enabling individuals to achieve self-integration, social integration, and ultimately self-actualization.

Religion relates to Maslow's hierarchy of needs at all levels. At the physiological level, where individuals are mainly concerned with satisfying their basic needs for food and water, religions offer hope at times of famine and drought by the intermediary of prayers and ritual performances. When the need is for safety, religions provide, besides prayers, a wide range of individualized protections such as charms or crucifixes that can be worn on the body for constant protection, and family and community rituals at times of crisis. Further up Maslow's scale, religions can provide social integration and self-esteem by incorporating individuals into smaller or larger groups of like-thinking people, bonded by their common faith. And finally at the level of self-actualization, religion may be (though it need not be) the very medium through which people achieve their peak experiences and achieve the wholeness of mind about which Maslow writes.

Religions thus cater to needs at all levels. We have called our book *The Social Ecology of Religion* because human needs occur in two spheres of life, both of which are incorporated into Maslow's scheme. These spheres are constituted by society and the environment.

On the social side, our needs concern our relationships with other people. Children need the support of loving parents. Kinsfolk are dependent on each other in numerous ways. At times of death and mourning we need the support of friends and relatives. At times of crisis we all need others. Religions have a vital role in relation to social needs in all parts of the world.

On the environmental side, human needs are directly related to the richness or poverty of the land on which people live, the availability of the resources of food to ordinary people, the climate and the level of rainfall. We have all seen films of people living in drought conditions in Africa, barely alive. For such people, their basic needs are terribly urgent. More normally, people in poor habitats have to work hard to provide themselves with food for the whole year, and the question of obtaining food is at the center of their interests and their rituals. In such conditions, high rates of mortality prevail, and so we find an expressed need for children, a dislike of childlessness; in these conditions religious rituals are aimed at increasing fertility.

How does this functional, need-oriented approach to religions relate to their history? Our approach to religion can be called "vernacular." We are interested in the common person rather than the theologian or what he studies—the higher reaches of religious thought. As a result, we are as hamstrung as any historian who tries to plot the history of the common man. Such is not the history that we find in the history books. A very important study has been made of vernacular history in Great Britain by the Cambridge group of social historians.[10] They have, by careful reconstruction from parish and other records, been able to piece together details of the relative wealth and poverty of people in bygone centuries, of their family size, and of their longevity. Equivalent studies have been done in a number of other countries, such as France and the United States. There are long-term studies of some religious groups such as the Hutterites[11] or the Amish.[12] Many of them try to link up pressures on land, or on food supply, with patterns of disease, natality, and mortality, and these factors have the advantage that they are relatively easy to document accurately. These are the kinds of data that may, eventually, be able to give us some substantial insight into how religions have played their part in history, affecting people's ability to respond to environmental crises; to earthquakes, floods, famines, and pandemics; as well as to social ills such as international and civil wars. Besides these evils, there are the everyday difficulties and personal disasters we all face from time to time. Religions have played their part in keeping people sane and stable. And most often there are the normal life events we have referred to, in which a million times a day religions have their part to play and have done so since the evolution of human culture itself.

We thus see religions as an integral part of vernacular history, as a strand woven into lives of individuals, families, social groups, and whole societies. Religions are like technology in that respect: ever present and influential to people's ability to solve life's problems day by day. If today the agnostic Westerner feels that religion is on the wane, then we should not forget that historically religions have been hugely important, just as now they are close to the roots of violent social tensions in the Middle East, whether in Iraq, Israel, or Lebanon. And we should also remember that a waning of religiosity in one generation can be followed by a regrowth, in different circumstances, in the next. It is certainly premature to conclude that religions as forces in the world and as forces in individual lives are a thing of the past. An interesting book, published in 1988, on the prevalence of mystical healing cults in New Jersey,[13] indicates a growth of spiritual movements related to human needs in the United States. The west of England, around the town of Totnes in Devon, is inundated with people seeking new forms of religious awareness and integration into modern life. These are the new religions. Elsewhere the old ones continue with renewed vigor, as in Russia, Poland, and the other former Communist bloc countries of Eastern Europe, and indeed the whole of the Near and Middle East and most of South East Asia. We have both in recent years visited Japan and been surprised to find how actively the old Japanese religion of Shinto is pursued today: shrines of this ancient faith are visited by many thousands of Japanese who attach small paper petitions to the thin branches of sacred trees. In Japan, despite mainstream Buddhism and ancient Shinto, there are literally thousands of new religions. Catholic churches continue to have packed congregations every Sunday in Southern Europe, as do Orthodox ones in Greece, especially on the patronal feast days of each church. It seems to be mainly in the northwest of Europe, in Scandinavia, and in parts of the United States that religion remains in the doldrums, mainly in areas where the rejection of religion has occurred for a number of reasons, some of which we can discern. On the intellectual level, some individuals have undoubtedly rejected religion as a source of true knowledge as a result of the impact of Darwinian biology in particular and science more generally. The culture of science and technology, in Western industrial society, has been put to work by commerce to promote individual solutions to individual problems. This has weakened the corporate "Gemeinschaft" and with it the collective religious supports which in bygone times brought people together in shared hardship. People in affluent populations who can use technology to solve their problems do not, it seems, need religious supports as much and can manage without them for the most part.[14] This very exception indicates what religion does for people in the rest of the world: it meets their needs and helps them cope with life's difficulties.

Morality and Religion

We can distinguish general morality, a kind of general mutual considerateness that forms the basis of all morality, from religious morality, the more precise rules and conventions of morality embodied in religions.* We have already stated that religions deal with people's needs. In the field of morality, they deal with social needs. The most primary and essential need for a person in society is to feel that he or she is a worthy member of that society. The feeling of worth or esteem has been remarked by sociologists. The work of Goffman (e.g., *The Presentation of Self in Everyday Life*)[15] shows how important it is for individuals to create a socially acceptable impression. Harré's *Social Being*[16] builds up a picture of humans as creatures whose satisfactory and sane existence is based on making adequate impressions and performing adequately or even well in society. In this sense our whole personality is a social product.

Being a moral agent, and being seen to be one, is a vital ingredient of achieving social acceptance and being a full member of a social group. In the religious community, performing the appropriate actions is important. In a churchgoing community, it is good, right, and proper to go to church, and a person who does not do so is to that extent frowned on and marginalized. If the appropriate rituals are not performed in such a group, the individuals concerned lose a certain degree of social esteem among the practicing members. Doubts arise over their membership of the religious community, and over the certainty with which they can be called on to reciprocate unselfishly or altruistically in times of need. Eventually, if they actually break central rules, they may be ostracized or rejected, unless the moral principle of forgiveness is invoked, as it may well be if they show signs of reform and a return to the fold.

The answer to the question we posed in chapter 1, "Why religions?," is thus becoming clearer. Religions express the social and moral integration of individuals into their communities, inform them how to think correctly and behave properly, and give them support at times of crisis. In all these ways, they fulfill the needs of individuals. They perform social and psychological functions. If we see human beings as intelligent creatures living in complex social groups, with long life spans that include a number of life crises, always in a world subject to natural disasters and diseases, we can explain why religions exist in terms of the social functions they perform in relation to the life cycle of individual persons, and between one person and another, always in the context of the prevailing features of the natural environment.

In the chapters that follow we shall adopt a life cycle approach to demonstrate how closely religions track the major events of life, and how deeply they are concerned with them and the environment in which they

* Durkheim (1899, trans. 1975) distinguished between morality and religion as follows: "The precepts of . . . morality are identical with those of religion, except that they do not rest on a system of obligatory beliefs. Those collective beliefs which are not religious are similar in all respects to properly recognized dogmas, except that they are not necessarily translated into a system of definite practices." (From W. S. F. Pickering [1975], *Durkheim on Religion,* Routledge and Kegan Paul, London, p. 93.)

occur. From conception to death, religions have teachings about how we should behave, how we should make decisions, what is the right thing to do and what is wrong. Religions are the arbiters of moral behavior in the most basic things we do. Many people are born for religious reasons. Islam in the Middle Eastern context exhorts its followers to be fruitful; Buddhism in Sri Lanka regards abortion as sinful. In the case of circumcision, our bodies are mutilated in the name of religion. At marriage, Christians all over the world take vows, sometimes a wife vows obedience, often the couple vows to be faithful and always to remain together until death intervenes. At death, a series of social links is broken and a period of grief begins; religions come to the fore all over the world to handle this situation, which is often beyond the capabilities of those most closely involved to handle on their own.

Things Can Go Wrong

We are in danger of presenting religions as nice, tidy, well-adapted systems of thought and practice. Nothing in human life is very tidy, and religions are no exception. We have already referred to disagreements over doctrine, but these can be regarded as a sign of healthy debate, even if they pass most of the religious populace by. However, things can go seriously wrong by any ordinary human standard in religious groups. When murder or suicide occurs on a grand scale we need to ask whether something has gone wrong. It is not always the case. The mass suicide of the Jews at besieged Masada in A.D. 73 was an act of religiously inspired heroism, not something gone wrong. However, the same cannot be said for the mass suicide of the inhabitants of Jonestown, Guyana, in 1978, who were a breakaway sect of white and black Americans (for a full account see Hall and Galanter).[17] They had vowed to kill themselves if ever the authorities tried to destroy their way of life. The founder of the sect was the Reverend Jim Jones; his church was called the People's Temple of the Disciples of Christ. According to reports in the mid-1970s, this sect, both before and after the move to Guyana, lived under a regime based on moral pressure and psychological constraint emanating from Jones, a charismatic individual who demanded complete loyalty from his followers. These were for the most part poor blacks, but there were also many middle-class whites.

As time went by, rumors of sexual excesses and drug addiction in the Guyana community alarmed relatives of converts in the United States, and the case for an investigation was taken up by U.S. congressman Leo Ryan, a man with a reputation for rooting out injustice. He went to Guyana with a number of the formally constituted "concerned relatives" and journalists, despite an arrangement that there would be no publicity. They visited the People's Temple, interviewed members, met Jones, and stayed the night. During the visit a number of members of the Temple

3.3. The scene after the mass suicide by members of the Christian Assembly of God at Jonestown, Guyana, in 1978. Cyanide was prepared in orange juice and drunk by adults, who sprayed it into the throats of children using syringes.

expressed a desire to leave. Jones was angered. At the airstrip, shortly before departure, Ryan and four of his party were shot and killed by a sect member, after which the majority of the people on the twenty-seven-hundred-acre settlement gathered together and committed mass suicide by cyanide poisoning, according to a prearranged plan. The number of bodies found was 912, including that of Jim Jones himself, his wife, and his son. These events took place on November 18, 1978 (fig. 3.3).

In the early part of 1993 the town of Waco, Texas, hit the headlines. Four U.S. federal agents and six members of a heavily armed religious cult were killed and a further number wounded in a gun battle. The sect, calling themselves the Branch Davidians, an offshoot of the Seventh Day Adventists, was led by a man called David Koresh, aged thirty-three, who claimed to be Jesus Christ, the Lamb of God, and to be impervious to death, though he was killed in the conflagration. The sect itself had its origins in 1929 when Victor Houteff, a prominent Seventh Day Adventist in Los Angeles, developed his own following and moved to Texas.

His group shared a farm and had their own school and printing press. At the beginning of the Second World War, Houteff changed the group's name to Davidians and insisted on a noncombative role for members in the war effort. He died in 1955 and was succeeded by his wife, Florence, who predicted that Christ would return on April 22, 1959. The cult split after the Second Coming failed to materialize, and a further split occurred in 1984, when Koresh headed the Branch Davidians. It appears he kept his sect in submission while taking privileges for himself, including having multiple wives. He decided to stockpile weapons against the day when the world came to an end, forseeing a need to defend the group and its ample food stores. However, this plan was interrupted when federal law enforcement agents tried to storm his fortress. As with Jim Jones, David Koresh reacted unfavorably to the interest of the law-enforcement agencies. He tightened his grip on his followers and prepared them for a long period of resistance. He spoke of dying for his beliefs and encouraged his followers to do likewise. At one stage during the following weeks he told his lawyer that he would not leave until he had deciphered the Seven Seals of the Bible's Book of Revelation.

The siege that ensued lasted fifty-one days. On Monday, April 19, the FBI finally ended the siege, sending in tanks with battering rams to make holes in the fortress walls, through which tear gas was poured to drive the occupants out. The FBI apparently believed that this scheme would work, and that the tear gas would cause at least the women and the twenty-five children to leave. In fact only nine of the ninety-five American, British, and Australian converts escaped. The rest, either voluntarily or through coercion, including all the children, remained inside the building which burned to the ground, having been set alight by cult members, in the space of less than an hour. Altogether eighty-seven people, including Koresh, died in the conflagration.

On Wednesday, October 5, 1994, yet another cult destroyed itself. This time it was the Order of the Solar Temple. Twenty-two bodies were found in a concealed underground chapel beneath a barn in the picturesque village of Cheiry, in the canton of Freibourg, Switzerland. Another twenty-five bodies were found forty-five miles away in two burnt-out chalets at Granges-sur-Salvan, near Martigny. There were also four deaths at Morin Heights, near Montreal in Quebec, Canada. Many of the victims were professional, well-to-do people. They had been drugged, their hands tied, shot in the head and, in some cases, suffocated. The cult's forty-six-year-old leader, Luc Jouret, who founded the quasi-Christian cult in 1984, was not among them. He had used members' money to stockpile weapons for future use during the chaos that would occur at the end of the world. This would take the form of a nuclear cataclysm, and a fallout shelter had been constructed.

Why the cult chose this particular day to self-destruct is not known, but the event had been carefully planned and executed. In the underground chapel the bodies were laid out fanwise in a circle, with their heads facing out. They were dressed in bright colors. On the wall was a picture of Luc Jouret as Jesus, holding a chalice, with a red rose above his head. Adjoining the chapel was a hall of mirrors. A former member of the sect said that the members believed they could become better people, more virtuous and clean-living, than the rest of the world. Like the People's Temple in Guyana and the Branch Davidians in Texas, the Order of the Solar Temple consisted of people who had turned their backs on the world and were finally at the mercy of their charismatic leader.

If there is a lesson to be learned from these incidents, it is that religious fervor knows no bounds, that religious persuasion is a mighty force, and that the very same beliefs that motivate good behavior in many people can, in the confines of a closed cult, become obsessive and highly dangerous.

We have ended on a note of caution—things can go wrong—to avoid giving the impression that all is well with religions and with the world. But our main theme is a positive one: To recapitulate the ideas of part I, we began by asking why religions, as a curious and complex part of all human cultures, should exist in the first place, why they should have developed during history and be so much a feature of life today. We suggested an answer in terms of the way they organize the lives of ordinary people, rather than in their answers to abstract questions or some vague relationship to society as a whole. Looking at earlier studies of religion in the anthropological literature we found nothing quite like this approach. There have been analyses framed in terms of the development of ideas (e.g., from magic to religion), in terms of social process, in terms of functionalism, and in terms of the development of particular ideas in time and space. Our approach relates the success of religions to their ability to meet human needs during the course of the life cycle, from conception to death. Because of the universality of the life cycle, we expect that religions will survive the onslaughts of modernism, which worships at the altar of consumerism and materialism. It seems unlikely that material things can perform the role religions perform all over the world. In part II we take apart the human life cycle and see just how involved religions are, everywhere, in organizing and making sense of it.

We start by examining the social ecology of religions in relation to conception. That is to say, we ask how religions organize and manage the fundamental biological process of conception in relation to the social world and the physical environment. In relation to the social world conception inevitably involves two people, and societies, through their religions, often attempt to ensure that the two are in a permanent and stable partnership and one that is recognized by their families and friends. This is because conception is not a nonsocial thing; it leads on to birth and the incorporation of a new member into the group. In relation to environmental factors, we see religions concerned with the question of whether or not to interfere with conception, and here the level of resources available and the costs of raising a child become very important, leading to difficult decisions and moral dilemmas.

Notes

1. Welch, H. (1972). *Buddhism under Mao.* Harvard University Press, Cambridge, p. 482.

2. Vanderpool, H. Y. (1986). "The Wesleyan-Methodist tradition." In Numbers, R. L., and Amundsen, D. W. (eds). *Caring and curing: Health and medicine in the Western religious tradition.* Macmillan, New York, p. 339.

3. O'Connell, M. R. (1986). "The Roman Catholic tradition." In Numbers, R. L., and Amundsen, D. W. (eds). *Caring and curing: Health and medicine in the Western religious tradition.* Macmillan, London, p. 139.

4. Lumsden, C. J., and Wilson, E. O. (1983). *Promethean fire.* Harvard University Press, Cambridge, Massachusetts.

5. E. O. Wilson (1978). *On human nature.* Harvard University Press, Cambridge, Mass., p. 178.

6. Reynolds, V., and Tanner, R. E. S. (1983). *The biology of religion.* Longman, London.

7. Geertz, C. (1968). *Islam observed.* Yale University Press, New Haven, Connecticut.

8. Harris, M. (1980). *Culture, people, nature* (3rd ed). Harper & Row, New York. Italics added.

9. Maslow, A. H. (1987). *Motivation and personality.* Harper and Row, New York.

10. Wrigley, E. A., and Schofield, R. S. (1981). *The population history of England: 1541–1871.* Edward Arnold, London.

11. Hostetler, J. A., and Huntington, G. E. (1974). *The Hutterites in North America.* Holt, Rinehart and Winston, New York.

12. Hostetler, J. A. (1970). *Amish society.* Johns Hopkins University Press, Baltimore.

13. McGuire, M. B. (1988) *Ritual healing in suburban America.* Rutgers University Press, New Brunswick, N.J.

14. Acquaviva, S. S. (1979). *The decline of the sacred in industrial society.* Blackwell, Oxford.

15. Goffman, E. (1969). *The presentation of self in everyday life.* Penguin, Harmondsworth, England.

16. Harré, R. (1979). *Social being: a theory for social psychology.* Blackwell, Oxford.

17. Hall J. R., and Galanter, M. (1989). *Cults: Faith, healing and coercion.* Oxford University Press, New York.

PART II

Religion and the Life Cycle

4

Conception and Contraception

How do religious rules affect human action? The method we have adopted in part II to answer this question is to use a life-cycle approach. There are other possibilities, but we have found that focusing on the life cycle enables us to see the effects of religions on human behavior in the clearest possible way. We shall therefore take the various parts of the human life cycle from conception to death and at each point ask the question, "How do a person's actions become affected, channeled, or controlled by the fact that he or she belongs to a particular faith or religious group with particular beliefs and practices?"

So, to begin at the beginning, we start with conception of the individual and ask, How does membership in a religious group affect the chances of conception? Any pair of parents may have a religion and insofar as they do, this religion will provide them with information about how and when it is appropriate, correct, and moral to conceive. These rules will affect the biological chances that conception will actually occur and therefore will affect the coming into existence of a new individual.

Religions, as we have shown, establish a rapport with ordinary people by providing them with rules of how to live their lives and explanations of their more mysterious life events. One of the greatest mysteries has always been the nature of conception, and there have been all manner of speculations about how and when it takes place. The Aranda of Central Australia believed that intercourse was not enough to ensure conception; there had to be spirit involvement too. A woman walking across the semiarid desert scrubland where the Aranda lived would feel a spirit enter her body. Looking around, she would notice a certain rock nearby, and that rock would be the spirit that had entered her. This in turn would have implications for the child's name, the spiritual clan group to which it must belong at birth, and the animals which would be taboo and must not be killed or eaten by it during its life.

The idea that there is a spiritual component to human (or indeed all) life as well as a physical one is widespread. Christians very often believe that God breathes the spirit of life into the child, and children are referred to as "gifts from God." As late as the 1880s a widely read U.S. handbook on pastoral medicine written by a Catholic doctor stated, "We must maintain that the human embryo is endowed with the rational soul at the very instant of conception and that the impregnated human fetus is an individual human being.[1] This can be seen as an extension of the idea of the Virgin Birth as a necessary precondition for Christ's divinity, leading to the muddled but profound belief that all children come from God.[2] In subsequent discussions of abortion, arguments have revolved around *when* the fetus becomes an individual; for some it occurs at conception, for others later. In some religions, notably Hinduism and its offshoot Buddhism, the entering spirit is not new, but is the reincarnation of a spirit that has already been, maybe many times, on its earthly round and is doomed to continue so until it achieves its own annihilation, extinction, or nirvana.

In the fourth century some Christian writers considered that it was no longer necessary to procreate as the world was complete and ripe for its temporal end and eternal salvation. In their view procreation was not the sole or sufficient justification for marriage and the cult of virginity developed. The apocryphal Acts of Thomas exhorted newly married couples to abstain from "this filthy intercourse lest ye become pure temples and are saved from afflictions, manifest and hidden, and from the heavy care of children . . . and he shall be without care and without grief and without sorrow."[3] At best, marriage preserved from sin those who could not endure asceticism. From the sixth to the eleventh century coitus interruptus attracted little attention.[4] This was backed up by constant reference to the troubles caused women by marriage. There was no praise for large families in early sermons or on gravestones.[5]

On the other hand, Jewish religious leaders have observed the need for Jews to propagate,[6] regarding propagation as a proper natural fulfilment of the divine creative plan.[7] Medieval Jewry saw its preservation as dependent on a high birth rate,[8] so that the idea of reproduction was experienced as a moral obligation.[9]

Age of Marriage and Conception

The age at which marriages may be contracted and consummated is laid down by various religions. No age limits have been fixed for the marriage of Muslims, and quite young children may be married. A well-known example is that of Muhammad's wife Aisha, who was married to him

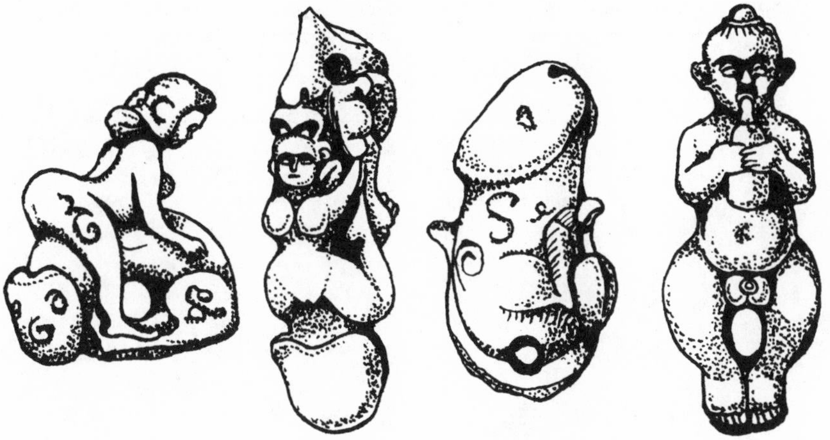

4.1. Small Buddhist fertility charms purchased in 1980 at the Rachanata temple in Bangkok. They are worn around the neck by women wishing to conceive.

when still a nine-year-old child playing with toys.[10] It is the custom not to hand over the girl to her husband until she has menstruated, rather than going by age alone. The tendency for girls to be married at the earliest possible time continued at least until the midtwentieth century to be the norm in some Muslim village communities[11] unless such marriages were precluded by other considerations.[12] Naturally, prepubertal marriage cannot produce conception, and hence the overall rate of marital conceptions will be reduced.

Hindus relate the age of the prospective bride to the age of her husband. An eight-year-old bride is regarded as suitable for a man of twenty-four years according to the Laws of Manu and even younger wives are allowed for distinguished suitors.[13] Traditional Jewish law recommended twelve years as a minimum age for the marriage of a woman and thirteen years for a man, but such minimum ages have been modified in Western countries by civil law, which in Israel for example raised the minimum age for a woman to seventeen years in 1960, while giving no minimum age for a man.

Premarital Conception and Christianity

In Christianity the minimum age acceptable for marriage has varied from time to time and place to place but has never been as low as in Muslim and Hindu countries. As a result, biological maturity precedes age of marriage and we have the phenomenon of premarital conceptions. To see whether Christianity in Britain has had any noticeable effect on restraining premarital sexual intercourse we can compare the dates of weddings

Table 4.1. Premarital Pregnancy in Seven English Parishes, 1550–1849

	1550–99		*1600–49*		*1650–99*		*1700–49*		*1750–99*		*1800–49*	
	A	*B*	*A*	*B*	*A*	*B*	*A*	*B*	*A*	*B*	*A*	*B*
Aldenham (Herts)	6	27	12	75	8	48	9	45	17	51	25	63
Colyton (Devon)	31	79	41	163	14	64	15	50	41	128	53	121
Hartland (Devon)	13	48	32	138	43	176	48	153	95	207	56	132
Easingwold (Yorks.)	0	—	5	26	4	41	8	62	32	108	11	38
Alcester (War.)	1	6	18	75	7	80	16	89	19	82	14	73
Banbury (Oxon)	10	33	23	140	8	81	43	162	73	237	0	5
Hawkshead (Lancs.)	0	—	25	116	19	95	16	70	44	97	44	95
Total	61	193	156	733	103	585	155	631	321	910	203	527
Live births less than 9 months after marriage	31.6%		21.3%		17.6%		24.6%		35.2%		38.5%	

Source: Laslett

Note: Since premarital sex is forbidden by Christianity, the table reveals the degree to which religious injunctions on intercourse were adhered to in the various periods.

A = Baptisms before 9 months. *B* = Total baptisms.

and the dates of baptisms for the first child in parish registers. In seven parishes for which records are available from 1550 to 1849 (table 4.1), premarital pregnancies, shown by baptisms recorded within nine months of marriage, fell during the sixteenth and seventeenth centuries but rose again during the eighteenth and nineteenth.[14] This can be seen from the percentage figures in the bottom line of table 4.1, and in the right-hand columns for births and baptisms in table 4.2.

A further study concluded that more than one sixth of all brides in English rural and semirural parishes between the late sixteenth and early nineteenth centuries were pregnant at marriage. Further, the proportion of pregnant brides increased after 1700 (table 4.2).

It was during the seventeenth century that the influence of the new, more puritanical form of Christianity appears to have brought down the premarital pregnancy rate substantially (fig. 4.2). It is only then that it can be postulated that religion had much effect on restraining premarital sexual intercourse and thus the level of conception.

Data from other areas show quite different patterns. In a Swiss valley with a strong Catholic tradition dictating premarital chastity for both men and women despite long engagements, there appears to have been virtually no premarital conception.[15]

By contrast, an interesting comparative study of Tippecanoe County, Indiana,[16] showed that 9.9 percent of religiously celebrated marriages and 21 percent of civil weddings were followed by the birth of a live child

Table 4.2. Births and Baptisms Registered in English Parish Records Within Nine Months of Marriage

		Births		*Baptisms*	
Period	*Area*	*No.*	*%**	*No.*	*%**
Pre–1700	South			84	15
	Central	85	27	158	16
	North			116	30
Post–1700	South	176	47	141	38
	Central	135	37	299	32
	North	289	44	372	38
Total		685	41	1,170	31

Source: Hair, P.E.H. (1966). "Bridal pregnancy in rural England in earlier centuries." *Population Studies,* 20, 233–43.

Note: Note the increased proportion of pregnant brides after 1700.

* = Percentage of all births and baptisms recorded in parish records.

within seven calendar months of the marriage, unlike premarital conception rates in the strongly Mormon state of Utah, where religion is a motivating force in the lives of many people and premarital sexual intercourse is regarded by them as an extremely grievous sin. In Indiana, where chastity norms are prescribed by a variety of denominations but less often observed in practice, and in Denmark, which has a long tradition of sexual intercourse during the engagement going back several centuries despite the Lutheran church's efforts to establish a chastity code, the situation is very different. The data in table 4.3a show the lowest incidence of

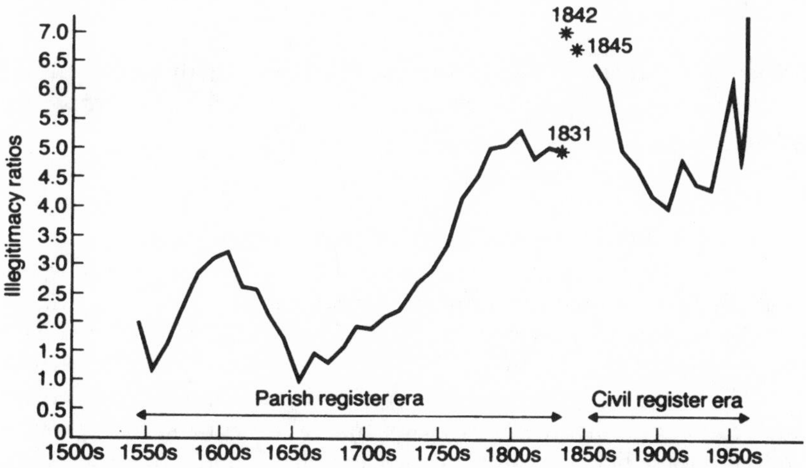

4.2. Illegitimacy ratios in England, 1540s to 1960s. Note the sharp decrease during the Cromwellian era. (Laslett).

Table 4.3a. Comparative Rates of Premarital Conception in Areas with Different Religious Proscriptions on Premarital Intercourse

	U.S.		*Denmark*	
Indices	*Utah County, Utah*	*Tippecanoe County, Indiana*	*City of Copenhagen*	*Entire Country*
I. Illegitimacy rate	0.9	2.9	11.2	6.6
II. Premarital conception rates				
(a) Child born within first six months of marriage	9.0	9.7	24.2	32.9
(b) Child born within first nine months of marriage	30.9	23.9	30.5	44.3

Source: Christensen

Note: The data conform to expectations.

Table 4.3b. Type of Marital Ceremony Chosen by Those with Premarital Pregnancy

Type of Ceremony	*Utah County, Utah* %	*Tippecanoe County, Indiana* %	*Copenhagen, Denmark* %
Civil	16.6	21.0	37.0
Religious	1.1	9.9	13.5

Source: Christensen

premarital pregnancy to have been in Utah. In all three places, a far higher proportion of premarital pregnancy occurred among those who had civil as against religious weddings (table 4.3b).

Obligation to Have Marital Intercourse

Most religions, certainly the major ones, require or have in the past required a husband to have intercourse with his wife. The Laws of Manu state of Hindus that "reprehensible is the husband who approaches not his wife in due season." Jewish law[17] stated that the wife could not be deprived of her rights to coitus except by her consent and that it was forbidden to force her. Roman Catholic canon law[18] stated that each spouse was bound to render marital dues to the other. The Koran states, "Your women are to you as cultivated land; come then to your cultivated land as

4.3. In this scene at a Buddhist fertility shrine in Bangkok, a woman is praying that she will conceive. In front of her are a number of small spirit shrines and red tin penises. (Knodel, J., and Chayovan, N. [1990]. "Contraceptive initiation patterns in Thailand." *Population Studies,* 44, 257–71.)

ye wish" (Sura 3.223). Buddhism is less verbally specific but can be seen in other ways to favor marital intercourse and the production of children. For example, young Thai Buddhist wives pray for fertility in front of a spirit shrine surrounded by large tin penises (fig. 4.3). The concern for fertility was sufficiently strong in nineteenth-century Japan for itinerant Buddhist monks to be fully occupied in carrying portable fertility shrines around the countryside on their backs (fig. 4.4). Finally, we know that Australian wives visited sacred sites to perform certain fertility rituals.[19]

The Timing of Sexual Intercourse

Religions do not only concern themselves with explaining how and why conception takes place but have rules that affect, positively or negatively,

4.4. An itinerant Buddhist monk in nineteenth-century Japan with a portable fertility shrine on his back.

the chances that conception will occur. One of the most important ways in which religions can affect the fertility of sexual intercourse is by making statements about times at which sexual intercourse is preferred and times at which it is forbidden.

Biologically ovulation occurs around the midpoint between two successive menstruations. In order for a mating to be fertile, the sperm needs to meet the egg after its emergence from the ovary during its passage down the fallopian tube. In order for a mating to be fertile, the sperm has to be present in the fallopian tube between the tenth and the fifteenth days of the menstrual cycle. Only if it is present at that time can fertilization take place and the subsequent process of implantation and embryonic development follow.

These biological facts have never been precisely understood by those who, in bygone ages, formulated religious rules pertaining to times of sexual intercourse. However, ordinary observation is enough to show that certain times in the menstrual cycle are more fertile than others. Thus without understanding the detailed biology of reproduction, religions have in fact been able to produce rules relating to the preferred times for fertile reproduction and for "safe" periods.

If a religion has a rule that sexual intercourse must occur during the period in which we know that matings are likely to be fertile, then this religion is clearly promoting reproduction. Correspondingly if a religion has a rule that matings should not occur during that period, then this religion is decreasing the chances of reproduction. In fact, many religions seem to encourage sexual intercourse in the fertile period by forbidding or restricting it during menstruation.

The Jewish code forbids coitus for seven days after the cessation of the menstrual flow and for a short period before to create a minimum total period of monthly abstinence of twelve days.[20] Intercourse at the end of this period of abstinence is regarded by orthodox Jews as a religious obligation.[21] Since this period lasts a minimum of eleven days, it is likely to be followed by increased coital activity with potentially enhancing effects.[22] The Muhammadan taboo on coitus is limited to the period of the menstrual flow, and this must be followed by a ritual cleansing (Koran, Sura 2.222). The traditional Roman Catholic view has been that there is no official objection to coitus during menstruation. Hindus state that the four days after the appearance of the menses are unfit for intercourse, as are the eleventh and thirteenth days.[23]

By directing intercourse away from the menstrual period religions are concentrating it around the fertile period and thus promoting the likelihood of conception. However, once a child has been born, religions often *restrict* intercourse until it is well established, perhaps because the birth of another child too soon after the first will reduce the milk (and maternal energy) available to the first, thus increasing the chances of its becoming sick or dying.

There are Islamic taboos on intercourse while the mother is nursing, and the Koran (Sura 2.233) lays down that children should be nursed for two full years. The Jews in the first centuries A.D. obliged the husband to practice coitus interruptus during the entire period of nursing.[24]

Further restrictions on intercourse relate to religious festivals wherein sexual activity is prohibited. During the Middle Ages, devout Christians were forbidden intercourse for three forty-day periods in the year, on Saturdays and Sundays, and on major feast days as well as for three days before taking Communion, so for such people marital intercourse was only possible on some 160 days in the year.[25] Restriction on Sunday intercourse was probably widespread to a much later date,[26] and in relation to the taking of Communion it was still present recently.[27] Lent is still a period in which no religious weddings are celebrated and in which there is abstinence from marital relations among the devout; there is traditionally self-denial of various kinds during Lent among both Protestants and Catholics in Europe, and the timing of births has been related to this religious event.[28]

There are no such restrictions during the Muslim holy month of Ramadhan, when men are encouraged to have intercourse with their wives at night (Koran, Sura 2.183) as a comfort from their daytime fasting. Hindus, however, have been said to avoid coitus during some religious festivals and fast days as well as on new and full moon days, the eleventh day after the full moon, and often specific days of the week such as Saturday, Sunday, and Monday. Restrictions have also been reported for days when the husband shaves and has a bath, days of sowing in the fields, and days of solar and lunar eclipses. A devout couple would avoid intercourse on as many as 120 days in the year besides observing any restriction imposed by menstruation.[29]

Failure to Conceive

Failure to conceive by a wife is a very serious matter in many Third World cultures, and religions have rules to deal with this. Very often a sterile wife incurs shame and ignominy; she is thought to be a victim of evil spirits or ancestral malevolence or to have committed a sin for which she is being punished. In Judaism and Islam she can be divorced on grounds of infertility. In Hinduism and Islam, another wife may be taken. Hinduism also allows for a barren wife to be superseded after eight years of marriage, as well as one whose children have died after ten years and one who bears only daughters after eleven years (Laws of Manu IX, 8). However, it may be that the wife is fertile and her husband infertile. In such cases, in Hinduism, he cannot be divorced (Laws of Manu IX, 70).

Traditional Judaism allows arrangements to be made for the annulment of a marriage which cannot be consummated. This is also the case in traditional Christianity, which in addition allows for the annulment of a marriage in which either partner refuses intercourse or is newly incapacitated from having marital intercourse by some condition. More importantly, traditional Judaism can invoke the "levirate," which requires a marriage between the widow whose husband has died without offspring and the brother of the deceased, or the giving of a formal release by his family so that she can remarry.[30] All these measures would tend to increase the likelihood of conception.

Subsequent Conceptions

We would expect logically that religious rules concerned with promoting fertility would favor intercourse for newly married women, whereas there might be rules which tended to restrict intercourse in the case of women who had already had a certain number of children or perhaps in the case of those women who had just given birth to a child. Such rules would make good sense because even though, on the one hand, it is important for reproduction to occur, on the other hand an excessive number of births lessens the chances of survival of offspring already born. However, we have not found explicit rules to restrict intercourse by women who already have a number of children, although even among some of the most intensely religious Amish, who are enjoined to have as many children as God provides, some sort of restriction tacitly occurs.[31]

By what other means then have religions devised rules to slow the overproduction of children? Islam states clearly that children should be nursed for two full years (Koran, Sura 2.233), and recent historical data have shown that ordinary Muslims (and also Hindus) in Pakistan and India nursed continuously for an average of twenty-one months[32] and indeed may still do so. There is little contemporary evidence for any Western association between Christian values and prolonged nursing.

Christian Pressure for the Use of Wet Nurses

However, in seventeenth-century France it was generally held that sexual relations could "corrupt the milk of the nursing mother, reduce the supply and even make it disappear if she had the misfortune to conceive again."[33] Some non-Christian societies (e.g., Muslims) have overcome the restrictions on a husband's sexual relations while the mother is nursing by allowing the husband to marry more than one wife. As stated, the Jews in the first centuries A.D. obliged the husband to practice coitus interruptus during the entire period of nursing.[34] The seventeenth-century Christian church for doctrinal reasons was unable to accept coitus interruptus as a solution, let along authorize the husband to have intercourse with other women, and it found a convenient solution to the husband's sexual needs by encouraging the practice of "putting babies out to nurse," thus permitting the resumption of sexual relations.

Biologically, nursing the child can hold back ovulation and hence the conception of another child. Data from seventeenth-century France show that women who put their children out to nurse had higher fertility rates than those who did not (table 4.4). Also, the interval between births was shorter for those whose nursing was terminated by the death of their children than those whose children survived (table 4.5).

It also seems likely, to complicate matters further, that the practice of wet-nursing increased or even doubled the infant mortality rate among urban families.[35] The church gave support for this practice, advising that "the wife should, if she can, put her children out to nurse, in order to provide for the frailty of her husband by paying the conjugal due, for fear that he may lapse into some sin against conjugal purity."[36]

Thus, in biological terms, two contrary effects resulted from the implementation of the church's moral rulings. First, because, presumably, the environment of the wet nurse was less favorable than the home environment (as has been reported more recently for Uganda and Jamaica), infant mortality was increased; and second, there was an increase in fertility caused by the earlier resumption of ovulation and sexual relations.

Table 4.4. Average Number of Births per Annum for Married Women, Depending on Whether or Not They Put Their Children Out to Nurse

	Women's Age Groups (yrs)						
	15–19	*20–24*	*25–29*	*30–34*	*35–39*	*40–44*	*45–49*
Not putting children out to nurse	0.429	0.530	0.490	0.421	0.300	0.132	0.016
Putting children out to nurse	0.545	0.589	0.603	0.501	0.417	0.116	0.023

Source: Lachiver, M., Dupaquier, J. (1969). "Breast Feeding and Fertility." ***Annales: Economie, Société, Civilisation,*** p. 1399.

Note: Note the higher fertility level of the women putting their children out to nurse.

In Islamic cultures breast-feeding wives tend not to engage in sexual intercourse with their husbands until their children have been weaned. The net effect of this sexual avoidance has been to increase the coital rate of other wives in polygynous households.[37] Does polygyny increase fertility? Islam has always allowed and encouraged polygyny. The Islamic origin of plurality of wives came after the battle of Badr (A.D. 624) in which a few of the limited number of existing Muslim males died. These men and their wives had left their families in order to follow Muhammad to Mecca. They had changed their religion and, as a result, the widows

Table 4.5. Fertility by Type of Marriage and Age Among Ngwa Igbo Women, Nigeria, 1974

	Age-Specific Fertility Rates per 1,000 Women		*Mean Live Births per Woman*	
Age Groups (years)	*Monogamous Wives*	*Polygynous Wives*	*Monogamous Wives*	*Polygynous Wives*
15–19	93.5	69.8	0.198	0.128
20–24	331.4	246.3	1.442	0.902
25–29	363.4	270.0	2.954	1.986
30–34	364.0	257.8	5.239	2.773
35–39	273.7	149.1	6.947	5.579
40–44	181.8	158.3	6.642	5.292
45–49	82.6	26.8	7.716	5.741

Source: Ukaegbu

Note: The lower fertility rates for polygynous wives can be explained by the ease with which males can divorce their polygynous wives under Islamic law. The women therefore spend less of their fertile lives in a sexual union.

Table 4.6. Births, Birth Rates, and Total Fertility for Israeli Jews and Moslems (per 1,000 females)

	Jews			*Muslims*		
	Births	*Birth Rates*	*Total Fertility*	*Births*	*Birth Rates*	*Total Fertility*
1950–54	42.0	31.0	3.88	—	—	—
1955–59	43.6	25.6	3.56	6.7	46.3	8.17
1960–64	45.7	22.5	3.39	9.3	51.7	9.23
1965–69	53.3	22.5	3.36	11.8	51.0	9.22
1970–74	65.7	24.3	3.28	17.4	49.5	8.47
1975–79	71.9	23.6	3.00	19.4	44.5	7.25
1980–84	72.9	21.8	2.80	19.4	37.0	5.54
1985–89	74.0	20.6	2.79	21.1	34.9	4.70

Source: Encyclopedia Judaica Yearbook (1990–91). Keter, Jerusalem.

could not go home. The small community of Muslims now had to create a means of coping with a sudden problem of the large number of unattached women.[38] This, at least, is the historical basis for polygyny in Islam, and clearly it increases overall fertility where there is a shortage of men. But in terms of births per woman, polygyny has been shown to produce lower fertility[39] (table 4.5). Why should this be so?

One reason relates to age. To have multiple wives is certainly prestigious but is also expensive in the time and effort involved in negotiations and maintenance. Nowadays specific cash outlays are involved. Polygynists thus tend to be older men. This lowers fertility as a result of lower coital frequency, lower sperm count, and lower sperm mobility.[40] Nevertheless (see later discussion) Muslem communities almost everywhere have a higher fertility rate than their non-Muslim neighbors. For example, in Israel the birth rate was twenty to twenty-one per thousand females in the mid-1980s, whereas the birth rate of Moslems living in Israel averaged thirty-five per thousand females (table 4.6).

Hindu Restrictions on the Remarriage of Widows

The Hindu scriptures state (Laws of Manu IX, 94) that the bride must be considerably younger than the bridegroom, that all women must eventually marry, and that the bride must be a virgin. There is a restriction on the remarriage of widows but not of widowers, with the result that a high proportion (up to 28.8 percent) of married women become husbandless before the end of their procreative life span[41] (table 4.7).

The Laws of Manu state that a virtuous wife who remains chaste after the death of her husband reaches heaven even if she has no son (Laws of Manu V, 160). The idea that widows cannot remarry as a general rule

Table 4.7. Married and Widowed Women in India, 1961

Years of Age	*Married* (%)	*Widowed and Not Remarried* (%)
15–19	69.5	0.5
20–24	91.8	1.83
25–29	94.2	2.9
30–34	91.4	6.4
35–39	87.0	11.1
40–44	77.7	20.7
45–49	69.7	28.8

Source: Indian Ministry of Information and Broadcasting, 1964.
Note: Note the steadily higher proportion of widows.

probably derives in part from the older practice that widows of royal castes and sometimes Brahmins sacrificed themselves on their husbands' funeral pyre (suttee), a practice which was made illegal by the British in 1829.

However, this religious ban on the remarriage of widows applied less strictly to low-caste Hindus, and the majority of younger widows remarried.[42] Nevertheless, a large proportion of widows remained "socially sterile" for religious reasons. This religious restriction on the remarriage of widows has long been the object of reform in India. It was particularly abhorrent to Mahatma Gandhi, who wrote, "Widowhood imposed by religion or custom is an unbearable yoke and defiles the home by secret vice and degrades religion."[43]

Relaxation of widow remarriage rules in recent years has been associated with a declining trend in mortality so that husbands are less likely to die during their wives' reproductive lives. Remarriage of widows also decreases the demand for young girls in the marriage market. The effect of the relaxation of religiously based restrictions has probably been an increase in the conception rate in rural India; this has, however, been met by a nationwide government sponsored contraception program.

Contraception

It is probably true to say that no society has been absolutely noncontraceptive, either in its legitimate or illegitimate marital practices or in the private behavior of copulating couples.

Besides affecting the chances of conception by rules about birth spacing, frequency of intercourse, and remarriage, a potent and frequent topic of debate in some but not all religions is contraception. Christianity has the most heated debates of all, and this is no doubt because it is the religion most closely associated with the developed modern world in which contraceptives are affordable by all. Contraceptive rules in various countries and cultures exist for mothers with young babies, unmarried teenagers, or people who are not in a social position to be able to rear offspring successfully, such as, in some societies, adult men and women who are not married to each other. What are the rules in different religions?

Much Hindu teaching is strongly pro-natalist. The begetting of a son has always been regarded as a primary religious duty (Laws of Manu II, 28) and ensures the salvation of the father (Laws of Manu IX, 137–38). Hinduism has no explicit teachings on contraception and no centralized institutions through which to make such declarations. However, the rules imply that Hindus should not practice contraception until a son has been born *and prospered*.

Buddhism is as quiet about contraception as it is about the whole question of marriage. An inquiry among Sinhalese Buddhist monks[44] showed that those who were well educated found no inconsistency between Buddhist ideology and contraceptive practices and, indeed, did not view the issue as a matter of intense religious concern. However, less well educated priests in village monasteries were in almost complete agreement that contraception was wrong according to Buddhist teachings on the grounds that prevention of birth was tantamount to killing, but their conviction was not strongly expressed. A further aspect of Buddhist anticontraception belief is that a prevented potential birth is the prevention of a rebirth, the working out of a dead person's religious destiny, and should not be interfered with.[45]

A more recent study in Thailand[46] has shown that contraceptive practice has increased from 15 to 68 percent in the last two decades, while the total fertility rate has fallen by two thirds. Northern Thai Buddhists spearheaded the use of contraception before marriage, while data for Muslim Thais show less contraceptive use than for Buddhists (see table 4.8 and fig. 4.5). Buddhists also use contraception sooner after childbirth than Moslems.

Islam has a strong procreative orientation which comes from a belief in the active providence of Allah. The number of children that should or should not be born is in Allah's dispensation (Koran, Sura 42.48–49). Certainly marriage is recommended and the unmarried are told to restrain themselves (Koran, Sura 24.32–33), while husbands are as already stated enjoined to use their wives as "land to be cultivated" (Koran, Sura 2.223). Islam has no contraceptive tradition of wide currency. Abstinence was no part of the life of the Sufi ascetics, of whom many, including Al-Ghazali, were married. A traditional view would be that any restriction of the number of potential children would show a lack of piety. Modern views, however, have supported contraception on the basis that Muhammad did not oppose coitus interruptus (this was, for example, first stated by the Mufti of Egypt in 1937).

The effects of urbanization and education on the fertility rate of Muslims as well as Christians could be seen in Lebanon before the recent

Table 4.8. Percentage of Ever-Married Thai Women Aged 15–49 Who Used Contraception Before First Pregnancy

Religiolinguistic Ethnicity	*Women Married Less Than*		*All Ever-Married Women*
	5 Years	*10 Years*	
Thai-speaking Buddhists			
Central Thai	53	42	23
Lao	30	23	11
Northern Thai	81	70	36
Southern Thai	30	24	11
Total	45	36	19
Moslems			
Thai-speakers	—	—	13
In south	(9)	14	8
Outside south	(47)	38	22
Total	23	24	13
Malay-speakers	(3)	(1)	1
Total	18	18	10

Source: Knodel and Chayovan

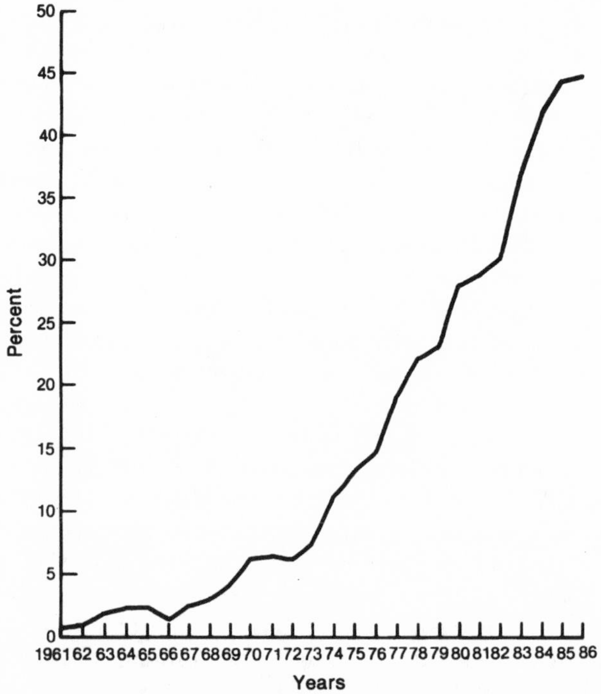

4.5. Percentage of married Thai women using contraception before pregnancy, by year of first marriage.

civil war. Among the rural (uneducated) population the Christian rate was 6.51 per ever-married couple and the Muslim rate 5.94. However, among the urban (educated) the Christian rate was 3.41 and the Muslim rate 4.68.[47]

The Christian attitude to procreation is largely unstated as the New Testament has none of the procreative directness of the Koran. It has exerted a moral force toward the stability of marriage and has heightened the importance of children as immortal souls received by their parents in sacred trust.

Christian stress on the nuclear family, the involvement of a few people in a predominantly permanent relationship, has led to an emphasis on respect for the individual personality and on affection as the most important ingredients in personal relations. Since the earliest Christians could not have had the assurance of the support of their extended families because of their conversion to a new religion, their need for intimate personal relations was intensified; personal security came from the religiously supported nuclear family and to a lesser extent the Christian community. Children came to be considered more directly important as filling out the couple's experience of a full life as well as providing them with economic support in later life; this was an important reason children were cared for and wanted.[48]

The early Christian church was ambivalent toward sexuality, increasingly stressing abstinence in relation to religious vocations while affirming the goodness of procreation within marriage and the sinfulness of "fornication." Early theologians proclaimed that nonprocreative marital intercourse, including coitus interruptus, was a form of sin against nature. Almost all sixth- to ninth-century penitentials were opposed to contraception, and some authors imposed a penance equal to that of homicide.[49]

The first codes of Roman Catholic canon law appeared in the twelfth century, and official teaching against birth control became established, prohibiting not only methods but positions for marital intercourse deemed contraceptive.[50] Aquinas classed contraception as worse than fornication, seduction, rape, incest, and sacrilege. Canonists treated contraception together with sodomy as crimes against nature.[51]

The Orthodox church still condemns nonprocreative sex but does apply its doctrines in a more flexible manner than the Roman Catholic church. The latter holds procreation to be an obligation in marriage involving "heroic" marital abstinence when there are medical, psychological, or social objections to impregnation. In general, traditional Christianity does not *actively* promote contraception because of its concern with family and children. Catholicism actively forbids it in mechanical forms, although "rhythm" methods may be used.

Catholic theology holds a fundamental premise concerning the nature of marriage. Marriage is the lawful contract between man and woman in which the primary purpose is the generation and education of offspring, and the secondary purpose is mutual help and the allaying of concupiscence. St. Augustine, who might perhaps be described as the founder of Christian moral teaching about marriage, held that any deliberate avoidance of conception made a wife into a prostitute and destroyed thereby the idea of marriage itself (*De moribus manichaeorum* II: 189n.). This approach to the relationship between men and women tends to increase fertility or maintain it at high levels, if unchecked by other ideas. The Catholic church backs up this ruling on the nature of marriage by asserting that the moral obligation of humans corresponds to the precepts of natural law, first to preserve life and second to perpetuate humankind.[52]

There is historical evidence that the Roman Catholic church has never had a marked influence on the sexual behavior of its followers. It would be implausible to conclude from the very low numbers of illegitimate births in twelfth-century French villages that an extremely long period of continence was successfully imposed on young people of the church until such time as they married.[53] In seventeenth- and eighteenth-century France the birth of the first child was closely related to the date of marriage, but subsequent births seem to have been planned to occur either after the harvest or after grape picking, depending on their parents' occupations.[54] Even the highly fertile Hutterites seem to have initiated their pregnancies during periods of lighter work loads between 1758 and 1964.[55] Perhaps it is unwise to talk of natural fertility and more useful to consider the question of quasi-rational measures of birth adjustment.[56]

Even when Catholic doctrine allows the planned limitation of marital intercourse to the supposed nonfertile period in the wife's menstrual cycle, officially it should not be indulged in for any pleasurable purpose. Any such restriction of intercourse can only be lawful under an overriding moral consideration of a medical, social, or economic nature. So this limited acceptance of a form of contraception is no way out for those Catholics who want to have sexual relations for reasons of mutual pleasure. At the same time there is nothing in Catholic moral doctrine by which the faithful have an obligation to procreate, and some moral theologians have stated that "it seems much more important to make sure that their consent (to periodic continence) is truly mutual and that they are able to practice it without serious danger to chastity or marital harmony and family welfare. . . . Married people are almost always the best judges of the reasons they may have for spacing children or limiting their family by these means."[57] This more moderate view was certainly not that of earlier Catholic moral theologians, as shown in the Encyclical *Casti Connubii* (Pius XI, 1931), which is quite clear that "every attempt on the part of the married couple during the conjugal act or during the development of its natural consequences, to deprive it of its inherent power and to hinder the procreation of a new life is immoral." Catholic doctrine does not, however, support the mere multiplication of children as the result of heedless overindulgence of married couples' sensual appetites.

Parents are expected to apply their natural rationality to the necessity of restraint.

This seems to be a "counsel of perfection," and it has undoubtedly been applied by numbers of intelligent, well-disciplined, and believing Catholics. However, canon law has always delighted in the intricacies of human relations, and it would seem that contraception was encouraged in illicit relationships, since the punishment was increased if the relationship was fertile.[58] A seventeenth-century religious text states that the "fornicating woman who, acting from repentance over the crime she has committed, moves her body away so as not to receive the male seed and not consummate the fornication which had begun" is exempt from guilt.[59] But where a culture in which Catholicism is the major religion favors a continuing and active sexuality and expects a high fertility rate, these doctrines scarcely determine the actions of any but the smallest minority, for instance in such countries as Brazil and Guatemala. Disobeying these religious rulings is seen as part of human frailty, while on the other hand any interference with its consequences is seen as a willful defiance of divine law. Such attitudes have contributed to the low success rate of most attempts to reduce the population growth of many Catholic Third World countries.

These contradictions and conflicts in Catholic doctrine on birth control reflect the fact that Roman Catholicism is a centralized faith with a unitary head, yet is at the same time practiced both in countries that remain extremely poor, for instance in much of South America, and in others that are comparatively affluent, such as Italy or Spain. In other words, a centrist dogma has to try to preach to countries and cultures on both sides of the demographic transition, that is, those practicing, for secular reasons, a high fertility regime and those who have achieved the level of affluence to be able effectively to reduce family size. No doctrine or dogma, however God-given, can hope to cover these two very different social and economic contingencies, and Catholicism, forced to decide, remains essentially backward-looking. It continues to condemn the use of any physical or chemical barrier to conception, but it allows periodic continence as contraception by the avoidance of the fertile period.

Catholics in developed countries do in fact practice contraception widely, and Catholic–non-Catholic differentials in completed family size have largely disappeared. There has for some time been a well-documented increasing trend in the United States for Catholic women to use unapproved methods of contraception (see tables 4.9 and 4.10). As table 4.9 shows, the period of most marked change was the 1960s, following Vatican II in 1963. Much of this change began among the more educated Catholics,[60] but the trend now covers Catholics at all social levels. Similar trends have been documented in European countries such as Belgium, the Netherlands, France, and Germany. In every case the decline in adherence to papal doctrine and the increased use of all kinds of contra-

Table 4.9. Percentage of U.S. White Catholic Women Aged 18 to 39 Who Have Never Used Any Method of Contraception, or Who Most Recently Used the Rhythm or Some Other Method

Most Recent Method	*1955*	*1960*	*1965*	*1970*
None	43	30	21	18
Rhythm	27	31	28	14
Other	30	38	51	68
Percentage total	100	100	100	100
Number of women	787	668	846	1,035

Source: Westoff and Ryder

ceptives have accompanied the general pattern in these countries of decreasing family size with increasing affluence. Nevertheless, church rulings do have some effect on Catholic practice since there is a continuing higher level of nonuse of mechanical contraception among U.S. Catholics than among Protestants.[61]

The end of high Catholic fertility has been signaled in a number of studies relating to Europe and the United States. It has recently been shown[62] that among non-Hispanic Catholic whites in the United States in the 1980s, Catholic total fertility rates were about one quarter of a child lower than Protestant rates (1.64 versus 1.91) (table 4.11). Their study showed later and less frequent marriage as an important determinant of the low Catholic birth rate. By contrast, Mormons and devout Protestants had high fertility rates, while those with no religious affiliation had the lowest rates of all.

However, nonuse in other parts of the world may result from other factors. Sri Lankan Catholics in their surrounding Buddhist culture prefer the "rhythm" method out of concern for the virtue of natural things.[63] The Mormons until the midtwentieth century held that birth control was

Table 4.10. Percentage of U.S. White Catholic Women Not Conforming to Church Teaching on Birth Control, by Age Group

	Age of Women				
Year of Birth	*20–24*	*25–29*	*30–34*	*35–39*	*40–44*
1916–20				28	45
1921–25			30	46	43
1926–30		37	40	52	50
1931–35	30	40	50	50	
1936–40	43	54	68		
1941–45	51	74			
1946–50	78				

Source: Westoff and Ryder

Table 4.11. Total Fertility Rates for Non-Hispanic White Women Aged 15–39 Years, by Frequency of Church Attendance, U.S., 1977–1987

	Catholic				
	All Regions	*Northeast*	*South*	*Midwest*	*West*
All	1.64	1.59	1.51	1.82	1.65
Weekly	1.69	1.58		2.10	
Less Often	1.62	1.57	1.58	1.69	1.78
	Protestant				
	All Regions	*Northeast*	*South*	*Midwest*	*West*
All	1.91	2.06	1.91	1.88	1.89
Weekly	2.24	2.58	2.00	2.31	2.43
Less Often	1.75	1.77	1.87	1.64	1.68

Source: Mosher et al.

wrong and that the only legitimate preventive was "absolute abstinence." Their birth rate up to the 1920s was eleven to twelve births per thousand higher than the national crude birth rates.[64]

Religion, Population Density, and the Control of Fertility

How do religious rules on contraception tie in with population density? How can we understand the encouraging of births by Catholicism in the slum conditions of Rio de Janeiro? Or Islam's similar indifference to the poverty of Karachi, Bandung, and Cairo, or the Hindu lack of sexual controls in Calcutta and Benares? These religious views or tendencies seem to foster high infant mortality rates and inadequate living conditions for their followers. However, it may be unreasonable to imagine that the Roman Catholic church has much influence in countries such as Brazil and Mexico, or to take its negative attitude to contraception in isolation from its equally well known views on the permanence of marriage and the virtues of chastity. These countries have taken early marriage and high fertility rates for granted for centuries. It is difficult for a centralized religious system such as Roman Catholicism to divide its moral doctrines so that it permits contraception in some areas and forbids it in others. Adjustments have to take place in other ways, for example, in age at marriage. There is also, as we have seen, a lot of variation in how individuals choose to interpret the central dogmas. As has been shown, people tend to have the number of children they think appropriate and then in one way or another cease reproduction.[65]

Thus Roman Catholic encouragement of fertility and its record in effectively influencing its members to this end have been most uneven. In some countries such as the Netherlands and Britain, Catholics have a low birth rate and in others such as Guatemala the rate is very high. If Roman

Catholicism has any influence, it is certainly obscured by economic, personal, and social influences.

In summary, we can see that the subject of conception in relation to religious rules and practices is a complex matter. Marriages may be encouraged before as well as after puberty; if the latter, one result is a greater or lesser number of premarital or extramarital or "illegitimate" conceptions, and this we see especially in Christianity. Religions that emphasize chastity and/or Puritanical forms of Christianity tend to have low rates of illegitimate conceptions despite later marriage.

Rules concerning the timing of sexual intercourse greatly affect conception rates. If religions ban sex during periods of menstruation, they increase the likelihood of conception. In the past, sexual intercourse was banned during periods of austerity, as during Lent in Christianity. Hinduism too has periods of abstinence. Muslims, however, do not forbid sex during their religious festivals.

Hindus and Muslims restrict the chances of rapid reconception after a birth by rules emphasizing prolonged nursing. The Christian invention of "putting babies out to nurse" in the seventeenth century increased the female fertility rate and reduced the interchild interval, but at the same time seems to have been associated with increased child mortality.

Remarriage rules occur in Judaism and Christianity, in cases where the marriage is not consummated. Judaism also has special arrangements for the remarriage of widows. Hinduism is strongly pro-natalist for younger wives but traditionally has not allowed the remarriage of widows. Recent opposition to this, however, together with lower mortality rates in all age groups, increases the likely conception rate.

Contraceptive rules vary both between and within religions. Hinduism is pro-natalist for sons, and therefore must be anticontraceptive in the early stages of marriage. Buddhism is anticontraceptive to the extent that this is believed to interfere with the rebirth of human souls in their progressive reincarnations. Islam is traditionally pro-natalist but coitus interruptus was never tabooed and may be practiced whenever this is felt to be appropriate. Mainstream Christianity is emphatic on the virtues of limited reproduction and tends to lay emphasis on the need for interparental love as expressed in sexual activity; where it opposes contraception, this is because the practice divorces sex from its true purpose. This is most clearly seen in the continued Catholic taboo on mechanical means of contraception, but there is no taboo on the rhythm method. Nevertheless, sex is not for pleasure as such, and people wishing to restrict their family size should, if devoutly Catholic, refrain from sex. At the present, however, we have noted evidence that Catholics, and doubtless all other Christian denominations, are less and less influenced by centralized dogmas and are tending to act in breach of these. We conclude that religious rules have to be viewed very much in their secular contexts and not given too much weight in determining actual outcomes in the matter of sexual activity and consequent conception rates.

In the next chapter we move on from the first stage of the life cycle, conception, to the next, pregnancy, and discuss first of all the issue of life or death for the *conceptus*, for before birth itself is allowed to happen people the world over have considered, and still consider, whether they want the baby or not. And religions have an important part to play in determining both the decision and the outcome. Many births are, of course, wanted and a cause for rejoicing. But if a birth is not wanted and yet it is allowed to happen, there is still time to act; infanticide was common in the past and is still frequently practiced outside Western cultures at the present time, illegal though it may be. Religious rules may forbid it or may govern the circumstances in which it is permitted. Finally there are life-and-death decisions to be made where the mother's life is at risk, and we shall also look at these.

Notes

1. Cappellmann, C. F. N. (1882). *Pastoral medicine.* In Kelly, D. F. (1979). *Emergence of Roman Catholic Medical Ethics in North America.* Pustet, New York, p. 12.

2. Warner, M. (1976). *Alone of all her sex: The myth and cult of the Virgin Mary.* Weidenfeld and Nicolson, London, p. 24.

3. Klijn, A. F. J. (1962). *The Apocryphal Acts of Thomas.* Leiden, p. 71.

4. Flandrin, J.-L. (1969). "Contraception, marriage and sexual relations in the Christian West." *Annales: Economie, Société, Civilisation*, 1370–90, p. 29.

5. Patlagean, E. (1969). "Birth control in the early Byzantine empire." *Annales: Economie, Société, Civilisation*, 1353–69.

6. Dorff, E. N. (1986). "The Jewish tradition." in Numbers, R. L., and Amundsen, D. W. (eds). *Caring and curing: health and medicine in the Western religious tradition.* Macmillan, New York, p. 29.

7. Zahavy, Z. (1960). "Birth control is ungodly." *Jewish Digest*, June, 53.

8. Gordis, R. (1955). *Judaism for the modern age.* Farrar, Straus and Cudahy, New York, p. 253.

9. Simons, J. (1986). "Culture, economy and reproduction." In Coleman, D., and Schofield, R. (eds). *The state of population theory.* Blackwell, Oxford.

10. Glubb, J. B. (1970). *The life and times of Muhammad.* History Book Club, London.

11. Monteil, V. (1952). *Revue des Études Islamiques.* 20, 37–48.

12. Levy, R. (1969). *The social structure of Islam*, Cambridge University Press, London.

13. Philippe, P. (1974). "Amenorrhea, intrauterine mortality and parental consanguinity in an isolated French-Canadian population." *Human Biology*, 46, 405–24.

14. Laslett, P. (1977). *Family life and illicit love in earlier generations.* Cambridge University Press, Cambridge.

15. Friedl, J., and Ellis, W. S. (1976). "Celibacy, late marriage and potential mates in a Swiss isolate." *Human Biology*, 48, 23–25.

16. Christensen, H. T. (1960). "Cultural relativism and premartial sex norms." *American Sociological Review*, 25, 31–39.

17. Ganzfried, S. (1928). *The code of Jewish law*. Star Hebrew Book, New York.

18. Arregui, G. M. (1927). *Summarium theologiae moralis ad recentum codicem iuris canonici accomodatum*. El Mensajero del Corazon de Jesus, Bilbao.

19. Kaberry, P. M. (1939). *Aboriginal woman, sacred and profane*. Routledge, London. Berndt, R. M., and Berndt, C. H. (1964). *The world of the first Australians*. Angus and Robertson, London.

20. Lev. 18:19, 20:18.

21. James, W. H. (1986). "Dizygotic twinning, cycle day of insemination and erotic potential of Orthodox Jews." *American J Human Genetics*, 39(2), 542–44.

22. Gardin, S. K. (1988). "The laws of Taharat Hamishpacha: Potential effects on fertility." *J Biosocial Science*, 20(1), 9–17.

23. Chandrasekaran, C. (1952). "The cultual component of sexual abstinence in Indian life." Proceedings of the Third International Conference on Planned Parenthood, pp. 73–79. Delhi.

24. Noonan, J. T. (1966). *Contraception: A history of its treatment by Catholic theologians and canonists*. Harvard University Press, Cambridge, pp. 69–70.

25. Bieler, L. (ed). (1963). *The Irish Penitentials*. Dublin Institute for Advanced Studies, Dublin.

26. May, G. (1931). *Social controls of sex expression*. Morrow, New York.

27. Puzo, M. (1972). *The godfather*. Book Club, London.

28. Nurge, E. (1970). "Birthrate and work-load." *American Anthropologist*, 72, 1434–39.

29. Chandrasekaran, C. (1952). "The cultural component of sexual abstinence in Indian life." Proceedings of the Third International Conference on Planned Parenthood, pp. 73–79. Delhi.

30. *Encyclopaedia Judaica* (1971). Vol. II. Keter, Jerusalem, pp. 122–31.

31. Resseguie, L. J. (1974). "Pregnancy wastage and age of mother among the Amish." *Human Biology*, 46, 633–39.

32. Potter, R. G., et al. (1964). "Application of field studies to research on the physiology of human reproduction: Lactation and its effects upon birth intervals in eleven Punjab villages, India." Symposium on Research Issues in Public Health and Population Change. University of Pittsburgh, Pennsylvania.

33. Flandrin, J.-L. (1979). *Families in former times: Kinship, household and sexuality*. Cambridge University Press, Cambridge.

34. Noonan, J. T. (1966). *Contraception: A history of its treatment by Catholic theologians and canonists*. Harvard University Press, Cambridge.

35. Bardet, J.-P. (1973). "Enfants abandonnés et enfants assistés à Rouen dans la seconde moitié du XVIIIe siècle." In *Hommage à Marcel Reinhard*. Societé de démographie historique, Paris.

36. Fromageau, G. (1733). *Dictionnaire des cas de conscience*. Paris.

37. Dorjahn, V. R. (1958). "Fertility, polygyny and their interrelations in Temne society." *American Anthropologist*, 60, 838–60.

38. Watt, W. M. (1968). *Muhammad at Medina*. Oxford University Press, Oxford.

39. Ukaegbu, A. O. (1977). "Fertility of women in polygynous unions in rural eastern Nigeria." *J Marriage and the Family*, 39, 397–404.

40. Davidson, J. (1948). "Protestant missions and marriage in the Belgian Congo." *Africa*, 18, 120–28.

41. *Annual Statistics*. (1964). Government of India. New Delhi.

42. Dandekar, K. (1959). *Demographic survey of six rural communities*. Gokhale Institute of Politics and Economics, Asia Publishing House. Bombay.

43. Gandhi, M. K. (1922–24). *Young India*. Ganesen, Madras.

44. Ryan, B. (1953). "Hinayana Buddhism and family planning in Ceylon." Paper presented at Milbank Memorial Fund Conference. New York.

45. Ling, T. O. (1969). "Buddhist factors in population growth and control: A survey based on Thailand and Ceylon." *Population Studies*, 23, 53–60.

46. Knodel, J., and Chayovan, N. (1990). "Contraception initiation patterns in Thailand." *Population Studies*, 44, 257–71.

47. Hawthorn, G. (1970). *The sociology of fertility*. Collier-Macmillan, London, p. 99.

48. Lorimer, F. (1954). *Culture and human fertility*. UNESCO, Paris, pp. 189–91.

49. Noonan, J. T. (1966). *Contraception: A history of its treatment by Catholic theologians and canonists*. Harvard University Press, Cambridge, pp. 161–64.

50. Kelly, D. F. (1979). *The emergence of Roman Catholic medical ethics in North America: An historical methodological bibliographical study*. Edwin Mellen Press, New York, pp. 19, 31.

51. Noonan, J. T. (1966). *Contraception: A history of its treatment by Catholic theologians and canonists*. Harvard University Press, Cambridge, pp. 260–61.

52. Davis, H. (1946). *Moral and pastoral theology*. vol 1. Sheed and Ward, London, p. 126.

53. Braudel, F. (1990). *The identity of France*. vol 2. *People and production*. Collins, London, p. 195.

54. Arbellot, G. (1970). "Cinq paroisses du village XVIIe–XVIIIe siècle." *Etudes de démographie historique*, p. 225.

55. Surbey, M. K. (1986). "Seasonality of conception in Hutterite colonies of Europe (1758–1881) and North America (1858–1964)." *J Biosocial Science*, 18(3), 337–45.

56. Voland, E. (1989). "Differential parental investment: Some ideas on the contact area of European social history and evolutionary biology." In Standen, V., and Foley, R. (eds). *Comparative socio-ecology: The behavioural ecology of humans and other mammals*. Blackwell, Oxford, p. 394.

57. Ford, J. C., and Kelly, G. (1963). *Contemporary moral theology*. vol II. Mercier, Cork, p. 430.

58. Flandrin, J.-L. (1969). "Contraception, marriage and sexual relations in the Christian West." *Annales: Economie, Société Civilisation*, 1370–90. p. 29.

59. Sanchez, T. (1607). *De sancto matrimonii sacramento*. Book 9, dispute 19, question 7. Antwerp.

60. Westoff, C. F., and Ryder, N. B. (1977). *The contraceptive revolution*. Princeton University Press, Princeton.

61. Mosher, W. D., and Goldscheider, C. (1984). "Contraceptive patterns of religious and racial groups in the United States, 1955–76: Convergence and distinctiveness." *Studies Family Planning*, 15(3), 101–11.

62. Mosher, W. D., Williams L. B., and Johnson, D. P. (1992). "Religion and fertility in the United States: New patterns." *Demography*, 29(2), 199–214.

63. Laing, J. E. (1987). "Periodic abstinence in the Philippines: New findings from a national survey." *Studies Family Planning*, 18(1), 32–41.

64. Bush, L. E. (1986). "The Mormon tradition," In Numbers, R. L. and Amundsen, D. W. (eds). *Caring and curing: Health and medicine in the Western religious tradition*. Macmillan, New York, p. 412.

65. Davis, K. (1967). "Population policy: Will current programs succeed?" *Science*, 158, 730–39.

5

Infanticide and Abortion

In chapter 4 we looked at religious rules and attitudes to conception and contraception and tried to interpret them in terms of whether the societies concerned had gone through the period of fertility transition or not. Here we turn to infanticide and abortion. Conception has now occurred and a new life has begun. Life is regarded in all societies as a precious commodity—often the most precious. Many cultural rules are concerned with the preservation of human life. There are additionally, at the start of life when the infant is helpless, strong biological mechanisms by which most mammals, especially primates, protect and nurture their infants. The mother–infant relationship is based on a set of powerful biological patterns of behavior which normally ensure that the infant does not starve or get lost or injured. Not only mothers but other females and also males show protective responses to infants in animal societies.

It is against this background that we now consider the following questions: Why do rules permitting or even exhorting infanticide and abortion in human societies exist? The simplest, "armchair" answer would be that humans plan their families according to their needs and resources. This uses a "rational" model of man: He takes nature into his own hands rather than being subject to natural forces. Is there in fact a positive relationship between the purposeful destruction of new viable human life and the survival of those already in existence, or of future children, planned but as yet not conceived? What are the rules and how does religion in particular make them effective? We begin by looking at some pretransition societies.

Infanticide in Small-Scale Hunting and Gathering Societies

There is some evidence from small hunting and gathering communities to indicate that people only keep the children they can rear without damaging their own survival. The Australian Aborigines have a record of widespread infanticide, and moreover they have on occasions articulated reasons for their practices: "Me bin keepem one boy and one girl, no good keepem mob, him too much wantem tuckout"[1] and "too much young fellow, no good two fellow pickaninny."[2] The Aborigine belief in reincarnation, according to Malinowski (presenting the data of others who wrote earlier than he), served as an excuse for the practice of infanticide.[3] For these nomadic people, living often in very uncertain conditions, a mother could only carry a single child and would kill or arrange to have killed any subsequent children until the first one was able to fend for itself. There is plentiful evidence of the extent of this practice.[4] In Aborigine society there did not appear to be any distinction between male and female babies as regards infanticide. It is a matter of birth spacing and the main consideration is the effect on the mother's mobility.

Even after a period of relative security, the possibility of famine and enforced long migration would make any attempt to save the life of a baby born very soon after its predecessor a danger to the more valuable life of its mother. In these circumstances infanticide is (or was) seen by the Aborigines as functionally advantageous. It even carried with it "a certain natural propriety . . . often regarded as a moral action and, to some extent, compulsory, although it is clear that it caused much sorrow at least to the mothers involved."[5]

5.1. A Japanese Buddhist–Shinto belief holds that girls born in the Year of the Horse will be difficult to marry off. Early neonatal mortality rate in 1906 and 1966, which were such years, was significantly higher for girls.

While it produced sorrow, it was at least socially sanctioned and involved no danger to the mother, who had already survived childbirth. Abortion would have been less certain to succeed and would have posed a danger to the mother. Also, abortion might terminate a pregnancy which might produce a needed child should earlier children have died by the time of this birth. These may be the factors promoting infanticide rather than abortion in the Aborigines.

Other hunting societies have also been shown to practice infanticide. Only rarely, however, do we have quantitative data. One in which we do, however, is that of the Netsilik Eskimos in the early part of this century[6] (table 5.1).

Finally, let us quote from Chagnon's study of the Yanomamö Indians of South America. A long quotation is given because of its unusual clarity and detail. The Yanomamö hunt and gather food and, in addition, they grow crops.

> As is apparent, there are more males in the Yanomamö population than females. This demographic fact results from the practice of selectively killing female babies: female infanticide. The Yanomamö also practice

Table 5.1. Infanticide Rates in Individual Netsilik Eskimo Women of Different Ages, c. 1920

Current Age of Mother	*Total Children Born to Her*	*Children Killed*
60	12	7 girls
45	4	0
26	3	0
65	11	4 girls
29	4	2 girls
50	10	4 girls
40	6	2 girls
30	3	2 girls
20	1	0
40	5	1 girl
60	7	1 girl
65	7	1 girl
45	11	7 girls
29	5	1 boy, 1 girl
35	7	2 girls
55	10	3 girls
26	4	1 girl, 1 boy
Totals	108	40 (= 27% of those born)

Source: Rasmussen

Note: The Netsilik were a hunting society who practiced infanticide to control population numbers.

male infanticide, but because of the preference to have a male as their first child, they unknowingly kill more females than males. The Yanomamö have only three numbers: one, two and more-than-two. They are accordingly, poor statisticians. They are quite unaware of the fact that they do kill more female babies, and every time I questioned them about it, they insisted that they killed both kinds—"more-than-two" of both kinds.

A child is killed at birth, irrespective of its sex, if the mother already has a nursing baby. They rationalize the practice by asserting that the new infant would probably die anyway, since its older sibling would drink most of the milk. They are most reluctant to jeopardize the health and safety of a nursing child by weaning it before it is three years old or so, preferring to kill the competitor instead. Kaobawä's wife, Bahimi, killed a new-born male shortly after I began my fieldwork. She later told me, quite tearfully, that it would have taken milk away from Ariwari, Kaobawä's favorite child. Ariwari at the time was over two years old, but Bahimi refused to wean him. Sometimes a child is killed simply because the mother doesn't feel that she can care for it properly and that it would be an inconvenience to have to tend a baby. I once saw a plump, well-fed, young mother eating a large quantity of food that would have been suitable to give to an older infant. Her emaciated, filthy, and nearly starved child—about two years old—kept reaching out for the food. The mother explained that the baby had gotten a bad case of diarrhea some time ago and had stopped eating. As a consequence, her milk had dried up. She refused to attempt to feed it other foods because "it did not know how to eat other foods." When I insisted that she share her food with the child, he ate it ravenously. In short, she was letting the baby die slowly of starvation. I have similar accounts from missionaries who have also witnessed cases such as this.

Male babies are preferred because they will grow up to be warriors and hunters. Most men make known their wishes to have a son—even to the point of insinuating that the wife ought to deliver a male or suffer the consequences. This is always done in a subtle way, usually by displaying signs of anger or resentment at the thought of having a daughter that constantly eats without being potentially an economic asset or guardian of the village. Many women will kill a female baby just to avoid disappointing their husbands. The Yanomamö also practice abortion in a very crude but effective way. The pregnant woman will lie on her back and have a friend jump on her belly to rupture the amnion. Sometimes abortions are effected because the woman does not want to kill the baby after it is born. In other cases a man will order his wife to abort if he suspects that somebody else conceived the child.

Several techniques are used to kill a newborn child. The most common method is to strangle it with a vine so as not to touch it physically. Another common method is to place a stick across the child's neck and stand on both ends of it until it chokes. In some cases the child is not given the stimulus to breathe and is simply abandoned. Finally, some women throw the child against a tree or on the ground and just abandon it without checking to see if it was killed by the injuries sustained. One of the New Tribes Missionaries discovered a female baby in 1964 that had

> been discarded in this fashion and brought her home with him. The baby's face was badly bruised on one side, but she survived. The missionary subsequently adopted her legally and is raising her in England.[7]

Infanticide in Pastoral Societies

A somewhat different picture appears in pastoral societies such as the pre-Islamic Arabs, who tended to kill girl children. Their own justification for this was not the hardship of transporting babies in desert conditions since they could carry young children on their camels and donkeys. In their patrilineal societies daughters married into other lineages and were lost in an economic sense to their parental families. Marriage did involve the acquisition of bride wealth in the form of livestock, and decisions to kill girl children thus involved consideration of the immediate loss of a child set against the long-term cost of rearing a girl to marriageable age. Lost too would be the social bonds she could create by the marriage she would one day make.

Whereas hunters and gatherers have little property, agnatic (patrilineal) nomads have disposable herds necessitating the survival of male relatives for inheritance; as property increases, the need for sons increases with it. The early Arabs are recorded as having a religious reverence for their patriclans in which a kinsman's blood was of great importance. All the duties of kinship were part of their religion and a clan god maintained the enduring sanctity of the clan bond.[8] Religion thus sanctioned the male-centered organization of these societies and by regarding women as second-class it also sanctioned female infanticide.

Muhammad and the Prohibition of Infanticide

The Islamic view of female infanticide is quite clear: the practice is forbidden. Muhammad made several straightforward statements that the care of daughters is a cause for glorifying Allah and referred to them in the Koran as "Allah's daughters." He accompanied this by stating in the Koran that "the female child buried alive shall be asked for what sin she was put to death" (Koran, Sura 6.141, 6.152). This has been taken by some Islamic theologians as specific disapproval of female infanticide.[9]

This change in attitude toward female infanticide enforced by Muhammad cannot obviously be explained in terms of any prospective advantages to the new Muslims from an expansion in the female population. Muhammad's institution of this change occurred before the migration to Medina in A.D. 622 and the establishment of a settled Muslim community. The First Pledge of allegiance to the Prophet from his Meccan nucleus of twelve men that they should not steal, commit fornication, nor kill their offspring[10] occurred when the future was far from clear. It was not the result of any clearly evident economic factors. It was initiated by the Prophet for other reasons and later became part of the dogma of Islam.

Muhammad himself was an orphan and possibly he was influenced by this personal experience. He knew that his own life was an act of God's providence. His father had died before he was born; if his father had died a few months earlier, the Prophet knew that he himself would not have been conceived.[11] He believed he was born fatherless by God's grace, and this shaped his thinking. Muhammad repeatedly refers to the wonder of procreation as one of the awesome signs of God—"We have created man of an extract of clay. . . . Blessed be Allah, the best of creators" (Koran, Sura 23.12–24)—so it is not surprising that he initiated this change of attitude toward a custom which was common in his day.

While no doubt he was a man who considered violence at times when it served his purpose, he also showed a consistent trait of compassion based on his own experiences as an orphan. He took part in some twenty raids or battles[12] among which was the battle of Uhud in which he was wounded. He ordered the execution of all the men of the Jewish Qurayzah clan, and of two popular singers who had presumably satirized his activities after the surrender of Mecca. And he organized the treacherous killing of some Khaybar Jews under the cover of an embassy.[13] But such behavior was less out of keeping with the times than his concern for orphans. Orphans are mentioned twenty-three times in the Koran as against some thirty times in the very much longer Old Testament and not at all in the New Testament.[14] Effective Christian concern for orphans is manifested later as a result of the church's insistence on legitimacy.

After the establishment of the Islamic community as a religious state, the avoidance of infanticide meant more mouths to feed in difficult economic circumstances. This was particularly so as the people had cut themselves off from their own lineages and clans by becoming members of the new religion and so had lost the possibility of getting food and labor and other support in the traditional ways. This was certainly a difficult period, and when the Muslims had reached the limits of their first expansion out of Arabia, the ruling class reintroduced female infanticide for a time because of the high male death rate from war and murder. This had left a surplus of high-born by unmarriageable women who could not by law be married to men from their recently conquered dominions.[15]

It is always necessary to remember that, for Muslims, Muhammad's words written down in the Koran are not merely his own, but the literal words of God, and as such have had power to modify Muslim behavior down the centuries. Though there have been times of neglect, there has also been a constant tendency for leaders to go back to "the word of Allah." Today there is no public comment on neglect of girl babies, and from this we have concluded that it no longer occurs in these societies.

This was not so in the past. Earlier data from Algeria suggested a certain degree of failure to register the births of females[16] and a similar practice in Egypt.[17]

These changes of attitude and practice can probably be interpreted best as a result of several factors. Initially, Muhammad's own ideas arose from the special circumstances of his life, in part as a reaction against the old rules of kinship. Later thinking attributed to the Prophet may have been concerned with promoting marriage and the family, and stimulating growth of the Muslim community from within, by increasing the birth rate as much as possible.

Carthaginian Sacrificial Infanticide

In the latter half of the fourth century B.C. not only were the priests at Carthage sacrificing children but these were preferentially firstborn ones. Diodorus Siculus[18] records that some nobles had substituted bought children for their own with the result that the priests, to punish them, had demanded an offering of five hundred infants of registered noble birth to be sacrificed to Baal Hammon, their chief god. Sacrifices by the aristocracy appear to have been a regular feature of their religious practices, and from archeological evidence it has been estimated[19] that 20 percent of the firstborn children of the wealthy were sacrificed.

It is known that the Carthaginians had comparatively small agricultural resources on which to base their economy and its trading expansion, and that these had been reduced by progressive soil erosion, possibly resulting in malarial undrained swamps and the decline of the timber forests which sustained their trading fleets. Other societies have killed infants as a means of population control, but in the case of Carthage it is hard to see the phenomenon purely as an effort to correct a demographic or ecological imbalance.

The Carthaginians did not just kill off "spare" children: they killed off the "best" ones. Firstborns tend to be more successful than later children. Other religions have had the idea of a jealous god that has to be placated but have sacrificed animals; not so the Carthaginians. Perhaps the reason may lie in the internal instability of Carthage. The city depended on a mercenary army and a priesthood not recruited from the nobility (in contrast to Rome and Greece), hence potentially at least at odds with the ruling class. At times of crisis the rulers may have been unable to resist outrageous demands by the priests and may have been forced to shed their very lifeblood in the supposed interest of their state, though definite evidence on this point is lacking. Nevertheless, we have to note that, whether of firstborns or others, infant killing has the same effect, and the link with reduced resources of food and timber must not be ignored.

This is not an isolated example of sacrifice of firstborns. The Nayars of southern India were reported at one time to have sacrificed their firstborn sons to the goddess of smallpox.[20] Extreme measures doubtless arise from economic, political, or social crises, and religions can act as intermediary agencies formalizing the necessary unpalatable action. In certain conditions the increase in birth spacing and decrease in family size resulting from these measures could make sense, and these events have been associated with rather abrupt changes—for the worse—in ecological circumstances.

Infanticide and Religiously Supported Status

Some societies have developed complicated systems of status differentiation supported by religious myths; the Hindu caste system is the most conspicuous example. Written into Hindu religious belief and practice is the caste structure: An ancient hierarchy of endogamous groups related to each other by social interdependence.

Subcaste members endeavor to better their position by arranging upcaste marriages for their daughters. It has been understood for some time that such a system can result in a surplus of women in the top part of any of these subcaste systems, and this has frequently been overcome by female infanticide[21] together with polygyny among the powerful, while the men at the lower end of a subcaste as a result tended to marry women of subcastes inferior to their own. The surplus of high-born unmarried women cannot be married to men of lower castes than they without involving their families in complicated issues of religious pollution, and there were few roles in Hindu society which unmarried women could perform.

The importance of caste in restricting marriage appears to have been particularly strong in Rajputana, resulting in large-scale infanticide of female babies, as early British administrators noted when the first censuses showed, in some cases, twice as many men as women. The 1852 census of Mysore showed, for instance, that the Thakoor caste had 10,695 male and 5,865 female children, and that out of every thousand of the Thakoor population, there were at least 42 fewer girls than boys below the age of twelve. A census for some villages in Kathiawar made in 1845 shows that the ratio of males to females was more than two to one in many cases.

The methods used were starvation, poisoning, strangling, exposure, burial alive, or drowning in milk after a prayer had been offered that they might be reborn in the form of a boy. This in itself indicates that any simple population reduction was not the object of the exercise: births *were* wanted but they had to be male. However, we should note that infanticide will always increase birth *spacing*, consequently increasing the survival prospects of existing children.

A Victorian study of Hinduism[22] showed that Bengali Brahmins had daughters who never lived with their husbands and often had annual abortions. Abortions were also induced by young widows, who were not allowed to remarry. Astrologers professed to be able to state the sex of the unborn child and abortion followed female diagnoses since the birth of a female was regarded as a misfortune.

The British administration waged a long campaign against these practices based on the Christian premise that they were no less than murder, without really understanding the Hindu preference for sons, let alone the problem for parents of trying to raise too many children. Some figures related to the government's campaign are included in table 5.2. While it took many years for these practices to be reduced so that they were at least no longer so obvious, some measures were immediately successful. A police detail quartered in one village in which there was a massive imbalance between girls and boys was apparently responsible for the survival of ten out of thirteen girls born in the next year.[23]

The Government of India Census Report for 1901 shows that the deliberate killing of female babies had been stopped by then. However, there remains the phenomenon of "benign neglect." Dubois[24] commented that "many a girl is allowed to die unattended when medical aid would be at once called in if the son were attacked." Today antenatal scanning techniques and sonograms are frequently used to determine the

Table 5.2. Consequences of the British Colonial Government's Campaign Against Female Infanticide

(a) Census figures on which the government campaign against female infanticide was based

	Children Under 10 Years	
Year	*Male*	*Female*
1834	979	394
1837	968	264
1841	1,650	826

(b) Census figures after the government campaign against female infanticide

	Persons Under 20 Years	
Year	*Male*	*Female*
1850	3,844	3,423
1851	3,901	3,598
1852	3,919	3,686

Source: Pakrasi, K. B. (1970). *Female Infanticide in India.* Editions Indian, Calcutta.

Note: Data from Kathiawar, India.

sex of unborn children with a view to abortion. In rural India female infanticide is still practiced and is generally condoned by the authorities. The reason always given is the high-cost dowry which fathers are obliged to pay on the marriage of the daughter. Sons, on the other hand, bring in wealth at marriage.

Abortion and the Human Soul

Both Hinduism and Buddhism, with their beliefs in an almost endless succession of lives, have every reason to oppose the idea of aborting a potential human being already started on another turn on the Wheel of Existence. The teachings of the Gautama Buddha state that "rebirth takes place when a father and a mother come together, and the one to be born is present."[25]

In Thailand a Buddhist who induced abortion was seen as not only impeding an individual's rebirth but also disobeying the prohibition against the taking of life.[26]

A parallel study in Sri Lanka[27] quoted a Buddhist as saying: "If a dead 'soul' wishes to be born into your family, it would be a terrible sin to prevent its birth. We will pay for such acts in our next life. Children that are to be born to you must be allowed to be born. That is how life goes on. We cannot and should not prevent this."

Both these religions have the concept of the cycle of rebirth by which humans can achieve release from suffering. To prevent a fetus from coming to term by abortion would be to interfere with this process, to injure a living creature, and thus to commit a sin for which one would in due course have to suffer in turn. However, in Buddhism there also exists an idea of divorcing oneself from sexual activities altogether, so that there was often in the past a pronounced reluctance to marry. Abortions were sometimes obtained by young Burmese girls who had conceived, in preference to a forced marriage.[28]

Ancient Greece

Infanticide and abortion were accepted in ancient Greece[29] in the fourth and fifth centuries B.C. when they were not only legitimate but even recommended. It was accepted not only in Sparta but also in Athens that weak and crippled infants were to be destroyed for the good of the state. There was also no moral objection to the destruction of the fetus for reasons of the common good.

Aristotle wrote (*Politics* vii, xvi) not only that deformed children should be disposed of but that children born to unsuitably matched parents, particularly those over age for optimum breeding and those surplus to the needs of the state, should be destroyed as well. That he was thinking within the accepted margins of contemporary religious ideas is shown by the fact that he recommended daily visits by pregnant women to the shrines of the deities controlling childbirth. In his own words:

> With regard to the choice between abandoning an infant or rearing it let it be lawful that no crippled child be reared. But since the ordinance of custom forbids the exposure of infants merely in order to reduce numbers, there must be a limit to the production of children. If contrary to these arrangements a copulation takes place and a child is conceived, abortion should be procured before the embryo has acquired life and sensation; the present of life and sensation will be the mark of division between right and wrong here.[30]

In other words, he was calling for slower reproduction but, failing that, for early abortion.

The Greek ideal of health was expressed by Plato as perfect physical and mental balance.[31] The sick, the crippled, and weaklings were inferior people and attention should only be given to them if their condition were likely to improve. If a man's condition were hopeless, or his disease incurable, the physician should not touch him. Treatment would be senseless since the goal, the restoration of health, was unattainable.[32] Thus the chronically ill Greek patient was burdened with odium as well as sickness.

The Hippocratic oath, sworn by Apollo the Physician and his students, stated that a physician would not involve himself in abortion or give a deadly drug to anyone.[33] There thus appears to be a contradiction in Greek thinking, although the oath may in fact have been composed and taken only in later times as there is no record of its being used in the pre-Christian era[34] even though Hippocrates himself lived in the fifth century B.C. It may have been a statement of desirable reforms by Orphic and Pythagorean philosopher–physicians who objected to the callousness of the Greek ideal of health.

Japan: Abortion and Astrology

What we have seen so far is, except in the case of Islam, a tolerance for infanticide in particular circumstances. Islam, the most pro-natalist faith, has not, by and large, permitted infanticide. In other cases, in particular in India, female infanticide, for economic and status reasons, continues to be widespread. Abortion has probably never been widespread in premodern societies because of the dangers involved.

With the coming of modern technology and the fertility transition, the whole situation is transformed. Slowly, abortion becomes, in the secular world, not only possible but safe and finally acceptable. At the same time, infanticide becomes a crime. Japan is known as a country in which after World War II modernization occurred more rapidly than elsewhere, perhaps because of the total breakdown of traditional ideas. Wholesale abortion for secular economic and health reasons is common in modern Japan. Yet, curiously, this is still a country in which fertility can be markedly influenced by astrological assumptions. It was widely held for instance that girls born in 1906 and 1966, both the Year of the Horse, would grow up to be bad natured and hence difficult to marry. This idea was reflected in birth statistics. In the earlier of these two years (1906) the sex ratio of officially reported births was 107.6 males to 100 females, compared with a long-constant sex ratio ranging between 104 and 105 males to 100 females.[35] While it is possible that some parents, eager to avoid the Horse stigma, "adjusted" the birth dates of their female children in that year, this difference may have been caused in part by the conscious neglect of girl babies.

In the latter year (1966) the overall birth rate dropped precipitously from an expected 18.7 per 1,000 population to an actual 13.7 per 1,000. At the same time the induced abortion rate rose from an expected 30.6 per 1,000 births to 43.1 per 1,000. Early neonatal mortality of girls (including accidents, poisoning, and violence) rose from 5.17 per 100,000 live births in 1965 to 7.78 in 1966. No such massive increase occurred in births of boys, for whom the comparable figures are 6.20 (1965) and 6.94 (1966);[36] see table 5.3a and b).

Japan, a country with Buddhism as one of its two principal religions (the other being Shintoism), became after the Second World War the most officially permissive country in the world for abortions. Indeed the custom of making offerings for the souls of aborted babies has become common. The 1952 Amendments to the 1948 Eugenic Protection Law

Table 5.3a. Induced Abortion Rates in Japan, 1965–67

	Observed	*Expected (per 1,000 births)*
1965	33.8	33.0
1966	43.1	30.6
1967	28.0	28.8

Source: Kaku

Note: In 1966, the Year of the Horse, more abortions were recorded than expected on the basis of previous data.

Table 5.3b. Early Neonatal Mortality Rates in Japan, 1965–67, as a Result of Accidents, Poisoning, and Violenc

	Boys	*Girls*	*Total (per 100,000 live births)*
1965	6.20	5.17	5.70
1966	6.94	7.78	7.34
1967	4.33	4.13	4.23

Source: Kaku

Note: Note the sharp increase in female mortality in 1966, the Year of the Horse. According to superstition, "Horse" girls grow up to be "bad-natured," and hence difficult to marry off.

authorized abortions for economic as well as health reasons. Potts et al.[37] have inferred from a comparison of the Ryukyu Islands, where abortion remained illegal, with Japan proper that the decline in fertility in mainland Japan would have resulted from illegal abortions even if it had not been legalized there.

The Buddhist attitudes to abortion in Thailand and Sri Lanka noted earlier, with their traditional concern for human life and the concept of rebirth, might, one would expect, have made themselves felt on the Japanese abortion issue. There was little evidence, however, of effective concern. In the case of Shintoism there would be few moral difficulties, as Shintoists believe that the fetus does not have a spirit until it has seen the light, so that the technique of abortion is considered to be sending "from darkness into darkness."[38] In any case, it seems that the modern Japanese have no effective religious or ethical attitudes that abortion is improper, judging by the ease with which abortion has become a regular feature of postwar life and has become institutionally legalized.[39]

The Infanticide of the Abnormal and Treatment of Twins

Not only is infanticide a crime in the affluent West, but Christian attitudes support this view, even in the case of retarded or deformed children. Their presence in contemporary industrialized society in large numbers constitutes a considerable social and economic burden on both families and the state. *Ethical abhorrence of infanticide occurs against a background of general affluence.* In the Christian West, it is particularly among the more religiously motivated that survival of an abnormal child is more easily accepted. A study in Pennsylvania[40] showed Catholic mothers more easily accepted retarded children than non-Catholics. It was concluded that this was because Catholic belief gives explicit absolution from any feeling of personal guilt by its insistence that every child is a special gift of God bestowed on the parents. Also, birth of a retarded child may be seen as a unique test of religious faith.

In less affluent societies abnormal children have been at best regarded as inauspicious, at worst as a sign of their mother's involvement with sorcery.[41] This is the case in some African societies, for example among the Sukuma of Tanzania, who seek to find out which of their ancestors is displeased enough to cause such a birth. Traditional societies are unlikely to see such a birth as a chance happening. In such cases, religious procedures exist to determine the cause of the misfortune. This can include the killing of infants born in an abnormal way, or who later develop in what is considered to be an abnormal way. The Sukuma have been recorded[42] as having killed children born by breech presentation and those who cut their upper teeth first. The South African Kgatla killed children born by breech presentation by smothering them with manure immediately after birth, as they were regarded as evil omens.[43] The Sudanese Mandari[44] killed babies born with extensively marked bodies, and in the past males born with one or no testicles were abandoned on anthills. There are numerous further examples of such practices.[45]

Twins have received special treatment in the religious practices of a wide variety of peoples[46] either because they were seen as assets or because they represented dangerous powers or forces. The Nupe of Nigeria[47] considered that twins were lucky and a sign of divine benevolence, representing a special incarnation, a concentration of the "kinship soul." There were annual sacrifices on their birthday and their homes had a twin shrine. The Mandari of the Sudan[48] welcomed twins but recognized that their delivery presented a greater danger for the mother and children than a single birth and that their life expectancy was lower. As they were seen to be signs of the "Spirit of the Above" and in a precarious position, special rituals were performed. In these cases twins received above average care throughout their lives. The sickness of one may have resulted in similar medical treatment of the other. Among the Nuer[49] they were regarded as having a single soul which survived if one of them died.

In other cases twins were regarded as dangerous. Among the Kavirondo of Kenya[50] anyone looking at young twins might be afflicted with eye disease, giving rise to prolonged avoidance and to their ritual seclusion in their mother's hut for several years during which period even the rubbish might not be removed from inside the hut. At the same time, paradoxically it would seem, their birth was a blessing of fertility which was celebrated and communicated to other people through the performance of specific rituals.

Among the Tallensi of Ghana[51] twins were not greeted with joy but they were not destroyed, nor regarded as sacred, nor was the mother subject to moral censure or ritual penalties. No woman wanted to bear twins as it was believed that twins might not be complete human beings at birth, and this view was supported by the expectation that at least one of a pair of twins would die.

In the affluent West, twins are diagnosed before birth, and so come as no surprise. Each twin is given as much care as would be lavished on a singleton, and there is no neglect or expectation that one will die. Nevertheless, few parents relish the idea of twins, and the reason is that they play havoc with the careful plans parents may have made to have, say, two or three children over a period of years, at regular intervals. Twins can cause real financial hardship, but after the perinatal period their welfare is not in doubt.

The Ancient Jews and Modern Jewish Thought

In early Talmudic times, abortion was not considered a transgression unless the fetus was viable, whereas the infanticide of a child at birth made the killer guilty of murder. Talmudic scholars held to the view that Biblical references to all kinds of harm referred to the woman and not to the fetus, basing their conclusion on the idea that murder could only be done on a live human being.

However, all abortion was subsequently prohibited when Talmudic scholars argued from the laws concerning abstention from sexual relations with one's wife. These were forbidden when they were likely to hurt the fetus, and the perpetrator was a "shedder of blood." The great Jewish writer Josephus (A.D. 38–100) stated that "the Law has commanded us to raise all children and prohibited women from aborting or destroying seed; a woman who does so shall be judged a murderess of children for she has caused a soul to be lost and the family of many to be diminished."

In matters such as the probability of a mental or physical defect of the child due to the mother's illness, or the aftereffects of use of drugs such as thalidomide, the general tendency among Jewish liberals in Christian countries such as Britain is that abortion can be justified in the interests of the mother's mental health, but much depends on the stage of the pregnancy. The liberal Jewish viewpoint extends therapeutic abortion to a wide range of circumstances, including excessive mental anguish.[52] Traditionally Israel prohibited abortion unless the mother's health was in danger, reflecting the fact that in classical rabbinic Judaism medicine was essentially prophylaxis and not therapy.[53] Today abortion is legal in Israel but as Teichman et al.[54] have shown it can be associated with considerable emotional stress. Outside Israel, Jewish women have often been the most liberal of all religious groups, largely accepting abortion as justified in a range of circumstances beyond that of the health of the mother. A recent study in Canada[55] has argued, however, that consideration needs to be taken of traditional texts in the modern situation, since these continue to influence the attitudes and behavior of orthodox community members.

Islam and Abortion

Islam, in line with its generally strong procreative orientation,[56] regards abortion as entailing the loss of a life. Thus it is not reasonable to perform it for any less pressing need than the saving of a life; such attitudes represent the continuation of the same themes which have already been described for Judaism and Christianity, and they have come out of the same cultural environment.

While Islamic jurisprudence regards the fetus as a person, there has been some divergence of opinion. The most prolific and perhaps the most famous of Islamic philosopher–theologians, Al-Ghazali, a married man who attempted to become a Sufi mystic, considered abortion at any time to be a crime that became graver and graver as the pregnancy advanced. However, most Islamic scholars have defined two phases of intrauterine existence, before and after the instillation of life, normally occurring at four months.

In Islamic law abortion is an offense punishable by the payment of compensation. The actual rules are as follows: When a man marries a woman, he "buys" the future contents of her womb. He is entitled to the equivalent of full adult compensation after four months for willful abortion. Up to four months he is entitled to one tenth of the full sum.[57] Similarly, a share of the property of a father who dies while his wife is pregnant is kept aside until his widow's pregnancy is completed so that her child can inherit. In practice perhaps only Islamic law truly regards the fetus as a human being by giving the unborn child such economic rights.

However, in Islam, as in other religions, abortion becomes more common with Western-style education. A study in Lebanon showed[58] that almost no traditionally educated Muslims had abortions but the numbers rose proportionately with Western education, and the number of Western-educated Muslims who had had abortions in the Islamic community studied actually exceeded the numbers for Western-educated Christians. Economic security, even in Islam, thus does seem to go along with a shift of beliefs and practices, and a Western-style education can be seen as a link in the chain of events by which this comes about.

The Christian Community and Abortion

Since Christianity sprang from a Judaic background, it is not surprising that it followed Judaic lines of thought. The destruction of the fetus was considered sinful from the start since Christians considered all forms of human life to be sacred. So it was ruled early that intercourse during pregnancy could be a sin partly because of the danger of causing abortion,[59] and partly because the object of coitus was to procreate and conception had already taken place. These views were generally held at least until the eighteenth century.[60] Tertullian argued that abortion was synonymous with murder because of the presence of a soul in the fetus,[61] but Augustine made a distinction between a formed and an unformed fetus.[62]

Abortion was made punishable according to canon law in the West by the Council of Elvira (c. A.D. 300) and in the East by the Council of Ancyra in A.D. 314. The canon law penalty for anyone procuring abortion, automatic excommunication, dates from the legislation of Popes Sixtus V and Gregory XIV in the late sixteenth century.

Early Christian thought also held to the Judaic view that the life of the mother had priority over that of the unborn child. Tertullian[63] wrote, "Sometimes by a cruel necessity, whilst yet in the womb, an infant is put to death when, lying in the orifice of the womb, he impedes parturition and would kill his mother if he is not to die himself . . . of the necessity of such harsh treatment I have no doubt."

The Christian attitude to abortion can be seen against the need to maintain the community's population growth, dating from the original small but expansionist Christian groups isolated in either hostile or indifferent societies. This was combined with high losses from war and disease and emigration related to missionary movements. This attitude is still held in new Christian communities in Africa and in those small, closed Christian sects in the New World, such as the Amish, the Hutterites, and the Doukhobours, and to a lesser extent the Mormons until the modern period.

Historically the African independent churches have opposed abortion. Longmore[64] described a case in which the minister of an African church was forced to resign because his daughter had procured an abortion with the help of his wife but without his knowledge. His own proven noninvolvement in his daughter's abortion was insufficient for his congregation not to demand his excommunication. Abortion would generally be regarded as wholly repugnant to African Christians of all denominations, though it is certainly resorted to, particularly in urban areas among women who cannot afford to remain pregnant.

Increasingly in the modern period the Christian, and especially the Roman Catholic, church has become the repository of a moral doctrine which is out of touch with the need for careful family planning in order to cope with life in affluent societies. In Europe, by and large, Catholic dogma is circumvented by recourse to non-Catholic clinics. In urban contexts in developing countries this may not be possible. This has meant that abortion has had to be resorted to illicitly by practicing Catholics. The situation is made worse by the Catholic ban on most forms of contraception. It has been estimated that bungled abortions accounted for more than 40 percent of female hospital admissions in Santiago, Chile, and that one third of all pregnancies ended in abortion.[65]

In the official Roman Catholic view any induced abortion is the equivalent of murder irrespective of duration of the pregnancy. This is the belief of Jehovah's Witnesses, too.[66] In contrast, many Protestant theologians have made a distinction between the period when the fetus is unable to survive independently (abortion allowed) and when the fetus could survive on its own (abortion not allowed).

In most developed countries religious opposition to the legalizing of abortion seems only to have been a delaying factor, but opposition will continue to come from vociferous pressure groups of Christians and others who form what is popularly called the "prolife" lobby.

The background to this attitude is the same as the Judaic view that a soul is lost, that it is a violation of the fundamental human right to life itself, and that the age of the fetus cannot affect matters since "it is probable that embryonic life is human from the first moment of its 'existence.'"[67]

A continuing number of surveys have shown this view to have been widely questioned. Christian conservatives are more likely than liberals to oppose abortion (fig. 5.2). Frequent church attendance has been correlated with disapproval of abortion even among nurses and social workers.[68] A study in Canada concluded that more than any other factor, a decline in religious values and beliefs would contribute to liberalized attitudes toward abortion and that socioeconomic characteristics were

5.2. A Christian antiabortion rally in the modern United States.

more important in shaping a woman's attitudes toward abortion than *situational variables*, such as accidental pregnancy, contraceptive practice, and desired or expected number of children.[69]

A study among clergymen[70] found that a more liberal attitude to abortion was correlated with a more liberal attitude to sex and women generally. Opposition to abortion is positively correlated with fundamentalism.

A study of abortion in Louisiana, in a predominantly Catholic community,[71] showed a high degree of conservatism toward abortion. A study in Northern Ireland[72] showed that Roman Catholics were less likely to have abortions than Protestants, and that for both religious communities abortion was primarily a middle-class phenomenon. Roman Catholic women, however, were more likely to be left without adequate social support during this time of great personal stress because of the hostile attitude of their church; this influenced the willingness of community members to assist them, as well as deterring them from asking for their help.

Religious and Other Dilemmas

Say "optimal" family size is two or three children but to achieve this means adopting sinful measures, what is to be the actual day-to-day practice? This kind of dilemma currently affects millions of people. Here and there, all over the world, individuals, parents, small groups, states, nations, and even world religions are considering their attitudes in the light of modern conditions. The trend in more affluent countries has been toward small family size and more permissiveness concerning abortion. Infanticide meanwhile has been condemned, and the widespread practice of adoption has provided an alternative solution to the problem of unwanted children.

We should note that the changes that have taken place, and are taking place, are doing so because of changes in ways of thinking that begin with a few breakaway individuals who provoke debates and discussion. Finally they can lead to changes in norms and laws. There may be a long period of agonizing personal choice, but times of change necessitate making choices. This is the process by which cultural change comes about where it is not the imposed result of external conquest or internal oppression. To ignore the complex interplay of choices and dilemmas is to fail to understand how existing cultural features can modify and be modified by prevailing economic and other trends. Religions have had to accommodate to new conditions to a greater extent in some places than in others. The study of abortion shows that religious attitudes may not keep pace with other aspects of culture and may have more or less success in thwarting secular ideas of "progress." To the extent that modern states combine new secular ideas with older religious ones, they present people with moral dilemmas about how to act in matters that have major economic consequences. Nowhere is this clearer than in the matter of how to decide on abortion in modern, densely populated, industrialized Christian societies. Moral dilemmas are finally resolved by changes in attitudes and actions of individuals, and these lead, over time, to changes in religious beliefs.

But let us move on now to happier events: to birth itself, and childhood up to adolescence. We shall see in the next chapter how deeply religions are involved in the arrival of a new human being, and how the infant is surrounded by religious influences. In particular, religious organizations have taken an interest in orphans and unwanted children. Following birth, children remain subject to religious influences during childhood, and in late childhood or around the time of puberty both boys and girls in different parts of the world are subject to rituals, often including circumcision or other genital mutilations, which carry deep religious significance. We shall look at these events and try, not necessarily successfully, to understand them.

Notes

1. Willshire, W. H. (1895). "On the manners, etc., of the natives of Central Australia." *J Anthropological Institute*, 24, 183–85.

2. Smyth, R. B. (1878). *The aborigines of Victoria.* Government Printer, Melbourne.

3. Malinowski, B. (1913). *The family among the Australian aborigines.* University of London Press, London.

4. Krzywicki, L. (1934). *Primitive society and its vital statistics.* Macmillan, London.

5. Fisher, R. A. (1930). *The genetical theory of natural selection.* Oxford University Press, Oxford, p. 200.

6. Rasmussen, K. (1931). "The Netsilik Eskimos." In *Report of the Fifth Thule Expedition: 1921–24.* Gyldendalske Boghandel, Copenhagen.

7. Chagnon, N. A. (1977). *Yonomamo—the fierce people.* Holt, Rinehart and Winston, New York, pp. 75–76.

8. Smith, W. R. (1901). *Lectures on the religion of the Semites.* Black, London, p. 47.

9. Watt, W. M. (1968). *Muhammad at Medina.* Oxford University Press, Oxford.

10. Is'haq, Ibn. (1955). *The life of Muhammad*, Guillaume, A. (trans.). Oxford University Press, London, p. 199.

11. Cragge, K. (1971). *The event of the Koran.* Allen and Unwin, London, p. 28.

12. Watt, W. M. (1968). *Muhammad at Medina.* Oxford University Press, Oxford.

13. Is'haq, Ibn. (1955). *The life of Muhammad*, Guillaume, A. (trans.). Oxford University Press, London.

14. Cruden, A. (1769). *A complete concordance to the Old and New Testament or a dictionary and alphabetical index to the Bible.* Warne, London.

15. Darlington, C. D. (1969). *The evolution of man and society.* Allen and Unwin, London, p. 350.

16. Breil, J. (1959). *La population en Algérie.* Imprimerie Nationale, Paris, pp. 74ff.

17. Mboria, L. (1938). *La population de l'Egypte.* Pro Caccia, Cairo.

18. Diodorus Siculus. (1946). *The library of history.* Heinemann, London, 20, 14:5–60.

19. Weyl, N. (1968). "Some possible genetic implications of Carthaginian child sacrifice." *Perspectives Biological Medicine*, 12, 69–78.

20. Sherring, M. A. (1872). *Hindu tribes and castes.* Thacker Spink, Calcutta, p. 81.

21. Dumont, L. (1970). *Homo hierarchicus: The caste system and its implications.* Weidenfeld and Nicolson, London. Dickermann, M. (1979). "Female infanticide, reproductive strategies and social stratification: A preliminary model." In Chagnon, N. A., and Irons W. (eds.). *Evolutionary biology and human social behaviour: An anthropological perspective.* Duxbury Press, Duxbury, Massachusetts.

22. Wilkins, W. J. (1975). *Modern Hinduism.* B. R. Publishing, Delhi, pp. 167–68.

23. Chevers, N. (1870). *A manual of medical jurisprudence.* Thacker Spink, Calcutta, pp. 752, 759.

24. Dubois, J. A. (1972). *Hindu manners, customs and ceremonies.* Oxford University Press, Oxford, p. 606.

25. Suriyabongse, L. (1954). "Human nature in the light of the Buddha's teachings." *J Siam Society*, 42, 11–22.

26. Hanks, J. R. (1968). "Maternity and its rituals in Bang Chan." Cornell Thailand Project Report Series. vol 6. Cornell University Press, Ithaca, New York, p. 16.

27. Ryan, B. (1953). "Hinayana Buddhism and family planning in Ceylon." Paper presented at Milbank Memorial Fund Conference. New York.

28. Nash, J., and Nash, M. (1963). "Marriage, family and population growth in Upper Burma." *South-Western J Anthropology*, 19, 251–66.

29. Monpin, R. (1918). *L'avortement provoqué dans l'antiquité.* Vigot, Paris.

30. Aristotle. (1962 ed.). *Politics.* Sinclair, T. A. (trans.). Penguin, Harmondsworth, England, pp. vii, xiv.

31. Plato. (1953). *Republic.* Heinemann, London, V.

32. Plato. (1953). *Republic.* Heinemann, London, III, p. 408.

33. Hippocrates. (1957). *Oath.* Heinemann, London, p. 299.

34. Scribonius Largus. (1887 ed.). *Compositiones Medica.* Leipzig.

35. Tak, J. van der. (1974). *Abortion, fertility and changing legislation: An international review.* Lexington Books, Lexington, Massachusetts.

36. Kaku, K. (1975). "Increased induced abortion rate in 1966: An aspect of a Japanese folk superstition." *Annals Human Biology*, 2, 111–15.

37. Potts, M., et al. (1973). *Abortion: A study in medical sociology.* Cambridge University Press, London.

38. Calderone, M. S. (1958). *Abortion in the United States.* Hoeber-Harper, New York, p. 149.

39. Goode, W. J. (1963). *World revolution and family patterns.* Free Press, New York, p. 340.

40. Zuk, G. H., et al. (1961). "Maternal acceptance of retarded children: A questionnaire study of attitudes and religious background." *Child Development*, 32, 525–40.

41. Buxton, J. (1973). *Religion and healing in Mandari.* Oxford University Press, Oxford, p. 250.

42. Cory, H. (1951). *The Ntemi: Traditional rites of a Sukuma chief in Tanganyika.* Macmillan, London.

43. Schapera, I. (1966). *Married life in an African tribe.* Faber, London, 223–25.

44. Buxton, J. (1973). *Religion and healing in Mandari.* Oxford University Press, Oxford, p. 250.

45. Krzywicki, L. (1934). *Primitive society and its vital statistics.* Macmillan, London.

46. Lagercrantz, S. (1941). "Über willkommene und unwillkommene Zwillinge in Afrika." *Ethnologiska Studier*, vol. 12–13, Gothenburg.

47. Nadel, S. F. (1954). *Nupe religion.* Routledge, London, p. 26.

48. Buxton, J. (1973). *Religion and healing in Mandari.* Oxford University Press, Oxford, pp. 144–49.

49. Evans-Pritchard, E. E. (1956). *Nuer religion.* Oxford University Press, Oxford, p. 131.

50. Wagner, G. (1949). *The Bantu of the North Kavirondo.* Oxford University Press, London, pp. 194, 325–29.

51. Fortes, M. (1949). *The web of kinship among the Tallensi.* Oxford University Press, London, p. 271.

52. Levine, R. R. (1968). "Judaism and some modern medical problems." *J Medical Society New Jersey*, 65, 638–39.

53. Wolf, A. J. (1976). "Judaism on medicine." *Yale J Biological Medicine*, 49, 385–89.

54. Teichman, Y., et al. (1993). "Emotional distress in Israeli women before and after abortion." *American J Orthopsychiatry*, 63(2), 277–88.

55. Feldman, P. (1992). "Sexuality, birth control and childbirth in orthodox Jewish tradition." *Canadian Medical Association J*, 146(1), 29–33.

56. Hathout, H. (1972). "Abortion and Islam." *J Medical Libanais*, 25, 237–39.

57. Hathout, H. (1972). "Abortion and Islam." *J Medical Libanais*, 25, 237–39.

58. Yaukey, D. (1961). *Fertility differences in a modernizing country.* Princeton University Press, Princeton, New Jersey, p. 31.

59. Clifford, J. J. (1942). "The ethics of conjugal intimacy according to St. Albert the Great." *Theological Studies*, 3, 1–26.

60. Amort, E. (1752). *Theologia moralis appendix ad tractatum de matrimonio.* Augustae Vindelicanum.

61. Tertullian. (1884 ed.). *De anima.* Clark, Edinburgh.

62. Augustine. (1847 ed.). *De Conjugiis Adulterinis: Seventeen short treatises.* Parker, Oxford.

63. Tertullian. (1884 ed.). *De anima.* Clark, Edinburgh.

64. Longmore, L. (1959). *The disposessed: A study of the sex-life of Bantu women in and around Johannesburg.* Cape, London, pp. 136–37.

65. Ehrlich, P. R., and Ehrlich, A. H. (1972). *Population, resources, environment: Issues in human biology.* Freeman, San Francisco, p. 291.

66. Cumberland, W. H. (1986). "The Jehovah's Witness tradition." In Numbers, R. L., and Amundsen, D. W. (eds). *Caring and curing: Health and medicine in the Western religious tradition.* Macmillan, New York, p. 480.

67. *New Catholic Encyclopedia.* (1967). McGraw-Hill, New York, pp. 1, 29.

68. Hertel, B., et al. (1974). "Religion and attitudes to abortion: A study of nurses and social workers." *J Scientific Study of Religion*, 13, 23–34.

69. Balakrishnan, T. R., et al. (1972). "Attitudes toward abortion of married women in metropolitan Toronto." *Social Biology*, 19, 35–42.

70. Price-Bonham, S., et al. (1975). "An analysis of clergymen's attitude toward abortion." *Rev Religious Research*, 17, 15–27.

71. Schneider, G. T. (1974). "Abortion in a predominantly Catholic community." *J Louisiana Medical Society*, 126, 323–25.

72. Compton, P. A., et al. (1985). "Family size and religious denomination in Northern Ireland." *J Biosocial Science*, 17(3), 137–45.

6

Birth and Childhood

In the preceding two chapters we looked at conception and then abortion and infanticide with respect to the role that religion played in organizing these events that affect the survival chances of individuals in the very earliest phases of the life cycle. Assuming that conception has been successful and that neither abortion nor infanticide is being practiced, we now come on to the event of birth itself and the subsequent years up to adolescence.

The new infant is of great importance to its family and the social group; this importance is generally very well understood, and in most societies the arrival of the new infant is regarded with great interest and joy. It is also a matter of great social interest to others apart from the child's family itself; it is of interest to the whole community in small-scale societies and to the widely ramifying branches of the family and its friends in larger ones. At the same time birth is a dangerous period even in advanced societies; early infancy is often the period when mortality achieves its highest levels before old age.

Life-and-Death Choices During Parturition

In any birth there may be complications during labor and there may be such difficulties that decisions have to be made whether the mother's or the infant's life is to be saved. What do religions have to say about this matter? Let us start by examining the extent to which those present at the birth, midwives or others, can legitimately interfere with the birth process by making and following through religiously sanctioned decisions about

6.1. A Christian child's prayer, accompanied by wooden angels, manufactured in the Philippines.

survival. Judaism holds that when there is a question of saving the mother or the child, the latter should be destroyed on the grounds that the more viable life receives preference if a choice has to be made.[1] In regard to abortion, the Jewish stance varies between those stating that even the aborting of a deformed fetus is tantamount to murder[2] and those who state that only after the fortieth day does the unborn fetus have the right to life.[3] Islam holds to the same view, stating "Only if conservation of the pregnancy entails a definite danger to the life of the mother is the foetus sacrificed, for the mother is the 'root' and the foetus is the 'branch.'"[4] Buddhists, too, consider that abortion is permitted when it is necessary to save the life of the mother,[5] and Hindus take the same view. The Catholic belief is that both mother and child have a right to life, neither has a better right than the other,[6] and it is morally indefensible to sacrifice the child in order to save the life of the mother, even when this sacrifice is judged to be the only means of doing so; there have been a series of decrees from the Holy Office to this effect (1884, 1889, 1895, 1898, 1902). In a late nineteenth century U.S. manual on pastoral medi-

6.2. In Italy children of Roman Catholics have silver keys hung around their necks to protect them from convulsions.

cine, it was stated that a priest had a duty to perform a cesarean section if that meant saving the life of the child once the mother had died. The same manual advised against the use of wet nurses as they were usually fallen women who replaced lazy mothers who wished to gossip at tea parties and was opposed to use of chloroform for the mother during childbirth as it was "better to educate the woman to bear the pain which will increase her love for her child."[7]

Giving Birth and Traditional Religious Influences

Religious rituals connected with childbirth and the protection of infants are known from Egypt as far back as the sixteenth century B.C., involving incantations and the use of protective amulets;[8] the former were probably used as lullabies when the child was sick or listless and thus felt to be threatened by evil forces.

In Buddhist Thailand,[9] prior to a birth, offerings were made to the family's protecting spirit and to the ancestors. The husband prepared a ceremonial gift for the midwife to ensure the use of her private magic. She might string a holy thread from which she hung magical signs around the house. Delivery should take place in a favorable astrological alignment during which the midwife says magical words.

The Hutterites use their own lay midwives in accordance with their belief in Christian communal self-sufficiency; the infant mortality rate in such cases is not significantly different from that of births delivered by physicians inside or outside the community,[10] probably because midwives detect and refer a large number of complicated pregnancies to physicians in time.

Midwifery in many cultures has technical and magicoreligious aspects corresponding, respectively, to the natural and supernatural worlds of knowledge and experience. In Thailand, Buddhists, according to Hanks,[11] believed the resources of the supernatural world are freely and easily accessible to everyone. He writes, "The closer an enterprise was to the margin of life and death, the larger the supernatural element." Thus in Thailand a professional midwife developed a large clientele as a result of success, which was thought to be a combination of her skill in physical matters and her detailed astrological knowledge, brought into play to help the delivery.

In Hinduism confinement is considered to be ritually unclean; thus it follows that the lying-in room in the past was often badly appointed, commonly a closet or an outside shed with as much air as possible excluded to prevent impurities from escaping.

Hindu midwives, since they were in contact with impurity, were of low caste; the idea of impurity together with poverty led to the use of dirty or old clothes and towels during the delivery, because such items had to be thrown away afterward. Indeed a midwife was likely to change into dirty clothes prior to delivering a child.[12] It is not surprising that

Western medical opinion of the Hindu midwife, who was often both illiterate and ignorant, was a low one; a Western observer wrote that the midwife was "dirty in habits, careless in work and often callous to suffering, bold in treatment with the courage born of gross ignorance . . . which causes untold mischief to her patients."[13]

Religious Concern for the Newborn Baby and Its Mother

In all cultures there is concern for the newborn child, and any danger or anxiety often prompts by religious rituals. The child in danger of death is quickly baptized in Christianity, not to cure it but to ensure its membership in the Christian community. Christian respect for new life is not comprehensive, however. Studies by historical demographers have shown that economic hardship can lead to rejection and neglect. For example, studies of infant and child mortality in seventeenth- to nineteenth-century Germany show that stepchildren were penalized at the expense of children born to a new marriage, and that there was a bias toward the care of daughters during periods of economic stress.[14] The newborn baby in Burma was often wrapped in a monk's orange robe as a protection against misfortune.[15]

Many cultures isolate the mother at the birth of her child as well as for a period afterward, in order to protect them from malevolent forces and to prevent them from contaminating others. In traditional Hinduism, the house in which a woman has been delivered and those in it were considered unclean for ten days, during which time they did not have contact with those outside; then the room was cleaned to purify it and all clothes used during that period were thrown away. The mother did not become completely pure until after a further ceremony of ritual purification forty days after delivery for a girl baby and thirty days for a boy; this period was shorter for lower castes.[16]

Some Muslim societies not only segregated mother and child but subjected them to constant heat as well as washing them night and morning for forty days.[17] This heating of the mother and child was also found in Hinduism, where it was specifically related to ritual uncleanness; a fire was kept burning all the time in the closed room so that there might even be a shortage of oxygen.[18] It can be seen that some of these ceremonies have positive health implications, others negative, since they either bring in hygienic elements, or prevent the mother and child from being exposed to outside infections, or bring in germs and provide them with ideal conditions of spread.

In traditional societies, the mother, child, or both are likely to have a number of potions to drink and charms to wear which are thought to be protective against known and unknown dangers (fig. 6.3). Even if the mother-to-be is taken to a Western-type maternity hospital in a developing country, it is still likely that she will be given such potions and

6.3. An Afro–Arab father and children from the East African coast. Each of them is wearing amulets containing quotations from the Koran.

amulets; even if she does not have them prior to the birth, they will be brought in by visitors at the first opportunity. In some modern African hospitals the systems of Western medicine and traditional magicoreligious practices often run parallel, so that they are combining with or even competing with each other. After a birth the traditional system is most likely to get the credit for success from the family, as well as the mother herself, because they understand the purpose and the means of the traditional procedures best. Even in the maternity ward of a modern European hospital the new baby is occasionally still given a crucifix to wear, both as a lucky charm and as a Christian symbol.

There are interesting parallels between the ostensible indifference of contemporary Western society to directly employed "magical" protection and the attitude of the Mbuti pygmies of Zaire, who show similar indifference; neither feel much need for special ritual protection of infants and both are concerned very much with the present rather than the future as regards physical health. Among the Mbuti "there is no apparent concern for any supernatural dangers and no precautionary steps taken."[19] Perhaps life in communities which are constantly changing membership, as happens to greater or lesser extent among nomadic pygmies and in the West, is associated with the absence of the prolonged magicoreligious rituals which are so often found when the child will be a member of a ramifying and deeply entrenched local kinship system.

The Concept of Illegitimacy and Infant Mortality

The principle of legitimacy in any society creates a social bond between the child and the rest of society through its family or clan. The rules of legitimacy are written into most religious rule systems and wherever they are strongly enforced, those who violate them, as well as their illegitimate children, suffer punishment.

Hindu Indian society has such strong concepts of legitimacy that the Laws of Manu contain no reference to illegitimacy even as a possibility to be punished by legislation. Enormous social difficulties ensue if there are such occurrences in the higher castes, where neither premarital sexual relations nor adultery is tolerated; degradation of status and excommunication from one's caste almost certainly follow. Much depends in such cases on the relative status of the caste and whether it is isolated from castes of adjoining status. Dumont[20] stated that it was "a universal principle that the illegitimate child has a status markedly inferior to that of legitimate children" and Hinduism certainly shows itself to be the extreme example of this situation. We should note that here we are describing the situation not only of a deserted unmarried woman and her child, but also of the offspring of less than legal unions that contravene subcaste endogamy and the ideas of ritual purity involved in this. Such unions are, or were, common enough to create subcastes which had distinct but inferior status.[21] In one known case of cross-caste marriage the way out of the situation was for the whole family to leave their caste and become Christians.[22]

There are further situations in which a girl conceives a child outside the common range of illegal and illegitimate unions. For a Hindu to conceive a child by a Muslim may be seen as beyond any possibility of legitimation. Such cases have resulted in the killing of the child and the subsequent suicide of the woman involved.[23] Many Hindu women abducted by Muslims during the 1948 partition disturbances were unwilling to seek repatriation as their ritual impurity could not be removed in such a way that they could ever be legitimately married within their own subcaste.

In Islam matters are very different. It is sufficient for the father to acknowledge cohabitation with a wife or concubine to establish the legitimacy of the child.[24] Since concubinage is lawful in Islam, it is not necessary for the mother of a child to be married to its father for it to be declared legitimate. But there is a distinction short of illegitimacy between the children of wives and those of concubines, the former having more rights within the family structure, such as inheritance of property, than the latter.[25]

The principle that a child born in wedlock is legitimate if the mother's husband acknowledges paternity clearly indicates the social rather than biological definition of the word. In the Islamic Shafi and Maliki schools of law, a man can acknowledge as legitimate a child conceived before his marriage, and one conceived up to four years after his marriage has been terminated. In Hanifi law the period is two years provided that his wife has not remarried. Thus the stigma of illegitimacy is largely absent in Islam and can be legally substantiated in very few cases; the general procreational atmosphere of Islam makes it unlikely that a father or mother will deny responsibility for a child.

In difficult cases interesting anomalies can occur. In one case, a Catholic Sukuma chief of Urima in Tanzania had a daughter only. Being a woman, she could not succeed to his position. To solve the problem, she bore a son in a love affair, and this son was then regarded as the lawful heir to the chiefdomship. The fact that the chief was a Catholic with a monogamous church marriage made him unwilling to follow the traditional practice of taking a second wife or wives in the hope of begetting a son.

In general, Christianity imposes penalties on unmarried mothers and their children. Often an unmarried mother-to-be does not have adequate social support during her pregnancy and the same often still applies to mothers without husbands after the birth. Even if the material aspects are catered for, in many areas in Christian countries a stigma remains. In some such countries the death rate of illegitimate infants is or has been higher than that of legitimate children.

Table 6.1 gives relevant data for Montreal during the eighteenth century; the death rate is a staggering 92.1 percent. A later study in New York[26] found the death rate per thousand deliveries to be 24.9 for the unmarried, as opposed to 13.2 for the married. A study in Italy (see table 6.2) showed that over a series of years the death rate for illegitimate children born alive was substantially higher than for legitimate children. A study in North Carolina (table 6.3) showed that in the white community both the perinatal and postneonatal mortality rates for illegitimate children were substantially higher than for legitimate ones. Among nonwhite illegitimate children there was a marked increase in the postnatal mortality rate.[27] A German study (table 6.4, see also Maier[28]) showed that in a large sample of deaths between birth and one year of age, more deaths due to prematurity occurred among illegitimate children (37.3%) than among legitimate ones (26.8%).

A study in California[29] comparing the health of spouseless and married mothers currently raising children found the spouseless substantially worse for both chronic conditions and functional disability as well as in their self-evaluation of their own health. Both mother and child can be seen to be at risk in this study.

Table 6.1. Mortality of Illegitimate Children Received as Foundlings into the Montreal General Hospital, 1760–71

Year	*Received*	*Died*
1760	17	12
1761	28	28
1762	37	36
1763	20	17
1764	26	24
1765	20	20
1766	31	27
1767	28	25
1768	30	29
1769	25	21
1770	29	27
1771	24	24
Total	315	290

Source: Fortier

The Church of Scotland in the preindustrial past made considerable effort to compel people to conform to its teaching. Seventeenth-century kirk sessions regularly publicly punished fornicators and adulterers. By the eighteenth century public humiliation had increasingly given way to commutation paid according to a more-or-less fixed tariff. By the nineteenth century this was rare but not unknown, since it survived in Lewis until midcentury.

Illegitimacy from 1855 until the 1890s did not fall generally below 8 or 9 percent of live births with wide variations. Ross and Cromarty were below 5 percent, whereas Kirkudbright and Dumfrieshire were between

Table 6.2. Mortality Rates Among Legitimate and Illegitimate Children, Italy 1950–65

Year	*Legitimate*	*Illegitimate*
1950	62.3	107.8
1955	49.9	81.0
1960	43.2	69.7
1965	36.0	36.2

Source: Nodari, R., and Pirovane, G. (1970). "Sulla mortalita infantile: Raffronte dei dati statistici referiti ai bambini nati nel matrimonio e fuori del matrimonio." *Minerva Pediatrica,* 22, 1254–56, 1449–51.

Note: The higher rate for illegitimate children can be attributed to poorer maternal and social support for the infant.

Table 6.3. Perinatal and Postneonatal Mortality Rates by Color and Legitimacy, North Carolina, 1957–66

	1957–61		*1962–66*	
Color	*Perinatal*	*Postneonatal*	*Perinatal*	*Postneonatal*
White				
Legitimate	30.7	5.5	29.2	5.1
Illegitimate	49.5	9.5	43.0	7.5
Nonwhite				
Legitimate	54.1	20.3	50.7	19.6
Illegitimate	60.0	28.9	57.9	27.7

Source: Scurletis et al.

Note: Note higher rates among illegitimate children.

14 and 18 percent. These higher rates do not seem to have related to the absence of church discipline but to the absence of familial control, the lack of cottages attached to farms, and the availability of jobs for unmarried female labor.[30] However, in England, at least, the parish priest's income depended in large part on his acceptability to his parishioners, and he must have hesitated before setting down in the church records the illegitimacy of children born to parishioners who might otherwise be accepted as married for all social purposes.[31]

The wave of religious austerity that occurred in Sweden from the midseventeenth century, and periodically subsequently, did not have any effect on the illegitimacy rates. Betrothal determined the legitimacy of children born before the religious marriage ceremony took place. Betrothal occurred in various forms outside church regulations; it was legally indispensable that there should be some sort of stable relationship. As early as the 1850s several commentators pointed out that religious revival had caused a decline in the illegitimacy rates in certain areas, but it

Table 6.4. Causes of Death in Legitimate and Illegitimate Infants, Bavaria, 1960–62.

Cause of Death	*Legitimate (%)*	*Illegitimate (%)*
Prematurity	26.8	37.3
Inborn factors and malformation	18.9	14.5
Birth injuries	9.4	7.0
Other causes	44.9	41.2
Total (%)	100.0	100.0
N	15,419	2,534

Source: Steichele, D. F., and Herschlein, H. J. (1964). Die Bedeutung der Proteolyse bei geburtshilflichen Defoibrininierungsblutungen und die Therapie mit Trasyel. *Archiv für Gynäkologie*, 199, 475–95.

was subsequently found that these same localities had low rates before the revivals occurred.[32]

In societies where the social system does not provide any advantages for the male to marry, and apparently religious injunctions are few or ineffective, illegitimacy is so common that few specific disadvantages accrue to such children or their mothers. Caribbean rates of illegitimacy have often exceeded 50 percent,[33] as neither the man nor the woman had much, if anything, to gain from any formal arrangement beyond the culturally sanctioned consensual union,[34] at any rate until late in life after the child rearing years were over. Late marriage might, in some cases, legitimize children born previously. By Roman Catholic law, all children born of parents who subsequently marry are legitimate.[35]

The Survival of the Child and Religious Inferiority

Hindus, even including those of Hindu origin who have later been converted from Hinduism to Islam, Buddhism, or Christianity, are much concerned with matters of purity and pollution. In the caste structure, those who are the most polluting and least pure are members of the lower castes and are allocated jobs which often put them into biologically unhygienic conditions.

On the other hand, the higher Hindu castes pay considerably more attention to regular cleanliness. Brahmin women bathe and put on clean clothes before cooking food; their kitchens are regularly cleaned for them and contact with refuse is reduced to a minimum. If contact occurs, it is followed by a thorough cleansing. However, in villages all cleaning jobs are relegated to the untouchables so that the more "clean" a person aspires to be, the less will he handle dirt, even to remove it. As a result the

Table 6.5. Infant Mortality Rates (per 1,000 Population) by Communities in Bombay City, 1938–47

Period	*Hindus (Lower Castes)*	*Hindus (Upper Castes)*	*Muslims*	*Indian Christians*	*Parsees*	*Europeans*
1938–39	332	272	247	236	111	174
1939–40	257	217	182	197	100	68
1940–41	232	209	187	169	95	39
1942–43	245	196	179	190	92	55
1943–44	261	193	181	193	84	53
1944–45	253	204	199	189	68	47
1945–46	286	186	166	164	80	26
1946–47	308	185	189	179	72	37
Average rate	272	208	191	190	88	62

Source: Chandrasekhar

floors of the moderately but not very rich (who could rarely afford domestic help) were sometimes actually dirtier than the homes of the despised poor.[36] Thus we cannot assume that the concern of all the higher castes for purity meant that they would in fact inevitably be cleaner in biological terms than those in lower castes. But since the lower castes were obliged to undertake occupations as lavatory cleaners, grave diggers, dung collectors, and so on, they were overexposed to infections. The data on death rates show that the lower castes also had higher rates of infant mortality. From 1938 to 1946 in Bombay the lower castes had an average infant mortality rate of 272 per 1,000, as against 208 for the higher castes;[37] see table 6.5. This differential continues at the present time.

The Survival of Unwanted or Orphaned Children

Christianity and Judaism have always been concerned about the survival of all children. The Old Testament expresses concern about orphans (Ps. 68, Deut. 16 and 26), and the Talmud mentions in particular the rights of female orphans, who have a clearly stated claim for support.[38] In Jewish law, if there is no parental estate, the community has the obligation to support orphans by providing communal funds for a boy to rent and furnish a house and for a girl to be given clothing and the minimum dowry necessary for marriage. The Christian archpriest Datheus is recorded as having started a foundling hospital in Milan in A.D. 787, the earliest record of such an institution. Early Christians adopted unwanted infants into their families, and provision was often made for abandoned infants left at church doors from the earliest times. In this approach Judeo-Christianity is deliberately involved in saving the lives of children who would frequently have fallen sick and died from lack of care otherwise.

From the earliest days, Christian institutions for foundlings have often been run by religious orders created for that purpose (fig. 6.4). Many foundling homes were established during the Middle Ages, but the most successful organization of this work was started by St. Vincent de Paul, who established the Paris Hospice des Enfants Trouvés about 1640. Although these institutions were designed for aiding the survival of unwanted children, their record of doing so was occasionally very poor.[39] The institution run by the St. Vincent de Paul order in Paris took in more and more foundlings from the late seventeenth century onward, so that by the third quarter of the eighteenth century about a third of all babies born in Paris found their way there. Even in the best of these institutions a third died within the year, and in the worst 90 percent died. It was much the same in the foundling hospitals and workhouses of London at that time, which have been described as highly effective infanticide agencies.[40] Behind the abandonment of children there often lay the most serious economic deprivation, hardship, and hunger. In Limoges between 1726 and 1790 children were increasingly abandoned during periods of

6.4. A foundling wheel on the outside wall of a Roman Catholic orphanage at Nahia, Brazil. The mother is depositing her child together with a note to the orphanage about the child, some clothes, and money on a revolving shelf. When she turns it, the baby will enter the orphanage and she herself will not be seen.

food shortage. Parents made decisions on which child to abandon in terms of the allocation of investment, which allowed them some leeway for exerting a strategically differentiated influence on the God-given fate of their children.[41]

The taking of another's child as one's own is clearly shown as having occurred in ancient Israel (see the stories of Abram and Hagar [Gen. 16:2] and of Jacob and Bilhah [Gen. 30:3]). But adoption was not a legal arrangement in old Judaic law. There was no recognized way of creating a kin relationship artificially by a legal act or fiction, but the law did allow for guardianship under conditions which were parallel to those of adoption except for inheritance, which required a specific testamentary disposition.[42] Thus guardianship appears to have been an individual act of charity or self-interest in Jewish religious tradition and did not involve any institutions specifically catering to unwanted children. The Lubavitch movement is an extreme orthodox Jewish sect opposed to even formal legal adoption. Their objections are based on a strict interpretation of Jewish law. Parents lavish a great deal of physical affection upon their children, by doing the same to their adopted children a couple would automatically have forbidden contacts with members of the opposite sex to whom they are not blood relatives.[43]

However, the state of Israel does now have a provision for legal adoption[44] which states that "an order under this act does not affect the consequences of the blood relationship between the adoptee and his natural parents so that the prohibitions and permissions of marriage and divorce continue to apply. On the other hand, adoption as such does not create new such prohibitions and permissions between the adopted and the adoptive family." This law thus has the effect of creating those ties between the adopters and the child which are usually recognized as existing between natural parents and their child, thus allowing for intestate succession. And it permits marriage between an adopted child and a member of the adopting family.[45]

Hindu religious law makes it imperative for a man to adopt a son if he has no natural children "because a son delivers his father from the hell called Put" (Laws of Manu), and such an adopted child inherits from his adoptive father, even to the extent of being relieved of any religious obligations to his natural parents. The ceremony of adoption consists of the transfer of paternal dominion over the child. However, there does not appear to be any provision in Hindu law for the adoption of, or provision for, foundlings in a more general context.

Both Greek and Roman law allowed for adoption in order to continue the family line and it was possible for foundlings to be incorporated into families; there were no provisions for the care of unwanted children by the city-state or religious institutions.

Adoption of a kind seems to have existed in pre-Islamic Arabia. When a man married the chief woman in a household, he automatically became "father" of any sons or daughters living with her.[46] Muhammad may have thus "adopted" Zaid bin Harithah, a slave, when he married the latter's owner, Khadija, rather than later, as is sometimes assumed, when Zaid refused to return with his natural father, who had come to Mecca to ransom him. Although Zaid was regarded as "ibn Muhammad," he was not regarded as a legitimate, inheriting son. Thus it happened that Muhammad at his death was survived by three daughters only.

Islamic law seems to favor nonadoptive relationships, for adoption gives no right of inheritance. Certain verses from the Koran are regarded by the orthodox as grounds for refusing to recognize adoption as having any binding legal consequences. This is especially so in regard to property transmission:

> To orphans restore their property
> (When they reach their age),
> Nor substitute (your) worthless things
> For their good ones; and devour not
> Their substance (by mixing it up)
> With your own. For this is Indeed a great sin.
> (Koran, Sura 4.2)

Let those (disposing of an estate)
Have the same fear in their minds
As they would have for their own
If they had left a helpless family behind.
Let them fear Allah, and speak
Words of appropriate (comfort).
(Koran, Sura 4.9)

Those who unjustly
Eat up the property
of orphans, eat up
a Fire into their own
Bodies: they will soon
Be enduring a blazing Fire.
(Koran, Sura 4.10)

Therefore, despite the form of adoption referred to previously, the particular Muslim view of paternity has meant that there are few instances in which an adopted child can be called wholly legitimate.[47]

Muslim canon lawyers have given considerable attention to the care of orphans when widows are left without sufficient means to keep themselves and their children. The Koran gives a general injunction about the care of orphans (Suras 2.218, 4.2, 93.6 and 93.9), perhaps deriving from Muhammad's own childhood difficulties. These arose out of contemporary social conditions in which the care of orphans fell upon the head of the clan, who might be unwilling or unable to support them. As soon as Muhammad's followers moved to Medina and formed an independent community, this responsibility would have fallen on the Prophet himself as their head. There were a great many widows with children, because the sect had suffered high losses of men at the battle of Badr. Muhammad's strong feelings about the care of orphans are shown in Sura 4.11 of the Koran, which states that those who misuse the property of orphans go to Hell. In addition, since the giving of charity is one of the Five Pillars of Islam, there are pious institutions (*waqf*) in most Muslim communities which provide for the poor, including orphans.

In general, then, we can see that some major world religions become actively involved with children who have no parents or whose parents cannot or will not look after them, usually increasing their immediate, and in many cases long-term, chances of survival. Foundling homes represent one way in which religiously motivated groups may take over responsibility for these children and look after them. What determines the precise outcome in any particular situation is the way in which religious, ethical, and moral ideas evaluate the life of children and instruct their adherents accordingly.

Religion and the Education of Children

Religious ideas dominated in the rearing of children more in the past than nowadays, in Western society at least, but they still play a major role in countries which have not yet fully accepted or been affected by the secularizing effects of much contemporary social change. Thus in the mid-twentieth century the Saudi Arabian government was approached by the United Nations with the proposition that child welfare advisers should visit the country, to which it replied that the Koran was completely adequate as a guide to child rearing and that no further advice was needed.[48]

In Islam the mother has a particular responsibility for the child during its early years. The length of this period varies between the different schools of law, but it is often until the child is seven years old, when the father takes over responsibility; even if there has been a divorce, children usually stay with the mother until this age. In the early years, therefore, Muslim children are assured of not being separated from their mothers by divorce.

In traditional Judaism the young child is an incomplete member of society and as such gets relatively less attention from the father than from the mother, as in Islam. As soon as the baby starts to talk, his mother teaches him religious blessings and some simple Hebrew words so that from the earliest years he is steeped in the atmosphere and spirit of Judaic learning. Formal education begins between the ages of three and five when the boy is first taken to the Jewish Torah teacher, who teaches him respect for the Book, to hold it in awe and to aspire to be a rabbi. The child learns by mechanical repetition and memorization which do not demand any understanding of the text, and in this respect Judaism is very similar to Islam with its village Koranic schools.

In both these religions the basis of the correct life is taken to be knowledge but not necessarily understanding of the scriptures. It is on this early introduction to religious ideas that future obedience to the dictates of the Torah and Koran is based. These ideas tend to remain even after those children are grown up, and even when they may have lapsed from the practices of their faith.

In the past there has been in most Christian communities some compulsory learning of the catechism as an essential basis for living, but it has never had the intensity and exclusiveness of Judaic and Islamic teaching, nor the effect of causing people to follow a particularly detailed set of religious injunctions.

Only in small, socially exclusive sects such as the Amish and Hutterites has the learning of the Bible some degree of the same intensity. Even there, however, most injunctions in the Bible are not assimilated to the depth experienced by Muslims, whose relatively short holy book with its specific injunctions is learned very thoroughly by most children exposed to the traditional type of teaching. Among the Amish there is rather a shared use of the Bible as an important source of knowledge and belief.

It is difficult to obtain evidence of the effects of specific religious differences in upbringing on morbidity or mortality rate, but such differences probably do exist. A study in German cities[49] showed that Roman Catholics were more likely than Protestants to purchase playpens and harnesses for restricting the mobility of their children. It is possible to speculate that this would lead to Catholic children's experiencing fewer acci-

6.5. A Navaho child in its cradle board. The father chants: "I have made a baby board for you. May you grow to a great old age. Of the sun's rays I have made the back, of the black clouds I have made the blanket, of the rainbow have I made the bow, of sunbeams have I made the side loops, of lightning have I made the lacings, of sun dogs have I made the footboard, of dawn have I made the covering, of black fog have I made the bed."

dents, but no data are available. In the case of Navaho infants, it has been suggested that the great extent of physical restraint affects the personality, at any rate in childhood (see fig. 6.5).

If we can assume that culture is transmitted by education in the widest sense of the word, then religions have been responsible for a large part of the educational process in all societies. While much of this education was related to religious issues, matters outside religion were commonly taught within a religious framework. Until comparatively recently most people have looked at the world through religiously tinted spectacles acquired during childhood. Once formal education begins, even today, it is often at first partly religious. The level of religious indoctrination of the young depends on the level of religious interpretation of everyday life within the school. It provides a formal scheme of reasoning for what people are doing; it governs the child's outlook in a general fashion in line with the way of life of the surrounding society.

The rearing of children in some parts involves hammering into their heads their religious duties and obligations as part of their cultural heritage. By this means the Hindu child comes to accept the ideas of ritual purity and impurity through which the caste system operates. The Muslim child learns Islamic practices concerning matters such as personal hygiene, especially washing, and the Jewish child learns such things as the dietary restrictions of the Talmudic code. These matters will be pursued in following chapters.

Rearing the Child Away from the Family

Missionary schools are a good example of formal and forceful separation of the growing child from the home environment for most of the year. Catholic missions among the Yanomamö Indians of Venezuela have taken six- to seven-year-old children into schools where they cannot be visited by their parents. It has been commented that the "emotional shock of living away from parents in such an exotic and insensitive environment will lead to serious developmental and emotional problems, crises of identity and personality disturbance that could be avoided,"[50] even if the changeover from primitive isolation to incorporation into the periphery of Latin-American society is more or less inevitable. The Wai-Wai of Guyana provided a very similar case.[51]

Removal of children from their families is not, in such cases, an unfortunate accident; it is foreseen and planned. The Father Divine movement in the eastern cities of the United States taught a denial of family ties and responsibility toward the family[52] which resulted in physical and emotional neglect of children by their parents which led to considerable insecurity and behavioral disorders in some children. The degree of emotional disturbance when children are reared away from home can lead to a loss of personal security which in turn can affect general health and impair reproductive capacity in later life unless self-confidence is restored. The so-called Moonies provide a further example.[53]

Childhood Behavior and Supernatural Sanctions

The growing child in every society is taught not only how to "behave" itself properly but the moral justifications for this, which are often expressed in religious terms. The idea that sin, disease, and misfortune are connected has a long history as well as widespread contemporary acceptance. It is during childhood that moral ideas are instilled. The Christian child is taught to honor his mother and father and later not to steal or covet the property of others.

For Muslims, the Koran as the literal word of God obliges the growing child to follow a wide range of social practices divinely laid down. Muslim mothers in Java[54] told their children stories from the Muslim tradition, informing them that God created the world and will punish them if they misbehave. All Muslims base their lives on the necessity of fulfilling the Five Pillars: first, affirmation of faith in God and Muhammad His Prophet; second, praying in the prescribed way five times per day; third, making a pilgrimage to the holy places at Mecca once in a lifetime; fourth, fasting during the holy lunar month of Ramadhan; fifth, giving of alms.

By the time a boy is eight, he will accompany his father to the mosque, where he will learn a system of prayers involving drill-like movements which can, from a biological viewpoint, be seen as valuable physical exercise. He will see his elders practicing daylight fasting during the holy month of Ramadhan and learn about the pilgrimage to Mecca. By adolescence the Muslim child will have accepted these rules of fasting and migrating as being basic premises around which his life should revolve.

The Hindu code of Manu is quite explicit in connecting disease with sinful acts, and this remains the basis of contemporary Hindu law, although with not quite the same divine authority as the Koran holds in Islamic law. A wide range of disorders, minor ailments as well as major diseases, is explained in terms of punishment for crime, such as dyspepsia for the theft of cooked food and consumption for the killing of a Brahmin.[55]

Thus the child learns at an early age that the social order in its day-to-day workings is supported by religious sanctions. In many cases he will envisage God and the spirits arrayed against dissenters and disturbers of the moral balance of society. The Sukuma in Tanzania see the misfortunes of the family as necessitating divination to find a cause which can be put right so that normality can resume; the child sees these processes in action. Many Christians, at least in their prayers, try to find a reason for their misfortunes and seek help or forgiveness; no one prays more fervently than a Christian child who feels that he or she has sinned.

Even when society's overall moral pattern cannot be seen as related to a particular religion, the behavior of children is often controlled by their recognition of an informal implied contract with God. Some Western parents are quite explicit in using this as a moral control. For example, one American mother stated that her daughter was "deathly afraid of being punished—not by me, but we've always told her that any little girl who tells a lie, God always does something terrible to them and she's deathly afraid of that."[56]

A study in Tennessee among white Americans[57] showed that this use of religious sanctions occurred with some frequency and with evident effects on the child's behavior and personality. These Tennessee parents used this method to gain control over their children. Another study in the Bahamas[58] suggested that those parents who feared the supernatural inflicted more physical pain on their children or the children in their charge than those who did not have this fear.

Where children were brought up in the exclusive Protestant environment of a sect such as the Mennonites[59] this alliance with God was the accepted approach to life and in no way could threats of divine punishment be seen as an abnormal reaction. The authority of God figured powerfully in Mennonite life, and parents saw themselves, and were seen, as intermediaries between God and their children.

The Circumcision of Boys

The circumcision of boys is carried out as a religious ritual by both Muslims and Jews. There is no mention of circumcision in the Koran, and it was probably adopted without question by Muhammad from an existing Arab custom; there are several traditions about his support for the practice. It is generally regarded as an essential part of the Islamic faith. It is usually performed with elaborate ceremony by a religious specialist but often under conditions which are far from hygienic. A mass Muslim ceremony in Pangani, Tanzania, in 1956 involved the use of a used razor blade by unwashed hands. No dressings were used, the air was dusty, and the ceremony drew in large numbers of flies. Islamic laws provide no guidance as to how and when the ceremony should be carried out, or whether any children may be excused on the grounds of ill health. Muslims appear to have given less attention than Jews to the medical complications of circumcision. The dangers of an unsterile knife used in ritual circumcision have been amply illustrated in a case in Cyprus in which there were five deaths from tetanus among twenty-three boys circumcised by a nonmedical operator.[60] There are great variations in the age at which circumcision is carried out in Islam. Perhaps the orthodox view is that it should be performed in the tenth year, just before the age when the boy can be punished for neglecting his prayers. Sometimes it is delayed so that expense can be saved by circumcising a group of boys together. In Dahomey it has been performed as early as the seventh day and among the Bosnians as late as the thirteenth year.

Judaism, on the other hand, offers specific guidance, defining when this operation must be performed or altogether abandoned. It is forbidden to circumcise a sick child before its recovery, or before the child is seven days old and "gains some strength." There is Talmudic recognition of what may be hemophilia since it is forbidden to circumcise a child if the two previous children have died from bleeding after their circumcision.[61] The obligatory sucking of the wound by the circumciser, which has now generally been replaced by the use of a number of glass or rubber suction appliances together with swabs, was in part an attempt to reduce the danger of infection. Judaism has paid considerable attention to the medical complications of circumcision arising from inept ritual operators,[62] by providing sterile environments in which it is performed. At least one U.S. hospital has a special operating theater with communication links to an adjoining visitor's room so the relatives can see and hear the ritual operation and its prayers.[63]

So both Judaism and Islam pay considerable attention to circumcision as a necessary rite, and of the two, the former seems to pay more attention to the biological issue of cleanliness. We can presume that the Jewish mortality rate from circumcision has always been lower than the Islamic, especially in tribal Islam.

While Christianity has no direct religious interest in circumcision, it has been forced to recognize the importance of the ritual as part of African initiation rituals when such people convert to Christianity. It may be a block to conversion if the young men do not feel truly adult without this ceremony. The Universities Mission to Central Africa in southern Tanzania tried to Christianize this local initiation rite by introducing a form of circumcision under hygienic conditions by a hospital dresser, but with little success.

Despite its infective dangers, there is the consideration that circumcision may be prophylactic against penile carcinoma. There is evidence that this disease is very rare[64] and there is a low incidence among Muslims as compared with Hindus.[65] A study in Macedonia[66] comparing non-Muslims with Muslims showed an incidence of 11.0 per thousand for the former and 2.7 per thousand for the latter. It has been suggested that circumcision has resulted in a lower incidence of cervical carcinoma in women, but it is possible that the incidence of this disease is also related to other factors, such as ritual washing of the genitals and frequency of intercourse.[67] In East Africa there is evidence of a higher incidence of penile and cervical carcinoma among uncircumcised Ugandans than among circumcised Kenyans.[68]

A study of the epidemiology of cervical carcinoma in Lebanese Christians and Muslims[69] showed, on the other hand, that cervical cancer was relatively as frequent in Muslim wives as in Christian wives, notwithstanding the different circumcision status of their husbands. In this study, 97.6 percent of Muslim men, but only 1.9 percent of Christian men, were circumcised. Case history study of 140 women with cervical cancer and 140 controls revealed association of the disease with the married state, early age at first marriage, low socioeconomic status, and no association with age at menarche or menopause. The author concluded that there was no reason to believe that in these populations any disease factor related differentially to either religion. A further study of uterine cancer in relation to male circumcision was made in Ethiopia.[70] Comparing the rate of uterine cancer in an Ethiopian (Muslim) hospital sample with the rate in Europe, Huber found the two rates to be the same (50 per 100,000 women) in the two areas, despite the fact that almost every male in the Ethiopian region studied was circumcised in early life.

The Circumcision of Girls

Female circumcision has been performed at various times and places throughout the world, but particularly in areas under Muslim influence in

Africa and in many indigenous African societies. There is no evidence that it occurred in early Egypt, but there is written evidence from Strabo and Herodotus[71] that it occurred there in later times.

This operation has been wrongly attributed to Islam for it antedates Islamic origin and does not occur in Saudi Arabia, Yemen, Iraq, Iran, and Turkey. It is not mentioned in the Koran, but there are traditions, based on alleged remarks of the Prophet, that it was an embellishment for a woman, while it was obligatory for a man. Although it is clear that clitoridectomy has no religious justification, it is regarded by most Sudanese Moslems as part of the discipline of the Muslim religion.[72] The justification for female circumcision is that it reduces sexual desire in girls and protects their morals by removing erogenous parts; it can also lead to constriction of the vaginal opening, which is considered more pleasurable for the husband. University students in Khartoum[73] regarded the practice of infibulation (closing of the entrance to the vagina by cutting and healing together)[74] as unjustified, but they continued to favor clitoridectomy, or *sunna* (meaning "duty" in Arabic) circumcision, suggesting that its justification was the protection that it gave from untimely pregnancy.

Once this rite has been performed, there may be complications beyond those connected with the actual operation, such as infections, injury to adjacent structures, and hemorrhage.[75] A Sudanese doctor[76] referred to the frantic struggling of girls who were forcibly held in the lithotomy position, so that what was actually cut and the extent of the operation could sometimes be uncontrolled.

The operation can result in complications for both marital partners later in life that arise from difficulties over the consummation of the marriage if the vaginal opening is too small. As a result coital injuries do occur, and rectal intercourse, prohibited by Islam, not infrequently occurs by default. Later there can be obstetric complications and the circumcised mother requires surgical assistance at birth. In recent years there has been much discussion of female circumcision. A valuable summary of the issues surrounding this topic can be found in the *Medical Anthropology Quarterly*; Gordon, in this volume, raises the modern issue of whether or not the traditional cultural relativism of anthropology is appropriate in the case of this particular custom.[77] In other words, can the anthropologist simply stand by and watch, describe, and record the events of female circumcision, or is there here a case for intervention?

The general context as far as Western anthropologists is concerned is the growing understanding of subjugation and abuse experienced by women in non-Western cultures. Such abuse is increasingly not tolerated in our own society. Is female circumcision a case of abuse? This raises complex issues because of the cross-cultural context. First, in countries like Sudan female circumcision is endemic; that is, it is practiced in villages all over the country. This is in contrast with actual physical abuse of women in our own culture, which is sporadic. However, it could be said that a general attitude of male supremacy is endemic in the West (or was until recently) and this is also true of Muslim countries such as Sudan. Should we, as Western anthropologists, intervene to try to eliminate what to us is a barbaric custom?

A closer examination of the subject reveals that there are in fact a number of varieties of the operation. The most minor, *sunna* ("duty"), is the removal of the clitoral prepuce by razor, knife, or smoldering stone and is really the only operation that can accurately be called "circumcision" since it involves cutting around the clitoris. The second form, excision or clitoridectomy, involves the cutting out of the whole clitoris as well as parts or all of the labia minora. In its varying degrees it is the most common form practiced in Egypt. In the Sudan excision is not performed, but a similar operation involves removal of the clitoris, the anterior or all of the labia minora, and slices of the labia majora. Even this is not the most extreme form of the operation, the so-called pharaonic form, also referred to as infibulation, which occurs in Sudan and Nubian Egypt. This involves complete removal of the clitoris, labia minora, and labia majora, with the two sides of the wound then stitched together, leaving a small pinhole opening for the drop by drop passage of urine and menstrual blood. The operation is done in a variety of ways, depending on where it is practiced. In rural settings, a small stick is often inserted to maintain the opening, and the two sides stitched together with thorns. Adhesives such as egg, oil, or wet cigarette paper are placed over the wound to promote healing. The girl's legs are often bound together for as long as forty days to ensure the desired tightly scarred aperture. In urban settings, stitching is likely to be done with catgut or silk sutures, and anesthesia and antibiotics are likely to be used.[78]

Many people are surprised to discover that even in the 1990s this operation is standard practice throughout rural and parts of urban Sudan and southern Egypt, and in many other parts of Africa. The most extensive medical survey of the practice was conducted between 1977 and 1981 by Dr. Asma El Dareer, with interviews of 3,210 women representing a random sample of households in northern Sudan. What the survey showed was that 98 percent of the women questioned were circumcised, 3 percent with the *sunna* procedure, 12 percent the intermediate, and 83 percent the pharaonic. The strongest predictor of type of operation was level of education. Of pharaonically circumcised girls 75 percent were from illiterate families, while educated families were more likely to opt for the milder forms. Over 90 percent of the operations in the Sudan were performed by *dayas*, or midwives, the rest by doctors, nurses, or old men and women who inherited the role.[79] In Egypt the incidence of genital operations was much lower, with estimates ranging from one third[80] to one half[81] of all women. Only in the south of the country were pharaonic operations performed.

Despite the trauma of the operation and its subsequent health complications the practice continues. An eyewitness account of the operation in a Sudanese village[82] related how, in the late 1980s, a young girl aged nine years was held down while the pharaonic operation was performed. The girl screamed throughout the operation, which was performed with a knife and other simple tools by an old woman. No men were present; the audience consisted of women. The atmosphere was routine, and a group of men who were sitting nearby outside the house did not interrupt their normal conversation during the episode. The anthropologist, an English woman, was very upset by this, the first such operation she had witnessed, and gave the girl some antiseptic lotion afterward for none was provided by the old woman.

The practice of clitoridectomy seems to be critical to the project of anthropology. Relativism is the watchword of anthropologists. Above all others, the anthropologist must suspend judgment, must try to understand the strange customs of the people she or he is studying, however abhorrent they may at first appear. Does this apply in the case of clitoridectomy? Should a Western anthropologist stand by and allow it to happen? If it were a rare thing, governments might well be so outraged by it that they would try to ban it and prosecute those involved in perpetrating it, as they do wife burning, self-immolation by widows, and female infanticide in India. All these are now illegal. But clitoridectomy occurs even more widely than in the Sudan and Egypt, being found in West Africa from Mauretania to Cameroon, across Central Africa to Chad, and in East Africa from Tanzania to Ethiopia, while infibulation is customary in Mali, Somalia, Ethiopia, and Nigeria. Many of these are non-Islamic settings and the practice probably antedates the coming of Islam to Africa.

It is thus a commonplace, fully accepted by the people in the places where it occurs. In our Western idiom it is not even a clear case of the subjugation of women for it is practiced by women, not men. We may hypothesize that it was first invented by men, to keep their women chaste, and that it remains part of the overall domination of women by men. Assuming this is so, what should a female Western, liberated, feminist anthropologist do about it? The answer seems clear enough on first principles: Try to stop it. Yet there are millions of clitoridectomies happening each year. At present the situation in the West is that the practice is now known about and widely discussed, and such pressure as can be exerted is being exerted on African governments and public health departments to bring it to an end. There is still a long way to go, however.

Clitoridectomy presents us with a further problem in this book. We argue throughout that religions give people a means to express and cope with the stages of the human life cycle. If this operation were a puberty ritual such as those that many young men and women undergo all over the world, often involving some suffering and pain, maybe with cutting of the skin or stinging by bees or some other such torture, then we could classify it as such. However, it is practiced several years before puberty, in late childhood. Why this should be so has not hitherto been explained. We suggest that it is really a puberty ritual but it is so severe that it cannot come at the time of puberty, when sexual activity is beginning. It has to occur earlier, and this leaves time for the scars to heal before sexual activity begins. If we regard it as a puberty ritual, we do have to ask ourselves why it should be so severe, what purpose is served, and for whom? We accept that it is part of the domination by men over women widespread in Africa and some other parts of the world. It seems to be the opposite of the approval and celebration of feminine sexuality found in some places, for example the Marquesas Islands or our own society. It seems to be based on the supposition, found in ancient Rome where infibulation occurred, and in so many other cultures at the present time, that women's sexuality has to be controlled and harnessed, primarily in the interests of their husbands, to prevent adultery. Clitoridectomy eliminates permanently the ability of a woman to have an orgasm, and it may go further, by preventing normal sexual intercourse completely. We thus interpret it as a puberty ritual of thoroughgoing male-dominant cultures.

However painful and however severe the aftereffects, we should not make the mistake of thinking that most African women themselves are against it. It is very widely regarded as a sign of mature womanhood to have had the operation. No self-respecting woman can do without it. A woman is unmarriageable until she has had it. After childbirth, when the vaginal opening has been enlarged to allow the birth, many women return to be stitched up again. In some areas of the Sudan and Nubian Egypt, the operation is invested with the form and symbolism of a wedding. The girl is adorned with gold and henna in the style of a bride, and a groom is exhorted to come forward. The operation is part of the ceremonial complex that leads to marriage and childbirth. The involvement of blood and genitalia foreshadows the young girl's future role as wife and mother.[83]

Although a circumcised girl may still be a child biologically, her status becomes that of a woman after her operation. She is no longer allowed to play outside or to socialize with boys her age, and she begins the task of waiting for a husband. She becomes subject to a strict code of modesty involving appropriate bodily covering, bashfulness and naïveté, and associated customs and beliefs relating to chastity, fidelity, separation, and seclusion.[84] There is honor involved in the operation, not just for the girl but for her whole family, whose collective honor is impugned if she does not have the operation. This may be the main reason for its continuance. This is also the main reason why Western agitation for its eradication has not been successful. Women's motives for wanting it to continue have been studied in Somalia.[85] Indeed, as Gordon shows, it has been to some extent incorporated into conventional medical practice, as physicians conduct 2 percent of urban operations, and *dayas* with government sponsored medical training perform about 35 percent.

Perhaps the most hopeful sign for those who want to see the custom eradicated is that where Western influences are strongest in urban centers in the Sudan, the incidence of pharaonic operations is dropping in favor of the intermediate form, while in urban Egypt a majority of the middle class now abstains from genital operations altogether.

To us in our culture, where both men and women strive for equality, are liberated sexually, and are able to enjoy sex to the full, these practices certainly seem abhorrent in the extreme. We feel that, whatever the normal relativist posture of anthropologists, faced with clitoridectomy there is no alternative but to do everything possible to have it made illegal and to prosecute those engaging in it so that it disappears completely. Its place in the cultures where it occurs has to be set against purely humanitarian and medical considerations. In the past, colonial powers have banned inhumane practices among their subject peoples. Today the colonial age is a thing of the past and so we are left with the pressure of public opinion to try to bring about change. As Gordon writes, "While relativism is a powerful descriptive tool for getting inside another culture, both the describer and his audience have cultural agendas that must be considered as well." From the point of view of religion and religious rituals, whether clitoridectomy is or is not thought of as a part of Islam, its functions in terms of puberty and marriageability cannot be considered without taking into account the loss of bodily function and the continued subjugation of women that it perpetuates.

From the biological point of view, the whole process of circumcision, for boys and girls, is very perplexing. Apart perhaps from the beneficial effects on penile and possibly cervical carcinoma, this cutting away of the skin around sensitive erogenous zones intimately concerned in the primary reproductive process seems to make little or no biological sense. It is hard, also, to come to terms with the possibilities it raises of infection and subsequent difficulties in sexual behavior and childbirth. Why then circumcision? Other religions manage without it and do not necessarily have alternative scarifications. The foreskin of the male cannot be biologically disadvantageous, or it would have been lost in the course of human evolution, eliminated by natural selection. The clitoris, arguably, makes reproduction more efficient by making sex more enjoyable for the woman. Why cut off or damage either of them? As often, clear answers are not to be found, although speculative reasons can be adduced, such as that reduced fertility can be advantageous in conditions where there is a need for increased birth spacing. For a while, no doubt, cultural rules can continue to operate (in this case literally) on the basis of traditional ideas, the adaptiveness or functionality of which may relate to bygone times. Or once-adaptive actions can come to serve new purposes. Just as face or body scars can be used as tribal markers indicating membership in the community, so can circumcision. It does also seem that part of the aim of female circumcision is to reduce the intensity of immediate sensual pleasure arising from genital stimulation. This is nowadays widely seen as an aspect of male control over women, a reflection of the dominant status of men in some African societies. Efforts to eradicate the practice, which some but not all men and women in the countries concerned find abhorrent (as do most or all men and women in countries where it does not occur), have met with only partial success at the present time.

In this chapter we have dealt mainly with the way religions become involved in the management of the preadolescent period, but toward the end of the chapter, with the discussion of circumcision, we came on to the period of adolescence itself and even took a forward look toward marriage and childbearing. These different phases of the life cycle can be distinguished analytically, but in real life they are all parts of a single complex. Our job in this book is to analyze, so we tease them apart, but they will always try to grow together again.

In the next chapter we do, however, go on to adolescence proper, a time typified in Western cultures by "Sturm und Drang," or a particularly high level of psychological tension. Here, clearly, is an area of human life for religions to enter into, and indeed very many societies (our own is something of an exception) do have rituals and other processes through which boys and girls must pass at adolescence.

Notes

1. Levine, R. R. "*Judaism and some modern medical problems.*" *J Medical Society of New Jersey*, 65, 638–39.

2. Jakobovits, I. (1965). *Jewish law faces modern problems.* Yeshiva University Press, New York.

3. Goldman, A. J. (1978). *Judaism confronts contemporary issues.* Shengold, New York.

4. Hathout, H. (1972). "Abortion and Islam." *J Medical Libanais*, 25, 237–39.

5. Ling, T. O. (1969). "Buddhist factors in population growth and control: A survey based on Thailand and Ceylon." *Population Studies*, 23, 53–60.

6. Davis, H. (1946). *Moral and pastoral theology*, vol 2. Sheed and Ward, London, pp. 166–67.

7. Capellmann, C. F. N. (1882). "Pastoral medicine." In: Kelly, D. F. *Emergence of Roman Catholic medical ethics in N. America.* Pustet, New York, pp. 39–40.

8. Erman, A. (1901). *Zauberspruche für Mutter und Kind aus dem Papyrus 3027 des Berliner Museums.* Abhandlungen der königlichen Akademie der Wissenschaften zu Berlin.

9. Hanks, J. R. (1968). "Maternity and its rituals in Bang Chan." *Cornell Thailand Project Report Series*, vol 6. Cornell University, Ithaca, New York, p. 92.

10. Converse, T. A. (1973). "Hutterite midwifery." *American J. Obstet Gynecol,* 116, 719–25.

11. Hanks, J. R. (1968). "Maternity and its rituals in Bang Chan." *Cornell Thailand Project Report Series,* vol 6. Cornell Univeristy Press, Ithaca, New York.

12. Bose, K. C. (1912). "Infantile mortality: Its causes and prevention." Proceedings of Second All-India Sanitary Conference, Delhi.

13. Lankester, A. (1924). *Lecture on the responsibility of men in matters relating to maternity.* Government of India Press, Simla, p. 5.

14. Voland, E. (1988). "Differential infant and child mortality in evolutionary perspective: Data from late 17th- to 19th-century Ostfriesland (Germany)." In Betzig, L. L., et al. (eds.). *Human reproduction: A Darwinian perspective.* Cambridge University Press, London, pp. 253–61.

15. Spiro, M. E. (1971). *Buddhism and society.* Allen and Unwin, London, p. 236.

16. Rose, H. A. (1907). "Hundu birth observances in the Punjab." *J Royal Anthrop Inst,* 37, 220–36.

17. Smith, M. (1954). *Baba of Kano: A woman of the Moslem Hausa.* Faber and Faber, London, p. 142.

18. Lankester, A. (1924). *Lecture on the responsibility of men in matters relating to maternity.* Government of India Press, Simla, P. 5.

19. Turnbull, C. M. (1966). *Wayward servants: The two worlds of the African pygmies.* Eyre and Spottiswoode, London, pp. 57–58.

20. Dumont, L. (1970). *Homo hierarchicus: The caste system and its implications.* Weidenfeld and Nicolson, London, pp. 115.

21. O'Malley, L. S. S. (1932). *Indian caste customs.* Cambridge University Press, Cambridge, pp. 94–95.

22. Archer, W. G. (1974). *The hill of flutes: Love, life and poetry in tribal India.* Allen and Unwin, London, p. 168.

23. Archer, W. G. (1974). *The hill of flutes: Love, life and poetry in tribal India.* Allen and Unwin, London.

24. Levy, R. (1969). *The social structure of Islam.* Cambridge University Press, London, p. 136.

25. Levy, R. (1969). *The social structure of Islam.* Cambridge University Press, London, pp. 79–80.

26. Pakter, J. (1961). "Out-of-wedlock births in New York City. II. Medical aspects." *American J Public Health,* 51, 846–55.

27. Scurletis, T. D., et al. (1969). "Trends in illegitimacy and associated mortality in North Carolina. 1957–66." *North Carolina Medical J,* 10, 214–21.

28. Maier, W. (1964). "Die Säuglingssterblichkeit chelich and unchelich Lebendgeborener: Todessursachen, Lebensdauer." *Archiv für Gynäkologie,* 199, 468–74.

29. Berkman, P. L. (1969). "Spouseless motherhood, psychological stress and physical morbidity." *J Health and Social Behaviour,* 10, 323–24.

30. Smout, C. (1980). "Aspects of sexual behaviour in 19th-century Scotland." In Laslett, P., et al. (eds.). *Bastardy and its comparative history.* Cambridge University Press, New York, pp. 192–216.

31. Laslett, P. (1980). "Comparing illegitimacy over time and between cultures." In Laslett, P., et al. (eds.). *Bastardy and its comparative history.* Cambridge University Press, New York.

32. Gaunt, D. (1980). "Illegitimacy in the 17th and 18th East Sweden." In Laslett, P., et al. (eds.). *Bastardy and its comparative history.* Cambridge University Press, New York, pp. 313–26.

33. Goode, W. J. (1960). "Illegitimacy in the Caribbean social structure." *American Sociological Review*, 25, 21–30.

34. Smith, M. G. (1962). *West Indian family structure.* Washington University Press, Washington. Clarke, E. (1957). *My mother who fathered me.* Allen and Unwin, London.

35. Macfarlane, A. (1980). "Illegitimacy and illegitimates in English history." In Laslett, P., et al. (eds.). *Bastardy and its comparative history.* Cambridge University Press, New York, pp. 71–84.

36. Myrdal, G. (1968). *Asian drama.* vol 3. Twentieth Century Fund, New York, p. 1607.

37. Chandrasekhar, S. (1959). *Infant mortality in India: 1901–55.* Allen and Unwin, London, p. 105.

38. *Encyclopaedia Judaica.* (1971). Keter, Jerusalem.

39. Fortier, B. de la. (1963). "Les enfants trouvés à l'hôpital général de Montréal, 1754–1804," *Laval Médical*, 34, 442–53, 35, 335–47, 36, 351–59.

40. Wrigley, E. A. (1969). *Population and history.* McGraw-Hill, New York, pp. 125–26.

41. Voland, E. (1989). "Differential parental investment: Some ideas on the contact area of European social hisotry and evolutionary biology." In Standen, V., and Foley, R. (eds.). *Comparative socio-ecology: The behavioural ecology of humans and other mammals.* Blackwell, Oxford, p. 392.

42. *Encyclopedia Judaica.* (1972). Keter, Jerusalem.

43. *Encyclopedia Judaica Yearbook.* (1974). Keter, Jerusalem, p. 302.

44. *Adoption of Children Law* (1960). Government Printer, Tel Aviv.

45. *Encyclopedia Judaica.* vol 2. (1992). Keter, Jerusalem, p. 302.

46. Watt, W. M. (1968). *Muhammad at Medina.* Oxford University Press, Oxford, p. 282.

47. Levy, R. (1969). *The social structure of Islam.* Cambridge University Press, London, p. 138.

48. United Nations Secretariat. (1949). *Annual Report.* New York.

49. Wendt, H. W. (1965). "Points of origin for infant ecologies: Religion and purchase of devices affecting pre-verbal mobility." *Psychological Reports*, 16, 209–210.

50. Chagnon, N. A. (1977). *Yanomamö—the fierce perople.* Holt, Rinehart and Winston, New York, pp. 159–61.

51. Guppy, N. (1958). *Wai-Wai: Through the forests north of the Amazon.* Murray, London.

52. Bender, L., and Spalding, M. A. (1940). "Behaviour problems in children from the homes of followers of Father Divine." *J Nervous Mental Diseases*, 91, 460–72.

53. Bromley, D. G., and Shupe, A. D. (1979). *Moonies in America: Cult, church and crusade.* Sage, Beverly Hills.

54. Geertz, C. (1960). *The religion of Java.* Free Press, New York, p. 179.

55. The laws of Manu. vol XI. (1969). Buhler G. (trans.). Dover, New York, pp. 49–53.

56. Sears, R. R., et al. (1957). *Patterns of child-rearing.* Row, Peterson, Evanston, Illinois, p. 380.

57. Nunn, C. Z. (1964). "Child control through a 'coalition with God.'" *Child Development*, 35, 417–32.

58. Otterbein C. S., and Otterbein, K. F. (1973). "*Believers and beaters: A case study of supernatural beliefs and child rearing in the Bahama Islands.*" *American Anthropologist*, 75, 1670–81.

59. Kurokawa, M. (1969). "Acculturation and mental health of Mennonite children." *Child Development*, 40, 689–705.

60. Gosden, M. (1935). "Tetanus deaths after circumcision." *Transactions of the Royal Society, Tropical Medicine and Hygiene*, 28, 645–48.

61. Jakobovits, I. (1961). "Medical spects of circumcision in Jewish law." *Hebrew Medical J*, 1, 258–70.

62. Shulman, J. (1964). "Surgical complications of circumcision." *American J Diseases of Childhood*, 107, 149–54.

63. Weiss, C. (1962). "Ritual circumcision: Comments on current practice in American hospitals." *Clinical Pediatrics* (Philadelphia), 1, 65–72.

64. Wolbarst, A. L. (1932). "Circumcision and penile cancer." *Lancet*, 1,150–53.

65. Bleich, A. R. (1950). "Prophylaxis of penile carcinoma." *J American Medical Association*, 143, 1054–57.

66. Kmet, J., et al. (1963). "Circumcision and carcinoma colli uteri in Macedonia, Yugoslavia: Results from a field study. 1. Incidence of malignant and premalignant conditions." *British J Cancer*, 17, 391–99.

67. Wahi, P. N., et al. (1972). "Religion and cervical carcinoma in Agra." *Indian J Cancer*, 9, 210–15. Terris, T., and Oalmann, C. (1960). "Carcinoma of the cervix." *J American Medical Association*, 174, 1847–51. Mitra, S. (1958). "Cancer of the cervix." *Cancer*, 11, 1190–94. Sorsby, M. (1931). *Cancer and race: The incidence of cancer among Jews.* John Bales, London.

68. Dodge, O. G., et al. (1963). "Circumcision and the incidence of carcinoma of the penis and cervix: A study in Kenya and Uganda Africans." *East African Medical J*, 40, 440–44.

69. Abou-Daoud, K. T. (1967). "Epidemiology of carcinoma of the cervix uteri in Lebanese Christians and Moslems." *Cancer (Philadelphia)*, 20, 1706–14.

70. Huber, J. (1960). "Uterus carcinoma and circumcision: Studies in Ethiopia." *Wiener. Medizinische Wochenschrift*, 110, 571–74.

71. Strabo (1950). *Geography.* Heinemann, London, vol. 14, 4, 9; Herodotus (1952). *History.* Heinemann, London, vol 2, 104.

72. Cloudsley, A. (1983). *Women of Omdurman: Life, love and the cult of virginity.* Ethnographica, London.

73. Nordenstam, T. (1968). *Sudanese ethics.* Scandinavian Institute for African Studies, Uppsala, pp. 95–96, 205–6.

74. Widstrand, C. G. (1964). "Female infibulation." *Studia ethnographica Uppsaliensia*, 20, 95–124. Dewhurst, C. J., et al. (1964). "Infibulation complicating pregnacy." *British Medical Journal*, 11, 1442. Gordon, D. (1991). "Female circumcision and genital operations in Egypt and the Sudan: A dilemma for medical anthropology." *Medical Anthropology Quarterly.* 5(1), 3–4.

75. Mustafa, A. (1966). "Female circumcision and infibulation in the Sudan." *Journal Obstetrics and Gynaecology, British Commonwealth*, 73, 302–6.

76. Hathout, H. M. (1963). "Some aspects of female circumcision." *Journal Obstetrics and Gynaecology, British Commonwealth*, 70, 505–7.

77. Gordon, D. (1991). "Female circumcision and genital operations in

Egypt and the Sudan: A dilemma for medical anthropology." *Medical Anthropology Q*, 5(1), 3–14.

78. Gordon, D. (1991). "Female circumcision and genital operations in Egypt and the Sudan: A dilemma for medical anthropology." *Medical Anthropology Q*, 5(1), 3–14.

79. El Dareer, A. (1982). *Women, why do you weep?* Zed Press, London.

80. Hosken, F. P. (1978). "Epidemiology of female genital mutilation." *Tropical Doctor*, 8(3) 150–56.

81. Rugh, A. (1984). *Family in contemporary Egypt*. Syracuse University Press, Syacuse, New York.

82. Parker, M. Personal communication.

83. Kennedy, J. G. (1970). "Circumcision and excision in Egyptian Nubia." *Man*, 5, 175–91.

84. Antoun, R. T. (1968). "On the modesty of women in Arab Muslim villages." *American Anthropologist*, 70, 671–97.

85. Dirie, M. A., and Landmark, G. (1991). "Female circumcision in Somalia and women's motives." *Acta Obstetricia Gynecologica Scandinavica*, 70(7–8), 581–85.

7

Adolescence

Initiation Rites for Adolescents

In small-scale societies studied by anthropologists the change to adolescence is usually marked by rituals of one kind or another whereby designated elders formally bring children out of the state of childhood by what are called *rites of passage*, and bring them into the adult world, where new rules apply, new forms of dress are used, and new kinds of behavior patterns are expected.[1] In nearly all such cases, religions play a major role in reorienting the child to his or her new status.

Where these rites occur they often concern themselves with both physical puberty and social status and recognize the movement from what is considered to be a presexual world, in which individuals are considered to be incapable of complete sexual relations (although they may in many cases have already indulged in sex play), to the sexual world of adolescence, in which sexual relations of certain kinds are expected to occur and are, in fact, actively promoted by the teaching of sexual techniques by older men and women.

For both boys and girls these rituals are often followed by a period of segregation in which the initiates learn the proper approach to teenage sex and also details of the adult society toward which they are now moving. Boys may be shown sacred objects (such as Australian bull roarers); taught the names of the gods and shown how humans impersonate them, as among the Hopi with their Kachina gods; toughened up by tribal scarification marking, as among the Nuer of the Sudan or the Iatmul of New Guinea (see fig. 7.2); or led to seek for personal visions, often in ways involving self-torture, as among the now extinct Mandan Indians (see fig. 7.3). Thus religions are deeply involved in the process of puberty rituals. The solemnity of the occasion as well as its instructional formality and learning processes impinge on the minds of all the participants; elaborate rituals and complicated symbols figure largely, justifying tribal myths, adult or masculine dominance, and other cultural features.

Regardless of the exact age at which thee rituals occur, the aim is to produce "proper" young adults, able to enter social maturity together with their age mates as the new and ascending generation of young adults. Thus what in our own society tends to be a shambles is handled by small-scale societies in a sensible way, inducing feelings of pride and social responsibility.

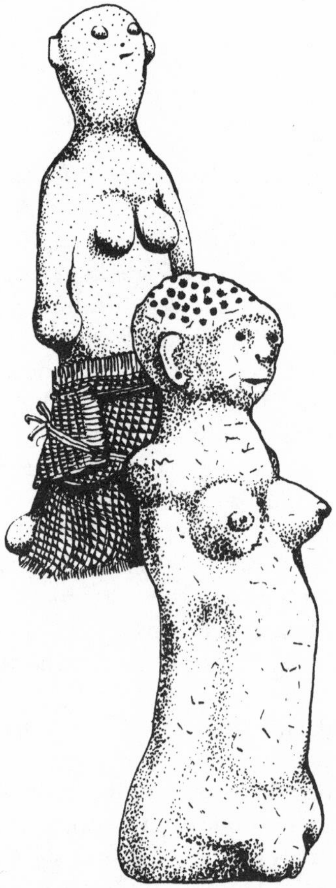

7.1. Zigua figurines from eastern Tanzania used in girls' puberty ceremonies as part of the instruction in their future wifely duties.

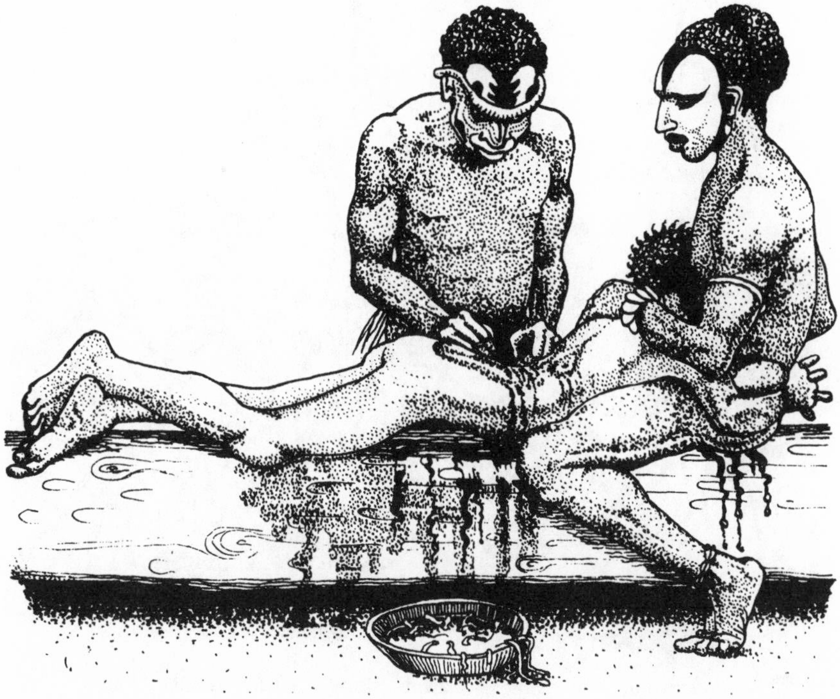

7.2. Initiation of a young man among the latmul of New Guinea. The novice is lying prone on an inverted canoe clasping his mother's brother, who acts as comforter and "mother." An initiator of the opposite moiety to that of the novice is cutting the latter's back with a small bamboo blade. In the foreground is a bowl of water with swabs of fiber to wipe away the blood. The white and black paint on the faces of the two men is a privilege of those who have killed a man. The band of opossum fur worn by the initiator is also a badge of homicide. (Bateson, G. [1936] *Naven: A survey of the problems suggested by a composite picture of a New Guinea tribe drawn from three points of view*. Macmillan, New York.)

Puberty Rituals for Adolescent Girls

Puberty ceremonies may occur before or after menarche and in some societies have the purpose of preparing girls for marriage, which follows soon afterward. Thus among the Bemba[2] the primary purpose was to make the girls marriageable—to make them grow and become women. In the opinion of the adult women involved in the Chisungu ceremony it was designed to change the course of nature by supernatural means. Thus the initiates received the magic associated with growth and nubility and obtained supernatural protection from the dangers associated with the physical onset of puberty, to make it easy for them to have intercourse safely with their future husband and to be safely delivered of their future children. The whole lengthy ceremony made the girl nubile in the

7.3. A scene from life drawn by G. Catlin among the now extinct Mandan Indians. In the Okipa ceremony the warriors sought a personal vision through self-torture. They were hung from thongs inserted through their flesh and were turned until they fainted. (Catlin, G [1841] *The manners, customs, and condition of the North American Indians.* London.)

eyes of the society and thus potentially fertile in a socially acceptable setting.

Although the initiators referred to "teaching" the initiates, Richards wrote that no direct instruction was given and that initiation neither gave additional knowledge and skill nor the right to use them. It was likely that the girls already knew about sex since the families lived in small huts and they would already have learned by observation and participation the elements of sex, the birth process, and child care.

What they did learn at puberty was the secret language of marriage, its etiquette, the rules and taboos of married life that a husband expected his wife to know. Richards wrote that "a girl may have little intellectual understanding of what is being done at the time of her (initiation), although she may be in a highly emotional state in which she is likely to be suggestible to the general emphasis laid on the importance of marriage and childbirth." Second, it taught not so much the technical activities of marriage but the socially approved attitudes toward them, and thus "the rite not only consecrates the woman's duties in the sense of making them seem honourable, but it is an occasion for the public affirmation of the legal obligations of marriage." The protracted Chisungu ceremonies made little use of the supplications common in our worship of supernatural beings, but they made great use of the exact performance of ritual acts and much use of elaborate symbolism and magic formulae; the girls were surrounded as they passed through these rituals with the penumbra of their community's religious understandings and practices.

Puberty Rites for Adolescent Boys

East African boys are initiated around the onset of puberty with the main purpose of inculcating tribal and religious values, economic skills, and sexual techniques. The initiates may well be segregated for a long period during which they receive intermittent instruction in the form of aphorisms and songs which are sometimes complicated and difficult to understand. Boys' initiations parallel those of girls since they are intended to prepare the ground for the assumption of adult roles (see fig. 7.1).

We may examine these rituals among the Zaramo of Tanzania,[3] where they are associated with circumcision and Islamic roles. There, and among the neighboring Zigua, the boys were segregated for three months during which they learned approved behavior through a number of couplets learned by rote, connected with roughly made, temporary clay figurines illustrating them, all of which were combined as teaching aids made for this purpose and had no sacred or secretive connotations.

The instruction placed considerable emphasis on sexuality, but stressed sexuality in the context of society and social obligation, the etiquette of sexual behavior in marriage rather than male pleasure per se. It also dealt with the boy's changed relationship to his mother and the relationship he could anticipate with his future wife and in-laws. The rituals and their symbolism presupposed that the boys were of an age when both sexual and social maturity were about to be reached.

Swantz[4] wrote that "it [the three-month puberty ceremony] is not the actual transition, biologically or socially; it is a form of preparation which emphasizes the male qualities of the growing boys." The rituals made the boys "clean" in their own eyes and in the eyes of society. That they were psychologically important is shown by the fact that it was found that boys who had their initiation delayed had become emotionally disturbed.

In any society where religion is tightly bound up with the culture there is no need for any formal training for the growing young to know what the religion is and how to support it. As the child grows and passes through adolescence, the religion is learned casually and concretely through following out examples set by others (see fig. 7.4), and "it persists on the basis of a constant rehearsal of its complicated dramas, woven as they are into the whole rhythm of social and cultural life."[5] Thus it is not correct to think of an adolescent's being "taught" a traditional religion in any formal sense. A Sukuma youth in Tanzania will see adults

7.4. In this Jewish family scene, children are growing up in a setting in which the family atmosphere is combined with readings from sacred literature and the consumption of alcohol on a modest scale.

consulting diviners and discussing the results; some of his relatives will wear amulets and others will have spirit shrines in their house compounds—no teaching is involved. Others will see sacrifices being performed and be involved as curious spectators on the edge of the family groups.

Over the years adolescents learn the framework of religious and magical thinking which they will use for the remainder of their lives—not as an optional, unimportant system broken down into a series of obligatory performances but as something into which most of the circumstances of their lives will fit. Among the most important ideas they will gain is that of causation. What are the effects that particular modes of thought may have on biological processes? The Azande of the Sudan provide a useful example since their ideas have been studied with great care.[6] Evans-Pritchard has shown that they believed that every event had an ascertainable cause but that this cause was only the proximate one. The Western-trained mind usually accepts this as sufficient, but for a Zande there were more distant events which also acted in a causal way, but which we would consider to be irrelevant.

The Azande adolescent grew up to accept that there were certain individuals who, by means of spells and psychic emanations, could cause injury to the health and property of others, and that there were objects (usually vegetable) which had the power, when used in combination with spells, to affect life and health. A Sukuma hospital dresser brought up with similar beliefs did not dispute that he had caught dysentery from drinking dirty water; his questioning over causation went on to considering *who* had caused him to drink that water.

Where there are ideas of causation which relate malevolent forces to the occurrence of sickness and death it is not surprising that magicoreligious means are sought to counteract them. Among the Azande, the local spirit diviner was contacted; by killing a chicken and seeing how it ran as it died, he interpreted how best to approach the problem, both socially and medicinally. While it is not possible to state that the physical materials used in counteractions had no physiological or psychological effects, the adolescent was certainly trained to seek in his illnesses and misfortunes a very roundabout cure, at least in terms of Western science.

These magicoreligious ideas can carry on long after this earlier conditioning has been superseded. For instance, the concept of witchcraft can survive even prolonged university training in the sciences;[7] however, students of the social sciences appeared to change their beliefs more radically, and Jahoda concluded that possibly these disciplines attracted more skeptical students who were in the process of changing their ideas anyway.

The Santals of Bihar and the Muria of Orissa (northeast India) traditionally permitted premarital sexual relationships. The Santals[8] from puberty enjoyed a period which lasted until marriage, in which boys and girls were under some obligation to pair off, but the pairings were not necessarily expected to develop into marriages.

In their relationships Santal adolescents are said to have had few anxieties. The idea of contraception in any form was treated with derision. Pregnancy usually led to marriage with the boy concerned if he acknowledged paternity and agreed to the marriage. If this did not happen and the girl's parents were not able to arrange a marriage by "purchasing" a husband, village elders sometimes enforced marriage with an old man as it would be unthinkable for the child to have no guardian clan spirit, apart from the fact that such a birth would defile the village spirits. Thus here religious sanctions ensured that no premaritally conceived child was without a social father. A considerable amount of premarital sexual intercourse did take place among the Santals, but premarital pregnancy did not constitute a social problem.

The Muria[9] not only had semipermanent sexual relationships between adolescents but had village dormitories in which teenagers cohabited with one another over a period of five years on average. This had the approval of the community and that of the tribal gods as well. Yet here things were very different. Premarital conception was seen as a social disaster bringing disgrace on the girl and financial penalty on the boy's parents. How then was conception avoided? The Muria themselves alleged that conception was prevented by the supernatural protection of the tribal gods over the village dormitories; they had a number of folk ideas about achieving contraception, such as the need for frequent change of partners, and they believed it helped to restrict intercourse to once or twice a week. There was no widespread use of coitus interruptus. They wrongly assumed that conception was most likely to take place shortly after menstruation. Yet Elwin gave details of 1,738 fertile marriages of which only 92 involved a definite premarital pregnancy; the reason for this shortfall is hard to discover except for the known fact that female reproductive physiological processes may take some years to function properly.[10] Low adolescent birth rates have been reported for a number of societies in which teenage coitus is widespread (e.g., in Timbuctoo);[11] this point was well discussed by Elwin with regard to a number of small-scale societies.

In the last two or three centuries, small rural communities in Western Europe allowed adolescents considerable but specified sexual freedoms, under a custom known as "bundling." This was not a situation of culturally endorsed general promiscuity as the relationships between these boys and girls were guided by both peer group and adult norms.[12] Religiously endorsed marriage was the almost inevitable culmination of such relationships, certainly if the girls conceived. The local church allowed or tolerated such liaisons on the grounds that no permanent harm was done if the girls did not become pregnant, and that it was probably better to have this period of sexual experimentation quasi-legitimized than wholly secretive. In these rural villages if a pregnancy occurred, the biological father was not likely to be in doubt or to disclaim responsibility and the families concerned would probably give their tentative approval to the relationship. The local Christian community, family, and church were interested in getting the couple married eventually even if the bride should be pregnant, or had given birth already, but typically the couple married before the first child was born.

Religious Teaching to Adolescents in Large-Scale Societies

The main world religions, in contrast with small-scale tribal forms, all give specific teaching to their growing children. Islam has long had village schools to teach children the Koran and Traditions of the Prophet by rote. Islam is a doctrinal faith, and any such religion must be to a greater or lesser extent in conflict with the day to day process of living; its universalism makes this inevitable. Geertz[13] has described the Muslim adolescent student or *santri* in Java as "merely a young man becoming adult in a religious environment, grown to maturity with the droning chants of Islam echoing in his ears."

The Buddhist system of teaching is also formalized in some areas, where each boy is initiated at least for a time into the Buddhist order of monks as a "novice."[14] A three-day ceremony, carried out with considerable pomp if his parents' finances allow, usually occurs when the boy has reached puberty. A few initiates stay in the monastery for a few days only, but some stay for more than a year. They should all stay there for three wet seasons as postulants, according to the Patimokkha (rules for the Buddhist monkhood, derived from Buddha the Gautama's teaching and the needs of the monasteries which developed in the centuries after his death).

The Buddhist novice learns the religious superiority of the male since only males are eligible to be novices. Even if he does not stay very long, he will certainly have learned the Five Precepts as the minimum requirements for anyone calling himself a Buddhist. The Five Precepts are abstention from killing (a prohibition which applies to all creatures including insects), stealing, illicit sexual relations, lying, and imbibing any intoxicant conducive to slothfulness. Further precepts add abstention from all sexual relations, taking food after midday, watching or participating in any theatrical entertainment, wearing jewelry or using perfume, sleeping on a high or ornate bed, and handling money. These further Precepts are the periodic (and if possible the permanent) aim of every Buddhist. The Precepts are repeated on the occasion of any prayer. These monastic obligations go far beyond those required of all but the strictest Christian orders.

The Influence of Religion in Multidenominational Societies

Membership of a community dedicated to a particular religion carries with it a characteristic pattern of belief so that members tend to support their religion's stand on moral issues. We have already shown how, in tribal societies and small communities, this influences patterns of thought if only because the growing child is exposed to little beyond the one approved pattern of living and thinking. To some extent this remains true of larger-scale Muslim, Hindu, and Buddhist societies. The same cannot be said of Western societies, which have wide alternative systems of thinking and acting from which adolescents can choose. How much does religious training influence the actions of adolescents in Western "Christian" societies?

There is little doubt that the usual adolescent processes of learning are augmented in religious matters if they are educated in a clearly demarcated denominational school. Such students may be favorably disposed to religion anyway.[15] Some results tend to show that these schools, whatever their denomination, produce more than a proportional share of students who have characteristics of closed-mindedness.[16]

Christianity is unusual among the religions of the world in that adolescents are often among the most active members of their denominations. A study in Greece showed that Christian activity peaked during adolescence and that this peak was not reached again later in life.[17] Other studies in the United States have, however, shown an overall increase in religiosity with age, despite a general decline in orthodoxy.[18]

Just as adolescence is found in some studies to be a time for increased Christian activity, it is also a pivotal time in which adolescents may become less favorably disposed to religion than they were as children. That they cease to practice and/or believe then seems to be attributable to conflicts between them and other members of their particular denomination, and also in their homes (Gosse's *Father and Son*[19] is eloquent on this subject).

It has been suggested that the religious enthusiasms of Christian adolescents are related to the anxieties caused by their ambivalent position in society. However, a study of U.S. Southern Baptist youths who responded to a religious appeal to come forward for conversion, rededication, and special service did not show any predisposing anxiety in these youths as compared with those who did not respond, nor did such anxiety as they had show any reduction as the result of this coming forward.[20] Another study[21] found that there was little to substantiate the hypothesis that Catholic adolescents wondered about fewer beliefs and thought they had fewer problems than non-Catholics. Thus we have the general picture of Christian adolescents being more or less interested and active in their faiths, and some not being religious at all in the conventional sense. Where the religious label applies, they are likely to follow the aims and ideas of their denominations with greater or lesser intensity. It is an oversimplification to distinguish between religious and irreligious adolescents; they are in a process of change, including changes of attitude to religion.

Religious Restriction on Adolescent Association

Even if a denomination does not actively involve itself in restricting association socially or by religious injunctions about the undesirability of such meetings, the preference many persons show for associating with others who share their views rather than with strangers logically produces patterns of association based on similarity of religious beliefs. In fact it will be shown in chapter 8 that even persons who do not actively practice their faith prefer to marry someone of the same faith, and this holds even in populations which have a generally very low level of religious involvement.

There is no doubt that some denominations do devote considerable direct and indirect effort to restricting association between their younger members and persons whom they consider to be "unsuitable" marriage partners, though this is not so effective in the wider world of the multidenominational city as it is in small, geographically restricted sects. Youth clubs, youth camps, youth services, and activities of all types bring adolescents together and this propinquity is the social matrix in which potential marriage partners select each other, only in part on the basis of shared beliefs.

While there is normally some degree of pressure to prevent interdenominational association and possible marriage, this pressure is particularly strong at the socially conceived "limits" of legitimate association. Here pure prejudice may emanate from religious belief and practice. Studies in the United States have shown that those with no religion are more likely to have a low level of prejudice in racial matters than those professing a religion.[22] In one study Catholic children were found to be anti-Semitic rather than generally race-prejudiced as a result of religious teaching about the Crucifixion.[23] In some periods the perjorative label "Christ-killers" has been a common form of Christian street abuse for Jews. Among Catholics it has been shown that anti-Semitism in students has diminished since the 1965 Vatican Ecumenical Council.[24] This council in its statement on non-Christian religions enjoins, "Remember the bond that spiritually ties the people of the New Covenant to Abraham's stock," continuing "God holds the Jews most dear for the sake of their Fathers," and concluding "this Sacred Synod wants to foster and recommend that mutual understanding and respect which is the fruit, above all, of biblical and theological studies as well as of fraternal dialogues." In particular, it refuted the view that Jews in general were killers of Christ and stated that no support can be given to any form of persecution.[25]

Judeo-Christian Thinking on Sin

In the past a widely held view has been that "keeping company" by couples intending to marry is potentially an occasion of sin. St. Alphonsus "would not permit a young man to go to the home of his betrothed more than once or twice . . . for I have rarely found one who does not sin in such a visit, at least in word or thought," and "I believe they ordinarily find it difficult to be outside the proximate occasion of sinning mortally."[26] Jewish rabbinical thought expressed in the Torah has similarly held that any sexual relations outside marriage are unlawful and, that being so, any meetings in private between individuals of opposite sexes are to be strictly prohibited.

So adolescent intersexual contact was traditionally discouraged in the Judeo-Christian tradition on the grounds that it might lead to a hasty and regrettable marriage, it exposed one to sexual temptation too early in life, and, for students, it imposed a strain on educational possibilities. As late as 1916 the Vatican forbade, even for pious purposes, dances which went on far into the night.[27] But this is today an isolated, anachronistic, and perhaps forgotten injunction. Many modern moralists appear to have greater confidence in the wholesomeness of the young, turning their attention to concern over the time and place of teenage associations, the availability of alcohol, the abuse of cars, and the time that adolescents are expected to be home.

The Stigma of Illegitimacy—a Restraint on Adolescent Coitus

In the preceding chapter we looked at the effects of illegitimacy on birth rates and mortality. Here we consider prevailing attitudes to illegitimacy as they apply to the young parent. Where the stigma of illegitimacy is very great, following the religious definition of all sexual relations outside marriage as immoral, as in Muslim Arab countries such as Egypt and Algeria, the illegitimacy rate is very low; where illegitimacy sanctions are slight, the rate is often quite high, as in Western Europe, where up to a third of all births in the 1990s occur out of wedlock.

The rules defining legitimacy and confining sexual relationships to marriage alone cannot be ascribed to prudishness. Such rules exist among Hindus who extol the virtues of sexual activity in all its many varied forms as a life-giving and joyous pastime that puts man into an almost divine condition. It is not sex that is tabooed but the breaking of category rules. Religious groups are in fact more concerned about illegitimate births than about mere sexual relations before marriage, because the former make public the fact that the rules are weak and threatened. Catholicism provides mechanisms of absolution such as prayer, confession, or sacrifice for the removal of the taints of minor sins. Absolution is available for those who feel that the sexual relations they have had before or outside their marriages are wrong. However, illegitimacy provides something of a problem. Various strategies exist to deal with the situation, but in general adolescents are warned not to get into it.

The disapproval of premarital conception in Christianity may perhaps be illustrated by the fact that couples in which the girl is pregnant tend to choose civil weddings rather than religious ceremonies. A study in Detroit showed that half the brides in civil weddings were already pregnant, as against less than a sixth in religious weddings.[28] There is no certainty that the former would not have chosen civil weddings even if they had not been pregnant, but the figures show that couples claiming religious affiliation to the Christian church had a premarital conception rate lower than that of all couples.[29]

What about attitudes to sexual activity? Adolescents involved in Christian institutions have been found to be generally less permissive in sexual matters than those not so involved. A study of U.S. Methodist youth leaders showed that 80 percent held to a standard which did not allow premarital intercourse, although at least a third approved of noncoital sexual activity.[30] Studies of sexual behavior among older adolescents showed that sexual liberality decreased in proportion to increased frequency of church attendance and that in general nonbelievers reported more liberal sexual attitudes and behavior than believers.[31]

Apart from the social problems resulting from premarital sexual relations, it may also be that there are desirable health consequences of observing such restrictions. It has been shown that women who have had sexual intercourse during adolescence face a higher probability of eventual cervical cancer.[32] The incidence of venereal disease (VD) and acquired immunodeficiency syndrome (AIDS) is also known to vary in proportion to the number of sex partners, and VD is at present widespread in the adolescent populations of the United Kingdom, United States, and other countries where, in general, religious controls are not strong.

Sexual Relations in Adolescence

Because of the social problems of pregnancy, the religious systems of most cultures have been more permissive about sexual intercourse for unmarried boys than for girls. In Western countries, frequency of sexual intercourse is, as expected, higher among males the less actively they are connected with religious groups. Pioneering work on this topic was done by Kinsey and his colleagues in the late 1940s in the United States. These showed that among males under the age of twenty years, active (i.e., churchgoing) Protestants and Catholics had rates of premarital coitus below average.[33] From this one may conclude that such religious sanctions as exist against premarital sexual intercourse were only effective in controlling young men's sexual behavior when they were devout. In Kinsey's sample of churchgoing and nonchurchgoing Protestant men between sixteen and twenty years without college education, the proportions reporting that they engaged in coitus were 70.4 percent and 90.5 percent, respectively. With college education the frequency for the churchgoing group fell to 27.3 percent and of the nonchurchgoing to 45 percent.

The effect of these religious and social restraints on sexual intercourse with socially acceptable girls was reflected by the high rates of visits to prostitutes by young single males, which varied between 48.2 percent for those without college education to 19.3 percent for the college-educated between sixteen and twenty years.[34]

In Western (as well as many other) societies, religious rules and attitudes to a greater or lesser extent restrict the sexual relationships of unmarried girls. This is more strongly the case in Hindu and Muslim societies and was also true in ancient Greece and Rome. With the approach of adolescence, social and therefore potential sexual contacts between boys and girls may be restricted if not totally prevented. In a modern Rajput community it was regarded as extremely scandalous for a young man and a girl to exchange glances publicly and they would be beaten if they were seen to do so.[35]

Most data for Western societies show that premarital sexual intercourse is most frequent among girls least actively connected with religious groups and lowest among those who are most devout.

Western societies from their Christian background have very generally transmitted the viewpoint that premarital sexual intercourse is potentially dangerous and damaging. This general attitude is translated into a prevailing feeling among devout adolescents that sex is sinful. This feeling is reinforced by a private sense of guilt and by public disapproval. Additional physical dangers are pregnancy, abortion, venereal disease, and AIDS; social dangers include forced marriage and legal difficulties. Moral objections from within and without are probably the principal factors restricting premarital intercourse in girls. To some extent such rules can be self-defeating. If a girl assumes that sexual intercourse will not take place within a particular association, she is more likely to become pregnant if intercourse does occur, since she will not have taken contraceptive precautions in advance.

While Judaism (Deut. 22:13–21) and Islam (Koran, Sura 24.2) and almost all Christian denominations judge coitus before marriage to be morally wrong, there has developed a double standard which disproportionately affects the girl. Many religions have expressed the no-sex rule in the form of a concern for the virginity of the girl at marriage, whereas the boy may even be expected to have sexual experience. Virginity rules have had, and continue to have, widespread support, and there is, in many cultures (Italy, parts of Africa, even Samoa), a preference among some men for virgin brides.

One effect of this double standard, maintained in part by religions, has been the development of a social distinction between "respectable" women who are marriageable and with whom sexual intercourse is a marital obligation leading to the birth of children and "unrespectable" women with whom men seek to have sexual relations and with whom marriage is more or less ruled out.

The Exposure to Sexuality in Adolescence

The exposure to adult sexuality in adolescence in the Western world is surreptitious. It is opposed by all the churches as pornographic, indecent, or immoral and is, in certain forms, against the law. The position of the Eastern faiths appears to be radically different.

In Hinduism it is not possible for the growing child to be unaware of adult sexuality; indeed it has an approved place in the religion since the male and female sexual organs are central in some temples and are a focus of worship. Some Hindu temples, such as Khajuraho (see fig. 7.5), are covered externally with copulating figures displaying a "languid and calculated eroticism."[36] The well-known Hindu text known as the Kama Sutra[37] spells out in great detail the desired and approved range of sexuality and instructs lovers on how to interact with one another.

Hinduism applauds marital sexuality and the child grows up within an ideology which is ostentatiously procreative to most Westerners, though for Hindus themselves, lacking Christian sex taboos, it expresses in physical form the union of the soul with the divine. Hindu adolescents

7.5. A sculpture from the Hindu temples at Khajuraho, India, dated from the tenth century A.D.

seeing the sexual imagery of temple paintings and sculptures as they grow to maturity think, perhaps, mainly of the physical and sensual aspects, but their religion makes them aware of complementary symbolic aspects. So we have in Hinduism an encouragement of marital sexuality that has never been overt in the Western world. Such a situation must contribute to encouraging adolescents to aspire to, or at least willingly agree to, an early date for their arranged marriages, if indeed they are not already betrothed before puberty.

Among Muslims, despite an external aloofness by women and the fierce condemnation of illegitimate sexuality, there is an equally open and divinely encouraged sexual activism for married couples. The Arab world has produced a number of erotic books, especially *The Perfumed Garden of Shaykh Nefzawi*,[38] which has for centuries had a wide currency in Islam. For present purposes, what is interesting in these books is not so much the ingenious variety of sexual practices described but the way in which they are included within the Islamic religious doctrine.

An Egyptian book about sex thus starts with the preamble "Praise to the Lord who adorned the virginal bosom with breasts and who made the thighs of women for the spear handles of men,"[39] while *The Perfumed Garden* starts similarly with "Praise be given to God, who has placed man's greatest pleasure in the natural parts of woman and has destined the natural parts of man to afford the greatest enjoyment to woman." This particular book is filled with numerous pious phrases and reflections such as "I, the servant of God, am thankful to him that no one can help falling in love with beautiful women; God, the magnificent, has said, 'Women are your field. Go upon your field as you like,' " and "I profited by this moment to admire the beauties of her vulva. The blessing of God the best creator, be upon it."

Sir Richard Burton noticed "the system of . . . teaching lads first arrived at puberty the nice conduct . . . of a branch of the knowledge tree which our modern education grossly neglects thereby entailing untold miseries upon individuals, families and generations."[40]

In small-scale societies we found that puberty ceremonies were widespread, sometimes with scarification rituals for social marking and other methods for toughening up or ensuring the bravery of young men. Instruction was included, conveying information on socially approved timing of sex, on marital duties and attitudes to sex, rather than on sex itself, which was well understood.

Whereas emphasis was heavily laid on sex in marriage for some small-scale societies, in others adolescent sex was the approved norm. In the latter case, we found that widespread promiscuity did not inevitably lead to the expected high premarital birth rates.

Coming on to larger societies and the major world religions, we found that they all tended to disapprove of premarital sex to a greater or lesser extent. We interpreted this in the light of the known facts of religious endogamy, and also of status considerations which in the case of the caste system were linked to Hindu ideas of purity and pollution. In Christian societies the situation was complex—some adolescents were unusually devout and were aloof from sexual activity, which was seen as sinful; others were permissive and even irreligious and might even be promiscuous. Despite modern contraceptive techniques, we noted higher rates of illegitimacy and premarital conceptions among the less devout, but this phenomenon was far more influenced by educational level: both the frequency of coitus and the rate of adolescent (premarital) pregnancy were lower in cases where education was more prolonged. We noted too a double standard for the two sexes. Boys were often far freer with regard to sex than girls before marriage, and prostitution was seen to play its part in making this possible.

Perhaps the most interesting contrast occurred within marriage itself, where Islam and Hinduism extolled the religious and virtuous nature of sexual activity, whereas in Christianity it remained a shadowy area. Oriental sex manuals, not so very long ago, were classed as "pornographic" in the West, and even now are so regarded by many devout Christians. The idea of sex in itself, even within marriage, as sinful is peculiar, among world religions, to Christianity.

In the next chapter we move on to consider marriage more fully. Marriage is the social legitimation of the reproductive process, whereby a man and his wife or wives care for each other and produce new members of the community. It begins with a fascinating and highly ceremonial occasion, involving transfers of wealth between the two families. Marriage is hedged about with taboos, and there are many rules governing the behavior of the married couple toward each other and toward others. Religions (as well as civil laws) play their part in restricting tabooed behavior and encouraging approved kinds. They also have roles to play in managing the stresses and strains of marriage and in dissolving marriages that fail. These and other aspects will be examined next.

Notes

1. Gennep, A. van. (1960). *The rites of passage.* Routledge, London.

2. Richards, A. I. (1956). *Chisungu: A girl's initiation ceremony among the Bemba of Northern Rhodesia.* Faber and Faber, London.

3. Swantz, L. W. (1970). "The Zaramo of Dar-es-Salaam: A study of continuity and change." *Tanzania Notes and Records,* 71, 157–64.

4. Swantz, L. W. (1970). "The Zaramo of Dar-es-Salaam: A study of continuity and change." *Tanzania Notes and Records,* 71, 157–64.

5. Geertz, C. (1960). *The religion of Java.* Free Press, New York, p. 177.

6. Evans-Pritchard, E. E. (1937). *Witchcraft, oracles and magic among the Azande,* Clarendon Press, Oxford.

7. Jahoda, G. (1968). "Scientific training and the persistence of traditional beliefs among West African university students." *Nature,* 220, 1356.

8. Archer, W. G. (1974). *The hill of flutes: Love, life and poetry in tribal India.* Allen and Unwin, London.

9. Elwin V. (1947). *The Muria and their ghotul.* Oxford University Press, Bombay.

10. Ashley-Montagu, M. F. (1957). *The reproductive development of the female with especial reference to the period of adolescent sterility.* Julian Press, New York.

11. Miner, H. (1953). *The primitive city of Timbuctoo.* Princeton University Press, Princeton, New Jersey.

12. Stiles, H. R. (1869). *Bundling: Its origins, progress and decline in America.* Munsell, Albany, New York.

13. Geertz, C. (1960). *The religion of Java.* Free Press, New York, p. 179.

14. Spiro, M. E. (1971). *Buddhism and society.* Allen and Unwin, London, pp. 234–47.

15. Remmers, H. H., et al. (1951). "Some personality aspects and religious values of high school youth." *Purdue Opinion Panel,* 10(3).

16. Quin, P. V. (1965). "Critical thinking and open-mindedness in public and Catholic secondary schools." *J Social Psychology,* 66, 23–30.

17. Sakellariou, G. T. (1938). "A study of the religious life of Greek youth." *Ereunai Psuchol Ergasteriou Thessaloniki,* 2.

18. Zaenglein, M. M., et al. (1975). "The adolescent and his religion: Beliefs in transition." *Revue Religious Research*, 17, 51–60.

19. Gosse, E. (1970). *Father and son.* Heinemann, London.

20. Cooley, C. E., and Hutton, J. B. (1965). "Adolescent response to religious appeal as related to IPAT anxiety scale." *J Social Psychology*, 67, 325–27.

21. Kuhlen, R. G., and Arnold, M. (1944). "Age differences in religious beliefs and problems during adolescence." *J Genetic Psychology*, 65, 291–300.

22. Burnham, K. E., et al. (1969). "Religious affiliation, church attendance, religious education and student attitudes toward race." *Sociological Analysis*, 30, 235–44.

23. Gruesser, M. J. (1950). "Categorical valuations of Jews among Catholic parochial school children." *Catholic University America Studies Sociology*, 34.

24. Ward, C. D. (1973). "Anti-Semitism at college: Changes since Vatican II." *J Scientific Study Religion*, 12, 85–88.

25. The Second Vatican Council. (1966). Constitution on the Church in the modern world. Secretariat of the Council, Vatican.

26. Alphonsus. (1905). *Praxis confessari in theologia moralis.* Rome.

27. Benedict XV. (1916). *Acta Apostolicis Sedis.* Rome.

28. Blood, R. O. (1969). *Marriage.* Free Press, New York, p. 145.

29. Blood, R. O. (1969). *Marriage.* Free Press, New York, p. 145.

30. Glass, J. C. (1972). "Premarital sexual standards among church going youth leaders." *J Scientific Study Religion*, 11, 361–67.

31. Sutker, P. B., et al. (1970). "Religious preference, practice and personal sexual attitudes and behaviour." *Psychology Reports*, 26, 835–41.

32. Rotkin, I. D. (1962). "Relation of adolescent coitus to cervical cancer risk." *J American Medical Association*, 179, 486–91.

33. Kinsey, A. C., et al. (1949). *Sexual behavior in the human male.* Saunders, Philadelphia, pp. 447–80.

34. Kinsey, A. C., et al. (1949). *Sexual behavior in the human male.* Saunders, Philadelphia, table 65.

35. Carstairs, G. M. (1961). *The twice-born.* Hogarth Press, London, p. 72.

36. Rowland, B. (1954). *The art and architecture of India.* Penguin, London, p. 164.

37. Burton, R., and Arbuthnot, F. F. (trans.) (1963). *The Kama Sutra of Vatsyayana.* Allen and Unwin, London.

38. Burton, R. (trans.) (1963). *The perfumed garden of the Shaykh Nefwazi.* Spearman, London.

39. Jalal Al-din Al Siyuti. (1990). *The book of exposition in the science of coition.* Carrington, Paris.

40. Burton, R. (1963). *The book of a thousand nights and a night.* Allen and Unwin, London.

8

Marriage

In this chapter we shall consider the institution of marriage with particular reference to how marriage is controlled by religious organizations or rules.

Every known society practices marriage in some form or other; every society makes some effort to bring the mating activities of its adult members under social control in order to establish rules for the orderly transmission from parents to offspring of material and nonmaterial things such as land and membership of clans. The object is to bring order to bear on essential processes such as rights of land use, rights of access to other individuals, and obligations to help with important tasks. A marriage is not to be construed as an event involving just the two persons concerned and their families; it is an institution which has widespread ramifications and involves large numbers of people.

The institution of marriage affects reproduction by making it "legitimate." The offspring of a legitimate marriage are often given prior access to the resources of the kinship unit and are accorded the full benefits of membership of this social group, whereas offspring born outside marriage may not have these advantages and may be short of food, medical care, or affection.

Marital Stability

In hunting and gathering tribes, there is often little emphasis on marriage as a lifelong arrangement. Among the Mbuti pygmies of Zaire[1] and the Hadza of Tanzania[2] betrothal and marriage were not tightly controlled,

8.1. In Greek Orthodox churches in Crete thin metal plaques are placed around certain popular icons testifying to the hope that the donor's prayers would be successful in the matter depicted. In this case a bachelor is praying for a wife.

couples wanted a "real" rather than an "empty" marriage, and divorce was common.

In less nomadic societies in which the community is settled on its own land and its members do not have to move frequently in search of their livelihood, more concern is shown for the survival of kinship groupings. Among the Sukuma of Tanzania the living, the dead, and the yet-to-be-born are one continuing family patriclan which can only be interrupted by the infertility of its male members or their failure to contract legitimate marriages. There is considerable social and religious pressure on men to marry and propagate descendants legitimately, as without such children clan ancestors are prevented from surviving in the memories and religious practices of their descendants. Such ancestors may turn malevolent and harm their remaining descendants within the extended family as a whole. The man who did not marry out of selfishness or poverty and had children in a series of love affairs was not carrying on his own patrilineage, for such children belonged to their mother's patrilineage.[3]

A relationship between a Sukuma man and woman is legitimized into marriage by the passage of cattle from his family to her family. These cattle represent a congeries of rights and obligations between the husband's family that receives the bride and the wife's family that gives her. It is not a transaction between the couple involved, although the man will have chosen a particular woman and she will have accepted him beforehand. Sukuma marriages are not undertaken lightly and in fact the divorce rate is low.

From the biological point of view it is not so much the absolute stability of marriages that affects child rearing as the relative stability of any given marriage in relation to the norms of the community. Depending on how much emphasis there is on marriage and its stability, the effects of illegitimacy will be greater or smaller. A Sukuma lover, if he makes an unmarried woman pregnant, not only has to pay compensation but gains no long-term advantages from his procreation.[4] He can, however, legitimize such a child before its birth by paying bride-wealth and marrying the woman. At a later stage he can pay cattle for each illegitimate child to the mother's family as compensation for the burden of rearing. Finally, he can pay bride wealth on behalf of an illegitimate son when the latter comes to marry. Only poverty would restrain a man from legitimizing his illegitimate children. Besides immediate there are long-term benefits of a spiritual kind, since a man can only become an ancestor if he has legitimate children. Most systems of ancestor recognition have within them positive inducements to marry and legitimize offspring even if this is delayed through poverty or irresponsibility until comparatively late in life. An ancestor cult can thus produce good care of and concern for children, and it is a sound reproductive strategy for individuals to work within it rather than outside it. This the Sukuma can do, however, even if they convert to Christianity or Islam.

In some societies such as the Tallensi of Ghana the authority of the ancestors was part of a system of social practice which worked to ensure moral relationships among members of a society predominantly organized through the structures of kinship. Agnatic ancestors provided the central scheme of reference and reasoning for the reproduction of Tale society; through their authority they gave sanction and support to the solidarity of lineage segments. Nonagnatic ancestors, in contrast, were recognized and provided a balancing sanction for the inevitable dynamic of individuality within such a highly organized society.[5]

Spirit Possession and the Survival of Marriages

In unsettled societies in Africa where there is considerable migration to work and husbands are separated from their wives, or when the husband or wife lives in an area such as an urban slum or in the mixed-sex labor lines of an agricultural estate or near a mine, separated from her or his family, the usual social methods of settling marital problems are lost and religion in the form of spirit possession may provide answers.

Spirit possession of women and accusations of witchcraft by their husbands occurred among the Nupe.[6] This served to assert the interdependence of the sexes and in fact conserved the existing pattern of relations between them. Although these phenomena appeared overtly to be highly disruptive of marriage, they really represented disguised conservatism and stability.[7]

Some stable African societies have well established systems of spirit possession in which ancestors "speak" through their descendants about the trouble particular individuals are bringing on themselves by their offenses against the unity and survival of the lineage. For such men and women the reason for their troubles in life is ascribed to the disapproval of their possibly even unknown ancestors. It is probable that this type of possession is increasing as more people become involved in personal troubles caused by social changes for which there are no traditional institutional solutions. Certainly possession occurs much more frequently in communities in or near urban–industrial areas than in traditional areas.

Spirit possession is particularly common in areas of coastal Tanzania and Kenya and in Somalia,[8] where wives suffer from the difficulties of urban life and have to manage without the support of their own extended families. This situation seems to be heavily loaded against the wife, who is particularly vulnerable to poverty if her husband does not support her adequately. In such cases the spirits of the family or of the locality in which the woman is living are invoked. The wife becomes possessed and is thus incapable of fulfilling her domestic obligations properly. The husband cannot negotiate directly with his wife as she is out of his world, and thus he has to organize her exorcism. During this exorcism the infesting spirit speaks through the wife, giving its reasons for troubling her and the price it expects to be paid to her (or the doctor in charge of the exorcism) if she is to be relieved of its presence. Thus she becomes the center of her husband's attention and he has to pay for her restoration to normality.

Possession occurred frequently in Sukuma communities near Mwanza town in Tanzania. In Dar es Salaam the urban witch doctor would lose clients by suggesting spirit exorcism, since the local Zaramo would have to go to their country homes for the ceremony. As a result, exorcism was common outside Dar es Salaam but not within the city, despite the fact that an estimated eight thousand urban dwellers visited witch doctors every day;[9] today the practice has become even more frequent. The 1963 initiations to the Buchwezi Spirit Society in Usukuma, Tanzania, included a majority of married, divorced, and widowed women. Thus religion in the form of involvement in a spirit cult can be seen to respond in a variety of ways to the particular needs of women with marital problems, in the case of the married women for the survival of their marriages and in the case of divorced and widowed women as a response to the loss of their husbands.

Hinduism and Marriage

Marriage in Hindu life has unique features since it is characterized by the obligation to marry within the caste or subcaste. In addition bachelors have lower religious status than married men and cannot perform certain rituals. The married state, not just the marriage ceremony, is regarded as sacred rather than secular. The Hindu scriptures state that "the husband receives his wife from the gods,"[10] and among Brahmins a wife is enjoined to treat her husband as a deity and to eat on the dining leaf from which her husband has already eaten, which for others would be considered impure. While polygyny is permitted when the first wife is infertile or has produced no sons, monogamy is held up as an ideal, typified by the mythical heroes Rama and Krishna.

The social requirements of Hindu marriage are so expensive that this most important of all family ceremonies is the principal cause of debt among Indian peasants. Although the religious injunctions of Hinduism apply more strictly to the higher castes, the wedding is, even among the peasantry, a ceremony of great complexity with a lengthy series of rituals and complicated, expensive prestations.

Hindu marriage is indissoluble under the Laws of Manu, and there is a religious ban on the remarriage of high-caste widows. The inducement to marry off daughters as early as possible is great; parents who had not succeeded in finding husbands for daughters past puberty were regarded as being guilty of a great sin.[11] The net effect of these attitudes and rules is to increase the birth rate, since reproduction begins at an early age, after the period of adolescent infertility (see chapter 7).

According to Klass, in Hinduism there is preference for virgin brides; the result (because marriage involves prepayments to the family of the bride) is that the older and wealthier men have younger virgin women as wives. The Laws of Manu state that twelve and eight are suitable ages for brides—or even earlier if necessary. The husband's age may render him less fertile and active than a younger man would be, but if older men are better able to care for their wives and children than younger ones, this arrangement can be advantageous to the girl. The youngest ages for brides have been found in the socially lowest endogamous units.[12]

Despite a general taboo, Hindu widows of lower castes have always remarried. However, we should note that it has been suggested that "remarriage" may not be an appropriate term for the Hindu practice, known in India as *natra*. Agrawal and Agrawal[13] have shown that Hindus see marriage as a sacrament that remains unbreakable even after death, although a widower or a man whose wife is barren or unable to bear a son may have a second wife. Some sacred books have advocated taking a second husband in certain cases. *Natra*, they write, should be seen not as remarriage but as a social alliance that allows for preserving the Hindu prohibition of remarriage. A wife's hope is usually to predecease her husband and thus avoid widowhood (see chapter 9), which is itself considered attributable to sins committed in a previous incarnation.

Again according to Klass, marriages are generally arranged by the parents even when some initial interest in a particular girl may have been expressed by a boy. The unmarried were seen as children who had little competence in the matter. Attempts to determine the desires of either the boy or girl have been described as rare and at best circuitous and perfunctory. Thus for Hindus marriage and first sexual experience are socially highly structured. A man's wife comes to him as a stranger, and their relationship in its initial phases is one in which sexual experience is combined with religious ideas and concepts of Hinduism learned in childhood.

In such delicate matters as obtaining socioreligious prestige from the marriage of a virgin daughter, a father is not likely to want to risk the uncertainties that arise from marrying her into a family of whom little is known. So it is important not only to marry her within the local subcaste (or higher) but within the range of families of whose habits one can be assured. It is also true that marrying into neighboring families keeps the cultivable land in large parcels; more food is grown as less land is taken up with boundary hedges and *bunds* (earth walls) between rice fields, and less time is spent getting to and from cultivable plots.

One is inclined to think that caste as a pervading institution must be in decline; human rights and democracy are guaranteed to citizens by Article 29 (2) of the Indian constitution, and all social disabilities were removed from the so-called Untouchables by Articles 15, 17, 25, 46, and other sections. The Westernized members of the upper classes have theoretically shed caste restrictions to a large extent, but they are still members of caste-minded families and find it useful to use caste to procure economic and social advantages. There have, however, been changes. In public health matters the provision of piped water and sanitation has reduced the biological significance of the idea of "impurity." The widespread use of public transport is incompatible with the idea of "contamination" from an endless succession of fellow travelers. Certainly some educated and urbanized middle-class Indians are changing, and they marry more widely outside the previously sacrosanct endogamous units, but they are still only a small minority.

With these changes we can see a rise in the age of marriage of women. Data available for 1986 for Nepal show that the mean age of marriage in 1986 was 15.8 years for Hindus, 18.9 years for Buddhists, and 14.6 years for Muslims.[14] We can expect a decline in the extent and closeness of consanguineous marriages as families gradually become more dispersed. But first marriages, except among a relatively small urbanized middle class, continue to be endogamous within the subcaste. We can also see the creation of new subcastes within which marriages will begin to take place, such as those of taxi drivers, and it may be that even "anti-caste" communities will discover to their chagrin they have become sub-castes when it comes to the marriages of their daughters.

Buddhism and Marriage: The Resort to Spirits

There are few references to marriage in Buddhist canonical texts, commentaries, and contemporary studies, except in terms placing it as a second-best institution, irretrievably inferior to the monastic life according to the demands of the Eightfold Path.

Marriage for Buddhists in some areas is celebrated by the public witnessing of a ceremony accompanied by a feast with a propitiatory offering to the village spirits.[15] It is the spirits which are particular to the area, together with those of the houses on both the mother's side and the father's side, that are held responsible for the personal protection of those who propitiate them at marriage ceremonies and in childbirth. Buddhism thus has a protective edifice of personalized spirits within the general structure of the prohibitions and injunctions of its faith. In chapter 4, we have discussed the possible effects of Buddhist ideas on conception, pointing out that Burma has an unusually low birth rate for an Asian country. The support of the spirits is secondary to the main Buddhist culture in Burma, and one study has shown that older persons, divorced and widowed, being conscious of the inevitability of rebirth, tend not to remarry, as "there exists at the level of values a Buddhist rationale for extreme hesitation in marriage and remarriage."[16] In the six north Burma villages studied, 80.6 percent of the widowed and divorced men and women did not remarry.

Jewish Attitudes Toward Marriage and Procreation

Judaism holds that marriage is for procreation and companionship and that this interpretation is based on biblical injunctions.[17] It is held that the Song of Songs, paralleling divine with carnal love, clearly had monogamous marriage in mind, as do numerous other biblical passages in Psalms and Proverbs. Jewish scholars have in general felt that although the Bible mentions polygyny, it has no overall religious validity and its survival in Indian and other Asian communities rests on local social conventions. To summarize a complex topic, Judaism emphasizes procreation, restricts the number of spouses to one at a time, disapproves of divorce but does not forbid it and allows remarriage, and combines the obligation to marry with an affirmative attitude to sexual passion, though immodest conduct is not allowed even between married couples.

Rabbinic literature as expressed in the Talmud typifies the sinner as the unmarried man who "spends all his days in sinful thoughts": "he who has no wife is not a proper man." Celibacy thus has no place in Judaism since it is not advocated as one of the biblical acts of self-denial[18] nor imposed on the priesthood.[19] There are many cases of scholars not marrying but it is often held that the aspiring scholar should marry first and then study.

Sexual desire is not evil or shameful in itself, as it is linked to the idea that without it men would not marry or beget children and that absence of children would diminish man as the Image of God. For orthodox Jews following the Scriptures, marriage is so important that in theory a man would be justified in selling a Torah scroll in order to get the money to marry. Again in theory, if he is not married by the age of twenty years God curses him; for a girl there is a danger that she will become unchaste if she is not found a husband. Marriage in Judaism is not a sacrament in the Christian sense since it is possible to dissolve it by divorce, but it is more than a legal contract since the wife is consecrated to her husband and forbidden to others. Thus we see in Judaism the factors of monogamous marriage and an acceptance of sexuality as morally good.

According to Dorff[20] Jewish thought holds that God created bodies as well as minds, emotions, and wills, and that the body is God's masterpiece. Man's duty is to have sexual intercourse with his wife independent of his duty to propagate, and this duty to fulfill the woman's sexual needs continues even after the man has propagated two children, one of each sex.

The Mishnah spells out specifically how often a man should offer to have sexual relations with his wife: "The times for conjugal duty prescribed in the Torah are: for men of independent means every day; for labourers only twice a week; for ass-drivers once a week; for camel drivers once in thirty days; for sailors once in six months."[21]

Early Christian Sexual Intercourse and Marriage

The Gospels tell us nothing about the physical aspects of marriage, and it is on St. Paul that the Christian interpretations tend to rely. He states:

> It is good for a man not to touch a woman, but for fear of fornication let every man have his own wife and let every woman have her own husband. Let the husband render the debt to this wife, [i.e., have sexual intercourse with her] and the wife also in like manner to the husband. . . . Defraud not one another, except, perhaps, by consent, for a time, that you may give yourself to prayers; and return together again, that Satan tempt you not for your incontinency.[22]

So it was not surprising that many early ecclesiastical writers took a very negative view of sexual activity both within and outside marriage. The ritualistic kissing in greeting by the early Christians was suspected by Athenagoras of being a highly erotic act, so it was classed as immoral to kiss for a second time after having enjoyed the first. John of Damascus even suggested that if Adam and Eve had obeyed God, human reproduction would have taken place in a less sinful manner.[23] St. Augustine was particularly severe: He held that sexual concupiscence was a vice and contamination and in no way to be considered as one of the benefits of marriage.[24] In his arguments against Manicheism he concluded that the only justification for sexual intercourse, which was evil, must be the procreation of children. Thus those who knew themselves to be sterile were not free from sin when they continued to have intercourse.[25] The idea of sex in itself as sinful has been a consistent theme of Christian moralists up to the present century.

The great theologian St. Thomas Aquinas held to much the same view, stating that "there are two ways in which married people are free from all sin in intercourse, to wit, by reason of procreating and by reason of rendering the debt; otherwise there is always sin in it at least venial."[26]

While the view that sexual intercourse was sinful unless aimed at procreation faded with the centuries, it did not disappear. In the early eighteenth century it was still maintained that sexual activity and pleasure were shameful but unfortunately necessary for human survival. Thus it would seem that sexuality in marriage must have been severely inhibited during this lengthy period of moral rulings. It made sexual intercourse during pregnancy sinful, likewise intercourse when a child was not wanted. And sex of all other kinds was sinful within as well as outside marriage.

Contemporary Christian Approaches to Marriage

While Catholic theologians have maintained for many centuries that the principal end of marriage is the procreation and rearing of children, it has now come to be accepted that the actual realization of these ends is not essential, nor indeed that the absence of procreative acts invalidates an enduring marriage.

The contemporary view is perhaps that the fundamental rights in marriage "embrace merely the acts by which the primary ends are achieved" and that "the essence of marriage, the fundamental marriage right, includes a right not only to procreative and educative acts but also the acts of mutual help (life partnership), the remedy for concupiscence (sexual fulfillment) and conjugal love."

Thus we see that there has been a turning away from the narrowly procreative idea of production of children as morally good in itself to the needs of married couples themselves. These new interpretations (if we disregard any wider social or economic considerations) are likely to have the effect of reducing fertility in modern contracepting marriages. The description of marital intercourse as "the remedy for concupiscence" seems derogatory, or at least depreciatory of sexual activity as having any positive value in itself. It is now widely considered as the embodiment of natural affections. It has also come to be considered as having a value in itself apart from its natural biological consequences. This is in effect advocating sex for its own sake and not for the purpose of producing children, that is, promoting nonreproductive sex and hence contraception.

Second, the stress on mutual help: "Cohabitation, community of board, use of material goods, earning a living and administering it, help of a more personal kind in the various circumstances of life, in psychic and bodily needs, in the use of natural faculties,"[27] as a part of the essential character of marriage lays emphasis on quality of care, not quantity of offspring.

Of conjugal love the moral theologians tend to avoid a specific definition, stating that it "is that virtue which effects a union of husband and wife by which they wish to give each other the marital benefits."[28] This should provide a satisfactory environment and promote the survival of any children who may be born, on a basis of love of a rational rather than romantic order; the latter is "too fleeting and uncontrollable to be the essence of permanent unions."[29] In general we conclude that these religious attitudes emphasizing parental harmony are conducive to the survival of such children as are born, of either sex, but are not in themselves procreative or conducive to the production of large numbers of children.

Establishing a Community: The Muslim Case

The move of the original Muslims from Mecca to Medina effectively isolated this small number of converts from their own clans. Their apostasy from their ancestral religion prevented any further marriages according to the currently accepted customs. The first Muslims were isolated socially, religiously, and geographically. Muhammad at the battle of Badr was able to field only three hundred fighting men of whom he lost sixteen.[30] At the battle of Uhud the following year the Muslims lost seventy men out of one thousand engaged. From the earlier battle there already existed the problem of the support of many widows and orphans. The battle of Uhud created an even greater number of bereaved, and it was impossible for these widows and orphans to return to their own families.

In a community used to feuding and fighting, as the pre-Muslim Arabs (who were a mixture of pagans, Jews, and Christians) had always been, there would often have been a surplus of women because men were killed in these persistent skirmishes. Available land, wealth, resources, and above all kinship obligations would, however, have ensured that such women and children were taken care of. Muhammad appears to have been worried by the problems of such a number of women without male support in a small religiously innovative community in an alien and often hostile environment, where the surviving men were in no position to marry further wives and care for their offspring because of the uncertainty of their own economic situation.

Thus it seems very probable that Muhammad needed actively to encourage a new and liberal kind of polygyny as a way of providing for widows and orphans. As we saw in chapter 5, he had always been greatly concerned with orphans because he himself had been one and had suffered from a difficult childhood.[31] He actually recognized that with some 10 percent of his fecund women as widows, the community's rate of expansion and the chances of establishing a sizable population for his new Islamic community would be reduced, as the early Traditions show.[32] In the words of Muhammad: "Marry women who are loving and very prolific for I shall outnumber the peoples by you."[33] Thus we see that one of the principal features of Islamic marriage originated with the issue of population size clearly in mind.

Muhammad was certainly strongly in favor of marriage and remarriage. The Koran has many references to marriage, and the Traditions give even greater support. Thus: "When the servant of God marries, he perfects half of his religion," and "Those of you who can support a wife should marry, for it keeps you from looking at strange women and preserves you from immorality." Adultery is discouraged by the long-standing practice of veiling Muslim women (see fig. 8.2), which is seen at its most extreme in Afghanistan and Saudi Arabia.

8.2. Veils of Muslim women take many forms, from complete covering to a wisp of cloth around the mouth and throat. These women illustrate varieties of veiling in contemporary Afghanistan (behind, standing) and Morocco (in front, seated). (Flandrin)

The principal innovation regarding marriage was that it was declared by a secular contract and not a religious rite, thus making it possible for all newcomers to marry into or within the "community" whatever their religion. This was also aimed at improving the position of women, who would thereby achieve a greater ability to rear children successfully. In the community of Islam, a marriage was valid by mutual consent before witnesses. The Koran laid down that a man might have up to four wives at a time[34] and that he must treat them with impartiality.

Muslim men may marry any woman except an idolatress.[35] In particular they may marry Christians and Jews, to whom the Scriptures have been revealed.[36] But Muslim women are allowed to marry believers only.[37] The prohibited degrees of kinship for marriage generally follow the Old Testament restrictions[38] but the Koran also forbids marriage to the divorced or widowed wife of one's father,[39] and to women who are sisters to each other.[40] A regulation unique to Islam prohibits marriage between persons who have been nursed by the same foster mother or between a foster mother and her fostered child.[41]

Slavery and Concubines in Early Islam

There were no barriers in Islam to having Muslim, Christian, and Jewish slaves as concubines but having unbelieving women was forbidden. A child begotten to a slave belonged to its father and was free. A man could not marry one of his own slaves except under certain conditions, for instance, if he were too poor to afford a free woman and had no slave of his own for a concubine.

Since the original Muslims mainly had contact with Christians and Jews these rules enabled their numbers to expand very rapidly. The automatic freeing of the children of concubine slaves must have led to a considerable increase in Muslim populations, and it is clear from the variations in physical appearance of some existing Muslim populations (e.g. in Arabia, Zanzibar, and along the coast of East Africa) that there has been a progressive mixing of the original Arab Muslims with neighboring populations over time, coupled with the spread of the Muslim religion by persuasion, adoption, conversion, and so on, to new peoples in new areas.

The Age of Marriage, Incidence of Divorce, and Place of Virginity in Islam

No age limits for marriage have been fixed by Islam and quite young children may be betrothed and married on the authority of their parents, but a girl is not handed over to her husband until after she has started to menstruate. Since the Prophet, in the Traditions, spoke approvingly of marrying virgins,[42] although he himself only did so once in a dozen marriages, there is a religiously supported preference for virgins.[43] The cost of their dowries is correspondingly higher and the expense of the extensive marriage celebrations can be very substantial. This being so, the husbands of virgin brides in Muslim countries tend to be older than their brides and moreover proportionately older than non-Muslim bridegrooms. In Libya the difference in age between Muslim and non-Muslim husbands not long ago was 9 years and in Iran 6.5 years.[44] This age factor would not of itself reduce the birth rate unless older men were appreciably less fertile than younger ones, and there is no evidence of this in the areas concerned; improved facilities for child rearing where the father is wealthy probably increase the survival rate of offspring. Table 8.1 shows the husband–wife age discrepancy in Shiraz, Iran, in the recent past.

A similar situation exists in Hinduism, in which the insistence on virgin and even prepubertal brides, especially in rural areas, is even stronger than in Islam. Large differences in age between bride and groom provoke no adverse comment. A study[45] has shown the same average age difference even among couples in a sample of urban Hindus but also indicated a general shift of both sexes toward later marriage. This can be seen by comparing older married couples with younger ones (table 8.2).

The study in Iran[46] showed not only that brides tended to have older husbands but that the proportion of couples divorcing in 1973 with fifteen or more years' age difference was about twice as great as the proportion divorcing with smaller age differences. An additional consequence of the taking up of young virgin brides by the older and richer men was thus higher divorce rates than among couples nearer each other in age.

Table 8.1. Husband/Wife Age Differentials for Couples Marrying in Shiraz, Iran, in 1956, 1966, and 1973

Years Husband Older than Wife	*Marriages (%)*		
	1956	*1966*	*1973*
0–4	21.6	18.0	29.6
5–9	33.1	32.1	39.7
10–14	27.1	29.7	19.7
15–19	10.3	12.2	6.4
20+	7.9	8.0	4.6

Source: Momeni

Note: In Muslim countries there is no stigma associated with wide differences in the ages of the bride and groom; on the contrary, the Muslim preference for virgin brides encourages such an age gap.

Table 8.2. Age at Marriage of Urban Hindus

Age at Marriage (in years)	*"Old Marrieds"* Husbands	*"Old Marrieds"* Wives	*"Young Marrieds"* Husbands	*"Young Marrieds"* Wives
10–13	—	12	—	2
14–15	—	4	—	5
16–18	6	7	—	12
19–24	13	4	19	14
25+	9	—	15	—

Source: Ross

Note: The age discrepancy is similarly marked in Hindus, but in this case the effect of urbanization is to promote later marriage.

The Islamic Polygynous Marriage

Islam requires the husband to act impartially toward his wives. This was at one time felt to relate only to material benefits and sexual access. Now it is increasingly felt that this requirement of equality of treatment has an emotional quality to it as well. The frequency of polygynous marriages has varied between 11 percent of all marriages in some Palestinian villages[47] to 1.9 percent in Algeria.[48]

These marriages have often been hard for husbands to manage.[49] Wives sometimes compete for the attention of their husband and for additional advantages for their children over the children of their cowives. On the other hand, when they work well, polygynous marriages are very satisfactory for the cowives. They gain advantages from the sharing of labor, from close friendships with one another, and from readily available help with child rearing.[50] Admittedly there is prestige in being one of several wives of a prominent and wealthy husband, but the competitive element is still present. In one such marriage the husband had to give each of his two wives identical household goods, such as stoves and freezers. Islam has always opposed any restriction on the principle of polygyny despite the considerable modernist pressure to abolish it as being deleterious to the status of women. Secular governments in Islamic countries have, however, done much to restrict it. Tunisia, for instance, outlawed it in 1957, while Syria insisted on prior judicial approval for a polygynous marriage in 1953 in order to protect the first wife financially. The reversion to fundamentalism in Iran, however, has restricted further moves toward liberalization.

Does polygyny have advantages for the children? The number of a man's wives shows his prestige and there may be benefits to the children deriving from this. Polygynous households have some advantages over monogamous ones: where a wife is ill or absent another is available for cooking and caring for children. The children may not encounter the wide range of parental styles from emotional deprivation to overstimulation which are characteristic of societies with monogamous marriages. As the Islamic polygynous husband is usually richer and more socially prominent than the monogamist, there are more money and more goods in the household as well as more people. Thus the children receive better facilities than in monogamous marriages. While the sexual arrangements tend to operate on a shift system, the domestic arrangements have an advantageous continuity rare in Western nuclear families.

The aim of many polygynous husbands in contracting more marriages is often prestige rather than increased sexual activity. This is shown in the reaction of some Sukuma tribesmen. On becoming Catholic and thus meeting the prohibition against taking extra wives, they become godparents to more children and thus achieve high status. One man had over a hundred godchildren, whom he provided with the same kinds of help as he would have given full sons and daughters, while they in their turn gave him the same help as would have been due to him as a full father (see fig. 8.3).

In many parts of Africa, there has been a decline of polygyny with the expense of keeping more than one wife under similar living conditions in urban industrial society, but in certain circumstances Islam may provide a moral background to a useful marital arrangement. Polygyny flourished among the younger, more educated white collar Luo living in Nairobi. It allowed them to maintain a nuclear family household in the city, and at the same time protect their land interests at home.[51] Polygyny may be an urban or a rural practice, or both. In Libya and Egypt there are no differences between urban and rural environments in this respect. In Syria it is more common in rural settings, while in the Arabian Gulf region it is more common in the cities.[52] In Somalia, polygynous marriages involve more than half the adult female population, and here it is an option primarily reserved for widows and divorcees.[53]

8.3. A modern wealthy African polygamist with his family.

Puritan Marriage: The Dominance of Reason and Moderation

In Islamic and Hindu societies we have found marriages to be arranged by families within a socioreligious conception of "right" marriage, often with little regard to the couples' prior ideas and personal wishes. In the case of early Puritan Christianity there was a much stronger emphasis on the individual. This emphasis, however, was placed in a general context of very restrictive beliefs regarding sexual indulgence and clear statements about the rights and wrongs of marriage. Let us take as an example seventeenth-century Puritans in America. Here, a Puritan's initial decision to get married was usually made by a man or woman without reference to any particular other person. The problem, once this decision had been made, was making a match with an equal in birth, religion, and education. This being so, it is not surprising to find that good Puritans controlled their affections even in their love letters; love for one's spouse required moderation because the highest love was to be reserved for God. Marriage was almost a statutory requirement in some places, at least to the extent that single persons were penalized. This occurred in both Massachusetts and Connecticut,[54] where single men and women had to live with families whose general pattern of living had received the approval of community leaders.

The Puritan New England sect was quite explicit about the way in which marriages were to be conducted. Sexual union constituted the first obligation of married partners to each other. The husband had a duty to support his wife and this was enforced by law. The couple were forbidden by law to strike each other, a rule which was supported by the courts on numerous occasions. Adultery in Massachusetts, Connecticut, and New Haven was a capital offense which appears to have been brought to court on three occasions only;[55] offenders were branded, whipped, fined, made to wear the letter *A*, or symbolically executed by being forced to stand on a gallows with a rope around their necks.

The duty of the wife was "to keep at home, educating her children, keeping and improving what is got by the industry of man." The couple's first duty was to give food, shelter, and protection to their children and indeed the courts enforced more care than the mere provision of food and shelter. Thus we see in the Puritan administered states of New England a very positive attitude to marriage with religiously motivated regulations to support it; the biological effects of this would be to promote the care of children.

Puritan ideas were also unusual in recognizing that relatives by marriage had equal status with those related by birth, because Puritans took literally the biblical statement that man and wife were one flesh. This definition extended the range of kinship obligations to all relatives through marriage. While we do not know the extent to which such help was provided, it must mean that the number of people who qualified for support was increased, but this reciprocally meant that any given person would be able to draw on a wide range of others for help. In effect it was just widening the kinship network, or the effective one, by equating the rights of affinal and lineal kin, a good example of group consciousness and one which should enhance the chances of both individual and group survival in difficult times.

Christian Pressure Against Concubinage and Infant Mortality

Before the sixteenth century in Continental Europe, concubinage was, like marriage, a comparatively long-lasting union within which it was relatively easy to bring up children. From then on the church campaigned continuously against it so that within a century it had virtually disappeared except among monarchs and the most powerful aristocrats, who maintained it for political as well as other reasons.[56] In the sixteenth century 50 percent of illegitimate births were the result of concubinage in the Nantes area of France, but by 1787 this had fallen to 2.5 percent. For children born out of wedlock the chances of survival became much lower than in the past. There was a steady increase in the number of children abandoned to public charity (see fig. 8.4). In France it became extremely rare for a girl to have more than one illegitimate child in the same parish. Such mothers were often driven out of their parish. By the seventeenth and early eighteenth centuries the rate of illegitimate births decreased

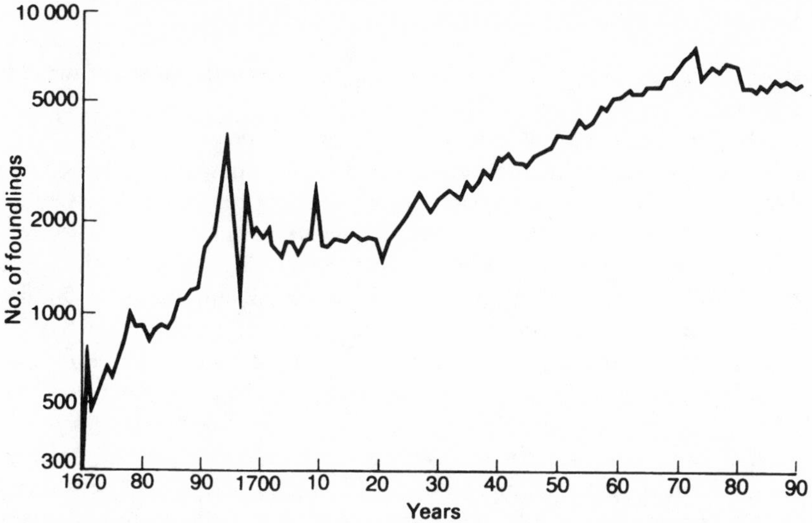

8.4. Graph showing the increase in the number of foundlings admitted to the Paris foundling hospital, 1670–1790.

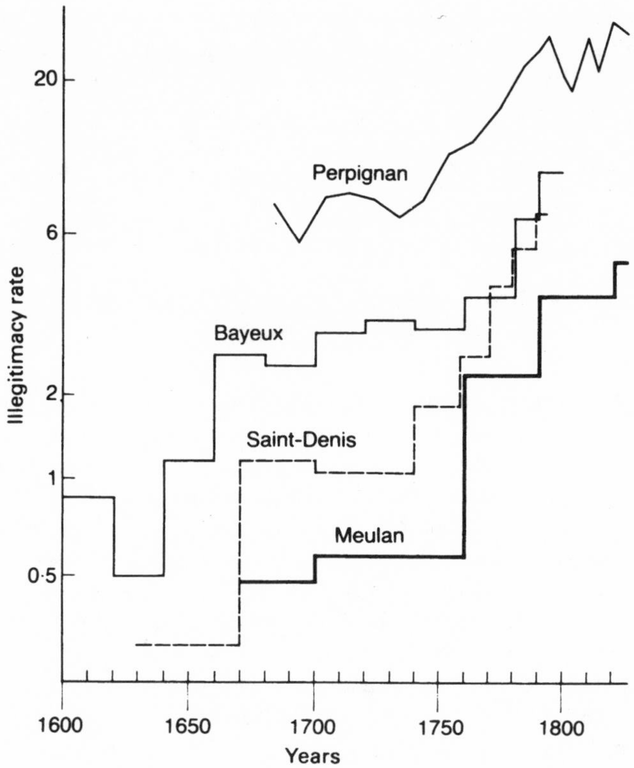

8.5. Trends in the illegitimate birth rate in four French towns. Note the relationship with fig. 8.4.

markedly in the rural areas and increased proportionally in the towns (see fig. 8.5).

Despite the redoubtable work of Christian innovators of charity such as St. Vincent de Paul, the mortality rate among such foundlings as were taken into the care of Christian religious orders remained much higher than that of children brought up by their parents, including those raised within concubinage in the sixteenth century. During the early eighteenth century 90 percent of foundlings died in Rouen; among poor children "assisted" by the town the death rate in the nursing stage was 38.1 percent; for those nursed by their mothers it was 18.7 percent.[57] For Lyons the death rates for foundlings were between 62.5 and 75 percent around 1771–73.[58] While the causal connection cannot be proved, it seems likely that the church's pressure for social and religious recognition of monogamous marriage, the Christianization of conjugal life, and the church's refusal to recognize concubinage resulted not only in the growth of illegitimacy but also in the raising of the death rate among the illegitimate young.

Choice of Spouse: The Phenomenon of Religious Homogamy

Most religions have rules to prevent their adherents from leaving their faith. The rules exist because it is felt, with some correctness, that to marry outside the faith leads to an even greater possibility that the children of such marriages will do likewise. Tertullian[59] stated that out-marriages were like fornication and that they created similar problems. Religious rules thus often favor homogeneity in the marriages of their adherents, so that like marries like. The justification for marriage within a faith is remarkably uniform in many religions. It has been well stated by the seventeenth-century New England Puritan Cotton Mather, who wrote of the justification that "it is lawful for all sorts of people to marry who are able with judgement to give their consent. Yet it is the duty of Christians to marry in the Lord; and therefore, such as profess the true reformed religion should not marry with infidels, papists and other idolaters."[60] And of the consequences, Increase Mather wrote: "Take heed how you dispose of your children. It may make us to dread to think what's coming, in that it is with us as it was with the Old World . . . the Sons of God are marrying with the Daughters of man."[61]

Even in the absence of positive injunctions, as in much of the modern United States, selection of acceptable spouses often involves similarity of religion as one of the many constraints. In the United Kingdom the proportion of religious intramarriages has been high, and in Ulster, Catholic–Protestant marriages are still today heavily proscribed, even physically dangerous, and can best be accomplished and maintained by emigrating to mainland Britain.

There are plenty of data that mixed religion marriages are more prone to divorce and separation than intramarriage.[62] Lehrer and Chiswick,[63] in a study of the 1987–88 National Survey of Families and Households in the United States, found that with the exception of Mormons and individuals with no religious identification, marital stability was similar across the various types of homogamous unions. Mormon marriages had significantly higher stability, while no-religion marriages had significantly lower stability. They also found that interfaith unions had generally higher rates of dissolution than intrafaith unions (see table 8.3). Earlier, a large U.S. study[64] showed that the children of mixed religion marriages were more likely to be arrested as delinquents than those born within a single faith.

Inbreeding coefficients for religious groups provide good evidence for the effects of homogamy within them. A study of religious endogamy in Beirut, Lebanon, found 88 percent of marriages to have been within the same religious community, whereas the expected proportion was 34 percent. Of these marriages 26 percent were consanguineous, most commonly of first cousins (63 percent).[65] The inbreeding coefficient and pro-

Table 8.3. The Effects of the Religious Composition of Unions on Marriage Dissolution, United States, 1987–88

Religion Variables	*Cox-Regression Coefficients and Standard Errors*	*Estimated Fifth-Year Dissolution Probabilities*
Both ecumenical Protestant, same NSFH code (benchmark)	—	0.20
Both exclusivist Protestant, same NSFH code	−0.078 (0.120)	0.19
Both Catholic	0.021 (0.119)	0.20
Both Jewish	0.336 (0.277)	0.27
Both Mormon	−0.493 (0.266)	0.13
Both other religion, same NSFH code	−0.443 (0.714)	0.13
Both no religion	0.714 (0.167)	0.36
Both ecumenical Protestant, different NSFH code	0.229 (0.152)	0.24
Both exclusivist Protestant, different NSFH code	0.522 (0.210)	0.31
Ecumenical Protestant, exclusivist Protestant	0.422 (0.128)	0.29
Ecumenical Protestant, Catholic	0.760 (0.130)	0.38
Exclusivist Protestant, Catholic	0.630 (0.177)	0.34
Intermarriage involving Jew	0.901 (0.248)	0.42
Intermarriage involving Mormon	0.832 (0.224)	0.40
Intermarriage involving other religion	0.855 (0.232)	0.41
No religion—ecumenical Protestant	0.510 (0.146)	0.31
No religion—exclusivist Protestant	0.682 (0.165)	0.35
No religion—Catholic	0.777 (0.169)	0.38

Source: Lehrer and Chiswick

Note: The right-hand column shows the probability that the marriage will have been dissolved in 5 years time.

portion of related marriages among the Amish have increased over time, from 0.004 and 37 percent in 1950 to 0.012 and 98 percent in 1985, because of multiple connecting paths, making 25 percent of these marriages between second cousins or closer kin.[66]

Religious Intramarriage

While most religions encourage the intramarriage of their followers, they also restrict the categories of kin who may be married either by absolute prohibitions (as for brothers and their sisters) or by allowing certain close categories with only special permission (as for cousins in Catholicism). Islam alone of major religions has encouraged cousin marriage as preferential for first marriages, and this has occurred very widely for many centuries.[67] This type of marriage extended to cross as well as parallel cousins,[68] and in communities where there were few children the result has been considerable inbreeding.[69]

This type of marriage occurs in widely divergent Islamic societies. The Koran (Sura 4.128) enjoins that marriage should be between "equals" and indeed refused to permit the marriage of a female slave with her owner unless she had been manumitted first. Why the emphasis on equality and (relatively) close kinship? One compelling reason is the acknowledged consequence of the Islamic system of inheritance, which can lead to the endless subdividing of land into smaller and smaller lots. Marrying a relative reduces this and also ensures that land will stay within the family.

Apart from these concerns, there are also social and other economic advantages to such marriages. The expenses and the prestige are shared by one set of relatives, and where there is prestige to be gained from discussing and publicizing a high bride price it is highly advantageous if very little money actually has to change hands, and the family *as a whole* loses none of it. The likelihood of divorce is also reduced because the patents-in-law of one spouse are the uncles and aunts of the other and there is thus a ramifying kinship network which can provide support in difficult times. In Mombasa, Islamic cousin marriages (including cross- and parallel cousins, unilateral and bilateral) are helpful in ensuring the success of as many children as possible. A child of parallel or cross-cousin marriage has advantages over other children. He or she is less likely to suffer from family instability. Whether the child is male or female, support under Islamic law and inheritance are assured, and the custom is more likely to integrate him or her into the family than to be a source of contention. Among the Nubians[70] it was found that in the current generation 45.1 percent had married their first cousins, although in the parental generation the proportion was 35.5 percent. While this degree of endogamy may be socially advantageous, there can be biological disadvantages if disadvantageous genes are present in the lineages concerned. It has been suggested that congenital malformations, stillbirths, and prenatal deaths tend to be higher in consanguineous unions,[71] though there are contrary findings and the correlation is not certain. On this point the Nubian data referred to showed that the average number of live-born children per first-cousin marriage was higher than for other types of marriage, but this may have been due to the fact that such marriages tended to last longer, because the child mortality rate also was consistently higher. The data showed 35.4 percent deaths of children in first-cousin marriages as against 27 percent of children born to more remote kin and to unrelated marriages.

In contemporary Lebanon the frequency of consanguineous marriages declines with the rise in the educational and occupational level of the husband, a trend also seen among Christians.[72] This decline is mainly in marriages between distant relatives, and this corresponds to the weakening of ties within the extended family. Consanguineous marriage has remained stable for first-cousin marriages in which economic advantages follow.[73] Besides the previous examples, taken mainly from Islam, religious intramarriage is well documented in Christian isolates such as the Amish. Hurd,[74] in a study of the "Nebraska" Amish, found that 47.4 percent of all marriages were between second cousins or closer, in a study covering four generations. In South India, among Hindus as well as Moslems, uncle–niece and parallel cousin marriages are especially common at the present time, as shown by a number of studies.[75]

Incest Taboos

Incest taboos are universal, prohibiting with varying degrees of horror, distaste, and penalties marriage and sexual relations between mother and son, father and daughter, and brother and sister. Such relationships are thought to damage the very essence of the family and the community of which it is part and are even thought of as being against the laws of nature itself. Among the Zigua of Tanzania, sex between mother and son is seen as witchcraft, between father and daughters as bestiality, but between brother and sister as something quite likely to occur; it reduces the marital chance of the woman but is not totally reprehensible in itself. One of the sanctions used to support incest taboos is the threat of deformity for the children born to such relationships. This does not imply any knowledge of genetics (i.e., the danger of excessive homozygosity), and such threats are a common sanction for a wide variety of norms.

This does not of course mean that malformation, diseases, and so on, associated with incestuous relationships are not the result of increased homozygosity, but it is a fact that often they are not; Bittles[76] has emphasized a number of other factors associated with incest that could lead to abnormalities, diseases, and death of the offspring. Among them the main ones are as follows: First, incest is often associated with low maternal age, and this in turn can mean an unprepared and inexperienced mother. Second, conversely, there is often an advanced paternal age, with a consequent greater likelihood of mutations in the male's sperm. Third, incestuous relationships have a positive association with mental subnormality of one or both parents, and this may be genetically transmitted. Fourth, incest tends in some societies to be associated with low parental socioeconomic status. Finally, incest can lead to a good deal of psychosocial stress for the mother, who may attempt to procure an abortion, so the fetus may be subject to various insults during pregnancy which become apparent after birth.

The incest taboo is often extended to relatives outside the nuclear family, but these extensions are not universally the same. Except for the primary incest taboos, there are many variations of the rules between societies and even within pluralistic societies. An absence of coincidence between biological distance and taboos makes it difficult to see them as

8.6. Among the Sukuma of Tanzania there occurred a marriage which was in breach of the normal exogamy rules. To propitiate the ancestors, a goat was sacrificed and divided, each "side" of the marriage eating the other side's part, thus separating the spouses.

having any universal genetic basis.[77] For instance, in many societies the terms *brother* and *sister* are used between the most distant relatives of the same generation but the taboo still applies. Use of the terms and the taboos is probably related more to ensuring the perpetuation of ramifying social systems than to preventing genetic malformations.

In some societies, when rather uncomfortably close marriages do occur, they can be "put right" by the carrying out of the appropriate socioreligious ceremonies. The Sukuma of Tanzania on such occasions sacrifice a goat, which is split in two, each half eaten separately by the close relatives of the marriage partners (see fig. 8.6). Incest within the nuclear family is generally punished very severely indeed.

Jewish Intramarriage

For Jews, marriage with non-Jews is both prohibited and invalid as a religious marriage should it take place. This law is based on biblical injunctions (Deut. 7:3–4) supported by rabbinic declarations. In Israel this is more than a purely religious ruling, for it is illegal to contract a religiously mixed marriage,[78] though there is no punishment if one is in fact contracted. This ruling is supported by other injunctions toward spouses, such as that they should have similar social background and age. Orthodox Jewish men are unlikely to intermarry with non-Jewish women, and orthodox Jewish women are even less likely than Jewish men to marry outside their faith. In Indiana, only 33.2 percent of the previously never-married, and 20 percent of the previously widowed, married non-Jews.[79] The Jewish maintenance of intramarriage rather than intermarriage can be seen partly as the result of the endogamous tendencies of other religious groups and partly of the Jewish tendency to maintain a somewhat exclusive social and economic life, reducing potential contacts with marriageable outsiders. A U.S. study has shown that the larger the Jewish community, the easier it is to organize communal activities and to maintain an organized intra-Jewish system. In smaller Jewish communities there is more intermarriage with outsiders.[80] A study of the genetic profile of South African Ashkenazi Jews found that they did not differ radically from those of Ashkenazi populations living in other parts of the world.[81]

Mixed Marriages and the Trend Away from Religious Homogamy

The conclusions of one lengthy study[82] showed that couples in mixed-religion marriages had fewer children than those who married within their own faith. Their children were less likely to finish secondary school, and very generally they rejected religion. The converse has also been shown, namely that the children of parents who attend the same church regularly stay at school longer.[83] The divorce rate of mixed-religion marriages tends, as we have seen, to be higher than for those who marry within their own faith. But it is well to remember that a religious difference between the spouses may be associated with other differences—for example, in socioeconomic, ethnic, or racial background—so that the difficulties in such marriages are unlikely to stem from religion alone.[84]

Some religions are so strongly opposed to the possibility of intermarriage that it would involve not only the loss of religious affiliation but the removal of those involved from their families as well. A Kenyan case, in which a woman who was a Muslim physiotherapist married a Hindu surgeon, resulted in the wife's father's placing a newspaper advertisement to state that this daughter was no longer a member of his family. In such cases the range of issues goes far beyond formal religious rules and involves deeper issues of pollution concepts and family name survival, so that only the most persistent and strong-minded of couples are likely even to contemplate such a marriage. Another Kenyan case initially involved the forced separation of the engaged couple by sending the Muslim girl to Britain for higher education, and it was only her persistent refusal to consider marrying anyone else that eventually allowed the marriage to the Hindu man concerned to take place.

For several decades, religious intermarriages have been becoming more frequent in the West. For example, a study in Switzerland[85] showed

Table 8.4. Catholic and Protestant Marriage Patterns in Switzerland, 1969–72 and 1979–82

Z values for religious intermarriage:		
	Bride	
Groom	*First Marriage*	*Higher Order Marriage*
A. 1969–72		
First marriage	0.236	0.336
Higher order marriage	0.348	0.361
B. 1979–82		
First marriage	0.300	0.312
Higher order marriage	0.386	0.387

Source: Schoen and Thomas

Note: The table shows that interfaith marriages became more common from the first period to the second.

that during the decade between 1969–72 and 1979–82 the number of Protestant–Catholic intermarriages increased from about one quarter to nearly one third (see table 8.4). Despite Judaism's prohibition of intermarriage, U.S. Jewish intermarriages are common, as are those of Catholics. There has been a steady decrease in religiously endogamous marriages in Canada, and a greater than 50 percent decrease among Mormons, Lutherans, and the Greek Orthodox. The lowest endogamy was found among Roman Catholics.[86]

An even more important cause of the increasing interreligious marriage rate in Western societies is the extent of mobility of the typical Western urbanite. Socioreligious association is often the sign of a stable community or at least a core of stability in mobile communities. Within modern cities, individuals tend to seek sectarian consolation because of the loneliness and instability of city living. A study[87] has shown that interreligious marriage rates tend to be higher for migrants into cities than long-term residents. Even when it occurs there is a consistent trend in mixed-religion marriages for one spouse to convert to the faith of the other, and wives convert more frequently than husbands. In the past some governments, as in Poland and Prussia, have decreed that the children of mixed-religion marriages had to follow the religion of the father. A U.S. study[88] showed conversions in the direction of the spouse with the higher social and professional status. Generally, intermarriage at the present rate is a recent phenomenon and has only been legal in Europe since the eighteenth century. Some countries, such as Poland, Lithuania, and Yugoslavia, prohibited religious intermarriage prior to the Second World War.

What conclusions can we draw about the institution of marriage, its structural rules, and the ways it influences the behavior of individuals? Marriage rules determine the legitimacy or otherwise of the young, and this can affect their chances of success, depending on how easy or difficult any given religious group makes it for parents to succeed when they are not married, or for the single parent (mother or father) to manage without a spouse. We noted that in some societies, generally those with a high degree of mobility, marriage tends to be unstable and there is little stigma to illegitimacy. In others, especially settled agricultural societies, marriage and legitimacy are focal issues and the problems raised by illegitimacy are greater. This tends to give legitimate children advantages over illegitimate ones.

Where changing social circumstances have imposed new stresses, as in newly urbanized communities, old marriage patterns have often broken down and religion in the form of spirit possession has been adapted accordingly.

Not all religions are promarriage for all members. Hindus and Jews are actively exhorted to marry and to have children, the former in particular to have sons. Buddhists place far less emphasis on marriage, and indeed many do not marry. In the case of Christianity a curious situation prevails: The religion tends to be in favor of marriage as the pathway to parental stability and it is proreproductive within marriage, but it is antisex. Sex in itself is, or was until recently, seen as sinful unless in the service of reproduction within marriage, though today some churches approve openly of sex between married partners even if not for child production. Christianity as a whole, in common with Hinduism and Islam, does not approve of sex per se outside marriage.

Islam provides an interesting case. Muhammad established a form of polygyny, at first to remarry widows whose husbands had been killed in battle. This practice, together with new rules about the case of orphans, a new rule that slaves could marry, another that the children of slave concubines were free, and one allowing marriage with women of other religions (mainly Christian and Jews), put Islam on a strongly expansionist tack. This whole program was, we know, based on a policy of politicoreligious expansionism. It was designed in the first place by one charismatic individual, but later was added to by many others.

Economic advantages for members of religious groups arose from the way Puritans treated their affinal kin as if they were lineal relatives, and from the practice of religious approval for cousin marriage, which kept property within the extended family. Both economic and psychological benefits arise from religious homogamy, that is, more or less clearly formalized rules enjoining marriage with a member of one's own religion or sect. Such benefits seem often to promote parental harmony, marital stability, and successful child rearing.

Celibacy and Sexuality

What do we mean by celibacy? To many laypeople undoubtedly the term implies a negative—a turning away from marriage and sex, a voluntary, self-imposed decision by a religious devotee not to engage in marriage and sexual activity (see fig. 8.7). The early pre-Reformation Penitentials, manuals for the guidance and administration of the Catholic church, give horrendous penalties for religious officials who deviated from celibacy. The Penitential of Finnian decrees, for a single act of fornication by a cleric, a year's penance on bread and water,[89] and in the so-called Roman Penitential a lustful intention calls for half a year on bread and water.[90] Nor are the celibacy rules concerned only with heterosexuality. The penalties for homosexuality are even greater. The Penitential of St. Columba states: "If anyone has committed fornication as the Sodomites did, let him do penance for ten years, for the first three on bread and water,"[91] while the Paris Penitential prescribes seven years for a layman.[92] The contemporary position is, however, different. While the sins may be the same as those listed in the works of past moral theologians, corresponding penalties are not given and the present training of Roman Catholic priests in the hearing of confessions emphasizes repentance and reconciliation with a minimal penalty, such as the saying of a few prayers, for even the most grievous sexual sin.

The Shakers went to great lengths to limit the possibilities of sexual contacts between their men and women members. Their Gospel of Christ's Second Appearing strictly forbids all private union between the sexes, in any place or under any circumstances, indoors or out. Brethren and sisters were not permitted to pass each other on the stairs. There were in all forty specific regulations to restrict contacts between the sexes.[93] On the other hand, rules concerning celibacy for the Catholic clergy may in certain circumstances be relaxed.

In the days when Iceland was Roman Catholic the clergy were not expected to practice celibacy. Jon, the last Catholic bishop of Iceland, who was beheaded in 1550 by the Protestants for refusing to accept the "new faith," had nine children by his concubine, Helga Sigordardottir.[94]

8.7. A procession of Cistercian monks, a celibate order of Roman Catholic men dedicated to a silent life of work and prayer within the boundaries of their monastery.

Celibacy and Spirituality

But the sexual side is only one aspect of celibacy; it is also a spiritual state. In this respect, celibacy is particularly associated with a state of extreme spiritual involvement and comprehension, such that it enables the individual to transcend the everyday passions and concerns of ordinary life and achieve enlightenment. This applies to Christian celibates and to the Buddhist celibates in the Mahayana northern school. Both Christianity and Buddhism stress the importance of sex and marriage for ordinary people, while denying them to those who seek the spiritual life. Thus if the flesh is denied, the spirit is felt by some Christian celibates to be freed. There is a greater possibility of service to the community, proximity to the Almighty, or attainment of the desired spiritual state.

Christian asceticism began to be influential in the third and fourth centuries in the form of moral purity, detachment from the world, and rejection of its pleasures. In this the early Christians went considerably beyond the New Testament pattern of self-denial since they idealized virginity, preaching contempt of the material world in general and of the body in particular. Eastern monasticism, especially in its earlier anchoritic form, emphasized the mortification of the flesh. Ascetics sought suffering for expiatory, propitiatory, or purificatory ends by abusing their bodies, which they thought to be the prison of their souls. Western monasticism on the other hand favored a disciplined life characterized by practicality and charity.[95]

Neither Judaism nor Islam has ever had any wide interest in celibacy. In the sense of being a holy state, celibacy falls at the opposite end of the spectrum from the Hindu orgiastic cults of Chakra Puja or Vamachari in which sex and especially incest are seen as purifying. Hinduism tends to consider that unrestrained sexual intercourse in the right social context is good and in keeping with the general fertility of nature. The Chinese religion of Tao holds sexual union to be a close form of contact with the divinity, perhaps even the most divine state of being. Indeed it is not really possible in Tao thinking to divorce sex from the whole pattern of life; sex is everywhere represented by the symbolism of the yin (female) and the yang (male), the elements of the two sexes, which find their expression in the trees, the fields, the rock pools, the weather, and all things natural and good.[96] In some Tao works[97] men (the yang element) must withhold their ejaculation as long as possible while they satisfy many women, but eventually they must ejaculate, as it is considered harmful to restrain oneself for too long. By contrast, the Christian and Buddhist celibates hold that sex deflects from preoccupation with matters divine, and celibacy may be defined, for the celibate, as a total dedication to God, or the Holy Trinity, and a giving of one's life to spiritual endeavor and helping others.

For the Christian, celibacy has been defined as the canonical state of abstinence from sex and hence marriage, freely undertaken for the purpose of dedicating one's life totally to God's service. For the Buddhist lamas, abstention from marriage and all sexual relations is a necessary detachment from the world as part of the process of conquering desire in order to achieve nirvana.

The Buddhist case of celibacy illustrates how culture presents its rules of inhibition. The Patimokkha, the monastic rules which monks recite twice a month on Buddhist Sabbath days, contains many regulations aimed at minimizing the occasions for interaction with females (see fig. 8.8). Hinduism similarly has celibacy in some extreme ascetic groups such as the Digambar Jains.[98]

Monks are even forbidden to touch their mothers. For example, if the mother of a monk should fall into a ditch, her son may offer her a stick but not a hand and has to think of himself as pulling out a log of wood. Nor may monks sleep under the same roof as a female animal. The main object of the rule is to lead to the suppression and ultimately the extinction of bodily and especially sexual desire. This, combined with such statements by the Buddha as that "it were better for you, foolish man, that your male organ should enter the mouth of a terrible and poisonous snake, than that it should enter a woman,"[99] must inhibit the sexual interests of any men who take their Buddhist faith seriously. Also the monk is sustained in his fidelity to celibacy by the fear of karmic retribution, punishment in hell and rebirth in a form delaying his final deliverance from desire, as well as by the fear of expulsion from the order and public disgrace.

8.8. Buddhist monks in Thailand receiving gifts of food in the early morning with downcast eyes and without speaking, from women devotees.

Celibacy for religious reasons must be considered a widespread contemporary and historical phenomenon. Aztec celibacy included both sexes; all Aztec priests were celibate;[100] the seducers of girls associated with temples and priests who failed to remain celibate were executed.[101] Inca celibacy was religious and confined to women.[102]

The feeling that sexual congress must by its very nature prevent the attainment of true religious states has been taken to extremes by certain groups such as the nineteenth-century Russian Skoptsy sect who castrated themselves en masse. This has also happened in the case of isolated individuals with fervent religious convictions.[103]

Celibacy and Reproduction

How effective is celibacy? What about illicit liaisons and illegitimate offspring? Quantitative data are hard to obtain, but some historical material does exist on the extent of celibate failure and public and institutional reactions to it. Celibacy for the Christian clergy was first written into canon law by the Council of Elvira in A.D. 306. The Council of Carthage, A.D. 419, extended the condition to include subdeacons. But the celibate condition was a constant source of difficulty, particularly in areas where the clergy could not be adequately supervised. In the eleventh century some clerical fiefs were virtually hereditary with parishes and bishoprics being passed from father to son, and it was then that Pope Gregory VII (1073–85) initiated the reaction to the lax observance of celibacy.

In general, during the commitment to celibacy in modern times as in the previous century, it is uncommon for the vow to be broken. When this occurs it is a subject of general distaste, and even scandal. Renan[104] testified strongly to the effective celibacy of the priests under whom he had studied for thirteen years as a seminarian.

The decision to be celibate is generally made in the late teens (see fig. 8.9), and effectively debars most of those who make it from reproduction. The trainee priest has a spiritual director with whom he works to control his spiritual and physical problems, including that of his sexual desire, principally by prayer rather than, in the past, by fasting and flagellation. If he fails he cannot become a priest.

The Social Contributions of Celibates

Christian celibates run a wide range of institutions which benefit the community in general and have done so from early medieval days. Indeed some orders are considered to have played an essential part in the development of medicine, and the place of the Society of Jesus in education is well known. Celibates in the religious orders administer both general and specialized hospitals for the old, the insane, alcoholics, and drug addicts

8.9. Young men dedicating themselves to a life of celebacy in the Roman Catholic church. They are seen here at the ordination ceremony.

and for childbearing. They also run homes for unmarried mothers, orphans, cripples, the homeless, and the disturbed and provide food and care for homeless transients. But celibates are not alone in doing this: both Islam and Hinduism run institutions for the help of the community but they are not run by celibates. Buddhist priests, perhaps the largest proportion of celibates in their societies in the world today, do very little social work and run few institutions. Buddhism is not greatly concerned with alleviating immediate physical suffering (although there is traditional Buddhist science of medicine and there are doctors). But some suffering is considered by Buddhists to be a necessary condition of human existence. For parentless children in Burma, however, there was the Social Service Sangha Association, which at one time had seventy-seven orphanages affiliated to Buddhist monasteries, catering to male orphans only. Nevertheless, it has been said that for the vast majority of Buddhist monks "social service is viewed not only as irrelevant but an obstacle to their quest for salvation."[105]

From our examination of marriage and celibacy, we consider next what follows after marriage. If things go wrong with the marriage, divorce may ensue, and religions are very concerned with the prevention or management of divorce. Where one spouse dies, the remaining partner may or may not want to remarry, and again religions are permissive or restrictive, giving guidance to those involved and in some cases specifying who the new partner shall be.

Notes

1. Turnbull, C. M. (1966). *Wayward servants: The two worlds of the African pygmies.* Erye and Spottiswoode, London.
2. Woodburn, J. (1968). "Stability and flexibility in Hadza residential groupings." In Blee, R., and DeVere, I. (eds.). *Man the hunter.* Aldine, Chicago.
3. Tanner, R. E. S. (1958). "Fertility and child mortality in cousin marriages." *Eugenics R*, 49, 197–99.
4. Cory, H. (1953). *Sukuma law and custom.* Oxford University Press/International African Institute, London.
5. Calhoun, C. A. (1980). "The authority of ancestors: A sociological reconsideration of Fortes' Tallensi in response to Fortes' critics." *Man.* 15(2), 304–19.
6. Nadel, S. F. (1952). "Witchcraft in four African societies: An essay in comparison." *American Anthropologist*, 54, 18–29.
7. Lewis, I. M. (1986). *Religion in context: Cults and charisma.* Cambridge University Press, Cambridge, p. 40.
8. Lewis I. M. (1989). *Ecstatic religion.* Routledge, London.
9. Swantz, L. W. (1970). "The Zaramo of Dar-es-Salaam: A study of continuity and change." *Tanzania Notes and Records*, 71, 157–64.
10. The laws of Manu. (1969). Buhler, G. (trans.). Dover, New York. Carstairs, G. M. (1961). *The twice-born.* Hogarth Press, London.
11. Srinivas, M. N. (1962). *Caste in modern India.* Asia Publishing House, London.
12. Klass, M. (1966). "Marriage rules in Bengal." *American Anthropologist*, 68, 951–70.
13. Agrawal, B. C., and Agrawal, S. K. (1972). "A note on Natra, the so-called 'remarriage' among the Hindus of Malwa." *Eastern Anthropologist*, 25(1), 73–80.
14. Aryal, R. H. (1991). "Socioeconomic and cultural differentials in age at marriage and the effect on fertility in Nepal." *J Biosocial Science*, 23, 167–78.
15. Spiro, M. E. (1967). *Burmese supernaturalism.* Prentice-Hall, Englewood Cliffs, New Jersey.
16. Nash, J., and Nash, M. (1963). "Marriage, family and population growth in Upper Burma." *South-Western J. Anthropology*, 19, 251–66.
17. Gen. 1:28, 2:18, 24.
18. Num. 6:2–8.
19. Lev. 21:1–15.
20. Dorff, E. N. (1986). "The Jewish tradition." In Numbers, R. L., and Amundsen, D. W. (eds.). *Caring and curing: Health and medicine in the western religious tradition.* Macmillan, New York.

21. Ketubbot, Torah, 5:6.
22. 1 Cor. 7:16.
23. Altenagoras (1972 ed.). *Legatio pro Christiani's.* Clarendon Press, Oxford, p. 32. John of Damascus (1955 ed.). *De fide orthodoxa.* Franciscan Institute, New York, vol. 4, p. 97.
24. St. Augustine, (1847 ed.). "De Nuptiis et Concupiscentia" and "De Bono Conjugali. In *Seventeen short treatises.* Parker, Oxford.
25. St. Augustine, (1847 ed.). "De Conjugiis Adulteris" and "De Bono Conjugali. In *Seventeen short treatises.* Parker, Oxford.
26. Ford, J. C., and Kelly, G. (1963). *Contemporary moral theology.* Mercier, Cork.
27. Pius XII. (1994). *Acta Apostolicis Sedis.* Rome.
28. McAuliffe, M. F. (1954). *Catholic moral teaching on the nature and object of conjugal love.* Catholic University of America Press, Washington, D.C.
29. Ford, J. C., and Kelly, G. (1963). *Contemporary moral theology.* Mercier, Cork.
30. Watt, W. M. (1968). *Muhammad at Medina.* Oxford University Press, Oxford.
31. Watt, W. M. (1968). *Muhammad at Medina.* Oxford University Press, Oxford.
32. Mishkatt Al-Masabih. (1963). *A collection of the most authentic traditions regarding the actions and sayings of Muhammad.* 2 vols. Robson, J. (trans.). Ashraf, Lahore.
33. Mishkatt al-Masabih. (1963). *A collection of the most authentic traditions regarding the actions and sayings of Muhammad.* 2 vols. Robson, J. (trans.). Ashraf, Lahore, Vol 2, p. 659.
34. Koran. (1960). Bell, R. (trans.). T. and T. Clark, Edinburgh, Sura 4:3.
35. Koran. (1960). Bell, R. (trans.). T. and T. Clark, Edinburgh, Sura 2:220.
36. Koran. (1960). Bell, R. (trans.). T. and T. Clark, Edinburgh, Sura 5:7.
37. Koran. (1960). Bell, R. (trans.). T. and T. Clark, Edinburgh, Sura 2:220. and 60:10.
38. Lev. 18:7–18. Koran, Sura 4:27.
39. Koran. (1960). Bell, R. (trans.). T. and T. Clark, Edinburgh, Sura 4:26.
40. Koran. (1960). Bell, R. (trans.). T. and T. Clark, Edinburgh, Sura 4:27.
41. Koran. (1960). Bell, R. (trans.). T. and T. Clark, Edinburgh, Sura 4:27.
42. Mishkatt Al-Masabih. (1963). *A collection of the most authentic traditions regarding the actions and sayings of Muhammad.* 2 vols. Robson, J. (trans.). Ashraf, Lahore, Vol 2, p. 659.
43. Momeni, D. A. (1972). "The difficulties of changing the age at marriage in Iran." *J Marriage and Family*, 34, 545–51.
44. Dixon, R. B. (1971). "Explaining cross-cultural variations in age at marriage and proportions never marrying." *Population Studies*, 25, 215–33.
45. Ross, A. D. (1961). *The Hindu family in its urban setting.* University of Toronto Press, Toronto.
46. Momeni, D. A. (1976). "Husband–wife age differentials in Iran." *Social Biology*, 23, 341–46.
47. Putai, R. (1958). *Kingdom of Jordon.* Princeton University Press, Princeton, New Jersey.
48. Seklawi, M. (1960). "La fécondité dans les pays arabes: Données numerique, attitudes et comportements." *Population.* 15, 846.

49. Lane, E. W. (1954). *Manners and customs of the modern Egyptians.* Dent, London.

50. Bohannan, P. (1992). *We the alien.* Waveland Press. Prospect Heights, Illinois.

51. Parkin, D. (1978). *The cultural definition of political response: Lineal destiny among the Luo.* Academic Press, London.

52. Chamie, J. (1986). "Polygyny among Arabs." *Population Studies*, 40, 55–66.

53. Johnson, N. E., and Elmi, A. M. (1989). Polygamy and fertility in Somalia." *J Biosocial Science*, 21, 127–34.

54. Massachusetts. (1636). Records. 1.186. Connecticut Records. (1636–37). 1.8.

55. Morgan, E. S. (1966). *The Puritan family: Religion and domestic relations in 17-century New England.* Harper and Row, New York.

56. Flandrin, J.-L. (1979). *Families in former times: Kinship, household and sexuality.* Cambridge University Press, Cambridge.

57. Bardet, J.-P. (1973). "Enfants abandonnés et enfants assistés à Rouen dans la seconde moitié du XVIIIe siècle." In *Hommage à Marcel Reinhold.* Société de demographie historique, Paris. pp. 28–29.

58. Garden, M. (1970). *Lyons et les Lyonnais au XVIIIe siècle.* Flammarion, Paris.

59. Tertullian. (1884 ed.). *Writings: Ad Uxorem.* Clark, Edinburgh. Vol. 2, p. 3.

60. Mather, C. (1853). *Magnalia Christi Americana.* Hartford, Connecticut. Vol. 2, p. 202.

61. Mather, I. (1685). *A discourse concerning the danger of apostasy: A call to heaven.* Boston, pp. 128–29.

62. Heiss, J. S. (1961). "Interfaith marriage and marital outcome." *Marriage and Family Living*, 23, 228–33.

63. Lehrer, E. L., and Chiswick, C. V. (1993). "Religion as a determinant of marital stability." *Demography*, 30(3), 385–405.

64. Zimmerman, C. C., and Cervantes, L. F. (1960). *Successful American families.* Pageant, New York.

65. Khlat, M. (1986). *Less mariages consanguinés à Beyrouth: Structures et conséquences biologiques.* Claude Bernard University, Lyons.

66. Khoury, M. J., et al. (1987). "Inbreeding and pre-reproductive mortality in the Old Order Amish. 1. Genealogic epidemiology of inbreeding. 2. Genealogic epidemiology of pre-reproductive mortality. 3. Direct and indirect effects of inbreeding." *American J Epidemiology*, 125, 453–83.

67. Patai, R. (1955). "Cousin right in Middle Eastern marriage." *South-Western J Anthropology*, 11, 371–90.

68. Tanner, R. E. S. (1964). "Cousin marriage in the Afro–Arab community of Mombasa, Kenya." *Africa*, 34, 127–38.

69. Tanner, R. E. S. (1958). "Fertility and child mortality in cousin marriages." *Eugenics Revue*, 49, 197–99.

70. Hussein, F. H. (1971). "Endogamy in Egyptian Nubia." *J Biosocial Science*, 3, 251–57.

71. Stern, C. (1960). *Principles of human genetics.* San Francisco. Stevenson, A. C., et al. (1966). "Congenital malformations." *Bulletin World Health Organization*, 34 Supplement.

72. Khlat, M. (1988). "Social correlations of consanguineous marriage in Beirut: A population based study." *Human Biology*, 60, 541–48.

73. Khlat, M. (1986). *Les mariages consanguinés à Beyrouth: Structures et conséquences biologiques.* Claude Bernard University, Lyons.

74. Hurd, J. P. (1985). "Kissing cousins: Frequencies of cousin types in Nebraska Amish marriages." *Social Biology*, 32(1–2), 82–89.

75. Rao, P. S. (1983). "Religion and intensity of inbreeding in Tamil Nadu, South India." *Social Biology*, 309(4), 413–22. Bittles, A. H., et al. (1990). "Interrelationships between consanguinity, religion and fertility in Karnataka, South India." In Landers, J., and Reynolds, V. (eds.). *Fertility and resources.* Cambridge University Press, Cambridge.

76. Bittles, A. H. (1981). "Genetic defects associated with human inbreeding." *Social Biology and Human Affairs*, 45, 145–47.

77. Murdock, G. P. (1949). *Social structure.* Macmillan, London, pp. 286–87.

78. Rabbinical Courts Jurisdiction (Marriage and Divorce) Law No. 5713–1973. Government of Israel, Tel Aviv.

79. *Encyclopaedia Judaica.* (1971). Keter, Jerusalem.

80. Rosenthal, E. (1968). "Jewish intermarriage in Indiana." *Eugenics Q*, 15, 277–87.

81. Lane, A. B., et al. (1985). "A genetic profile of the South African Ashkenazi Jewish population." *South African Medical J*, 68(13), 935–39.

82. Burchinal, L. G., and Chancellor, L. G. (1963). "Survival rates among religiously homogamous and inter-religious marriages." *Social Biology*, 41, 353–62.

83. Morgan, J. N., et al. (1962). *Income and welfare in the United States.* Michigan University Survey Research Center. McGraw-Hill, New York.

84. Monahan, T. P. (1973). "Some dimensions of interreligious marriages in Indiana. 1962–67." *Social Forces*, 52, 195–203.

85. Schoen, R. and Thomas, B. (1990). "Religious intermarriage in Switzerland." *European J of Population*, 6(4), 359–76.

86. Basavarajappa, K. G. (1988). "Spouse selection in Canada, 1921–78: An examination by age, sex and religion." *J Biosocial Science*, 20(2), 211–23.

87. Chancellor, L. E., and Burchinal, L. G. (1962). "Relations among interreligious marriages, migratory marriages and civil weddings in Iowa" *Eugenics Q*, 9, 75–83.

88. Salisbury, W. S. (1962). "Religiosity, regional sub-culture and social behaviour." *J Scientific Study Religion*, 2, 94–101.

89. Bieler, L. (ed.). (1963). *The Irish Penitentials.* Dublin Institute for Advanced Studies, Dublin.

90. McNeill, J. T., and Gamer, H. M. (eds.). (1938). *Mediaeval handbooks of penance.* Columbia University Press, New York.

91. Bieler, L. (ed.). (1963). *The Irish Penitentials.* Dublin Institute for Advanced Studies, Dublin.

92. McNeill, J. T., and Gamer, H. M. (eds.). (1938). *Mediaeval handbooks of penance.* Columbia University Press, New York.

93. Andrews, E. D. (1963). *The people called Shakers.* Dover, New York.

94. Tomasson, R. F. (1980). *Iceland: The first new society.* University of Minnesota Press, Minneapolis.

95. Amundsen, D. W., and Ferngreen, G. B. (1986). "The early Christian

tradition," in Numbers, R. L., and Amundsen, D. W. (eds.). *Caring and curing: Health and medicine in the Western religious tradition.* Macmillan, New York.

96. Rawson, P., and Legeza, L. (1979). *Tao: the Chinese philosophy of time and change.* Thames and Hudson, London.

97. Chang, J. (1977). *The Tao of love and sex.* Wildweed House, London, pp. 35–46.

98. Carrithers, M. (1989). "Naked ascetics in southern Digambar Jainism." *Man*, 24(2), 219–35.

99. The Book of the Discipline (1938–42). Homer, I. B. (trans.). Pali Text Society, London. 1:36.

100. Thompson, J. E. (1933). *Mexico before Cortes: An account of the daily life, religion and ritual of the Aztecs and kindred people.* Scribner, New York.

101. Bandelier. A. F. (1880). *On the social organisation and mode of government of the ancient Mexicans.* Peabody Museum Reports, 2, Harvard University Press, Cambridge, Massachusetts.

102. Rowe, J. H. (1944). "Inca culture at the time of the Spanish conquest." In Steward, J. H. (ed.). *Handbook of the South American Indians*, Smithsonian Institution, Washington, D.C.

103. Kushner, A. W. (1967). "Two cases of auto-castration due to religious delusion." *British J Medical Psychology*, 40, 293–98.

104. Renan, E. (1883). Souvenirs d'enfance et de jeunesse. Calman, L. (ed.). Levy Frères, Paris.

105. Spiro, M. E. (1971). *Buddhism and society.* Allen and Unwin, London.

9

Divorce and Widowhood

In this chapter we want to look at the opposite side of the marriage coin—marital breakdown in one form or another, through death or accident to a spouse or loss of other kinds, and remarriage.

Let us start with a consideration of divorce, that is, the termination of a marriage by either partner. This may in fact be impossible in some religions or very difficult, as in Roman Catholicism and the first marriages of high-caste Hindus. Or it may be a relatively simple matter as in some African societies where a wife has only to break a cooking pot and put it outside the door of the hut for her husband, on returning home, to discover that he has been divorced.

In tribal systems which are deeply concerned with the survival of the clan, the family, or the individual as a descendant, the infertile wife is the most miserable of women. Among the Sukuma a barren wife crisscrosses the tribal region seeking the reason for her condition in an endless series of consultations with traditional spirit investigators who might be able to tell her how to induce her ancestors to withdraw their malevolence so that she can conceive. The Sukuma marriage ceremony only initiates a marriage; it becomes a continuing and developing institution if children are born. The marriage then becomes part of the social and religious fabric of the community instead of remaining marginal.[1] Among these people infertility of the wife is cause for divorce irrespective of the length of the marriage.[2] To a lesser extent this is also true of incapacity of the husband to beget children. This situation is paralleled in many African tribal societies.

Where cultures and their religions are heavily procreative in tone, as in Islam or especially Hinduism, in which the husband has a direct reli-

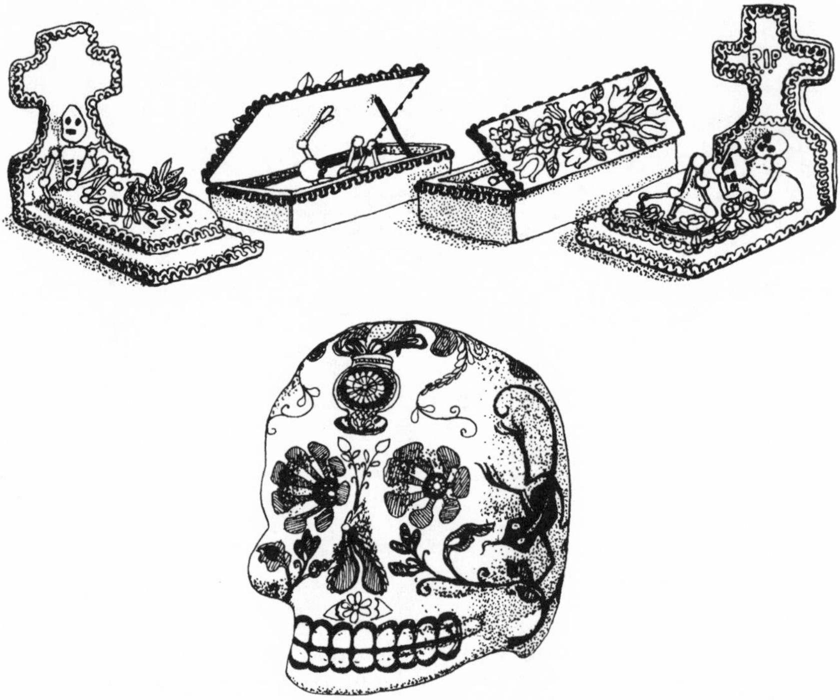

9.1. Sugar coffins, marzipan graves, and skulls are made to be eaten on All Souls' Day (November 2) in Mexico. In this way the family remembers its loved ones now deceased.

gious need for a son to prevent him from suffering in the next world, the position of the infertile wife is extremely uncertain and full of anxiety. In Hinduism, even if she is fertile but has produced only daughters her status is still low; she has failed in her main role as the producer of male children. The pressure is even greater on the wife of a prominent man. The status to which she aspires in both these religions is to be known as the mother of a son, a more important role than being known as the wife of a certain man.

Infertility has often been adequate grounds for divorce in Islam as well as among the lower castes in Hinduism. In Judaism it has similarly been a suitable ground for divorce provided that it is proved. According to Jebamoth VI:6 "If one married a woman and waited with her ten years without her bearing a child, he is not permitted to remain exempt from the duty of procreation. When he divorces her she may remarry and the second husband waits with her ten years" (The Talmud). In Christianity the infertility of either the man or the woman is no grounds for divorce, nor even for an annulment, since any assessment of infertility must come after consummation and it is the act of consummation that seals the marriage in the eyes of the church and of God. It may well be that in medieval and modern Christian agricultural communities this fact resulted in the high rate of premarital conceptions of many brides, as farmers and others would not risk being stuck with an infertile wife whom they could not divorce.

Many tribal societies, and indeed most societies (including sectors of the most urbanized Western ones), pay considerable attention to invoking the help of the Divine in making marriages fertile. The Lugbara of Uganda[3] have fertility shrines to which offerings were made if any wives or daughters of the lineage were barren, and in fact the Lugbara ancestor cult and similar cults in other African societies were concerned among other things with maintaining fertility. Prayers, sacrifices, and visits to the local witch doctor or medicine man were made by individuals seeking fertility.

Hinduism and Buddhism have always had special shrines in their temples for "problem-solving" purposes,[4] and some shrines are specifically devoted to curing barren women. Dubois[5] and El Saadawi[6] have suggested that Hindu and Muslim women subject themselves to sexual intercourse with the priest of the temple or the mullah in the hope of becoming pregnant. Alternatively the woman may offer to grant sexual intercourse to a certain number of pilgrims to the shrine as a thanks offering to the titular deity for his aid in becoming pregnant. All these methods are in fact religious solutions to the problem deeply felt by infertile wives, which they perceive as a danger to their marriage. But even where the danger of divorce is less real, wives and their husbands continue to want children. Visitors today to Greek Orthodox churches will see beside the more popular icons the plentiful little silver panels which testify to answered prayers, and numbers of these show they are expressing gratitude for babies born in answer to their prayers (see fig. 9.2). Some religions allow for the replacement of an infertile wife and Hinduism provides such a woman with religiously sanctioned support. Christianity, however, forbids the abandonment of an infertile wife.

Annulment of Unconsummated Marriages

The procedure of annulment has been favored by the Judeo-Christian religions because in their eyes the unconsummated marriage has never actually existed. In the same vein St. Paul refers to marital intercourse as the debt which the spouses owe to each other because of the marital contract. Roman Catholic theologians have held that unconsummated Christian marriages can be annulled on the ground of the impotence of the husband or the physical incapacity of either party to complete the marriage act. Some have gone beyond this to allow annulment for incurable incompatibility of temperament, as in the case of arranged marriages in France and Italy in the nineteenth century, when the bride could not

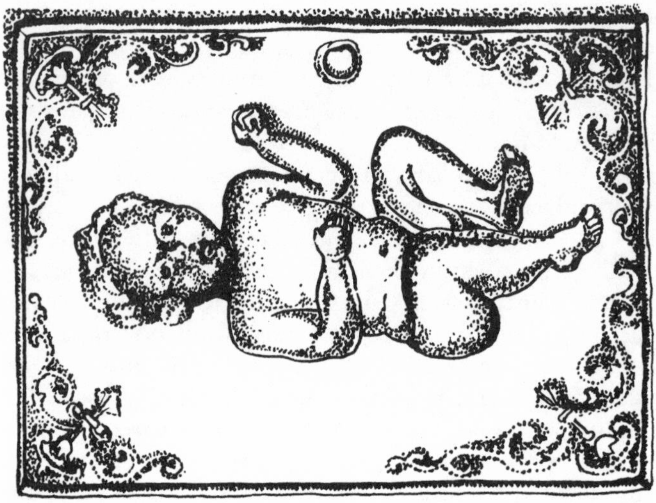

9.2. Another plaque of the kind shown in figure 8.1. This one expresses thanks that prayers for a child have been answered.

stand the sight of her new husband, or when she lived in dread of family discord after having been talked into a marriage by her family when she wanted another man, or even when her husband wanted another woman; or on the grounds that one party has obtained a civil divorce in order to marry religiously; and in situations in which the spouse is forced into marriage in order to keep a man or woman out of further sexual trouble or "incontinency" as it may be called. Finally there have been annulments on the grounds of contagious disease, where one spouse suddenly realizes that the other has venereal disease or leprosy, or for reasons of behavior, namely that one partner requires the other to perform an act of sexual perversion.

Islam provides[7] for the annulment of marriage if either party is sexually incapable of carrying out intercourse, which both husband and wife have the right to receive from each other. Islam has additional grounds for annulment where the marriage contract has not been fulfilled if the bride was described as a virgin when she was not, or if promises to pay the dowry before consummation were not kept.[8]

Judaism makes similar allowances for annulment on the grounds of defects or disabilities in the wife or husband that prevent "cohabitation." This term is somewhat wider in its possible interpretation than the mere absence of the ability to have sexual intercourse and goes beyond questions of dangerous and contagious diseases.[9]

Remarriage After Divorce in Hinduism

Divorce is not permitted in high-caste Hinduism but it occurs in lower castes. So any assertion of higher caste status requires the relinquishment of the opportunity to divorce.[10] Since traditional Hindu marriage was sacred and therefore indissoluble, this restrained the breakdown of marriages except by desertion; now a series of new laws has made the civil dissolution of a religious marriage possible under somewhat onerous grounds.[11] While the number of divorces has risen, Hindu marriage remains very stable. Studies of contemporary Hinduism often do not contain any description or details of divorce.

If divorce occurs under this new legislation it is tantamount to a reduction in caste status, and this itself prevents or certainly reduces the possibility of the divorce or of the divorcing person's remarriage, except lower down the socioreligious scale. Additionally there is a Hindu emphasis on the sanctity of first marriages which goes far beyond most concepts of a sacramental marriage: The husband is held in high religious esteem; divorce involves something approaching apostasy. Again this restrains divorce from the woman's side.

Furthermore, in Hinduism we see not only religious sentiment against divorce but a proscription against remarriage. Just as the remarriage of widows is scandalous, that of divorcees is even more so. The rejected or rejecting wife is expected to devote herself to sexual abstinence and the care of such children as she may have. We should recall, however, that these rules are characteristic of the higher castes only.

Islamic Divorce and Remarriage

Muhammad, according to the Traditions, did not approve of divorce, calling it the thing most hated by God.[12] Nevertheless the Koran gives the husband complete freedom to divorce his wife by simply saying, "I divorce you" three times.[13] Should the husband wish to remarry the same woman, she has first to be married to another man, and then redivorced[14] with three menstrual periods delay between each divorce and marriage.

The Koran contains many details of the procedure for divorce but few of the grounds for it. Since no justification for divorcing a wife is demanded by the Koran, the husband can do so without any reason other than his own caprice.[15] The only restraint on divorce by the husband is that he is required to pay the unpaid part of any marriage agreement with his wife's family, but alternatively the wife could encourage her husband to divorce her by agreeing to forfeit any part of the money that was still owed.

So there are restraints on Muslim divorce apart from the expenses of paying the bride price for a new wife. While it may have been possible for the richer man to divorce frequently, there are restraints that result from the fact that many Islamic marriages are alliances between two families. The poor subsistence farmer must always be circumspect in the use of his powers to divorce. Islamic countries generally have put secular legal restraints on the husband's religious right to divorce. From 1950 in Egypt husbands have had to give their reasons in court before a divorce can become effective, and both Algeria and Tunisia have ruled that divorces can only be decided in the courts. So the religious aspects of divorce, except where there is collusion between the parties, seem to be of diminishing contemporary importance, especially in the larger, modernizing North African states.

As Islam lauds the married state and most Islamic countries provide few if any roles for the unmarried or divorced woman who does not wish to remarry, it is certain that if they can they will remarry quickly after the obligatory delay. This is not the case with divorced women in Western countries. The younger divorced woman in the West may or may not decide to remarry, but there is normally a considerable time gap: 50 percent of divorcees in the United States were still unmarried two years after the divorces.[16]

Islam and Fornication

The killing of adulterous persons rather than mere divorce is often considered to be a specific characteristic of Islam so we shall examine the issue, since the biological effects of such a procedure are clearly profound. Muhammad's views on this subject appear to have changed during the course of his public life and the Koran reveals these changes when it is examined according to the probable time sequence of its verses and chapters. The avoidance of fornication (i.e., sexual intercourse between persons who are not either married or in concubinage) is the mark of the believer.[17] Proof of adultery requires four witnesses,[18] and if it is proved, the adulteress is to be confined in her house until she dies. But the text allows for repentance. Muhammad took a different line after suspicions arose among others about his own wife, Aisha, stating that fornicators should be beaten with a hundred strokes,[19] and he doubled the penalty for his own wives should they be involved.[20]

There is nothing in the Koran which authorizes the killing of an adulterous woman as such, and yet this appears to have happened frequently.[21] Much seems to rest on the "verse of stoning," not usually considered to be an original part of the Koran,[22] which states: "If a man and a woman who have reached years of discretion commit adultery, stone them in every case as Allah's punishment." This is one of a number of verses which the caliph Omar thought were contained in the Koran until he was convinced to the contrary by lack of evidence.[23]

It seems unlikely that there was ever such a harsh ruling, and if there was, we should note its inclusion of men. Possibly we have here a ruling used to cover a small residue of cases which involved complicated issues of honor which could not be resolved by the usual processes. The killings of adulterous women are not Islamic religiously imposed solutions in the Muhammadan sense, but arose from subsequent falsifications and distortions.

Christianity: Divorce and Remarriage

Almost all Christian denominations prohibit divorce for their adherents or allow remarriage only for what is regarded as the "innocent" partner. They actively discourage their members from breaking their marriage vows since these are based on the Gospel statement "What therefore God hath joined together, let not man put asunder."[24]

Although in earlier centuries various councils and divines wavered over the issues involved, it was from the sixteenth century Council of Trent that separation rather than divorce was allowed on the grounds of adultery, apostasy, cruelty, and heresy, but in all such cases the tie of matrimony was not broken so remarriage was forbidden.

In all this, Christianity has taken a different line from Judaism, which has always allowed divorce by the husband, though with certain restrictions.[25] For instance, barrenness of the wife had to be proved, and if there was premarital intercourse with the bride, this disallowed subsequent divorce.[26] Divorce was also disallowed in cases of insanity of the wife, or youthfulness that made it impossible for her to understand the implications of what would happen to her, and in addition a false accusation that she was not a virgin on her marriage disallowed her husband from subsequently divorcing her.[27] But there was no restriction on the wife's remarriage after divorce.[28]

The Christian hard line against accepting marital failure reinforced the structure of marriage. Before Christianity became a popular religion attracting enormous numbers of converts, the early Christians may well have encountered the same problems that faced Muhammad at an early date in his creation of the new Muslim community. It was logistically necessary to hold Christian marriages together so that the new communities could continue to exist and build up into further generations of Christian families. In later times Christian cultures have evidently maintained or reinforced the idea of marriage as a lifelong, indissoluble institution. There are differences between different Christian sects in this regard. In a recent study of Catholicism and Protestant marriages in the United States, Sander[29] found that both having a Catholic upbringing and being a Catholic now were correlated with lower frequencies of divorce than was the case for Protestant groups. The figures are shown in table 9.1.

Christian Sukuma women in Tanzania prefer to be married to Christians rather than traditionalists because of the added security which the Christian concept of marriage gives to their unions. By its stress on permanence in the eyes of God, Christianity reduces the strain of possible failure and contributes substantially to the persistence of the social and biological unit of society within which children are reared. Marriage is held in high esteem, and the security it brings is favored over the satisfaction of sexual desire and reproductive success.

In most religions, adjustment to marital problems has been required

Table 9.1. Divorce Statistics for White Non-Hispanic Men and Women by Religion and Year of Birth, 1987–91

	Men			*Women*		
Ever Divorced	*Before 1930*	*1930–1949*	*1950–1969*	*Before 1930*	*1930–1949*	*1950–1969*
Catholic upbringing	17.1%	33.3%	24.6%	13.7%	36.4%	29.8%
Baptist upbringing	32.1	39.1	36.7	23.8	44.4	43.4
Other Protestant upbringing	19.1	38.9	26.5	23.1	40.1	32.2
Catholic now	11.4	29.9	25.6	14.9	30.3	28.7
Baptist now	25.0	42.4	34.8	25.3	47.7	42.2
Other Protestant now	19.6	37.4	27.2	23.0	39.5	33.1
N upbringing	499	664	655	898	787	904
N now	488	627	608	899	781	866

Source: Sander

in the main from wives. This is less so in Christianity, where wives have a much higher standing than in Islam or Hinduism. Christian wives are further felt to gain a special ethical dignity from their forbearance, perhaps even suffering, in difficult marriages; this concept of "unselfish love" encourages marriage survival.

The Widowed and Remarriage: The Levirate

Let us now consider the phenomenon of widowhood. Where a man dies leaving a widow with or without children and the woman is still fertile but has no mate, some societies have developed social mechanisms to enable her to continue married life. One such is the "levirate," in which the woman is remarried to her dead husband's brother. This keeps her existing children and any future ones within the clan of the dead husband.

There is an ancient Semitic tradition given in the Bible[30] encouraging the brother "to marry her [the widow of a brother] and raise up seed to thy brother," so it is not surprising that in Judaism a brother had the obligation to marry such a widow, especially if his brother had died without offspring,[31] and had to release her formally before she could remarry anyone else. Indeed this rule has recently caused trouble in Israel, where the deceased husband's brothers may be living abroad. Legal provision has had to be made for Israeli women to be able to apply to the rabbinical courts for a formal release in cases where the brother was not traceable or refused to give it.

The Nuer of the Sudan practiced "ghost marriage," a form of levirate[32] in which the widow neither was inherited nor remarried but continued to be married to her dead husband while cohabiting with his brother until she died. Any children she bore to the brother carried her dead husband's name. The Nuer also had a further kinship fiction to ensure the survival of the name of a dead bachelor who had no male heir and, of course, left no widow to bear him male heirs through a brother. In such cases the lineage could marry a woman *to his name* in a properly legitimate marriage and whatever sons she might bear from whatever lover would carry the dead man's name even though he would not even have known the woman while he was alive; so he would survive as a social entity.

The levirate was at one time common in some Arab communities, where about half of all widows married their husband's brothers.[33] There are many advantages in such arrangements. As the widow is inherited by her husband's brother, she will not have far to go to her new husband's house and will stay together with her own children. If she refuses to be inherited, not only may she not have a home nearby on remarriage but her children will be lost to her and kept by her dead husband's clan. From the new husband's point of view, any property she inherits under Muslim law is available to him[34] and he also gets a new wife without having to pay more than a minimal marriage settlement for her.

In Musoma, Tanzania, despite the prohibition in 1929 of the levirate by local government regulations and the Christian church, it was still well in evidence thirty years later. Widows still found it to their advantage to enter the households of their late husband's brothers even as subordinate wives, and even if it meant breaking with their church. In Hinduism, where we have seen that upper-caste widow remarriage was generally discouraged, the levirate was encouraged and has occurred widely among lower castes.[35] Only in the form of the Nuer "ghost marriage" discussed earlier are the children of the widow reared in a truly fatherless family; contrast the situation in the West.

Remarriage of Widows in Hinduism

The best known aspect of the Hindu interdiction on the remarriage of upper caste widows was the custom of "suttee," in which widows immolated themselves on the funeral pyres of their husbands.[36] (see fig. 9.3). It is difficult to know how many widows killed themselves in this way though there exists a figure of 706 for the Bengal Residency in 1817.[37] The British attempted to stop the custom by the 1829 Act for the Prevention of Sati (Suttee), but it had little effect as there was no provision in that law for the remarriage of widows. To live on as a widow was regarded as morally wrong and it continued to be an intolerable existence: a widow's head was shaved, she wore white, she ate one meal a day

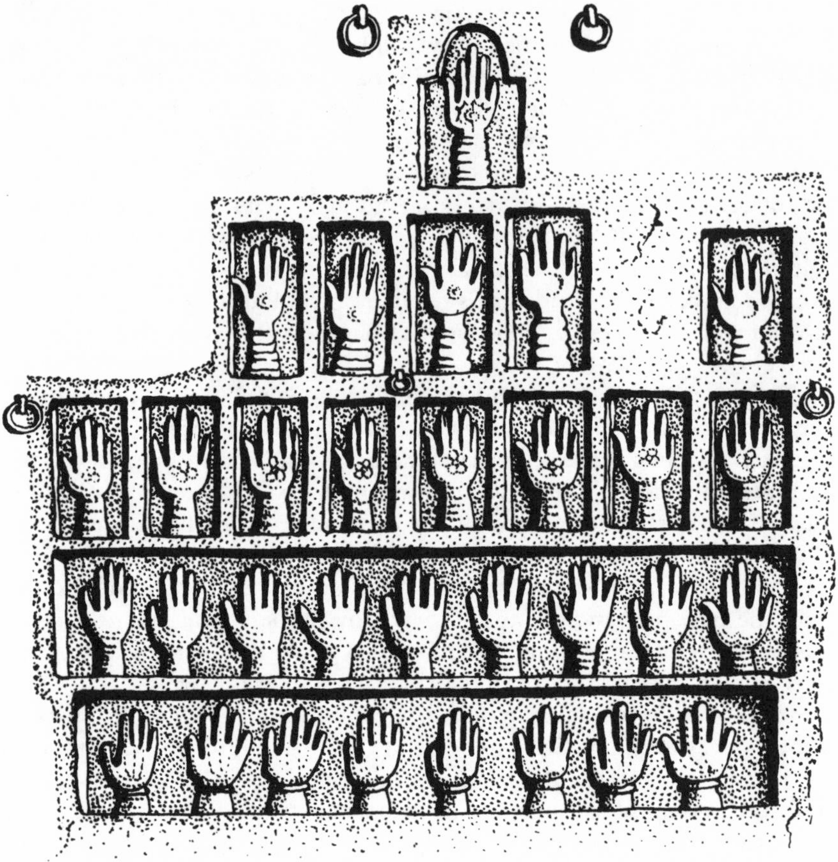

9.3. The suttee gateway to a Rajasthan palace has carved impressions of hands in commemoration of widows who had burned themselves to death on the funeral pyres of their husbands. Such women placed red ochre palm prints on the wall as they passed through on their last journey. These were later carved in relief so that the memorial should not be lost.

only, and she was avoided on all social occasions as an inauspicious omen (see fig. 9.4).

These customs may well have been generally followed for centuries[38] and have exerted considerable pressure on widows. Altekar[39] gave a figure of 2 to 10 percent of widows in priestly and noble families burning themselves to death in the areas where it was most common. One of his own sisters killed herself on the funeral pyre of her dead husband, a retired senior army officer, in 1946, and there have been still later cases. There was a famous case of suttee in Rajasthan in 1987. The widow, named Roop Kanwar, was eighteen years of age. Such self-immolating widows are still widely venerated as supreme examples of the wifely devotion expected of the best Hindus. In an especially venerated case, the widow who burned herself was still a young virgin.[40]

We have already discussed in chapter 8 the large age difference between Hindu husbands and wives and the fact that brides tend to be as young as the law and local opinion allow. Age for age, male mortality rate is in any case usually higher than that for females. Thus there will always be substantial numbers of widows in Hindu communities. While it is doubtful whether there are still any noticeable numbers of prepubertal brides (a group which in the past led to the existence of virgin widows), there is still the problem of large numbers of youngish widows. In 1901, eighteen of every thousand girls aged ten to fifteen years were widowed and the figure was ninty-two in the age group twenty to thirty years.[41] However attractive the marriage may be, it takes considerable courage and conviction for a Hindu man to marry a widow. There is a counter-pressure from her kinsmen favoring remarriage of widows in nonagricul-

9.4. A group of Hindu widows living communally and devoting themselves to prayer. Their costumes are decorated with the word *Rama,* the seventh manifestation of the god Vishnu.

tural castes because of the obligation on them to maintain her. A second counterpressure favoring widow remarriage is the possibility that she will have illicit sexual liaisons, leading to disapproval and harassment by male relatives and a social stigma on her and others too.[42]

As mentioned, some studies[43] have shown that the ban on widow remarriage is less strong in the lower castes, except where they are attempting to establish higher caste status. Remarriage is also more frequent generally than it has been in the past since families cannot afford to have unproductive women in the home. But there are further complications which can prevent the remarriage of widows because of its perceived inferior status and the general lowering of the religious status of all those involved in the arrangements. The relatives of the first husband will not wish to meet the relatives of the second husband of the divorced wife or widow, so the second marriage has to take place in a different village from the first one, but usually villages form communities and some relatives are present in all the local villages. If the two sets of relatives cannot be disentangled, then a remarriage may not be arrangeable.[44] In any case the new husband will be socially restricted as well as debasing his future family's ancestral purity and his reputation.

Christianity and the Widow

St. Paul[45] opposed the remarriage of widows except on the grounds that it would be better for them to marry than to burn and elsewhere[46] suggested that they had better remarry as otherwise "they learn to be idle, wandering about from house to house; and not only idle, but tattlers also and busybodies, speaking things which they ought not. I will therefore that the younger women marry, bear children, guide the house, give none occasion to the adversary to speak reproachfully."

Since first marriages were anyway regarded by St. Paul as a poor alternative to virginity, it is not surprising that second marriages were even more vehemently opposed. Athenagoras in the second century called them a form of adultery,[47] and St. Jerome wrote[48] even more strongly that young widows in remarrying were prostituting themselves "for a paltry and passing gain to pollute that precious chastity which might endure forever."

In modern Western societies we do not find clear-cut mechanisms for replacing the deceased partner of a marriage. It is left to the surviving individual to find a new partner if he or she wants to, and this can be difficult for a widow with a large number of children, or even a few. However, in the modern West the clear alternative for a woman is to pursue her own career. Women with successful careers may choose never to marry, or not to remarry if their husband dies, whatever age they may be.

However, in contemporary Christianity younger widows often do remarry. On the other hand, it is sometimes covertly felt that older women who have been widowed ought not to experience a new outburst of sexual feelings, or indeed expect to remarry, but to accept widowhood. These quasi-religious sentiments do nothing to provide the widow with economic support, and there are strong economic, as well as social and psychological, grounds for her remarriage, both for her own and for her children's welfare. Christianity is not helpful to widows. They are not encouraged by the church to remarry, least of all to remarry quickly, and there are no Christian organizations which cater particularly to the widowed, though this is the normal experience, late in life, of almost all married women. For such older people, their isolation and often loneliness do not constitute biological loss of fertility, since they are already post-menopausal. They can still perform grandparental functions. However, there is evidence of an increased mortality rate in that group. The mortality rate of bereaved women has been substantially higher than that of the nonbereaved of the same age and sex.[49] This heightened mortality rate has also been found for the younger widowed between twenty and thirty-four years of age in a United States study.[50]

We pursue our concern with older people in the next chapter. In many societies older people are a burden on the community, being less active and less productive than the young. Nevertheless, older people have more experience and are accorded respect. This is particularly true in cultures with ancestor cults, but also in places where the old have ritual control over funeral and mortuary rites. There are, however, situations in which the old are, or were in the past, encouraged to commit suicide, and we look at the most famous example, the institution of suttee, or self-immolation, by orthodox Hindu widows.

Notes

1. Tanner, R. E. S. (1958). "Fertility and child mortality in cousin marriages." *Eugenics R*, 49, 197–99. See also Tanner, R. E. S. (1958). "Ancestor propitiation ceremonies in Sukumaland, Tanganyika." *Africa*, 28, 225–31.

2. Cory, H. (1953). *Sukuma law and custom*. Oxford University Press/ International African Institute, London.

3. Middleton, J. (1971). *Lugbara religion*. Oxford University Press, London.

4. Bhardwaj, S. M. (1973). *Hindu places of pilgrimage in India*. University of California Press, Berkeley.

5. Dubois, J. A. (1972). *Hindu manners, customs and ceremonies*. Oxford University Press, Oxford.

6. El Saadawi. (1980). *The hidden face of Eve: Women in the Arab world*. Zed, London.

7. Russell, A. D., and Suhrawardy, A. A. M. (1925). *A manual of the law of marriage*. Kegan Paul, London.

8. Westermarck, E. (1914). *Marriage ceremonies in Morocco*. Macmillan, London.

9. *Encyclopaedia Judaica*. (1971). Keter, Jerusalem.

10. Kane, P. V. (1950). *Hindu customs and modern law*. University of Bombay Press, Bombay.

11. Government of India. (1955). Hindu Marriage Act. Delhi.

12. Mishkatt Al-Masabih. (1963). *A collection of the most authentic traditions regarding the actions and sayings of Muhammed.* Robson, J. (trans.). Ashraf. Lahore.

13. Koran. (1960). Bel, R. (trans.). T. and T. Clark, Edinburgh. Sura 2:229.

14. Koran. (1960). Bel, R. (trans.). T. and T. Clark, Edinburgh. Sura 2:230.

15. Russell, A. D., and Suhrawardy, A. A. M. (1925). *Manual of the law of marriage.* Kegan Paul, London. Aghababian, R. (1951). *Legislation Iranienne.* Paris.

16. Goode, W. J. (1965). *Women in divorce.* Free Press, Glencoe, Illinois.

17. Koran. (1960). Bell, R. (trans.). T. and T. Clark, Edinburgh. Sura 17:34 and 25:68.

18. Koran. (1960). Bell, R. (trans.). T. and T. Clark, Edinburgh. Sura 4:19–20.

19. Koran. (1960). Bell, R. (trans.). T. and T. Clark, Edinburgh. Sura 24:2.

20. Koran. (1960). Bell, R. (trans.). T. and T. Clark, Edinburgh. Sura 33:30.

21. Antoun, R. T. (1968). "On the modesty of women in Arab Muslim villages." *American Anthropologist*, 70, 671–97. Canaan, T. (1931). "Unwritten laws affecting the Arab women of Palestine." *J Palestine Oriental Society*, 11, 172–203.

22. Gibb, H. A. R., and Krammers, J. H. (1953). *The shorter encyclopaedia of Islam.* Brill, London.

23. Watt, W. M. (1967). *Companion to the Quran*. Allen and Unwin, London.

24. Matt. 19:6.

25. Westermarck, E. (1912). *The origin and development of moral ideas.* Macmillan, London.

26. Deut. 22:29.

27. Deut. 22.

28. Deut. 24:2.

29. Sander, W. (1993). "Catholicism and marriage in the United States." *Demography*, 30(3), 378.

30. Gen. 38:8. See also Deut. 26:5–6, Matt. 22:24, Mark 12:19, Luke 20:28.

31. *Encyclopaedia Judaica*. (1971). Keter, Jerusalem.

32. Evans-Pritchard, E. E. (1956). *Nuer religion*. Oxford University Press, Oxford.

33. Rosenfeld, H. (1958). "An analysis of marriage and marriage statistics for a Moslem and Christian village." *Internat Archives Ethnography*, 49, 32–62.

34. Gaudefroy-Demombynes, M. (1954). *Muslim institutions.* Allen and Unwin, London.

35. Karve, I. (1953). *Kinship organisation in India*. Deccan College Monograph Series, 11, Poona.

36. Altekar, A. S. (1956). *The position of women in Hindu civilisation*. Berarsidar, Benares.

37. Dubois, J. A. (1972). *Hindu manners, customs and ceremonies.* Oxford University Press, Oxford.

38. Dubois, J. A. (1972). *Hindu manners, customs and ceremonies.* Oxford University Press, Oxford.

39. Altekar, A. S. (1956). *The position of women in Hindu civilisation*. Berarsidas, Benares.

40. Carstairs, G. M. (1961). *The twice-born*. Hogarth Press, London. p. 74.

41. Government of India. (1902). *Census of India: 1901*. Government Printing Office, Delhi.

42. Kapadia, K. M. (1957). "A perspective necessary for the study of social change in India." *Sociological Bulletin*, 6, 40–49.

43. Dandekar, K. (1961). "Widow remarriage in six rural communities in Western India." International Population Union Conference, New York.

44. Mayer, A. C. (1965). *Caste and kinship in Central India*. Routledge, London.

45. 1 Corinthians 7:8–9.

46. 1 Tim. 5:13–14.

47. Athenagoras. (1972 ed.). *Legatio pro Christianis*. Clarendon Press, Oxford.

48. Jerome. (1963 ed.). *Epistola LIV*. The Westminster Press, Louisville, Kentucky.

49. Rees, W. D., and Lutkins, S. G. (1967). "Mortality of bereavement." *British Medical J*, 4, 13–16.

50. Kraus, A. S., and Lilienfeld, A. M. (1950). "Some epidemiologic aspects of the high mortality rate in the young widowed group." *J Chronic Diseases*, 10, 207–17.

10

Middle and Old Age

Religions Supporting the Elderly

A purpose served by many religions is ministering to the sick and to the aged, who often become sick as they get old (see fig. 10.2).

Judaism pays particular attention to the old. The Torah says: "Who is sure of heaven? He that honors the aged." Reverence and tender consideration for old age have an important place in Jewish life: "The old must be helped; their infirmities must be borne with patiently; their society is to be sought out." The aged who unite in their lives both piety and learning are made the object of singular veneration.[1] Buddhism makes no such provision for care of the aged, nor indeed for any form of social work. Christianity has been responsible for widespread institutional care of the aged through religious orders which regard this work as their particular vocation. Islam, with its insistence on charity as one of its five basic tenets, makes provision for some sort of general support for those who have no families. Islamic Egypt has large numbers of welfare societies, but the expenditure of these bodies for the care of the aged and beggars in 1960 was only 0.069 percent of their total expenditure of nearly 4 million Egyptian pounds, and only 914 persons are said to have benefited.[2] It seems that although these voluntary associations are expressed in a Muslim idiom, the movement they reflect is also a new development under the stimulus of sociopolitical events.

It is difficult to distinguish between the natural concerns of a family for the care of its own aged members and the moral requirements of religion. Institutionalized religious care for the old is often a response to a need in urban situations when families were, or are, no longer fulfilling

10.1. In this scene at a Shinto shrine in modern Japan a group of old men and women are seen praying. (Charlton et al.)

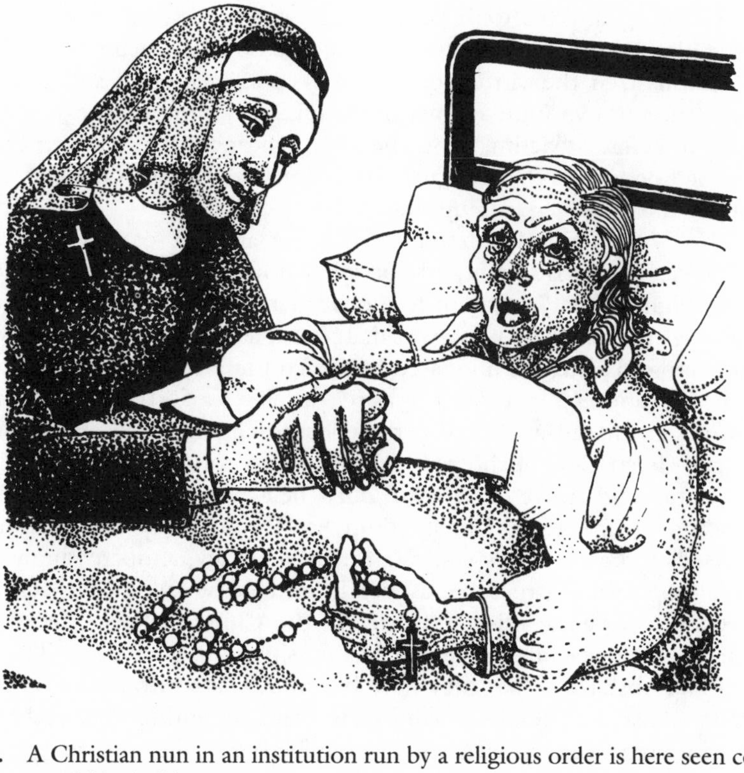

10.2. A Christian nun in an institution run by a religious order is here seen comforting an old bedridden woman.

their normal obligations. Christianity may have responded more institutionally to this problem than most religions because the nuclear family with its neglect of wider obligations largely arose within the geographical boundaries of urban medieval Christendom. Today Mother Teresa's response to the abandoned old and dying in Calcutta has received grateful attention and financial support from the Indian authorities because it is meeting this same need, unmet by other religions and secular institutions. Christian religious orders in particular seem to have the organization form and underlying motivation to develop this type of charitable work.

Why should this be so? Christianity, by its attitude to old people, puts forward or expresses the general value it holds about all human life. It lays stress on the value of *all* human life, human experience, and the significance of the individual and attempts to promote the health and happiness of all individuals, so it must logically do so for old individuals as well as younger ones. The value which it places on human life and which we see in the care of the old, which comprises a large part of the expenditure and time of Christian organizations such as the Salvation Army, is part of a general value system.

This is not, however, to suggest that religious concern for older folk exists wholly to maintain some kind of consistency about the value of life as a whole. Force of logic is not the driving force behind the Christian care for the aged. What we have is an expression of a sympathetic concern for the old and helpless in particular, enjoined by the teachings of Christ, who emphasized the virtues of self-sacrifice as well as of suffering and upheld the positive value of meekness, mildness, powerlessness, and the quality of being a "victim." It is the same sentiment that leads to care of unwanted pets and opposes cruelty to animals and vivisection as a whole even when it is of medical importance.

This is the opposite extreme from the attitude of some nomadic tribal societies of abandoning old people who are unable to keep pace, or the "benign neglect" of them found in many of the poorer subsistence economies of the present day world. In such areas all "soft" feelings, for young and old alike, are mitigated by the constant reality or possibility of actual starvation. We cannot ignore the level of control over food resources in the causation and persistence of religious rules about care of the aged. Even Christ exhorted his disciples to concentrate on the living (the young) and "leave the dead to bury their own dead."[3] Only with the increasing prosperity of Christendom has the intensity of age concern increased to present levels, and with it, incidentally, an increasingly aged overall population structure, as death rates have fallen as a result of improved medical facilities and care. In the Christian West, the old are probably now reaching a better health situation than ever. The one remaining obstacle is that they have become isolated from their families, have thus lost the benefits of family involvement, and tend to feel lonely and depressed. This obstacle must surely be resolved in the next century as it is so pressing. At the same time in some parts of the world, such as

Africa, poverty may increase steadily, with rising populations, and this will not give rise to any general improvement as far as the old are concerned. Their existence will remain as precarious as ever, and perhaps even more so, and their relative numbers in the vast populations of the Third World will not increase as they have in the West.

Old Age and Religious Involvement

While it is often assumed that religious involvement increases with the approach of death, this is not always so.[4] Among Christians in the West there appear to be a peak of church attendance around the time of retirement and a steady decline thereafter related to increasing infirmity, the absence of transport and inability to continue driving, and the dislike of being dependent on others for transportation to services.[5] Religious attitudes and feelings as such increase among those who already have an acknowledged religion;[6] these feelings can become more intense even though their institutionally oriented practices diminish.[7] This increasing divergence between faith and church attendance among the old can be balanced to a limited extent if religious services are brought to old folk in their private homes or in the institutions in which they live, by peripatetic priests or, more often, by religious services on radio and television. The social interactions associated with church attendance are very important in enhancing the quality of life for older people.[8]

Men appear to lose interest in Christianity in old age much more frequently than women. There is no rush to religious belief and practice among the terminally ill. The approach of death does not produce a large number of conversions or a return to earlier beliefs. Christianity has no last-minute influence on the dying, who are influenced more in their reactions by the religious practice of their whole lives and by the general socioreligious environment from which they come.[9]

Other religions tend to have a more active approach to the involvement of the old in religious practices. Elderly Buddhists observe the rituals more frequently than do those of other ages, particularly at the village level, where monastery ceremonies occur near to their homes. The higher attendance of older women there has been accounted for by their desire to be reborn as men.[10] Hinduism has the preferred state of *sannyasi* for the elderly; to achieve this they must detach themselves from their work and family responsibilities and become wandering ascetics.[11]

Ancestor Cults and Old Age

Certain religions in China and Africa use the "social fact" of an afterlife, in which retribution on the living by angry ancestors can occur, as the sanction for their moral belief system during life. In that sense the afterlife is, or can be, the basis of the rules promoting significant actions that occur during life, and realizing this helps us to understand the esteem in which older people are held in certain societies. They are close to ancestral status.

This attention and its significance show in the Chinese cemetery in Manila where the size of the tombs and the fact that some of the larger ones have electric fittings to allow their descendants to feast there in their memory testify to the importance of these practices in the life-style of the Chinese elite. These acres of tombs are so impressive that they are included on some tourist itineraries. The comparable tombs of the Roman Catholic cemetery nearby show almost no care of the graves at all after the initial months of grief, so that it has a deserted and derelict air.

In the tribal religions of preliterate societies which stress lineality, we often find the phenomenon of ancestor propitiation. The deceased members of a family have an influence on their descendants, and ceremonies are carried out to maintain beneficial contact with them and to placate their anger when it has affected the family's well-being. Thus it comes about that grandparents are seen as prospective ancestors, and as such it is considered unwise to anger them because of what they might do in revenge after their deaths.

Reduced Fear of Death Through Religion

Religions, through rituals, provide an orderly progress through life and into death. Believers know the stages involved and are given some self-assurance by ritual occasions; they become habituated to death by taking part in funerals or ancestor worship during their active lives (see fig. 10.3). Such events tend to be played down in Western societies, and it is known that close relatives of the deceased in countries like Britain and the United States have an increased risk of themselves dying after the death of a close relative.[12] An "orderly" death in which the deceased dies at home in the midst of his or her family has also been shown to have a less damaging effect on the bereaved close relatives, siblings as well as spouses, in a study in Wales (see table 10.1). The risk that close relatives will die during the first year of bereavement is almost doubled when the death causing bereavement occurs in a hospital rather than at home, and it rises to five times when the death happens at a site other than a caring institution or at home.[13] For the aged and infirm, therefore, other people's deaths need careful sociopsychological management, and religions are very often deeply concerned with this.

The religious concept of a "good death" is one in which the person dies in a properly sanctified state, for example, as Roman Catholics sometimes put it, "fortified by the rites of the Holy Church." The dying person is the center of rituals to put his own mind at rest and to concentrate it on the promise of the next world, while it is beneficial for the agitated survivors to be able to recite special prayers.

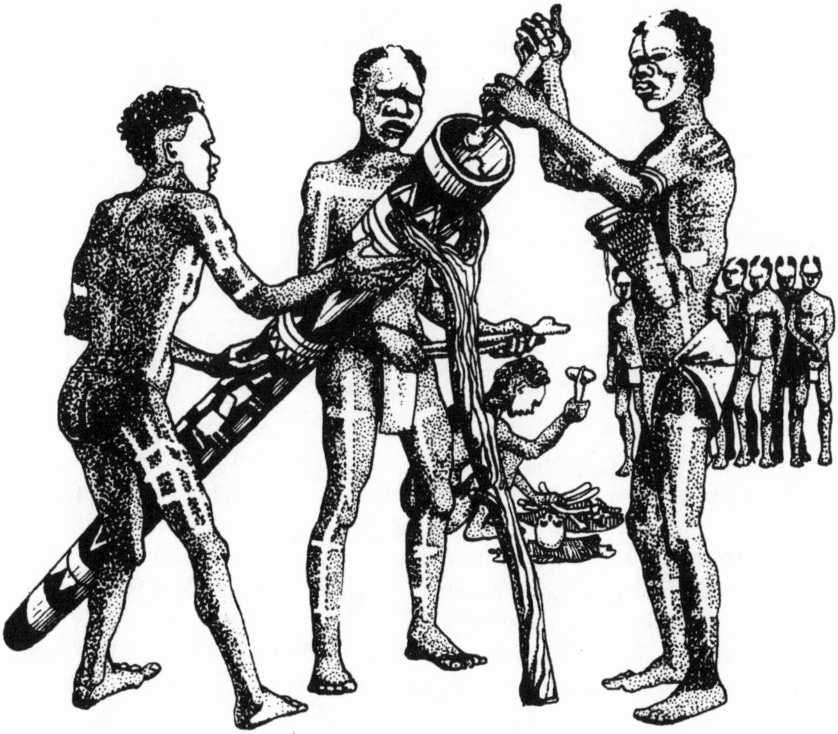

10.3. Aborigine tribesmen conducting the bone post ceremony in Arnhem Land, northeast Australia. The bones of a dead man are crushed up by his relatives and pushed into a hollow painting log, which is then erected as a permanent memorial.

Burmese Buddhists believe that an individual's position in his next incarnation can be influenced by his state of mind immediately prior to death, and to achieve this Buddhist devotions are recited at the deathbed by his friends, relatives, and, as often as possible, monks.[14] While these Buddhist and Christian ideas involve the dying in essentially restful rituals, Hinduism, at least for high-caste Brahmins, involves the removal of the dying man from his house and bed to be ceremonially purified outside on the ground by a priest and the nearest relative.[15]

In most cultures there is a proper way to die, usually surrounded by one's relatives and involved in the socioreligious ceremonies of one's faith. This idea sustains not only the aged but also the living. It is being increasingly recognized that death ceremonies are an essential part of the process of mourning, without which the surviving close kin have no accepted and successful way of working out their sorrow and their reintegration into society and a useful social life.

A part of the last rites in the Sukuma involves a farewell to the dying person in which all the relatives present touch the feet of the moribund

Table 10.1. Percentages of Deaths at the Sites Listed When the Death Was Followed by the Death of a Close Relative

	Years of Bereavement					
	1	*2*	*3*	*4*	*5*	*6*
Died at home	7.1	5.0	1.2	2.5	0.6	0.6
Died in hospital	12.6	3.7	3.8	4.0	2.0	1.0
Died in chronic sick unit	17.5	8.1	6.7	—	—	—
Died in old people's home	—	—	20.0	—	—	—
Died at other sites	37.5	—	20.0	—	—	—

Source: Rees and Lutkins

individual. In contemporary Western society touching by any except the most intimate relatives may have fallen into disuse because of fears of infection, or general distaste for being too closely associated with dying and death, and also the fact that those who are expected to die as part of a diagnosed disease or senility usually do so away from their families in an institution for the aged or a hospital. Such separation is unimaginable in most smaller-scale societies. For instance, among the Lodagaa[16] it is preferred that an individual should die sitting up in the arms of a close kinswoman.

In a study of religious orientation and its relationship to death anxiety, this was found to be lower in those with strong integral religious beliefs and greater in those with more expedient religious views.[17] Yates et al.[18] found that religious belief was an important source of support for patients with advanced cancer.

Suicide and Religion

Suicide is predominantly found, in our own kind of society, among the old and among men (see fig. 10.4). A recent study[19] has shown that whereas the male suicide rate fell sharply from 1960 to 1970, since then it has been rising, while during the whole of the 1960–1990 period female suicide rates have been falling (data from England and Wales). Although Durkheim's classic study of suicide concluded that lower rates correlated with church affiliation, some recent studies have not found a significant relationship.[20] A closer correlation was with low socioeconomic status[21] and with high internal migration and divorce rates.[22]

A study of religiosity and U.S. suicide rates confirmed the general hypothesis that religiosity deters suicide,[23] but this was qualified by a further study which concluded that a religious person's negative attitude to suicide could be modified by particular circumstances.[24] However, a British study found no significant differences between a group which had

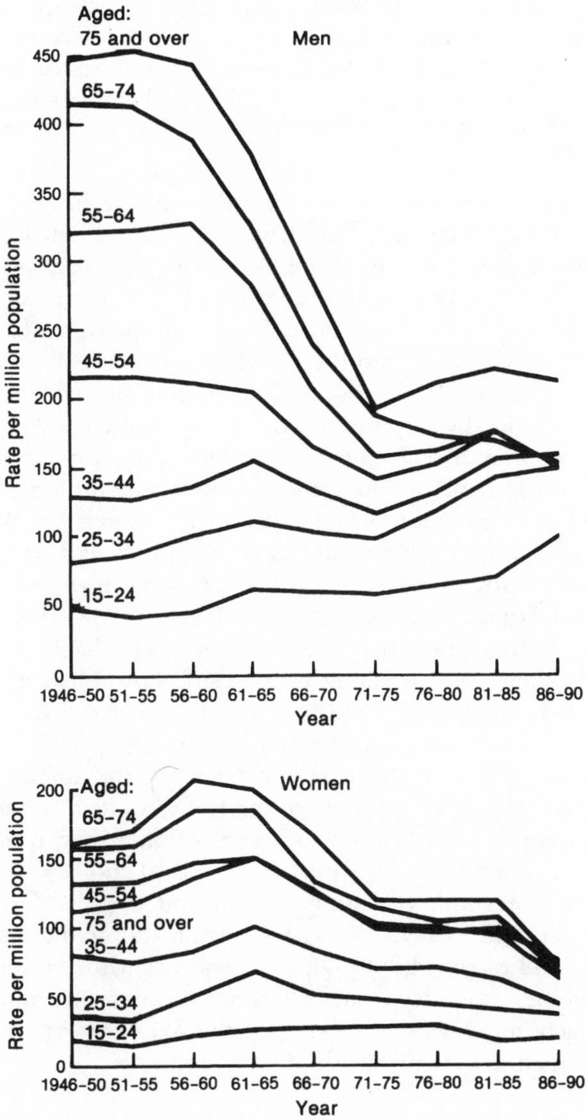

10.4. Recorded suicide deaths: Rate per million population by sex and age, 1946–90, England and Wales.

attempted suicide and a control group, concluding that suicide attempts may occur independently of religious attitudes.[25] According to Dublin:

> With advancing years habits become set, reactions run in established grooves, and forced changes become more difficult and disturbing. Impairments are accumulated, particularly of chronic and painful diseases. Many older people suffer from psychoses of one type or another, especially from depressions, and from feelings of loneliness and futility

> as relations with family and friends and productive work drop off. Economic insecurity is often a serious problem, as is also inability or unwillingness to tolerate hardships. Young people, when difficulties arise, can more readily work off their pent-up emotions without resorting to self-destruction. They have more and safer methods of relieving emotional tensions.[26]

Considerable attention has been paid to suicide in relation to religious belief and practice, and there have been several detailed studies of it.[27] Western religions have always taken a strong stand against it, even in old age. Early Christians mainly considered that God had sovereign power over life and humans therefore should not interfere in any way; life was not theirs to terminate and the self-killer was guilty of mortal sin and buried outside consecrated ground. This idea is still widespread: "The suicide prevents the divine purpose from being realised and interrupts his service to God. Man like all else must subserve the glory of God."[28] Suicide is certainly infrequent where the guidance and authority of religion are accepted without question and where the church forms the background of communal life and its duties are rigidly prescribed.

We have already discussed (see chapter 9) the now-infrequent custom in which Hindu widows destroyed themselves on their husband's funeral pyre, concluding that in the past this was probably confined very largely to the upper castes. Hindu women still, however, commit suicide more frequently than men,[29] and it is probable that the self-destruction by women is just one aspect of a certain concept of womanhood due to a number of specifically Hindu factors:[30] first is the inferior status of women, shown clearly in their lower survival rates at birth and in early childhood; second, a very early marriage is often arranged for them by their fathers without choice or with very restricted choice of bridegroom; third, the daughter-in-law is subordinated and oppressed by her husband's mother and father. We can contrast the traditional "socially embedded" kind of suicide of high-caste widows with the more general suicide of women nowadays, out of feelings of inferiority and not being wanted, which more closely resembles the Western type except that women, not men, are chiefly involved.

Altruistic Suicide and the Survival of the Reproductively Active

Finally, we should consider the situation in hunting and gathering societies in which such suicides as do occur tend to be for altruistic purposes[31] where the loss of an older life will allow others to survive. When an individual's needs and continued living begin to be a liability to the group, he or she may turn to suicide. Among the Eskimos it used to be that old people would kill themselves,[32] and other cases are well known and documented in which old folk who no longer could manage the nomadic existence were expected, and able, more or less passively to accept abandonment.[33]

The life cycle, for everyone, ends with death; in the next chapter we look at how religions "manage" this especially traumatic event. There are two aspects: the problem of coping with fear for the dying person and the management of grief by the surviving relatives. In both respects religions have since time immemorial provided explanations, hope, guidance, and other kinds of psychological comfort. Indeed, death provides the best evidence for the role of religions in giving meaning and significance to human life. Without religious beliefs life and death fail to make any sense and people in all parts of the world have invested death with a particular meaning, most often as a transition stage to a future existence. Here we see denial of the idea of termination of life, of any kind of absolute end. Religions, by denying the finality of death, give comfort to the dying and hope to the living.

On the darker side, religions also can bring about death, through a variety of magical means. We look at rules concerning the treatment of the dead, the phenomenon of martyrdom, and the religious wars and killings that have characterized the past and continue on into the present time.

Notes

1. Joseph, M. (1917). "Care of the aged." In Hastings, W. (ed.). *Encyclopedia of religion and ethics.* T. and T. Clark, Edinburgh.
2. Berger, M. (1970). *Islam in Egypt today: Social and political aspects of popular religion.* Cambridge University Press, Cambridge.
3. Luke 9:60.
4. Moberg, D. O. (1965). "Religiosity in old age." *Gerontologist*, 5, 78–87.
5. Barr, H. M. (1970). "Aging and religious disaffiliation." *Social Forces*, 49, 60–71.
6. Barrow, M. L. (1958). "The role of religion and religious institutions in creating the milieu of older people." In Scudder, D. (ed.). *Organised religion and the older person.* University of Florida Press, Gainesville.
7. Hinton, J. M. (1963). "The physical and mental distress of the dying." *Q J Medicine*, 32, 1–21. Young, G., and Dowling, W. (1987). "Dimensions of religiosity in old age: Accounting for variation in types of participation." *J Gerontology*, 42(40), 376–80.
8. Markides, K. S. (1983). "Aging, religiosity and adjustment: A longitudinal analysis." *J Gerontology*, 38(5), 621–25. Koenig, H. G., et al. (1988). "Religion and well-being in later life." *Gerontologist,* 28(1), 18–28. Mindel, C. H., and Vaughan, C. E. (1978). "A multidimensional approach to religiosity and disengagement." *J Gerontology*, 33(1), 103–8.
9. Wingrove, C. R., and Alston, J. P. (1971). "Age, aging and church attendance." *Gerontologist*, 11, 356–58.
10. Spiro, M. E. (1971). *Buddhism and society.* Allen Unwin, London. p. 218.
11. Dubois, J. A. (1972). *Hindu manners, customs and ceremonies.* Oxford

University Press, Oxford. Carstairs, G. M. (1961). *The twice-born.* Hogarth Press, London, pp. 96–97.

12. Krause, A. S., and Lilienfeld, A. M. (1959). "Some epidemiologic aspects of the high mortality rate in the young widowed group." *J Chronic Diseases*, 10, 207–17. Parkes, C. M., and Brown, R. J. (1972). "Health after bereavement: A controlled study of young Boston widows and widowers." *Psychosomatic Medicine*, 34, 449–61. Young, M., et al. (1963). "Mortality of widowers." *Lancet*, 2, 454–56.

13. Rees, W. D., and Lutkins, S. G. (1967). "Mortality of bereavement." *British Medical J*, 4, 13–16.

14. Spiro, M. E. (1971). *Buddhism and society.* Allen and Unwin, London, p. 248.

15. Dubois, J. A. (1972). *Hindu manners, customs and ceremonies.* Oxford University Press, Oxford, pp. 482–83.

16. Goody, J. (1962). *Death, property and the ancestors: A study of the mortuary customs of the Lodagaa of West Africa.* Tavistock, London, pp. 49–50.

17. Kraft, W. A., et al. (1987). "Religious orientation and assertiveness: Relationship to death anxiety." *J Social Psychology*, 127(1), 93–95.

18. Yates, J. W. et al. (1981). "Religion in patients with advanced cancer." *Medical and Pediatric Oncology*, 19, 121–28.

19. Charlton, J. et al. (1992). "Trends in suicide deaths in England and Wales." *Population Trends*, 69(13), 10.

20. Stack, S. (1981). "Suicide and religion." *Sociology Focus*, 14, 207–20.

21. Stack, S. (1983). "A comparative analysis of suicide and religiosity." *J Social Psychology*, 119, 285–86.

22. Lester, D. (1987). "Religiosity and personal violence: A regional analysis of suicide and homicide rates." *J Social Psychology*, 127(6), 685–86.

23. Martin, W. T. (1984). "Religiosity and US suicide rates, 1972–78." *J Clinical Psychology*, 40(5), 116–69.

24. Best, J. B., and Kirk, W. G. (1982). "Religiosity and self-destruction." *Psychological Records*, 32, 35–39.

25. Neal, C. D. (1981). "Religion and self-poisoning." *International J Social Psychiatry*, 27, 257–60.

26. Dublin, L. I. (1963). *Suicide: A sociological and statistical study.* Ronald Press, New York, p. 22.

27. Durkheim, E. (1932). *Sucide: A study in sociology.* Free Press, Chicago. Dublin, L. I. (1963). *Suicide: A sociological and statistical study.* Ronald Press, New York.

28. Davis, H. (1946). *Moral and pastoral theology.* Sheed and Ward, London, pp. 142–43.

29. Shah, J. H. (1959). "Causes and prevention of suicide." Paper read at Indian Conference of Social Work, Hyderabad.

30. Meer, F. (1976). *Race and suicide in South Africa.* Routledge and Kegan Paul, London.

31. Durkheim, E. (1932). *Suicide: A study in sociology.* Free Press, Chicago.

32. Nansen, F. (1893). *Eskimo life.* Longmans, London, p. 151.

33. Carr-Saunders, A. M. (1922). *The population problem: A study in human evolution.* Clarendon Press, Oxford.

11

Death

In this chapter we come on to the inevitable next stage of the life cycle, death itself. This involves the actual process of dying, a time after this for funeral and mourning ceremonies, dealing with the bereaved, and a subsequent period when the dead person is, or may be, psychologically or socially active among his or her descendants and others in the community.

Religions are very concerned with this crucial point of the life cycle; very concerned with ministering to the dying person, preparing him or her for the world to come, generally being involved with his physical needs and psychological feelings at this time, and likewise helping those people who are especially close. In many religions the body is left largely, or entirely, in the hands of religious organizations which have special ways of dealing with the situation.

Dying and death are key areas of focus for the religions of the Western world. One reason for this could well be that religions have lost much of their day-to-day significance for the living in modern Western society; there is a general lack of preoccupation with religion as an everyday consideration among the living. This, as we saw in the last chapter, extends into old age. Nevertheless it seems that at the time of death itself, even in modern Western societies, the services of local religious bodies are called in. The social services may to some extent be active until death, in care of the aged, but they are not adequate for the scale of the problem provided by death itself. Nor, it seems, is the wish to "face the facts" of a loved one's death necessarily fulfilled for the bereaved. We are not only concerned here with what religions do about dead people but with whether these activities help the survivors and make them better able to cope, to recover, and to resume productive and active lives. Despite its efforts, Christianity is not

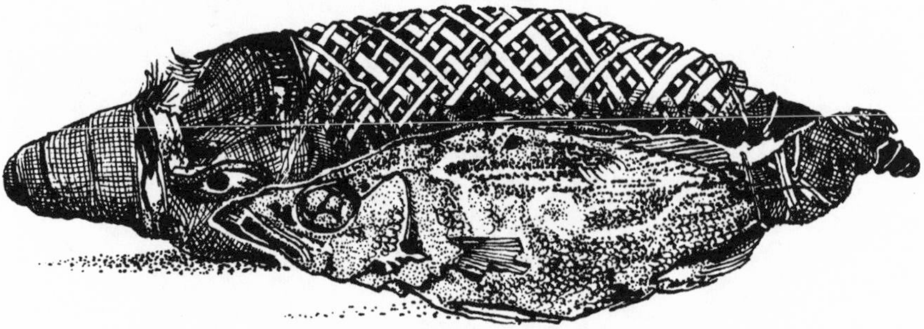

11.1. In ancient Egyptian tombs, food was provided in preserved form for the departed. These examples are a preserved crocodile (behind) and a fish (front).

always able to cope, as we shall see; Hinduism, Muslim, and tribal religions probably do better, and we shall suggest a reason for this.

Mourning Procedures and Funerals

What are the effects of death on the survivors? We can distinguish social and psychological effects. The death of a person who occupies an important place in the social structure of the group leaves a gap in the structure. Most deaths are among the aged, who in our society (though not in many others) are generally marginal. Less often, a person dies in the middle of his or her life cycle at the peak of his or her prime and social significance. The death of a child is, again, socially a marginal event.

Psychologically, things are different. In the case of a child's death there is the important question of bereavement of the surviving members of the family, which in our society tends to be severe. There is not a great social structure deficit here, but a major emotional upset. When a parent dies in his or her prime, bereavement is again severe, and the spouse and children have to be cared for. The psychological impact can still be sharp, though it must normally have been anticipated. The rituals surrounding death are as much for the living as for the dead person, and indeed biologically they are strictly for the living. Bereaved people feel a sense of grief; they do not necessarily comprehend a death and they may not know what to do about the situation. Therefore, religions need to have rules for the expression of grief, for the explanation of death, and for the management of situations which arise when people do not comprehend. The grief itself is given legitimate expression and religions have places and times when this should be done. They sometimes have rules about who in particular should grieve and how long they should grieve. The funeral is not only the method by which the body is disposed of and the final termination of that particular person's active life, but a message to the mourners.

Death has a wide range of psychic and psychosomatic effects on the bereaved (table 11.1). A comparative study of widows in two cities, Boston and Sydney, showed that grief can upset the stomach and is related to rheumatism, skin irritations, headaches, and asthma.

Table 11.1. Psychosomatic Grief Reactions of Widows in Boston and Sydney

Symptom or complaint	*Total widows (%)* *n = 375*	*Total controls (%)* *n = 199*
Neurological		
Migraine	4.8	3.0
Headache	17.6	9.0
Dizziness	9.1	4.5
Fainting spells	1.3	0
Blurred vision	13.7	7.5
Dermatological		
Skin rashes	6.1	2.5
Excessive sweating	9.3	5.0
Gastrointestinal		
Indigestion	9.9	4.5
Difficulty in swallowing	4.8	1.5
Peptic ulceration	2.1	2.0
Colitis	0.5	0
Vomiting	2.7	0
Excessive appetite	5.4	0.5
Anorexia	13.1	1.0
Weight gain	8.5	9.0
Weight loss	13.6	2.0
Genitourinary		
Menorrhagia	4.3	0.5
Cardiovascular		
Palpitations	12.5	4.0
Chest pain	10.1	4.5
Respiratory		
Dyspnea	12.0	4.5
Asthma	2.4	1.5
General		
Frequent infections	2.1	0
General aching	8.4	4.0
Neoplastic growth	0.8	0
Diabetes mellitus	0.8	0.5

Source: Maddison, D., and Viola A. (1968). "The health of widows in the year following bereavement." *Journal of Psychosomatic Research*, 12, 297–306.

The importance of the rituals of death is that they are socioreligious requirements which have to be carried out by the bereaved within the social context of friends, relatives, and neighbors who are less bereaved. The bereaved are not left alone to generate and multiply the psychosomatic symptoms of their grief, but are required to be active, and in many cultures there is a special role for bereaved persons over quite a long period, such as the forty-day mourning period for Muslims, at the end of which their recovery from bereavement is well advanced.

Most societies have prescribed mourning behavior which varies within a common theme: that the bereaved are in some ways abnormal and that this abnormality diminishes with time. Among the Buddhist Lepchas of Sikkim any married person in any way connected with the dead person had to abstain from sleeping with his or her spouse for three days after a death. On the death of a spouse, parent, or sibling, the survivors were debarred for a year from marrying. For affinal and classificatory relations this prohibition lasted for forty-nine days.[1]

There is little doubt that contemporary Western society has increasingly simplified mourning rituals, even removed them from the family context; families move too often and the nuclear family is too small to provide either the environment or the personnel for big family rituals. The bereaved are very often alone after the funeral, and it is tempting to see in this social isolation a direct connection with the physical symptoms shown in table 11.1.

Western cultures have abandoned many rituals which used to attend the transition into and through the state of being bereaved. Lacking these social supports, some bereaved people adopt roles which ensure that their society will be forced to accord them liminal status by becoming sick or by interpreting the features of their grief as symptoms. Such a person seeks help from other specialists, in particular the medical practitioner. Getting a prescription confirms the "patient" in his sick role, which provides him with the means to suppress some physiological manifestations of grief.[2]

The involvement of the bereaved in special activities from the moment of death is very obvious in some societies, particularly where families are extended. In Islamic societies the women of the bereaved family maintain formalized wailing from the time of death up to the burial, beating themselves, scratching their faces, tearing their clothes,[3] and even in some cases hiring professional wailing women.[4]

It is an ethnocentric mistake to assume that the behavior evoked is solely a reaction to the disruptions of social and emotional equilibrium caused by a particular death. Funerals provide occasions and materials for a symbolic discourse on life through different treatments of the dead detailing theories as to what happens in the afterlife. Each culture perceives different implications for the dead in losing their individuality. For Greek aristocrats not to be remembered was terrifying; for the Kraho there were stages in the loss of personal identity until they became stones; for the Merina their crushed bones merged into the family tombs; and for the Dowayo there was an association with a generic control over fertility benefiting groups rather than individuals.[5]

Religious Ideas as a Cause of Death

Religions approach the problems of "death management" where death arises from any cause whatever. There are also, however, instances where religions themselves cause death. They can bring death to individuals or to whole groups, and to old and young alike.

A case in point is snake handling, using poisonous snakes that have not been "milked" or had their fangs or poison sacs removed. Religious ceremonies using such snakes occurred among the Hopi Indians of the southwestern United States.[6] Young men had to go out before the snake ceremony, find and collected certain poisonous snakes alive, a dangerous business indeed. Then, at the time of the ceremony, the snakes were handled in a great variety of ways. The religious functionaries involved were men, often in their prime; they are reported to have avoided snake bites to a great extent, but we have no accurate data on the extent of bites and fatalities.

The members of some small Christian denominations such as the Holiness Churches of the southern United States until recently had their entranced members test their faiths by handling poisonous snakes, following the Gospel of St. Mark (16:18) (see fig. 11.2). They also applied torch flames to their bodies and drank strychnine.[7] In this study it is stated that although there had been widespread handling of poisonous snakes, very few people had been bitten; despite refusal of treatment, about thirty Holiness members are known to have died from snakebite since 1910.[8] G. W. Hensley, the initiator in 1909 of snake handling in Tennessee, died of snakebite. The practice of snake handling probably continues despite its legal prohibition in Tennessee, Kentucky, and Virginia.[9]

A further, well documented, but rather different way in which religion can cause death is through psychological suggestion. The subject, sometimes called "Voodoo" death, has been well reviewed by Cannon,[10] who concluded that "it may be explained as due to shocking emotional stress—to obvious or repressed terror." He found valid evidence of it in South America, Africa, Australia, New Zealand, the Pacific Islands, and Haiti. In many of the cases he cited, the death concerned followed upon the discovery by an individual that he or she had broken, sometimes inadvertently, a sacred taboo (e.g., eating a forbidden food). Death could occur either soon after or long after the breach. Cannon was concerned to assess the possibility that death was in fact an outcome of wholly physical, nonpsychological processes of poisoning or self-starvation. The latter was indeed often involved, but it was an outcome of the initial psychological shock. "The question arises," he wrote, "whether an ominous and persistent state of fear can end the life of a man." His interpretation of the underlying physiological process indicated that it could. He described how the sympathetic nervous system and the hormonal adrenal medullary system together could, if their action were prolonged, bring about a fall in blood pressure due to a reduction in the volume of circulating blood, which, together with reduction of food and water, could cause death as a result of "shock" in the surgical sense. One of the authors (V. Reynolds) observed a case of near-death from "witchcraft" in Uganda in 1962; the patient recovered, however, when he moved from his home community

11.2. Poisonous snake handling by the Reverend Doyle Morrisy, a member of a fundamentalist Christian sect in the southern United States.

to another village. This individual was a well-educated African who spoke fluent English. There are in addition a number of further studies relevant to this phenomenon.[11]

The Use of Corpses in Magical and Religious Rituals

The traditional Western picture of the witch and wizard using human ingredients in magic potions, boiled and stirred while chanting powerful spells, is well illustrated in Shakespeare's *Macbeth*: "Nose of Turk and Tartar's lips, finger of birth-strangled babe, liver of blaspheming Jew." There is indeed evidence that human ingredients were used in rituals in parts of Africa.[12] Some well-known cases of this use occurred in Lesotho, where at least sixty ritual murders occurred in a ten-year period[13] in which the victims were mutilated while still alive to supply the blood and flesh ingredients of magic medicines needed for the support of political power. Among the ancient Aztecs too, hearts were routinely taken from living victims for ritual purposes; likewise in the old West African Kingdom of Benin. In such cases, religions cause considerable loss of life.

The consequences of disease arising from the consumption of human tissues for ritual purposes is known from the New Guinea disease kuru studied among the Foré people.[14] This is a severe degenerative disease of the central nervous system affecting much of the population of certain areas, resulting in death within nine months of the appearance of the first symptoms. Foré women practiced ritual cannibalism of their dead kinsmen, particularly eating the brain tissues, which were squeezed into a pulp with the bare hands and eaten. With the decline of the practice after 1957 there has been a steady decline in the incidence of kuru.

This New Guinea case is interesting insofar as it involves eating dead relatives; thus it tends to keep this particular disease within the extended family and as a result was at first thought to be a genetic disease. In certain American Indian tribes, however, such as the Hurons and Iroquois, captives were regularly eaten either cooked or raw; indeed the latter ate the Jesuit priest de Brébeuf raw in recognition of his bravery under torture.[15]

Cannibalism of old people, who were killed and eaten by their relatives, was reported from East and South Asia during the nineteenth century. Early literature contains many references to this practice, as for instance among the Battak of Sumatra[16] and the Birhors of Central India.[17] While the explanation has been put forward that this occurred as an act of filial piety to retain within the family the powers of the old, it has been observed that "like so many other funeral customs which are supposed to comfort the dead this may be the survival of a practice which was originally designed to promote the selfish interests of the living."[18] There are a number of reasons why this might be so.

It has often been assumed that cannibalism is related to the religious beliefs of the eaters, but this need not always be so. In a detailed study of Azande cannibalism, Evans-Pritchard[19] concluded that the motive was simply a taste for human meat, sometimes accentuated by extreme hunger. But the author pointed out that this whole subject was full of hearsay, quoting the Azande's conviction that British doctors were cannibals who performed surgical operations to obtain meat. A variant of this view was often encountered by one of the authors (R. Tanner) in Tanzania, where it was widely believed that the parts of the body removed in hospital operations were used in the preparation of magical medicines. The other author (V. Reynolds) heard the view expressed in Uganda in 1962 that whites, in general, were cannibals from time to time.

There are different kinds of cannibalism, and we can distinguish at least three: First is commemorative cannibalism, in which male Trobriand Islanders exhumed and dismembered the bodies of related men and were expected to display their filial piety by sucking the decaying flesh off the bones.[20] Second is compassionate cannibalism, in which the Gimi women of New Guinea were expected to eat the dead bodies of their men in order to release the latter's individual spirits.[21] Third is fertility cannibalism among the Bimin-Kuskusmin of New Guinea, among whom male agnates honored the dead by eating morsels of their bone marrow to ensure the passage of the dead man's spirit to the ancestral world, thus recycling his procreative and ritual strength within his patrilineage.[22]

The Preparation of the Body for Disposal

An idea expressed in many religions is that the dead should not be left alone. This may in some societies have been or still be to prevent the use of the body for witchcraft. In other cases it ensures that the dead are always "properly" disposed of. Judaism has burial societies, and medieval Christianity had religious orders specifically dedicated to the disposal of dead people who had no relatives. Few religions, if any, have ever considered it proper that the dead should be disposed of without due preparation. When the dead are left unattended or disposed of in mass graves, it is usually because religious concern for the individual person has broken down under some kind of stress or disaster such as war, epidemic, or earthquake. Religions do not as a rule make provision for this, and their normal death customs are not appropriate for mass disposal.

We know that some death customs such as cradling the corpse, found in Java[23] and other places (see fig. 11.3), are quite extraordinarily dangerous to health. The Bontoc Igorot, a mountain people living in North Luzon, Philippines, have their dead placed on a chair under the house for several days and

> as a rule decomposition sets in well before the third day. Often the corpse swells greatly; the liquid escapes through the nose and the mouth. Insects also swarm around the corpse and a couple of women chase them almost continually with a kind of fan which they make for this purpose. Although the odour is at times unbearable, the people remain on the house-ground and eat their meals with no less appetite. One can imagine how it must have been when the corpse was kept on the death chair as long as ten days.[24]

In many parts of the world, the dead body is prepared for burial by being washed and dressed by special personnel. In Islam, body washers were entitled to keep the clothes of the deceased.[25] In Buddhism this job was done typically by relatives and always by men.[26]

11.3. Among the Kukukuku people in New Guinea a dead grandfather who has been smoke dried over the fire in the living hut for two months is surrounded by his family.

Among Buddhist societies we encounter some unhygienic religious practices concerning the dead. David-Neel[27] was an eyewitness of the custom of drinking tea out of a cauldron that had just held a corpse, during a funeral ceremony in Tibet. In Nepal, Faul[28] observed an unhygienic religious practice, which she described as follows:

> The two parts of Pashupatinath Stupa [a Buddhist shrine] lie on either side of the Bagmati River [in Katmandu, Nepal], connected by a bridge. Huge numbers of people come there to worship every morning. And, when there is no hope of recovery, it is there that the dying are taken to

the dying house. When their time is near, they are carried to the edge of the river, so that they may die with their feet in the holy water.

Such practices seem likely, if only occasionally, to spread infection. There are, of course, in hygiene-conscious societies, special washing practices after touching a dying person or a dead body. But not everywhere.

In many cases relatives and neighbors come to some form of lying-in, to say farewell or pay final respects to the deceased, and there is often a steady stream of visitors (see fig. 11.4). Even if death has been due to infection, relatives may be required or may want to kiss, touch, and otherwise handle the bodies of their loved ones. This heavy involvement of relatives will tend to spread any infection present along kinship lines, a process that hardly makes good sense in terms of positive kin selection. The West has seen a massive reduction of frequency of death from infectious diseases, so that the dead are more likely to be perfectly "safe" to those nearby. Yet many Westerners no longer seem able to touch dead bodies of any except their most beloved without extreme reluctance. The effort made by the Jewish and Christian religions to help those involved

11.4. This scene from the contemporary United States shows relatives of a deceased man paying their last respects at a funeral parlor.

see death as a necessary and not particularly dreadful part of life seems often to fail in modern Western society, where psychosomatic illness often follows a death (see earlier discussion and chapter 10). Almost the first thing we do with a dead person is to cover him or her with a sheet, as if the sight of a corpse were inappropriate, frightening, or even disgusting. Not so in societies in what we call the underdeveloped world or Third World, where general instability and high mortality rates make death, if not an everyday, at least a familiar event. We can therefore distinguish between "open" funeral customs and "closed" ones, meaning by those terms the extent to which feelings are openly expressed and given ritual expression or kept in check. In the former case the living and the dead mingle together in harmony; in the latter they remain at a hygienic distance from each other.

The Disposal of Dead Bodies

Dead bodies have to be disposed of and religions often provide the rules and personnel for this, even when the dead and their survivors are not specifically religious. From a biological point of view this process is important, since the corpse, even if not unhygienic at first, is bound to become so sooner or later.

Religions advocate particular methods of corpse disposal, the Hindus by burning and the Christians traditionally by burial, though nowadays very much by cremation too. These are adequately hygienic methods of disposal. However, in the Hindu case, there is not always enough wood to burn the body completely and as a result the Ganges receives large numbers of half-burned bodies (see fig. 11.5). With burial, in some non-Western societies, the soil may be too hard in the dry season, or the tools too inadequate, to allow for burial to be at a sufficient depth to eliminate all possibility of infection. Nomadic people often do not have the tools to dig graves. The Masai of East Africa expose their dead and never kill hyenas since they consume cadavers. The Parsees expose their dead in specially constructed "towers of silence," built well away from habitation. Neither society buries any human remains.

Until the growth of cities, Christian dead were traditionally buried in graveyards surrounding village churches, usually situated in the middle of housing. Each house had its own well or access to a communal well nearby. One of the authors (R. Tanner) lived in an old house in rural England with its own well directly downhill from a graveyard, which was less than fifty yards away. The through-put of water in a constantly used well can be expected to have had adverse health effects in the Middle Ages and later, especially for the transmission of cholera.

Even where we might wish to explain the burial of the dead near the living in religious terms, as for instance in a society with an ancestor cult stressing the need for communication between the dead and the living,

11.5. At Benares, India, bodies are dipped into the River Ganges prior to cremation. After cremation the remains are disposed of in the river.

there may also be more prosaic factors. The Sukuma of Tanzania bury their dead in their cattle pens, and their own explanation for this is only partly a religious one: they also state that the soil is softer there. They do not like the burial grounds provided by modern mission churches because the graves are not guarded and they are concerned that the newly buried body will be dug up by witches and wizards, or by hyenas.

Religious Attitudes to Autopsies

Every religion, as we have seen, has an idea of what is the correct attitude to the body of a deceased person. Judaism holds that respect for the dead prevents the mutilation of a body for dissection or postmortem examination. There has been divided rabbinical opinion as to whether dissection is permissible for the purposes of advancing learning and research. The anatomical needs of Israeli hospitals have at times been disproportionately met by the use of non-Jewish bodies. Thus, the refusal of permission for autopsies in New York City Jewish hospitals has not affected the 36 percent minimum quota of autopsies required for hospital accreditation because of the availability of the bodies of non-Jewish people dying in those hospitals.[29] In these New York Jewish hospitals the rate of refusal for permission for an autopsy was 62 percent among Jews and 38 percent among non-Jews. There have been occasional cases[30] in which relatives have sought to prevent an autopsy on religious grounds when it has been legally required in cases of unusual sudden death. In 1942 Chief Rabbi Kook forbade autopsies of Jewish bodies, but his successor, Rabbi Herzog, allowed autopsies designed to save future lives and in cases in which it would be humane to establish the presence of hereditary disease. In 1965 there were orthodox objections to this broad range of permissions so the use of autopsies was limited to saving future lives when there was an immediate possibility of doing so, for instance, in cases when several patients in the same hospital were suffering from an undiagnosed disease and one of them died. This ruling in fact resulted in a greater proportion of autopsies among non-Jewish corpses to reach the 36 percent quota.

In 1965, in Israel, there were "allegations of widespread abuse of the safeguards contained in the Law of Anatomy and Pathology,"[31] and the then Chief Rabbi Y. Nissim of the Sephardi and Head of the Rabbis of Israel and Chief Rabbi Y. Unterman of the Ashkenazi supported the orthodox agitation for strictly limited permission for autopsies (i.e., autopsies only allowed in cases where they would assist in saving the lives of other patients). In 1980 autopsies in Israel were severely curtailed after the Begin coalition government compromised on the law regarding anatomy and pathology in order to obtain conservative political support.[32] The contrast between the Christian and Jewish attitudes is striking here. Of the two, of course, Christianity is the newer faith; in the modern world its management of death is, as we have seen, deficient. It is hygiene-conscious rather than putting feelings first, and it has thus been able to absorb the ideas of autopsy by specially trained personnel and reap the benefits of the information so obtained for the improvement of care of the living.

Organ Transplants from the Dead

Dead people can help the living, increasingly in modern times, as their bodies can be used for replacement parts for other living people. This can happen during life or at the death of one person, giving a sick person a new lease of life. If a dead person acts as the donor of a kidney to a younger person, then in a very real sense he or she is responsible for the latter's reproductive success. This is a recent event so that one cannot expect religions to have developed a great deal of thought and practice concerning it. However, it does seem that religions have reacted differently to this use of dead bodies for transplantation.

The Jewish view is ambivalent: Many rabbinic authorities permit organ transplantation if the absolute and positive death of the donor has already been satisfactorily established. However, failed transplantation have also been condemned as "double murder."[33] This follows through the rulings against the mutilation of the dead that govern autopsies (discussed earlier); not only is the dead person wrongly mutilated, but so also is the recipient, especially when the transplantation fails.

The Roman Catholic view is that organ transplantation presents little moral difficulty provided that consent has been obtained from the donor or the legal custodian of the corpse, but the grant of a part is not a duty or an obligatory act of charity. Pius XII stated that financial circumstances and social status should not be related to availability of body parts and that it is best to refuse financial compensation for them.[34] In general the Christian world has adapted easily to these modern developments.

Suicide, Self-Destruction and Martyrdom

Suicide among the aged was discussed in chapter 10. Here we shall consider other kinds of suicide to see how religious affiliation affects the probability that a person will or will not take his or her own life in particular circumstances.

Suicide has in the past been an important characteristic of Japanese society, particularly toward the end of the Second World War in connection with the religions of Shintoism and Buddhism. Many Japanese believed that they had the religious obligation to die for their emperor as a divine figure and did so in banzai charges by groups of soldiers; very large numbers of Japanese committed suicide at the end of the war on Saipan and Iwo Jima when an estimated twenty-two thousand civilians died, mostly by suicide.[35] Kamikazi ("Divine Wind") suicide was practiced by pilots in their bomb-carrying aircraft. The cause was not only the shame of personal survival but the shame that survival would bring to their families.

The names of 4,615 kamikazi pilots who lost their lives in the Pacific war are inscribed in the Kannon temple in Tokyo.[36] These young men in early adulthood were steeped in the Japanese idea of honorable death as expressed in their traditional samurai philosophy and by their religion. These acts of suicide were the result of carefully pondered and prepared acts considered to be the only reasonable course of action for honorable men in the circumstances of personal and national extremity. The state religion of Shinto promised that those giving their lives in the service of the emperor would return as divine spirits to be worshiped in the Yasukuni Shrine. But many of these pilots were Buddhists, not Shinto. They came from a university background, and many do not appear to have paid much attention to any of the popular forms of religion which would assure their believers of happiness in some future existence; some indeed were openly skeptical.[37] It would not be correct to see Buddhism as a major motivational force in their suicides since this faith is essentially pacific. It could not be seen as endorsing the destruction of human beings by men riding bombs at them. Such a death would not be perceived as enhancing the killer's position in the next life as a stage nearer the extinction of self. We can conclude that these suicides are principally part of the Japanese military tradition and that they were only supported in part by Buddhist and Shinto ideology.[38] New Japanese religious cults have also produced mass suicides.[39]

There have been other examples of large-scale suicides of religious groups. The 960-strong Jewish community at besieged Masada in A.D. 73 killed themselves on the last night of the siege; only two women and five children hid and did not kill themselves.[40] In York in A.D. 1190, 150 Jewish men and women killed themselves to avoid further persecution.

However, Judaism distinguishes clearly between *suicide* and *self-destruction*.[41] The latter is the appropriate term here. Self-destruction should be undertaken willingly and is called *Kiddush ha-shem*, or sanctification of the (divine) name. It is the proper course of action if the person finds himself faced with an unavoidable threat to his or her religious principles. This is so clearly a part of the Jewish faith that medieval Jewish prayer books included a benediction to be recited before a Jew killed himself and his children, and special memorial lists were compiled to preserve the memory of those who had sacrificed themselves in this way.

Self-destruction by religious sects occurs also in Christianity, as in the case of Jonestown, Guyana (see fig. 3.3). The motivation here was complex, but certainly a strong component was the fear that the U.S. authorities were about to break up the sect, remove its leaders, and try to reintegrate the rest into the world from which, for various reasons, they had fled. Their unity was expressed in a fervent religious idiom; it was in that idiom that their self-destruction was accomplished.[42] The same applies to the incident at Waco, Texas, in 1993 and in Switzerland in 1994.

In other Christian cases a strong element of altruism underlying actions that brought about death, often on quite a large scale can be detected. Again, such cases can be considered to a great extent suicidal. For example, the story of the plague at Eyam in Derbyshire, 1665–66, illustrates this. When the disease began to appear there the rector, together with his nonconformist predecessor, urged his parishioners to stay put, pointing out the danger of scattering the seeds of infection among neighboring villages so far unaffected. So this village cut itself off from outside contacts and 260 people died in fourteen months, including the wife of the rector, out of a total population of about 350 people.[43]

This seems to have prevented the plague from spreading as virulently elsewhere. We can only guess at the strength of character of the rector which enabled this community to behave as it did, and we can only guess whether more people would have survived if they had dispersed, but the principal motive in this fatal self-abnegation was religious.

There are many other cases of Christian altruistic actions leading to death. Right from the earliest years of Christianity, Christians seem to have courted death in their care and treatment of the sick, particularly during plagues. Eusebius[44] writes about the A.D. 263 plague at Alexandria:

> Most of our brethren were unsparing in their exceeding love and brotherly kindness. They held fast to each other and visited the sick fearlessly and ministered to them continually, serving them in Christ. And they died with them most joyfully, taking the affliction of others and drawing the sickness from their neighbours to themselves and willingly receiving their pains. And many who cared for the sick and gave strength to others died themselves, having transferred to themselves their death.

There is little accurate information on early Christian deaths other than the names of martyrs, of whom there are somewhat less than 5,000. Some researchers have considered the number of martyrs small[45] and others large,[46] suggesting that there were 100,000 executed martyrs from the persecution by Nero (who was emperor A.D. 54–68), to the end of Diocletian's period as emperor in A.D. 305. Except for the persecution by Nero there may not have been any wholesale killing which could have greatly affected the birthrate. Some accurate figures come from Palestine, where, from the spring of A.D. 303 until Galenius' edict in A.D. 311, there were 44 killings, but for other totals there is no corroboration; it does seem that for the length of the period involved[47] the totals must have been modest.

Ecclesiastical records are filled with references to martyrdom such as that of the eighty clerics who petitioned the emperor Valens (A.D. 364–78) about the treatment of Christians. He, pretending to send them into exile, arranged for their boat to be set on fire so that they might even be deprived of burial.[48]

Later, the Inquisition is widely considered to have burned to death large numbers of those opposed to Roman Catholicism in the early Middle Ages. Some commentators have denied this, however, stating that it marked an improvement in the treatment of criminals and its procedures considerably diminished the number of those condemned to death.[49] Records have survived for Toulouse from 1307 to 1323.[50] During this period the Inquisition pronounced 930 sentences. Of these, only 42 individuals were given over to the secular authorities and burned; 307 were imprisoned, but of these only 9 were strictly confined; the remainder were allowed to live with their spouses under more or less communal living conditions. The secular authorities were far more active, on occasion burning Albigensian heretics in large numbers, 200 at Monsegur in 1244 and 80 at Berlaiges in 1248.

Religion and Communal Destruction

So far in our analysis of diseases and the ways in which they correlate to religious behavior, we have concentrated on disease as it is scientifically defined and on behavior that was certainly not intended to cause disease. However, if our study is on the biological consequences of religious behavior, then we have to include occasions in which it has caused the death of significant populations by violence or famine.

Historically we cannot know the extent of these demographic changes in exact terms. Records exist of religious wars and their consequences, but violence requires physical effort and it may be that the Crusades and the Wars of Islam's expansion, Hindu–Moslem recurring dynastic feuds, and so on, rate larger in history books than they may in the reality of numbers, if these could ever be available for analysis.

Indian history has produced many messianic movements which regularly have inspired a series of rebellions[51] causing loss of life, the most famous being the so-called Indian Mutiny of 1857–59, inspired by Hindu and Moslem anxieties over the practice of their faith which led to many deaths in battle, retribution, and starvation. Apart from collective British deaths of whole communities, as at Cawnpore and Delhi, Christian deaths were only a fraction of those incurred by the mutineers. Confrontations between Hindus and Moslems and between Sunni and Shia Moslems have a monotonous regularity which is almost ritualized violence.[52] Between 1923 and 1927 there were 112 Hindu/Moslem disturbances resulting in 450 known dead and at least 5,000 wounded. In one 1929 Bombay communal riot 154 were killed and nearly 1,000 were hospitalized.[53] These were but minor disturbances in comparison to the religious rather than the communal killings in the partition of India in 1947, where untold thousands died in the Punjab and over 3,000 bodies were collected from the Calcutta streets, as the result of one period of rioting.

There are examples enough in recent history such as the ritual elimination of Buddhist monks in Inner Mongolia in the earliest years of communism and the massacres of Sikhs and Hindus in India after the assassination of Indira Gandhi. The recent Iran–Iraq War, when seen from the Iran side with its theocratic political system, was largely fought by them on religious terms. Iranian conscripts went into battle impressed by the religious necessities of their sacrifices.

The Taborites of Bohemia were told by their preacher, Hisica, in 1420 that only their communities were to be spared from the imminent destruction of a corrupt society. Somewhat paradoxically their pursuit of a sinless existence led them to orgiastic sexual excesses, plundering, and murdering, which provoked their extermination in a Catholic campaign in 1421.[54]

A South African convert, Mhlakaza, had religious experiences which were not taken seriously by the missionaries. On his return to his homeland his ideas led to the prophecies made by his adopted niece, which the spirits of the ancestors gave to her. These spirits told her that the dead were preparing to rise again with wonderful new cattle, but first the Xhosa must kill their own cattle and destroy their corn since both were contaminated and impure and, further, they should not cultivate in the new season. To prepare for this great event they should build great new cattle enclosures and dig new deep grain pits as well as building new houses. Also she prophesied that the blind would see, the deaf hear, the crippled walk, and the old become young again.

The Xhosa were already in trouble over a lung sickness epidemic in their cattle and British colonial policies aimed at destroying Xhosa political and economic independence. These prophecies were partially a logical development of their existing religious concepts, and the common belief in the Christian notion of the resurrection.[55] Xhosa women were the warmest supporters of the prophet as they were anticipating getting crops without having to cultivate.[56]

The results of their belief in these prophesies were disastrous. Because of famine the population dropped by two thirds in 1857 alone, as probably 75,000 died, together with some 400,000 cattle which were slaughtered. More disastrously they were no longer able to cultivate 600,000 acres, and that cleared the way for white settlement.

The Taiping Rebellion (1851–64) has a special place in the history of religion as it reputedly caused more deaths in the ensuing civil war than any other in history. A partial convert to Christianity, Hung-Siu-Tseun, had an earlier moment of "illumination," which subsequently turned into a belief that he was the son of God and the brother of Jesus Christ.[57] He and his followers did not simply believe that the Manchu emperor had lost the Mandate of Heaven and therefore had to be replaced. They accepted a new and foreign source of transcendent legitimacy—God in Heaven— which supplanted the Confucian notion of kingship.[58]

His message of common property, higher status for women, and sexual puritanism promised to take his followers from their old life of low status and impoverishment to an assured position among the elect: a promise of both relief from the Manchu oppression and a coming era of social harmony. Its appeal to the alienated resentful peasantry of South China was very nearly successful, since his rebellion lasted for over a decade, occupying Nanking and threatening the survival of the Manchu.

The counterattack of the Manchu (in which Gordon of Khartoum participated as a mercenary general, earning the sobriquet Chinese Gordon) was to kill almost everyone involved. Travelers passing through the once-populous Yangtse province could go for days without seeing more than rotting corpses, smoking villages, and pariah dogs. Ningpo became a city of the dead with no trace at all of the half a million inhabitants save for the canals "filled with dead bodies and stagnant filth." Fifteen years of butchery and famine were to cost China somewhere between 10 and 20 million souls.

There have been earlier mass killings for religious reasons in China. In the seventeenth century Szechuan after the fall of the Ming dynasty, Zhang-Zian-Zhong proclaimed an independent kingdom and announced himself to be heaven's instrument of vengeance against a sinful humanity and, as a result, killed 1 million of his subjects.[59]

Further, more serious damage is likely to have been caused by sieges occasioned by religious wars in which whole communities died. Thus in the siege of the Saracen fortress of Damietta (Lower Egypt) in 1219, only three thousand Muslims survived of an estimated eighty thousand inhabitants because of starvation and disease when besieged by Christian crusaders.[60] As we come forward in history, larger numbers have been killed because of their religion with the invention of ever more efficient weapons and means of destruction, though this impression may be due in some measure to better historical records. The St. Bartholomew's Day massacre of French Protestants in 1572 probably totaled some ten thousand men, women, and children.[61] In this case, figures for Paris come from the payments paid to gravediggers who disposed of bodies floating down the Seine.[62]

Russian pogroms of Jews involved large numbers, for example three hundred killed in Odessa in 1905; eighty in Bialystoil in 1906; and during the period 1917–21, mainly by the White Ukrainian army, possibly as many as sixty thousand killed in 887 major and 349 minor pogroms.[63]

It is only with the Jewish Holocaust during the Second World War that we have more detailed figures. These are admitted to be incomplete[64] as only incomplete records are available of the actual numbers liquidated by Nazi Germany. Certainly something like 6 million Jews died, including in some cases the virtual obliteration of whole communities. The complexity of such events in social and political terms, their ideological implications, and their origins are vast and libraries have already been written about them.

The darker side of religions—religious wars in particular—is not the subject of this book, though we need to take note of the powerful reality of religious strife. To some extent it is not simply a case of religions at each other's throats, but of a much wider competition between different nations, states, or ethnic groups, or of people fighting for political or economic dominance. Religions can in such circumstances come to stand for the wider realities: They become social markers (see fig. 11.6).

We move on next to part III, to a consideration of another important role of religions in human life, namely the part they play in relation to sickness. Our main focus, on the life cycle, would be incomplete if we did not include religious concerns with what is perhaps the single most prevalent and most serious problem humanity has to face in its struggle for life, the very real phenomenon of disease. In much of the less developed world diseases are of the infectious kind, whereas in the developed world these have been largely eliminated (though new strains and new diseases appear from time to time) with the result that noninfectious diseases account for most deaths. Religions have rules for combating both kinds

11.6. During the Christian–Muslim fighting in Lebanon, a Maronite priest is seen shooting from a church wall. Another young Maronite has a picture of the Virgin Mary on the butt of his rifle.

of disease either directly by medicinal practices, indirectly through ritual, or obliquely by offering hope of recovery and faith in the will of God. Healing, both physical and psychological, is very much a part of religion. Historically, religious groups have been responsible for the growth of health care in our own society. There is also a widely accepted belief in a relationship between good ("clean") living and health, and association of sickness with sin, in Christian thought. We look at these ideas in both their ancient and modern contexts.

Notes

1. Gorer, G. (1938). *Himalayan village*. Michael Joseph, London, p. 361.

2. Parkes, C. M. (1985). "Bereavement." *Brit J Psychology*, 146, 11–17.

3. Gaudefroy-Dehombynes, M. (1954). *Muslim institutions*. Allen and Unwin, London, p. 171.

4. Lane, E. W. (1954). *Manners and customs of the modern Egyptians*. Dent, London, p. 517.

5. Humphreys, S. C. (1981). *Comparative perspectives on death.* Academic Press, New York.

6. Parsons, E. C. (1939). *Pueblo Indian religion.* Chicago University Press, Chicago.

7. Schwarz, B. E. (1960). "Ordeal by perpents, fire and strychnine: A study of some provocative psychosomatic phenomena." *Psychiatry Q*, 34, 405–29.

8. Alther, L. (1975). "The snake handlers." *New Society*, 34, 532–35. See also fig. 11.2.

9. Wilson, B. (1970). *Religious sects.* Weidenfeld and Nicolson, London. Galanter, M. (1989). *Cults, faith, healing and coercion.* Oxford University Press, New York, pp. 78–79.

10. Cannon, W. B. (1942). "Voodoo death." *American Anthropologist*, 44, 169–181, 189.

11. Barber, T. X. (1961). "Death by suggestion: A critical note." *Psychosomatic Med*, 23, 153–55. Johnson, H. M. "The Kahuna Hawaian sorcerer: Its dermatologic implications." *Archives Dermatology (Chicago)*, 90, 530–35. Lester, D. (1972). "Voodoo death: Some new thoughts on an old phenomenon." *American Anthropologist*, 74, 386–90. Lex, B. W. (1974). "Voodoo death: New thoughts on an old explanation." *American Anthropologist*, 76, 818–23.

12. Cory, H. (1951). *The Ntemi: Traditional rites of a Sukuma chief in Tanganyika.* Macmillan, London, pp. 35–36. Goody, E. (1970). "Legitimate and illegitimate aggression." In Douglas, M. (ed.). *Witchcraft confessions and accusations.* Tavistock, London, p. 219.

13. Ashton, H. (1952). *The Basuto.* Oxford University Press, Oxford.

14. Gajdusek, D. C. (1973). "Kuru in the New Guinea Highlands." In Spillang, J. D. (ed.). *Tropical neurology.* Oxford University Press, London.

15. Kenton, E. (1925). *The Jesuit relations and allied documents: Travels and explorations of the Jesuit missionaries in North America (1610–1791).* Albert and Charles Boni, New York.

16. Leyden, J. (1811). "On the languages and literature of the Indo-Chinese nations." *Asiatic Researches*, 10, 202.

17. Dalton, E. T. (1872). *Descriptive ethnology of Bengal.* Council of the Asiatic Society of Bengal, Calcutta. p. 220.

18. Westermarck, E. (1912). *The origin and development of moral ideas. Macmillan, London*, vol. 1, p. 390.

19. Evans-Pritchard, E. E. (1965). "Zande cannibalism." In Evans-Pritchard, E. E. (ed.). *The position of women in primitive societies and other essays in social anthropology.* Faber, London. Evans-Pritchard, E. E., (1965). *Theories of primitive religion.* Clarendon Press, Oxford.

20. Malinowski, B. (1929). *The sexual life of savages.* Routledge, London, p. 133.

21. Strathern, A. (1982). "Witchcraft, greed cannibalism and death: Some related themes from the New Guinea Highlands." In Block, M., and Parry, J. (eds.). *Death and the regeneration of life.* Cambridge University Press, London.

22. Lewis, I. M. (1986). *Religion in context: Cults and charisma*, Cambridge University Press, Cambridge, pp. 73–74.

23. Geertz, C. (1960). *The religion of Java.* Free Press, New York, p. 69.

24. Lambrecht, F. (1938). *Death and death ritual.* Publications Catholic Anthropological Conference, Washington, D.C., p. 342. See also Jenks, A. E.

(1905). *The Bontoc Igorot.* Government Ethnological Surveys Publications, No. 1, Manila.

25. Lane, E. W. (1954). *Manners and customs of the modern Egyptians.* Dent, London, p. 518.

26. Spiro, M. E. (1971). *Buddhism and society.* Allen and Unwin, London, p. 249.

27. David-Neel, A. (1977). *Magic and mystery in Tibet.* Abacus, London, pp. 33–34.

28. Faul, J. P. (1979). "I studied the monkeys in Kathmandu." *Today's Education*, 48–53, p. 51.

29. Jakobovits, I. (1961). "Medical aspects of circumcision in Jewish law." *Hebrew Medical J*, 1, 258–70. Jakobovits, I. (1961). "The religious problem of autopsies in New York Jewish hospitals." *Hebrew Medical J*, 2, 233–38.

30. Curran, W. J. (1977). "Religious objection to a medico-legal autopsy." *New England J Medicine*, 297, 260–61.

31. *Encyclopaedia Judaica*, vol. 10 (1971). Keter, Jerusalem, pp. 1, 182.

32. Geller, S. A. (1984). "Autopsy." *Mount Sinai J Medicine*, New York, 51(1), 77–81.

33. Rosner, F. (1971). "Transplant." *Encyclopaedia Judaica*, 15, 1337–40.

34. Paquin, J. (1967). "Organ transplant." *New Catholic Encyclopedia*, 10, 754–55.

35. Toland, J. (1971). *The rising sun: The decline and fall of the Japanese Empire, 1936–45.* Cassell, London.

36. Morris, I. (1975). *The nobility of failure.* Secker and Warburg, London, p. 459.

37. Inoguchi, R., and Nakajima, T. (1960). *The divine wind: Japan's Kamikazi force in World War II.* Bantan, New York, p. 80.

38. Okumiya, M. (1980). *Kamikazi and the Japanese.* New York.

39. Takahashi, Y. (1989). "Mass suicide by members of the Japanese Friend of the Truth Church." *Suicide Life-Threatening Behaviour*, 19(3), 289–96.

40. Yadin, Y. (1970). *Masada.* Weidenfeld and Nicolson, London.

41. *Encyclopaedia Judaica*, vol 10. (1971). Keter, Jerusalem, pp. 978–79.

42. Lasaga, J. I. (1980). "Death in Jonestown: Techniques of political control by a paranoid leader." *Suicide Life-Threatening Behaviour*, 10, 210–13.

43. Daniel, C. (1966). *The sotry of the Eyam plague.* Privately printed, Eyam.

44. Eusebius. (1890). *Church history.* Parker, Oxford.

45. Dodwell, H. (1684). *De paucitate martyrum.* Oxford.

46. Hertling, L. (1944). *Die Zahl der Martyrer bis 313.* Gregorianum, Rome, 25, 103–29.

47. Gregoire, H. (1951). *Les persécutions dans l'empire romain.* Royal Academy of Belgium, Brussels.

48. Socrates, S. (1891). *Ecclesiastical history*, Zenos, (trans.) Parker, Oxford.

49. Vacandard, E. (1908). *The Inquisition.* Longman, New York.

50. Maycock, A. L. (1927). *The Inquisition.* Constable, London.

51. Fuchs, S. (1965). *Rebellious prophets: A study of messianic movements in Indian religions.* Asia Publishing House, London.

52. Shaheed, F. (1990). *The Pathan-Muhajir Conflicts 1985–86: A national perspective.* Oxford University Press, Delhi, p. 196.

53. Pandey, G. (1990). *The Colonial construction of "communalism": British writings on Banaras in the 19th century.* Oxford University Press, Dehli.

54. Kaminsky, H. (1962). "The free spirit of the Hussite Revolt." In Thrupp, S. L. (ed.). *Millennial dreams in action: Essays in comparative history.* Mouton, The Hague.

55. Peires, J. B. (1989). *The dead will arise: Nongqawuse and the Great Xhosa cattle-killing movement of 1856–57.* Ravan Press, Johannesburg.

56. Soga, T. (1857). Comment on the Xhosa cattle killing movement. UPC. Mission Record.

57. Boardman, E. P. (1952). *Christian influence upon the idealogy of the Taiping Rebellion.* University of Wisconsin Press, Madison.

58. Wakeman, F. (1966). *Strangers at the gate: Social disorder in South China, 1839–61.* University of California Press, Berkeley.

59. Bernstein, R. (1982). *From the center of the earth: The search for the truth about China.* Little, Brown, Boston.

60. Oliver, S. (1894). *Historia Damiatana.* Bibliothek des literarischen Vereins in Stuttgart, Tübingen.

61. Erlanger, P. (1962). *St Bartholomew's Night.* Weidenfeld and Nicolson, London.

62. Weiss, N. (1888). "La Seine et le nombre des victimes parisiennes de la Saint Barthélemy." *Bulletin de la Société de l'histoire du Protestantisme Français,* 36, 341–74.

63. *Encyclopaedia Judaica,* vol 13 (1971). Keter, Jerusalem, pp. 694–701.

64. *Encyclopaedia Judaica* vol 8 (1971). Keter, Jerusalem, p. 889.

PART III

Religions and Disease

12

Faith and Sickness

In the previous chapters we have examined the ways in which religions have been involved in the normal processes of living—birth, marriage, and death. These processes can be socially controlled by rituals, and religions are constantly involved in managing the life events of their believers. In a sense, religions provide written or unwritten manuals which tell believers all they need to know to manage the normal course of their lives. Religions are handbooks, handbooks on moral behavior, parental investment, and death control.

However, life does not follow a normal pattern for long. Things go wrong. We are prone to accidents and illnesses. Some individuals die suddenly. Whole communities are subject to epidemics or famines. At such times people ask searching questions to which science can provide no answers: Why did this have to happen to *me*? What have *I* done to deserve this? Why has this catastrophe happened *here*?

Religions, in part, determine how individuals will cope with their crises, either by resignation ("God knows best; it is God's will") or by action (such as sacrifice). God is praised for the birth of a child, and by the same logic the sudden death of a child is His will. Religious belief can soften the blow of illness and even prolong life. Psychologists have been interested in the effects of religion on mental health, and many recent studies have concluded that religious practices have a positive impact.[1]

We need to remember that scientific medicine classifies every disease very largely by its physical symptoms and attempts to cure it either with drugs at the level of physical, chemical, and biochemical process, or by surgery. These methods have been enormously successful over the last two or more centuries. Life expectancy is now higher in the developed world

12.1. The grotto at Lourdes in the early twentieth century, showing crutches and other appliances hung up by those who have been cured there.

than at any time in human history. However, this has raised new problems and new contrasts. Within the developed world itself, many people suffer from new diseases that are the outcome of stress. Such illnesses may not be dramatic but they can be debilitating. People feel the need for therapy, and they obtain it in a variety of ways, mainly by recourse to healers who are not recognized by the official medical fraternity. This, as we shall show, is very much the case in the United States, which has perhaps the most advanced scientific medical profession in the world.

Also, it goes without saying that in the less developed countries of the world there is no such thing as scientific medicine as we understand it, or such medicine is only available to a minority who can afford it. In many African countries a disease such as typhoid fever is attributed to the anger of ancestors, the consequences of sin, the result of witchcraft or family quarreling. The common factor to these explanations is that they are social. In other words, the cause of sickness is sought in the social environment rather than the physical one. There is truth in this view as well as in the Western scientific belief: Social disruption or social isolation can be very debilitating and lead to lowered resistance to ever-present agents of disease.[2] Only recently has Western scientific medicine tried to take account of social factors in relation to sickness, but it is poorly equipped to do so, because doctors no longer have the time for individual patients, and they tend in any case to see them in the setting of the office rather than in their homes. This has left a psychological gulf which people are filling in all manner of ways, by recourse to a wide range of healers. In particular the medical profession has a blind spot in relation to how patients cope with severe injury and loss.[3]

Healing in the Modern City Context

One of the best modern studies of the range of alternatives chosen by ordinary people to deal with their health problems is that of McGuire.[4] This study took a cross section of middle-class people living in New Jersey, most of whom had steady jobs and ongoing marriages, and found them engaging in naturopathy, faith healing, transcendental meditation, occult therapies, psychosynthesis, and native American healing methods. Nearly half of these people considered themselves to belong to mainstream religions. Another study, which shows a U.S. population engaging in yoga, transcendental meditation, and Zen Buddhism, is that of Wuthnow[5] in California.

These modern somewhat mystical activities subserve personal needs within a social milieu. The choices a person makes are private, for example, choosing to visit a faith healer in relation to some intractable health problem, but they nevertheless relate to that person's social biography.[6] Social groups in which discussion of faith healing is commonplace, in which faith healing is an everyday occurrence people accept, provide the ground in which individuals who have never done it before will give it a try. Religious practices take hold in a stronger and more all-embracing way where they have a normative sanction. Faith in such settings has a power to influence that rational argument lacks. A good example of the effect of religious social factors on health is the Mormon prohibition of the use of tobacco and alcohol. Not only does this show up in lower mortality rates in Mormons than non-Mormons living in the same area, but mortality rates are lower in Utah, where Mormons comprise the majority of the population, than in Missouri, where they do not.[7]

Fringe healing groups cannot make much headway while they remain on the fringe. They lack priesthoods and institutional arrangements. They have no canonical literature to ensure uniformity or conformity to their rituals. Yet they remain popular and widespread in modern America. Prayer within these groups is a cathartic exercise occurring between like-minded people who give each other support at times of crisis and difficulty. By making their troubles public they achieve a catharsis not attainable in any part of the orthodox medical world nor, it seems, in the orthodox religious one. They also enable people to express their concern about their loved ones. For example, a worried New Jersey mother engaging in faith healing described how she was "soaking her daughter's eczema in prayer."[8] Again, the orthodox medical profession has no space for the worried relatives of a sick person, but the fringe faiths accept this aspect of illness and offer comfort and a hope of doing something to help. The difference from orthodox religion is also apparent: A mother could go to her local church and pray for her daughter in private but would be unable to make this the central concern of the priest and the whole congregation, whereas in a faith healing group this is precisely what she can do.

The most extreme forms of this personal involvement in group action are found in what have come to be called "cults."[9] A cult is a religious or semireligious set of ideas taken up by a social group, normally under the supervision and leadership of a charismatic individual. The disastrous movement led by the Reverend Jim Jones was a cult, the Moonies are a cult, and there are hundreds of other cults in modern society, especially in the United States, Japan, and Wales. Some are entirely beneficial to their members; others are (judged from outside) harmful. In the case of the latter, what seems to go wrong is that the allegiance demanded of followers by the leader is too extreme, and this may be accompanied by an attempt to control every aspect of their lives, including their sexual behavior. Cults can, however, be less extreme, and can bring a sense of security and meaning to people who have lost that in their ordinary lives.

Perhaps what modern religious healing groups do most of all is to put people back in charge of their health. The whole person is involved, in a social context, and can perform certain actions such as we see in yoga, or clear his or her mind as in meditation, or express fears and worries as we see in group therapy. Each of these various techniques brings its own kind of benefits, spiritual and physical, and these benefits are not obtainable through either orthodox medicine or orthodox churchgoing.

Fatalism

If a religion imparts fatalistic ideas, these lessen the efforts individuals make to overcome their diseases. Other individuals feel that they need not attempt to cure them. There is a saying of the Prophet Muhammad that as plague came from God, it must be seen as martyrdom. Death in battle and death from the plague were equally favored by God.[10] The Ottoman Empire was notorious for its fatalism when confronted with the plague. No effort was made to take precautions, to isolate victims, or to prevent the transmission of infection.[11]

Hinduism as a religious way of life teaches no gospel of mercy to those outside the caste into which one is born.[12] Since one's earthly condition is largely determined by one's previous existences and Hindus are religiously preoccupied with changing their own future existence, caste deadens the imagination to the state of mind of outcaste human beings.[13]

In modern conditions the fate of children with malignant disease can be thought to be in the hands of God and beyond the control of the treating physician.[14] This same fatalism has been said to lead to Moslems' having fewer emotional reactions to bereavement than those observed in Westerners.[15]

A study of the impact of genetic diseases on parents in a Moslem culture was made by Panter-Brick.[16] She studied thirty six Saudi families whose children suffered from neurometabolic disorders at a specialist hospital in Riyadh. All the parents believed God determined their fate in granting health or illness. One mother said, "the disease runs in my family. But only God knows why some children are fine and others are not." This excellent study deserves to be quoted at length:

> Parents . . . used religion as a vehicle for expressing their feelings ("*Insh'Allah*" or "God Willing" being one common expression). Many

> popular attitudes towards health and disease were rooted in the body of Islamic teaching elaborated in the *Qur'an*, narratives of the Prophet Mohammed's life (*hadith*) and the writings of theologians . . . They believed their burden was willed by God and should be borne patiently (*Qur'an* LVII vv. 22–23: "Naught of disaster befalleth in the earth or in yourselves but it is in the Book before We bring it into being. . . . [G]rieve not for the sake of that which hath escaped you"). This helped parents to overcome feelings of anger or helplessness. . . . [M]others would say "I must accept His will." The more devout families perceived suffering as a test of their faith. . . . Religion also made possible the denial of responsibility. . . . Lastly, religious beliefs allowed hope for the child's survival, and did not prevent parents from seeking a cure. According to an authoritative *hadith*, the Prophet said "O, servants of God, seek medical treatment. God has put a remedy for every malady, clear to whoever knows it and unclear to whoever does not know it."[17]

Christian thought at one time held that predestination alone explained why plague was irresistible; the role of providence offered the only effective consolation for those afflicted or threatened by the plague.[18] In the 1900s, in France, nuns who were deeply involved in medical work were suspected of having a guilty indulgence toward a fatalistic form of providentialism rather than interpreting illnesses or accidents as punishments for sin.[19]

Religion and Disease Within the Western Setting

In the United States, particularly in the midnineteenth century, there was widespread intense pietism, emphasis on religious feeling which acted as a stimulus to social reform[20] and to public health reform in the case of New York City. Two figures dominated this trend in public health attitudes, Dr. J. H. Griscom, a Quaker, city inspector, and principal health officer, and R. M. Hartley, a Presbyterian merchant who helped found the New York Association for Improving the Condition of the Poor, in 1842.[21]

Griscom, the son of a Quaker educator and philanthropist, argued that hygiene and physiological mechanisms had a spiritual as well as material content, holding that

> indulgence in a vicious or immoral course of life is sure to prove destructive to health. Our Creator afflicts us with diseases that we may know how frail and dependent we are. But he has also given us a knowledge of the laws which regulate our growth, and our lives, so that by attending to them and living purely and uprightly, we may avoid those diseases in a great degree.[22]

He drew habitually on arguments from design, taking the view that New York's mortality rates could not be a normal part of God's world because they were so high[23] and stressing the unnatural quality of city life. Neglecting to remedy these evils was culpable and an affront to God:

"Cleanliness is said to be next to godliness and if after admitting this, we reflect that cleanliness cannot exist without ventilation, we must then look upon the latter as not only a moral but religious duty."[24]

He produced a detailed and critical report on the city's sanitary condition,[25] and it has been contended that "this study already contains in essence the principles and objectives that were to characterize the American sanitary reform movement for the next thirty years."[26] He carried out his campaign for the state's involvement in improving the health of the city over two decades at legislative hearings and public meetings and through journals, consistently displaying the pietistic origin of his concern for public health. As a result, an increasing number of doctors became interested in public health problems.

Hartley in the long run was more influential than Griscom as the principal organizer and longtime director of his Association, and is considered to have been the shaper of America's first social welfare agency, leading its involvement in tenement and public health reform. His social activism was founded on the evangelical enthusiasm of his youth and despite his success in business in New York City, his spiritual commitment continued throughout his life; for example, an entry in his diary for 1856 stated: "At evening attended a sanitary lecture at the Cooper Institute. Today my mind has been pervaded with a deep seriousness and a desire to dwell on spiritual things."[27]

His association opened the first public wash-house in New York City in 1852 and, after a long campaign over their findings of a remarkably high infant mortality rate, the production and sale of milk came under legal control in 1862. He fought with others for the establishment of an effective professionally staffed City Board of Health in 1866.

Thus both these vigorous reformers were basically motivated by a religious commitment to saving and helping the unfortunate, with an assumption that there was a close relationship among environment, health, and morals.

Traditional and Modern Medical Ideas

Modern medicine is to some extent an outgrowth of Christian religious concern for human suffering, but its demonstrable effectiveness for human survival in terms of reduction of death rates is not much more than a century old. Prior to this, and still today in many parts of the world, even among those directly affected by modern Western medicine, local traditional religion and indigenous medicines are still used in the treatment of human misfortune. Traditional healers have attempted to solve health problems in many ways, for example, by herbalism (see fig. 12.2), exorcism, or the confession of sin, and have generally dealt with the whole person and his or her problems as a single unit, rather than

12.2. A contemporary scene at the marketplace in Zomba, Malawi. On sale are a variety of herbs, pangolin scales, snake skins, tortoise shells, imported cowrie shells, and various liquid medicines.

with the affliction alone as if it were to all intents and purposes separate from the person suffering from it.

It is now becoming recognized in the West that traditional "medicine men," whether diviners, diviner–herbalists, or shrine priests, can have an important place in any "Third World" public health system.[28] This view can be justified on the grounds that such practitioners have developed valid and successful skills in dispensing curative, preventative substances and in providing rehabilitative care; they often use an astute approach to human health; they belong to the same culture as their patients, sharing common beliefs, values, and symbols of communication with them; and they have skills in interpersonal relations, including counseling with sympathy, identification, and concern. Yet despite these advantages there has been little overall utilization of their services by Western doctors in the tropics.

In this relationship between traditional and Western medicine, it is important to remember that good doctors cure, rather than that cures make good doctors. Overall there is little doubt that Western drugs inspire considerable confidence, Western-style processing of illness, particularly as regards what is seen as the aloofness of medical personnel, generates much less. Peasants and the urban poor mainly have dealings with nurses and medical assistants, who often, because of the shortage of doctors, prescribe rather than refer cases on which they may not be competent to reach a diagnosis.[29] The choice may lie between the local traditional healer and a small Western-style bush dispensary with few medications often in short supply, and it is the former who in practice provides the health service for most of the population most of the time.[30]

Little recognizable ritual is associated with Western medical treatment, and medical examinations are usually both detached and cursory. Western medicine places the accent on the clinical and biological evidence, and this point of access closes off contact with the socioreligious forms of diagnosis used by traditional practitioners.[31] The Western system considers itself to be all-embracingly effective, so that it is far from ready to accept "untrained" traditionalists, who can nonetheless be surprisingly effective.[32] By concentrating on the purely physical, Western medicine fails to treat the social aspects of sickness. Cures can only be achieved under the most favorable environmental conditions.[33]

While Western medical outposts often have a mission-station basis, they nonetheless seem very secular to non-Western tribal groups. Sometimes the doctor in a hospital with religious backing may be in a position to bridge the gap. The patient can at least assume that there is a religious dimension to the treatment because of religious symbols associated with the doctor and staff: Religious dress may be worn; a crucifix or religious saying may be seen on the wall; or the hospital may be situated in the grounds of a church. However, this is still not the environment which they feel is sympathetic to the social problems surrounding their illness, and at worst they may experience such places as totally alien to their conception of sickness.

Traditional healers are, in many countries, relatively more common in towns than in more rural areas. Mwanza town in Tanzania had about ten times more diviner–herbalists in the mid-1950s than the surrounding countryside. The same situation prevailed in Nigeria in 1979 (table 12.1) and continues at the present time.

Table 12.1. Estimated Number of Traditional Medicine Men in Selected Nigerian Cities, 1973

City and State	*Population Estimate*	*Number of Medicine Men*
Lagos, Lagos	665,246	15,168
Ibadan, Western	627,379	14,304
Benin, Mid-western	100,694	2,296
Enugu, East Central	138,457	3,117
Kano, Kano	299,432	6,736

Source: Harrison

In East Africa and elsewhere Christian religious organizations have proliferated so that the modern person can get religiously related "health treatment" in a clearly Christian environment which does not have the status shortcomings of traditional treatments. A long queue of people waited to go through the laying on of hands for their health and other problems after a Legio Maria Mass in Nairobi in 1969, and both indigenous and foreign clergy are under constant pressure to use their religious powers if not to cure, at least to stave off misfortune.

The extent of cooperation between indigenous healers and governmental agencies varies from place to place, but overall appears to be low. Some Malaysian medicine men have attended government-sponsored elementary medicine and hygiene courses,[34] and in India there has been some cooperation in family planning.[35] What appears to have happened in Zaïre, and may well be the case elsewhere, is that traditional healers as locally powerful men are receiving de facto recognition from the political authorities and that in general they continue to practice, both because it is impossible to stop them and because these new states find it hard to provide the expensive alternative of even a minimal modern public health system.[36]

It is interesting to compare the healing practices of a Coptic (Christian) priest[37] and a Muslim sheikh[38] in Ethiopia. The people consulting both these religious practitioners of medicine were suffering from physical and mental illnesses and, as well, were seeking solutions to social misfortunes. In both situations, the cures were gradual and consisted of a combination of medical treatment and services offered by the two priests, supported by the confidence of the patients by virtue of their religious faith. Both priests had rigid methods which they applied to all persons who came seeking their help. The Coptic priest induced trance states by his dominating personality and his standardized and suggestive method of questioning. The Muslim sheikh was equally dogmatic in his therapy, stating that suffering could only be cured by faith in Allah and supporting this by hitting sufferers with his hand on the afflicted part of the body. According to Workneh and Giel,[39] these diverse religious therapies both appeared to "work." This raises the general question of what it is that cures disease and how far Western science, with its emphasis on pharmacological cures for so many symptoms, has, in departing from traditional methods, lost as well as gained.

Perhaps in important ways magicoreligious practices give their participants the conviction and the courage to carry on with their lives instead of giving way to despair (see fig. 12.3). It is here that we can consider one of the most important aspects of religion and its relationship to medicine: the question of the "miracles" which are recorded as having occurred at Roman Catholic shrines such as that of Our Lady of Lourdes.

The medieval concept of a miraculous cure was widespread and well supported by evidence. The tomb of St. Thomas Becket was associated with 1,141 miracles between circa 1171–1179; that of Godric of Finchale

12.3. A Sukuma witch doctor exorcising an ancestral spirit from a sick woman so that she can propitiate this ancestor, who will then withdraw the illness.

(who was never canonized) 244, that of St. Frideswide of Oxford 108, and that of Simon de Montfort 190, between 1265 and 1279. It is difficult to correlate miracles to particular shrines as there was considerable shrine hopping. One man is recorded as having visited eighty seven holy places and another moved from shrine to shrine for fourteen years.[40] Miracles, and the belief in miracles, continue into the present scientific era, for instance, at Medjugorge in the former Yugoslavia.

Pilgrimages

The best known pilgrimages are those to Mecca, Jerusalem, and Benares. However, modern Western Europe has no fewer than six thousand active shrines, which receive an annual total of 70 million religiously motivated visits, not counting those of tourists. Some such as Lourdes have more than 4 million visitors per year, while others have less than a thousand and are of only local significance. There are 937 Hispanic Latin-American pilgrimage centers drawing devotees from outside their areas.[41] In addition to Roman Catholic shrines such as those at Medjugorge, Fatima, and Lourdes, formal pilgrimages have been reestablished by High Church Anglicans and Lutheran congregations in Britain, Sweden, and other countries of Western Europe.[42]

All these pilgrimages involve the pilgrims in physical activities: climbing of mountains, crawling to the shrines, dipping of persons into water, drinking of water, kissing of icons, and so on. Such physical actions evidently give tangible expression to the underlying beliefs. The importance of pilgrimages lies in their psychosomatic consequences. The motives for going are complex, but few who go can fail to benefit in some way. The number of miracles at Lourdes accepted by medical authorities is extremely small in relation to the number of pilgrims. But there are other aspects that may be more important. As Garner[43] writes: "And so the sick leave Lourdes, still with their bodily ailments, all but a few. But they are cured—cured of despair, of sadness, of their inability to accept mortality. What is the definition of health? Optimum adaptation to one's environment. In this sense, nearly every pilgrim, bodily sick or not, who goes to Lourdes receives a benison of health."

Not all writers, however, have seen Christianity as a health-giving faith. Darlington,[44] for example, described the pre- and post-Christianization of Rome as follows:

> Christian ideas on cleanliness must be counted a step back from those of civilized people either pagan or Jewish. When Jerome came to Rome as an Illyrian immigrant he found a city with 9800 public baths. But he felt that these resorts of profane pleasure would be better converted to sacred baptisteries. The man who had bathed in Christ, in his opinion, needed no second bath.

And he added a footnote:

> Other factors helping in the decline of washing were perhaps the decay of the Roman aqueducts and the Christian idea that nudity and mixed bathing led to sexual promiscuity (whence the transference of the word bagnio in Italian to mean brothel). The Christian rejection of washing and tolerance of filth was to continue down to our own day. It was to devastate Christian cities with plague, generation after generation. Milder epidemics began in Rome with Marcus Aurelius but became more serious with Justinian in Constantinople. They continued, one disease replacing another, up to the last century in Europe. The damage was selectively disadvantageous to Christians in relation to Jews in the same cities; and also in relation to non-Christian cities, notably, as we shall see later, in Islam.
>
> The consequences have been far-reaching. Until recently rules of hygiene have always depended on religion for their enforcement in multiracial and stratified societies. The right rules have therefore been indispensable for any religion that was to expand into warm countries with dense populations. Christendom had thus been permanently deflected away from southern countries by its neglect of cleanliness, its opposition to nudity and washing.[45]

In a very thoughtful and carefully worded study, Vaux[46] analyzed the possible, and in some cases actual, interrelations between the Judeo-Christian commitment and health. He wrote:

> Religion may contribute to physical and mental health. Certainly in the deep meanings of well-being, good religion brings health. Salvation tends one's being toward health. But in a more profound sense, sound religion may render one weak rather than strong, dependent rather than independent, critical rather than adjusted, non-conformist rather than well-rounded, ecstatic rather than integrated, pain-bearing rather than tranquillized. In fact, at the radical heart of the Christian tradition, where prototypic man is crucified man, we find the notion that normative man, man at his best, is suffering man, broken man, pathetic man, dying man. In one sense the hale and hearty, robust man of our perennial Promethean mythmaking is the inversion of what our religion sees as ideal man. This man is pathetic, sympathetic and empathetic, dying into life. In normative personhood masculinity is graced by inclination toward the feminine. The Greek hero is not model humanity in this tradition. (p. 525)

Vaux continued his study with a consideration of the various ways in which religiosity can affect a person's will to go on living, by generating purpose in life, and how this in turn can affect survival, for example, by influencing how a patient progresses postoperatively or survives anesthesia. He contrasted the idea of the survival, after death, of the soul (as in Plato's account of the death of Socrates in the *Phaedo*) with the Christian idea of the resurrection of the body. Socrates faced death confidently; Jesus approached it with trembling and distress.[47] The following question is posed by Vaux:

> Does a Socrates-like confidence in immortality lead one to easily accept death, even to the extent of inflicting it on oneself? Does a Hebraic dread of death lead one to preserve life, cling to every modicum of vitality, undergird every effort of biomedical science to forestall, perhaps even defeat, this last enemy? (p. 591)

It was his belief that

> intrinsic beliefs about life after death are commitments to present health concerns. Depending upon whether immortality or resurrection controls the belief, we find varying positions regarding:
>
> (a) resistance to natural fate (epidemics, infectious disease, malnutrition, degeneration and ageing, death) through preventive medicine and public health programmes;
>
> (b) extending the life span through biomedical research and clinical therapeutics;
>
> (c) "willingness to die." Positions are found ranging from rage and resistance at one end of the spectrum through reluctant or peaceful acceptance, to pathological yearning for death at the other end of the spectrum. (pp. 531–32)

Medical Care in Medieval Islam and Hinduism

While it is true that medical institutions in the Christian world developed as part and parcel of specifically Christian charitable institutions, this was not the case with Islam. Hospitals in the Islamic world had become by the early ninth century more secularized institutions. In A.D. 821 a Moslem father wrote to his son advising him on his duties as a governor stating that he should set up hospitals for sick Moslems with people to attend them and doctors to treat them.

These hospitals were exclusively medical institutions usually run by a government official with a relatively secular orientation so that at least initially Christian and Jewish doctors were able to practice in them. They provided unprecedented care for the insane, and since orthodox Islam (except for Sufism) did not sanction exorcism, they replaced Christian supernatural healing with Galen's humoral pathologic practices. The consequence was the institutionalization of Galenism in these Islamic hospitals, bringing about a new era of medical professional expertise.[48]

Islamic medical texts were written in Arabic, but there was considerable intermingling of medical professionals of a variety of faiths. A striking example of this is the fact that in twelfth-century Cairo Ibn Jum a'i the Israelite was personal physician to Saladin, in which office the great Jewish doctor Maimonides succeeded him.[49]

While the origins of Islamic medicine and hospital care arose from Byzantine models,[50] their record is distinct since care of the sick was not carried out by religious orders. The first institutional care of the blind, the disabled, and lepers was provided by a hospice built in Damascus in A.D. 706 by the caliph Al-Walid as a philanthropic gesture. By the end of the century two hospitals had been founded in Baghdad under the auspices of the caliph Al-Rashid; from then on hospitals became a feature of all the main cities of the Islamic world.[51]

One of the basic requirements of Islam is the giving of alms, considered as religiously important as prayer, fasting, and the pilgrimage to Mecca. It is not surprising therefore that Islamic rulers welcomed the opportunity to build and equip new hospitals to fulfill their religious obligations as well as to testify to the wealth and grandeur of their regimes. Further, the services of these hospitals and their doctors were in the first instance supported by philanthropy and then by public funds and were provided free to all regardless of age, sex, or social standing.

We do not know what the demographic effects of these hospitals may have been on the populations they served, but we do know that the larger hospitals were also medical schools. These schools were responsible for raising both the standards and the quality of the medical profession within the Islamic empire, particularly as they employed Christian and other non-Muslim physicians and so were not closed off from new ideas by religious restrictions.

We also know that the patients in these hospitals were cared for systematically. Islamic medical treatment was based essentially on Greek ideas and consisted of therapy by exercises, baths, and diet predicated on the humoral theory introduced by Hippocrates and elaborated by Galen. If these treatments had no effect, a comprehensive materia medica was used and was widely available.[52] In addition, manipulations, bone setting, cauterizing, venesection and minor eye surgery were practiced. However, the development of major surgery was hindered by religious and traditional opposition to human dissection. The Adudi hospital in Baghdad, built in A.D. 981, had twenty four physicians who called daily on the patients, and at the Al-Nuri hospital in Damascus physicians were required to keep regular records of diet and medication after their daily rounds.

In the Al-Fustat hospital in Cairo built in A.D. 872, there were separate wards according to sex and the kind of illness or surgery involved. Separate baths for men and women were installed, and patients were required to wear special clothes provided by the hospital authorities while their clothes and valuables were kept in a safe place until their discharge. The Al-Dimnah hospital in Tunisia, built in A.D. 830, specially employed Sudanese women as ward attendants and nurses. Childbirth does not, however, seem to have been an occasion of institutionalized concern.

Medieval Hinduism also had religious institutions which carried out substantial medical work, but regrettably information about them is limited to a few surviving inscriptions on temple walls.[53] Details are known about a small hospital with fifteen beds attached to the Vishnu temple at Madhurantakam endowed by the Chola king Rajikesari Veerarajendra (A.D. 1063–69). Another temple, at Sriranganadha, had a dispensary for pilgrims in the thirteenth century, and during that period dispensaries and hospitals existed at the educational and religious centers of Kanchi, Draksharama, and Pithapuri.

The monasteries of southern India are known to have provided medicines and relief for the treatment of the sick, and the Kodia monastery in an inscription dated A.D. 1162 was described as a place for the treatment of diseases of the destitute and the sick generally, and for the distribution of food to the poor, lame, blind, and deaf. Perhaps we have in these medieval inscriptions evidence not so much that these Hindu charitable institutions cured the sick, but that they kept alive many who would otherwise have died of neglect.

Hindu Medicine Today

The Hindu Laws of Manu see physical ills as the result of evil acts committed in a previous incarnation: "Thus in consequence of a remnant of the guilt of former crimes, are born idiots, dumb, blind, deaf and deformed men, who are all despised by the virtuous." The adulteration of grain results in redundant limbs, the theft of the words of the Veda in dumbness, the stealing of clothes in leprosy, and the theft of a lamp in blindness. A Hindu patient has to settle this debt incurred in a previous life in order to be cured.[54] Thus the well-being of the individual cannot be found in social or economic reform.[55] These sufferers for the sins of a previous generation are also not allowed to sacrifice,[56] and indeed by their very presence they penalize the giver of a sacrificial feast.[57] Those who have genetic deformities or certain stated diseases are effectively prevented from marrying by very strong social and religious sanctions.

Besides the belief that the serious and predominantly genetic or constitutional diseases mentioned, arise from events during a prior incarnation, the Hindu view of health and sickness holds that there should be harmony and balance among the elements controlling the proper functioning of the body.[58] Any disharmony creates noninherited disease and is caused in the main by faulty diet and by immoderate or inappropriate behavior in physical, social, or economic matters; sexual excess; loose conduct with women; harshness in business dealings; intrafamilial quarrels over land; and activities of ghosts.

This concept of balance comes from the religious conviction that there is a cosmic order of the universe by which even the gods are governed,[59] a moral and physical order enforced by truth, righteous duty, and observance of religious rites in which the activities of sacrifice are connected with prevention and cure. Within this system of order under the great gods Brahma, Vishnu, and Shiva, there are localized cults, with goddesses often related to specific disorders such as smallpox, chickenpox, cholera, and boils.[60]

A study of medical care for a series of fatal illnesses in a rural Indian community in the Punjab[61] compared the proportion who had consulted Westernized physicians or auxiliary health workers with those who had gone to local spiritual healers and the practitioners of indigenous medicine (table 12.2). The youngest age groups had the lowest levels of any kind of medical care, and spiritual healers and practitioners of indigenous medicine dominated all terminal care. We cannot know how the course of any of the fatal illnesses might have been affected if the people concerned had seen another kind of healer than the one they did.

This study also showed that fewer females (49.1%) than males (60.5%) had some sort of medical care during their fatal illnesses and that generally they were seen by attendants of a low level of professional competence. As is also indicated (table 12.3), spiritual healers and practitioners of indigenous medicine were consulted more frequently in cases of infectious than noninfectious diseases.

A further study of the morbidity rate of children below five years[62] in Delhi showed that many of the patients had been treated by practitioners of indigenous medicine. Even when the families concerned were members of a contributory health scheme many still visited homeopaths and practitioners of indigenous medicine.[63]

A study of the personal health expenses in the North Arcot district of

Table 12.2. Medical Care of 615 Fatal Illnesses of Punjab Villagers, by Age

	Patients Receiving Medical Care from Local and Nearby Sources by Kinds of Medical Service								
Age	*Physician*	*Practitioner of Indigenous Medicine*	*Auxiliary Health Worker*	*Spiritual Healer*	*Total Patients Treated*	*No Medical Care*	*No Medical Care Other Than by Staff Member*	*Unknown*	*Number of Fatal Illnesses*
0–27 days	8	7	16	28	44	48	3	8	103
28 days–11 mos	17	45	42	39	86	18	6	6	116
12–23 mos	13	30	30	27	59	7	17	1	84
24–35 mos	8	9	13	10	19	2	2	—	23
36–47 mos	3	2	4	—	6	1	2	—	9
48–59 mos	2	1	1	1	3	—	1	—	4
5–14 years	2	5	7	5	12	4	1	1	18
15–44 years	26	17	29	16	48	6	4	—	58
45–64 years	29	32	32	11	57	14	3	—	74
65+ years	19	29	35	9	67	38	20	1	126
Total all ages	127	177	209	146	401	138	59	17	615

Source: Singh et al.

Note: Spiritual healers dominate the treatment of the young.

Table 12.3. Medical Care of 615 Fatal Illnesses in Eleven Villages of the Punjab, India, by Class of Disease

	Infectious Diseases	*Noninfectious Diseases*	*Injuries (B47–50)*	*Total*
Number of fatal illnesses	283	307	25	615
Patients receiving medical care from local and nearby sources:	226	167	8	401
Physician	63	64	—	127
Practitioner of indigenous medicine	108	67	2	177
Auxiliary health worker	111	91	7	209
Spiritual healer	98	46	2	146
No medical care	33	90	15	138
No medical care other than by staff member	23	34	2	59
Unknown	1	16	—	17

Source: Singh et al.

southern India showed (table 12.4) the high proportion of families who spent money on native and allopathic medicines, prayers, and offerings. The expenditure on health care of all types for the lowest-income groups was 7 percent of their incomes as compared with 2.5 percent for the highest-income groups.[64]

During the three decades since these studies were made, medical advances have improved the situation in rural India. However, increasing population pressure has meant that indigenous medicinal practices have continued to flourish.

Judaism and Medicine

It has been written:

> The medical principles of the early Hebrews, as enshrined in the Pentateuch, represent a notable advance upon contemporary theories of disease in that they repudiated magic completely, and sought to consider disease either from an empirical standpoint or else in terms of the personal spiritual relationship between the sufferer and his God. The principles of personal and social hygiene contained in the medical sections of Leviticus are unique in antiquity as rational assessments of pathology.[65]

Here, by way of example, is a short but typical section of Leviticus 13:

> And when a man or woman hath a plague [i.e., sickness] upon the head or the beard, then the priest shall look on the plague: and, behold, if the

Table 12.4. Proportion of Families Spending Money on Stocking Native and Other Medicines, North Arcot District, Southern India

	Percentage Stocking		
Income per Capita (Rupees)	*Native Medicines*	*Allopathic Medicines*	*Food Supplements and Tonics*
0–199	28.1	31.6	3.5
200–399	23.8	40.6	6.6
400–599	38.1	46.0	11.1
600 and above	30.0	64.0	25.0
Total	28.8	45.5	10.8

Source: Rao et al.

Note: Note the popularity of indigenous medicines among all income groups.

> appearance thereof be deeper than the skin, and there be in it yellow thin hair, then the priest shall pronounce him unclean: it is a scall, it is leprosy of the head or of the beard.
>
> And if the priest look on the plague of the scall, and, behold, the appearance thereof be not deeper than the skin, and there be no black hair in it, then the priest shall shut up him that hath the plague of the scall for seven days:
>
> And in the seventh day the priest shall look on the scall: and, if the scall be not spread in the skin, and the appearance thereof be not deeper than the skin; then the priest shall pronounce him clean: and he shall wash his clothes and be clean.[66]

Most of the ideas stated in the Old Testament were concerned with segregating those thought to have leprosy and proclaiming their uncleanliness. The Jews regarded leprosy as brought about by the sins of shedding blood, taking oaths in vain, incest, arrogance, robbery, envy, and benefiting from the misuse of sacred objects.[67]

If we compare the Hindu and Judaic views of sin and disease, an interesting contrast emerges. In the Hindu case, the sin was committed in an earlier incarnation, and thus the afflicted person is not a victim of his own wrongdoings; in the Jewish case, however, he is. Second, and more importantly for our analysis, is the fact that whereas many of the medical treatments in Hinduism, even in modern times, are what we in the West would consider somewhat magicoreligious, in the case of even ancient Judaism a more practical and prosaic medical text was available and treatment consequently more effective. Nor was there a discernible cost factor involved in the Judaic case, since from the outset it was the priest (rabbi) who was consulted, and his services were available to rich and poor alike. In any case there was no equivalent of the caste system in ancient Jewish society, nor any less concern for women and children than for men: All life was sacred and to be saved.

Epidemic and Personal Disease as the Result of Sinful Actions

Christianity developed its own theory of disease as either punishment for sins, possession by the devil, or the result of witchcraft.[68] A detailed study of the attribution of pre-Crusade illness showed that only 7 to 21 percent of sicknesses were attributed to the sins of the afflicted persons or their kin.[69] There was an awareness of a transcendental universe reacting to and causally affecting the earthly universe, permitting a religious interpretation of earthly events. Thus the Great Plague was attributed to sinfulness.[70]

The Fourth Lateran Council in 1215 under Pope Innocent III ordered physicians under pain of excommunication to exhort their patients to confess their sins and to abandon their care if they refused; this was ratified by the Second Council of Ravenna in 1311 under Pope Clement V.[71] The Council of the Church in Spanish America in 1555 referred to the earlier doctrine as still being valid, evidence of the church's involvement in medical care there after the conquest.

It was again mentioned in Pope Pius V's 1566 encyclical *Supra Gregem Dominicum*, which ordered physicians to leave patients if they refused to confess after three days warning, which was reinforced in the Roman Provincial Council in 1725 under Pope Benedict XIII giving bishops powers to excommunicate physicians should they dare to continue to treat such obdurate patients. These rulings may have been of greater importance in Spanish America where the church monopolized medical care for many centuries than in Europe where secular care was available.[72]

However, the early Christian Church, despite the emphasis on sin, should not be seen as having totally retarded medical progress. Early Christian sick were exhorted to see physicians as the servants of God.[73] Initially the priest worked beside the doctor,[74] and the two only became separated when disease ceased to be seen as something concerning the whole person. Clerical medicine lingered in areas where the parish priest was the only educated person,[75] just as it does today in some missionary dioceses. Today a Roman Catholic is guilty of serious sin if he fails to follow the informed opinion of his physicians.

The Black Death was widely regarded as a Holy punishment for the sins of the world.

> The Europeans were possessed by a conviction of their guilt. They were not so sure of what, exactly, they were guilty, but the range of choice was wide. Lechery, avarice, the decadence of the church, the irreverence of the knightly classes, the greed of kings, the drunkenness of peasants; each vice was condemned according to the prejudices of the preacher, and presented as the last straw which had broken the back of God's patience. . . . The European, in the face of the Black Death, was in general overwhelmed by a sense of inevitable doom.[76]

Ziegler makes the point that "the Black Death descended on a people who were drilled by their theological and their scientific training into a reaction of apathy and fatalistic resignation. Nothing could have provided more promising material on which a plague might feed."

There was no consistent secular search for the cause of the disease and the cure was left to the clergy, who in some areas, notably Germany, advised extreme penitence, giving rise to the flagellant movement. The rationale behind the movement was that since the pestilence was God's wrath, the only cure lay in demonstrating penitence, and this could best be demonstrated by public acts of self-punishment. Flagellants on the march moved in a long procession from two hundred to one thousand strong. Arriving at their destination, they formed a circle around the marketplace and into this circle came sick people from the area. Self-scourging then took place, until the flagellants were in a state of near-hysteria, using whips with nails in them to tear at their flesh and occasionally actually killing themselves (see fig. 12.4). One of the promises brethren had to make on joining the movement was not to change their clothes (they wore long skirts down to their ankles). It is hard to think of a more efficient method of spreading the plague than the practices of these people, which were specifically designed to eliminate it.

Sin

The association of disease with sin has been a constant theme. Mahatma Ghandi stated in 1934, "I share the belief with the whole world civilised and uncivilised that calamities come to mankind as a chastisement for their sins," just as the Mormons in 1832–33 regarded the cholera pandemic as divine chastisement for wickedness.[77] The Methodists viewed serious epidemics as the judgments of an all-wise powerful God.[78]

Some modern African sects such as the Christian Aladura of Nigeria hold that disease, besides being a natural phenomenon and caused by evil

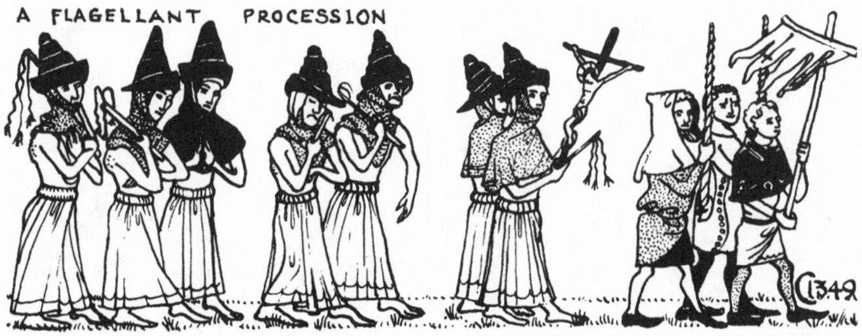

12.4. A procession of medieval flagellants in the fourteenth century at the time of the Great Plague.

agencies, "is a punishment for sins sent by God or His ministers and can only be cured by the moral repentance of the sufferer; to use medicine, even as a palliative, would deceive us as to our sin and so would be wicked."[79] The break of the Aladura with the Apostolic church in 1939–40 made this formulation even more explicit, and there was an exposition of their doctrine that sickness was the result of sin or unbelief of some kind. Peel concludes: "It is a mark of the secure hold of this institution on its members that they have so far acted to maintain the Church's institutional goal . . . that sin is the origin of sickness, both being traced to the Fall."[80]

Further, the Aladura believe that drugs and other human remedies weaken faith in Christ, that faith must not be "assassinated" by the bad example of leaders, and that denial of divine protection would send their people back to idolatry since "it is our common experience that fetish priests and witch doctors have both good and bad medicines."[81] During a smallpox outbreak in Ibadan, Nigeria, in early 1965, the head of the Aladura church said sanctified water was the best protection possible.

The 1938 constitution of the Aladura Church stated:

> It is forbidden to go to doctors or to use medicine of any kind . . . be it native or any (other). . . . We trust in heavenly healing in this Church. . . . The power of herbs has been ended, the power of medicine reduced to vanity, the power of incantation exterminated. The Lord laid down the spiritual water for everyone, and Christ is the rock of the water![82]

Christian Scientists state that illness is a state of mind and that the true believer should concentrate on prayer and refuse medical treatment. Mary Baker Eddy, the founder of the Christian Science church, taught that "materialist" healing was unnecessary for believers as only the action of the divine mind on the human mind could cure disease. Being ill is being in error, and the recommended therapy is prayer. Here are some quotations from her book *Science and Health* (1906):

> Christian Science reveals incontrovertibly that mind is all-in-all, that the only realities are the divine Mind and idea. (p. 109)
>
> Christian Science explains all cause and effect as mental, not physical. (p. 114)
>
> Christian Science eschews what is called natural science, in so far as this is built on the false hypotheses that matter is its own lawgiver, that law is founded on material conditions. (p. 127)
>
> We must abandon pharmaceutics, and take up ontology—"the science of real being." (p. 129)
>
> Treatises on anatomy, physiology, and health, sustained by what is termed material law, are the promoters of sickness and disease. (p. 179)

Small wonder, then, that orthodox medicine considers Christian Scientists to be problem patients![83] They are likely to seek medical help later than the average patient and to feel guilty about doing so. The actress Doris Day and her husband sang hymns when she was suffering from a tumor which nearly proved fatal.[84] A study of Christian Scientists in the state of Washington[85] estimated that at least 6 percent of all Christian Scientist deaths there were preventable in the sense that the condition would have been amenable to surgery.

Blood Transfusions

In Catholic ethics blood transfusions have always been approved and the donors have been praised for their charity (Pius XII 1960)[86] and are not necessarily at fault if they accept payment. Whether a doctor can give a blood transfusion without the approval of the patient or of those persons morally and legally responsible for him or her is another matter over which there has been both legal and moral debate. However, some Catholic moralists[87] have held that a fully conscious adult patient has the right to refuse a blood transfusion.

These discussions usually center on the Jehovah's Witnesses. This fundamentalist Christian sect expresses repugnance to transfusions on the biblical grounds that humans may eat anything "but flesh with the life thereof which is the blood thereof"[88] and its members regard transfused blood as being "eaten" in the sense that an infusion of blood supplies the body with nourishment.

United States hospitals have applied to the courts on many occasions to overrule a patient's objection to a blood transfusion[89] and to override the wishes of the parents of a sick child.[90] There are no cases in which doctors have been sued by those believers who have received blood transfusions against their religious beliefs,[91] but recovered patients have appealed against court rulings empowering doctors to give transfusions.[92] In Britain there have been court applications with reference to adult refusals[93] as well as acceptance of the fact that such patients have the right to die for their beliefs if they are fully aware of the implications of a refusal to accept such transfusions. A further United States case[94] held that where a patient had clearly expressed her wishes, absolving the doctors from any civil liability, and no minor children were involved, then the state had no right to interfere.*

Considerable ingenuity has been shown by surgeons in devising techniques for heart surgery using the patient's own blood so that they can operate without moral problems or extraordinary clinical danger. There

*The complicated issues involved are discussed in two wide-ranging editorials. See Rosam, E. D. (1991). "Patients' rights and the role of the emergency physician in the management of Jehovah's Witnesses." *Annals of Emergency Medicine*, 20(10), 1150–52. See also Fontanarosa, P. B., et al. (1991). "Managing Jehovah's Witnesses: Medical, legal and ethical challenges." *Annals of Emergency Medicine*, 20(10), 1148–49.

have been cases in which surgeons have refused to operate[95] once they have discovered that the patient would not accept blood transfusions, and other cases in which they have transfused against the wishes of their patients and even against their own understanding of the legal position. This has to be considered an important medical issue as the number of Witnesses is increasing and, while this sect provides no membership figures, those potentially liable to surgery cannot now be less than 2 million. There is no doubt that a number of Jehovah's Witnesses have died prematurely because of their beliefs rather than because of failure to operate under appropriate surgical conditions. In Denver, in a small community of seventy adults, 29% had refused blood transfusions for themselves and 46% had had "bloodless" surgery on themselves or a family member, but no evidence was found that any family member had died because of his or her beliefs.[96] Certainly there have been problems, as in a case of gastrointestinal bleeding which required the use of erythropoietin, which had to be dissolved in a small quantity of 2% human serum albumin. The patient consented after discussions between her doctors and church elders.[97]

Indeed, there are problems related to the beliefs of Jehovah's Witnesses, but it is possible that the problems are more anticipated than real. Most of the Denver sample expressed the view that they would sue any physician who wanted to enforce a transfusion. This issue of blood transfusions only arose after 1945 when their use became widespread,[98] and if the seventy-five hundred Jehovah's Witnesses in Britain are used as a means for calculating the extra risk, only one death in twenty five years is found to be attributable to a refusal.[99]

Euthanasia

Euthanasia has several related meanings.[100] These include action or inaction based on the direct intention to shorten the agony caused by fatal disease which could last months or years, through the planned withdrawal or omission of life-prolonging treatment. Most doctors admit that this possibility is a result of a new situation caused by the unusual progress of medicine. A United States study[101] showed that almost all Protestant doctors sampled were in favor of negative euthanasia, 80 percent indicating that they actually practiced it, but fewer Catholic doctors agreed. The points at issue are various. One view is that, if life is to be prolonged, there has to be some faint hope that a reasonably happy and significant existence may return to the sick person in an anticipated period.[102] The decision to prolong life must be primarily a medical one rather than an economic one, though the effect of further futile treatment on a family's finances often has to be considered. In cases of poverty the doctor in a state-supported hospital system can make decisions divorced from this economic aspect; such is not the case in places where medical care is private. A moral theologian may, however, hold that doctors should not strive officiously to keep alive someone who is dying whatever the financial aspects of the situation or may argue (with Hippocrates) that doctors should always strive to cure and hence prolong life. Confusion reigns! The idea of positive euthanasia—encouraging death for the "useless"—has certainly had a long history, starting with Plato,[103] who stated that those who were not physically healthy in the ideal state should be allowed to die. Thomas More[104] suggested that the incurably ill patient should "either dispatch himself out of that painful life, as out of a prison or a rack of torment, or else suffer himself to be rid of it by others."

The reemergence of the concept of eugenic efficiency and the modern idea of euthanasia were created by Francis Bacon,[105] who laid down the procedures to be followed. These principles have been outlawed by all modern states; only Nazi Germany practiced euthanasia on the incurably ill and mentally subnormal calling its program *Todesgnade*, the "boon of death," which is roughly equivalent in meaning to the Greek *euthanasia*. It is interesting to note that the state of Ohio passed a law referring euthanasia on demand to a committee of four.[106] This law was extended later to apply to malformed and idiot children before it was struck down by the United States Supreme Court as unconstitutional.

In the orthodox Jewish view there can be no shortening of life as all life has an equal and infinite value, and relief from suffering cannot be purchased at the cost of life itself.[107] The Jewish philosopher Maimonides stated that death by euthanasia should be legally codified as murder "whether (the victim) is healthy or about to die from natural causes."[108]

Has the policy of making euthanasia illegal been the result of Judeo-Christian influence or other principles? One is inclined to think that legal prudence may have had the dominant hand in restraining the possibility of making euthanasia legal. Even when the aim of any such law may be conceived of as being in the best interests of the incurable or subnormal patient, the opportunities for misuse are many.

However, behind this legal prudence lies the fact that Judeo-Christian tradition, starting with the biblical injunction "Thou shalt not kill the just and the innocent,"[109] has consistently condemned euthanasia and opposed it where it has actually occurred. Pope Pius XI issued a ruling[110] which stated: "If the state authorities not only fail to protect these little ones, but by their laws and decrees suffer them to be killed or even deliver them into the hands of doctors and others for that purpose, let them remember that God is the Judge and Avenger of the innocent blood that cried from earth to heaven." Such pronouncements have provided the religious backing for legal prudence.

In this chapter we have looked at the many ways in which faith has interacted with sickness and death to give people a clearer idea of how to deal with some of the most difficult of life's problems.

It is an interesting fact, however, that some of the things religions cause people to do can actually enhance the risk of disease for those people. Indeed, some of the worst diseases in history have been spread by people engaging in religious activities, in some cases to stop the spread of disease. We look in the next chapter at such topics as pilgrimages, missionary activities, and certain rituals in relation to their role, possible or actual, in the spread of diseases.

Notes

1. Crawford, M. E., et al (1989). "The relationship between religion and mental health/distress." *Review Religious Research*, 31(1), 16–22. See also the following studies: Ellison, C. G., et al. (1989). "Does religious commitment contribute to individual life satisfaction?" *Social Forces*, 68(1), 100–23; Idler, E. L. (1987). "Religious involvement and health of the elderly: Some hypotheses and an initial test." *Social Forces*, 66, 226–38; Johnson, D. P., and Mullins, L. C. (1989). "Subjective and social dimensions of religiosity and loneliness among the well elderly." *Review Religious Research*, 31(1), 3–15; Pollner, M. (1989). "Divine relations, social relations and well-being." *J Health and Social Behavior*, 30(1), 92–104; Poloma, M. M., and Pendleton, B. F. (1989). "Exploring types of prayer and quality of life: A research note." *Review Religious Research*, 31(1), 46–53; Ross, C. E. (1990). "Religion and psychological distress." *J Scientific Study Religion*, 29(1), 236–45. See especially Levin, J. S., and Schiller, P. L. (1987). "Is there a religious factor in health." *J Religion and Health*, 26(1), 9–35.

2. McGrath, J. W. (1988). "Multiple stable states of disease occurrence: A note on the implications for an anthropological study of human disease." *American Anthropologist*, 90, 323–24.

3. Sherrill, K. A., et al. (1988). "Adult burn patients: The role of religion in recovery." *Southern Medical J*, 81(7), 821–25.

4. McGuire, R. B. (1988). *Ritual healing in suburban America*. Rutgers University Press, New Brunswick, New Jersey.

5. Wuthnow, R. A. (1977). "A longitudinal, cross-national indicator of societal-religious commitment." *J Scientific Study Religion*, 16, 87–99.

6. Simons, J. (1986). "Culture, economy and reproduction." in Coleman, D., and Schofield, R (eds.). *The state of population theory*. Blackwell, Oxford. p. 259.

7. McEvoy, L., et al. (1981). "Life-style and death patterns of the Missouri Reformed Latter Day Saints members." *American J Public Health*, 71(12), 1350–57.

8. McGuire, R. B. (1988). *Ritual healing in suburban America*. Rutgers University Press, New Brunswick, New Jersey.

9. Galanter, M. (1989). *Cults, faith, healing and coercion*. Oxford University Press, New York.

10. Dols, M. W. (1987). "The origins of the Islamic hospital: Myth and reality." *Bulletin History Medicine*, 61(3), 367–90.

11. Slack, P. (1985). *The impact of plague in Tudor and Stuart England*. Routledge, London, p. 49.

12. Kipling, J. L. (1891). *Beast and man in India*. Macmillan, London, p. 4.

13. Shils, E. (1959). "The culture of the Indian intellectual." *Sewanee Review*, 67, 257–58.

14. Bahakim, H. M. (1987). "Muslim parents' perception of an attitude towards cancer." *Annals Tropical Paediatrics*, 7(1), 22–26.

15. Bedikian, A. Y., et al. (1985). "Saudi patient and companion attitudes toward cancer." *King Faisal Specialist Hospital Medical J*, 5, 17–25. Bedikian, A. Y., and Thompson, S. E. (1985). "Saudi community attitudes toward cancer." *Annals Saudi Medicine*, 5, 161–67.

16. Panter-Brick, C. (1991). "Parental responses to consanguinity and genetic disease in Saudi Arabia." *Social Science and Medicine*, 33(11), 1295–1302.

17. Panter-Brick, C. (1991). "Parental responses to consanguinity and genetic disease in Saudi Arabia." *Social Science and Medicine*, 33(11), 1295–1302.

18. Slack, P. (1985). *The impact of plague in Tudor and Stuart England.* Routledge, London, p. 40.

19. Leonard, J. (1977). "Women, religion and medicine." *Annales*, Sept.–Oct., 887–907.

20. Niebuhr, H. R. (1937). *The kingdom of God in America.* Harper and Bros., New York.

21. Rosenberg, C. E., and Rosenberg, C. S. (1968). "Pietism and the origins of the American Public Health Movement: A note on John M. Griscom and Robert J. Hartley." *J History Medicine*, 42, 16–35.

22. Griscom, J. H. (1847). *First lessons in human physiology to which are added brief rules of health: For the use of schools.* Roe Lockwood and Son, New York, pp. 132–33.

23. Griscom, J. H. (1857). *Improvements of the public health and the establishment of a sanitary police in the city of New York.* C. van Benthuysen, Albany, New York.

24. Griscom, J. H. (1850). *The uses and abuses of air: Showing its influence in sustaining life and producing disease.* Redfield, New York, p. 137.

25. Griscom, J. H. (1843). *Annual report of the internments in the city and county of New York for the year 1842, with remarks thereon, and a brief view of the sanitary condition of the city.* James van Norden, New York.

26. Rosen, G. (1958). *A history of public health.* M. D. Publications, New York, p. 238.

27. Hartley, I. S. (1882). *Memorial of Robert Milham Hartley.* Privately printed, Utica, New York, p. 288.

28. Ademuwagun, Z. A. (1969). "The relevance of Yoruba medicine men in public health practice in Nigeria." *Public Health Reports*, 84, 1085–91.

29. Alland, A. (1964). "Native therapists and Western medical practitioners among the Abron of the Ivory Coast," *Transactions New York Academy Sciences*, 26, 714–25.

30. Imperato, P. J. (1977). *African folk medicine: Practices and beliefs of the Bambara and other peoples.* York Press, Baltimore.

31. Bibeau, G. (1979). "The WHO in encounter with African traditional medicine: Theoretical conceptions and practical strategies." In Ademuwagun, Z. A., et al. (eds.). *African therapeutic systems.* Crossroads Press, Waltham, Massachusetts.

32. Lambo, T. A. (1971). "Problems of adjustment between traditional and modern methods of medical practice." In *The traditional background to medical practice in Nigeria.* Occasional Pub. 25. Institute of African Studies, Ibadan.

33. Hepburn, S. J. (1988). "Western minds, foreign bodies." *Medical Anthropology Q*, 2, 59–74.

34. Bolton, J. M. (1968). "Medical services to the Aborigines in West Malaysia." *Britsh Medical J*, 818–23.

35. Neumann, A. K., and Bhatia, J. C. (1973). "Family planning and indigenous medicine practitioners." *Social Science and Medicine*, 7, 507–16.

36. Janzen, J. M. (1974). "Pluralistic legitimation of the therapy systems in contemporary Zaire." *Rural Africana*, 26, 105–22.

37. Giel, R., et al. (1968). "Faith healing and spirit-possession in Ghion, Ethiopia." *Social Science and Medicine*, 2, 63–79.

38. Workneh, F., and Giel, R. (1975). "Medical dilemma: A survey of the healing practice of a Coptic priest and an Ethiopian Shiek." *Tropical and Geographical Medicine*, 27, 431–39.

39. Workneh, F., and Giel, R. (1975). "Medical dilemma: A survey of the healing practice of a Coptic priest and an Ethiopian Shiek." *Tropical and Geographical Medicine*, 27, 431–39.

40. Finucane, R. C. (1977). *Miracles and pilgrims: Popular beliefs in medieval England*. Dent, London.

41. Nolan, M. L. (1991). *The European roots of Latin American pilgrimage*. Greenwood Press, New York.

42. Nolan, M. L., and Nolan, S. (1989). *Christian pilgrimage in modern Western Europe*. University of North Carolina, Chapel Hill.

43. Garner, J. (1974). "Spontaneous regressions: Scientific documentation as a basis for the declaration of miracles." *Canadian Medical Association J*, 111, 1254–64.

44. Darlington, C. D. (1969). *The evolution of man and society*. Allen and Unwin, London.

45. Darlington, C. D. (1969). *The evolution of man and society*. Allen and Unwin, London.

46. Vaux, K. (1976). "Religion and health." *Preventative Medicine*, 5(4), 522–36.

47. Mark 14:36, Luke 22:44.

48. Dols, M. W. (1987). "The origins of the Islamic hospital: Myth and reality." *Bulletin History Medicine*, 61(3), 367–90.

49. Rahman, F. (1984). "Islam and medicine: A general overview." *Perspectives in Biology and Medicine*, 27(4), 585–97.

50. Runciman, S. (1933). *Byzantine civilization*. Arnold, London.

51. Hamarneh, S. (1962). "The development of hospitals in Islam." *J Historical Medicine*, 36, 366–84.

52. The medical formulary of Al-Kindi. (1966). Levey, M. (trans.). University of Wisconsin Press, Madison. Elgood, C. (1951). *A medical history of Persia and the Eastern Caliphate*. Cambridge University Press, Cambridge.

53. Reddy, D. V. S. (1941). "Medical relief in medieval South India: Centres of medical aid and types of medical institutions." *Bulletin History Medicine*, 9, 385–400.

54. Nichter, M. (1983). "Paying for what ails you: Sociocultural issues influencing the ways and means of therapy payments in South India." *Social Science and Medicine*, 17(14), 957–65.

55. Goheen, J. (1958). "India's cultural values and economic development." *Economic Development and Cultural Change*, Oct. 2, p. 2.

56. The laws of Manu. vol III. (1969). Buhler, G. (trans.). Dover, New York, pp. 151–55.

57. The laws of Manu. vol III. (1969). Buhler, G. (trans.). Dover, New York. pp. 161, 177.

58. Opler, M. E. (1963). "Cultural definition of illness." *Human Organization*, 22, 32–35.

59. Kane, P. V. (1946). *History of Dharmasastra*. Bhandarkar Oriental Research Institute, Poona.

60. Dube, S. C. (1956). *Village India*. Routledge and Kegan Paul, London.

61. Singh, S., et al. (1962). "Medical care in fatal illnesses of a rural Punjab population: Some social, biological and cultural factors and their ecological implication." *Indian J Medical Research*, 50, 865–79.

62. Malhotra, P., and Prasad, B. G. (1966). "A study of morbidity among children below 5 years of age in an urban area in Delhi." *Indian J Medical Research*, 54, 285–314.

63. Seal, S. C. (1964). "Morbidity survey of contributory Health Service beneficiaries. Part II." *Indian Council of Medical Research*, New Delhi.

64. Rao, P. S. S., et al. (1973). "Personal health expenses among rural communities of North Arcot district." *Indian J Medical Research*, 61, 1100–9.

65. Harrison, I. E. (1979). "Traditional healers: A neglected source of health manpower." In Ademuwagun, Z., et al. (eds.). *African therapeutic systems*. Crossroads Press, Waltham, Massachusetts.

66. Lev. 13:29–34.

67. *Encyclopaedia Judaica*. (1971). Keter, Jerusalem.

68. Ackerknecht, E. H. (1971). *Medicine and ethnology: Selected essays*. Johns Hopkins University Press, Baltimore.

69. Kroll, J., and Bachrach, B. (1986). "Sin and the etiology of disease in pre-Crusade Europe." *J History Medicine*, 41(4), 395–414.

70. Ziegler, P. (1970). *The Black Death*. Penguin, Harmondsworth, England.

71. Sigerist, H. E. (1960). "The special position of the sick." In M. I. Roemer (ed.). *H. E. Sigerist on the sociology of medicine*. M. D. Publications, New York.

72. Guerra, F. (1969). "The role of religion in Spanish-American medicine." In Poynter, F. N. L. (ed.). *Medicine and culture*. Wellcome Institute, London.

73. Amundsen, D. W., and Ferngreen, G. B. (1986). "The early Christian tradition." In Numbers, R. L., and Amundsen, D. W. (eds.). *Caring and curing: Health and medicine in the Western religious traditions*. Macmillan, New York, p. 58.

74. Zweig, S. (1931). *Die Heilung durch den Geist*. Leipzig, p. 12.

75. O'Connell, M. R. (1986). "The Roman Catholic tradition." In Numbers, R. L., and Amundsen, D. W. (eds.). *Caring and curing: Health and medicine in the Western religious traditions*. Macmillan, New York, pp. 119–20.

76. Ziegler, P. (1970). *The Black Death*. Penguin, Harmondsworth. England, p. 36, 39.

77. Bush, L. E. (1986). "The Mormon tradition." In Numbers, R. L., and Amundsen, D. W. (eds.). *Caring and curing: Health and medicine in the Western religious traditions*. Macmillan, New York, p. 401.

78. Vanderpool, H. Y. (1986). "The Wesleyan-Methodist tradition." In Numbers, R. L., and Amundsen, D. W. (eds.). *Caring and curing: Health and medicine in the Western religious traditions*. Macmillan, New York, p. 334.

79. Peel, J. D. Y. (1968). *Aladura: A religious movement among the Yoruba.* Oxford University Press, London, p. 129.

80. Peel, J. D. Y. (1968). *Aladura: A religious movement among the Yoruba.* Oxford University Press, London, pp. 134–35.

81. Peel, J. D. Y. (1968). *Aladura: A religious movement among the Yoruba.* Oxford University Press, London, p. 132.

82. Turner, H. W. (1967). *African Independent Church.* vol 2. Oxford University Press, Oxford, p. 142.

83. Hoffman, L. (1956). "Problem patient: The Christian Scientist." *Medical Economics*, 33, 265–83.

84. Hotchner, A. E. (1976). Doris Day: Her own story. W. H. Allen, London, p. 196.

85. Wilson, G. E. (1956). "Christian Science and longevity." *J Forensic Science*, 1, 43–60.

86. Pius XII (1960). *Papal teachings. The human body. Christ the model of blood donors.* St. Paul Press, Boston, Massachusetts.

87. Haring, B. (1972). *Medical ethics.* St. Paul Publications, Slough, England, p. 39.

88. Gen. 9:3–4, Lev. 17:10–14.

89. Georgetown Coll. 331 Fed. 2d. 1000 Misc. 2180. 1964.

90. Illinois S. Ct. 104 NE 2 769. 1952.

91. Schechter, D. C. (1968)."Problems relevant to major surgical operations in Jehovah's Witnesses." *American J Surgery*, 116, 73–80.

92. Moore, J. L. (1964). "Religion and blood transfusions." *J Medical Association Georgia*, 53, 304.

93. *Lancet.* (1960). 6, 976.

94. Brooks Estate 205 NE 2nd 435. 1965.

95. Minuck, M., and Lambie, R. S. (1961). "Anesthesia and surgery for Jehovah's Witnesses." *Canadian Medical Association J*, 54, 1187–91.

96. Findley, L. J., and Redstone, P. M. (1982). "Blood transfusion in adult Jehovah's Witnesses: A case study of one congregation." *Archives Internal Medicine*, 142(3), 606–7.

97. Pousada, L., et al. (1990). "Erythropoietin and anaemia of gastrointestinal bleeding in a Jehovah's Witness." *Annals Internal Medicine*, 112(7), 552.

98. Cumberland, W. H. (1986). "The Jehovah's Witness tradition." In Numbers, R. L., and Amundsen, D. W. (eds.). *Caring and curing: Health and medicine in the Western religious tradition.* Macmillan, New York.

99. Drew, N. C. (1981). "The pregnant Jehovah's Witness." *J Medical Ethics*, 7(3), 137–39.

100. Firth, R. (1981). "Euthanasia." *J Royal Anthropological Inst*, 45, 1–4.

101. Williams, R. H. (1969). "Our role in the generation, modification and termination of life." *Archives Internal Medicine*, 124, 215–37.

102. Rhoads, P. S. (1968). "Moral considerations in the prolongation of life." *J South Carolina Medical Association*, 64, 422–28.

103. Plato. (1953). *The republic.* Heinemann, London. p. 460.

104. More, Thomas. (1965). "Utopia." In Surtz, E., and Hexter, J. H. (eds.). *Collected works.* Yale University Press, New Haven, Connecticut. p. 187.

105. Bacon, F. (1905). *Collected Works.* Routledge, London, pp. 106, 487.

106. Flood, P. (1956). *New problems in medical ethics.* Series III. Mercier, Cork.

107. Jakobovits, I. (1971). "Euthanasia." In *Encyclopaedia Judaica.* vol 6. Keter, Jerusalem, pp. 978–79.

108. Maimonides. (1949). *Code.* Yale Judaica Series, New Haven. Yad, Roze'ah 2:7.

109. Exod. 23:7.

110. Pius, XI. (1931). *Casti connubii.* Catholic Truth Society, London.

13

Religions and the Enhanced Risk of Disease

Infectious diseases need certain conditions in which to thrive. Most are not happy with very small populations. By and large, whether viruses or larger organisms are involved, they need big populations in order to survive, because in small populations one of two things is likely to happen: Either they wipe out the host population and hence themselves, or they produce immunity in the population and the population survives while the disease agents die out.

So infectious diseases tend to do best where they occur in large communities, especially where there is a shifting population, and in situations where individuals are moving around rather rapidly into new areas, where there are new people arriving and the disease agents can find new hosts. Therefore religious occasions which in any way bring people together are likely to promote conditions in which infectious diseases thrive, whereas aspects of religion which tend to cut people off from each other or close group frontiers are likely to be antagonistic to the entry from outside of infectious diseases.

Besides infectious diseases, there are diseases of other kinds—deficiency diseases and genetic diseases. These too may be enhanced by religious practices. For example, the total vegan upbringing of young children by the Black Hebrew community in Israel[1] was shown to have caused growth retardation and these children suffered a wide range of deficiency diseases. Similarly, the overall refusal of the Faith Assembly in Indiana to use medical assistance has resulted in significantly higher infant and maternal mortality rates.[2] With respect to genetic diseases, inbreeding among the Amish produces a large proportion of defective traits.[3]

Let us now return to infectious diseases and look at some examples.

Plague

An extremist Protestant group, the Flagellants,[4] toured towns in Europe in the Middle Ages trying to atone for the wrath of God manifested by the Black Death. They whipped themselves severely before appreciative and understanding crowds. Here is a good example of religious activity that helps to spread infectious disease. Plague took on two forms: initially it was bubonic, transmitted by rat fleas, but later it became pneumonic, spread by droplet infection. Pneumonic plague spread rapidly where many people were gathered together in one place, and so the penitents spread the disease widely as they went about atoning for it. Their numbers were often large;[5] a single monastery in the Low Countries provided accommodation for twenty-five hundred flagellants in six months and fifty-three hundred visited Tournai in two and a half months. Whatever good they may have done in awakening people's consciences, they spread the plague to young and old alike.

Plague had reached Europe from the East in 1348. It was considered to have been sent by God as retribution for the wickedness of the present generation. Langland[6] wrote that these pestilences were for "pure sin." It has been estimated that about a third of the European population died.[7]

While "infection" of some kind was recognized as the mode of transmission of the plague, with some civil authorities trying to prevent its spread by keeping travelers away or quarantining them, its widespread and virulent attacks and high mortality rate, against which nothing appeared to be effective, made it almost inevitable that there would be general support for both religious explanations and reactions.

St. Bridget of Sweden, visiting Rome in 1349, stated that the proper method of tackling the epidemic was to avoid extravagant clothes, give alms freely to the needy and celebrate special Masses in honor of the Trinity.

Pope Clement VI ordered a jubilee year in 1350 granting special indulgences to all who made the journey to Rome; it has been estimated that very large numbers came from all over Europe and later returned home, thus spreading the infection into areas not previously touched. He also gave indulgences (remission of time to be spent in purgatory) to priests ministering to the plague stricken,[8] which inadvertently had the same consequences.

The Corporation of London suggested in 1563 that householders attend church daily during the plague epidemic to give public displays of repentance for sin.[9] Some Puritan divines in England opposed precautions against plague.[10]

It is difficult to see what the Christian institutions of the time could in fact have done to slow the spread of the disease and aid the sick, given the existing state of medical knowledge, but we can see that Christian reactions in many cases must have furthered the disease by encouraging large gatherings and the movement of penitential groups across whole countries.

Later some Christians recognized that plague was spread by contact and restricted movement. At the village of Eyam two clergymen convinced their parishioners that they could contain their infection by having no outside contacts.[11] The Swedish Lutheran bishop Laurentius Paulinus in 1620 stated that spreading of the plague by commercial travelers should be equated with murder.[12]

Outside Christianity there are many other examples of religious actions that can increase the opportunities for spread of plague. One such is the practice of keeping live rats in certain Hindu temples (see fig. 13.1), another is the making of pilgrimages.

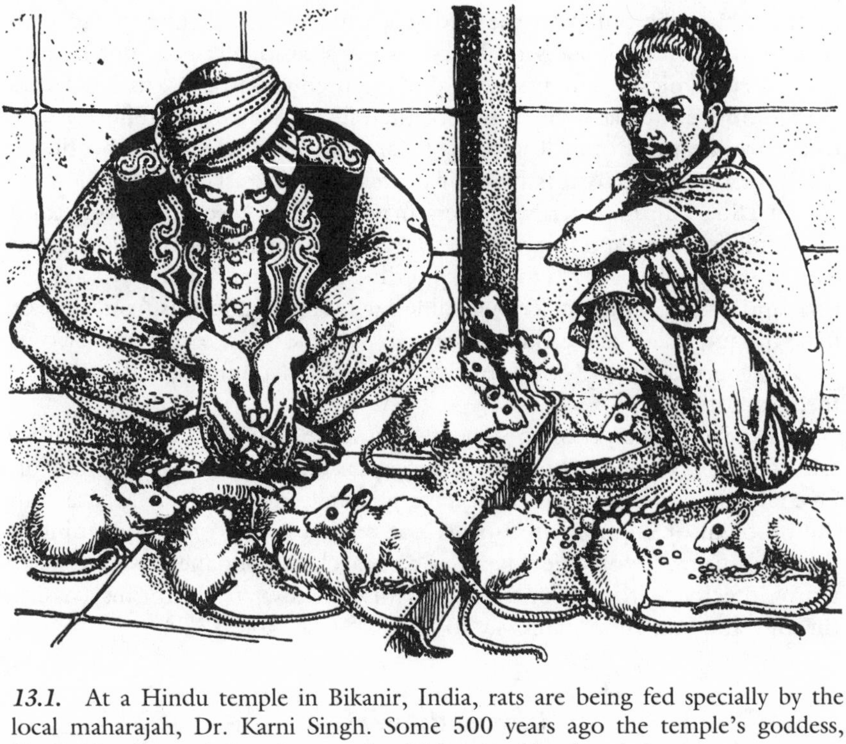

13.1. At a Hindu temple in Bikanir, India, rats are being fed specially by the local maharajah, Dr. Karni Singh. Some 500 years ago the temple's goddess, Karni Ma, directed that the rats should be worshiped and there are now more than 100,000 rats in the temple.

Religious Pilgrimages

Best known of the world's religious pilgrimages is the one to Mecca. It is no exaggeration to state that the whole of Saudi Arabia is mobilized to provide for the temporary influx of Moslem pilgrims who each year visit Mecca. Within the small area around Mecca devoted to the pilgrimage by 1974 four transport companies alone were providing 2,550 cars and 2,957 buses with another 2,000 ordered.[13]

The preventive medical problems of the pilgrimage to Mecca have increased with the enormous rise in the number of pilgrims who arrive by air. In the quite recent past the time it took to arrive at Mecca ensured that the weaker pilgrims never arrived at all, the incubation period for some diseases had passed before they entered the country, and those who did arrive were to some extent acclimatized. The use of modern transport has created unmanageable congestion in Mecca which has resulted in problems of inadequate sanitation, noise, and physical exhaustion, so that the pilgrimage has become for many as much a physical as a spiritual experience.

Pilgrimages to Mecca in the 1800s involved about thirty thousand persons per year, involving journeys at least as long as those undertaken by the Christians but with the added feature of sexual intercourse with African slaves. Pilgrimages to Mecca were occasionally accompanied by cholera epidemics.[14] The first well-documented occurrence, in 1831, has been estimated to have killed half of the pilgrims in Mecca. Pilgrims still today drink water from the spring of Zam-Zam and take home bottles of this holy water to be drunk by their nearest and dearest.[15]

In 1863 pilgrims carried cholera from India to Mecca, and one third of the ninety thousand pilgrims are thought to have died; the disease was subsequently relayed by returning pilgrims to Mesopotamia, Syria, Palestine, and Egypt. The last serious epidemic involved pilgrims from Odessa in 1907 and killed more than twnety-five thousand; a recent minor outbreak occurred in 1974 among some Nigerian pilgrims, killing about three hundred.

The size of the problem is clearly immense. During 1973 there were said to be 1,290,364 pilgrims at Mecca, excluding local Saudi Arabians. Overall standards of health care have generally improved at Mecca, but the problem of pilgrim infection is not related only to the end-point of the pilgrimage. Before the advent of air travel, the Sudanese were consistently infected with a wide variety of diseases by West Africans passing through the Sudan on their way to Mecca[16] (see table 13.1).

Indian Pilgrimages

The connection between cholera and numerous Hindu places of pilgrimage was first noticed in the nineteenth century when the mortality rate

Table 13.1. Deaths from Infectious Diseases in Zalingei District, Sudan, Which Have Been Attributed to West African Pilgrims on the Way to Mecca

Year	*Disease*	*No. of Deaths*
1927	Relapsing fever	10,000
1929	Smallpox	359
1940	Yellow fever	1,627
1944/45	Relapsing fever	754
1949	Smallpox	Epidemic
1950/51	Cerebrospinal meningitis	9,741
1951/52	Smallpox	Epidemic
1952/53	Smallpox	578
	Relapsing fever	Epidemic
1958/59	Smallpox	90
1960/61	Cerebrospinal meningitis	892

Source: El Tayeb

Note: The effect of bringing new strains of infection into a relatively immobile population can be disastrous.

was seen to escalate after pilgrims had traveled to celebrate astronomically calculated religious festivals.[17] Apart from the major religious fairs each province has large numbers of minor fairs that attract many thousands every year (table 13.2). The major festivals on the upper Ganges and elsewhere draw travelers from all over India.[18]

Every twelfth year there are large gatherings of Hindu pilgrims at Hardwar and Allahabad on the Ganges between February and early April, in which enormous crowds collect for a few days. Every one of these gatherings from 1879 until 1950 was followed by a cholera outbreak (table 13.3). Since that time inoculations have become compulsory and the custom of installing mobile lavatories at these fairs has become standard. Pilgrimages outside the Ganges valley have also been associated

Table 13.2. Religious Fairs Held Annually in the United Provinces, India

Attracting a Gathering of:	*Number of Fairs*
Less than 5,000 people	3
5,000 to 10,000	143
10,000 to 25,000	142
25,000 to 50,000	41
50,000 to 100,000	58
100,000 and over	12

Source: Banerjea

Note: Religious fairs have been linked to increased incidence of infectious diseases such as cholera.

Table 13.3. Cholera Mortality Related to Kumbha and Ardha-Kumbha Religious Fairs in the United Provinces, India

Year	*Fair*	*Mortality*
1879	Hardwar	35,892
1882	Allahabad	89,372
1885	Hardwar	63,457
1888	Allahabad	18,704
1891	Hardwar	169,013
1894	Allahabad	178,079
1897	Hardwar	44,208
1900	Allahabad	84,960
1903	Hardwar	47,159
1906	Allahabad	149,549
1909	Hardwar	21,823
1912	Allahabad	18,894
1915	Hardwar	90,508
1918	Allahabad	119,746
1921	Hardwar	149,667
1924	Allahabad	67,000
1927	Hardwar	28,285
1930	Allahabad	61,334
1933	Hardwar	1,915
1936	Allahabad	6,793
1938	Hardwar	70,622
1942	Allahabad	7,662
1948	Allahabad	52,604

Source: Banerjea

with cholera as with the Madras epidemic in 1875–77 in which known deaths amounted to 357,430.

It is indeed hard to think of a more effective way of spreading a water-borne disease than the religious practices of these Hindu pilgrims (fig. 13.2). "Water is not only being drunk as part of the religious ceremony by all the pilgrims, but it is also taken back with them in bottles and drunk by their relatives very soon after their return home." On one pilgrimage "two sufferers in the last stages of cholera were taken out of the pool and died immediately afterwards."[19]

While a particular Hindu pilgrim may perhaps visit only a single center and do so only once in a lifetime, there are large numbers of persons who make a living out of the pilgrimages as beggars or priests, moving from one center to another. They are almost perpetually on the move.[20] It has also been noted that most pilgrims have scant material resources and are isolated from the home society with its rules of health; they huddle together with their fellow pilgrims, providing ideal conditions for the spread of many different types of infections.[21]

13.2. Hindu pilgrims engaging in ritual washing in the River Ganges at Benares, India.

Most particularly in the Islamic and Hindu cases there seems to be a strong element of compulsion to go. In Islam, the requirement is stated in the Koran, and it is a once-in-a-lifetime command. Hindus, by contrast, make more frequent pilgrimages to the Ganges and in the case of local "fairs" may go annually. The early Christians, like the Muslims, made their journey to Jerusalem once only.

Missionaries as Sources of Infection

While we have already discussed the movements of large numbers of pilgrims to a limited number of religious sites, it must not be forgotten that small numbers of people dedicated to particular religions have always gone beyond their usual places of residence to seek religious truth or to carry that truth to those who have not yet heard it.

Such religious migrants have a long history. The early Buddhist missionaries traveled afar to spread their faith from its heartland in the Ganges valley to the farthest parts of Asia. Under Ashoka's patronage the Third Buddhist Council in 225 B.C. initiated a well-documented missionary movement[22] that sent monks to Kashmir, Sind, Mysore, Ceylon, and Bengal.

The Buddhist faith, with its doctrines of detachment from all earthly involvement, has enabled monks to wander in a way which was later paralleled by the travels of the wandering friars of medieval Christianity. A great period of Buddhist interchange began after the mid fourth century A.D. with Indian monks visiting China[23] and Chinese monks visiting India.[24]

While we do not know what infections these early travelers may have carried, we can assume that their travels had some medical significance as we do have parallel evidence from contemporary records of Christian missionaries carrying diseases from and back to their countries of origin. Missionaries on furlough to the United States (table 13.4) have been shown to have high levels of intestinal protozoa and helminths[25] as well as icteric[26] and viral hepatitis, which in United States missionaries was found to have a rate of 1,301 per 100,000 as against 24.2 for the United States domestic population.[27]

Not only have missionaries reduced their own health by travel, they have also affected the health and survival of those they have sought to convert. Among the South American Indians this phenomenon in its modern form can be seen in Brazil. Isolated mission stations now have airstrips from which the missionaries themselves come and go, and by means of which visitors drop in on short trips from the United States. A Yanomamö village of 179 people suffered 40 percent mortality in 1974; as a result the village had no children below the age of ten years, as they had died of infectious diseases brought in by missionaries and other airborne visitors. Chagnon[28] writes: "The only thing that had changed . . . was the initiation of contact with the foreigners downstream whom they had been visiting regularly to obtain machetes. Rerebawä, in reflecting on what was happening, commented introspectively: "When I was a boy we did not have epidemics like this. It did not begin until foreigners started

Table 13.4. Parasites Found in U.S. Missionaries on Leave

	No. Examined	*% with Helminths*	*No. Examined*	*% with Protozoa*
Below 19 years	1982	27.0	1752	39.1
Over 19 years	2889	16.2	2563	39.0

Source: McQuay

Note: In this way missionaries can act as routes of transmission to new, unresistant populations.

coming here.' " The Wai-Wai of Guyana have also suffered from the diseases brought in by missionaries,[29] as have many other native South American peoples.

Infection from the Practice of Cannibalism

If individuals eat a fellow human being who is suffering from certain transmissible diseases at the time of death, there is the likelihood of their being infected, depending on how the human food is prepared. In New Guinea the disease kuru has been found to be associated with cannibalism. We include it here because of its religious associations. Kuru is a severe degenerative viral disease of the central nervous system affecting women and children and, more recently, adult men, known to medical science only since 1957. It results in death within three to nine months after the appearance of the first symptoms. Among the Foré-speaking people, where the disease occurred until the recent decline of cannibalism, human flesh was eaten because people liked its taste, but they did not kill in order to eat the flesh of their victims.[30]

While the flesh of leprosy and dysentery victims was not eaten, the flesh of kuru victims was especially preferred. The disease was regarded as caused by witchcraft. Most women were cannibals, observing few restrictions on eating anyone except close relatives, whereas among men it was less common as they believed that cannibalism robbed them of their vitality and protection from arrows in tribal warfare. Overall, men seldom ate the bodies of women because women, both living and dead, were believed to be physically dangerous to men and were avoided in many circumstances. Women prepared the corpses for eating, working bare-handed, squeezing raw brain tissue into pulp manually, and ultimately eating the cooked flesh.

For a time kuru was thought to be a genetic disease because of its pattern of family recurrence. The gene was thought to be female sex–linked and rarely penetrant in adult males, but it was clear that this could not be the only explanation as the high frequency of kuru (it was the major cause of death among the Foré) could not have been maintained in the face of such a high rate of gene loss (see fig. 13.3). In fact, kuru mimicked a genetic disease. It is now thought to be caused by an infectious, heat-resistant virus that passes from person to person through peripheral routes such as open sores, and the respiratory tract and through eating practices. The virus moreover was present in its highest concentration in the brains of the victims—a concentration of over 1 million infectious doses per gram.[31]

Diet

A good diet heightens resistance to disease; a poor one lowers it. How do religious dietary rules affect resistance?

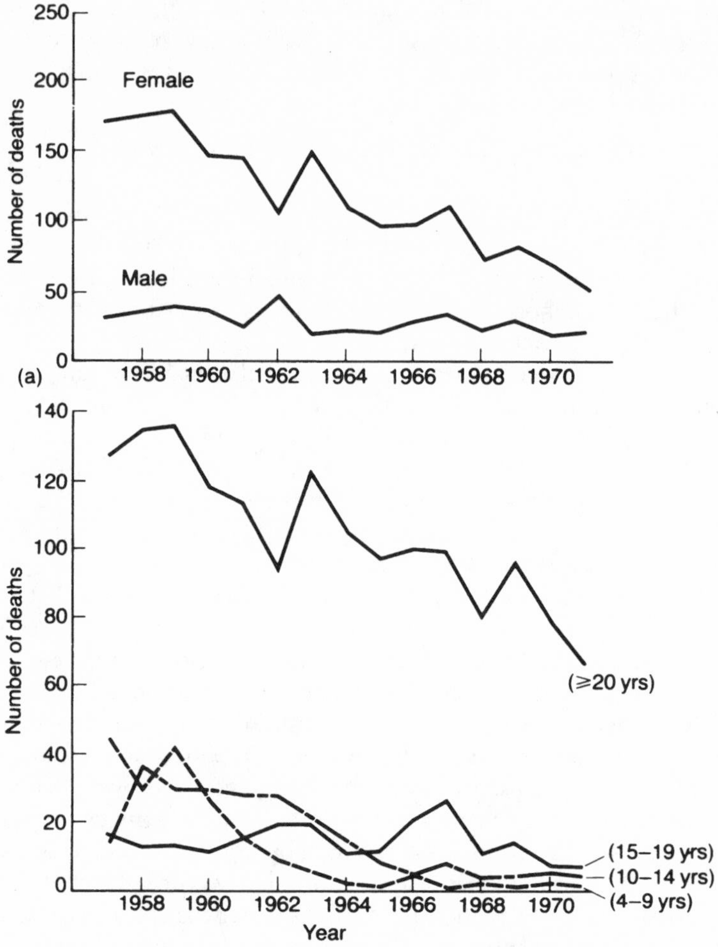

13.3. Number of deaths caused by kuru. Distribution (a) by sex and (b) by age. This uneven distribution gave a clue to the cause of the disease (see text).

Some religions divide the year into periods of deprivation and/or periods of plenty and revelry. Thus in the Muslim holy month of Ramadhan, days of austerity alternate with revelry and feasting at night. The devout Muslim fasts for thirty days during daylight hours and suffers more from lack of water than lack of food in areas where the holy month occurs in the hottest part of the year; he can eat and drink what he likes during the night. There are widespread exemptions for the old or sick, for travelers, for pregnant women and nursing mothers. Such periods of controlled fasting have no deleterious effects on health.

The fasting rules of the Ethiopian Orthodox (Christian) church seem to go beyond this and can become a health hazard. They prohibit eating before midday and the eating of any food of animal origin except fish at any time during the 110 to 150 annual days of fasting. One result of this extensive fasting is injera gastritis, a stomach complaint caused by the required diet of baked flour pancakes. Lasting effects are especially visible in the six months to three years age group of children, who receive about 25 percent less than adequate total protein during fasting and especially suffer from the virtual elimination of milk and animal protein sources. This change for the worse in the already inadequate diet of the poor, particularly the children, has been described as "ominous."[32]

In other societies such as the Orang Asli of West Malaysia[33] we again find religious food taboos with a restriction on the intake of animal protein; this chiefly affects the protein intake of women of childbearing age and children. This is combined with the fact that men eat first and whenever there is a general shortage of food in this community it is the women and children who must go hungry. When a large animal is killed, the flesh is taboo to younger women and children so that only men and women *past* childbearing age benefit from this short-term protein boost. The rationale for these animal taboos is curious and complex. All animals are believed to have spirits, and those of the stronger animals are more powerful. Disease is caused by a spirit attacking the body. The weaker members of society (women and children) are more easily attacked so they must only eat the small animals with weaker spirits.

In Zen Buddhism, Western-style, diet is sometimes related to the practice of Zen macrobiotics[34] in which the best diet for creating a spiritual awakening or rebirth is largely a cereal–vegetarian diet combined with the avoidance of many fluids. This diet is believed to help in achieving a general state of well-being. It is regarded as a prevention and even cure for cancer, mental disease and heart trouble, and medical consultation is not advocated.[35] An American promoter of the regime states: "We shall demonstrate the macrobiotic preparation of delicious aesthetic meals that cure all illnesses (present and future) giving at the same time longevity and youthfulness to everybody, at no expense and with no special training."[36] In the opinion of the United States Council of Foods and Nutrition individuals who, for long periods, rigidly follow Zen macrobiotic diets are in danger of serious nutritional deficiencies, including scurvy,[37] anemia, hypoproteinemia, hypocalcemia, and actual starvation; malnutrition in infants who were found to be receiving only 40 percent of the nationally recommended dietary intake[38] is on record (fig. 13.4).

There are other diseases of development which are to some extent caused by religious rules. Kwashiorkor is a widespread disease in parts of Africa, resulting almost entirely from the absence of sufficient protein in the diet of the child. This absence of protein is, in parts of East Africa, the result of religious taboos on the consumption of meat, chicken, and eggs by children and also by their mothers. This debilitating condition may be fatal per se or the precondition for other diseases. The Baganda, for instance, do not allow their women to eat meat of any kind, and they subsist largely on cooked bananas (*matoke*) and vegetables. This is given as a staple diet to children and often leads to kwashiorkor.[39]

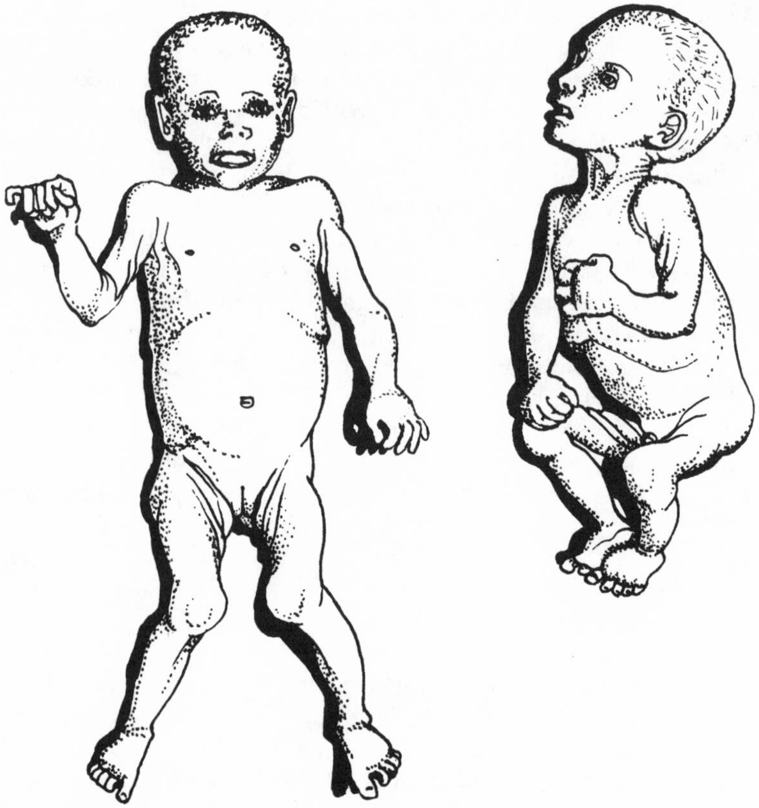

13.4. Severe nutritional disorders in children fed on macrobiotic diets. Roberts, I. F. et al. (1979). "Malnutrition in infants receiving cult diets: A form of child abuse." *British Medical J.* 1, 296–98.

Purification and Prayer

Whereas washing is normally thought of as a cleansing activity and may in many cases be so, such is not always the case and much may depend on the precise circumstances at the time. A good example is that provided by Islam. The Koran commands: "O you who believe! when you rise up to prayer, wash your faces and your hands as far as the elbows, and wipe your heads, and wash your feet to the ankles" (Sura 5:7), echoing the command referred to in the Old Testament (Exod. 40:32) which the Lord gave to Moses, to wash before going near to the altar. Thus, today, the followers of Islam, before each prayer session (and there are up to five every day, though actual participation varies for each person according to circumstances) wash in the prescribed way if the situation permits. This practice can promote hygiene. For instance, in the Grey Street mosque in Durban and many others, washing takes place in an anteroom beside the main prayer room, and there is a continuous supply of piped running

13.5. A typical scene outside a mosque where water for preprayer washing of the hands, face, and feet comes from a standing rainwater tank.

water so that any disease agents from infected devotees are rapidly dispersed into the drains. By contrast, in mosques in rural areas of Yemen and Bangladesh, the water for washing comes from water storage tanks, and all those who wash before prayer run the risk of contracting infections from guinea worms,[40] schistosomes,[41] or any other disease agents present in the water (fig. 13.5).

Washing is often associated with religious pilgrimages. Many Roman Catholics (and not a few others) journey to Lourdes, in France, mainly during the warm weather from April to October. There they visit the grotto where Bernadette saw her vision of the Virgin; many of them are sick and go to Lourdes in search of miracle cures. Besides the grotto, there is the nearby holy spring which has been channeled into baths in which those seeking cures dip themselves or are dipped.

The scene at the baths is described by Marnham.[42] Those who have come to immerse themselves first join one of the long lines. They then change clothes in a cubicle and walk down some steps into a stone tub. Those on stretchers are carried down by teams of *brancardiers.* At the far end of the tub are a small Madonna and prayer cards in nineteen languages. The prayers are recited, and then the supplicant leans back, to be lowered into the water by the brancardiers. "Early in the day (the water) is clean and freezing. Later, as the pilgrims pass through it, it becomes warmer. It is changed once, at midday."

There are altogether thirteen tubs which at peak times handle an average of eighty five pilgrims an hour. For instance, on August 14, 1978, 1,800 men and 4,750 women were bathed. Pollution of the water has been investigated on several occasions. A devout theory holds that microbes die in Lourdes water; words to this effect appeared in a recent *Guide to the Grotto*. This claim was based on tests carried out in the 1930s, which found Lourdes water to be polluted with colon bacillus, staphylococcus, streptococcus, pyocyneus, and other microbes but showed that experimental animals were unaffected by these bacilli when derived from Lourdes water. Undoubtedly pollution is present in the water, but evidently this fact is not a consideration for those whose faith renders it utterly pure.

Contact with Religious Objects and Infection

Some religions involve their faithful in touching and kissing holy objects (see fig. 13.6), or drinking and eating from certain utensils. Muslims as part of their pilgrimage to Mecca kiss the stone in the *kaaba*; Catholics

13.6. Kissing a crucifix outside a contemporary Russian Orthodox monastery at Pskouo-Petcherski, Russia.

kiss the feet of a wooden Christ during Good Friday services. In the latter case an altar server with a cloth wipes the wood between kisses. Muslims wash the exposed parts of their bodies prior to praying in the mosque, and in Yemen the cisterns containing the water for washing outside mosques have been found to harbor snails infested with schistosomiasis.[43] Similarly *Bacterium coli* has been found in the bowls containing blessed water at the entrances to Catholic churches in Perugia into which church-goers dip their fingers to cross themselves before going into the church.[44]

In such practices it can be assumed that harmful microorganisms are deposited on the objects of devotion by some of the devotees, and that these microorganisms are transferred to subsequent touchers. The sharing of a communion cup from which some Christian denominations drink wine has come under experimental study, using simulated conditions, for the possibility of transfer of infections.[45] In this study, the wiping of the edge of the cup between drinkers was found to be remarkably ineffective in lowering the bacterial count, but another study[46] found that it reduced the bacterial count by about 90 percent (see table 13.5).

In the study by Hobbs and colleagues the bacteria recovered from a test cup after a simulated communion service included species of *Bacillus, Micrococcus, Neisseria, Staphylococcus,* and *Streptococcus.* The communion wine killed certain microorganisms within two to three minutes, but *Microbacterium avium* was undiminished after an hour and *Staphylococcus pyogenes* was completely protected by the saliva droplets in which it was suspended. More recent studies have held that the communion cup cannot pass on either hepatitis B virus or human immunodeficiency virus (HIV),[47] and it has been shown that there are only very rare examples of HIV being spread by means other than injection, intercourse, or transfusion, or across the placenta during pregnancy.[48]

The study by Gregory and associates concluded that both the common communion cup and its contents could serve effectively as vehicles

Table 13.5. Effect of Wiping and Rotating the Chalice on Numbers of Organisms Recovered from the Drinking Surface

Experiment No.	*1*	*2*	*3*	*4*	*5*	*6*
1 Drinking from same place	485	2,700	1,700	7,820	9,200	1,670
2 Drinking from different places	910	3,020	3,320	7,840	4,290	5,200
3 Drinking from same place and wiping	215	125	320	790	1,730	2,300
4 Drinking from different places and wiping	765	305	465	920	9,440	80

Source: Hobbes et al.

Note: The experiment shows wiping to be effective in reducing bacterial infection, whereas rotating the cup increases the chance of infection.

for the rapid transmission of infectious microorganisms, suggesting that the practice might be dangerous if an infected person were to participate in the communion ritual. Tuberculosis could, for example, be transmitted in this way. The study by Hobbs and associates concluded that tuberculosis would not be a significant hazard except possibly if an excessively salivating individual were at the beginning of the communion line! Medical opinions are thus divided. We should recall, however, that virulent new strains of tuberculosis are making a comeback at the present time, so that vigilance remains essential.

In this chapter we have shown how religious practices, wholly accidentally, have spread and may continue to spread infectious diseases. There is far less evidence that religions can enhance the incidence of noninfectious diseases. One recent study which did show this deserves mention, however. In a survey of 28,169 Chinese Americans[49] it was shown that they died significantly earlier than matched white controls if they had one of the particular diseases associated with their birth year phase. Chinese astrology holds that a person's birth year phase makes him or her especially susceptible to death from certain causes. For example, if the phase is Earth, he or she is particularly susceptible to tumors. This study showed that such people did in fact die 1.3 to 4.9 years earlier than controls if they had "their" kind of disease. The explanation appears to be largely psychosomatic: that is, an element of fatalism or loss of the will to live speeds up the course of the disease.

Notes

1. Shinwell, E. D., and Gorodischer, R. (1982). "Totally vegetarian diets and infant nutrition." *Pediatrics*, 70(4), 582–86.

2. Kaunitz, A. M., et al. (1984). "Perinatal and maternal mortality in a religious group avoiding obstetric care." *American J. Obstetrics Gynecology*, 150, 826–31.

3. McKusick, V. A. (1973). "Genetic studies in American inbred populations with particular reference to the Old Order Amish." *Israel J Medical Science*, 9, 1276–84.

4. Leff, G. (1967). *Heresy in the later Middle Ages.* Manchester University Press, Manchester.

5. Cohn, N. (1962). *The pursuit of the millennium: Revolutionary messianism in the Middle Ages and its bearing on modern totalitarian movements.* Mercury, London.

6. Langland, W. (1957). *Piers Ploughman.* W. W. Skeat. (ed.). Oxford University Press. Oxford.

7. Ziegler, P. (1970). *The Black Death.* Penguin, Harmondsworth, England.

8. Amundsen, D. W., and Ferngreen, G. B. (1986). "The early Christian tradition." In Numbers, R. L. and Amundsen, D. W. (eds.). *Caring and curing: Health and medicine in the Western religious traditions.* Macmillan, New York, p. 96.

9. Slack, P. (1985). *The impact of plague in Tudor and Stuart England.* Routledge, London, pp. 30, 31.

10. Ottosen, P.-G. (1988). "Fighting the plague in 17th- and 18th-century Sweden." In A. Brändström and L. G. Tedebrand. (eds.). *Society, health and population during the demographic transition.* Almqvist and Wiksell, Stockholm, pp. 309–22.

11. Daniel, C. (1966). *The story of the Eyam plague.* Privately printed, Eyam.

12. Ottosen, P.-G. (1988). "Fighting the plague in 17th- and 18th-century Sweden." In A. Brändström and L. G. Tedebrand. (eds.). *Society, health and population during the demographic transition.* Almqviot and Wikoeil, Stockholm, pp. 309–22.

13. Bushnak, A. A. (1978). *The Hajj transportation system. Hajj Studies.* vol. 1. Croom Helm, London.

14. Pollitzer, R., and Swaroop, S. (1959). *Cholera.* World Health Org. Monograph, Series 43, Geneva.

15. Omar, W. (1958). "The Mecca pilgrimage is no longer a hazard." *Medical J Malaya*, 13, 187–90.

16. El Tayeb, E. M. (1976). *Health problems in the Sudan associated with the Mecca.* Diss., Ross Institute, London

17. Sen, H. (1903). "Cholera in the district of Puri with a special account of the epidemic during 1901." *Indian Medical Gazette*, 38, 135–38. Also see Anderson, S. (1904). "Cholera epidemic in Puri town and district, July 1902." *Indian Medical Gazette*, 39, 48–51.

18. Bhardwaj, S. M. (1973). *Hindu places of pilgrimage in India.* University of California Press, Berkeley.

19. Rogers, L. (1926). "The conditions influencing the incidence and spread of cholera in India." *Proceedings Royal Society Medicine, Epidemic Section*, 19, 59–91.

20. Swaroop, S., and Raman, M. V. (1951). "Endemicity of cholera in relation to fairs and festivals in India." *Indian J Medical Research*, 39, 41–49.

21. Banerjea, A. C. (1951). "Note on cholera in the United Provinces (Uttar Pradesh)." *Indian J Medical Research*, 39, 17–40.

22. Thapar, R. (1961). *Asoka and the decline of the Mauryas.* Oxford University Press, London.

23. Wieger, L. (1929). *Textes historiques.* Mission Press, Hsienhsien.

24. Bagchi, P. C. (1950). *India and China: A thousand years of Sino–Indian cultural relations.* China Press, Bombay.

25. McQuay, R. M. (1967). "Parasitologic studies in a group of furloughed missionaries. I. Intestinal protozoa. II. Helminth findings." *American J Tropical Medicine*, 16, 154–66.

26. Frame, J. D. (1968). "Hepatitis among missionaries in Ethiopia and Sudan." *J American Medical Assoc*, 203, 819–26.

27. Kendrick, M. A. (1974). "Viral hepatitis in American missionaries abroad." *J Infectious Disease*, 129, 227–29.

28. Chagnon, N. A. (1977). *Yanomamö—the fierce people.* Holt, Rinehart and Winston, New York.

29. Guppy, N. (1958). *Wai-Wai: Through the forests north of the Amazon.* Murray, London.

30. Glasse, R. (1967). "Cannibalism in the kuru region of New Guinea." *Transactions New York academy of Sciences*, 29, 748–54.

31. Gajdusek, D. C. (1973). "Kuru in the New Guinea Highlands." In Spillan, J. D. (ed.). *Tropical neurology.* Oxford University Press, London.

32. Knutsson, K. E., and Selinus, R. (1970). "Fasting in Ethiopia: An anthropological and nutritional study." *American J Clinical Nutrition*, 23, 956–59.

33. Bolton, J. M. (1972). *Food taboos among Orang Asli in West Malaysia: Potential nutritional hazard."* American J Clinical Nutrition, 25, 789–99.

34. Ohsawa, G. (1965). *Zen macrobiotics: The art of longevity and rejuvenation*. Ohsawa Foundation, New York.

35. Ohsawa, G. (1965). *Zen macrobiotics.: The art of longevity and rejuvenation*. Ohsawa Foundation, New York.

36. Ohsawa quoted by Sherlock, P., and Rothschild, E. O. (1967). "Scurvey produced by a Zen macrobiotic diet." *J American Medical Association*, 199, 794–98.

37. Sherlock, P., and Rothchild, E. O. (1967). "Scurvy produced by a Zen macrobiotic diet." *J American Medical Association*, 199, 794–98.

38. Robson, J. R. K., et al. (1974). "Zen macrobiotic dietary problems in infancy." *Pediatrics*, 53, 326–29.

39. Welbourn, E. M. (1955). "The danger period during weaning: A study of Baganda children who were attending Child Welfare Clinics near Kampala, Uganda." *J Tropical Pediatrics*, 1, 34–46, 98–111, 161–73.

40. Underwood, P., and Underwood, Z. (1980). "New spells for old: Expectations and realities of western medicine in a remote tribal society in Yemen, Arabia." In Stanley, N. F., and Joshe, R. A. (eds.). *Changing disease patterns and human behavior*. Academic Press, New York.

41. Farooq, M., and Mallah, M. B. (1966). "Behavioural pattern of social and religious water-contact activities in Egypt-49 Bilharziasis project area." *Bulletin World Health Organisation*, 35, 377–87.

42. Marnham, P. (1980). *Lourdes: A modern pilgrimage*. Heinemann, London, p. 93.

43. Olivier, L. and Ansari, N. (1967). "Epidemiology of Bilharziasis." In Mostofifk, F. K. (ed.). *Bilharziasis*. Springer Verlag, New York.

44. Losito, P. (1946). "Church hygiene: Microbic content of holy water in various churches of Perugia." *Bull Soc Ital Bio Sp*, 22, 463–65.

45. Gregory, K. F., et al. (1967). "Infection hazards of the common communion cup." *Canadian J Public Health*, 58, 305–10.

46. Hobbs, B. C., et al. (1967). "Experiments on the communion cup." *J Hygiene Cambridge*, 65, 37–48.

47. Gill, O. N. (1988). "The hazard of infection from the shared communion cup." *J Infection*, 16(1), 3–23.

48. Kingston, D. (1988). "Memorandum on the infectious hazards of the common communion cup with especial reference to AIDS." *European J Epidemiology*, 4(2), 164–70.

49. Phillips, D. P., Ruth, T. E., and Wagner, L. M. (1993). "Psychology and survival." *Lancet*, 342, 1142–45.

14

Religions and the Reduced Risk of Disease

A study by Friedman and Rosenman[1] showed higher rates of coronary artery disease in "type A" people, who were characterized by forceful driving personality, competitiveness, and adherence to deadlines, than in "type B" people, who lacked these traits. Christian beliefs, if taken seriously, should make people less desperately competitive, or at least not more so. Christian churchgoers have indeed been found to have less heart disease than nonchurchgoers.[2] From the point of view of diet, Christianity, which regards gluttony as sinful, tends to reduce the intake of fats and sugars; likewise Islam, which has prayers involving physical exercise five times a day, must be conducive to fitness. Buddhism, which emphasizes the value of a contemplative life, disapproves of cut-throat competition, teaches meditation, and suggests a slow pace of life and a friendly, cooperative attitude to the business of making a living, appears to enable its followers to avoid the stress syndrome discussed. Overall it seems that religiosity and religious stability seem to protect against the competitiveness, aggressiveness, and impatience typical of "type A" behavior.[3]

Some forms of cancer are known to be environmentally induced. Such, for example, is lung cancer, which is caused by inhaling tobacco smoke into the lungs; the smoking habit also increases the incidence of heart disease. Religious groups, such as Mormons, who taboo or object to smoking have a low incidence of lung cancer.

Use of Left and Right Hands

Religious rules on which hand is to be used for excretory and/or sexual activities are widespread in Hinduism and Islam. In general the left hand is used for these purposes while the right is appropriate for eating and culinary actions. Thus, Islamic teaching has it that "one must neither eat nor drink with the left hand for these are Satan's manners," and that "one holds the genitals with the left hand."[4] Again "many of the Arabs will not allow the left hand to touch food in any case except when the right hand is maimed."[5] Regarding the Almighty himself: "Allah has nothing left-handed about him since both his hands are right hands."[6]

Hindu beliefs follow the same general rules. The sacred Laws of Manu state: "He who desires to be pure must clean the organ by one application of earth, the anus by applying earth three times, the left hand alone by applying it ten times" (V, 136). This seems a clear indication of the idea that the left hand is actually dirtier and in more need of cleaning than the penis or the anus. As regards sex instruction, the Hindu husband learns: "He should then with his wife get on the bed with his face toward the east or the north. Then, looking at his wife, let him embrace her with his left arm, and, placing his right hand over her head . . . next, let him place his (left) hand on her vagina."[7]

Finally, exclusion of the left hand from cooking and eating is prevalent in many African peoples, for instance in rural Tanzania and in West Africa.[8] What is perhaps most remarkable is the apparent absence of any such emphasis, or even mention, in Christianity or Judaism. It is as if these religions had overlooked a practice by which they could have immensely benefited themselves over the years. Although the *general* idea of hygiene has been promoted by these religions, they might, nonetheless, have been expected to embrace the idea of handedness just discussed.

Leprosy

Ancient Jewish law forced suspected lepers to live apart from the settlements of healthy people. The contribution of medieval Christianity to leprosy control was the institutionalization of this separation. From the old Judaic precepts the idea of contagion gradually became the motive power in the development of an entire system of preventive measures, at first largely limited to lepers and persons suspected of having leprosy.[9] The recognition of the contagious nature of leprosy led to the gradual development of compulsory regulations to prevent the spread of the disease. Leprosy by the sixth century was sufficiently common in southern France and the Mediterranean littoral for the Council of Lyons in A.D. 583 to promulgate an edict putting rigid limitations on the free movement of lepers. Other regulations prohibited them from going barefoot on public roads or touching articles for sale and insisted that they make their presence known by blowing horns or shaking rattles. At church lepers were segregated. Nevertheless Gregory IX in 1494 ruled that leprosy

14.1. A Christian nun bandaging the hand of a victim of leprosy in present-day East Africa.

was not cause for the dissolution of a marriage, and that in the case of a couple of whom one only had leprosy, the other was obliged to have sexual intercourse.

The Christian church became prominent in the establishment of leprosaria and remains a distinct factor in the gradual elimination of the disease (see fig. 14.1). The influence of the church made leper colonies less oppressive than the term suggests,[10] since lepers were to be kept at the expense of the church and were under the care of their bishops.[11] Lepers were not absolutely confined, and these colonies received a large measure of public support from prominent men since it was believed that the prayers of lepers on behalf of others were of particular value.

Buddhism and Leprosy

In the early history of Chinese Buddhism no monastery was without its medical specialists, and they were active for centuries in institutions such as hospitals and orphanages because of the Buddhist limitless compassion for all created beings. In A.D. 653 Buddhist and Taoist monks and nuns were forbidden to practice medicine, but government neglect left the hospitals in Buddhist control for some years. During this period such hospitals were known as Compassion Pastures, but in A.D. 845, as part of the great dissolution of the monasteries under Wu Tsung, they were transferred to lay control when they became known as patient compounds. Some Buddhist divines are known to have been active in medical work. The Indian monk Narendrayasas, who died in China in A.D. 589, established leprosaria in the dynastic capital, and the Chinese monk Chih-Yen taught and nursed in the leper colony where he died in A.D. 654.[12]

The fast in daylight hours of Moslems for the month of Ramadhan follows the lunar calendar so that on occasions Moslems in the northern hemisphere may fast for as long as eighteen hours every day for a month. Fasting has been a matter of some interest in relation to health. In young Moslems it has been shown that there are significant increases in the intake of protein and carbohydrates together with the reduction in the number of meals taken, and an increase of family meals, leading to a significant increase in body weight.[13]

In a study of pregnant women none had a completely normal set of biochemical values at the end of a day of fasting, but there were no differences in the pregnancy outcome.[14] One study concluded that an obese patient with diabetes mellitus should find the fast highly beneficial.[15] In both Britain[16] and Kuwait[17] Moslems have to change their drug dosage timings during Ramadhan. Many Jews discontinue medications during the eight days of Passover.[18] It has been ruled that eyedrops do not but nose drops and enemas do break the fast rules.[19]

Church Attendance and Health

Medical surveys have occasionally tried to relate health to frequency of attendance at religious services. A study in Washington County, Maryland,[20] compared women attending church less than twice a year with those who went at least once weekly. The former had trichomonads in 17.8 percent of the sample, compared with 12.4 percent in the latter. Cytological changes that suggested or confirmed cervical cancer occurred in 1.88 percent of the former, compared with 0.64 percent of the latter. Such results may be related to earlier conclusions showing a negative correlation between frequency of extramarital coitus and frequency of church attendance.[21]

A further survey in the same area of the United States[22] found that those who went to church once a month or more had a rate of 84 in 100,000 for newly reported active tuberculosis, while in those who attended twice a year or less the rate was 138. Several studies have found that a high frequency of church attendance is associated with lower blood pressure levels[23] and on a less testable level that religious commitment was inversely associated with blood pressure.[24]

These conclusions were followed up in a further study,[25] which

Table 14.1. Numbers of Deaths and Death Rates from Selected Causes by Usual Frequency of Church Attendance Among Persons 16 Years or Older, Washington County, Maryland

	Usual Frequency of Church Attendance		
	Once or More per Week	*Less than Once Weekly*	*Relative Risk for Less Frequent Attenders*
1963 Census population	24,245	30,603	
*Artriosclerotic heart disease**			
Deaths	38	89	
5 year rate per 1,000	8.52	18.12	2.1:1
Pulmonary emphysema			
Deaths	18	52	
3 year rate per 1,000	0.74	1.70	2.3:1
Cirrhosis of the liver			
Deaths	5	25	
3 year rate per 1,000	0.21	0.82	3.9:1
Suicide			
Deaths	11	29	
6 year rate per 1,000	0.45	0.95	2.1:1
Cancer of the rectum			
Deaths	13	17	
5 year rate per 1,000	0.54	0.56	1:1
Cancer of the colon			
Deaths	27	28	
5 year rate per 1,000	1.11	0.91	0.8:1

Source: Comstock and Partridge

*Among white females only, aged 45–64 in 1963. Other figures are for both sexes.

Note: In all except the last case the risk is greater for less frequent attenders.

showed (table 14.1) a relatively higher risk for certain diseases among infrequent church attenders than among regular churchgoers. A more recent, carefully controlled study in Melbourne, Australia, of patients with colorectal cancer has shown that self-reported or perceived "religiousness" was a statistically significant protective factor against colorectal cancer, reducing the incidence to 70 percent of that in nonreligious patients.[26]

Can anything be concluded from this broad range of associations? It seems likely that the seriously ill would progressively fail to attend services rather than maintain their previous regularity, but in one study[27] there were no such diminutions. It must, however, be the case that some bedridden patients who can no longer attend church services are visited at home or in the hospital by the clergy. The reported relationship between religious attendance and life satisfaction remained significant despite controlling for the fact that the sick were not capable of getting to church. Comstock, who has specialized in this type of study, concludes that whatever the mechanism of association, it could still prove useful in identifying groups at increased risk of suffering from a number of important diseases. Others have found that being actively involved in religion decreases the number of reported mental and physical symptoms.[28]

The Health of the Clergy

If the rules and practices of a religion have any effects on the health of its followers, then those who adhere most strongly should show these most clearly. The expectation of life for the Christian clergy appears to have been longer in the nineteenth century than that for the general population of males of the same age distribution (table 14.2). Many factors undoubtedly contribute to these findings, quite apart from the beneficent effects of income, diet, regular employment, and good housing. For instance, longevity might also be influenced initially by selective recruitment of healthy individuals to the clergy; aspirants to the Roman Catholic priesthood often receive both physical and mental health examinations.

The average life expectancy of Roman Catholic missionaries has been found to be fourteen years less than the average in their home countries, with variations between temperate Asian and tropical and subtropical African countries.[29]

A study designed to discover the effects of Christian monastic life on health[30] compared the nutrition of Benedictine monks in Holland who

Table 14.2. Annual Mortality Rates (Percentage) for Clergymen as Compared with the General Population, in England/Wales and Prussia

	Age Group		
	25–45	*45–65*	*25–65*
England and Wales			
General male population 1863–71	1.15	2.52	1.84
Clergy in general 1860–61	0.52	1.72	1.04
Church of England clergy 1860–61	0.48	1.72	1.02
Protestant ministers 1860–61	0.54	1.58	1.01
Roman Catholic priests 1860–61	0.97	2.69	1.57
Prussia			
General male population 1776–84	0.97	2.59	1.68
Protestant ministers 1801–33	0.58	2.00	1.18

Source: Stüssi, H. (1873–75). "On the mortality of the clergy." *Journal of the Institute of Actuaries and Assurance*, 18, 343–52. Quoted in King, H., and Bailor, J. C. (1969). "The health of the clergy: A review of demographic literature." *Demography*, 6, 27–43.

Note: In both countries mortality rate was lower among the clergy.

Table 14.3. Medical Data for Trappist and Benedictine Fathers and Brethren

	Trappist Monks			*Benedictine Monks*		
Data	*Fathers*	*Brethren*	*Both*	*Fathers*	*Brethren*	*Both*
Number	96	84	180	102	66	168
Average age (years)	48	53	50	47	37	42
Average height (m)	1.69	1.66	1.68	1.71	1.70	1.70
Average weight (kg)	79	72	76	69	65	67
Obesity* (no. of cases)	40	23	63	23	7	30
Average blood pressure						
Systolic (mm Hg)	147	147	147	136	136	136
Diastolic	83	80	82	85	83	84
Number with diastolic hypertension ≥ 100	9	4	13	7	3	10
Number with myocardial infarction	1	—	—	—	—	—
Number with angina pectoris	2	1	3	3	1	4

Source: Groen et al.

* An individual was classified as obese when his weight was equal to more than 110 percent of the normal for his age and height.

Note: The diet of the Trappists is vegetarian and frugal, whereas the Benedictine diet is both omnivorous and more generous. Trappists nevertheless weighed more and had higher systolic pressure, on average, than Benedictines.

Wednesday Sep 07 06:22 AM

lived on a mixed "Western" diet with that of Trappist monks in Belgium who had a frugal vegetarian diet (table 14.3). More obesity occurred among the Trappists, against expectations. However, it has been noted[31] that the Trappist diet is not uniform internationally, in line with the differences between the manual working brethren and the largely sedentary, contemplative fathers. Another study[32] concluded that the prolonged consumption of a diet low in animal protein had no deleterious effects on the health of a Trappist community.

A further study showed that markedly reduced coronary heart disease mortality rate in a sample of monks was associated with a higher than average cancer mortality rate.[33] In a recent study of morbidity (see table 14.4), 134 Trappist and Benedictine monks living in Dutch monasteries were found to suffer less than the general population from heart disorders, asthma, and bronchitis but to be twice as likely to suffer from sinusitis, migraine, arthritis, and rheumatism.[34]

In conclusion it can be seen that there is no easy answer to the question, Do clergy have especially good health? There are differences among denominations, in disease patterns as well as in life expectancy. In general we have seen that clergy do tend to have good life expectancy, but that

Table 14.4. Self-Reported Morbidity Among Trappist and Benedictine Monks in the Netherlands, 1991

Morbidity Indicator	Prevalence (%)	Age	
		SMR*	95% CI†
General health perceived as less than good	19.7	0.65	0.42–0.87
One or more subjective health complaints	85.3	1.10	0.99–1.17
One or more chronic conditions‡	49.6	1.00	0.83–1.18
Heart disorder	1.5	0.23	0.06–0.93
Asthma/chronic bronchitis	2.3	0.28	0.09–0.83
Sinusitis	11.5	2.37	1.44–3.75
Migraine or serious headache	6.1	2.35	1.18–4.54
Arthritis, rheumatism, arthrosis	24.6	2.24	1.63–2.98

Source: Mackenbach et al.

* SMR, standardized morbidity ratio. This is the ratio of the "observed" to the "expected" number of cases of ill health among monks; the expected number was calculated on the basis of age-specific or age- and education-specific prevalance rates among the general male population.

† Cl, confidence interval.

‡ From a list of 23 conditions. Only specific conditions for which the 95% confidence interval of the SMR did not include 1.00 have been listed.

the mortality rate from heart diseases is high, especially among Catholic priests.

The Health of Nuns

Kunin and McCormack[35] found that both systolic and diastolic blood pressure were lower for nuns than for controls in both a white and a black group (table 14.5). A twenty-year study showed that their blood pressure remained virtually the same while that of women living in the community increased progressively over the same period.[36]

It has been known for some time that there is an increased relative frequency of breast cancer in nuns, while marriage appears to increase the frequency of cervical cancer. A study of death rates in Verona from 1769 to 1839[37] found a ratio between cancer of the breast and uterus in the proportion of 1:4 for married women as compared to a 3:1 ratio for single women other than sisters, and a ratio of 9:1 for sisters.

Another study[38] found only three cases of cancer of the cervix in Canadian nuns in a total of 140,000 pathological reports of malignant tumors of the uterus. Similar negative results are recorded from Germany[39] and Chicago.[40] However, British nuns eating little or no meat had an incidence of breast and colon cancer which was not significantly different from that of the general population.[41]

Table 14.5. Mean Systolic and Diastolic Blood Pressures, Adjusted for Age, in Nuns and Working Women (Controls), Both White and Black.

Group	Blood Pressure (mm Hg) Systolic	Blood Pressure (mm Hg) Diastolic
Whites		
Controls	124.9	76.0
Nuns	121.2	71.2
Blacks		
Controls	129.6	79.0
Nuns	122.4	71.7

Source: Kunin, C. M. and McCormack, R. (1968). "An epidemiologic study of bacteriuria and blood pressure among nuns and working women." *New England J Medicine,* 278, 635–42.

Note: Note the lower blood pressures in the nuns.

Disease and Some Smaller Christian Denominations

It is known that alcohol and tobacco contribute substantially as causative factors in certain diseases that affect the liver and respiratory tract. For this reason we are interested in the disease profiles of the Seventh Day Adventists and the members of the Church of Jesus Christ of Latter Day Saints (Mormons), which prohibit the use of alcohol and tobacco.

Some 70 percent of the population of Utah are Mormons. Cervical cancer in Utah is 26 percent below the national average; this lower occurrence is accounted for by the Mormons having rates 50 percent below the national and Utah non-Mormons averages.

A study of cancer of the colon in Utah showed the Mormon rate to be 37 percent below and non-Mormons 15 percent below the national average. There may be environmental as well as religious factors particularly, as there is little difference in meat, fat and fiber consumption between the Utah population and the United States population as a whole.[42] A recent study of county cancer mortality rates in the United States found that high concentrations of Mormons were associated with the lowest rates, in contrast with the rates for active Jews, which were the highest.[43]

The Mormon church proscribes the use of tobacco and alcohol, but from 1929 total abstinence has only been required for church leaders as a prerequisite for being in good standing.[44] An analysis of cardiovascular disease deaths showed that Mormons had a 35 percent lower mortality rate than the national rate, while Utah non-Mormons' rates were not significantly different. There were similarly lower rates for hypertensive and rheumatic heart diseases.[45]

A much wider study of Californian and Utah Mormons showed that the age adjusted death rates for active Mormon men aged thirty five to sixty four years was 38 percent below the national average, and their remaining life expectancy was seven years greater than for United States whites.[46] The California Mormons were found to have low rates of cancer incidence.[47]

Two additional factors for the assessment of these correlations between health and religion should be considered. First are nonreligious factors which could have had these consequences. For example, in comparing Utah Mormons with non-Mormons it has been shown that Mormon wives had had fewer hysterectomies and breast X-rays, more often lived in rural areas, and were exposed to fewer occupational hazards.[48]

The second important issue is the question of causal factors. There are some clear and simple correlations which appear to have general validity. All four well-known Christian sects, the Amish, the Seventh Day Adventists, the Hutterites, and the Mormons, have well observed rules against smoking and their lung cancer rates are strikingly low.[49]

However, in most cases the situation is more complicated and we lack a clear understanding of the causal connection between dietary habits and diseases. Further, a study of Californian Seventh Day Adventists[50] showed that only a proportion of the membership obeyed the dietary rules (table 14.6). Such considerations must be taken into account when evaluating correlations between disease and religious practice.

For example, a thirteen-year follow-up study of age-adjusted mortality rates for 22,940 Californian Seventh Day Adventists (SDAs) and 112,725 non-SDAs showed low comparative rates for leukemia in males

Table 14.6. Percentage of Raised and Converted Seventh Day Adventists Obeying Dietary Rules Compared with Practices of Nonmembers (All Over 30 Years of Age)

<table>
<tr><th></th><th colspan="3">Males</th><th colspan="3">Females</th></tr>
<tr><th></th><th>Raised SDA</th><th>Converted SDA</th><th>Non-SDA</th><th>Raised SDA</th><th>Converted SDA</th><th>Non-SDA</th></tr>
<tr><td>N</td><td>210</td><td>253</td><td>417</td><td>228</td><td>266</td><td>404</td></tr>
<tr><td>Percentage of:</td><td></td><td></td><td></td><td></td><td></td><td></td></tr>
<tr><td>Non-smokers</td><td>93</td><td>62</td><td>35</td><td>98</td><td>81</td><td>74</td></tr>
<tr><td>Non-drinkers</td><td>93</td><td>55</td><td>28</td><td>98</td><td>88</td><td>70</td></tr>
<tr><td>Non–meat eaters</td><td colspan="2">56</td><td>2</td><td colspan="2">52</td><td>1</td></tr>
<tr><td>Non–fish eaters</td><td colspan="2">64</td><td>16</td><td colspan="2">68</td><td>17</td></tr>
<tr><td>Non–coffee drinkers</td><td colspan="2">82</td><td>17</td><td colspan="2">82</td><td>14</td></tr>
<tr><td>Non–tea drinkers</td><td colspan="2">90</td><td>38</td><td colspan="2">89</td><td>34</td></tr>
<tr><td>Non–milk drinkers</td><td colspan="2">17</td><td>15</td><td colspan="2">19</td><td>21</td></tr>
</table>

Source: Wynder et al.

Note: The table demonstrates that many of the religious prohibitions are violated by members.

Wednesday Sep 07 02:21 AM

(0.54:1) but not in females (1.01:1), a high rate for stomach cancer in males (1.41:1) but not for females (0.89:1), and a low rate for colorectal cancers in males (0.62:1) and females (0.58:1).[51] Such figures demand a complex interpretation.

This study showed that 93 percent of men born Seventh Day Adventists had never consumed alcohol and that of the men who did drink only 1 percent of born members and 9 percent of converts had taken one or more drinks per day for twenty years or more. The proportions for women were 1 percent and 1 percent, respectively. Similarly none of the born and 13 percent of the converted members had smoked sixteen or more cigarettes per day for twenty years or more, with the proportions for women being 0 percent and 2 percent, respectively.

The distribution of cancer between the Seventh Day Adventists and the controls showed that for men the observed percentages were lower than the expected values and the differences were statistically significant and particularly striking for cancers of the bladder, lung, mouth, esophagus, and larynx. The risk of lung cancer was half that of demographically similar populations.[52] For women there were statistically significant differences for cancer of the cervix. Subsequent studies[53] of Californian Seventh Day Adventists have confirmed that their cancer mortality rate is considerably below that of the general population. Fruit consumption has recently been shown to have a strong and statistically significant association with low rates of lung cancer in a large sample of 34,198 Californian SDAs; however, the rate of smoking in this sample was a mere 4 percent, indicating this as a likely causal factor.[54]

Although a large share of this reduction in cancers is due to the very high rates of cancer mortality known to be related to smoking, there are numerous other differences. Other characteristics of the Seventh Day Adventists themselves and/or their life-style may be involved besides their dietary habits, smoking, and so forth. A study[55] of the background and life-style of Seventh Day Adventists states that they are by no means representative: the proportion of college-educated persons, for example, is twice that of the general population. However, adjustment for education did not wholly eliminate the mortality differences, and it was suggested that an important variable may be their total dietary pattern. Their typical lacto–ovo–vegetarian diet has about 25 percent less fat and 50 percent more fiber than the average nonvegetarian diet and the unsaturated to saturated fat ratio is about double the average.[56] Studies have revealed significant differences in their fecal microbial flora.[57] Lack of coffee consumption could account for a proportion of their reduced bladder cancer risk[58] and perhaps have other beneficial effects on health.[59] Subsequent studies have shown that vegetarian diets do not necessarily provide all-around health protection; they have good to fair effects on blood pressure, coronary artery disease mortality rate, and diabetes, but fair to poor effects on risks of breast cancer, cancer of the colon, and osteoporosis.[60] The consumption of meat, eggs, milk, and cheese by SDAs did not have a negative association with any cause of death.[61] It has been concluded that the Seventh Day Adventist dietary pattern is significantly related to a reduction in certain diseases, and in the case of coronary heart disease to delaying its appearance,[62] but that these effects are caused at least in part by life-style and social factors and not by diet alone.[63]

In respect to the beneficial effects of a vegetarian diet, it has been found[64] that the blood pressure of Seventh Day Adventists, both systolic and diastolic, was significantly lower than that of nonmembers, and there was a gradient toward increasing blood pressure with increasing egg intake,[65] and a higher diastolic blood pressure in those drinking tea and coffee.

Finally, a recent Norwegian study found that the expected low incidence of cancer rates in Seventh Day Adventists disappeared when all SDAs were included in the survey regardless of extent of religious activity. It was only the zealous members of the faith who had lower rates.[66]

Miracles

Miracle reports of the twelfth to fifteenth centuries came from shrines which were faith-healing centers. They were the place of last resort for those who had already tried the limited range of secular possibilities.

In examining the miracles attributed to five English saints from 1150 to 1220, some were doubtless explicable in terms of luck, emotion, and benign illnesses, but there is no clear explanation for the sudden, total disappearance of crippling physical disabilities or the restoration of speech, vision, and hearing to the previously deaf, blind, and mute.[67] During the twentieth century charismatic revival in the United States many thousands of testimonials to divine healing cures were published,[68] and the concept of faith healing is very much alive today.

Religions and Techniques for the Prolongation of Life

Prayer for the prolongation of life and the avoidance of suffering is ubiquitous, and it is only recently with the growth of concern for, and scientific research into, psychosomatic diseases that interest has been shown in the possibility that prayer is an effective agent for the reduction of pain and the lengthening of life. Galton made a quantitative study of the "success" of prayer, positing that because the British monarchs had more regular prayers said for their welfare than anyone else in Britain, they should have lived longer than the average citizen; he found that their life expectancy was in fact lower than the average.[69] Perhaps it is quality rather than quantity that counts!

Some purposive praying for specific patients paired with unprayed-for controls has been attempted under clinical observation. A small British study of chronically ill patients initially showed that those prayed for did better than the controls, but subsequent pairs showed that the controls did better. The authors thought this might be accounted for by the prayer group's waning interest in the patients.[70] A small American study in which the sick and the prayer group did not know each other and the latter were kept up to scratch by reminders showed a marked delay in the deaths of the sample in comparison with those in the control group.[71]

It is only recently that any large-scale testing of the therapeutic effects of intercessory prayer has taken place, where controlled observations were made in a coronary care unit population (see table 14.7). A total of 393 patients tested by a double-blind protocol* were followed for ten months: 192 in the intercessory prayer group and 201 in the control group. At entry into the unit there were no statistical differences between the two groups, but during the prayer period the intercessory prayer group had a significantly lower severity score ($p < 0.01$), and under twenty six categories of medical analysis the intercessory prayer group did better in twenty. The prayed-for group also spent a shorter time in the intensive care unit and used fewer medications after discharge.[72]

The Christian Churches and AIDS

The appearance of acquired immunodeficiency syndrome (AIDS) is a matter of concern to all those involved in charity and concern for moral values. Despite the horror of this pandemic there has been no particularly Christian response to AIDS over and above the charity already obligatory for all Christians. In the past, many religious orders were founded for specific purposes stimulated by local conditions. In the case of AIDS, this does not appear to be happening. Existing resources and personnel are heavily involved in caring for their own members, and they may not have enough resources for a major new initiative. However, there is nothing to prevent such a development to meet this new crisis in the future. Mother Teresa's concern for those dying on the streets of Calcutta is just such an example, which led to the development of a specialized order with thousands of nuns for the care of the terminally ill. In the United States there is a new AIDS sufferers support program, CARA (Care and Resources for People Affected by AIDS), but it is a lay organization of volunteers.

The Christian churches take clear moral views on AIDS, which depend on the situations in which the disease is caught. As in Islam, Buddhism, and Hinduism (except possibly for Tantrism, which holds that extreme sexual licence is a necessary precondition for freedom), they take a straightforward biological view of "natural processes." Homosexual anal intercourse is against the order of nature and is totally wrong, and therefore to advocate condoms for gay men would be to condone

*In a double-blind experiment, neither the experimenters nor the subjects know which category they fall into. Thus in this case the prayed for did not know they were being prayed for.

Table 14.7. Results of Intercessory Prayer: New Problems, Diagnoses, and Therapeutic Events After Entry

	Intercessory Prayer Group		*Control Group*		
	%	*No.*	*%*	*No.*	*p*
Antianginal agents	11	21	10	19	ns
Unstable angina	10	20	9	18	ns
Antiarrhythmics	9	17	13	27	ns
Coronary angiography	9	17	11	21	ns
VT/VF	7	14	9	17	ns
Readmissions to CCU	7	14	7	14	ns
Mortality	7	13	9	17	ns
Congestive heart failure	4	8	10	20	<0.03
Inotropic agents	4	8	8	16	ns
Vasodilators	4	8	6	12	ns
Supraventricular tachyarrhythmia	4	8	8	15	ns
Arterial pressure monitoring	4	7	8	15	ns
Central pressure monitoring	3	6	7	15	ns
Diuretics	3	5	8	15	<0.05
Major surgery before discharge	3	5	7	14	ns
Temporary pacemaker	2	4	1	1	ns
Sepsis	2	4	4	7	ns
Cardiopulmonary arrest	2	3	7	14	<0.02
Third degree heart block	2	3	1	2	ns
Pneumonia	2	3	7	13	<0.03
Hypotension (systolic < 90 torr)	2	3	4	7	ns
Extension of infarction	2	3	3	6	ns
Antibiotics	2	3	9	17	<0.005
Permanent pacemaker	2	3	1	1	ns
Gastrointestinal bleeding	1	1	2	3	ns
Intubation/ventilation	0	0	6	12	<0.02
Days in CCU after entry	2.0 ± 2.5		2.4 ± 4.1		ns
Days in hospital after entry	7.6 ± 8.9		7.6 ± 8.7		ns
No. of discharge medications	3.7 ± 2.2		4.0 ± 2.4		ns

Source: Byrd

Note: In a carefully controlled study, the results of prayer for cardiac patients in a hospital were studied in relation to new problems for patients, diagnoses, and improvements in health after entry. For 20 of 26 conditions, the prayed-for group did better than the not-prayed-for group. In some cases the results were statistically significant (final column).

ns = not significant

p = probability

immorality of a particularly distasteful kind. Indeed, anal intercourse with a wife would produce the same moral reaction should the Catholic church be asked for a canonical ruling. Fundamentalist Christians view the AIDS epidemic as a historical cosmological event, a sign of the end of the world. The Reverend Jerry Falwell has claimed that AIDS is God's punishment for homosexuals, and that the People of God, the good people, have to be protected from the stigmatized sinners, homosexuals, prostitutes, and promiscuous heterosexuals.[73] AIDS has been referred to as "Jerry Falwell's revenge."[74] Islamic attitudes toward AIDS are related to the "indecencies" mentioned in the Koran (Sura 7.33), so that it is seen as God's punishment for sexual deviants.

Infection from a prostitute would be seen as the consequence of an immoral act, and it would be equally immoral to use condoms to prevent the possibility of such an infection.[75] Infection that resulted from contaminated needles in heroin "main-liners" would be ruled as a relatively minor sin and infection from a spouse or contaminated blood would involve no implication of moral failure.

It is difficult to see how there could be any change in these moral viewpoints. Should Christian moralists conclude that since men and women frequently engage in immoral sexual intercourse, they should be advised to protect themselves from the consequences of their activities?[76] Some Catholic leaders have described promiscuity as both immoral and suicidal and have called for a moral renaissance.[77]

On the other hand, there has been no change in the view that AIDS sufferers should be helped and perhaps helped in special ways as lepers from the medieval period to the time of Father Damien have been helped.[78] Cardinal O'Connor of New York is not a hypocrite when he condemns homosexuality from the pulpit while spending one day per week as a nurse in an AIDS clinic for the terminally ill.[79] Certainly this type of example is very necessary to ensure that such sufferers are not stigmatized in hospital care by those who have the ethical obligations of their professions to fulfill.[80]

Catholicism and Drug Addiction

It is generally considered that religion is a more effective control over alcoholism than any medical therapy. More alcoholics have been cured by religious conversion than by all the medical programs combined.[81] The strongest predictor of abstinence from alcohol, tobacco, and all drugs combined was a high degree of professed religious belief[82] and commitment to Christ.[83] This also correlates with parental involvement in religious practices.[84] Within Christianity there are substantial differences in the use of alcohol. The inhabitants of the Western Isles of Scotland have alcoholism as a social problem, and a recent study of islanders showed that a substantial majority of Protestants either did not drink at all or only drank on special occasions. Few Catholics were abstainers and those with no religion drank more regularly than those in any other category.[85] In the United States Protestant students appear to drink less than the average,[86] and overall the more religious youth appear less likely to smoke, use soft drugs, and drink alcohol.[87] In the United States there has been a noticeable reduction in alcohol use by adolescents when they have joined charismatic sects.[88]

Judaism has a clear record of low alcohol abuse. Israel was the lowest of twenty one countries in per capita alcohol consumption,[89] and had a low rate of cirrhosis of the liver compared to the United States and France.[90] Sobriety appears to be a Jewish characteristic, not only in the United States (among adults),[91] but among students as well over several generations.[92]

So much for the question of diseases and sickness in relation to religious faith and religious practices. We end part III here. We have in this section seen something of the complexity of the relationship between religions and diseases—often the context is that of human beings struggling with diseases in a context of imperfect knowledge of their causes and modes of transmission.

In the last chapter we summarize the main points that have come out of our studies and try to get a picture of religions in relation to human life as a whole, why they are with us, what functions they perform and needs they fill, and why they are unlikely to disappear in the future.

Notes

1. Friedman, M., and Rosenman, R. H. (1974). *Type A behavior and your heart.* Fawcett Crest, New York.

2. Comstock, G. W., and Partridge, K. B. (1972). "Church attendance and health." *J Chronic Disease*, 25, 665–72.

3. Levin, J. S., et al. (1988). "Religion, type A behavior and health." *J Religion and Health*, 27(4), 267–78.

4. Tamiya, ibn. (1950). "Iqtidâ al-sirât al-mustaqim, muhâlafat 'ashâb al-jah;afim." Cairo. Rusd, ibn. (1355AH). *Bidâyat al-mujtahid wa nihayat al muqtasid.* Cairo, p. 52.

5. Lane, E. W. (1954). *Manners and customs of the modern Egyptians.* Dent, London, p. 150.

6. Tabari, Muhammad ibn Jarir. (1879). *Annales*, Leiden, p. 56.

7. Avalon, A. (1963). *The great liberation.* Ganesh, Madras.

8. Leonard, A. J. (1906). *The lower Niger and its tribes.* Macmillan, London.

9. Singer, C., and Sigerist, H. E. (1924). *Essays in the history of medicine*, presented to K. Sudhoff. Oxford University Press, London.

10. Walsh, J. J. (1928). *The Catholic Church and healing.* Burns, Oates and Washbourne, London.

11. Mercier, C. A. (1915). *Leper houses and medieval hospitals.* Lewis, London.

12. Needham, J., and Lu Gwei-Djen. (1969). "Chinese medicine." In Poynter, F. N. L. (ed.). *Medicine and culture.* Wellcome Institute, London.

13. Frost, G., and Pirani, S. (1987). "Meal frequency and nutritional intake during Ramadan: A pilot study." *Human Nutrition Applied Nutrition*, 41A, 47–50.

14. Malhotra, A., et al. (1989). "Metabolic changes in Asian Muslim pregnant mothers observing the Ramadan fast in Britain." *British J Nutrition*, 61(3), 663–72.

15. Ebbing, R. N. (1979). "Muslims, Ramadan and diabetes mellitus." *British Medical J*, 2(6185), 333–34.

16. Aslam, M., and Healy, M. A. (1986). "Compliance and drug therapy in fasting Moslem patients." *J Clinical Hospital Pharmacy*, 11(5), 321–25.

17. Aslam, M., and Assad, A. (1986). "Drug regimens and fasting during Ramadan: A survey in Kuwait." *Public Health*, 100(1), 49–53.

18. Chusid, E. L., et al. (1982). "Selecting respiratory medications during the Passover holiday." *Chest*, 81(4), 524–25.

19. Rispler-Chaim, V. (1989). "Islamic medical ethics in the twentieth century." *Journal of Medical Ethics*, 15(4), 203–4.

20. Naguib, S. M., et al. (1966). "Relation of various epidemiologic factors of cervical cancer as determined by screening." *Obstetrics and Gynecology*, 28, 451–59, (1966). "Epidemiologic study of trichomoniasis in normal women." *Obstetrics and Gynecology*, 27, 607–16.

21. Kinsey, A. C., et al. (1953). *Sexual behavior in the human female*. Saunders, Philadelphia.

22. Comstock, G. W., et al. (1970). "The non-official census as a basic tool for epidemiological observations in Washington County, Maryland." In Kesler, I. I., and Levin, M. L. (eds.). *The community as an epidemiologic laboratory: A casebook of community studies*. Johns Hopkins University Press, Baltimore.

23. Graham, T. W., et al. (1978). "Frequency of church attendance and blood pressure elevation." *J. Behavioural Medicine*, 1(1), 37–43. Walsh, A. (1980). "The prophylactic effect of religion on blood pressure levels among a sample of immigrants." *Social Science and Medicine*, 148, 59–63. Larson, D. B., et al. (1989). "The impact of religion on men's blood pressure." *J Religion and Health*, 28, 265–78.

24. Levin, J. S., and Vanderpool, H. Y. (1989). "Is religion therapeutically significant for hypertension." *Social Science and Medicine*, 29(1), 69–78.

25. Comstock, G. W., and Partridge, K. B. (1972). "Church attendance and health." *J Chronic Disease*, 25, 665–72.

26. Kune, G. A., Kune, S., and Watson, L. F. (1993). "Perceived religiousness is protective for colorectal cancer: Data from the Melbourne Colorectal Cancer Study." *J Royal Society Medicine*, 86, 645–47.

27. Comstock, G. W., and Partridge, K. B. (1972). "Church attendance and health." *J Chronic Disease*, 25, 665–72.

28. Hannay, D. R. (1980). "Religion and health." *Social Science Medicine*, 14A, 683–85. Cohen, D. I., et al. (1985). "Social networks, stress and physical health: A longitudinal study of an inner-city elderly population." *J Gerontology*, 40(4), 478–86.

29. Boldrini, M., and Ugge, A. (1926). *La mortalita del missionari*. Catholic University, Milan.

30. Groen, J. J., et al. (1962). "The influence of nutrition and ways of life on blood cholesterol and the prevalence of hypertension and coronary heart disease among Trappist and Benedictine monks." *American J Clinical Nutrition*, 10, 456–70.

31. Groen, J. J. (1964). "De levenswijze der Trappisten en haar invloed op het ontstaan van coronaire hartziekten en het cholesterolgehalte van het bloed." *Voeding*, 25, 310–13.

32. Mirone, L. (1954). "Nutrient intake and blood findings of men on a diet devoid of meat." *American J Clinical Nutrition*, 2, 246–51.

33. Keys, A. (1961). "Further observations on monastic cholesterol." *New England J Medicine*, 264, 1005.

34. Mackenbach, J. P., Kunst, A. E., de Vrij, J. H., and van Meel, D.

(1993). "Self-reported morbidity and disability among Trappist and Benedictine monks." *Amer Journal of Epidemiology*, 138(8), 569–73.

35. Kunin, C. M., and McCormack, R. C. (1968). "An epidemiological study of bacteriuria and blood pressure among nuns and working women." *New England J Medicine*, 278, 635–42.

36. Timio, M. (1985). "Study of nuns supports stress factor in blood pressure increase with age." *Family Practice News*, 15(9), 87.

37. Rigoni-Stern, D. (1844). "Nota sulle ricerche del Dottor Tanchou intorno la frequenza del cancro." *Ann Univ Med*, 110, 484–503.

38. Gagnon, F. (1950). "Contribution to the study of the etiology and prevention of cancer of the cervix and cancer of the uterus." *American J Obstetrics and Gynecology*, 60, 516–22.

39. Schomig, G. (1953). "Die weiblichen genitalkarzinome bei sezueller enthaltsamkeit." *Strahlentherapie*, 92, 156–58.

40. Towne, J. E. (1955). "Carcinoma of the cervix in nulliparous and celibate women." *American J Obstetrics and Gynecology*, 69, 606–13.

41. Kinlen, L. J. (1982). "Meat and fat consumption and cancer mortality: A study of strict religious orders in Britain." *Lancet*, 946–49.

42. Lyon, J. L., and Sorenson, A. W. (1978). "Colon cancer in a low risk population." *American J Clinical Nutrition*, 31, S227–S230.

43. Dwyer, J. W., et al. (1990). "The effect of religious concentration and affiliation on county cancer mortality rates." *Journal of Health and Social Behaviour*, 31(2), 185–202.

44. Bush, L. E. (1986). "The Mormon tradition." In Numbers, R. L., and Amundsen, D.W. (eds.). *Caring and curing: Health and medicine in the western religious traditions.* Macmillan, New York.

45. Lyon, J. L., and Sorenson, A. W. (1978). "Colon cancer in a low risk population." *American J Clinical Nutrition*, 31, S227–S230.

46. Enstrom, J. E. (1978). "Cancer and total mortality among active Mormons." *Cancer*, 42, 1943–51.

47. Enstrom, J. E. (1980). *Health and dietary practices and cancer mortality among California Mormons.* In Cairns, J., and McElheny, R. K., (eds.). *Cancer incidence in defined populations.* Gold Spring Harbor, New York.

48. West, D. W., et al (1980). "Cancer risk factors: An analysis of Utah Mormons and non-Mormons." *J National Cancer Institute*, 65, 1083–95.

49. Troyer, H. (1988). "Review of cancer among 4 religious sects: Evidence that life-styles are distinctive sets of risk factors." *Social Science Medicine*, 26(10), 1007–17.

50. Wynder, E. L., et al. (1959). "Cancer and coronary artery disease among Seventh Day Adventists." *Cancer*, 12, 1016–28.

51. Phillips, R. L. (1980). "Cancer among Seventh Day Adventists." *J Environmental Pathology and Toxicology*, 3, 157–69.

52. Najman, J. M., et al. (1988). "Religious values, practices and pregnancy outcomes: A comparison of the impact of sects and mainstream Christian affiliation." *Social Science and Medicine*, 26(4), 401–7.

53. Lemon, F. R., et al. (1964). "Cancer of the lung and mouth in Seventh Day Adventists." *Cancer*, 17, 486–97.

54. Fraser, G. E., et al. (1991). "Diet and lung cancer in California Seventh Day Adventists." *American J Epidemiology*, 133(7), 683–93.

55. Phillips, R. L. (1975). "Role of life style and dietary habits in risk of cancer among Seventh Day Adventists." *Cancer Research*, 35, 3513–22.

56. Hardinge, M. G., et al. (1958). "Nutritional studies of vegetarians. III. Dietary levels of fiber." *American J Clinical Nutrition*, 6, 523–25. Hardinge, M. G., et al. (1962). "Nutritional studies of vegetarians. IV. Dietary fatty acids and serum cholesterol levels." *American J Clinical Nutrition*, 10, 516–24.

57. Finegold, S. M., et al. (1977). "Fecal microbial flora in Seventh Day Adventist populations and control subjects." *American J Clinical Nutrition*, 30, 1781–92.

58. Cole, P. (1971). "Coffee-drinking and cancer of the lower urinary tract." *Lancet*, I, 1335–37. Cole, P. (9173). "A population-based study of bladder cancer." In Doll, R., and Vodopija, I. (eds.). *Host environment interactions in the etiology of cancer in man*. International Agency for Research on Cancer, Lyon, France.

59. Reynolds, V., and Tanner, R. E. S. (1983). *The biology of religion*. Longmans, London.

60. Dwyer, J. T. (1988). "Health aspects of vegetarian diets." *American J Clinical Nutrition*, 48, 712–38.

61. Snowdon, D. A. (1988). "Animal product consumption and mortality because of all causes combined, coronary heart disease, stroke, diabetes and cancer in Seventh Day Adventists." *American J Clinical Nutrition*, 48, 739–48.

62. Fonnebo, V. (1985), "The Tromso heart study: Coronary risk factors in Seventh Day Adventists." *American J Epidemiology*, 122(5), 789–93; Fraser, G. E., (1987). "Ischemic heart disease risk factors in middle-aged Seventh Day Adventist men and their neighbors." *American J Epidemiology*, 126(4), 638–46; Fraser, G. E., (1988). "Determinants of ischemic heart disease in Seventh Day Adventists: A cross-sectional study showing significant relationships." *J Chronic Disease*, 34, 487–501.

63. Fraser, G. E. (1988). "Determinants of ischemic heart disease in Seventh Day Adventists: A review." *American J Clinical Nutrition*, 48, 833–36.

64. Armstrong, B. et al. (1977). "Blood pressure in Seventh Day Adventist vegetarians." *American J Epidemiology*, 105(5), 444–47.

65. Snowdon, D. A. (1988). "Animal product consumption and mortality because of all causes combined, coronary heart disease, stroke, diabetes and cancer in Seventh Day Adventists." *American J Clinical Nutrition*, 48, 739–48.

66. Fonnebo, V., et al. (1991). "Cancer incidence in Norwegian Seventh Day Adventists, 1961–1986." *Cancer* 68(3), 666–71.

67. Gordon, E. C. (1986). "Child health in the Middle Ages as seen in the miracles of five English saints: A.D. 1150–1220." *Bulletin History Medicine*, 60(4), 502–22.

68. Harrell, D. E. (1975). *All things are possible: The healing and charismatic revivals in modern America*. Indiana University Press, Bloomington, p. 87.

69. Galton, F. (1883). *Inquiries into human faculty and its development*. Macmillan, London, pp. 277–94.

70. Joyce, C. R. B., and Welldon, R. M. C. (1965). "The objective efficacy of prayer." *J Chronic Diseases*, 18, 367–77.

71. Collipp, P. J. (1969). "The efficacy of prayer: A triple-blind study." *Medical Times*, 97, 201–4.

72. Byrd, R. C. (1988). "Positive therapeutic effects of intercessory prayer in a coronary care unit population." *Southern Medical J*, 81(7), 826–29.

73. Copello, A. G. (1989). "A world suffering with AIDS: Community or ideology: Reflections on illness and health." In Hallman, D. G. (ed.). *AIDS issues*. Pilgrim Press, New York.

74. Weber, T. P. (1986). "The Baptist tradition." In Numbers, R. L., and Amundsen, D. W. (eds.). *Caring and curing: Health and medicine in the Western religious traditions.* Macmillan, New York.

75. Sweemer, C. de (1989). "AIDS: The global crisis." In Hallman, D. G. (ed.). *AIDS issues.* Pilgrim Press, New York.

76. Somfai, B. (1989). "AIDS issues: Confronting the challenge." In Hallman, D. G. (ed.). *AIDS issues.* Pilgrim Press, New York.

77. Hume, B. (1987). "AIDS: Time for a moral renaissance." *The Times,* Jan. 7, 10.

78. Lynch, A. (1989). "AIDS-related suffering: Therapy, healing or?" In Hallman, D. G. (ed.). *AIDS issues.* Pilgrim Press, New York.

79. Woodward, J. (ed.). (1990). *Embracing the chaos: Theological responses to AIDS.* Society for Promoting Christian Knowledge, London.

80. Steinbrook, R., et al. (1985). "Ethical dilemmas in caring for patients with AIDS." *Annals Internal Medicine,* 103, 787–90.

81. Kovel, J. (1976). *A complete guide to therapy: From psychoanalysis to behavior modification.* Pantheon, New York. Larson, D. B., and Wilson, W. P. (1980). "Religious life of alcoholics." *Southern Medical J,* 73, 723–27.

82. Khavari, K. A., and Harmon, T. M. (1982). "The relationship between the degree of professed religious belief and the use of drugs." *International J Addictions,* 17(5), 847–57.

83. Dudley, R. L., et al. (1987). "Religious factors and drug usage among Seventh Day Adventist youth in North America." *J Scientific Study Religion,* 26(2), 218–33.

84. Cancellaro, L. A., et al. (1982). "The religious life of narcotic addicts." *Southern Medical J,* 75(10), 1166–68.

85. Mullen, K., et al. (1986). "Religion and attitudes towards alcohol use in the Western Isles." *Drug Alcohol Dependency,* 18(1), 51–72.

86. Burkett, S. R. (1980). "Religiosity, beliefs, normative standards and adolescent drinking." *J Studies Alcoholism,* 41(7), 662–71.

87. Vener, A. M., et al. (1977). "Traditional religious orthodoxy, respect for authority and non-conformity in adolescence." *Adolescence,* 12 (45), 43–56.

88. Galanter, M. (1981). "Peer group influence on adolescent alcohol use: The psychiatric impact of charismatic sects." *Bulletin New York Academy Medicine,* 57(5), 370–77.

89. Hyman, M. M., et al. (1980). *Drinkers, drinking and alcohol-related mortality and hospitalizations.* Rutgers Center of Alcohol Studies, New Brunswick, New Jersey.

90. Masse, L., et al. (1976). "Trends in mortality from cirrhosis of the liver: 1950–1971." *World Health Statistics,* Report 29, 40–67.

91. Glassner, B., and Berg, B. (1980). "How Jews avoid alcohol problems." *American Sociological Reviews,* 45, 647–64.

92. Perkins, H. W. (1987). "Parental religion and alcoholic problems as intergenerational prediction of problem drinking among college youth." *J Scientific Study Religion,* 26(3), 340–57.

15

General Conclusions

In this book, we have been concerned with what religion does for or to people, how it shapes their decisions and their lives, and in particular how it solves problems and dilemmas relating to everyday life. We have not been concerned with issues that rightly belong to philosophy or theology; questions about whether religions are good or bad, right or wrong, means of salvation or delusions for the woolly minded. We have not entered the arena of science versus religion, nor taken any stand on the question of which religion is best. In the traditions of sociology and anthropology, we have noted the existence of religions and religious practices, and we have tried to explain them in terms of human needs.

Human needs are themselves subject to much academic debate. What exactly are our needs? Most would agree on what Malinowski[1] called our "basic" needs—for warmth, food, sex, and so on. But there remains a further set of needs, the so-called derived needs, that can be equally pressing, such as the need for a higher standard of living, leading eventually to a felt need for items that can best be called luxuries. Religions cater to needs at all levels, but perhaps mostly at the more basic level. However, as our book has shown, the concept of needs, while essential to our analysis, is not sufficient to explain what religions appear to be doing in the world. What is missed in relating religions to needs is the environment, which has two dimensions, one physical and the other social.

On the physical side, human needs are directly related to the richness or poverty of the land on which people live, on the availability of the resources of food to ordinary people, on the climate and the level of rainfall. We have all seen films of people living in drought conditions in Africa, barely alive. For such people, their needs are terribly urgent. More normally, people in poor habitats have to work hard to provide themselves with food for the whole year, and the question of providing food is at the center of their interests and their rituals. In such conditions, high rates of mortality prevail, and so we find an expressed need for children, a dislike of childlessness, and religious rituals aimed at increasing fertility. We have seen in the previous pages how strongly religions can emphasize fertility and large family size in poor countries. The secular reason is that to be a parent of many children is to be rich, to have social support and material support in later years. To be without children is a sad fate in much of the Third World. It is only in affluent Westernized societies that we find a reduction in the stress laid by religions on the need for married couples to have children. Protestant Christianity is extremely unusual in lacking any emphasis in the marriage ceremony on fertility, emphasizing the relationship between the husband and wife, and regarding a childless marriage as a full and complete entity. In much of the world such a marriage can be dissolved by the husband, who will seek a fertile wife.

There is a second set of needs that concern our relationships with other people. Children need the support of loving parents. In most societies, kin are dependent on each other in numerous ways. At times of death and mourning we need the support of friends and relatives. At times of crisis we all need others. Religions have a vital role in all parts of the world in relation to social needs.

Skeptics may argue that religions are in fact self-interested, rather than interested in the lives and feelings of ordinary people. One line of argument runs as follows: Religions are like firms; in that they compete with each other. That is why they take an interest in births, marriages, and deaths—because they want to ensure recruitment and continuity. Just as ordinary commercial firms argue that their products are superior, give better value, than rival products, so religions argue that their particular concepts of goodness and salvation and their particular rituals are best. This is a view that has a certain element of truth in it, but it misses a lot. Primarily, it looks at what religions are doing from the sociological and economic end of things, and consequently it ignores the view from below, from the point of view of the individual.

As far as individuals are concerned, religion is something inherited from parents or acquired from friends or teachers. It offers ways of thinking about life, and rituals in which the thinking is embedded. Take for instance the phenomenon of baptism. Baptism is a ceremony or ritual, taking different forms in different sects of the Christian church, by which a baby (or in some sects an adult) becomes incorporated into the faith, becomes a Christian. Without such a ceremony the child is not considered a member of the faith and is not eligible for salvation. So important was baptism in eighteenth-century Catholicism that a special baptismal syringe was devised to baptize an unborn child, while still in its mother's womb, in cases where the mother was dying in childbirth (see fig. 15.1).

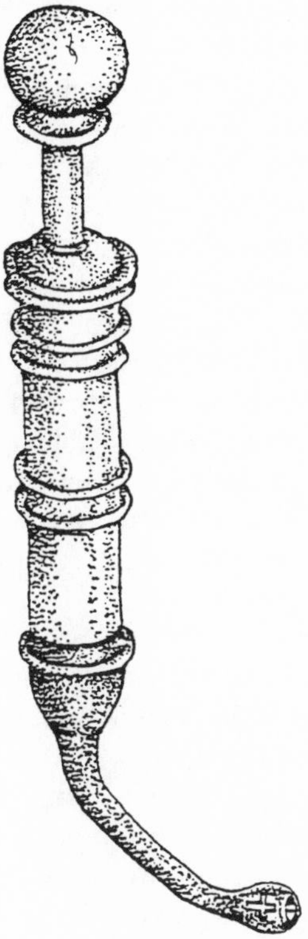

15.1 Baptismal syringe for use on children dying in the womb.

Nothing could illustrate the importance of religion better than the baptismal syringe. The baby is going to die as well as its mother, but it must not die unbaptized, because its soul must be made eligible for salvation.

Normally, of course, baptism is a happy event, and not only is a soul prepared for enlightenment but a person is brought into the church. From the point of view of the parents, this involves a commitment to bring up the child in the ways of the faith as best they can. But the event also marks the entry of the child into the local religious community, a group of like-minded people who can act as a social support mechanism in times of need and provide a source of friendship and comfort. The infant, without knowing it, joins a group who will help if called on and will also monitor his or her behavior in ways that may prove upsetting and embarrassing at times in the future. The network of relationships established by joining a religious community has a negative as well as a positive side, and this can lead to its rejection in later years, a common enough phenomenon in Western societies. In more traditional societies, participation in the religious rituals of the society is an ordinary part of life for everyone, and rejection does not exist as a possibility.

We have looked at the involvement of religions in the human life cycle in the pages of this book and there is no need to repeat what was said earlier. Here we seek for generalities about the involvement. Other species manage without religions, yet they pass from birth to death easily enough. What is it about humans that brings religion into the events of life? Primarily, it seems, humans have a need to endow their life events with meaning. This issue has been discussed at length by one of the authors in an earlier work.[2] Meaning, in this sense, is the significance of our actions in the social settings of everyday life. It is the difference between folding your hands in the course of after-dinner conversation and folding your hands in church. Meaning is present in all the things we do. Without it, we would not be able to interact socially. Even basic actions, such as eating, dancing, or singing, have social meaning—they take place in particular settings, to which particular rules apply, and are understood by others in socially conventional ways. For example, we do not take food from someone else's plate without asking, even if we are hungry and he or she is not. We do not burst into song on the bus. And there are closely prescribed places and times for dancing, as well as ways of doing it acceptably, which can in some settings and at certain times in history be very formal indeed.

Religions provide some of the background ideas and rituals that help to fill the lives of those who are religious with meaning. In a traditional society such as that of a group of Australian Aborigines, people are wholly enmeshed in a religious view of the environment. There are spirits in particular places, and in animals, that affect how one moves around and exploits the surrounding landscape. In our own society religions have become optional but have the same functions nonetheless. The difference is that there are secular alternatives. Rationalists can reject religion and then seek meaning in terms of global consciousness, or animal rights, and this may lead them to give up eating tuna, or meat of all kinds, just as an Aborigine will not eat the meat of a red kangaroo if that is his or her spirit animal.

Our book has looked primarily at the passage of human life rather than the physical environment as such. The passage of life is not something that occurs in isolation. Just as ecology is the study of the physical environment, so socioecology is the study of the social environment and the physical environment together, and how individuals interact with them. The meanings of human life are strongest in the social domain. Every relationship, in every human society, has its particular significance for the people concerned. Being a brother, or a father, or a niece has a different meaning in that it means different things and implies different relationships in different societies. For example, in Karnataka, a state in south central India, Hindu uncles even today regard their nieces as preferred marriage partners. In patrilineal societies in many parts of the world, both the biological father and his brother are called "father" by the child and have the same rights and duties toward him or her. These relationships, however defined, become from time to time during life the foci of particular events. If the Hindu uncle decides to take his niece to be his wife, then at the marriage ceremony a very complex set of religious rituals, expressing religious meanings are enacted. These have the effect of validating and legitimating the marriage, which is thenceforth not a mere living together of a man and a woman but an indissoluble bond that gives the man, the woman, and the offspring of the union a clear set of places in society and, most importantly, explains to them who they now are and what they must henceforth do if they are to continue to be fully integrated members of society.

Those certainties are largely lost to the individuals who make their own way through life in modern societies. For them (and many would have it no other way) everything is to be decided from first principles. The difficulty they encounter is what Sartre called *angoisse*—a poignant uncertainty that they are doing, or have done, the right thing. Of course, for Sartre, a committed atheist, *angoisse* is a necessary part of being a modern, thinking human being. Indeed, for Sartre, the only valid morality is that which comes from rational, considered thought. The difficulties of life must be faced up to and there is no escape through religion. Should a man, he asks, join the army and go to war for his country or stay at home and look after his ailing, possibly dying mother? The decision must be made by weighing up the consequences of each line of action. There is no question of asking a priest for guidance or seeking the solution in prayer. All ways of opting out of making a personal choice by having recourse to external agencies, be they supernatural, other people, or general principles, are excluded. The man must decide on his own.

This counsel is at the opposite end of the spectrum from that which a religious person would give. The more devout and committed the religious person, the more he or she will be inclined to counsel recourse to either ritual or prayer or both. Hindus, caught on the rack of unemployment in a country without state benefits, give what little they have for offerings to the temple gods in the belief that this will enhance their employment opportunities. Childless Hindu women pray before the lingam stone in their local temple for the gift of a child. Moslems seek help from Allah five times a day with their current problems and decisions. Christians and Jews take their problems to their God.

Again, for the atheist who wants to decide matters for himself or herself, there is no question of having children baptized. That would be to capitulate to the church, to enter the community of those who put their faith in God, to set one's offspring off in life in that particular direction, reducing their autonomy, putting them at the mercy not so much of supernatural powers as of those who believe in supernatural powers. Many parents who were themselves brought up in a religious setting in the West and who have since become disenchanted and lost their faith do not baptize their children, in order to save them from the suffering they themselves have had to endure and which they now regard as wholly unnecessary.

The price of autonomy is a loss of a sense of community, of shared understandings and access to a set of comforting meanings in times of trouble. When it is argued that religions give false answers to problems, and therefore a rational approach is better, we should not overlook that for many people, including those of the highest intelligence, there come times of personal crisis in which any beliefs or answers are better than none. When a spouse or a child dies suddenly, unexpectedly, the human psyche is put under immense strain and recovery or even survival can depend on making sense of the events concerned. Religions are tailor-made to provide the sense that we seek at such times. Rejecting religion means that recovery has to be achieved by recourse to rationality, but rationality has nothing to say about such things, and recovery can thus be very difficult indeed.

It is thus in their ability to deal with life and death events that religions find their true place in the scheme of human meanings. They bring with them the weight of tradition, a sense of certainty. In traditional societies there are no alternatives to the religious ways of doing things. Whereas in the West we have both religious and secular weddings, there is only one kind of wedding in traditional societies, though it may vary from a very simple ceremony to a very elaborate one depending on the social status of those involved. Whereas we in the West find our way through the trials and tribulations of adolescence as best we can, Masai boys have special rituals and undergo special tests to prove their manhood, girls are inducted into the mysteries of sex by the older women, and after the ceremonials are over they can legitimately live together, conceive a child, and marry. This is not a version of the romantic fallacy. We are not claiming, as Margaret Mead for example wrongly claimed, that adolescence can be an uncomplicated time in other societies. That would not be true anywhere. Life among the Masai is as difficult in its ways as life in the West. But the difficulties do not include the problem of whether a person is a child or an adult. Masai society has a ritualized way of making that clear to the young people themselves and to the rest of society.

That, as we see it, is what religions are all about. They are about defining who we are and what we can and cannot, should and should not, do in the range of situations life presents us and those we live among as we pass from the cradle to the grave. Why then are we in the West not more religious than we are? Why have we lost this most useful way of dealing with life and its problems? That would be the subject of a different book and is a topic about which much has been said and written already. The rise of science, the rise of individualism, the success of technology, the ever increasing commercialism and industrialization of our societies, the failure of church leaders and ministers to modernize their ideas, the poverty of the church itself, all have contributed to a decline in the status of the church and its leaders in the West. In other parts of the world this has not happened. Islam is gaining strength in many of the poorer countries of the modern world, often by rejection of the West and its values, which have not brought prosperity to those countries or their people. Hinduism, Buddhism, and Judaism remain strong though less expansionist than Islam. There are millions upon millions of people in the modern world who, though economically poor by Western standards, have none of the problems of self-identity we have, do not wonder how to manage the social aspect of their lives, and never ever experience the pangs of loneliness. Even in Calcutta, the poorest of cities, there are qualities of people's lives we in the West can envy.

Because Westernized man is just as much in need of mental, social, and physical homeostasis as his less affluent Eastern and Southern counterparts, we can expect, and indeed find, him developing new and alternative ways of dealing with the problems of ontological being. Drawing from religious movements that have reached the West in the form of books and lectures we find in our cities today small groups of proponents of almost every faith ever known, from Zen mysticism to veganism, to Christian fundamentalism, to asceticism, to communalism with or without free love. What happens in New Jersey, detailed by McGuire,[3] happens in some form or other in all big cities. People have come together in small groups in the modern industrialized world to provide mutual support for one another; to listen to each other's stories; to comfort each other in bereavement and other crises such as loss of job, divorce, or an illness of someone they love; to help each other with their problems; to empathize; and to try to build up from a level of shared experiences to a level of trust and mutual confidence. Here we see the very beginnings of new, somewhat spiritual, and potentially religious awakenings. These people, often college educated and in professional occupations, feel that rational, science-based culture has let them down, and they have discovered this at times of emotional crisis, when to their surprise they were unable to cope with the situation that developed around them. Often, a chance meeting or conversation triggered the move into a more spiritual direction. In some cases the results are dramatic—a return of mental tranquillity and a new ability to face life. We know from studies of what have been called "cults" that such conversions can at times lead to deleterious or even disastrous results when individuals become too bonded to charismatic leaders, such as Reverend Moon in the United States or Reverend Jones in Guyana, who could be said to exploit them. But this does not have to happen. More often, it seems, such groups are viable and develop a quiet and respectable life of their own, failing to produce scandals or hit the headlines in any way. These are the little grass-roots beginnings that can develop, given particular circumstances, into sects and even religions. Such developments, should they occur, tend to take the form of a structuring up of the group as numbers expand, followed by the formation of a hierarchy of controlling individuals, a set of rules for members, and attempts to define the group in opposition to other such groups by particular stress on its unique beliefs or activities rather than those it shares with other such groups. Fringe healing groups have, at the outset, no priesthoods, no institutionalized forms of worship, and no canonical literature, but these are the directions in which they must move if they are to resist fragmentation as numbers of converts grow or converts are drawn from a wider social class background and other ethnic groups. Thus religious communities develop. We can expect to see the development of such groups in the next century in the West, using the ideas of the Eastern and even African religions as much as those of Christianity. Eventually one or more major new faiths could arise, perhaps combining personal fulfillment and emotional strength with an ecological and global consciousness.

In the meantime, in the rest of the world, religions are jostling for supremacy here and there, and elsewhere the older faiths reign supreme. It is only when one travels that one realizes how alive religion is in many parts of the world—Catholicism in South America, Buddhism and Shinto in Japan, Hinduism in India, Christianity of all kinds in Africa. Atheism and agnosticism as we know them are not common on a global scale, and it would be ethnocentric of us to think they were the phenomena of the future, that religions were doomed to disappear as Western values came to predominate. The West itself may have things to learn in the coming century.

Notes

1. Malinowski, B. (1944). The scientific theory of culture. Oxford University Press, Oxford.

2. Reynolds, V. (1980). The Biology of human action. Freeman, Reading.

3. McGuire, R. B. (1988). Ritual healing in suburban American, Rutgers University Press, New Brunswick, New Jersey

INDEX

THE TRIUMPH OF EVOLUTION

Niles Eldredge

THE TRIUMPH OF EVOLUTION AND THE FAILURE OF CREATIONISM

A PETER N. NEVRAUMONT BOOK

A W. H. Freeman / Owl Book

HENRY HOLT AND COMPANY NEW YORK

Henry Holt and Company, LLC
Publishers since 1866
115 West 18th Street
New York, New York 10011

Henry Holt® is a registered trademark
of Henry Holt and Company, LLC.

Portions of this text have been previously published in the author's
The Monkey Business: A Scientist Looks at Creationism (Washington Square Press).

Library of Congress Cataloging-in-Publication Data

Eldredge, Niles.
The triumph of evolution: and the failure of creationism / Niles Eldredge
p. cm.
Includes index.
ISBN 0-8050-7147-4 (pbk.)
1. Human evolution. 2. Creationism. I. Title.

GN281.4.E45 2000
599.93'8—dc21 99-058515

Henry Holt books are available for special promotions and
premiums. For details contact: Director, Special Markets.

First published in hardcover in 2000 as
A Peter N. Nevraumont Book by Nevraumont Publishing Company, Inc.

First Owl Books Edition 2001

A W. H. Freeman / Owl Book

Designed by Tsang Seymour Design, Inc.
New York, New York

Printed in the United States of America

10 9 8 7 6 5 4 3 2 1

Dedicated to the inspired and unflagging efforts of Eugenie Scott and her entire staff at the National Center for Science Education—frontline defenders of quality science education in America.

CONTENTS

In the Beginning
Religion, Science, . . . and Politics

That the United States and the rest of the modern world are fundamentally a secular, technologically based society (albeit one generally committed to the free and unfettered practice of religion) is nicely brought out by the Y2K doomsday myth so widely adopted as we approached the recent millennial date: January 1, 2000. The dark scenario of widespread shortages and other societal malfunctions born of computer glitches, after all, was universally seen as delivered not by a vengeful, wrathful God, but rather by us humans.

Early programmers had assumed (if they thought about it all) that their shorthand, two-digit system of keeping track of yearly dates would long since have changed by the year 2000. In sharp contrast, previous millennial myths saw doom and destruction as God's payback for our sins—still our fault, of course, but with punishment meted out by God, not by errant machines. Likewise, we thanked the techno-fixers—not a merciful God—that the worst of the Y2K problem was handily cut off at the pass. That we were able to blame computer programmers, and not God, for what seemed to so many as impending doom and still manage to concoct a millennial scenario of darkest catastrophe just as all our forebears crossing the previous millennial divide did, shows us how far we have—and haven't—come.

But if the doomsday scenario this time was completely secularized, nonetheless the advent of the Millennium has intensified contact between science and religion—much of it in the spirit of conciliation, though some of it with continued mistrust and hostility. Currently more than several hundred college courses specifically address "science and religion." The Templeton Foundation annually awards a sum in excess of that carried by a Nobel Prize in recognition of the furtherance of closer ties between science and religion. In 1999, for example, the award was $1.24 million compared to the more modest $978,000 handed out by the Nobel Committee in 1998 (though in fairness it must be said that there is only one Templeton Prize, whereas there are several Nobel Prizes). Numerous colloquia on science and religion have been held—some sponsored by religious institutions, such as the Vatican, and some by decidedly secular institutions, such as the American Association for the Advancement of Science. Television shows and, of course, many books and articles have been in full cry as well.

I see several distinct ways in which science and religion are variously engaged either in potentially fruitful dialogue, or at daggers drawn or simply as ships passing in the night. The latter relationship is simply stated: in most nations—technologically advanced or impoverished, agrarian Third World alike—there is little day-to-day contact between the realms of science and religion. That is as true of the United States as it is of most of the nations of Europe, South America, Asia, and Africa. In countries where forms of Christianity predominate, for example, the overwhelming mainstream has, for well over a century, viewed the relation of science and religion as essentially neutral: each constitutes an important sector of society, but each does a vastly different job.

From this perspective, the role of religion is spiritual, moral, and social. Science, on the other hand, is there to discover the workings of the universe—and to lead to technological advance. This is why so many scientists (such as my friend and colleague, paleontologist Stephen Jay Gould) advocate a polite going of separate ways—a sort of benign acknowledgment that each exists, but can and should have little to do with one another. That is the general stance that I myself have adopted in my earlier works on creationism in American society—a sort of "rendering unto Caesar" division of labor that would minimize conflict but at the same time not look for any particular close resonance between the two domains.

But others insist that there is either resonance—or inherent conflict—between the domains of science and religion. I believe my colleague Margaret Wertheim[I] is right when she says that, in Western culture, historically speaking, the supposed warfare between science and religion has been greatly exaggerated. Indeed, most of the formative figures in the emergence of modern science were deeply religious and thought (as Wertheim has observed) that they were discovering the "mind of God" every bit as much as some modern physicists appear to think they are. Yet it is undoubtedly true that with the Darwinian revolution of the mid-nineteenth century—with the certain knowledge gained by some newer branches of science that the Earth is very old, has had a very long history (and especially that life on Earth is almost as old), and has had a history of change—has collided very deeply with conservatively held traditional religious beliefs in Judeo-Christian circles.

There are, indeed, many people who believe literally that the notion of biological evolution is the work of the devil.[2] As detailed here, I have spent over twenty years talking with, debating, and reading the literature of creationists—roughly, people who believe that God created the heavens and Earth, and all living things according to accounts in Genesis. I remain convinced that their unrelenting hatred of the very idea of evolution stems from their concept of morality: where morals come from, and why people behave in a moral fashion (when they do). The argument is simple: the Bible says that "mankind" was created in God's image. If that is not true, if instead we are descended from the apes, then there is no reason whatsoever to expect humans to behave in a godlike, moral fashion. We would, instead, be expected to behave like "animals." The conviction is deeply held.

Thus, in some quarters, it is simply not possible to assign to science the task of cosmology while giving religion the role of articulating a moral and spiritual understanding of what it means to be a living human. It is not possible because the two are seen as inseparable: morality flows automatically and solely from the manner in which humans were "created" in the first place. From this perspective, religion (meaning, specifically, certain forms of religion—especially conservative Christianity, but also conservative strains of Islam and Judaism[3]) are fundamentally at odds with at least some forms of the scientific enterprise.

In the United States especially, creationism is associated not only most closely with aspects of Christian Fundamentalism, but with conservative (mostly, if not exclusively, conservative Republican) politics. And though I document this charge fully in later chapters of this narrative, I cannot emphasize enough at the outset that politics is the very essence of this conflict. It is the belief that evolution is inherently evil—a belief that stems from religious interpretation, *and therefore poses a threat to the hearts and minds of the populace,* that, I am convinced, motivates the vast majority of the creationists. Thus the issue is about what is to be taught in the public schools, and the arena in which the battle takes place goes far beyond local school board meetings and classroom confrontations: it includes bills passed by state legislatures and opinions handed down by the Supreme Court of the United States. It includes judgments passed by statewide school boards, such as the decision to downgrade the teaching of evolution in the statewide syllabus in Kansas late in the summer of 1999—a mandate issued after the first text of this narrative had already been written. On the face of it, then, creationism is a political issue—and has been at least since Clarence Darrow defended John Scopes against the prosecutorial zeal of William Jennings Bryan in Dayton, Tennessee, on July 10–21, 1925.

Are there creationists who are religiously motivated but are not at the same time social and political conservatives? There must be, but in twenty years I have yet to encounter a single such person. Are there creationists, politically conservative or not, whose main concern does lie in the apparent moral implications of evolution and what it means especially to their own personal lives—whose main goal is not to influence what other people's kids are taught in school? Again, probably so. But the vast majority of active creationists do not restrict their activities to preaching to the converted, though they do plenty of that as well. They are motivated primarily to see that evolution is not taught in the public schools of the United States.

In any case, what creationism is *not* is a valid intellectual argument between opposing points of view. That battle was fought—with evolution emerging triumphant—in the latter half of the nineteenth century. Some twenty years ago, it was fashionable for creationists to claim that their views are not a religious, but rather a legitimate *scientific,* body of "knowledge." I will be taking a long hard look at the central claims of this so-called scientific creationism—the wolf in sheep's clothing concocted in the 1970s that deliberately removed religious rhetoric from the cant of creationism—a move calculated to bypass any objections based on the First Amendment to teach such patently religiously inspired material in a public school science class. No one was fooled. The best comment I have ever heard anyone make about scientific creationism came from Judge William Overton, who presided over the famed Arkansas trial in 1981: If this stuff is science, why do we need a law to teach it? The law in question was Arkansas's then recently passed "equal time" bill mandating that two competing versions of science ("evolution science" and "creation science") were equally valid, both deserving time and attention in the curriculum. Framed as an intellectually valid debate between supposedly opposing legitimate sets of scientific claims, instead scientific creationism was a shallow ploy. Intellectually, the debate has been dead since 1859—and evolution was triumphant!

Yet the debate rages on, and though tactics have changed, and once again creationists have become more open in acknowledging their religious motivations (often preferring now to claim that the idea of biological evolution is really a form of religious belief, rather than scientific theory), nonetheless the same old arguments *against* the validity of evolution as a scientific concept are still being trotted out. And thus, once more unto the breach, it becomes necessary to defend the integrity of evolution as a well-established body of knowledge and theory in science—intellectually triumphant not only within biology, or science generally, but within the intellectual framework of Western culture generally.

The newest, and by far most successful, voice in the creationist firmament belongs to Phillip Johnson, Boalt Professor of Law at the University of California, Berkeley. As we shall see in some detail (especially in Chapters 5 and 6), Johnson claims to have introduced something new into the debate: his conclusion that science in general, and evolutionary biology perhaps in particular, is rooted in what he calls philosophical naturalism, meaning that scientists think that the material world—matter and energy—is all that exists, and that an explanation for all natural phenomena necessarily entails only, well, natural phenomena. In other words, Johnson says that science is intrinsically and inherently atheistic. What, he says, if God really does exist, moreover the kind of proactive God in whom Johnson himself professes belief—one who is involved with details of everyone's daily life? Shouldn't the scientific enterprise be concerned that, given that possibility, the explanation of natural phenomena in terms of cause and effect that is the daily stuff of science might be hopelessly misguided if a divine agency outside the system were really pulling all the strings? Johnson finds it absurd that science could afford to ignore so cavalierly what might possibly be the real mover and shaker behind absolutely everything that happens.

Johnson turns a deaf ear to the obvious rejoinder: science is a human enterprise devised to experience in systematic ways the material universe. Everyone (including Johnson) agrees that a physical universe exists (actually, some people, though none of them creationists, have expressed doubt over even this proposition). We humans can directly experience that material world only through our senses, and *there is no way we can directly experience the supernatural.* Thus, in the enterprise that is science, it isn't an ontological claim that a God such as Johnson envisages does not exist, but rather an epistemological recognition that even if such a God did exist, there would be no way to experience that God given the impressive, but still limited, means afforded by science. And that is true by definition.

Johnson has a string of admirers drawn from academe, including philosophers and various scientists—among the latter, biochemist Michael Behe. I have met several of them and have "debated" both Johnson and Behe on college campuses (albeit only one time each). As I will recount in later chapters, beyond Johnson's charge of "philosophical naturalism" there is literally nothing new in their antievolutionary rhetoric. Their central thesis—that there are phenomena in the natural world of such great complexity that they simply cannot be explained by recourse to known natural processes—is exactly the same argument that was thrown at Darwin by the cleric St. George Jackson Mivart (1827–1900), one of the first and most ferocious critics of Darwin's *On the Origin of Species.* Mivart asserted that the human eye is simply too complex a structure to have evolved gradually and piecemeal, and therefore must instead be the intricate handiwork of a Creator.

Johnson, along with conservative members of Congress (such as House Republican Whip Tom DeLay) assert we are in the midst of a "culture war." Given the ethnic and cultural diversity that is the United States, given the highly secularized flavor of our big and blowsy society as epitomized by our attribution of Y2K doom at the Millennium to humans and *not to a vengeful God,* this proclaimed culture war is unilaterally declared by some segments of conservative Christian society in the population. But they are powerful, and they are continuing to have major impact. And that is why I feel I must once again pick up the cudgels to rail against these creationists—odd as it may seem, given that they have nothing new to say, and given that all the important issues as *intellectual issues per se* were resolved fully in the nineteenth century.

I take up this task because I am convinced that the integrity of science education in the United States and abroad is directly threatened by such nonsense. The issue is *not* whether any one particular student *believes* in evolution. But, as I develop throughout this book, it very much does matter that soon-to-be-adults living (and voting) in a technologically driven world know something about the ways their fellow humans gather knowledge about the natural world. Kids, in other words, need to be taught what science is all about—and that includes being exposed to the grandest conclusions of science. Not only do we need to continue to produce homegrown scientists, but also we need in this secular age to produce new generations of citizens who are conversant with science enough to make intelligent decisions in the polling place. Pretending to young minds that we cannot tell the difference between good science and bad, between the real and the bogus, not only sends a horribly distorted message about the very nature of science, but also makes evident to most students that adults don't care much about the truth. I write this book because those who see a necessary conflict between science and religion—and a "culture war" over the hearts and minds of the American populace—are doing their best to destroy quality science teaching in the United States.

There are still other ways in which science and religion commingle in modern American life—ways that see at least potential common ground, rather than inherent conflict, or simply benign nonintersection. In a major aspect of this common-ground approach, we are treated to visions of physicists contemplating the mind of God, and some theologians looking for God in scientific data. I once read an account of a meeting in which the consensus was reported to be that if the rate of expansion of the universe is greater than the escape velocity of stars fleeing the center of the universe from the Big Bang, then the universe is a singularity, literally a once-in-all-time phenomenon—as such casting doubt on the existence of God; if, instead, expansion rate is lower than escape velocity, expansion will slow down and the universe will eventually collapse back in on itself and, presumably, burst forth again, perhaps in an endless series of big bangs and implosions. This scenario suggested to the assembled scientists and theologians that perhaps a supernatural being lay behind the universe after all. When meant, as most of them are, in the spirit of ecumenicism, such exercises can do little harm, but I seriously wonder if they will ever shed much light on the nature either of God or of the universe.

Then there is the fact that many Western scientists, despite the common preconception, are themselves religious. In addition, many ordained clergy are also Ph.D.-holding, practicing scientists. Together these facts show that, to many, there is far from an intrinsic barricade between science and religion, though most religious scientists, no doubt, compartmentalize their workaday experiences from their religious beliefs and practices. Once again, whatever the nature of positive interactions in the personal lives of scientists or of the content of their professions and their religious beliefs, I see as yet no sign of any lasting benefit to either science or religion—except for the happy knowledge that the two can coexist within a single human breast.

I have held out what I take to be the best for last. For though I write this book determined to fight off the grimmer, darker messages attacking science in the name of religion, I really do see an as yet undervalued, as yet largely unexamined arena where lies, I think, some real hope for resonance between science and religion—and by "religion" I mean absolutely all religions that have ever existed of which we have any knowledge at all.

Creationism is just one of the two important social issues that have intersected my life as an evolutionary biologist. The other one is the horrendous loss of species—an event now gripping the planet that some have called the Sixth Extinction. Human beings are laying waste the world's ecosystems, and in so doing driving something like thirty thousand species of microbes, fungi, plants, and animals extinct every year. That's by far the fastest rate of ecosystem destruction and species loss since the time when the dinosaurs and so many other kinds of life were abruptly erased 65 million years ago—the result of a collision between Earth and extraterrestrial objects, and huge volcanic eruptions as well.

I have explored the question, How have humans entered the extinction business? In a series of three books, several articles, and a major exhibition at the American Museum of Natural History. I have proposed that culture became more important than traditional biological adaptations in the way ancestral humans approached the general problem of making a living. But the real change came when humans invented agriculture—and instantly became the first species in the entire 3.8-billion-year history of life to stop living inside local ecosystems. Among many other consequences, this move, clever as it was, took the normal controls off our population size, and we have skyrocketed from some 6 million people ten thousand years ago at the dawn of agriculture, to over 6 billion now. And that is the problem: 6 billion people, vying for unequally distributed wealth, are wreaking ecological havoc all over Earth.

And I have learned something more: people's concept of the gods or God change over time as well. And when examined in detail, concepts of God seem to dovetail remarkably well with my Western analysis of the relation of a given people to the natural world. I have come to see that religious traditions in general—and concepts of God in particular—reveal a lot about how people see themselves, and how they see themselves fitting into the natural world. It turns out that, naturally enough, people do tend to have a pretty clear idea of who they are and how they fit into the natural world in a functional sense (it's just their stories of how they got that way that tend to be fanciful!).

Thus a history of concepts of God should yield a pretty interesting human ecological history. And it suggests something more: if it is indeed the case, as I firmly believe it is, that this mounting loss of species and the accompanying topsoil loss and lack of adequate supplies of fresh water constitute some of the direst threats facing humanity right now, practitioners of the world's religions, many of whom are already aware of the environmental threats to their own lands, can potentially stand as the greatest source of good for the planet. Here, then, is a true millennial issue: a set of environmental problems besetting humanity at the year 2000, but a problem in which science and religion, instead of acting as enemies, stand a good chance of working together within the larger body politic to effect some truly positive measures. And though I plan to explore this positive side of the interaction between science and religion in book length form elsewhere, I cannot resist ending this present anticreationist tract with a preliminary exploration of these themes, which I do in the final chapter.

So far, I've talked about other people's views, and though I've made it clear that I am an evolutionary biologist not about to buy the possibility that people didn't evolve but rather were created by God sometime within the last ten thousand years, I have not revealed my own religious position. Here it is: I am a "lapsed Baptist." Along with many others, I see myself as an agnostic because "atheist" is too definitive, implying one can know something that is in principle unknowable. I will say that I am extremely skeptical that the kind of all-knowing, all-caring, all-doing God pictured in some circles exists. On the other hand, I think that concepts of God—*all* concepts of God—are about something, and of course I am not about to quarrel with anyone's personal interpretation of any one of those particular concepts of God. At the end of Chapter 7, I'll have more to say on this.

I confess also that I have personal reasons to become involved in the fight against creationism. One day in August of 1979, I received a phone call from a member of the Iowa Education Department. He wanted to know if I really had said that I thought that it would be a good idea to teach creationism alongside of evolution in high school classrooms.

I was appalled. I told him I had never said any such thing, and he replied that, in a typescript of an interview conducted by one Luther Sunderland with me in my office at the American Museum of Natural History, I was quoted as saying precisely that. Sunderland, an engineer by trade, had come to my office, representing himself as a "consultant" (how official that title was I never learned) to the New York State Board of Regents as they were conducting a curriculum review. He was really a lobbyist for creationism—and by all odds the most clever and successful creationist spokesman in the eastern United States in the late 1970s and early 1980s. Sunderland had sent me the typescript of our recorded conversation—with the invitation to change anything I felt was inaccurate or simply didn't like. The problem was, he left immediately for Iowa and introduced the uncorrected transcript into a legislative study session before I had received my copy and had a chance to edit it. The damage was done, and I felt humiliated as I listened to the Iowa official gently tell me that, however earnestly honest scientists try to be, they have to be aware of the political fallout of their remarks.

I was furious, of course, for letting Sunderland dupe me.[4] But it was a valuable learning experience: I learned right then that *the entire issue of creationism* (then largely masquerading as scientific creationism) *is purely a political battle*—for the hearts and minds of the nation's youth. I also learned that all was considered fair in the creationist wars. Determined to even the score, I wrote a piece for the journal *The New Republic* ("Creationism Isn't Science") in 1981—a brief salvo that caught the eye of a prescient young editor who invited me to expand it into book format. The result was *The Monkey Business* (1982), the forerunner to this book, written to set the record straight, and to provide ammunition to the hands of the nation's beleaguered high school biology teachers and their students—and for anyone else who might want a road map to help them navigate through creationist rhetoric—and what to say in reply.

In short, scientists cannot afford to shy away when broad social issues intersect their professional lives. I truly wish this updated and expanded version of my earlier consideration of creationism were not necessary. We simply have other, better things to do: more interesting things to think about in evolutionary biology and ecology, as well as pressing problems brought on by the calamitous decline of ecosystems and loss of species all around us to solve. But creationism *is* here, so we must fight! Evolution is triumphant in the intellectual realm, but it is still under siege in the political arena of the United States at the Millennium.

Telling the Difference
Science as a Way of Knowing

A favorite ploy of creationists as they argue to inject their particular brand of religion into the classroom is that, when you get right down to it, science and religion are alternative belief systems, and to be fair we should just get up in front of the kids, dispassionately recount both versions, and let the kids decide which version of events appeals to them more. They want us to tell our children that there is no way to distinguish between accounts of the origin and history of the universe, of the Earth, and of life derived from religious tradition as recounted in the Bible, on the one hand, and the latest thinking on these subjects in science, on the other. Insisting that there is no intrinsic difference between scientific and other forms of explanation—calling both, instead, alternative belief systems—cuts to the very heart of the creationist threat to educational integrity: if we tell kids there is no difference, they don't stand much of a chance of grasping the rudiments of science and how it is done.

Testability lies at the very heart of the scientific enterprise: if we make a statement about how things are—for instance, how the Earth originated, and how all the world's living species have come into being—we must be able to make *predictions* about what we logically should observe in the material world if that statement is true. Repeated failure to confirm predicted observations means we have to abandon an idea—no matter how fondly we cherish it, or how earnestly we may wish to believe it is true.

The history of science is littered with discarded ideas—notions of how things are that were simply not borne out by continued investigation. Science is far from being a belief system, for in science no idea is sacred. No statement is the ultimate truth. It is in the very nature of things that precious few ideas put forth to date in science have entirely withstood the test of time. Biological evolution is one of those ideas. So is the idea that the Earth is round.

Facts and Theories: Is the Earth Really Round?

When Ronald Reagan injected creationism into the 1980 presidential campaign, he took a familiar route. Referring to evolution, he told reporters (after speaking to a group of fundamentalist clergy in Dallas, Texas), "Well, it is a theory, a scientific theory only, and it has in recent years been challenged in the world of science and is not yet believed in the scientific community to be as infallible as it once was believed."[1]

Beyond the fascinating commingling of politics, religion, and science, Reagan's remark picked up a standard creationist ploy when he said that evolution "is a theory, a scientific theory only." It is true that most of us in normal, daily life use the word "theory" to mean a tentative, sketchy notion about why or how something happened. All of us, for instance, have our own "theories" on why a band of southern Republicans in the House of Representatives fought so hard to oust Bill Clinton as President of the United States, or why the United States has been fighting in the Balkans—or why so many suburbanites love to drive SUVs. This is standard usage.

But creationists, including some who claim bona fide scientific credentials, have exploited the vernacular connotation of the word "theory," in effect saying that scientists use this word in precisely the same colloquial way. Thus, if evolution is "only a theory," our confidence in it ought to be less than if it were, say, a fact. Theories turn into "harebrained ideas" with ease. "Theory" is a bad word: to call an idea a theory is to impugn its credibility.[2]

Yes, theories in science are ideas: a theory may be a single, simple idea or, more usually, a complex set of ideas, as, for example, the Alvarez hypothesis invoking extraterrestrial impacts to explain the mass extinction of dinosaurs and a myridad of other organisms event at the end of the Cretaceous Period some 65 million years ago. There is no hard-and-fast way of telling a hypothesis apart from a theory; like lakes and ponds, and rivers and streams, theories and hypotheses differ in some vague way only by their size. Theories are generally grander, more encompassing than more narrowly focused hypotheses. But I have seen some mighty big ponds and some rather small lakes in my time.

Some theories are good and have withstood the test of time well. The idea that all organisms, past and present, are interrelated by a process of ancestry and descent—evolution—is such a theory. On the other hand, some theories have stood the test of time poorly and are no longer credited with much explanatory power. Spontaneous generation—the idea that organisms sprang from inorganic beginnings de novo, and are not all interrelated—has long been discarded as a useful scientific notion. It is taught in schools today, if at all, only as a historical curiosity.

Philosophers of science have argued long and hard over the differences among facts, hypotheses, and theories. But the real point is this: they are all essentially the same sort of thing. All of them—be they facts, hypotheses, or full-blown theories—are *ideas*. Some ideas are more credible than others. If the overwhelming evidence of our senses suggests that an idea is correct, we call it a fact. But the fact remains that a fact is an idea.

Let's take a concrete, if extreme, example that brings home this point very clearly. Consider the statement "the Earth is round." Is it a fact, a hypothesis, or a theory? A prominent creationist with whom I once spoke took offense at my suggestion that dismissing evolution as a credible notion was no different in principle from denying that the Earth is round. To him, and to most of us, that the Earth is round is a fact—something we all know to be true, something we take for granted. But why do we all think that "the Earth is round" is a fact? How many of us can perform a critical experiment to show that the Earth really is round? How many of us have ventured high enough into the upper reaches of the Earth's atmosphere that we could really see the Earth's curvature? Most of us have seen photos of the Earth taken from satellites, from spaceships, and from the moon. Clearly the Earth is round. But the relatively few vocal "flat-Earthers" have a counter even for this: to them, the spectacular achievements in space of the past half century are all an elaborate hoax—nothing more. To them, all the photos of the "Big Blue Marble" taken from satellites, space stations, and the moon itself are fakes.

Now, if the Earth is round, it is probably safe to assume it has always been so—at least since the dawn of human history, when we can pick up a written record of humanity's views on the question.[3] Yet the roundness of Earth was certainly not generally accepted as fact when Columbus set sail with his fleet of three ships. Indeed, many people thought it was a harebrained idea, and that Columbus was about to sail over the edge of what was patently a flat Earth. Only after the globe had been safely circumnavigated a number of times without a single ship dropping off the world's side did the roundness of the Earth start to take on the dimensions of credibility we deem necessary for a notion to become a fact.

Yet Eratosthenes, a Greek living in Ptolemaic Egypt in the third century b.c., showed that the Earth could not be flat with a simple yet conclusive experiment. His predecessors had already suggested the Earth is round because it casts a curved shadow on the moon. And ships sailing toward an observer appear on the horizon from the top of the mast down, also suggesting that the Earth is curved. Hearing that the sun shines directly down a well at Syene (now Aswan, Egypt) at noon on the summer solstice (the longest day of the year), Eratosthenes measured the angle between the sun's rays and a plumb bob he lowered down a well in Alexandria, some 600 miles north of Aswan, precisely at noon. That there was an angle at all in Alexandria was inconsistent with the idea that the Earth is flat. Eratosthenes could explain the phenomenon only if he envisaged a ball-shaped Earth. Using simple trigonometry, he calculated the circumference of the Earth to be the equivalent of about 28,000 miles, a respectable approximation to the 24,857 miles our modern instruments give us today. Columbus was aware of this and of later calculations, and he used them in his navigation.

Is the proposition that the Earth is round a fact, a hypothesis, a theory, or a downright falsehood? Obviously, it is an idea that has been variously considered all four. It was first called a wild idea, then a necessarily true conclusion (albeit accepted by only a few Greek savants); its respectability as a credible idea grew with the Renaissance. Now most of us proclaim it as fact—inasmuch as all attempts to disprove it have utterly failed. Flat-Earthers notwithstanding, we now even have direct confirmatory photographic evidence that the Earth is a sphere. But a round Earth is still an idea, albeit an extraordinarily powerful idea.

So what of Ronald Reagan's remark that evolution is "only a theory"? The answer is this: all of science is only a theory. And to label an idea as a theory in science is really a compliment, not a pejorative: for an idea to be called a theory in science, it has to have already passed many hurdles—and to look like it has a really good shot at being right.

Evolution: How Good an Idea Is It?

The common expression "evolutionary theory" actually refers to two rather different sets of ideas: (1) the notion that absolutely all organisms living on the face of the Earth right now are descended from a single common ancestor, and (2) ideas of *how* the evolutionary process works—how, for example, do new species arise from old ones, and what processes actually underlay the reduction from four toes to but a single digit on the front feet of horses during the course of their 50-million-year evolutionary history? When scientists think about evolution in the first sense—i.e., has it actually happened—they strongly agree that it has, and many pronounce evolution in this first sense to be a fact. On the other hand, though biologists are in agreement on many of the basic mechanisms of the evolutionary process (the second sense of the expression "the theory of evolution"), many of the details are still being debated, as is healthy and normal in the unending human endeavor that is science.

Creationists love to gloss over this rather clear-cut, simple distinction between the idea that (1) life has evolved, and the sets of ideas on (2) how the evolutionary process actually works. Indeed, they like to pretend that disagreements and debates among biologists on the mechanisms of evolution somehow cast doubt on the first proposition—the fundamental idea that all life has evolved, that all species are descended from a single common ancestor in the remote geological past. That is exactly the import of Ronald Reagan's remark quoted earlier.

I will keep these two separate senses of evolution entirely distinct. In the remainder of this chapter and in the next, I will examine two grand predictions about what we should observe in the natural world if it is true that life has evolved. After demonstrating that the simple assertion that all species on Earth are interrelated passes all tests to falsify it with flying colors—and therefore that the theory of evolution in the first sense is as highly corroborated as any notion in science possibly can be—I will turn in Chapter 4 to a consideration of evolution in the second sense: what science has to say about *how* life evolves.

The First Grand Prediction: Evolution Did Happen

Creationists are fond of pointing to the obvious fact that events that happened in the past are not subject to experimental verification or falsification, or to direct observation. After all, goes the creationist cry, no one was there at the beginning of the Cambrian Period to witness firsthand the supposed initial burst of evolutionary activity leading to the rapid evolution of complex animal life. How can we study something scientifically that has already happened? Creationists also note that few reputable biologists seem willing to predict what will happen next in evolution. And after all, says the creationist, if evolution is truly a scientific theory, it must be predictive—in the narrow sense of "making statements about what the future will hold" (and, of course, inherently untestable to biologists living in the moment). According to this creationist interpretation of science, that biologists neither can nor will predict the evolutionary future is strong evidence that the very idea of evolution isn't really scientific at all.

All this fancy rhetoric beclouds the simple meaning of "predictivity" in science. All that "predictivity" really means is that if an idea is true, there should be certain consequences—certain phenomena that we would expect—*predict*—to find if we looked. We should be able to go to nature—to the physical, material world—to see whether or not these predicted phenomena are really there.

So, in this spirit, we simply ask, If the basic idea is correct that all organisms past and present are interrelated by a process of ancestry and descent that we call evolution, what should we expect to find in the real world as a consequence? These observable consequences are the predictions we should be making—not guesses about the future.

Prediction 1: The very idea of evolution—descent with modification—implies that some species are more closely related to each other than they are to more distant relatives. Therefore, we would predict that the living world is organized into groupings of closely similar species that are in turn parts of larger groups of more distant relatives that share fewer similarities, that are in turn parts of still larger groups with definite, if fewer, similarities. Eventually, the largest grouping of all—*all of life*—should be united by the shared possession of one or more characteristics. In other words, if evolution is true, the living world should be organized in a hierarchical fashion of groups within groups—a direct reflection of how closely related to one another each organism is.

In a very real sense, this prediction was discovered to hold true long before the idea of evolution was commonly accepted as the explanation for how the living world is organized. For at least a century before Charles Darwin (1809–1882) published *On the Origin of Species by Means of Natural Selection,* in 1859, biologists had recognized that life is organized into distinct groupings arranged in a natural, hierarchical fashion. The famous Swedish naturalist Carl von Linné (1707–1778)—more familiarly known simply as Linnaeus—had published the tenth edition of his *Systema Naturae* a full 101 years earlier, in which he outlined his scheme of classification of living things. Biologists today are still using the Linnaean hierarchy, which Linnaeus established as *a natural system, before the idea of evolution had been generally accepted.* (Linnaeus, like most other biologists before Darwin, was himself a creationist.) Linnaeus saw natural groupings of different kinds of plants within his Kingdom Plantae, and of different kinds of animals within his Kingdom Animalia. Biologists since Linnaeus's time have greatly refined his work, cataloguing hundreds of thousands of additional species and adding to the categories of Linnaeus's original classification scheme, but the basic hierarchical structure of Linnaeus's scheme remains—as it is simply a reflection of how biological nature is organized.

Darwin came along and simply showed why the Linnaean hierarchy exists—why it must be there if life has evolved. The Linnaean hierarchy, even though its rudiments were recognized almost a century before Darwin's epochal book, is a necessary consequence—a *prediction*—of what the structure of the living world must look like if all of life has descended from a single common ancestor.

Let's look at this prediction from a different perspective—literally, from the bottom up: Because there are a lot of *differences* between, say, bacteria, pine trees, rats, and humans, if evolution has actually happened, it must be the case that as new species arose from old, changes in the genetic, anatomical, and behavioral properties of organisms appeared from time to time. Later descendants would inherit these changes, while ancestors (whether survivors to the present, or found as fossils) would, of course, lack these new features. Because there are millions of species on the planet, we know that if evolution has occurred, there must be a process of lineage splitting—diversification—going on. The more recent the evolutionary diversification, the more similarities ought to be shared by organisms.

Here, a simple analogy drawn from human affairs is illuminating. Consider the work of patient monks in the Middle Ages who laboriously copied manuscripts from remote times and thus saved us from knowing even less than we do about our ancient past. From time to time a monk would make a minor mistake as he copied—a happy circumstance, it turns out, for historians whose job it is to track down the development of modern versions of ancient texts, for each undetected mistake was faithfully copied by later generations. Here we have descent: manuscripts being copied, and the copies being copied later. We also have modification: an early manuscript, free of errors, resembles its descendants to varying degrees. *An error introduced into a copy is passed on to all subsequent copies.* The result: the subsequent copies of manuscripts share more novelties (newly introduced items of change) than their earlier models do. If the copying in general has been accurate, all manuscripts will be fundamentally the same. But the differences between the manuscripts will be arranged such that later manuscripts will have more of the same changes than they have in common with earlier manuscripts.

Now, consider the possibility that two monks copy the same manuscript, and each introduces a different mistake. The two manuscripts are moved to separate monasteries, there to be copied—in isolation from each other—

over and over again by succeeding generations of monks. We now have two separate "lineages" of manuscripts. Within each lineage, all manuscripts have some unique peculiarities in common, and each succeeding manuscript has, in addition, more in common with its "descendants" than with the "ancestor." Both lineages converge at the ancestral manuscript, and the two lineages share all those features of the original that have not been modified by errors in copying over the ensuing centuries.

This analogy (though now rendered obsolete by scanners and copy machines) with biological evolution is entirely apt: manuscript historians predict that manuscripts copied in single, isolated monasteries are bound to share more errors in common than they will with other manuscripts copied elsewhere; thus, the history of manuscript transmission through the ages can be studied. Even when they don't know the exact chronological history of the copying process, manuscript historians can tell which of two manuscripts was copied first because of the distribution of errors in them.

The monk analogy applies in force to biological evolution: the very idea of evolution implies that each species will tend to have some features unique to itself, but each species must also share some similarities in structure or behavior with some other species. Furthermore, each group of similar species will share further features with other groups of species, and this common group must share features with still other groups. This pattern of sharing similarities with an ever widening array of biological forms must continue until all of life is linked up by sharing at least one similarity in common. And thus we arrive back at the first grand prediction of the very idea that life has evolved: the patterns of similarities in the organic world are arranged like a complex set of nested Chinese boxes.

We can go ourselves to nature and easily test this fundamental prediction. Does it work? Take any species—for example, the domestic dog *(Canis familiaris)*—and trace its relationships with other organisms. If this fundamental prediction of evolution is correct, there must be additional species that more or less resemble dogs—and of course there are: coyotes and various species of wolves. Somewhat more distant in terms of similarity, and hence relationship, we see that dogs are united with foxes and some extinct forms known only from fossils because all share some peculiar features of the middle ear. Members of this group (zoologists call them the Family Canidae) share other similarities (particularly of the ear region) with bears, raccoons, and weasels. In turn, all these creatures share carnassial teeth (in which the last upper premolar and first lower molar are bladelike and shear past each other like a pair of scissors) with cats, civets, and seals—the group zoologists call the Order Carnivora. Carnivores, it turns out, share three middle-ear bones, mammary glands, placental development, hair, and a host of other features with a number of other organisms, including humans. These organisms we call mammals. Mammals share with birds, lizards, snakes, and turtles an amniote egg, with its protective, enveloping tissues. Amniote animals share with frogs and salamanders the property of having four legs.

The kinship of dogdom widens as we see that some creatures, including all dogs, carnivores, mammals, and tetrapods, share backbones and other features with various sorts of animals we call fish. These animals, collectively, are the vertebrates. The circle widens to embrace progressively more groups: dogs, fungi, rose bushes, and amoebas have fundamentally similar (eukaryotic) cells. The eukaryotes are a massive, basic division of life, but they don't include bacteria and certain kinds of algae, for these are simpler yet, lacking the complex structures of the true eukaryotic cell. But bacteria and blue-green algae fall neatly into the fold when we look at the basic chemical constituents of all cells. RNA (ribonucleic acid), which copies the structure of the genetic material (DNA, or deoxyribonucleic acid) and sees to it that genetic information is translated into proteins, is found in all living things. And there, from a dog focal point, we have a quick rundown of the interrelatedness of all of life, as well as a capsule summary, at the same time, of the Linnaean hierarchy.

We started with dogs. We could have started with cats. The results would have quickly turned out the same (dogs and cats being so closely related). Had we started with ourselves, *Homo sapiens* (literally "wise mankind"), we would have found a nested grouping of ever widening similarities, starting with the great apes, then humans, apes, and Old World monkeys, and then that group (Anthropoidea) together with New World monkeys. Adding the lemurs and other prosimians, we would have found what zoologists call the Order Primates. From then on, the branch quickly melds with the dog line: primates, like carnivores, are mammals; mammals are amniotes; and so on.

Had we started with roses, the example would have taken longer to reach the same point of interrelatedness: roses share properties with various berries (Family Rosaceae), which share properties with other plants. All flowering plants are united by virtue of their shared mode of reproduction. All plants photosynthesize. Roses meet dogs only at the level of the Eukaryota. But the point is, they do meet. Thus this basic first prediction—the very notion that life has evolved—is confirmed: life, all life, as diverse as it is, is linked in a hierarchical arrangement of similarities. This must be so if evolution has occurred. This, indeed, is what we find.

More than 200 years of intense biological scrutiny leaves abundantly corroborated the fundamental idea that life has evolved. All organisms, including ones newly discovered on a daily basis, readily fall into this scheme. But it is even more important to see that the basic notion of evolution is inherently testable—hence inherently scientific. *Had we failed to find this nested pattern of similarities interlinking all forms of life, we would, as scientists, be forced by the rules of the game to reject the very notion of evolution.*

Ironically, creationists are no different from the rest of the citizenry of the United States in enjoying the myriad practical fruits of this first grand prediction of evolution: the application of predictions of similarity in essential fields of medicine and agriculture, not to mention the even more recent use of DNA testing in criminal law. For we routinely predict that, if we study a particular aspect of an organism—say, its digestive enzymes or the fine internal structure of its teeth—we will find exactly the same pattern of similarities already seen between this organism and others when biologists before us examined the hair, skulls, and fingernails. In other words, we predict that patterns of similarity of unexamined properties of organisms will agree with patterns already seen in more readily observable features. This must be so if evolution is a viable notion because life has had one single, coherent history.

This special notion of predictivity is vital to biomedical and agricultural research, which are the better-known areas of applied comparative biology. Not long ago, the news media carried a report entirely typical of the logic and structure of this kind of research. A doctor in Tennessee found that thiamine (one of the B vitamins) has a great positive effect in the treatment of lead poisoning. He performed his initial experiments on calves. Switching over to rats, he was disappointed to find the results weaker and less dramatic. Obviously, he told his interviewer, we should try thiamine on monkeys and apes suffering from lead poisoning. Why would he want to do that?

The good doctor was predicting that our own physiology (after all, it is treatment of lead poisoning in humans that motivated the research) would be more similar to the physiologies of monkeys and apes than to those of calves or rats. (Though because we share a more recent common ancestry with rats than with cows, I would predict that unfortunately his results with rats have greater implications for the treatment of lead poisoning in humans than do his results with calves.) Patterns of similarity seen in previous experience lead us to predict the existence of other, as yet unexamined, similarities. We expect the results of using thiamine as a treatment for lead poisoning in humans to be more similar to its effects on monkeys and apes than on either calves or rats, simply because we have known for centuries that we share more features with apes and monkeys than we share with any other sort of creature. It is this predictive feature of evolution, then, that underlies the entire rationale of biomedical experimentation on animals other than humans to assess the value and safety of various compounds to alleviate human ailments.

This simple prediction—that there is one grand pattern of similarity linking all life—doesn't *prove* evolution, but only because science proceeds by falsifying—*disproving*—statements we make about how the universe is structured and how it behaves. But we gain tremendous confidence in our statements if, after hundreds of years, everything we have devised to test an idea fails to falsify it. And so the failure of scientists to disprove evolution over the past 200 years of biological research means that the fundamental idea that life has evolved really is one of the few grand ideas of biology that has stood the test of time. This basic notion of evolution is thoroughly scientific in the strictest sense of the word, and as such is as highly corroborated and at least as powerful as the notion of gravity or the idea that the Earth is round, spins on its axis, and revolves around the sun. In the realm of science—and indeed in grander arenas of human knowledge and wisdom—evolution truly is triumphant.

The Fossil Record
Evidence of the Evolutionary History of Life

There is a second grand prediction that flows from the simple thesis that all life has descended from a single common ancestor—i.e., has evolved. Prediction 2: There should be a record of the evolutionary history of life preserved in the rock record, and that record should reveal a general sequence of progression from smaller, simpler forms of life up through the larger, more complex forms of life over long periods of time.

That there must be a history to life is obvious from the very idea of evolution: just as a family tree genealogy recreates the "begats" of remote ancestors—great grandparents, grandparents, and parents up to the current generation, all living in (overlapping) time periods from the past to the present—so too does the evolutionary notion of ancestry and descent among species imply the passage of time. Just how much time is necessary for evolution to have produced the full array of more than 10 million species, ranging from bacteria to tigers, is not intrinsically predictable (but it is, as we shall soon see, ascertainable through the techniques of geology and paleontology). But the very idea of evolution automatically invokes the passage of time every bit as much as does the notion of human family history.

Why would we predict there to be a general sequence from the simpler and usually smaller forms of life—single-celled organisms like bacteria—up to the multicellular creatures like us? Why not assume, instead, that everything arose virtually at once, or indeed progressed the other way down—from humans or elephants first, to bacteria last? Indeed, one of the stories of creation as recounted in Genesis calls for the creation of the Earth in just six days—and of all life in just two of those days—implying that the historical record of life should show everything appearing at exactly the same time, except we humans, who arrived a day later.

Despite recent claims of possible fossilized evidence of life brought down to the Earth in a Martian meteorite, we still have no definitive proof that life exists elsewhere in the universe. Until we have positive evidence to the contrary, in other words, we must assume (as Darwin did) that life arose here on Earth. Moreover, the proteins and the macromolecules that are the very foundation of living systems must have been formed from naturally occurring chemical precursors. Though experiments performed since the 1950s have been successful at synthesizing amino acids (the basic constituents of proteins) from such naturally occurring compounds as ammonia and methane, all the biochemical steps that led to the formation of the first organism—i.e., a system with the capacity to exist, buffered against a hostile environment, with the chemical wherewithal to reproduce (presumably with the chemical RNA first)—have yet to be deciphered. But clearly, if life arose naturally from prebiotic chemical constituents, the first living organisms must have been even simpler than the bacteria that abound around us and in a very real sense still run the world's ecosystems today. If life arose from nonlife, in other words, it would have to have been in a simple structural form. It could hardly have arisen, spontaneously, as an elephant.

Another way to look at this prediction is to think about the first grand prediction, which was discussed in the previous chapter. As we saw, the very concept of evolution yields the prediction that a grand pattern of similarity, through a complex set of nested groups arranged in hierarchical fashion, must in the end embrace absolutely every form of life known to exist—or to have existed in the past. And we saw that this prediction is abundantly verified by biological experience. The simplest forms of life on Earth right now are bacteria, which lack the truly complex cell structures found in other single-celled organisms, as well as in fungi, plants, and animals, but which nonetheless have biochemical pathways and, crucially, RNA and DNA every bit the same in basic structure as is found in the rest of the living world, including in our own bodies. In a very real sense, we can think of bacteria, the simplest known living things, as the least common denominator of all living systems, and as such in all probability remnants of the earliest forms of life ever to have graced our planet.

I now turn to a condensed review of the fossilized record of life—one that abundantly confirms our second prediction about the basic sequence of life on Earth, starting with primitive bacteria and bringing us up to the complex flowering plants and mammals (including humans) that were, as one would expect, much more recent arrivals on the planet. Much of creationist rhetoric is directed against the fossil record: creationists repeatedly claim that the fossil record of the history of life is *not* in accord with the general notion of evolution, and for this reason it is important to review the fundamentals of life's history as revealed not in the Bible, but in the rocks.

I have an additional motive in mind as I recount the story of life on Earth over the past 3.5 billion years. I have been a professional paleontologist for over three decades. Throughout my career I have been wresting from fossils clues about *how* life evolves—as we have seen, the second grand meaning of the phrase "theory of evolution," and the subject to which I turn in Chapter 4. I think of the fossil record—all 3.5 billion years of it, the last half billion chockablock full of wonderful complex animals and plants—as a series of "experiments" already performed by the evolutionary process. For I see hauntingly similar stories in the history of life—stories told by Cambrian trilobites, Permian corals, Jurassic dinosaurs, and even by our own ancestors in the rich fossil record of human evolution over the most recent 4 million years. The hauntingly similar histories of all these different kinds of creatures, spread out over a half billion years of geological time, form patterns in very much the same sort of way that a physicist's experiments in the cloud chamber of a linear accelerator reveal evanescent traces of the behavior of a subatomic particle—patterns that tell the physicist about the mass, charge, and other attributes of these otherwise unseeable bits of matter. My Devonian trilobites living 380 million years ago have left similar traces, as have all the other species that we are fortunate enough to have found in the fossil record of the evolution of life. And so I will—as we work our way up the history of life, with our eyes glued on our major prediction that life has had a rich history that confirms the general prediction that it has proceeded from simple to complex—also stop to point out clues that will help us when we turn in Chapter 4 to consider that second major aspect of the theory of evolution: our understanding of what factors cause life to evolve.

In the Beginning . . .

We have a very good idea when the Earth was formed: about 4.65 billion years ago, most likely as a coalescence of gas, dust, and larger rocky particles. Three lines of evidence converge on this date: (1) the actual age of the oldest moon rocks collected, brought back to Earth, and analyzed; (2) the actual age of the oldest meteorites found (presumed to have formed in the asteroid belt at the same time the Earth was formed); and (3) the location at which the curve of dates of rocks on Earth projects back to "time zero." All these direct dates are ascertained from measurements of the ratio of remaining atoms (isotopes) that decay into daughter atoms at a statistically constant rate (see Chapter 5 for more on these techniques, and for a discussion of creationist attacks on atomic physics).

James Hutton (1726–1797), a Scottish physician and gentleman farmer who essentially founded the modern science of geology, predicted that we would never find the oldest rocks that had ever been on Earth. Hutton saw the evidence for a continual cycle of mountainous uplift, followed by erosion forming particles that would ultimately themselves be fused into rock, uplifted, and once again eroded. As Hutton (1795) put it, he saw "no vestige of a beginning, no prospect for an end." Hutton realized that there would be little chance for the Earth's oldest rocks to escape the forces that are continually tearing away and transforming rocks in our dynamic Earth. And he was right: the oldest rocks we have found to date—some 4.0-billion-year-old igneous rocks from Canada, fall a half billion years short of the actual age of the origin of the Earth.

Now, one of the most arresting facts I have ever learned is that life goes back as far in Earth history as we can possibly trace it. Fossils are found only in sedimentary rocks—i.e., rocks formed by the aggregation of particles of mud, silt, sand, or lime. Metamorphic and igneous rocks are simply formed in the wrong environments—especially under conditions of higher pressure and temperature—so whatever remains of organisms they may originally have contained is obliterated. But some of the oldest sedimentary rocks so far discovered—3.5-billion-year-old rocks in Australia—contain the fossilized remains of simple bacteria. And in even older rocks (3.8 billion years old), geochemists have found forms of carbon atoms (isotopes) considered by biochemists as a fingerprint of the presence of life. In other words, in the very oldest rocks that stand a chance of showing signs of life, we find those signs—those vestiges—of life. Life is intrinsic to the Earth!

One of creationism's fondest lines of attack on evolution is the claim that science has not yet fully solved the riddle of how life originated. But, as Charles Darwin himself proclaimed in his *On the Origin of Species*, the question of the origin of life is separate from the issue of what happened to life after it did arise. The earliest fossils we have are of very simple, mostly rod-shaped bacteria—far advanced over the simplest of molecules capable of self-replication that must have constituted the earliest forms of life.

But consider what a bacterium is compared to all other forms of life. Bacteria are prokaryotes: they lack the nuclei typical of the cells of all other organisms—from single-celled creatures (the protoctists) such as amoebas, up through the multicellular plants, fungi, and animals. The nuclei of the cells of these more complex organisms house most of their DNA—the genetic material that serves the dual functions of running the basic machinery essential for staying alive and replicating itself in the reproductive process—allowing, in other words, the equally essential process of reproduction of the organism to occur. DNA is the template from which RNA copies genetic information, in turn taking it to the ribosomes, where amino acids are assembled according to that information to form proteins. It is the proteins that run the cell, catalyzing chemical reactions and forming the building blocks of the cell itself.

These more complex organisms (i.e., the single-celled protoctists, plants, fungi, and animals) almost always have not one, but two, copies of each gene organized along pairs of chromosomes in the nucleus of each cell. Bacteria have a simpler setup: since there is no nucleus, the single-stranded genetic material is simply disseminated in strands in the body of the organism. Thus, complex as they are, bacteria are fundamentally far simpler than all other organisms that have ever existed on Earth.[1]

Thus, evolution predicts that the simplest kinds of organisms we know should be the oldest ones we find in the fossil record. And that is exactly what we do find.

In addition, at the very earliest stages of life's existence on Earth, we meet up with a theme—a recurrent pattern—that is utterly typical of life's entire 3.8-billion-year history, a theme that will figure prominently in my account of the evolutionary process in the following chapter: almost without fail, whether we are considering ancient bacteria 3.8 billion years old or the evolution of the human lineage in the last 4 million years, we find that significant events in life's history are correlated with significant events in the physical history of the Earth's atmosphere, oceans, and lands. For example, there is mounting geochemical evidence that the Earth was bombarded by many extraterrestrial objects—apparently comets—at the same time that the moon was pockmarked by its own bombardment 3.8 billion years ago. Some geologists have speculated that this tremendous comet bombardment supplied most of the water we now have on the Earth's surface—water so essential to life, trapped here by our gravitational field, but lost on the atmosphere-lacking moon, which lacks sufficient mass to keep gases and water molecules around it. Others think that primitive forms of life itself[2] might have been brought to Earth during this bombardment. Comets, after all, are "dirty snowballs," and the organic chemical compounds that are the basic constituents of life are common in outer space.

Still others think that whatever life might have existed on Earth *before* this monumental cometary bombardment 3.8 billion years ago may well have become extinct—meaning that life may well have developed not once, but twice, on Earth. Clearly we need to know more about the details of early Earth history to resolve these questions. But the very fact that these issues exist shows two very important things about science:

First, the great amount we have learned about both the very earliest stages of the Earth and life on Earth allows us to pose the questions in the first place. When I was in graduate school in the 1960s, pre-Cambrian paleontology was in its infancy. When Darwin was writing in the mid-nineteenth century, paleontologists knew absolutely nothing about the history of life before the appearance of the earliest forms of animal life (which we now understand happened about 535 million years ago). Now we see an increasingly rich early fossil record—one restricted to bacteria for at least its first 1 *billion* years—but rich enough for us to get some definite ideas of what the earliest phases of life's evolution were like.

Second, we see the creative side of the scientific mind at play. New questions arise from the analysis of data, and of repeated patterns in the history of life. The reason why anyone would speculate that the massive cometary bombardment 3.8 billion years ago caused an extinction of the Earth's earliest life forms is simply that there is now consensus in the scientific world that much later—65 million years ago—a smaller-scale cometary bombardment killed off the last of the dinosaurs, as well as many other marine and terrestrial species. We now understand that extinction caused by physical disaster is a fact of the history of life; if it could happen 65 million years ago, why not 3.8 billion years ago?

Thus science is a form of human knowledge, and like every other branch of human knowledge, it grows. We have definitive rules—canons of judgment—by which we decide which ideas are probably valid and which are not. We need good hard evidence, detectable by our senses. Obviously, not every idea of those I have mentioned about what happened to life 3.8 billion years ago on Earth can possibly be true at one and the same time. The evidence to date is tantalizing but scant, so we leave the ideas out on the table, certain that one day we'll garner even more evidence—geological, molecular, fossil—to focus the picture even more clearly, and to narrow the range of possible answers. We may even come up with still newer ideas. As we shall see in later chapters, creationists like to call the changeability of scientific conclusions the Achilles' heel of science, but the growth of knowledge—scientific or otherwise—absolutely depends on keeping a collective mind open to all (rational!) possibilities, weeding through them as the evidence mounts, before a consensus on what really happened is reached. And then it is on to the next exciting problem!

Bacteria still rule the Earth. We tend to overlook that fact, since for all intents and purposes bacteria are invisible. We know them mainly because they cause infections. But they do so many other things as well. One small example: were it not for bacteria living in the hindguts of termites, most cellulose—especially in arid regions of the Tropics—simply would not be broken down. Without decay, the world would soon be literally choked with dead wood. Some bacteria (the so-called blue-green algae) photosynthesize, among other things adding to the world's supply of oxygen. Others are vital for the cycling of nitrogen, carbon, and sulfur through the world's ecosystems.

We also overlook bacteria because of the old-fashioned tendency to call the earliest stages of life the Age of Bacteria, followed by the Age of Invertebrates, the Age of Fishes, the Age of Reptiles, the Age of Dinosaurs, the Age of Mammals, and then finally the Age of Mankind. It has been traditional in evolutionary circles to stress the progressive aspects of life's history, so when something new comes along (e.g., complex animal life), there has been a tendency to focus on the new, forgetting about the earlier forms of life that are still very much present. It is abundantly evident, though, that the evolution of new, including more complex, forms of life by no means implies that the earlier, simpler, more primitive forms are thereby somehow rendered obsolete. They do not, as a rule, become extinct, and their presence is as important in the world's ecosystems today as it ever was.

Evolution, as my colleague Stephen Jay Gould likes to say, is much more like a richly branching bush than like a simple ladder of progressive change. When new, often more complex life forms evolve—finding a role, and thereby surviving, but by no means supplanting the forms of life that preceded them—they enrich life's diversity by being added to the mix of what was already there. Thus the second grand prediction of life—that more complex forms of life necessarily evolve from, and thus come later than, more primitive forms—does *not* include (as some creationists have claimed) the idea that later, more "advanced" forms are necessarily superior to, or drive to extinction, earlier, more primitive forms of life.

After bacteria, the next major step in life's history was the evolution of the eukaryotic cell—the complex type of cell with its own discrete nucleus housing pairs of gene-bearing chromosomes that is shared by many singled-celled organisms (such as amoebas), as well as all fungi, plants, and animals. The oldest known fossils of eukaryotes are single cells recovered from sediments approximately 2.2 billion years old. In the summer of 1999, scientists reported finding chemical traces typical of eukaryotic organisms that are even older: some 2.7 billion years old, though to date, no actual fossils of eukaryotic organisms that old have been found. Note that, just as we would predict, these earliest eukaryotic organisms are the remains of simple, single-celled protoctists—i.e., not more complex, multicellular plants, fungi, or animals. Thus, just as we would expect, the next major step in the evolutionary history of life was to go from the relatively simple structure of a bacterial cell to the more complex structures of the eukaryotic cell—but still at the level of single-celled organisms, and *not* at the even more complex level of organization of multicellular organisms (fungi, plants, and animals).

Biologist Lynn Margulis has proposed an explanation for this great evolutionary step—one that, like the notion of a round Earth, was greeted with disbelief and even derision as a crackpot idea when she first proposed it in 1967. But her idea is so powerful, with so much corroborating evidence supporting it, that by the 1980s and 1990s, it had become common knowledge—a powerful, abundantly confirmed hypothesis that itself has virtually turned into a fact. Margulis proposed that the eukaryotic cell arose as a symbiotic fusion of two (or more) different kinds of bacterial cells. "Symbiosis" literally means two forms of life living together in close association for each other's mutual benefit. Generally, the association is so close and intense that the forms simply must live together, and sometimes it is so close that the two different life forms seem to be one single organism. Lichens, for example, are symbiotic associations of algae and fungi.

The cells of eukaryotes contain organelles—miniature systems outside the nucleus, embedded in the cytoplasm and performing various metabolic roles. The ribosomes, for example, are the sites for assembly of proteins, controlled by transfer RNA that has copied the instructional sequences from the DNA of the cell's nucleus. Mitochondria, another kind of organelle, are the sites where respiration (chemical extraction of energy from food) occurs. In plants, cells are additionally equipped with chloroplasts, organelles in which the chemical reactions of photosynthesis occur. One of the more surprising results of molecular biology was that *both mitochondria and chloroplasts have their own DNA*—single-stranded, very much the way DNA occurs in bacteria. Margulis proposed that mitochondria and chloroplasts were originally free-living bacteria that invaded other bacterial cells and, in effect, specialized in energy production while other parts of the newly evolved eukaryotic cell specialized in other tasks. The other parts of the eukaryotic cell may also have arisen as separate bacterial invasions, though the evidence is by far the most persuasive for the chloroplasts and mitochondria because they still have their own separate complements of DNA and RNA. And, sure enough, mitochondrial DNA replicates as the rest of the cell divides.

Biologists quickly came to accept Margulis's thesis on the origin of chloroplasts and mitochondria once it became clear that the DNA of these organelles is always present and bears no resemblance or connections with the DNA of the nuclei of eukaryotic cells. There is simply no other rational explanation for the arrangement of DNA within all eukaryotic cells. Cellular fusion—evolutionary symbiosis taken to its final conclusion—accounts for the basic division of labor of the organelles of the eukaryotic cell.

What prompted this major evolutionary advance: the origin of the eukaryotes? Though here again we cannot be sure, recent work by Caltech geologist Joseph Kirschvink and his colleagues strongly suggests that the world underwent a truly bizarre and extreme climatic event around the time eukaryotic life evolved. Kirschvink calls it "snowball Earth": The geological evidence is persuasive that, around 2.2 billion years ago, continental glaciers started growing as extensions of the polar ice caps. But, unlike more recent glacial events, Kirschvink has found that these massive sheets of ice reached all the way into the Tropics—and probably right down to the equator 2.2 billion years ago.

Did snowball Earth somehow *cause* the evolution of the eukaryotes sometime over 2 billion years ago? We simply do not know enough about either the physical or the biological events back then to be sure. But it is a tantalizing possibility: the approximate correlation in timing of a major step in life's evolutionary history with one of the most severe climatic episodes ever to occur on Earth strongly hints of a connection between these events.

Once the single-celled eukaryotes had evolved, there were no major advances in evolutionary history for some 1.5 billion years. Though undoubtedly the single-celled protoctists diversified, their fossils are difficult to find, and we have relatively few samples over this 1.5-billion-year interval to give us insights into the nature of eukaryotic single-celled life during this period. Life remained small and relatively simple; the larger and more complex animals, plants, and fungi had yet to appear.

The Cambrian Explosion

Creationists are very fond of the Cambrian explosion, the relatively abrupt appearance of complex animal life that marks the beginnings of a rich and dense fossil record. Creationists say that the second grand prediction of evolution—that life has evolved in an orderly fashion, with simpler forms preceding more complex—is violated, even downright falsified, by the early Cambrian fossil record. Paleontologists, on the other hand, see this explosion as a fascinating example of the phenomenal speed at which evolution can work. What is this Cambrian explosion exactly, and how well does it conform to our prediction that simpler forms of life precede the more complex?

As geologists in the late eighteenth and early nineteenth centuries began the job of mapping the sedimentary rocks of Europe and North America in earnest, they saw that all the rocks lying below what they called the Cambrian System ("Cambria" was the Roman name for Wales, where Reverend Adam Sedgwick [1785–1873] first studied and named rocks of this age) seemed devoid of fossils. In contrast, from the Cambrian on up, fossils of complex life—first marine invertebrate animals like corals, brachiopods, mollusks, and trilobites; and later vertebrate life (fishes); and even later, invertebrates (insects), vertebrates (amphibians; later, reptiles; still later, birds and mammals), and plants on land—became consistently abundant.

Some of the oldest of these fossils in the Cambrian are of trilobites, the most primitive group of the Phylum Arthropoda (literally "jointed-legged ones"), which also includes crustaceans (crabs, barnacles, shrimp), millipedes, horseshoe crabs, spiders, and insects. That arthropods, as all biologists agree, are much more complicated animals than, say, sponges or corals presented a puzzle: Why are some of the oldest forms of animal life that are found in the fossil record also some of the most complex?

Thus was born the riddle of the Cambrian explosion—made even more puzzling after Darwin convinced the scientific world that life had indeed evolved in an orderly fashion. Paleontologists speculated that there must be an interval of time missing, or that all the traces of even more ancient life—traces that would have recorded the transition from single-celled eukaryotes to simple animals such as sponges or corals—had been obliterated by erosion and metamorphism.

Though it is true that the vast majority of so-called Precambrian rocks are indeed metamorphic or igneous, nonetheless there are sequences of sedimentary rock that lie below fossiliferous Cambrian rocks. These really *ought* to produce forerunners and precursors to the abundantly preserved hard-shelled invertebrates that show up in such profusion in Lower Cambrian rocks. And sure enough, diligent searching and collecting, primarily in the latter half of the twentieth century, has—as we would predict from the simple idea of evolution—shown that there was complex life before the Cambrian trilobites, brachiopods, mollusks, and sponges burst upon the scene.

Geologists have recently discovered that perhaps as many as three or four more prodigious "snowball Earth" glaciations occurred over a 200-million-year interval beginning about 800 million years ago. We find, for the very first time, the fossilized remains of large organisms that lived right after the last of these stupendous glacial events had subsided some 600 million years ago. Best known from the Ediacara Hills of the Flinders Range of Australia, elements of this so-called Ediacaran fauna of the Vendian Period (600–540 million years ago) have been found in such far-flung places as Newfoundland, the Charnwood Forest of England, and Namibia in southern Africa. The fossils come in a variety of shapes and sizes,[3] and frankly, the paleontological world has yet to reach complete consensus on what these Ediacaran fossils really are: Are they true animals, primitive versions of later forms of life? Are they instead lichens, as has been suggested? Or are they a form of life that flourished and then became utterly extinct—leaving it very difficult for us to figure out exactly what manner of beast they were?

On the other hand, many of the Ediacaran fossils are very similar to well-known forms of invertebrate life. *Spriggina,* for example, looks to most of us paleontologists very much like a segmented worm and, with its rather well developed head region, perhaps a forerunner to Cambrian trilobites. Likewise, I see no problem in relating others—indeed the vast majority—of the Ediacaran fauna to various groups of cnidarians, also known as coelenterates (especially sea pens—soft-bodied relatives of corals), and it is well worth noting that cnidarians (which include corals, anemones, and jellyfish, which lack true organ systems) are among the simplest, most primitive forms of animal life on the planet. Still others (e.g., *Tribrachidium*) remind me forcibly of echinoderms (which include starfish and sea urchins, especially the later-occurring (in the Cambrian Period) edrioasteroids, a now long-extinct group of echinoderms. Though some paleontologists still disagree, for my money I think we will eventually conclude that many, if not all, of these fossils Ediacaran are closely related to the corals, echinoderms, worms, and arthropods that they seem to resemble.

Thus, predictably, we have begun to fill in the gaps; we now know that the advent of complex multicellular animal life did not occur overnight (nor in a single biblical day), but rather took place in a succession of events spanning 160 million years. But what of that relatively sudden, abrupt appearance of trilobites and other complex forms of animal life at the base of the Cambrian?

Recent research, initially mostly on fossil faunas in Siberia, has led to the discovery of a variety of generally small shell-like forms that, like their Ediacaran predecessors, are difficult to assign to well-known groups with utter certainty. They look, for the most part, like mollusks—snails, clams, and cephalopods being later, more familiar molluscan examples. But then, sometime around 540 million years ago, we begin to find an array of fossil remains of what were quickly to become some of the dominant elements of marine life for hundreds of millions of years. Trilobites, for example, make their appearance, as do brachiopods (bivalved creatures unrelated to the bivalved clams; brachiopods still exist in modern seas), as well as early mollusks and calcareous spongelike creatures known as archaeocyathids.

First impressions—including those of the early geologists—see this as an instantaneous explosion of a vast assortment of invertebrate life forms. We now know that trilobites and other sorts of Cambrian life did not show up absolutely all at the same time all over the world; rather, it apparently took a good 10 million years for the familiar faunas of the lowermost Cambrian rocks to become fully established.

I have walked up a dry creek bed in the White-Inyo Range on the California-Nevada border, carefully observing and collecting while climbing a rock sequence near the very base of the Cambrian. I'll never forget finding exactly what my geologist guide had told me I would: that, in the lowest (therefore oldest) sediments, I would see only trace fossils—meaning the sedimentary structures formed as animals moved through, or walked on top of, the bottom muds of that ancient sea. Some of these traces were clearly made by animals as complex as trilobites. But where were their skeletal remains, which as we walked up the hill, all of a sudden became common and easy to find and collect? Either there was something peculiar about the chemical environment when the lower sediments were accumulating—something that prevented skeletal material from surviving long enough to become buried and eventually preserved as a fossil—or the skeletons were too thin and delicate to make it all the way to the burial-and-preservation stage.

I simply don't know, in this particular case. But it is clear that the ability to grow to large sizes and to secrete hard material like calcium carbonate to build a tough external skeleton—the sort of skeleton that readily becomes fossilized—was severely hampered by the chemistry of the ancient seas. One particularly attractive notion (the Berkner-Marshall hypothesis), well supported by geochemical measurements, is that there simply was not enough oxygen dissolved in seawater until about 540 million years ago—enough, that is, to support the metabolic requirements of large-bodied, multicellular organisms, including their ability to secrete hard external skeletons.

So it seems likely that the ancestors of the major groups of invertebrates had already diversified to some extent *before* they had grown very large and had developed external exoskeletons. Indeed, that is what I think the Ediacaran organisms are telling us (though some of these did reach respectable sizes, albeit apparently without forming truly well mineralized exoskeletons). Recall, too, that it was the coral-like forms that dominated life in the Ediacaran seas.

The invertebrate phyla alive today—and alive since Cambrian times—show a nice evolutionary gradation from simple to complex. Simplest are the sponges, which lack true tissues, having only a few different types of cells. The cnidarians (corals, anemones, various sorts of jellyfish and polyps) come next in the spectrum of complexity: these animals have two distinct layers of tissues in their bodies, though they lack true organs. More complex are such phyla as the flatworms, which have eyes and excretory organs, for example, but lack segmentation or a true body cavity. Still more complex are the brachiopods and bryozoans; the segmented worms, mollusks, and arthropods; and the echinoderms and chordates (the latter is our own group, but some chordates are still considered invertebrates[4]).

Once inside the Cambrian, we find no direct succession through time of the simplest invertebrates up through the most complex. There is no sequence by which sponges enter first, followed by corals, then flatworms (never, in any case, found as fossils), then brachiopods, worms, trilobites (arthropods), and so on. There are two reasons for this lack of succession, implicit in what we have seen so far. First, it is pretty clear that these groups had already diversified—evolved—from each other sometime during the Vendian—prior, that is, to the time when many of these groups, roughly at the same time, presumably for geochemical reasons, attained the ability to secrete salts into their outer coverings, giving them hardened skeletons for the first time. That, I think, is one of the main lessons of the Ediacaran fossils.

Second, no biologist would ever propose that sponges gave rise to corals, which gave rise to flatworms, which gave rise to mollusks, which gave rise to . . . , and so on ad infinitum—like the long list of "begats" in Genesis. For if you look at the small larvae of all these groups, similarities quickly become evident that have suggested to biologists over the years how the actual ancestors in this grand evolutionary radiation really looked. Larvae are small, and they are soft-bodied—just as are some of the fossils we are only now beginning to recover from Vendian sediments. The hard-bodied invertebrates that began showing up in profusion some 540 million years ago were already well differentiated and diversified, and they were descended from much smaller, soft-bodied forms that had evolved sometime in the 100 million or so years after the last-documented snowball Earth—well before, that is, the base of the Cambrian.

In the old days my predecessors predicted the existence of what they called the Lipalian interval—an interval of time just before the Cambrian during which the great radiation of invertebrate animal phyla took place. The problem was, they couldn't find it. Now we've found it, and we have dubbed it instead the Vendian. As paleontological techniques become ever sharper, we almost certainly will find more direct evidence of the pattern of this great invertebrate diversification—one that, if it ever becomes good enough, will show that the less complex groups (such as the ancestral sponges and cnidarians) actually did precede, even if not by much, the more complex groups like mollusks and arthropods.

After the Radiation: The Pulse and Pace of Evolutionary History for the Last 540 Million Years

Once complex marine animal life finally became established some 540 million years ago, and all the major groups except the vertebrates (in the form of primitive fish[5]) had appeared, patterns of evolution become far easier to trace in the rocks. Once again we find a simple agreement between the fossil record and evolution's second grand prediction—that simpler, more primitive forms precede their evolutionary, more complex, descendants. We also see the beginnings of a repeated set of patterns to life's evolution that are still going on around us today—patterns that have much to tell us about *how* life evolves.

Let us consider the pulse and pace of evolution—the typical evolutionary patterns—that we begin picking up in the Cambrian Period, at the beginning of the Paleozoic Era. Five hundred million years ago, life was still restricted to the seas (at least as far as we know; bacteria were undoubtedly also living in fresh waters and terrestrial environments, but the record of these ancient environments is poor to nonexistent). Marine life was both plentiful and richly diverse—with trilobites, brachiopods, the spongelike archaeocyathids, primitive echinoderms (starfish relatives), and primitive mollusks especially common. In one justly famous quarry in British Columbia, an astonishing array of soft-bodied animals discovered in the Burgess Shale[6] has shown us how incredibly diverse early life in Cambrian seas was, also showing us that most marine deposits, no matter how richly fossiliferous, contain the remains of only easily preserved organisms—i.e., those with hardened skeletal parts.

Paleontologist Allison R. ("Pete") Palmer, formerly of the State University of New York at Stony Brook, and since retired from the U.S. Geological Survey, has documented a succession of faunas in Cambrian rocks of the western United States. Palmer was impressed by the tendency of entire groups of trilobites to flourish, and in particular to evolve many different species relatively quickly—species that would persist for millions of years before sudden environmental change (Palmer thought it was the rising of sea level) would disrupt these nearshore shallow-water ecosystems, abruptly driving many species extinct. Palmer called each of these successive evolutionary and ecological episodes a biomere.[7]

Palmer's work (primarily in the 1960s and 1970s) was the first of its kind in the modern era to expose the fundamental nature of the organization of the fossil record for the last half billion years of life on the planet. The pattern of rapid evolutionary diversification, followed by long intervals of great ecosystem stability with very little evolutionary change detectable within species, followed (after millions of years) by physical disruption of ecosystems and loss of many species to extinction, and then followed by another burst of rapid evolutionary change, is absolutely typical of evolutionary patterns on land and sea for as long as complex animal (and, later, plant) life has been on Earth.

Indeed, this pattern can be found virtually everywhere in the fossil record of the history of life. For example, paleontologists Carlton Brett and Gordon Baird[8] have documented eight successive intervals very reminiscent of Palmer's biomeres—but this time from the Middle Paleozoic of the Appalachian region of eastern North America. Each of their recognized intervals lasts 5–7 million years—an aggregate total time of some 45–55 million years. Brett and colleagues estimate that between 70 and 85 percent of the species are present throughout their respective intervals, and only some 20 percent, again on average, make it through to the next succeeding interval. Their name for this type of repeated pattern in the history of life is coordinated stasis.

There are many other examples: dinosaur faunas of the Mesozoic, mammalian faunas of the Cenozoic, marine Cenozoic faunas—even the great Rift Valley sequences of eastern and southern Africa, where our own evolutionary drama was played out—all show exactly the same pattern: (1) great ecological stability, with great evolutionary stability of animal and plant species, followed by (2) physical disruption of ecosystems, with high rates of species extinctions, followed by (3) rapid evolutionary proliferation of descendant species. But we should not lose sight of the fact that the new species replacing the old ones are always different, equipped with newly evolved adaptations. Nowhere is this characteristic sequence of events more obvious than in the details of human evolution in Africa, which fit this pattern exactly, as we shall shortly see. In the African case, the same pattern goes by the name "turnover pulse," coined by paleontologist Elisabeth Vrba, who was the first to pinpoint the importance of this pattern in the evolution of African mammals, including our own hominid ancestors.

Here is another pattern that has great potential significance for understanding *how* the evolutionary process works—the subject of the next chapter: during the long intervals of time between environmental disruption, extinction, and the rapid subsequent development of new species, ecosystems and species themselves are remarkably stable. Little or no evolutionary change accumulates in most species during these periods of quiescence—a phenomenon not greatly remarked on by biologists until my colleague Stephen Jay Gould and I discussed it in the 1970s, calling it stasis.

All the great biologists and geologists prior to Darwin were, in some sense at least, creationists. Evolution had yet to gain scientific credibility up through the first half of the nineteenth century, and most educated Europeans were religious as a matter of course. In the early 1800s, the great French biologist-geologist-paleontologist Baron Georges Cuvier (1769–1832) recognized no fewer than 32 separate divisions of the fossil record of life—in a crude, beginning way, seeing the history of life very much as we see it now—as a succession of extinctions followed by proliferation of new ecosystems with new species to fill the roles vacated by their extinct predecessors. Cuvier thought that the proliferations were independent creations by God (unlike modern-day creationists, who follow Genesis literally and see only a single creative episode for all of life); it is the triumph of the Darwinian-inspired evolutionary perspective that allows us to see them for what they really are: evolutionary responses to ecological change. And it was Cuvier who, despite creationist interpretation, was among the first to draw attention to these all-important patterns of stability and what he called revolutions.

Global mass extinctions leave far more devastation in their wake than the regional pattern variously dubbed biomeres, coordinated stasis, and turnover pulse—and produce far greater evolutionary results. The greatest extinction (so far!) to have hit Earth's biota took out at least 70 percent—and possibly as much as 96 percent—of all species living on Earth, according to paleontologist David M. Raup, formerly of the University of Chicago. That was some 245 million years ago, at the end of the Permian Period—an event that changed the complexion of life so deeply that early paleontologists (long before Darwin) used it to divide the Paleozoic Era (Ancient Life) from the Mesozoic Era (Middle Life).

But it is not just individual species that succumb to extinction in these massive, global extinction crises. When global extinction events strike, they tend to take out so many species that entire families, orders, and even classes—the larger units of the Linnaean hierarchy—disappear. And on the other side of the line, when whatever caused the extinction event itself passes, life rebounds, and entire new families, orders, and even classes of animal and plant life become established. Let us look at some examples of these larger-scale evolutionary changes.

Ammonoids are coiled (almost always, though there are exceptions), externally shelled cephalopod mollusks—close relatives to the living pearly nautilus of the South Pacific. (Other living cephalopods include squids and octopi.) Ammonoids evolved in the Devonian Period from nautiloid ancestors; they became extinct at the end of the Mesozoic Era, in the fifth great mass extinction, which occurred some 65 million years ago.

The ammonoid shell, like that of the pearly nautilus, is divided by a series of partitions. These partitions (called septa) intersect the outside shell wall and leave a characteristic pattern of hills and valleys that is especially visible on fossils in which the outer shell has been worn away. It is these suture patterns that show so much evolutionary change during the course of ammonoid history. And though there are some collateral groups of ammonoids, by far the dominant groups were the Paleozoic goniatites, the

Triassic ceratites, and the Jurassic and Cretaceous ammonites. The earliest ammonoids, the goniatites, had the simplest sutures, expressed as smooth lines arrayed in peaks and valleys (or "saddles" and "lobes," to use the terms of ammonoid paleontology). The later ceratites had secondary crinkles on the lobes but not on the saddles. The last great group—the true ammonites—had crinkles on both the lobes and the saddles. [see Figure 1]

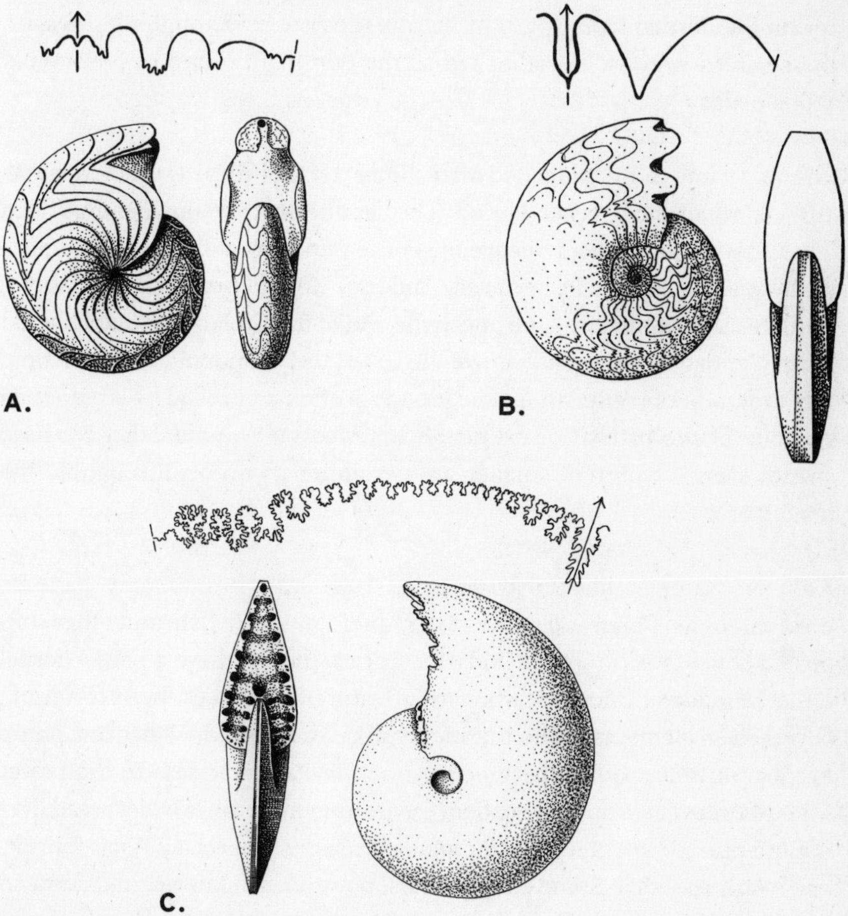

FIGURE 1 The three basic kinds of ammonoid suture patterns, showing suture pattern on the side of the shell, a view of a septum, and the outline of the suture pattern. **A.** The Mississippian goniatite *Imitoceras.* **B.** The Triassic ceratite *Meekoceras.* **C.** The ammonite *Placenticeras.* From Easton, 1960, pp. 441, 448, and 461.

Now here is progressive evolution in the old, classic sense, for anatomical complexity increases through time in ammonoid history. But consider the timing and the circumstances behind these events: all but one genus (small group of species) of goniatites became extinct at the Permo-Triassic extinction event at the end of the Paleozoic. But those few related goniatite species gave rise to the first of the ceratites, which rapidly radiated in an explosive evolutionary proliferation of species. Soon, as Triassic ecosystems began to regain the normal look typical of marine ecosystems throughout the ages, the ceratites were well established as the dominant group of ammonoid cephalopods.

The very same thing happened after the next major mass extinction event, at the close of the Triassic Period. The ceratites became extinct, but from one surviving ammonoid lineage the entire vast array of the still more complexly sutured ammonites evolved. And they were to proliferate and thrive until the next extinction—the one at the end of the Cretaceous that ushered in the Cenozoic Era—finally drove the last of the ammonoids to extinction. The evolution of entire large-scale groups is often controlled by larger-scale versions of the pattern of extinction followed by evolution that we have already seen is typical of smaller-scale evolutionary events throughout the history of life.

Another example that illustrates such large-scale evolutionary patterns involves corals. Corals are related to sea anemones, jellyfish, and other soft-bodied cnidarians (Phylum Cnidaria). Corals, though, have a hard external skeleton made of calcium carbonate, a feature that makes them commonly preserved elements of the marine fossil record from the Paleozoic on up to modern times. Corals became common in Paleozoic seas in the Lower Middle Ordovician, as limy seafloor environments became widespread over the interiors of the great continental landmasses, especially Asia, Europe, and North America. Some earlier corals, however, are known, and some in the Cambrian of Australia look very like the modern corals we have today—the Scleractinia, also known as hexacorals for their sixfold symmetry of septa supporting the soft tissue of the coral polyp itself.

But the dominant corals of the Paleozoic Era—corals that often formed massive reefs—had a fourfold symmetry to their internal septal arrangements.

Moreover, their skeletons were formed from the mineral calcite, the more stable atomic arrangement of calcium carbonate than the delicate aragonite form of calcium carbonate. The big problem in coral paleontology always was, How did the modern scleractinian corals—found first in Lower Triassic rocks—evolve from the Paleozoic corals, which were last seen in the Upper Permian? How did the mineralogical change (calcite to aragonite) occur? And how, after hundreds of millions of years of fourfold symmetry, did six-sided symmetry evolve? [see Figure 2]

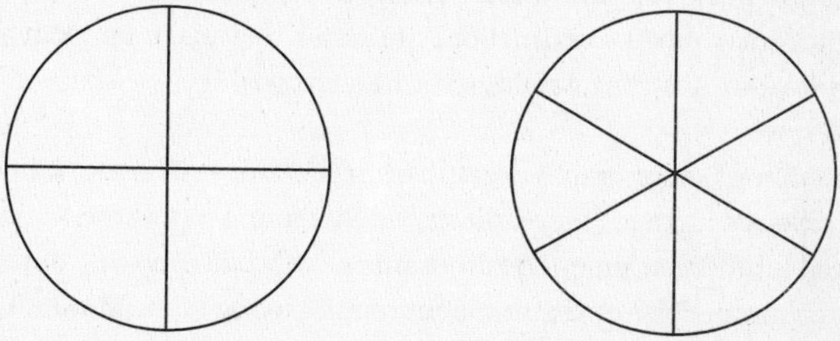

FIGURE 2 Coral: Four-fold symmetry vs. Six-fold symmetry.

The answers to these puzzles are a bit different from what we just saw in ammonoid evolution; in that example, evolutionary advances in complexity occurred in small groups of species that somehow managed to survive when most of the older ammonoids became extinct. The corals present a somewhat different evolutionary story: We now understand that scleractinian corals did not evolve directly from the Paleozoic rugosans or tabulates. We now understand, instead, that the nearest relatives of scleractinian corals are actually the naked sea anemones (which show the same pattern of six-sided internal symmetry). It now seems that the early Cambrian corals were part of a sixfold-symmetry lineage that persisted—largely as naked anemones that have left only a few fossil traces in the Paleozoic, but a lineage that was nonetheless always there, throughout the Paleozoic. When the older forms of corals died out in the great Permian mass extinction event, one branch of the sixfold-symmetry (anemone) lineage independently acquired the ability to secrete calcium carbonate—albeit in the form of aragonite, not calcite.

Thus evolution seems very much to involve the reinvention of the ecological wheel: when the Paleozoic corals became extinct, a related branch of cnidarians independently evolved the ability to secrete calcium carbonate, thereby evolving into what can only be described as the general coral niche, and producing so many species that zoologists classify them as the Order Scleractinia. In that sense, the Orders Rugosa and Tabulata of the Paleozoic were replaced by the Order Scleractinia. But note, too, that the Scleractinia almost certainly would not have evolved had not the Rugosa and Tabulata been driven to extinction. This is the evolutionary phenomenon that paleobiologist Stephen Jay Gould has called contingency: had those Paleozoic corals not succumbed to extinction, the corals that make up today's Great Barrier Reef in Australia would never have evolved.

Here's an even more graphic example: In the Upper Triassic, a little over 200 million years ago, the earliest mammals and the earliest dinosaurs appeared for the first time. The dinosaurs clearly had evolved from the very similar, but more primitive, thecodont reptiles living in the Middle Triassic. The mammals had evolved from a different branch of the reptiles: the synapsids, reptiles with but a single hole in the side of the head (as opposed to the two holes characteristic of snakes and lizards, crocodilians, birds, dinosaurs, and still other diapsid reptile groups). Indeed, the evolution of mammals from the "mammal-like" reptiles (therapsids) is one of the best-documented examples of macroevolution ever encountered in the fossil record. Especially known from South Africa's great Karroo System of sediments spanning the Permian and Triassic Periods, the sequence of fossils progresses upward from creatures with undifferentiated tooth rows and a single middle ear bone right on up through very mammalian-looking animals with teeth differentiated into incisors, canines, and molars, and with three middle ear bones.[9] The Karroo sequence—like nearly all other segments of the fossil record of life's history, is separated into distinct biomere-like zones, and the changes in early mammalian evolution take place in the same sort of pattern of stability followed by extinction and then evolutionary advance that is seen in all other parts of life's evolutionary story.

But it was the dinosaurs, not the mammals, that evolved into a rich array of small, medium, and large species—some herbivores, some scavengers, and some, of course, carnivores. In the great extinction event that closed the Triassic Period, the dinosaurs were cut back severely, but they did not succumb completely to extinction. They bounced right back—in an evolutionary sense—and once again held, as it were, most of the important jobs in the world's terrestrial ecosystems. Though they suffered vicissitudes throughout their 150-million-year reign, nonetheless it was always the dinosaurs, not the mammals, that were able to evolve more species and to diversify, playing a wide variety of roles in Earth's ecosystems.

No one knows why it was always the dinosaurs, and never the mammals, that were able to evolve such a wide assortment of body sizes and ecological types. But finally, at the end of the Cretaceous Period 65 million years ago, the last of the dinosaurs finally did succumb to the environmental horrors thrown up by the collision between Earth and one or more comets—and, the thinking now goes, by the correlated outpouring of vast columns of lava on the other side of Earth, in peninsular India.

So, after a long reign in which evolution repeatedly refreshed their diversity, suddenly the dinosaurs were gone. The mammals, which had diversified into several distinct lineages, but which had not developed anything like the diverse array of ecological types that the dinosaurs had, managed to hang on through the mass extinction event at the Cretaceous-Tertiary boundary. In the words of famed Harvard paleontologist Alfred Sherwood Romer (1894–1973), mammals had remained "the rats of the Mesozoic" (personal communication), definitely playing second fiddle to the dinosaurs and the other ruling reptiles.

It took only a few million years—the characteristic lag seen after all major mass extinction events—before the mammals suddenly burst forth in a blaze of evolutionary activity. All of a sudden, huge lumbering herbivorous mammals appeared on the Paleocene landscape; by the Eocene, recognizable ancestors of all the modern groups of mammals had evolved. The death of the dinosaurs did not cause mammals to evolve; they had already evolved long since. But it did bring about the evolution of mammalian *diversity:* the Orders Carnivora (carnivores), Cetacea (whales), Artiodactyla (deer, antelope, cattle, etc.), Perissodactyla (horses, camels, rhinos, etc.), Rodentia (rodents), Lagomorpha (rabbits), Chiroptera (bats), and so on, all date back to the Eocene. The earlier Paleocene mammals largely died off, and only a few of the modern mammalian groups date back to the Mesozoic—groups, interestingly enough, such as our own order, Primates. That's right; we belong to one of the earliest, most primitive mammalian orders.

But it is, as I have already remarked, human evolution that most clearly disturbs creationists, and it is our own story that serves as perhaps the most dramatic and relevant of all examples of evolution. Human evolution perfectly fits the picture of ecosystem stability and disturbance, and the extinction and rapid evolution of species. We are like all other living creatures: until the invention of agriculture, like all other species, local populations of *Homo sapiens* and species ancestral to us had niches in the local ecosystems—initially in Africa, and later around the world. So it should come as no surprise that patterns in human evolution match perfectly the sorts of patterns seen in Paleozoic trilobites, Mesozoic dinosaurs, and early Tertiary mammals.

Spurred on by the intense interest in human evolution, paleoanthropologists have by now amassed a rich fossil record that is especially dense and illuminating for the past 3.5 million years or so. I can hardly do justice to the full story here;[10] rather, I will focus on the basic story of increase in brain size in human evolution, which along with increase in overall body size and the (largely earlier) adoption of an upright bipedal posture, is perhaps the most arresting feature of *progressive* evolution in hominid evolution. There simply is no doubt that brain size increases as we travel up through the rock record of human evolution in Africa. The tale of the skulls is creationism's worst nightmare.[11] And just like all other evolutionary patterns encountered in this chapter, the story is not one of gradual progressive change, but of episodes of evolutionary change following environmental disruption and, at least in one instance, extinction of earlier species.

I'll focus on just three critical phases to illustrate the point. Paleontologist Elisabeth S. Vrba of Yale University has noted the very same sort of biomere-like patterns in Africa seen by Palmer, Brett and Baird, and so many other paleontologists elsewhere throughout the past half billion years of life's evolutionary history; her term for the pattern is "turnover pulse." In a nutshell, Vrba has found that there was a dramatic worldwide drop in mean temperature of some 10 to 15°C that took place between 2.8 and 2.5 million years ago (no evidence of actual glacial ice in the northern continents of Eurasia and North America has so far shown up for this pre–Ice Age global cooling event). The effect of this cooling on the ecosystems of eastern Africa was a while in coming, but just about 2.5 million years ago, there was an abrupt change, from moist woodlands to a much drier, open grassland habitat.[12] Though some species were able to survive in wet woodlands elsewhere, and others, such as antelope that were already adapted to open grasslands, moved in (while still others, such as impalas, simply survived because they are adapted to both sorts of environments), the cooling effect wrought such drastic ecological change that many animal species simply became extinct. And because ecological disruption can trigger extinction as well as evolution (through speciation; see Chapter 4 for more on this), many new species evolved quickly as the new, open grassland ecosystem emerged.

Now, the dominant hominid species—in fact, the *only* hominid species we know about from the interval 3.0–2.5 million years ago—was *Australopithecus africanus* (literally "southern ape of Africa"). (So far, this species is known mainly from southern African deposits, where evidence of the same ecological events first worked out for eastern Africa has now been found.) *Australopithecus africanus* stood upright; males were no more than 4 feet in height and weighed no more than 100 pounds. Their pelves are distinctly more humanlike than apelike—part of the evolutionary change associated with the assumption of upright posture and bipedal walking. Their teeth are also distinctly more humanlike than apelike. And though some paleoanthropologists have claimed to see human features in the folds of the brains (endocasts) of this species, the actual brain size is firmly within chimpanzee range: about 400–450 milliliters in volume. For comparison, the average brain size of a modern human is approximately 1,350 milliliters.

Australopithecus africanus disappeared from the fossil record of southern Africa about 2.5 million years ago,[13] a presumed victim of extinction. Yet, just at 2.5 million years ago, we find (in both eastern and southern Africa) the remains of not one, but two, new lineages of fossil hominids. And we also find the first stone tools! Dramatically—if not really surprisingly—patterns of human extinction and evolution fit in *exactly* with the total picture of ecosystem disruption, extinction of many species, and the evolution of new, savanna-adapted species in their stead.

One of these two new lineages was the "robust" australopithecines, a fascinating lot indeed. The males had large sagittal crests for the insertion of massive jaw muscles needed to work their impressive lower jaws stocked with enormous molars for grinding their plant food. Though to the untrained eye the skulls of the several different robust australopithecines look somewhat gorilla-like, their brain size was about the same as that of *Australopithecus africanus*, and unlike any ape, they retained the structure of the pelvis and long bones inherited from their ancestors; in other words, robust australopithecines were true upright and walking hominids.

But they were definitely not our direct ancestors. Rather, they were an evolutionary side branch—ecological specialists obliged by their dental adaptations to eat tubers, nuts, fruits, and other vegetable materials. And, like other ecological specialists, the robust australopithecine lineage shows very rapid rates of evolution—with at least five different species occurring in Africa in a 1-million-year period (2.5–1.5 million years ago). The flip side of the rapid evolutionary rates of ecological specialists is their characteristically very high rates of extinction: none of the species of robust australopithecines so far discovered lasted very long.

The other lineage featured a more gracile anatomy: thinner bones, no massive crests on the head, smaller teeth—in other words, a skeletal anatomy far more like our own than like that of the robust australopithecines. The major difference between these newly evolved gracile hominids and their *Australopithecus africanus* predecessors was a significant increase in the size of the brain—to the vicinity of 700–750 milliliters. For this and other reasons, paleoanthropologists regard these as the earliest members of our own genus—the genus *Homo*. The earliest species, first occurring right at 2.5 million years ago in eastern Africa, was *Homo habilis*.[14]

Equally dramatic as the skulls themselves is the presence—again right at 2.5 million years ago—of the earliest definite signs of material culture. Here, at the very beginnings of the archeological record, we find the first stone tools—first discovered by the Leakeys in Tanzania's Olduvai Gorge.

Crude as they were, these ancient implements are thrilling, for they mark the first physical evidence that we can point to showing the departure, among our ancestors, from a purely biologically based to a learned behavioral (i.e., cultural) base for wresting a living from the surrounding local ecosystems in which they lived.

There is no question that the evolutionary events occurring just before and after 2.5 million years ago in Africa—events that were triggered by a global cold snap that disrupted Africa's ecosystems—had an enormous impact on human evolution, as well as on the evolution of many lineages of antelopes, pigs, birds, and so on. Without that "turnover pulse" (as Vrba refers to it), we simply would not be here today contemplating our own "origins," as the creationists like to put it.

But that's not all: the first Ice Age glaciation event—when huge sheets up to half a mile thick crept down from the northern polar regions to cover much of Eurasia and North America—also had its evolutionary effects, including on human evolution in Africa. For at just about this time, we find the earliest remains of what Ian Tattersall calls *Homo ergaster* (see Tattersall and Schwartz, 2000)—early African forerunner to the justly famous *Homo erectus,* which was first discovered in Java by the Dutch physician Eugene Dubois (1858–1940) near the end of the nineteenth century.

The thing about *Homo ergaster* is that, already by 1.5 million years ago, our ancestors had come to look very much like us. The best-preserved specimen discovered so far is the nearly complete skeleton of the so-called Nariokatone boy—thought to have been around 11 years of age at time of death. At full maturity, paleoanthropologists estimate he would have attained a full height of 5 feet 11 inches; in other words, he would have been as tall as the average present-day American male. As Ian Tattersall has put it, "from the neck down" *Homo ergaster* and *Homo erectus* were essentially modern in their skeletal anatomy. But not so their skulls—which contained a brain that, at about 1,000 milliliters, on the one hand was significantly larger than that of *Homo habilis,* but on the other hand still fell far short of the 1,350 milliliters that is the average volume of modern members of our own species, *Homo sapiens.*

In other words, as we move up in time through the African fossil record, we find species in our lineage with progressively larger brain sizes: from the 450 milliliters of the early australopithecines, through the 750 milliliters of the earliest members of the genus *Homo,* through later species *(Homo ergaster)* with brains of about 1,000 milliliters, finally culminating in the appearance of our own species, *Homo sapiens,* also in Africa, which evolved perhaps as much as 150,000–200,000 years ago, the oldest fossils occurring at about 120,000 years ago.[15]

So there it is: creationism's worst nightmare in a nutshell. There is a wonderful gradation of fossil human remains spanning an interval of the last 3 million years in Africa—so-called missing links occurring all the way as we go from something rather apelike (though human in its ability to walk upright) right on up through the appearance of modern human beings. We now see that successful early human species—like absolutely all other kinds of successful species that have been on Earth over the past 3.5 billion years—remained anatomically stable as long as their ecosystems remained stable. Physical environmental change, destabilizing those ecosystems, sent ancestral hominid species to extinction and spurred the evolution of new species just as it did in so many other plant and animal species of the ancient African landscape.

The evidence is just too good: ironically, the fossil record of human evolution is one of the very best, most complete, and ironclad documented examples of evolutionary history that we have assembled in the 200 years or so of active paleontological research. And, as we shall see (in Chapter 6), creationist attempts to punch holes in this incredibly well documented history of human evolution are simply puerile and downright wimpy.

The examples of evolutionary history presented in this chapter illustrate typical large-scale patterns in the history of life. Each shows us that evolutionary novelties—the appearance of the truly new—come at some point later in time than the appearance of the simpler, less complex anatomical structures. There is sense to the history of life—a sense made evident by the simple postulate that life has evolved. And that is the triumph of evolution.

What Drives Evolution?
The Evolution of Evolutionary Theory

If life has evolved, and if some kinds of evolutionary change can happen sufficiently rapidly to be observed during one person's lifetime, we should be able to go to nature to observe the change, to measure its tempo, and to test ideas about why and how it happens. And we should be able to simulate some kinds of evolutionary change experimentally on laboratory organisms, and even use mathematics and computers to run evolutionary experiments on an even more abstract level. This is the second meaning of the expression "evolutionary theory"—i.e., *how* does life evolve?—and the focus of discussion in this chapter.

That breeders can radically alter the anatomical and behavioral properties of animals and plants,[1] and geneticists can experimentally alter their fruit flies and guinea pigs, shows that small-scale evolutionary change can and does take place in brief intervals of time—obviously a circumstance consistent with the basic notion of evolution. Creationists often concede that such small-scale changes are possible, but they insist that these changes are not the stuff of large-scale evolutionary change between "basic kinds." But creationists are whistling in the dark.

The purpose of this chapter is to show precisely how evolutionary processes taking place in relatively small scales of space and time connect to larger-scale entities, processes, and events to produce the entire history of life—from the smallest incremental evolutionary change to the vast spectrum running from the simplest bacteria on up through the complex fungi, plants, and animals—from, in other words, the small-scale changes of so-called microevolution on up through the larger-scale changes often referred to as macroevolution. For, as we have already seen, this tremendously diverse array of life, spanning at least 3.5 billion years of Earth history, is all connected by a pattern of nested sets of genetic and anatomical similarity that can rationally be explained only as the simple outcome of a natural shared descent with modification. The only alternative is the decidedly vague and inherently untestable (thus inherently unscientific) claim that it simply suited a supernatural Creator to fashion life in this way.

Yet I have another motive in writing this chapter as well. I want to explore further the very nature of the scientific enterprise. It is no secret that scientists often disagree—sometimes over rather fundamental issues of their discipline.[2] So in this chapter I adopt a historical approach to reveal the growth of understanding of how the evolutionary process works, based on a prodigious growth of knowledge of all things biological (and geological) since the mid-nineteenth-century days when Darwin first convinced the thinking world that life has indeed evolved. But the road to enhanced knowledge and understanding is often bumpy, and I will reveal the arguments—and their resolutions—as I proceed.

It is also no secret that evolutionary biology still has its share of healthy disagreement. This is somewhat less true at the Millennium than it was, say, in the 1970s and early 1980s, since much has been accomplished since then. But there is still quite a lot to be resolved.[3] In particular, I will trace the growth of understanding of the evolutionary process with two goals in mind: first, to see how notions of *discontinuity* (so important to creationists, who insist there are no connections between "created kinds") have been incorporated into evolutionary thinking since the initial emphasis (going right back to Darwin) on *continuity*—among organisms within species, between species, and indeed in all of life. What discontinuities interrupt the continuous evolutionary spectrum from bacteria to redwood trees? What causes these discontinuities?

I also want to explore how we arrived at what I see as the greatest remaining source of conflict within evolutionary biology: the answer to the question, What actually drives the evolutionary process? As we shall see, all evolutionary biologists readily acknowledge that natural selection is the mechanism underlying adaptive change in evolution, and therefore the main ingredient of the evolutionary process that has produced the amazingly diverse array of life on Earth. And evolutionary biologists also agree that the evolutionary process is complex, involving ecological and physical environmental factors in addition to the genetic components that underlie the origin and maintenance of genetic variation, as well as selection for stasis and adaptive change.

Yet evolution is a phenomenon so rich and varied in its scope that biologists of many different disciplines come to look at the process from a variety of points of view. And therein lie some of the most exciting aspects of the study of evolution, and the source of many of the conflicts within the field. For example, the geneticist focuses, perforce, on short-term changes in the genetic composition of localized populations, while the paleontologist looks at a far broader sweep of evolutionary history: the fates of entire species and of even larger-scale groups. It is as impossible for me, a paleontologist, to study the generation-by-generation changes wrought by natural selection in my Devonian trilobites as it is for a geneticist to discover the patterns of regional ecosystemic disruption, followed by extinction and evolution of entire species. The job, clearly, is to integrate these multiscalar phenomena, and we're still not entirely there. But we've made a lot of progress—not just from Darwin's day, but even in the past twenty years.

Thus here is my millennial characterization of the grand dichotomy within evolutionary biology—stated in exaggerated form (with acknowledgment that many evolutionary biologists are already comfortable with some middle ground): On the one hand, some prominent evolutionary theorists tend to focus almost solely on natural selection. They see—correctly—that natural selection is the central process in evolution. But they tend to stop right there. The most extreme form of this position lies in the work of Oxford University biologist Richard Dawkins, author of the notion of the "selfish gene." Dawkins thinks that genes are in a constant competitive struggle among themselves to see their faithful copies represented in the next and succeeding generations. Evolution simply flows out of this competitive struggle.

Dawkins's characterization of natural selection is an extreme version of Darwin's original formulation in *On the Origin of Species* (1859):

> As many more individuals of each species are born than can possibly survive; and as, consequently, there is a frequently occurring Struggle for Existence, it follows that any being, if it vary however slightly in any manner profitable to itself, under the complex and sometimes varying conditions of life, will have a better chance of surviving, and thus be *naturally selected.* (p. 5)

In other words, Darwin saw that organisms compete for resources (mostly food—his "Struggle for Existence"), and that competition has implications for who reproduces. The genetic recipes for competitive success for organisms in the real world will tend to be passed along differentially, and when conditions change, other variant forms instead will be "selected."

However the Dawkins version of natural selection differs from Darwin's,[4] the main point here is that any evolutionary theory that focuses almost exclusively on natural selection—any evolutionary theory that does not specify the conditions that in effect turn natural selection on and off—is by definition an incomplete evolutionary theory. In a nutshell, Dawkins says that (1) natural selection amounts to competition among genes for representation in succeeding generations, and (2) since natural selection is the motor of change, the entire history of life flows from this fundamental first principle.

Thus Dawkins sees the primary impetus for evolutionary change as arising from the genes themselves. That's one of the two extreme answers to the question, What drives evolution? Here's the other: nothing substantial happens in terms of accruing adaptive evolutionary change *unless and until physical events upset the ecological applecart, leading to patterns of extinction and evolution of species.* This, it is obvious, is the position I tend to favor strongly—obvious in view of the condensed account of the 3.5-billion-year evolution of life that I gave in Chapter 3.

To my mind, the primary control over the evolutionary process lies in the events occurring in the physical world. I see a continuous spectrum from local ecosystem disturbance—with little or no evolutionary response—on up through the gross patterns of extinction and evolution occasioned by the five most severe episodes of mass extinction that have struck the planet in the last half billion years. I have deliberately stated these two starkly different views of the underlying causes of evolution in extreme terms. I now hasten to add that there is much merit in both: both have direct and very powerful relevance and application to the specific domains from which they arose, and which they endeavor to explain. The Dawkins gene-centered version is especially powerful on the small-scale level of generation-by-generation change within populations, and it is, in addition, a vital component of the underlying theoretical structure of the subdiscipline of sociobiology. On the other hand, it is useless as a general evolutionary theory covering the large-scale events in the history of life.

Then again, though, emphasis on large-scale climatic and other physical events yields an evolutionary perspective that does take the large-scale biological historical events into account, but is weak in terms of explaining the internal dynamics of selection (and other genetic phenomena) on smaller scales. Clearly, we need a general evolutionary theory that brings both elements into play. The remainder of this chapter, through its historical account, will seek to build to such a pluralistic view—with the recognition that there is still much work to be done. This is, after all, science, and science is a learning process. We have come a very long way, but there is still much more to be learned.

The Evolution of Evolutionary Theory

Darwin relied on a barrage of patterns to convince his readers that life had evolved. These included the grand pattern of nested resemblance absolutely linking up all forms of life, as well as patterns in the geographic and geological distribution of organisms. But it is generally supposed that Darwin succeeded where others before him had failed in establishing the credibility of the very idea of evolution because he supplied, as well, a plausible mechanism to explain *how* life evolves.[5]

We have already encountered Darwin's original exposition of the principle of natural selection: in a nutshell (once again), because more organisms are born each generation than can possibly survive and reproduce,[6] and because organisms vary within local populations (and those variations are heritable), on average, those organisms best suited to coping with life's exigencies are the most likely to survive and reproduce. It follows as a logical necessity that the heritable recipes for success (what we now understand to be the genetic information underlying more successful adaptations) will tend to be passed along differentially to the next succeeding generation.

It is important to realize that Darwin's theory—pangensis—about how organisms tend to resemble their parents (in stark contrast to his views on how life evolves) was later shown to be false. In Darwin's time, there was no science of genetics, indeed no concept of the gene. Darwin's views on inheritance belong in the same realm of outmoded scientific concepts as the idea of a flat Earth, or the notion that the sun revolves around our planet. His theory of inheritance envisioned various organs of the body each contributing "gemmules," little forerunners of each cell type in the body, which congregate in eggs and sperm and develop into parental replicas in the offspring. We now know that the same information that serves as a recipe for development in the fertilized egg is found in *each*[7] of the billions of cells in any vertebrate organism's body. Darwin knew nothing of this, but as it turned out, his ignorance was sublimely irrelevant to the problem he was really interested in tackling: evolution.

In other words, the knowledge that organisms show variations, that those variations are heritable, and that population sizes are inherently limited was sufficient for Darwin (and his contemporary, the naturalist Alfred Russell Wallace, 1823–1913) to formulate the notion of natural selection. It doesn't matter, it turns out, how the mechanisms of heredity actually work to understand how natural selection works. This point was not fully grasped by biologists: Many early geneticists, at the dawn of the twentieth century, thought that their discoveries of the fundamental principles of genetics somehow cast doubt, or rendered obsolete, the concept of natural selection. It took several decades of experimentation and theoretical (including mathematical) analysis to show not only that there was no conflict inherent between the emerging results of the new science of genetics and the older Darwinian notion of natural selection, but that the two operate in different domains. The principles of inheritance work within single organisms—two organisms, in the case of sexual reproduction. In contrast, natural selection involves differential reproductive success among large numbers of genetically varying organisms within a reproductive population.

Darwin touched off a storm when he published *On the Origin*. Today's creationism is, in some sense, merely an echo of that distant thunder. But many of the biologists who were immediately convinced *that* life had evolved took sharp issue with Darwin's notions on *how* life had evolved. Natural selection seemed to some a bit too brutish, too materialistic. And still other biologists were attracted to alternative theories on how life might have evolved. Foremost among the competing theories was Lamarckism.

Jean-Baptiste Lamarck (1744–1829) was a French zoologist active a half century prior to the appearance of Darwin's book. A great zoologist convinced of the interconnectedness of all life, Lamarck is generally remembered today (largely in scorn) mostly for one tiny fragment of his intellectual edifice: he thought that evolutionary change occurred when an organism developed a new capability, or underwent a slight modification, during the course of its lifetime, and subsequently passed the newly acquired trait along to its offspring. The classic conflicting scenarios of "how the giraffe got its long neck" (with apologies to Rudyard Kipling) demonstrate the differences between the Lamarckian notion of the inheritance of acquired characteristics and Darwinian natural selection.

The Lamarckian version sees individual proto-giraffes stretching their necks, craning for leaves in tree canopies, and passing on their slightly distended necks to the next generation. In contrast, the Darwinian view invokes variation in neck length within a population of proto-giraffes and imagines a situation in which competition for leaves high up in tree canopies selectively favors those with the relatively longer necks. These longer-necked giraffes tend to survive and leave more offspring, and little by little the average neck size of the proto-giraffe lineage increases.

It is a testimony both to Victorian biology's ignorance of genetics and to the persuasiveness of Lamarckian-inclined biologists that Darwin allowed Lamarckian notions to creep into later editions of *On the Origin*, though he steadfastly maintained his preference for natural selection. But in the

1880s, just after Darwin's death, the German biologist August Weismann (1834–1914) propounded what we now call the Weismann doctrine: that germ cells (eggs and sperm) create the physical body, and that the process is a one-way street. Nothing that happens to the body turns around and affects the germ cells. Characteristics developed during an organism's lifetime simply cannot be transmitted to offspring. Weismann, in other words, claimed to have refuted Lamarckian notions of evolution.[8]

In any case, Weismann had convincingly removed Lamarckian notions from biology just when genetics was in its birth throes in the early years of the twentieth century, when three biologists nearly simultaneously discovered the works of the Austrian monk Gregor Mendel (1822–1884). Mendel's famous experiments with peas implied that the factors that underlie the inheritance of features—say, blue or brown eyes, or wrinkled or smooth pea skins—are particulate, since there is a marked degree of independence and shuffling of these characteristics that seem to follow simple laws when careful breeding experiments are performed. Within a decade, the science of genetics was up and running, and important discoveries, such as that genes lie in linear arrays on chromosomes in the nuclei of all but the simplest cells, had already been made.

All the rapid advances made in the heady days of early research in genetics seemed to challenge Darwin's idea of natural selection. In fact, most biologists concentrated on such fields as genetics and the equally rapidly advancing field of physiology, spurning evolutionary biology altogether as old-fashioned. And the biologists who were left to ponder the mysteries of evolution professionally in the early decades of the twentieth century were troubled: how could Darwin's scheme of natural selection, which he saw as working on a smoothly gradational field of variation, be reconciled with the idea that genes are separate particles, each producing its own characteristic? And what of the Dutch botanist Hugo de Vries's (1848–1935) notion of mutations, in which large-scale changes in the flower of the evening primrose would suddenly appear?

"Mutations" came to be the official term for what the breeders had for years more informally termed "sports'"—the unexpected, quirky appearance of new features not inherited from parents or, for that matter, grandparents.[9]

Mutations are the source of all true novelty, it seemed, but they also seemed to be large-scale effects, not the minor new forms of variation required by the classical Darwinian view.

In the context of the new genetics, natural selection seemed to be in trouble. Many conflicting versions of evolutionary theory sprang up in the first two decades of the twentieth century, some of which not only violated Darwinian principles but also were inconsistent with the new genetics.[10] By the 1920s, biology had drifted rather far from the Darwinian fold, though evolutionists were quick to rally around the flag when the call went out for expert witnesses (who actually never ended up on the stand) for the Scopes trial.

Thus, just when the Scopes case came bursting onto the national stage, evolution was a relatively minor area of biological research taken as a whole and was, as well, fraught with difficulties. Some paleontologists in the 1920s still clung to Lamarckian notions (despite Weismann's valiant efforts to debunk Lamarckism), while others adopted vitalism, a mystical notion that saw evolution as an inner-directed drive to perfection. But it was the apparent conflict between genetics and Darwin's notion of natural selection that was the real stumbling block.

It was the work of three mathematically gifted geneticists—the American Sewall Wright (1899–1988) and the Englishmen J. B. S. Haldane (1892–1964) and Sir Ronald Fisher (1890–1962)—that resolved the apparent incongruities between the mechanisms of inheritance and the principle of natural selection. By the late 1920s, it had become clear that many mutations have relatively minor effects, that some genes play a role in forming more than one characteristic, and, most importantly, that most characters are formed by the action of more than one gene. The old black-white, brown-blue, wrinkled-smooth, either-or dualities in the theory of inheritance had given way to the view that a spectrum of variation (in height, say, or number of head hairs) could nonetheless be under genetic control. All of a sudden, there were no longer any formal objections, from the genetics quarter, to the notion of natural selection working to preserve the most beneficial of a spectrum of variation in each generation.

All this came from genetics, despite complete ignorance of the biochemical "anatomy" of genes—the structure of DNA. The biochemical basis of inheritance was still a black box, but at least what geneticists had learned circa 1930 no longer seemed to render natural selection an impossibility. The way was thus cleared for a rapprochement between genetics and evolutionary theory. Wright, Fisher, and Haldane made important contributions—essentially founding the field of population genetics, in which the effects of selection, mutation rate, and random genetic drift[11] could be studied by mathematical formulas and the analysis of experimental results.

But it was the Russian-born geneticist Theodosius Dobzhansky (1900–1975), an immigrant to New York in the 1920s, who really put it all together. Trained as a naturalist (actually, as a beetle specialist), Dobzhansky took up the study of fruit flies, which had already yielded such stunning experimental results in Thomas Hunt Morgan's (1866–1945) laboratory at Columbia University in the first decade of the twentieth century. In the 1930s, Dobzhansky began a long series of studies of natural populations in the wild of fruit fly genetics—a series that continued right up to his death in 1975.

In 1937, Dobzhansky published his first major book, *Genetics and the Origin of Species,* a title with a deliberate reference to Darwin's greatest book, published so long before. And the bridge Dobzhansky built involved far more than a literary allusion. In the book, Dobzhansky effectively argued for the central role played by natural selection in changing the genetic composition of populations of organisms in nature.

Darwin emerged completely vindicated: natural populations seem to possess ample amounts of genetic variation. But this variation, as Darwin himself had noted, seems highly organized: local populations within a species differ from place to place, reflecting adaptation to slightly different environments. The average length of a sparrow's wing, for example, is longer in warmer climes than in populations situated high up the slopes of mountain ranges. The physiological explanation is simple: shorter wings radiate less body heat, a distinct advantage in colder climates. Natural selection, then, preserves the variants within species that are best suited to the precise ecological conditions of each local habitat over the entire range of a species.

Dobzhansky's book accomplished a lot more than finishing the fusion between genetics on the one hand, and the original Darwinian vision of adaptation through natural selection on the other. In his first chapter, Dobzhansky pointed out that, if that were all to the story, the world of living creatures would look a lot different to us than it does. Looking around us, we see populations of different species of birds, mammals, trees, and shrubs. Thinking of the denizens of my own backyard for a moment: The gray squirrels all look pretty much alike (despite some underlying genetic variation), and they look very different from their close relatives, the eastern chipmunks. Likewise individual specimens of the several species of oaks and maples all look a lot alike—and quite different from other, closely related tree species.

In other words, Dobzhansky looked around and saw *discreteness* in the living world. He saw gaps between species—gaps that simply wouldn't be there if natural selection, working on a spectrum of variation within one enormous species population, were all there is to the evolutionary process. Natural selection, Dobzhansky knew, would be expected to produce a continuous array of variation, since populations—and entire species—are adapted to the specific environments of each and every locale.

Dobzhansky, moreover, had the first insights on how the hierarchical structure of living systems is related to the evolutionary process. At the level of the genetics of individual organisms, he realized that genes are particulate and discrete, as are their variant versions (alleles). (What we have learned about the structure and composition of DNA and RNA in the years since Dobzhansky wrote his book only bears this point out further.) At the second level, however—the population level—things are completely different: here we enter the realm of relative gene frequencies, in which selection (and genetic drift) shift frequencies of genes in a continuous, gradational manner. Here lies the real reason why Darwin could formulate accurately his theory of natural selection without knowing the first thing about genetics: the two processes—inheritance and changing gene frequencies through natural selection and genetic drift—take place at completely different levels of biological organization.

There is a third, even higher level, in which populations of organisms are aggregated into larger arrays that we call species. Dobzhansky (and his contemporary, American Museum of Natural History biologist Ernst Mayr,

1904–) conceived of species essentially as the largest collections of organisms that are capable of mating with each other. And these reproductive communities, these species, are for the most part discrete entities. At this higher level, once more we confront gaps and discreteness.

Darwin of course saw the same gaps, but because his primary goal was to convince the world that life had evolved, he quite naturally stressed the evidence for continuity, downplaying discontinuity as much as an honest man like he possibly could. After all, he was trying to overthrow a worldview that was beautifully summarized in two of my favorite quotes from pre-evolutionary, pre-Darwinian days: (1) "Species tot sunt quot ab initio faciebat Infinitum Ens (meaning "There are as many species as originally created by the Infinite Being"), by Carolus Linnaeus, the great botanist and founder of the modern scheme of classification, writing in *Systema Naturae* (1758); and (2) "Species have a real existence in nature, and a transition from one to another does not exist" (a statement from British philosopher William Whewell, writing in *History of the Inductive Sciences*, 1837).

Both statements acknowledge the reality and discreteness of species and maintain that species are not interconnected by a natural process of evolution. Darwin obviously felt that, to establish that species are connected in an evolutionary sense, he had to deny, in a very real sense, their discreteness. That there are gaps between species was plain enough to Darwin, but he chose to explain the gaps purely by invoking the extinction of intermediate forms.

Dobzhansky thought otherwise. He thought that gaps between species are the direct result of the evolutionary process itself. In answer to the question of why the living world is cut up into an array of (some 10 million) more or less discrete species, Dobzhansky maintained that partitioning of pools of genetic information would help focus a species' adaptations to the environment: one large species, spread out over a variety of environments, would contain the genetic information pertinent to each localized environment. And that information would spread (in a process called gene flow). To focus more narrowly on a subset of environments, it would be helpful, Dobzhansky thought, to interrupt that gene flow, to partition that vast array of genetic information—in short, to make two species where there once had been but one.

Dobzhansky also spoke of a natural trade-off inherent in the genetics of natural biological systems (i.e., populations and species): in general, it is best not to focus adaptations (and underlying genetic information) too narrowly, lest the environment change and extinction loom. On the other hand, a continuous array of genetic information would not support adaptive focus on any subset of environmental conditions.

That is why Dobzhansky's book is best remembered for its analysis of the origin of new species. Ironically, Darwin never did discuss the origin of species in his book of that name. For reasons just discussed, to Darwin, the "origin of species" was essentially synonymous with the term "evolution" itself. The simple accumulation of anatomical change over thousands and millions of years was what Darwin had in mind when he thought of new species arising from old. Occasionally, he realized, species would somehow become fragmented, such that what was once a single species would leave two (or even more) species, each newly embarked along slowly divergent, separate pathways. But to Darwin, such divergence was little more than a special case of natural selection molding far-flung populations along somewhat different lines, until their differences appeared so great that we would be obliged to call them different species.

Dobzhansky and other biologists in the 1930s recognized that species are something more than mere collections of organisms similar in their anatomical and behavioral properties. They are also breeding communities; in fact, it is their interbreeding, and consequent sharing of genetic information, that makes their component organisms so similar in the first place. Years of observation in the field and experience in the lab and breeder's pen showed that most species cannot be successfully mated even with their closest relatives. More to the point, even when such hybridization is technically possible—when the species are found together in the wild—hybrids are nonetheless rare, or altogether absent; i.e., even if they can interbreed, they don't. Lions and tigers in India (yes, there still are a few lions in India) have been in close contact in some places within human memory, yet, insofar as I am aware, the "tiglons" produced in some zoos have never been seen in the wild.

How do new reproductive groups—new species—originate? Dobzhansky's thoughtful discussion of the origin of what he called isolating mechanisms has settled the issue. The behavioral and anatomical differences between species are what keep them from interbreeding. These differences usually evolve when a species is so far-flung that some of its populations become isolated from the main group. In other words, normal adaptive differentiation (as with wing length in sparrows), plus prolonged geographic isolation (when no mating between the two divisions of a species takes place), starts the ball rolling. If divergence has proceeded far enough, when two groups that used to be members of the same species once again come into contact, genetically based anatomical, physiological, and behavioral traits have become so differentiated that the groups no longer interbreed.

Ernst Mayr, an ornithologist working at the American Museum of Natural History in New York, published *Systematics and the Origin of Species* (1942) a few years after Dobzhansky's book appeared. Mayr knew that naturalists even before Darwin were aware of a general pattern in nature in which a species' closest relative typically lives in an adjacent region—not in the same area. Victorian naturalists called such species vicars (in the sense that they either replaced or represented one another geographically) or germinate ("twin") species. In a sense, such species are just slightly different versions of the same thing. The scarlet tanager of eastern North America, for example, is "replaced" in the West by the equally striking, if differently colored, western tanager.

Darwin used the patterns of geographic variation and vicariant species as part of his argument that life must have evolved. In contrast, Dobzhansky, Mayr, and other evolutionists of the 1930s and 1940s emphasized the importance (in fact, the utter necessity) of geographic isolation for disrupting an ancestral species to produce two species where once there had been but one. To these later workers, evolution is descent with modification all right, but it is produced by a one-two combination of adaptive change plus occasional episodes of disruption, creating the great array of different species we see all around us today. Thus by the early 1940s, we finally had a theory of how natural selection effects genetic change, and how accumulated genetic change plus geographic isolation yields reproductive isolation—a new species derived from an older, ancestral species. Biologists had finally added the all-important aspect of species-level discontinuity to the spectrum of continuous variation generated by natural selection.

But what of the large-scale changes in evolution? The work of Fisher, Haldane, Wright, Dobzhansky, and Mayr (and, of course, their many colleagues) spoke directly to the evolution of the sorts of differences between, say, lions and tigers. The conclusion that the kind of adaptive change within species underlies the differences we see between closely related species has long since seemed so voluminous and incontestable that even today's creationists accept microevolution. Patterns of evolutionary change within species seem no different in principle—just milder in degree—from the sorts of changes we see between closely related species. All evolutionary changes are produced by natural selection working each generation on the variation presented to it. Could this simple process also account for all the changes among the larger groups of animals and plants—between, say, reptiles and mammals?

Let us return just for a moment to the grand pattern of nested sets of resemblance linking up absolutely all species on Earth. Closely related species are classified in the same genus, and related genera are put in the same family. Families are lumped together in the same order, and related orders are grouped into the same class. This is the Linnaean hierarchy that was devised, long before Darwin's day, to encompass the nested pattern of similarities that define groups of organisms—a pattern naturalists had observed in the organic world since Aristotle. But, we must ask, what exactly are these genera, families, orders, and so on? It was clear to Darwin, and it should be obvious to all today, that they are simply ever larger categories used to give names to *ever larger clusters of related species*. That's all these clusters, these higher taxa, really are: simply clusters of related species.

Thus, in principle the evolution of a family should be no different in its basic nature, and should involve no different processes, from the evolution of a genus, since a family is nothing more than a collection of related genera. And genera are just collections of related species. The triumph of evolutionary biology in the 1930s and 1940s was the conclusion that the same principles of adaptive divergence just described—primarily the processes of mutation and natural selection—going on within species, accumulate to produce the differences we see between closely related species—i.e., within genera. Q.E.D.: *If adaptive modification within species explains the evolutionary differences between species within a genus, logically it must explain all the evolutionary change we see between families, orders, classes, phyla, and the kingdoms of life.*

This highly reasonable inference still demanded cogent exposition. In his *Tempo and Mode in Evolution* (a book begun in the late 1930s but not published until 1944), George Gaylord Simpson (1902–1984), a vertebrate paleontologist also at the American Museum of Natural History, attempted to show that all the major changes in life's evolutionary history could be understood as a by-product of these newly understood principles of genetic change. To undertake this task, Simpson had to confront that greatest and most persistent of paleontological bugbears: the notorious gaps of the fossil record.

Darwin and his evolution-minded successors in the paleontological ranks preferred to explain these gaps away: they blamed the incompleteness of the geological record of the events of Earth history. According to this explanation, the lack of abundant (creationists say *any)* examples of smoothly gradational change between ancestors and descendants in the fossil record merely bears witness to the gaps in the quality of the rock record. True enough, but not entirely so, said Simpson, to his everlasting credit.

Simpson thought the fossil record has a great deal to say about how evolution occurs—its pace and style, its "tempo and mode." After all, it is in the enormous expanse of geological time that the evolutionary game has actually been played. But to make a such a claim is also to assert that the fossil record is at least complete enough to be taken seriously. Thus the gaps had to be confronted. And since gaps there certainly are, they must at least in part be a product of the evolutionary process, if not merely the artifacts of a poor geological record.

It is the gaps in the fossil record that, perhaps more than any other facet of the natural world, are dearly beloved by creationists. As we shall see when we take up the creationist position, there are all sorts of gaps: absence of gradationally intermediate transitional forms between species, but also between larger groups—between, say, families of carnivores, or the orders of mammals. In fact, the higher up the Linnaean hierarchy you look, the fewer transitional forms there seem to be. For example, *Peripatus,* a lobe-legged, wormlike creature that haunts rotting logs in the Southern Hemisphere, appears intermediate in many respects between two of the major phyla on Earth today: the segmented worms and the arthropods. But few other phyla have such intermediates with other phyla, and when we scan the fossil record for them we find some, but basically little, help. Extinction has surely weeded out many of the intermediate species, but on the other hand, the fossil record is not exactly teeming with their remains.

Simpson knew this but preferred a view of evolution consistent with the emerging principles of genetic change over the alternative posed by German paleontologist Otto Schindewolf (1896–1971). Schindewolf interpreted the gaps in the fossil record as evidence of the sudden appearance of new groups of animals and plants. Not a creationist, Schindewolf believed all forms of life to be interrelated, but he felt that the fossil record implies a saltational mode of evolution—literally, sudden jumps from one basic type (called a Bauplan, or fundamental architectural design—conceptually if tangentially related to creationists' "basic kinds") to another. Simpson and his peers scoffed at such an idea, and rightly so, since little evidence emanating from genetics laboratories even remotely hinted at how such sudden leaps could occur. And the cardinal rule of science—that all ideas must be testable—held sway: the prevailing theory and evidence of genetics of the 1930s (and genetics hasn't changed all that much since) were against large-scale, sudden switches in the physical appearance of descendant organisms. Schindewolf's views were at odds with nearly all that was known of genetics in the 1930s. His saltational explanation of the gaps was impressive—but wrong, as far as Simpson was concerned.

Simpson thought that most of the fossil record amply supports Darwin's view—that species slowly but surely—*gradually*—change through time, such that new species arise from old by imperceptible gradations over time. There is plenty of evidence, he felt, to show that 90 percent of evolution involves the gradual transition from one species to the next through time. When there were gaps between closely related species and genera—in other words, when new species appear abruptly in the fossil record with no smoothly intergradational intermediates between them and their ancestors—Simpson was (like Darwin) content to blame the gaps on the vagaries of preservation inherent in the formation of the fossil record.

In contrast to his treatment of species, Simpson did acknowledge that the sudden appearance of new groups—those ranked rather high in the Linnaean hierarchy, and what the creationists call basic kinds—implies something *true* about how evolution works. If evolution were always a slow, steady change from species to species, Simpson pointed out, the transitions between major groups would typically take millions of years, and we should expect to find some fossil evidence of the transitional forms. Not finding them very often, he deduced, implies that evolution sometimes goes on rather quickly—in brief, intense spurts. The presence of some intermediates (such as *Archaeopteryx,* the proto-bird) falsifies Schindewolf's saltational notions. But the relative scarcity of such intermediates bespeaks a major mode of evolution producing truly rapid change—a mode Simpson called quantum evolution. In physics, a quantum is a sudden, definite shift in state, a jump from one state to another without intermediates, an either-or proposition. The fossil record mimics these sudden changes in state, as is shown, for instance, by the evolution of whales from terrestrial mammalian forebears.

Whales first appeared in the Eocene, some 55 million years ago. They are primitive—for whales. But the earliest specimens look like whales, and it is only their general mammalian features that tell us they must have sprung from another group of terrestrial mammals in the Paleocene.[12] Bats are another example: a perfect specimen from the Eocene of Wyoming is primitive—for bats—but anyone looking at it will see at once that it is a bat, and evidence for its derivation from a particular kind of insectivorous Paleocene mammal still hasn't turned up.

Simpson's specific theory about how these sudden shifts come about in the course of evolution is no longer accepted in all its details, mainly because Simpson himself effectively retracted the idea in his sequel, *The Major Features of Evolution,* published in 1953. The original idea of quantum evolution envisioned a small population rapidly losing the adaptations of its parental species, going through a shaky phase, and then luckily hitting on a new set of anatomical and behavioral features suitable to life in a new—radically new—ecological niche. Simpson supported his theoretical stance with the solid structure of genetics, but he later dropped the notions of "inadaptive" and "preadaptive" phases. Why he did so reveals the power of the very idea of natural selection.

The tide of thinking in genetics was simply running against notions of genetic change that didn't specifically include natural selection. Early in the 1930s, for instance, the geneticist Sewall Wright spoke about the fate of genetic information among different breeding populations (he called them demes) within a species and of the role that chance plays in determining the composition of the next generation. Wright was not wholly infatuated with natural selection as the only agent of evolutionary change. Although his concept of genetic drift as a random factor in evolution was accepted by his peers, it was a grudging acceptance. It is only recently that his shifting-balance theory, in which the differential success of such breeding populations is a major issue, has once again begun to be taken seriously.

Both notions pay but little heed to the narrow, restricted version of natural selection, which is differential reproductive success of individuals within breeding populations based on their relative abilities to cope with life's exigencies. But by and large, Dobzhansky's book, plus Mayr's and Simpson's and a host of shorter technical publications in the late 1930s and 1940s, came close to asserting that the only significant force underlying genetic, hence evolutionary, change is natural selection. By 1953, Simpson himself saw his original concept of quantum evolution as too far removed from the consensus. He modified quantum evolution to mean merely an extremely rapid phase of change, governed throughout by natural selection as a small population invaded a new habitat.

By the early 1950s, the gist of evolutionary theory said that genetic change is largely a function of natural selection working on a field of variation presented to it each generation. New features from time to time appear, ultimately brought about by mutation. Most mutations are harmful; some are neutral, or even beneficial. The neutral or beneficial mutations hang on and one day might prove to be a real advantage as the environment provides new challenges to the organisms. In any case, as the environment changes (as all environments eventually do), it does so generally slowly. Natural selection preserves the best of each generation, and their genes make up the succeeding generation. Through time, through enough generations, selection wreaks tremendous changes. And occasionally habitats divide and species fragment, following separate adaptive histories. Hence, species multiply. Given enough time (and remember that geologists tell us that the

Earth is fully 4.5 billion years old), all manner of change will accrue: species keep on giving rise to new species, and adaptive evolutionary change accumulates. The more species, the more adaptive change—and the greater the evolutionary divergence. Genera, families, orders, classes, and phyla—all owe their genesis (as it were) to the simple processes of mutation, natural selection, and speciation.

Thus, by 1959, the centennial year of the publication of Darwin's *On the Origin of Species,* the essence of Darwin's vision had been integrated with the science of genetics. The importance of the evolution of new species, producing a discontinuous array of adaptive diversity, had been added, though it was already being downplayed somewhat and was soon to be ignored almost completely by a major, gene-centered branch of evolutionary biology that developed in the 1960s and 1970s. Though most evolutionary biologists were congratulating themselves and each other that, not only had Darwin been vindicated but also in effect a complete evolutionary theory had already been achieved, post-1959 developments were soon to belie that conclusion.

Evolutionary Biology at the Millennium

The molecular revolution that began with the famous discovery by Watson and Crick (and unheralded partners, such as Rosalind Franklin) of the structure of DNA has had a pronounced, if subtle, effect on evolutionary biology during the last forty years of the twentieth century. Indeed, in a sense history replayed itself, as some molecular geneticists thought that the new understanding of the molecular structure of the gene somehow alters the older formulations of population genetics. But, as we have seen especially with the work of Theodosius Dobzhansky—who so clearly saw that the genetic processes of inheritance take place at the level of the individual, whereas natural selection and genetic drift take place within populations of individual organisms—any new knowledge of the chemical structure of genes can only enrich, rather than supplant, the understanding of evolutionary processes that has accumulated since the days of Charles Darwin.

And molecular biology has indeed enriched evolutionary discourse. For a while, controversy erupted over ways in which molecular processes could themselves bias the transmission of forms of genetic information,[13] suggesting to some biologists that fundamental concepts of the evolutionary process would have to be modified in light of the new science of molecular genetics. Among the more subtle impacts of the molecular revolution in evolutionary biology, however, was the emergence of one of the main strands of evolutionary thought of the past forty years, which was mentioned at the outset of this chapter:[14] the approach to evolution epitomized by Richard Dawkins's concept of the selfish gene. This explicitly gene-centered movement began right after the Darwinian centennial, with the publication of two critical papers by geneticist William Hamilton (in 1964), and especially American biologist George C. Williams's influential book *Adaptation and Natural Selection* (1966). Williams's work attempted to inject greater rigor into evolutionary analysis and maintained that natural selection works strictly for the "good of the individual"—i.e., not for the good of the species, as evolutionary biologists had been wont to assume, rather uncritically, off and on ever since Darwin.

Perhaps the most important aspect of this work has been the development of the field of sociobiology. To Darwin the presence of altruism, in which organisms act to benefit others in their populations, is a bit of a conundrum: if, he reasoned, the continual struggle for existence constantly pits organisms against each other for survival (and ultimately for reproductive success), what advantage could there be in *helping* other organisms? Hamilton's twin papers in 1964 went far toward resolving this problem, which was emerging as a real difficulty, given the renewed emphasis on individual selection (as exemplified by Williams's book in 1966).[15] Hamilton showed by mathematical analysis that the more genes any two organisms share, the more it is to their own benefit (i.e., in terms of seeing their own genes make it to the next generation) to cooperate with their relatives.

Social systems, of course, rely on cooperation among their members. The entire field of sociobiology—spearheaded by Harvard evolutionary biologist E. O. Wilson—sprang from the realization that altruistic behavior is expected to be correlated with degrees of genetic relatedness. This construct works particularly well with social insects, which are characterized by peculiar genetic systems in which nestmates share even higher percentages of their genes than the 50 percent genetic similarity typical of siblings.

Sociobiology is only one conspicuous example of the focus of post-1959 evolutionary research. There have also been detailed examinations of natural selection in the wild, as well as numerous studies documenting the intense evolutionary interactions among different species in local ecosystems.[16] The major journal devoted to evolutionary biological research in the United States—*Evolution*—greatly expanded the number of pages published annually during the last half of the twentieth century. Modern evolutionary biology, focused on genes and natural selection, is alive and well, and it has fully incorporated molecular genetics into its fundamental structure.

Indeed, we now know that genetic, evolutionary change in natural populations is occurring constantly, and at least in some instances the genetic flux is so great that the problem is to reconcile it with one of the great patterns in the evolutionary history of life briefly encountered in Chapter 3: stasis. How can genetic change be so common and so rapid within populations, while species as a whole tend to remain fairly stable over millions of years? Then, too, though some geneticists have turned their attention to the speciation process to great effect, on the whole the focus on within-population genetic change has tended to downplay the significance of the discontinuities between species that had been added to the evolutionary discourse by Dobzhansky and Mayr just before World War II. But those gaps are real, and they are created by the evolutionary process. And both these problems—stasis and the creation of gaps between species by the very process of speciation—came together in the theoretical postulate known as punctuated equilibria, part of a second major stream of evolutionary research that developed in the 1960s. This field of research stresses the larger-scale patterns in the history of life, many of which were encountered in Chapter 3.

In the 1960s, I was one of a number of graduate students interested in evolutionary paleontological research. Most of us were enrolled in Columbia University's Geology Department, for though our primary interests were distinctly biological, invertebrate paleontology had traditionally been a field of geological investigation. And it was invertebrates that caught the eyes of most of us, since invertebrate fossils are found in great profusion in the Paleozoic, Mesozoic, and Cenozoic strata of the world; often, many thousands of specimens can be collected that span millions of years. And one thing that evolutionary theory had long since made abundantly clear is that evolution through natural selection works on variation within populations of organisms. We also understood that geographic variation is an important ingredient of the evolutionary process, and many marine formations crop out over truly vast areas on the world's continents.

So naturally we thought it would be far easier to study evolution if we had large samples of brachiopods or clams or snails—or, in my case, trilobites. Studying evolution would be a snap, we thought: all we needed to do was drive from outcrop to outcrop, plotting out patterns of within-population and geographic variation, tracing evolutionary history directly as it unfolded before our eyes as we sampled up through successfully younger layers of fossiliferous rock. Basically, the evolutionary pattern we expected to find was Darwin's originally predicted pattern: slow, steady gradual change within species as we looked up the geological column.

At first, I was frustrated. Collecting trilobites from New York west to Iowa, from southern Canada south through Virginia, sampling populations that spanned at least 6 million years, I could find very few differences among the hundreds of specimens I found. Despair began to creep in, as I thought my first major piece of paleontological research was turning out to be a failure. As I struggled to find some signs of gradual evolution within my lineage of Devonian trilobites, it finally became clear to me that stability was the norm, the rule in the history of my species lineages of trilobites.[17] All around me, others were finding great stability in their species lineages of fossils as well.

Yet evolution was nonetheless plainly occurring: new species of trilobites, distinguished by small but consistent differences between samples, occasionally did appear. When I placed my data on a series of maps representing five successive slices of time, a pattern of geography leaped out, instantly suggesting that my trilobites were evolving through the general process of geographic speciation, as described by Theodosius Dobzhansky and Ernst Mayr. I described these results in the journal *Evolution* in 1971, and a year later my fellow graduate student (since gone on to the Harvard faculty) Stephen Jay Gould and I developed a general model of evolution based on my trilobites, his snail examples, and what we took to be fundamental patterns of (1) stasis and (2) geographic speciation that we thought were demonstrably the rule rather than the exception in the evolution of species throughout the history of life (see Eldredge and Gould, 1972).

The gaps between species are especially important here, given creationist claims that gaps between species (and higher taxa) are sufficient to disprove the very notion of evolution. Though some of my samples of Devonian trilobites do preserve some transitional states between ancestral and descendant species, by and large what we paleontologists see is the persistence of stable species for millions of years, followed by the appearance of other, usually quite similar species. Sometimes there is a clear geographic component to the pattern, but very often we find these species occurring one on top of the other in the rock column. Sometimes the two (i.e., ancestral and descendant species) overlap in time, but very often they do not.

How could we explain these gaps—these quick changes from one set of anatomical features to another? Easily: Gould and I realized that standard geographic speciation theory as developed especially by Dobzhansky and Mayr was sufficient. Geographic isolation leading to reproductive isolation need not take long to occur: our estimate was from five thousand to fifty thousand years, and some geneticists immediately commented that speciation could go on a lot faster than that. Speciation can be a rapid process—and one *altogether too quick to show up in detail in the fossil record*. The layers of sediment that entomb the fossil record are simply too episodic, too inherently gappy themselves, to record the passage of every successive year—or decade—or century—of geological time. In other words, the naturally occurring gaps between closely related species in the modern fauna and flora, directly caused by the process of fissioning known as speciation, typically happens so quickly that rarely do we catch it in midstream when we scour the fossil record for insights on how evolution occurs.

But that's not all. When we published our paper on punctuated equilibria in 1972, although Gould and I claimed the pattern was very general—typical of species up and down the fossil record since time immemorial—we nonetheless did not realize that many species in regional ecosystems stay in stasis together for long periods of time. Likewise, we did not take into account that other major aspect—the larger pattern of coordinated stasis, or turnover pulse—that (as we saw in Chapter 3) is a dominant theme in the history of life over the past half billion years. In other words, *we did not realize that the pattern of species lineage stasis and speciation that we called punctuated equilibria was happening to the vast majority of the species lineages living in close proximity in local and regional ecosystems.*

Stasis and evolution (adaptation through natural selection in conjunction with the speciation process) typically happen simultaneously within many separate lineages of animals and plants, from Cambrian trilobites on up through Pliocene-Pleistocene hominids—the fossil record of our own human evolution. Stability is the norm until a physical environmental event (such as a spurt of global cooling) disrupts regional ecosystems sufficiently that a threshold is reached, and relatively suddenly many species become extinct. Only after such spasms of extinction do we find much evidence of speciation—i.e., actual evolutionary change.

What, then, drives evolution? To my mind, and to many of my colleagues as well, it seems clear that nothing much happens in evolutionary history *unless and until physical environmental effects disturb ecosystems and species.* Competition among genes or organisms for reproductive success is important but in and of itself insufficient to create the dominant patterns we encounter when we examine the history of life.

It is also important to recall Dobzhansky's early message on the hierarchical structure of genetic (i.e., evolutionary) systems. Dobzhansky saw that genes are parts of organisms, which are in turn parts of local populations, which are in turn parts of species. Species, in turn, are parts of larger-scale systems—the higher taxa such as families, orders, and so on, of the Linnaean system. This nesting of genes up through higher taxa, in the functional, dynamic sense of evolutionary theory, constitutes what I call the evolutionary hierarchy—or perhaps better, Dobzhansky's hierarchy.

Ecological systems, too, are hierarchically structured: local ecosystems are connected (through the flow of matter and energy between populations of organisms, each with a different niche) to form regional systems, which themselves are parts of large-scale (e.g., subcontinental) systems, and so forth. All the world's ecosystems are actually joined into one grand global system.

Putting this all together with what we have seen about patterns in the history of life, and with what we have learned about the evolutionary process from the study of genetics and ecological processes yields the outlines of an evolutionary theory that I believe best takes everything into account. Here, in very rough and simple form, is my thumbnail sketch of how evolution works: [18]

On the smallest scales, with little or no environmental disruption and little ecological perturbation, local populations of different species within local ecosystems undergo normal processes of mutation and natural selection, but selection will for the most part be for the status quo. However, different populations of the same species living in adjacent ecosystems will undergo slightly different mutational and selection histories, and in this way genetic diversity within a species as a whole may increase through time.

Ecological disruption of local ecosystems (e.g., damage by fires, storms, oil spills) kills off many individuals within local populations and triggers the normal processes of ecological succession, with pioneer species dominating early assemblages, and species characteristic of later (mature) stages coming in later. Ecosystems are reassembled through recruitment from outlying populations, adaptations already in place are utilized, and little if any evolutionary change occurs.

Longer-term regional ecological disruption (as, for example, when glaciers invade temperate zones from the higher latitudes) disrupt ecosystems even further; in response, species engage in habitat tracking, collapsing toward the Tropics in search of suitable (recognizable) habitat. Yet even in these times of great environmental change, ecosystemic disruption, and displacement of species, natural selection remains dominantly stabilizing as long as species can continue to identify and occupy suitable habitat (which is why many species remain in stasis even during times of momentous environmental stress, as was typical, for example, in the Pleistocene of North America and Eurasia).

Only when environmental stress reaches a threshold—when ecological systems are so severely stressed that they can no longer survive—and when habitat tracking is not an option for many species, does extinction begin to claim many regionally distributed species, clearing the way for rapid speciation events in many separate lineages. This is what is going on at the boundaries between Palmer's Cambrian biomeres, and between the episodes of Brett and Baird's coordinated stasis, and what constitutes, as well, Vrba's turnover pulses (all of which I discussed in Chapter 3). According to the fossil record, most evolutionary change in the history of life occurs in conjunction with these physically induced episodes of ecological stress and extinction. Here, natural selection becomes strongly directional, as new species, with new adaptations, develop rapidly.

Finally, at the grander geographic scales—up to and including the entire Earth—environmental disruption is so severe, and extinction occurs on such a great scale, that entire large-scale arrays of species—taxa such as families, orders, and classes—may go extinct, triggering, as we saw in Chapter 3, the rapid diversification of other lineages, which in many cases are clearly ecological replacements for the lineages that had succumbed to extinction (e.g., see the coral example of Chapter 3).

This is how I—one evolutionary biologist out of many—see the evolutionary process. Microevolution and macroevolution differ only as a matter of scale, as we have seen from the connectedness of all life, and from the sliding scale of events—from the simplest, smallest evolutionary changes up through the enormous effects wrought as the aftermath of global mass extinctions.

I have placed this "sloshing bucket" model of the evolutionary process before you here at the end of this chapter on the evolutionary process not because I insist it is the absolute truth, or anything near the final word on how the evolutionary process works. Quite the contrary: though I suspect most of my colleagues will find much to agree with in this (very abbreviated) sketch of my version of how evolution works, *it is the very strength of the scientific enterprise in general—and of evolutionary biology in particular—that many of my colleagues will not wholeheartedly agree with the foregoing model.*

Creationists claim this is a defect of evolutionary biology—this lack of complete consensus among ourselves. On the contrary: that is its very strength. We have come a long way since Darwin, but we still have a way to go before we can find ourselves in total agreement on all details of how the evolutionary process works. Indeed, realist that I am, I know that day will never come.

We do all agree that life has evolved. We do all agree that the reason why organisms tend to fit their environments so well is that their anatomies, physiologies, and behaviors have been shaped by natural selection, working on local populations living resource-limited lives within the confines of local ecosystems. And we are coming ever closer to agreeing that whatever phenomena of stability and genetic change take place within local populations, gaps between species arise primordially through speciation. It has become, as well, increasingly apparent that speciation events do not take place randomly with respect to one another, but rather are regionally concentrated in bursts that follow close on the heels of environmental disruption of ecosystems and extinction of numbers of species; that is, the data of paleontology are clear on the point that most speciation (and extinction) events involve many unrelated plant and animal lineages, living in association in regional ecosystems, in relatively brief spans of time.

In other words, we agree on a lot of things. But there's still a lot about which we cannot all agree, so work will go on. But it is good, honest work, empirical at base. It is, in short, the very antithesis of the a priori doctrinaire ravings of creationists.

Creationists Attack: I
Scientific Style and Notions of Time

Creationists think that the entire content of the preceding chapters is false—whether maliciously or naïvely or even satanically motivated, in any case thoroughly false. Creationists passionately believe that evolution is the root of much moral decay and downright evil in modern society, and that it must be opposed at all costs. And most creationists still reject the notion that the Earth itself is very old and has had an even longer and equally intricate history as life itself has had.

So what do creationists have to say about the foregoing—the rules of evidence that belong to the empirical-analytical world of science (as opposed, for example, to the rules of evidence and argumentation in a court of law?)[1] Creationists have not yet managed to propose (let alone compile convincing empirical evidence in favor of) a creation model alternative to the well-established patterns and generalizations of geology and evolutionary biology. Indeed, some creationists are willing to admit that theirs is a crusade against evolution prompted by religious beliefs and are often willing to concede that God is by definition supernatural—and therefore not open to empirical investigation in the first place.[2] So the central strategy of all creationist literature has always been to debunk evolution, thereby leaving creationism as the sole standing survivor, constituting the "truth" of the matter. To creationists, it makes abundant sense that, if evolution could somehow be shown to be fatally flawed—to be false—then their version of the history of the cosmos would be instantly established as the correct one.

As far as science is concerned—as the preceding chapters make abundantly clear—though the inevitable disagreements still pervade geology and biology, there are no credible scientific alternatives to an essentially Darwinian view of evolution through natural selection.

So let us pick up the gauntlet and see how well the creationists have mounted their attack on scientific method; on nuclear physics (e.g., in terms of the radiometric dating of rocks); on astrophysics (age of the Universe); on the formation of the geological column and the interpretation of geological history; and, of course, on the evolution of life—the patterns of its history, and what science says it has learned about how the evolutionary process operates. For the moment let's play their game, conceding for the sake of argument that it is indeed an either-or matter, and see who wins on intellectual grounds alone.[3]

By far the closest thing to a clear, concise, and definitive version of what creationists believe to be a rational alternative to the tenets of historical geology and evolutionary biology comes in the formal codifications of "creation science," the form of creationism invented with the explicit goal of injecting creationism into public school curricula under the cloak of science. And though I will use the writings of "creation scientists" as by far the most convenient means of tabulating and analyzing the tenets of creationism as a whole, I will say at the outset that creation science isn't science at all. Creation scientists have not managed to come up with even a single intellectually compelling, scientifically testable statement about the natural world—beyond, that is, hypotheses that have long since been tested and abandoned by science, in many cases as long ago as the nineteenth century. Creation science has precious few ideas of its own—positive ideas that stand on their own, independent of, and opposed to, counteropinions of normal science. And as we shall see, the few ideas that can be construed as scientific are fatuous.

Scientific creationism forms the basis of the bills passed in the 1980s by the legislatures and signed into law by the governors of Arkansas and Louisiana. It is extreme and virulent. It insists that the Earth and all of its life were created in six twenty-four-hour days by the act of a supernatural Creator. Scientific creationists may have failed to contribute anything of substance to the intellectual pursuit—open to all—that is real science, but they have met with some considerable success in promulgating their views in the process of educating U.S. schoolchildren, as well as in the political arena that surrounds that all-important process. And that is reason enough to take a long, hard look at what these people are saying.

What Are Scientific Creationists Saying?

When debating creationists, scientists are bombarded by a number of challenges that creationists have culled from scientific writings on the natural world. The arguments typically take the following form: "All right, let's see you explain this one!" Hurling challenge after challenge, jumping from atomic physics to zoology, creationists eventually wear the opposition down with their compendia of nature's enigmas. One of their favorites, for example, is the bombardier beetle, darling of creationists because its intricate defense system (bombardier beetles forcefully eject hot fluids when threatened) is impossible (for creationists) to imagine evolving through a series of less perfect, intermediate stages—and, they say, impossible for an evolutionist to prove. Some intrepid evolutionists take them up point by point, and there was a lively exchange on the bombardier beetle in the summer 1981 issue of *Creation/Evolution,* a journal devoted to combating the creationist effort. But such compendia of cases quickly become tedious, and in the end they demonstrate nothing.

Evolutionists admit at the outset that they are puzzled by some of nature's products, and, in any case, as scientists they are in no position to prove anything. But some general themes recur in the literature of scientific creationism—both general objections to what they persist in calling "evolution science," accompanied by countless examples, and statements that make up the corpus of creationist thought on how things have come to be as they are. The bombardier beetle, for example, is but one of the many cases of the general argument that intermediate stages between an anatomical structure and its supposed precursor are impossible, could not be produced by natural selection, and do not, in any event, show up in the fossil record—once again, the hydra-headed problem of gaps.

Other general objections include the argument that apparent design in nature is a prima facie case for a Designer; that complex molecules, anatomical structures, and behaviors cannot have arisen by chance, the probabilities of a natural process forming them being remote; and that the evolution of the complex from the simple violates more fundamental scientific laws—particularly the first and second laws of thermodynamics. To creationists, something cannot come out of nothing (their version of the first law), and once begun, a system inevitably declines and cannot become more complex (their précis of the second law).

These and other sorts of objections, with their myriad examples, are interwoven with various direct pronouncements to form the "creation science" model. Prominent creationist authors such as Duane Gish and Gary Parker (from the Institute for Creation Research, or ICR, in San Diego) have supplied bits and pieces from which we might cobble together a scientific-creation model, but the scientific-creation model given by lawyer Wendell R. Bird in the December 1978 issue of *Acts and Facts* (published by the ICR) is the best place to start, since it provided the basis of the definition of creation science as spelled out in Arkansas Act 590. Bird's list of seven points succinctly summarizes the scientific creationist position, and I will use it as a springboard for discussing all the major creationist claims in the remainder of this chapter and in the following chapters. Bird's scientific-creation model is as follows:

> (1) Special creation of the universe and earth (by a Creator), on the basis of scientific evidence. (2) Application of the entropy law to produce deterioration in the earth and life, on the basis of scientific evidence. (3) Special creation of life (by a Creator), on the basis of scientific evidence. (4) Fixity of original plant and animal kinds, on the basis of scientific evidence. (5) Distinct ancestry of man and apes, on the basis of scientific evidence. (6) Explanation of much of the earth's geology by a worldwide deluge, on the basis of scientific evidence. (7) Relatively recent origin of the earth and living kinds (in comparison with several billion years), on the basis of scientific evidence.

Compare Bird's statement with the language of Arkansas Act 590, which defines creation science as follows:

> (It) means the scientific evidence for creation and inferences from those scientific evidences. Creation-science includes the scientific evidences and related inferences that indicate: (1) Sudden creation of the universe, energy and life from nothing. (2) The insufficiency of mutation and natural selection in bringing about development of all living kinds from a single organism. (3) Changes only within fixed limits of originally created kinds of plants and animals. (4) Separate ancestry for man and apes. (5) Explanation of the earth's geology by catastrophism, including the occurrence of a worldwide flood. (6) A relatively recent inception of the earth and living kinds.

Quick comparison shows Bird's model and the definition of creation science in the Arkansas law to be virtually identical. The law merely combines Bird's first and third points into one statement (part 1 of the statute) and substitutes a statement about the insufficiency of mutation and natural selection to produce life's diversity for Bird's misuse of the second law of thermodynamics as its second point. All the rest is the same—even the order. Thus Bird's statement of the scientific creationist position is especially important because it has served as the basis for legislation and contains the elements of what creationists would like to see added to the science curricula of all secondary schools in the United States—unless, of course, school boards can be persuaded to drop the subject of evolution entirely from the official curriculum in biology, as happened in the summer of 1999 for the entire state of Kansas. And that is why I choose Bird's statement as a structural guide to my examination—and refutation—of the creationists' nonsensical claims.

Creationists as Theoretical Physicists

In *Evolution: The Fossils Say No!* (1973), Duane Gish (at the time Associate Director of the ICR and Professor of Natural Science, Christian Heritage College) laments: "The reason that most scientists accept evolution is that they prefer to believe a materialistic, naturalistic explanation for the origin of all living things" (p. 24)—thus anticipating Phillip Johnson's supposedly original attack on philosophical naturalism by some twenty years. But as we have already seen, it is not so much a matter of scientific preference than of necessity: scientists are constrained to frame all their statements in naturalistic terms simply to be able to test them.

When a scientific-creation model such as Bird's, or the definition of such a model enacted as a state law, avers that the origins of the universe, the Earth, and life were the acts of a supernatural Creator, it is automatically excluding itself from the realm of science. (The law changes Bird's "Creator" to "creation," but "creation," especially "from nothing," must directly imply a Creator, as all the creationist literature openly admits.) Gish has admitted, "We do not know how the Creator created, what processes He used, *for He used processes which are not now operating anywhere in the natural universe* [Gish's emphasis]. This is why we refer to creation as special creation. We cannot discover by scientific investigations anything about the creative processes used by the Creator" (1973, p. 40). Thus creationists in effect acknowledge at the outset that creationism in any guise really isn't science at all. One would think that this alone would be enough to keep creationism out of the science curricula of schools. It's simply a matter of definition—of what is science and what is not. By its very definition, scientific creationism cannot be science.

Creation of something from nothing, creationists say, is supernatural. "Matter can be neither created nor destroyed" is the popular cant rendition of the first law of thermodynamics. Creationists like Henry Morris say that evolutionists (meaning, simply, scientists) cheat when they admit they don't know how the universe started. Whence all those particles of matter? Creationists deride the "who knows? maybe it was always there" shrug of an answer that most scientists give. The ultimate origin of matter—beyond any specific theory of a Big Bang origin of the universe and development of the various kinds of atoms, molecules, stars, and galaxies—really is a mystery about which only a few theoretical cosmologists have claimed to have any inklings. Scientists admit when they don't have the faintest idea why or how something happened, and the ultimate origin of matter—at least so far in the annals of science—is a beautiful example. But the creationists know.

The second law of thermodynamics—that all systems tend toward decay and disorder (increase in entropy)—is a great favorite of scientific creationism. Claiming that the Creator first created the Earth and all its life, then set the first and second laws into motion, creationists see the "law of inevitable decline" as the fatal objection to evolution. Evolution is the development of the complex from the simple, they say—precisely the opposite of what you would predict from the second law. Henry Morris (who used to direct the ICR), in *The Scientific Case for Creation* (1977), has a graph (p. 6) showing the creationist expectation: after a perfect beginning, things have gone downhill on Earth—the second law working in its inexorable fashion.

Morris dismisses an apparent exception to the second law: At the moment of fertilization, a human egg is a single, microscopic cell. That cell divides, its daughter cells divide, and so on. The adult human consists of billions of cells. But we are not gigantic multicellular eggs. During development, cells differentiate and take on different forms. They are grouped into specialized tissues, and these tissues are grouped into organs. Creationists admit that adults are, in a basic sense, more complex than the eggs from which they sprang, though, as we have already seen, each cell has the same basic genetic information in its DNA as is contained in the original fertilized egg. To creationists like Morris, however, the process of development from egg to adult does not violate the second law of thermodynamics, because it is only temporary. Death is inevitable, and with it, decay. The second law triumphs in the end.

And, biologists point out, so it will in evolution. It is as certain as anything in science that the sun will not last forever. If, in another 15 billion years, the sun becomes a red giant in its dying days, the Earth will be consumed. In any event, burn out the sun, and the source of our energy is gone. Life will, inevitably, cease to exist. The law will win out. In fact, the vast majority of species that ever lived are already extinct. Some species appear to last for millions of years, but the overwhelming conclusion from the fossil record is that no species can last forever, regardless of what eventually happens to the sun. So, the second law is working here too.

All this is, in a very real sense, merely playing with words, the way the creationists do. Yes, all systems will run down—if there is no fresh input of energy into them. In other words, *the second law applies only to isolated systems.* And the Earth is no isolated system: Plants trap only a fraction of the sun's energy that comes our way; the energy is trapped in the form of sugars, which form the base of the food chain sustaining all animal life. The atmosphere, oceans, and rocky surface of the Earth's crust retain some solar energy in the form of heat. All the rest is reflected back out to space (with a minute amount bounced back again from the moon and artificial satellites). The system isn't running down; it is, instead, open with this continual influx of solar energy. Life uses only a fraction of this available energy; far more is available than is actually used.

In sum, the second law of thermodynamics applies to closed systems—i.e., systems in which no additional energy can enter. In contrast, the developing human embryo—from fertilized egg up through a newborn infant—has a continual supply of energy, from the mother through the placenta. After birth, energy derived from eating and drinking takes over, and in this sense the human body is an open, not a closed, system. The same is true of ecosystems receiving sunlight and sustaining living processes, including the forms of genetic exchange and modification underlying the evolutionary process.

Faced with this argument—that the second law applies to closed, rather than open, systems—Morris and colleagues have simply rewritten the second law, not with the language of mathematics appropriate to the task, but with pseudoscientific jargon. Creationists claim (falsely) that the second law applies to all systems, and they speak mysteriously about systems that require an "energy conversion mechanism" and a "directing program." In the words of Stanley Freske (writing in the spring 1981 issue of *Creation/Evolution,* p. 10), "Creationists are not showing that evolution contradicts the second law of thermodynamics; instead, they are saying that the second law, as accepted by conventional science, is incorrect and insufficient to explain natural phenomena. They insist that something else of their own making must be added—namely a divinely created directing program or a distinction between different kinds of entropy."

Creationists' use of the second law as a general falsification of evolution is a wonderful example of bad science, and (because at first they didn't realize that the law applies only to closed systems) of desperate attempts to salvage their notion. Nothing about this smacks of the scientific; it is, rather, the all-too-human attempt to preserve a pet idea at all costs—even if it requires bending the rules of normal science to serve one's own ends.

Of Time and the Navel

Creationists say that the universe, the Earth, and all of life are young. All were created within the last few thousand years or so. Henry Morris, R. L. Wysong, and other creationist apologists have devoted many pages to attacking the notion that the universe, the Earth, and life are billions of years old. And they have assembled "scientific evidence" purporting to show that the Earth is only a few thousand years old. It is when they have confronted the rock record that scientific creationists have most vehemently attacked the integrity and judgment of scientists. In their discussions of historical geology, creationists have more than amply demonstrated their capacity for cleverly distorted "scholarship." And it is in their efforts to propound an alternative explanation for the observations of geologists that creationists reveal themselves for the pseudoscientists they really are.

The notion that the Earth has had an extremely long history is one of the great intellectual achievements of human thought. Though there had been occasional flashes of insight throughout history, there was no real need to consider the possibility that the world was vastly older than popularly imagined until the late eighteenth and early nineteenth centuries, when a few men began patiently examining the intricacies of the great sequences of rock strata in Europe. The Greek traveler and historian Herodotus remarked on the seashells he found on Mediterranean hillsides around 400 b.c. Many centuries later, Leonardo da Vinci understood the fossilized shark teeth he found in the surrounding Italian hills to be exactly what they appeared to be: the remains of ancient sharks inhabiting a sea of long ago. But the common conception of fossils up through Renaissance times saw them as petrified thunderbolts—or the work of the devil, who put fossils in the Earth to mislead us all. Today, according to Henry Morris, Satan's role is still perceived in this vein, as it is no less than the devil himself underlying the "well-nigh universal insistence that all this must have come about by evolution" (1963, p. 77).

Creationists accept fossils for what they are: dead remains of once living organisms. Creationists believe that dinosaurs existed, though some think they were wiped out in Noah's Flood, and others contend that Noah had some dinosaur couples on the Ark. In other words, creationists believe that fossils are real all right, but they simply aren't as old as evolutionists insist they are.

When confronted with the evidence that the universe, the Earth, and life really are vastly older than they would like to believe, creationists admit that things certainly *look* old. But, they say, this appearance of old age is illusory. Instead of blaming the devil for tricking us by making the Earth and its living inhabitants seem old (the explanation preferred by their intellectual forebears in the Middle Ages), they blame . . . the Creator! When the Creator made the world, they say, he made it *appear* as if the Earth and life really did have a long history. He had to have done things this way, creationists assert, simply because the universe had to be set in motion: light from distant stars had to have reached the Earth by the end of the sixth day, and rivers had to be already running in their courses. In short, the system had to be up and running at the very moment of creation. But light from distant stars, and streams running in their channels, look as if they've been there a while. It takes time for light to travel interstellar distances or for streams to carve their channels. Often creationists say the Creator's design included a sort of instant history for the universe, the Earth, and life; after Creation, natural processes (such as the laws of thermodynamics) were set in motion, so light continues to reach us from distant heavenly sources, and streams continue to carve their channels.

The idea of evolution had already been "in the air" before Darwin finally published *On the Origin* in 1859. Many people found the notion of evolution disturbing. One such person was Philip Gosse, a clergyman who beat Darwin to the punch with a book of his own, which he called *Omphalos,* the ancient Greek word for "navel," published in 1857. Gosse developed an elaborate argument that it was God's intention to give the Earth a *semblance* of history, just as he gave Adam a navel even though Adam was not born of a woman.

Gosse included fossils in his catalogue of items God created to make us think that the Earth and life are truly old. Many of Gosse's fellow clergymen reacted in horror to this picture of a deceitful God, little better than a nasty devil playing tricks on us. It seemed incomprehensible to most rational minds that a Creator-God would endow humanity with the ability to think, and at the same time take such elaborate steps to fool us. When scientific creationists today claim that the Creator's efforts automatically established an apparent history, they are reverting to Gosse's *omphalos* argument, though of course they deny that the Creator made this mere semblance of history simply to fool us. Rather, they say, it is just the way he had to do it. Either way, it doesn't make a great deal of sense.

What is the evidence that the universe, the Earth, and life are vastly older than the six thousand years Archbishop Ussher (1581–1656) computed from the pages of Genesis? The first inklings came when the Danish physician Niels Stensen (1638–1686, who wrote in Latin and used the Latinized version of his name, Nicolaus Steno) made a few commonsense generalizations about sedimentary rocks in the mid-seventeenth century. Steno saw that most of the layered rocks of the Earth's crust are formed of minute grains of sand, clay, lime, and other mineral substances. He knew that streams carry such particles and discharge them into lakes and seas and that such particles could be observed accumulating in such places in the present day. From these elementary observations, Steno framed the law of superposition: sedimentary beds accumulate from the deposition of particles; the lower beds form first, the upper beds being piled later on top of the lower beds. Thus, beds lying above other beds must be younger than the lower beds.

Creationists do not wholly dispute Steno's law in principle, though their thesis that all the miles of thick sediments were formed during the forty-day Noachian deluge amounts to a rejection of Steno's simple proposition: it would simply be impossible to accumulate the vast thicknesses of sediments deposited since the Cambrian (let alone even earlier geological eras) in a layer-by-layer orderly fashion in such a minute period of time as forty days. Nor do creationists deny that some rocks are metamorphosed (altered by heat and pressure into crystalline form) while others are igneous, cooled from a molten mass such as volcanic lavas. What they *do* reject is the complex chain of observation and reasoning begun in the late eighteenth century and based on the start by Nicolaus Steno.

The late-eighteenth-century physician and farmer James Hutton, as I noted in Chapter 3, essentially founded the modern science of geology when he methodically applied observation, common sense, and a knowledge of present-day processes to explain how the physical features of his Scottish landscape might have formed. Hutton was a Plutonist: he believed that some rocks, such as the lava flow forming King Arthur's Seat, a rock formation at Edinburgh, had cooled from a once molten mass. His opponents were Neptunists, led by the German geologist Abraham Werner (1750–1817), who believed that all rocks, including granites and lavas, schists and sediments, had precipitated out of an ocean that had encircled the globe in primordial times. That controversy died in the first half of the nineteenth century, when it was conclusively shown that some rocks must have cooled from a molten state and that some such igneous rocks (particularly lava flows) lay above older rocks that must have formed from true sediments. Neptunism, as an explanation for the formation of the sequence of rocks in the Earth's crust, is the geological equivalent of the idea of pangenesis, the theory of inheritance adopted by Darwin and other nineteenth-century biologists. Both neptunism and pangenesis are now thoroughly outmoded.

But Hutton prompted another controversy, one that the scientific creationists claim is still alive. Hutton used observations of what was going on in nature around him in the present to interpret the events of the past, just as Steno, Leonardo da Vinci, and Herodotus had done before him. A conflict soon arose: Huttonian geologists saw the action of wind and rain eroding rocks and sending particles rushing downstream to be deposited in lakes and ocean basins as proffering an open vista of long periods of gradual change. Their opponents, such as the French scientist Baron Georges Cuvier and the English clergyman William Buckland (1784–1856), saw it otherwise: called catastrophists, they interpreted geological history as a series of sudden, even violent, happenings, interspersed with periods of quiescence. As I mentioned in Chapter 3, Cuvier thought that the fossil record of life revealed not one but an entire series of separate creations. Buckland saw the physical history of the Earth as a series of cataclysmic events, the last one being the Great Flood of Genesis.

Modern creationists, of course, reject these rather complex notions of catastrophism, calling merely for a single creation of the world and all living "kinds," then catastrophic flood, and then the resultant configuration of things more or less as we see them today. Creationists see themselves as neocatastrophists, and they impugn evolutionists as uniformitarians.

We owe the concept of uniformitarianism primarily to the English geologist Charles Lyell (1797–1875), who followed Hutton's lead and developed a truly coherent science of geology. Lyell, who was to prove so influential on Darwin, yet who rejected evolution until his later years, spoke of the uniformity of geological processes in his famous *Principles of Geology*, published in the years 1830–1833. Creationists today, presumably out of simple ignorance, have utterly misconstrued the modern understanding of Lyell's uniformitarianism. As Stephen Jay Gould and others have pointed out, uniformitarianism meant at least two things to nineteenth-century geologists. It meant that we can seek to understand events of the Earth's past by studying processes of change still going on around us today. It also implied that slow processes, such as the erosion and deposition of sediments, further indicate that all events in Earth history occur at uniform, and usually rather slow, rates. According to this second meaning of uniformitarianism, great changes are the result strictly of the gradual accumulation of minute changes over formidably long periods of time; in this second sense, "uniformitarianism" is a virtual synonym of "gradualism."

The first of these ideas attached to the word "uniformitarianism" is simply common sense—a cardinal assumption if we are to do science at all. The laws of nature that we observe operating today were operative in the past as well. In other words, water has run downhill and the Earth has revolved around the sun ever since there has been an Earth, water, and hills. This is merely the naturalistic assumption, the requirement that all scientific explanations be couched in terms of processes that we have reason to believe are operating in nature, now and in the past—a notion totally counter to the creationist position that different rules were in force at the time of creation, and processes we see operating today were invented by the Creator only after he had created. This first meaning of uniformitarianism is simply another way of stating how all of science is done.

The other meaning of uniformitarianism, however, is another kettle of fish entirely. When creationists say (as they did in Arkansas Act 590) that they are catastrophists while evolution scientists are uniformitarians, they mean that they believe that events of the past were often, if not always, sudden, violent, and cataclysmic. They have the Great Flood specifically in mind, of course. But geologists long ago abandoned this second meaning of uniformitarianism—that all changes in Earth history were the product of infinitesimally minute changes gradually accumulating through time. For well over a century now, we have spoken of the Ice Ages in the recent geological past, when four times huge ice fields have grown over the continents of the Northern Hemisphere. Volcanoes and earthquakes are both infrequent and sudden in their action, and many wreak huge changes. And the invocation of an asteroid impact as the trigger to the ecological collapse that ended the Cretaceous world and wiped out perhaps as many as 50 percent of all living species was a catastrophe par excellence.

Indeed, as we have seen, it is now becoming fashionable to view everything from the evolution of species to the mass extinctions and subsequent proliferations that pepper life's history as a sequence of episodic change—not the slow, steady, gradual change this second meaning of uniformitarianism implies. No, indeed, creationists cannot justifiably claim that they, and they alone, recognize that events in the history of the Earth and its life frequently reflect episodic events rather than slow, steady, progressive change, as Wendell Bird and the Arkansas legislature would have it. Creationists do stand alone as anti-uniformitarians because only they attack uniformitarianism in its first sense: only creationists are willing to suspend natural laws, as we think we understand them today, to frame an ad hoc explanation of the Creator's acts in bringing the universe, the Earth, and life into existence a few short thousands of years ago. But such a stance does not allow them to claim as their own the valid part of the old catastrophism: the notion that the nature of historical events is frequently more episodic than gradual.

The Geological Timescale

One of the most important weapons in the creationist arsenal is the assertion that the entire scheme of Earth history worked out by geologists is based on faulty logic, or circular reasoning. Henry Morris, for example, says, "Most people do not realize that the very existence of the long geological ages is based on the assumption of evolution" (1977, p. 32), and, "How can the fossil sequence prove evolution if the rocks containing the fossils have been dated by those fossils on the basis of the assumed stage of evolution of those same fossils? This is pure circular reasoning, based on the arbitrary assumption that the Evolution Model is true" (p. 35).

This is the essence of the creationist attack on the notion of a truly old Earth: how do geologists "tell time"? they ask, and then they tell you that, despite what you might think, most rocks cannot be dated directly by measurement of the amount of radioactive decay of various atoms. (This is true.) Instead, they say, geologists use fossils to tell time: they arrange their fossils according to a supposed evolutionary sequence, they correlate rocks all over the world using this supposed sequence, and then they turn around and claim that the fossil record proves evolution. Some creationists have even maintained that when fossils are found out of the "proper" sequence, they are ignored—a charge which is nothing short of a vicious lie. If geologists and paleontologists really were as stupid and self-deceiving as creationists claim, their activities would be as circular and worthless as creationists say they are. The crux of the creationists' argument is that the myth of the geological column and geological timescale is upheld against all contrary evidence by geologists and paleontologists who wish to preserve evolution at all costs. This is a serious charge and is, of course, false.

The truth is that the basics of the geological column—the thick sequence of strata containing the outlines of events in Earth history—as well as most of the basic divisions of geological time, were established well before Darwin published *On the Origin* in 1859. And in fact, to the extent that they held any publicly expressed opinions on the subject, *the geologists who established the basic sequence of divisions of geological time back then were creationists.* The charge that the sequence of subdivisions of geological time—with the Paleozoic, Mesozoic, and Cenozoic Eras as the main divisions of the past half billion years or so—is a ploy to support the false doctrine of evolution is simply untrue. "Paleozoic," "Mesozoic," and "Cenozoic," mean, respectively, "ancient life," "middle life," and "recent life," referring to the animals and plants fossilized in these rocks, the sequence of which was worked out independently of any notion of evolution.

How was our knowledge of the geological column developed? Creationists point out the indisputable fact that in no single place on Earth—even in cases like the Grand Canyon, or the thick sedimentary sequences exposed in such mountain chains as the Alps, Rockies, and Andes—has the full geological column been preserved and exposed. Portions are always missing. In the 1820s and 1830s, explorer and gentleman geologist Roderick Impey Murchison (1792–1871) and Cambridge professor of geology and clergyman Adam Sedgwick set out to study the sequence of strata lying below the Old Red Sandstone, a set of strata widely exposed in the British Isles, now known to be Devonian in age. Using Nicolaus Steno's rule that lower rocks are older than those lying above them, Sedgwick studied the sequence of rocks in Wales from the bottom up. Murchison, meanwhile, working some distance away, was tracing a sequence of layers downward from the Old Red Sandstone. Murchison paid particular attention to the occurrence of fossils in the rocks, while Sedgwick concentrated more on the mineral content.

Both men worked by documenting the physical position of the strata—i.e., which strata overlay which. Each worked out a sequence of position of the rock layers of their areas by examining exposures and noting which beds lay above and below which others. Murchison confirmed that his rocks underlay the Old Red Sandstone; Sedgwick showed that he was studying rocks that lay below Murchison's—rocks that were the oldest of the sedimentary sequence in Wales. Sedgwick called his rocks Cambrian after Cambria, the Roman name for Wales. Murchison called his rocks Silurian for the Silures, an ancient tribe of the region.

The two men, friends and colleagues at first, soon entered into a bitter dispute. As Murchison kept tracing his sequence downward while Sedgwick worked his way up the sequence, they eventually met in the middle; that is, they soon found themselves discussing the same rocks. Each claimed that the intermediate rocks in dispute belonged to his sequence, and the argument was not resolved until 1879, when geologist Charles Lapworth (1842–1920) named all the rocks between Sedgwick's original Cambrian and Murchison's Upper Silurian beds the Ordovician (after the Ordovices, yet another ancient tribe). Today we still recognize the Cambrian, Ordovician, and Silurian as the three oldest subdivisions (periods) of the

Paleozoic Era. Anyone can still go to southwestern England and Wales and examine the physical sequence of rocks that led to the definition of these three geological periods. It is the physical what-lies-on-what observations that provide the real basis for studying geological time.

Now, it is certainly true that we call some rocks in the United States and elsewhere around the world Cambrian, Ordovician, or Silurian. And it is here that scientific analysis—the testing of hypotheses by seeing if predicted patterns actually occur in nature—comes into play. William Smith (1769–1839), a British surveyor, showed the way. Creationist Henry Morris calls Smith's technique old simply because it was invented almost two hundred years ago (i.e., also prior to the general acceptance of any idea of evolution)—as if the age of an idea has anything to do with its validity. (On those grounds, it is time to get rid of the ideas that the Earth is round and revolves around the sun.)

Smith was surveying the terrain for one of the ambitious canal projects brought on by the Industrial Revolution. Climbing the hills of the English countryside bordering the projected path of the canals, Smith noted that the fossils he saw always occurred in the same order. He could stand on the side of one hill and predict what he would find on the same level on the next hillside, on the basis of his experience with the order of fossils. He could predict, if someone showed him a suite of fossils, which fossils would be found below them and what one could expect to find above them. From this experience, Smith found he could take a mixed collection of fossils and tell the collector, correctly, what the sequence of fossils had been as they lay in the rocks.

There is no assumption of evolution here. It is simple observation: fossils occur in the same general sequence everywhere they are found. When pronouncing two bodies of rock strata—no matter how widely separated they may be—to be roughly equivalent in age (correlative) on the basis of their fossils, there is no evolutionary presupposition whatsoever. The only assumption is that identical, or nearly identical, fossils are the remains of organisms that lived at roughly the same time, wherever they might have lived. This is the basis, for instance, for stating that rocks of Cambrian, Ordovician, and Silurian age occur in the United States as well as in Great Britain, where they were originally studied and named.

We have found Cambrian and Ordovician trilobites and other fossils in the United States—called Cambrian or Ordovician because they are, in some instances, dead ringers for the British fossils. Moreover, these fossils in the United States occur in the same basic sequence as the ones Sedgwick and Murchison found early in the nineteenth century in the rocks of England and Wales. So the correlation of rocks—i.e., saying that two bodies of rock are approximately the same age—is *not* based on the assumption that evolution has occurred. Rather, it is based on simple empirical observation of the order in which fossils occur in strata and on the standard procedures of scientific prediction (i.e., that the same geological sequence will be found around the world) and testing by further observation (which has abundantly corroborated the prediction in over 150 years of subsequent geological field research).

Today we even have an independent means of cross-checking our assumption that similar fossils imply rough equivalence of age for the formation of two or more bodies of rock, for now we have radiometric dating as an independent check.

Geologists quickly saw the potential for the direct chemical dating of rocks soon after Marie Curie (1867–1934) discovered radioactivity. Geochemists, following close on the heels of atomic physicists and chemists, know that unstable nuclei of some kinds of atoms (i.e., isotopes of some elements) emit radiation at statistically constant rates, and in so doing these atoms are transformed into another isotopic form. If we know the original amount of the "parent" and "daughter" isotopes at the time a rock was formed, and if we know the rate at which the parent isotope decays to its daughter isotopic form, we can measure the current ratio of daughter to parent and thus calculate how long ago the rock was in its initial state.

Aha! cry the creationists, lots of assumptions there! How do we know that decay rates are constant? The answer is that laboratory experiments have repeatedly shown that extremes of temperature and pressure fail to alter decay rates,[4] so we continue to have confidence in the theory of radioactive decay—just as we assume that gravity has always been in operation as we observe it today.

Just look at the results. We can take a sample of rock—say, a granite from Nova Scotia. We know it must be Devonian in age because it intrudes rocks containing Devonian fossils but is itself overlain by slightly younger sediments, as judged by the fossil content. Someone from a geochemical lab takes several samples and analyzes the age by three different decay paths between different isotopes of uranium and lead. The ages all come out to be about 380 million years, with a small plus-or-minus error factor of a few million years. (A few million years sounds like a huge error, but a couple of million years one way or the other is a small error compared with the huge age calculated. Saying "380 million years plus or minus 2 million" is like thinking back a year ago and saying you cannot remember whether something happened on the nineteenth or the twentieth of May).

Now, someone from another lab comes along, samples the same Nova Scotia granite, and gets the same results. Then someone else dates a different Devonian granite—one, say, from Greenland—also associated with Devonian fossils. Sure enough, the process works. Rocks predicted to be nearly the same age on the basis of their fossil content always turn out to be nearly the same age when radiometric dates are obtained. And rocks predicted to be older or younger than others always turn out to be older or younger—by the predicted number of millions of years—when dated radiometrically. In short, by now we have literally thousands of separate analyses using a wide variety of radiometric techniques. It is an interlocking, complex system of predictions and verified results—not a few crackpot samples with wildly varying results, as creationists would prefer to have you believe.

Perhaps the most dramatic demonstration of the validity and accuracy of modern geological dating comes from the deep-sea cores stored by the thousands in various oceanographic institutions. The direct sequence is preserved in these drill cores, of course, and the microscopic fossils in them allow the usual this-is-older-than-that sort of relative dating to be done. We can also trace the pattern of changes in the orientation of the Earth's magnetic field: as you go up a core, some portions are positively charged, and others are negative. Major magnetic events, reflecting a flipping of the Earth's magnetic poles, are recognizable, and the sequence of fossils, the same from core to core, always matches up with the magnetic history in the same fashion from core to core.

Then, when we obtain absolute dates from the cores (usually by using oxygen isotopes), we find that the date of the base of the Jaramillo event (one of the pole-switching episodes) *always* yields a date of some 980,000 years ago. The dates are always the same (again, with a minor plus-or-minus factor). They are always in the right order. They are always in the tens or hundreds of thousands of years for the most recent dates, and in the millions of years farther down the cores. There is such a complex system of cross-checking the independent ways of assessing age—all pointing to the same results—that I must remind myself that scientists cannot claim to have the ultimate truth.

We have as yet found no rocks directly dated at 4.65 billion years, the estimated age of the Earth. Recall that this is James Hutton's original prediction, as he correctly surmised that the ravages of time preclude the survival of the most ancient crustal materials. The oldest rocks that have been found so far are just about 4 billion years old. The oldest moon rocks, as well as stony meteorites, however, do yield dates of around 4.5 billion years, as already mentioned, agreeing well with the extrapolated age predicted by geochemists of 4.65 billion years for the age of the Earth—a prediction made long before we sent someone to the moon to pick up some samples.

No, the creationists' attack on geological time simply won't work. There are far too many independent lines of evidence—none of which is based on the assumption of, let alone an underlying commitment to, the idea of evolution—that amply confirm what geologists thought must be so 150 years ago: the Earth simply cannot be a mere ten thousand years old. This is no story concocted by a Creator as part of his creative process. The Earth really is extremely old. And, of course, the universe is even older—15 billion years or so, an estimate based on the speed of light and the calculated distance between the center of the universe and its most remote objects.[5] Appearances may be deceiving, of course. The Creator could be only making it look this way. But, leaving a Creator aside as science must, the mundane calculation of modern astronomers is 15 billion years.

But the creationists do not give up. Morris has written that even if the world were as old as geologists say, evolution still would not be proven—which, of course, is correct. Yet most creationists still passionately care that the Earth be proven to be young, and that all the features of the geological record be interpretable as essentially the product of one single event—Noah's Flood. Creationists flatly accuse geologists of covering up the facts to preserve their pet theory of evolution. They point to "polystrate fossils" (their term), by which they mean fossils (usually trees) that are standing vertically and therefore must be sticking up through millions of years of time—if the evolutionists can be believed. Here they pretend that geologists insist that sedimentation rates must always be slow, steady, and even, instead of the truly rapid rates that are sometimes observed. Polystrate trees show every sign of extremely rapid burial, generally when rivers flood over their banks.

But the creationists' favorite ploy to discredit the notion that there is an orderly sequence of rocks and fossils in the Earth's crust lies in their distortion of large-scale rock displacement, which geologists call thrust faulting. Creationists point to areas of the Earth where the fossils seem to be out of sequence, and this is true: in mountain belts, geologists sometimes find older rocks lying on top of younger rocks—in apparent contradiction of Steno's law of superposition. For example, Permian trilobites have been collected way up the slopes of Mount Everest, in rocks lying on top of much younger (Cretaceous) limestones.

Creationists say that a convenient ad hoc explanation—one that they find incredible—is advanced to explain away this "fatal flaw" of historical geology: the concept of massive thrust faulting. Faults are zones where two bodies of rock move past each other. For example, the area of coastline in California west of the famous San Andreas Fault is moving northward relative to the other side of the fault; the San Andreas actually marks the place where the entire Pacific plate is sliding past the North American plate. In other faults, rocks drop down, sliding past other blocks of rock that remain elevated. Africa's famed Rift Valley System is such a place, where the valley floor (with Olduvai Gorge and the Serengeti Plain) is formed by massive blocks of rock dropping down past the higher ground to the west and east. Another kind of fault forms the category in question here: thrust faults occur when regions of rock are crumpled up in the process of mountain building. Sometimes the crumples fracture, and sheets of rock are literally thrust up over other rocks. Large-scale thrust faults are found only in regions of mountain building, where the crust of the Earth has been severely deformed.

Creationists have been uncharacteristically silent so far on the notion of plate tectonics (earlier known as continental drift), a theory that seeks understanding of many features of the Earth in terms of huge slabs of the Earth's crust (plates) changing their position with respect to one another over the course of geological time. For example, peninsular India is reconstructed as part of the Southern Hemisphere supercontinent Gondwana for much of geological time, breaking off only about 70 million years ago and eventually running into Eurasia (about 20 million years ago), and in so doing buckling and thickening the crust and forming the Himalayas. Part of the enormous energy that such processes involve has produced large-scale horizontal movements, in which sections of the Earth's crust have moved many miles laterally. All true mountain belts are folded, like the pleats of an accordion, so mountain belts are all more narrow now than they were as deep basins, when they were accumulating their hugely thick sequences of sediments. It was the crumpling and occasional breakage of those accordion-like pleats of rock that sent Permian strata sliding above Cretaceous rocks on what is now Mount Everest.

Creationists, true to their ways, try to debunk specific examples of thrust faults to show that the whole idea of such faults is an invention by scientists to save their precious idea of an orderly succession of rocks in the geological column. The creationists' favorite example is the Lewis thrust in Montana, where Precambrian (1-billion-year-old) rocks lie on top of fossiliferous Cretaceous rocks only about 90 million years old.

Do paleontologists really invoke overthrusting just to save their story? Are there no independent ways to demonstrate that massive dislocation of strata has occurred? Well, there are—the main one being that, along all faults, in places where both sides of the rocks are exposed, there is (naturally enough) a zone of pulverized rock caused by the scraping of the two rock masses against each other. In addition, slickensides, essentially scars of the movement, are typically seen on the faces of the rock on both sides of the fault. [see Figure 3]

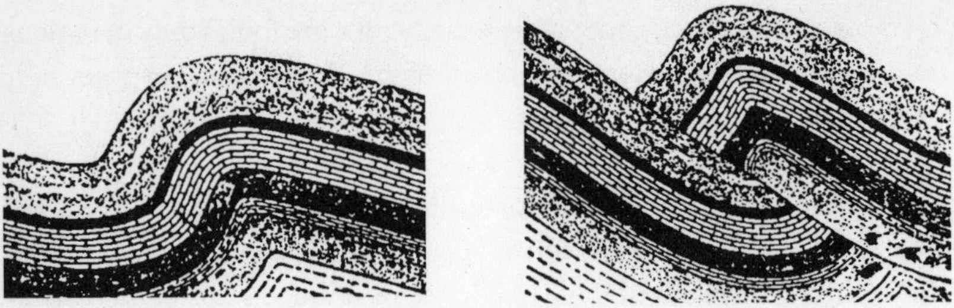

FIGURE 3 Development of an overthrust in side view. **1.** Pressure begins to fold a series of rock strata. **2.** With further pressure, the fold breaks, and the rock strata to the right slide over the sequence on the left–leaving older rocks lying on top of younger ones in some parts of the thrust. From Hills, 1953, p. 125, fig. 80.

How do creationists deal with the evidence of thrust faulting? With distortion—and some very poor scholarship. I have a creationist book (J. G. Read's *Fossils, Strata and Evolution,* 1979) that is devoted almost solely to the overthrust problem. In it the author says, in effect, overthrusts are a real phenomenon, mentioning the zones of pulverized rock as tell-tale signs of a real overthrust. So far, so good—though Read fails to mention that the way his "real" examples of overthrusts were first detected was by the anomalous occurrence of fossils, and *not* by the recognition of a thin layer of pulverized rock.

The next step for Read and other creationists (such as Henry Morris) is to turn to what they consider phony examples—the truly massive cases such as the Lewis overthrust, which are the only ones they care about—as they promise to falsify the reality of the geological column in general. Picture after picture (in Read's book) shows the Precambrian rocks sitting over Cretaceous shales in Montana—all without a trace, so they claim, of physical deformation.

What do real geologists have to say about the Lewis overthrust? According to geologist Christopher Weber, who has examined the creationist literature on the Lewis overthrust in some detail, the oft-repeated claim that there is no physical evidence of faulting between the Precambrian and underlying Cretaceous of the Lewis thrust is simply false. Weber (1980) writes:

> Whitcomb and Morris [in *The Genesis Flood* (Morris and Whitcomb, 1961, p. 187)] lift the following words from this article [i.e., a professional geological report by C. P. Ross and Richard Rezak, *The Rocks and Fossils of Glacier National Monument,* 1959]: "Most visitors, especially those who stay on the roads, get the impression that the Belt strata (i.e., the Precambrian) are undisturbed and lie almost as flat today as they did when deposited in the sea which vanished so many million years ago."

But, Weber continues, if we read the rest of Ross and Rezak's paragraph, we find that Whitcomb and Morris quoted it out of context:

> ". . . so many million years ago. Actually, they are folded, and in certain places, they are intensely so. From points on and near the trails in the park, it is possible to observe places where the Belt series, as revealed in outcrops on ridges, cliffs, and canyon walls, are folded and crumpled almost as intricately as the soft younger strata in the mountains South of the park and in the Great Plains adjoining the park to the east."

Even more damning is the thin layer of shale said to occur between the two rock units, evidence of thrusting (as crushed rock) in some areas, but evidence of tranquility (undeformed strata) in the case of the Lewis overthrust, as far as creationists are concerned. Such thrusting, less widespread than creationists would have us believe, and always confined to zones of mountain building where rocks are ordinarily highly disturbed, are not the ad hoc saviors of evolution. Like any other proposition in geology, overthrusts are based on physical evidence, though fossils out of sequence help geologists spot overthrusts in the first place.

The Noachian Deluge and the Fossil Record

In an exception to their tactic of simply trying to debunk science, creationists have made definitive statements—alternative explanations about how things have come to be as we find them today, statements we can actually test—when using the biblical Great Flood to explain the occurrence of all sedimentary rocks and fossils over the face of the Earth.

Although the only research this notion is said to have directly inspired (as far as I know) was a couple of abortive "arkeological" expeditions to Mt. Ararat, nonetheless the creationist position can be examined on its own merits.[6]

Charles Schuchert (1858–1942), an eminent geologist and paleontologist at Yale University in the early twentieth century, published the *Atlas of Paleogeographic Maps* of North America toward the end of his productive career; the book appeared posthumously in 1955. Thumbing through these maps, anyone can see that today we are in a relatively unusual period of Earth history: the continents today are abnormally dry. The more usual condition by far is for the seas to be flooded over most of the continental interiors. Schuchert's maps reveal a kaleidoscopic pattern of flooding and emergence during the last half billion years as the seas waxed and waned over the continent. Wherever the seas appeared and lasted for some time, they left a covering of bottom sediments; when the seas withdrew for any length of time, erosion would set in and take away the upper parts of the blanket of sediments. And some places—where the seas never reached—never did accumulate a sedimentary record. The upshot: no place on Earth can possibly be expected to have a continuous and complete sedimentary record—of the last ten thousand years, of the last million years, of the last billion years.

So here we have it: a sedimentary rock record, in some places tens of thousands of feet thick (as in the Andes) and in other places totally absent (as over parts of central Canada, where erosion has removed what little amount of sediments ever did cover the granitic core of the North American continent). Geologists explain the uneven distribution of sediments by normal processes of sediment deposition and erosion: deposition where the seas covered the land, erosion when the rocks of the crust are exposed to the atmosphere. Scientific creationists see the entire sequence as the result of one cataclysmic deluge.

Creationists have adopted, with little sign of comprehension, the geological notion of facies. The facies concept points to the simultaneous development of different environments and habitats in different parts of the world. Walking from the seashore inland on the eastern and western coasts of the

United States, for example, takes one from marine habitats, to beaches, then perhaps to lagoons, then to marshes, coastal forests, swamps, and mountains. If all were preserved, each habitat would look different in the rock record, and certainly the kinds of animals and plants preserved as fossils would be different from habitat to habitat. So far, so good. Geologists have been aware of this for years: different kinds of rocks, with utterly different fossil content, may nonetheless be contemporaneous because they were formed in different environments that existed on Earth at the same time.

Creationists claim that this ecological zonation will automatically produce the general order of life that paleontologists have found in the entire fossil record—the fallout of one enormous flooding event. Trilobites, brachiopods, and other invertebrates should appear first: after all, they were already living on the bottom of the sea. Simple, spherical organisms will tend to sink faster than more complex invertebrates, so we have "hydrodynamic selectivity" in addition, to help put the simple creatures at the bottom of the sedimentary pile. Living on land, amphibians, reptiles, birds, and mammals will be buried later by the Great Flood and thus will appear higher up in the rock record, as the seas filled up and encroached on the land. The more clever and advanced the terrestrial animal, the more successful one would predict it to be (according to creationists, that is) in avoiding the calamity of drowning, so dinosaurs are found in lower beds than mammals (actually, not by much!) and humans appear only in the uppermost layers of the sedimentary record.

That is the creationists' answer: ecological zonation, hydrodynamic selectivity, and relative success at fleeing to higher elevations—three points of "explanation" of the sedimentary and fossil record according to the scientific creationist model of a single, worldwide flood. Furthermore, since conditions would have been chaotic during the flood, naturally we would predict some exceptions to the general sequence. This is the cream of creationist pondering over how the fossil record has been formed.

Never mind that the record is, in places, tens of thousands of feet thick, with abundant evidence that much of it (such as limestones and finely laminated shales) must have formed exceedingly slowly. Never mind that careful geological mapping in Colorado and Wyoming, for instance, shows perfectly clearly how marine rocks—with clams, snails, ammonites, mosasaurs, and other creatures of the Cretaceous briny deep—grade laterally into terrestrial dinosaur-bearing beds of the same age in Montana. Here is true ecological zonation: Cretaceous animals, both vertebrates and invertebrates, living side by side and not piled on top of one another. And here's another example: I am intimately familiar with Devonian rocks in New York State that reveal fish that had occupied streams and ponds and are now preserved in the present-day Catskill and Pocono Mountains, and that were contemporaneous with shellfish living offshore in the marine waters of western New York and Pennsylvania.

The creationists' argument simply makes no sense. Too many geologists have climbed over those rocks and have seen how they overlie one another. Geologists for the most part don't care very much about the biological subject evolution; that is, they haven't in the past, and as far as I can tell, they still don't care much about it today. What they passionately do care about is the history of the Earth, and of one thing they are certain: the Earth has had a history, a tremendously long and complex history. To disparage the work of geologists over the past two hundred years, to try instead to foist on the naïve the charade that there is no tremendous rock record and that the people who have strived so arduously to understand it are merely fools, is as cavalier an act as I have been sorry to witness. No, it is the creationists—not the geologists—who distort the truth, freely slinging mud at all who cross their peculiarly myopic view of the natural world.

Creationists Attack: II
The Origin and History of Life

The English peppered moth, *Biston betularia,* has been a longtime favorite example in the evolution section of zoology texts, and it has been equally prominent in creationist literature attacking evolution. According to the traditional evolutionary account,[I] this moth species comes in two basic colors: mottled white, and black. The mottled white form beautifully matches the lichens on many English trees; the black moths stand out against the background and are easier targets for moth-hungry birds. During the Industrial Revolution, when pollution from the factories killed the lichens and the trees reverted to the darker color of natural bark, all of a sudden it was the white form that was conspicuous. Black moths soon outnumbered white ones, until comparatively recently, when the crusade against air pollution has once again tipped the scales back in the white variety's favor: the lichens are back in force, and now it is the black moths whose life expectancy is the lower of the two. Here, evolutionists assert, is adaptive evolution—natural selection monitoring environmental change. The moths best suited to prevailing conditions are, on average, more likely to survive and reproduce. The peppered moths provide a beautiful case of small-scale evolution.

It comes as no surprise, then, to find these English moths well represented in creationist literature, too. And it was only a minor departure from their usual course to see that, rather than trying to debunk the example, creationists such as Gary Parker and Duane Gish accept the facts of the moth story—of course, claiming that it somehow supports the creation model.

But I was not prepared to find creationists—particularly Parker and Gish, perhaps the two most eloquent creation "biologists"—actually accepting the moths as examples of small-scale evolution by natural selection! *Modern creationists readily accept small-scale evolutionary change and the origin of new species from old.* That, to my mind, is tantamount to conceding the entire issue, for, as I recounted at some length in Chapter 4, there is utter continuity in evolutionary processes from the smallest scales (microevolution) up through the largest scales (macroevolution).

How can creationists admit that evolution occurs while sticking to their creationist guns and denying that evolution has produced the great diversity of life? Creationists simply insist that the sorts of examples of evolution that biologists give have nothing to do with the wholly new, the truly different. The creationist model is clear on this point: the Creator created "basic kinds," each kind replete with its own complement of genetic variation. Creationists see nothing wrong when they admit that natural selection and reproductive isolation have worked *within* each basic kind, sorting out this primordial variation to produce various specialized types. Creationist R. L. Wysong, a veterinarian, likens the process to the production of the panoply of dog breeds by artificial selection—the great array of different dogs all springing from the same ancestral pool of genetic variation.

Creationists deny that mutations fill the bill as the ultimate source of new variation. Mutations, they claim, are nearly always harmful and are in any case exceedingly rare—precisely the arguments seen as a serious intellectual challenge to Darwinian theory in the earliest days of genetics, until their resolution in the late 1920s and early 1930s. With the advent of molecular biology, genetic variation within species has been shown to exceed by far all previous estimates, and most mutations are small-scale and neither especially harmful nor beneficial when they occur. It fits the evolutionary view of the world that mutations are random with respect to the needs of organisms: mutations don't occur because they help an organism; rather they are mistakes in copying the genetic code—in this sense, no different from the mistakes monks occasionally made when copying medieval manuscripts. That some of these biological mistakes may ultimately prove beneficial is all evolutionists have ever claimed.

Kinds and Kinds: Creationists and the Hierarchy of Life

If evolution (according to creationists) goes on within but not between kinds, the creationist notion of "kind" becomes rather important. Creationists such as Parker and Gish openly admit that kinds, or basic kinds, are, well, kind of hard to define. The word "kind" has no formal meaning in biology; "kind" to a biologist, if it meant anything at all, would probably mean "species." Here is what Gish has to say about basic kinds; please take the trouble to read his words carefully, for they pose the crux of the creationist position on biological history and present-day diversity and are, at the same time, self-contradictory:

> In the above discussion, we have defined a basic kind as including all of those variants which have been derived from a single stock. We have cited some examples of varieties which we believe should be included within a single basic kind. We cannot always be sure, however, what constitutes a separate kind. The division into kinds is easier the more the divergence observed. It is obvious, for example, that among invertebrates the protozoa, sponges, jellyfish, worms, snails, trilobites, lobsters, and bees are all different kinds. Among the vertebrates, the fishes, amphibians, reptiles, birds, and mammals are obviously different basic kinds. Among the reptiles, the turtles, crocodiles, dinosaurs, pterosaurs (flying reptiles), and ichthyosaurs (aquatic reptiles) would be placed in different kinds. Each one of these major groups of reptiles could be further subdivided into the basic kinds within each.
>
> Within the mammalian class, duck-billed platypuses, opossums, bats, hedgehogs, rats, rabbits, dogs, cats, lemurs, monkeys, apes, and men are easily assignable to different basic kinds. Among the apes, the gibbons, orangutans, chimpanzees, and gorillas would each be included in a different basic kind.
>
> When we attempt to make fine divisions within groups of plants and animals where distinguishing features are subtle, there is a possibility of error. Many taxonomic distinctions established by man are uncertain and must remain tentative.

> Let us now return to our discussion of evolution. According to the theory of evolution, not only have the minor variations within kinds arisen through natural processes, but the basic kinds themselves have arisen from fundamentally different ancestral forms. *Creationists do not deny the former, that is, the origin of variations within kinds, but they do deny the latter, that is, the evolutionary origin of basically different types of plants and animals from common ancestors* [emphasis mine]. (1973, pp. 34–35)

Gish, of course, cannot possibly mean what he literally says in this passage. He says that "variation" occurs within basic kinds but not between them and proceeds to define such groups as reptiles and mammals as basic kinds. By his very words, then, bats, whales, humans, and the rest of the mammals (and he does acknowledge that human beings are mammals!) he cites could have arisen as variations within the basic mammalian kind. But he then defines these subgroups of mammals as themselves constituting basic kinds, which, according to creationist tenets, means they *cannot* have shared a common ancestor. Bats beget bats, whales beget whales, and so forth, but Gish's words imply that there is no common ancestral connection between these subunits of mammals within the larger, enveloping mammalian basic kind. But if Class Mammalia is "obviously" a basic kind, why can't we see whales and bats as arising simply from variation within a created kind? These statements, of course, are inconsistent at best and nonsensical at worst. One cannot but agree that creationists indeed have trouble with the notion of basic kinds.

What a contrast with the evolutionary position! Evolutionary biologists ever since Darwin have seen that all life is neatly connected within the Linnaean hierarchy: all life, in other words, is intricately nested in ever larger arrays determined by shared genetically based anatomical features. Closely similar species are grouped together, and they form genera with other, only slightly more divergent species; genera sharing unique features form families; families uniquely sharing features form orders, and so forth. All of life fits into this natural arrangement (i.e., not an artificial and arbitrary human construct). And, as we saw at length in Chapter 2, it was Darwin who realized first that a *hierarchical nesting of all living forms must necessarily be the result if evolution—descent with modification—is correct.*

Furthermore, there is no obvious place to draw some sort of dividing line, and to say that smaller groups of species below this line are connected by some sort of natural evolutionary process—but that there are no connections among the larger groups. The reason why Gish himself, try as he might, couldn't do it is simply that it cannot be done. If you admit that dog varieties all belong to one species, and that there is a connection among dogs, coyotes, and wolves, you cannot just stop there; you must also concede (as we have already seen) that, *by the very same token,* dogs share certain similarities with bears and weasels, and these three, as a group, share still other similarities with hyenas and cats, with which they constitute the mammalian Order Carnivora. And, of course, it goes on from there, until all of life falls into this natural organization that is the very imprint of evolutionary history.

Gish points out that "division into kinds is easier the more the divergence observed"—whatever that might truly mean. What is obvious, instead, is that the closer we come to humans, our own species *Homo sapiens,* the smaller the basic kinds Gish and other creationists wish to recognize. The invertebrate groups Gish lists are huge: worms include at least five phyla, snails constitute an entire class of mollusks (comparable at least to the vertebrate classes, such as birds and mammals), and trilobites are an arthropod class. Protoctists (single-celled eukaryotic microorganisms) include many different phyla.

The message is clear: let the paleontologist talk about evolution within the trilobite "kind." Trilobites arose early in the Cambrian Period, some 540 million years ago, and they are last found in rocks approximately 245 million years old. During their roughly 300-million-year sojourn, we know of thousands of species that are classified into numerous families, superfamilies, and orders. But, apparently to creationists, if you've seen one trilobite you've seen them all, and all the changes paleontologists have documented in this important group of fossils are just variation within a basic kind.

I cannot agree. Trilobites are as diverse and prolific as the mammals, and examples of evolutionary change linking up two fundamental subdivisions of the Class Trilobita are as compelling examples of evolution as any of which I am aware. Airily dismissing 350 million years of trilobite evolution as variation within a basic kind is actually admitting that evolution, substantial evolution, has occurred.

But the real reason why creationists care little about trilobites is that they are really worried about only one basic kind: humans. I suspect that creationists would gladly define the rest of life as a single basic kind (and thus allow evolutionary connections among all forms of life) as long as people were singled out as a separate, unique basic kind. After all, Arkansas Act 590 makes a special point of defining a separate ancestry for humans and apes as part of creation science. Yet the degree of biochemical similarity between humans and chimpanzees is greater than 98 percent! It is a source of great satisfaction, I must admit, that with all the attention paid to the biology and fossil record of our own species, as we saw at some length in Chapter 3, it is far easier to demonstrate connections between our own species—the "basic kind" *Homo sapiens*—and the living great apes and fossil hominids, than it is to show connections between the major divisions of trilobites.

We are now in a position to compare the scientific-creation model of the origin of life's diversity with the scientific notion of evolution. Creationists say there can be variation within kinds (microevolution) but not between kinds (macroevolution—"real evolution" to Gary Parker). Biologists assert that there has been one history of life: all life has descended from a single common ancestor; therefore one process—evolution—is responsible for the diversity we see. Creationists insist on two separate theories: (1) the creation of these nebulous basic kinds by a supernatural Creator, followed by (2) microevolution producing variation within those basic kinds. They admit they have no scientific evidence for the first phase.

There is a commonly followed maxim in science (often called Occam's razor) that the simpler idea in general is to be favored over a more complex one when there is no compelling reason to proceed otherwise. The dualistic structure of the creation-science model is a vastly more complicated notion (however barren this structure might be of actual concrete ideas, not to mention evidence) than the simple notion that all life has descended from a single common ancestor—no matter how rich and complex may be the ideas about how that process has worked to produce life's history and present-day diversity.

Oh, Those Gaps!

Creationists love gaps, lack of any obviously intermediate forms between dogs and cats, insectivores and bats, lizards and birds, fishes and frogs, and so on, and better yet the supposed absence of intermediates in the fossil record. Gaps, to creationists, are the Achilles' heel, the fatal flaw, of biological evolution.

Evolutionary biologists remain unperturbed by the gap problem for several very good reasons: (1) The evidence of connectedness and continuity—whether on a small scale between closely related (often nearly indistinguishable) species, or on larger scales—is simply much better than the creationists claim. In addition, (2) as we saw in Chapter 4, beginning with Dobzhansky's work in the 1930s, evolutionary biologists have come to realize that *the evolutionary process itself—especially via speciation—automatically creates a measure of discontinuity*. And, as Darwin himself noted, (3) many species that would appear as intermediates are now extinct: for example, the australopithecine species, as well as *Homo habilis, Homo ergaster,* and *Homo erectus* are now all extinct, so anyone who would claim close evolutionary connections between chimps and humans (based for example, on their remarkably high percentage of shared genes)[2] nonetheless does not have the benefit of lots of intermediate species, since those intermediates are now extinct. Fortunately, we do have them in the fossil record! Finally, as Darwin also pointed out, (4) we cannot possibly expect to find the remains of all species that have ever lived, for several reasons: the sedimentary record itself is too discontinuous ("gappy"), much has been destroyed by erosion already, fossils tend to be destroyed by chemicals in the groundwaters percolating through rocks (not to mention the ravages of metamorphism), most sediments remain deeply buried and thus inaccessible, and for the most part only animals and plants with tough tissues (e.g., shells, bones, wood) are likely to be fossilized in the first place. With all those things to go against it, the fossil record emerges as a true marvel, and it has produced many series of intermediates, some of which were encountered already in Chapter 3. Let's consider one additional, classic example—one that shows up time and time again in zoology texts and creationist tracts alike: the Mesozoic reptile-bird known as *Archaeopteryx*.

The case of *Archaeopteryx* makes it clear that one person's intermediate is another's basic kind, or failing that, outright fraud. Paleontologists point to examples from their own work, and creationists respond by refusing to accept the examples as intermediates. To evolutionary biologists, *Archaeopteryx* is beautifully intermediate between advanced archosaurian reptiles and birds. In contrast, creationists don't say that *Archaeopteryx* is a fake; to them, it's just another bird. It isn't.

Archaeopteryx comes from Upper Jurassic limestones of Bavaria. The seven known specimens are about 150 million years old. Zoologists have known for years that birds are effectively feathered reptiles (dinosaurs, actually), because there are so relatively few anatomical differences between birds and living reptiles, and even fewer between birds and the archosaurian reptiles (including dinosaurs) of Mesozoic times. Birds have some evolutionary specializations not found in reptiles: in addition to their uniquely constructed wings, they lack teeth and have feathers, four-chambered hearts, and horny bills.

Gish says of *Archaeopteryx*, "The so-called intermediate is no real intermediate at all because, as paleontologists acknowledge, *Archaeopteryx* was a true bird—it had wings, it was completely feathered, it flew. . . . It was not a half-way bird, it was a bird" (1973, p. 84). In other words, since evolutionists classify *Archaeopteryx* as a bird, then a bird it is, not some kind of intermediate between reptiles and birds. Semantic games aside, it is certainly accurate to see birds as little more than feathered archosaurs. Feathers, wings, and a bill are three evolutionary novelties that *Archaeopteryx* shares with all later birds, and these new features are the ones that allow us to recognize the evolutionary group birds. But all living birds lack teeth and bony tails, and they have well-developed keeled breastbones to support strong flight muscles. *Archaeopteryx* lacks such a keel but still retains the teeth and bony tail typical of its reptilian ancestors.

The reason why *Archaeopteryx* so delights paleontologists is that *evolutionary theory expects that new characteristics—the "evolutionary novelties" that define a group—will not appear all at the same time in the evolutionary history of the lineage.* Some new characters will appear before others. Indeed, the entire concept of an intermediate hinges on this expectation. Creationists imply that any intermediate worthy of the name must exhibit an even gradation between primitive and advanced conditions of each and every anatomical feature. But there is no logical reason to demand of evolution that it smoothly modify all parts simultaneously. It is far more reasonable to expect that at each stage some features will be relatively more advanced than others; intermediates worthy of the name would have a mosaic of primitive retentions of the ancestral condition, some in-between characters, and the fully evolved, advanced condition in yet other anatomical features. *Archaeopteryx* had feathered wings, but the keeled sternum necessary for truly vigorous flight had not yet been developed in the avian lineage. And *Archaeopteryx* still had the reptilian tail, teeth, and claws on its wings.

Creationists point to some living birds that, while still young, have poorly developed keels or claws on their wings (as is the case with the South American hoatzin). They also point to Cretaceous birds, younger than *Archaeopteryx*, that still had teeth. Here is the height of twisted logic: creationists say, "Look here—there are some modern and fossil species of birds with some of the supposed intermediate or primitive reptilian features that are out of the correct position in time." Instead of interpreting these birds as primitive links to the past, creationists see them as somehow a challenge to *Archaeopteryx* as a gap-filling intermediate.

The whole point about intermediates, though, is that ancestral features are frequently retained while newer features are being added to another part of the body. It was not for another 80 million years or so that birds finally lost their teeth—though they had lost their tails in the meantime. That juvenile stages of descendants often show features of their adult ancestors, as in the hoatzin's juvenile claw, prompted the German evolutionary biologist Ernst Haeckel's (1834–1919) famous nineteenth-century maxim "ontogeny recapitulates phylogeny," meaning that the evolutionary history of an animal is in a sense repeated in its development from egg to adult. Bluster as they might, creationists cannot wriggle away from *Archaeopteryx*.

Creationists Confront Human Evolution

The case the creationists care about most—and quite possibly the *only* case they care about—is the origin of humans, *Homo sapiens*, us. And it is indeed ironic that delineating humans as a basic created kind separated by profound and unbridgeable gaps from the living great apes and extinct species of hominids is a task of Herculean proportions, a challenge that so far has evoked only a feeble response from creationism's leading exponents. Creationists have had pitifully little to say about this, their worst nightmare: the overwhelming genetic and anatomical evidence of connections between humans and the great apes (and, through the apes, with the rest of life), and the dense and rich fossil record of human evolution.

What do the creationists say about human evolution? Creationists such as Gish and Parker agree with anthropologists that younger fossils are very modern in appearance, though they don't admit that anatomically modern human fossils from southern Africa are over a hundred thousand years old, and that modern humans arrived in Europe around thirty-five thousand years ago. They also like to revive the old canard that, with a necktie and coat on, a Neanderthal man would pass unnoticed in the New York subways. I sincerely doubt it, since most paleoanthropologists have generally concluded that Neanderthals were a distinct species.

Skipping back 3 million years or so, we find various species of the genus *Australopithecus,* whose name means (as creationists fondly point out) "southern ape" and thereby, on linguistic grounds alone—automatically, in the creationist book—is a form of ape and no member of the human lineage. Assessing zoological relationships on such etymological grounds is rather dubious, to say the least, but the creationists' claim that "it looks like an ape, so call it an ape" greatly insults these remote ancestors and collateral kin of ours. They had upright posture and a bipedal gait, and some of them, at least, fashioned tools in a distinctive style. No apes these, but rather primitive hominids looking and acting just about the way you would expect them to so soon after our lineage split off from the line that became the modern great apes.

But it is the fossils of the middle 1.5 million years I just skipped over that make creationists writhe. Here we have *Homo erectus,* first known to the world as *Pithecanthropus erectus* (literally "erect ape-man"), based on specimens from Java, and as *Sinanthropus pekinensis* ("Peking man") from China. Now known from Africa as well (in the form of the closely related species,

Homo ergaster), the *Homo erectus* lineage lived virtually unchanged for over 1.5 million years and was, by all appearances, a singularly successful species. *Homo erectus* had fire and made elaborate stone tools, and its brain size was intermediate between that of the older African fossils and the later, modern-looking specimens. Specimens of *Homo erectus* don't look like apes, yet they don't look exactly like us, either. To most of us, *Homo erectus* looks exactly like an intermediate between modern humans and our more remote ancestors.

What do creationists do with *Homo erectus*? No problem: *Homo erectus* is a fake in the creationist lexicon. Gish asks us to recall Piltdown, that famous forgery—evidence of skulduggery in the ranks of learned academe. And what, the creationists ask, about *Hesperopithecus haroldcookii* ("Nebraska man"), described years ago on the basis of a single tooth, which later turned out to have belonged to a pig? (Scientists do make mistakes, and pig and human molars are rather similar, presumably a reflection of similar diets.) So it is, they say, with *Homo erectus*. According to Gish, the Java fossils were just skullcaps of apes wrongly associated with a modern human thighbone. And the original Peking fossils are now gone, apparently lost by a contingent of U.S. marines evacuating China in the face of the Japanese invasion of World War II. Hmmm, very suspicious, say the creationists. Never mind the casts of the originals, the drawings and photographs plus detailed written descriptions of these fossils published by the scholar Franz Weidenreich. And never mind that the Chinese have since found more skulls at the original site, or that Richard Leakey has found the closely related species, *Homo ergaster*, beautifully preserved in East Africa.

That the best the creationists can do with the human fossil record is call the most recent fossils fully human, the earliest merely apes, and those in the middle—the intermediates, if you will—outright fakes is pathetic. Humans are about the worst example of a basic kind that creationists could have chosen. The irony is great: the case toward which all their passion for producing propaganda is ultimately directed—how *we* got here—is about the most difficult one I can think of to support the model of creation.

Creationists on the Fossil Record: A Final Note

It would certainly be helpful to the creationist cause if all organisms could be shown to have appeared at the same time in the rock record—the result of one grand creative act by God—or, failing that, at least a grand commingling of extinct and modern forms of life all deposited together by Noah's Flood. Thus creationists have taken great delight in the supposedly human footprints alongside bona fide dinosaur tracks in the Cretaceous Glen Rose Formation, exposed in the channel of the Paluxy River in Texas. Here, they proclaim, is direct evidence that humans and dinosaurs roamed the Earth together, just as it was written in *Alley Oop*. Gary Parker is quite suave as he describes fitting his own feet into these impressions. But none other than a creationist (B. Neufeld, in his article "Dinosaur Tracks and Giant Men," 1975) has blown the whistle on these tracks. Alas for the creationist cause, they aren't footprints at all; the few "human" impressions visible these days do not show any signs of "squishing" of the sedimentary layers either at the edges or directly beneath the "tracks" (as the dinosaur prints, incidentally, clearly do). And, according to Neufeld, during the Great Depression it was a common local practice to chisel out human footprints to enhance tourist interest—a practice akin to the recent fabrication of Bigfoot footprints in the Pacific Northwest. Need anything more be said about the quality and trustworthiness of creationists' dealings with the fossil record?

Sparring with Luther Sunderland

Earlier I said that creationists are poor scholars at best and at worst have been known to distort the words and works of scientists. Throughout the creationist literature, one sees repeatedly statements such as this from Gary Parker:

> Famous paleontologists at Harvard, the American Museum, and even the British Museum say we have not a single example of evolutionary transition at all. (1980, p. 95)

This statement is untrue. We have already encountered Luther Sunderland as the creationist who lured me into confrontation in the first place (see Chapter 1) and the man who bragged that he convinced Ronald Reagan's speechwriters to inject a bit of skepticism about evolution into a presidential election campaign. Sunderland interviewed prominent paleontologists at various museums and universities. I was one of them. Some of us tried to discuss some procedural difficulties in recognizing ancestors,[3] also admitting that the fossil record is full of gaps. Nothing new there. All the paleontologists interviewed later told me that they certainly did cite examples of intermediates to Sunderland.

Sunderland then wrote letters to newspapers and testified in various venues (e.g., to the Iowa State legislature, as already mentioned) that the paleontologists he interviewed admitted that there are no intermediates in the fossil record. In 1984, Sunderland published *Darwin's Enigmas: Fossils and Other Problems.* Later he went on to write *Darwin's Enigma: Ebbing the Tide of Naturalism,* copyrighted in 1988 but first printed in August of 1998. Sunderland says that his 1998 book "presents the substance of these interviews through the use of short excerpts and summaries of the replies to the questions" (p. 13).[4] It is worthwhile taking a look at what Sunderland is up to here, and I'll do so by picking out the most egregious thing he has me saying—or has to say about me. My actual opinions on all the other distorted issues with which Sunderland saddles me (and my paleontological colleagues) in the course of his book are, of course, revealed in the pages of this book, though not in the format of a rejoinder specifically to the work of Luther Sunderland. I will single out here the worst case—one that creationists are still using in their writings and debates (including on the Internet), and one that has defenders of evolution wondering if I *really* said what Sunderland has me saying in his book.[5]

The issue, once again, is gaps—the supposed lack of intermediates in the fossil record—and revolves around what I purportedly said about horse evolution or, rather, about an exhibit on horse evolution that had been on continual display at the American Museum of Natural History for many years. Photos of this exhibit were routinely reproduced in zoology textbooks for much of the twentieth century. Here is Sunderland's version of what I said to him about that exhibit:

> I admit that an awful lot of that has gotten into the textbooks as though it were true. For instance, the most famous example still

> on exhibit downstairs (in the American Museum) is the exhibit on horse evolution prepared perhaps fifty years ago. That has been presented as literal truth in textbook after textbook. Now I think that that is lamentable, particularly because the people who propose these kinds of stories themselves may be aware of the speculative nature of some of the stuff. But by the time it filters down to the textbooks, we've got science as truth and we've got a problem. (1998, pp. 90–91)

So there you have it: Sunderland has me slamming my curatorial predecessors at the museum for misleading the public. A few pages later, Sunderland gets back to me and the horses and makes a serious charge about *my* integrity; please bear with this rather lengthy quotation, as it reveals the heart and soul of creationist tactics:

> When scientists speak in their offices or behind closed doors, they frequently make candid statements that sharply conflict with statements they make for public consumption before the media. For example, after Dr. Eldredge made the statement about the horse series being the best example of a lamentable imaginary story being presented as though it were literal truth, *he contradicted himself.* The morning of the beginning of the Seagrave's [sic] trial in California he was on a network television program. The host asked him to comment on the creationist claim that there were no examples of transitional forms to be found in the fossil record. Dr. Eldredge turned to the horse series on display at the American Museum and stated that it was the best available example of a transitional sequence. On February 14, 1981, Sylvia Chase, host of the ABC television program "20/20," questioned him on this subject as follows:
>
> Sylvia Chase: "Dr. Niles Eldredge, Curator of the Department of Invertebrates of the American Museum of Natural History, is one of many scientists vigorously opposed to the creationists. I asked him for evidence (of evolution)."

> Dr. Eldredge: "Ahh, the horse is a good example. Here is an effectively modern horse which is a million years old, but we can all recognize it as a horse. And as we go deeper in lower layers of rock, back further in time, we excavate successfully more primitive horses. Here's one that is two-million years old. They are becoming progressively less and less obviously horse-like till we get back 60 million years ago, and here is the ancestor of the rhinoceros—or very close to the ancestor of the rhinoceros.[6] So that when the creationists tell us that we have no intermediates between major groups, we point to a creature like the dawn horse and say 'Here we have an exact intermediate between horses and the rhinos.'" *So, in 1981, after joining the anti-creationist campaign, Dr. Eldredge repeated a scenario for a nationwide audience that in 1979 he had called "lamentable"* [italics mine]. (pp. 94–95)

Now, I have no idea whether the words Sunderland puts directly in my mouth are accurate, verbatim accounts of what I actually said; some of this doesn't sound particularly like me, and after all, I have only Luther Sunderland's word for it—and he is, in effect, calling me a liar. But let's assume I actually said everything that he quotes me as saying in these two passages. If so, the reader might well be inclined to agree with Sunderland—that I was talking out of both sides of my mouth, blatantly contradicting myself—and even believe that I did so for the ideological purpose of defeating creationism, after I had joined the anticreationist campaign.

Well, there is no doubt that I am a thoroughgoing anticreationist, and one of the major reasons is the falsely malevolent light in which creationists cast evolutionary biologists: if we are not just plain stupid fools, then we are liars who say one thing to each other and quite another to the world at large.[7] But here, for the record, was what I was talking about—first with Luther Sunderland, and then with Sylvia Chase:

Eldredge with Sunderland (1979): As codeveloper with Stephen Jay Gould of the theory of punctuated equilibria, I was very sensitive to any and all claims made, past and present, by my paleontological brethren to the effect that evolution is a phenomenon of slow, steady, gradual, and progressive change *both within species through time and also between successions of species through time.* My problem with the old horse exhibit is that it depicted horse evolution as linear and gradual, though I must also say that nothing in the old text said anything whatsoever about gradual evolution. Still, it was a fair inference that that is what the take-home message would be. Remember, this was still the early days of trying to get paleontologists to reexamine their data, and to see whether or not species—of horses, dinosaurs, corals, whatever—were as typically stable as my trilobites. I am, in this connection, extremely gratified to report that, unsurprisingly, now that the work has been done (post-1979), the predominant patterns of horse evolution fit the patterns of stasis followed by extinction and speciation that I have discussed (in Chapters 3 and 4) as being utterly typical and general for all of life. In short, my outburst to Sunderland was on the subject of evolutionary gradualism—*not* on the question of anatomical intermediates.

Eldredge with Chase (1981): The dead horse that Sunderland and all other creationists beat is, of course, not stasis versus gradualism, but the existence of anatomical intermediates, especially if they exist in perfect stratigraphic order. I am here to tell you that my predecessors had indeed unearthed and mounted a wonderful series of skeletons, beginning with the Eocene *Hyracotherium* (the so-called dawn horse), with its small size, four toes on the front feet, five on the back feet, shortened face, and generalized perissodactyl teeth suitable for browsing, not grazing. Climbing up the Tertiary stratigraphic column of the American West, we find the horses becoming progressively bigger, with fewer toes (modern horses have but one on each foot) and more complicated teeth. The horses of the Pliocene are essentially modern.

This is not a made-up story. Those fossils are real. They are in the proper order, and they are a spectacular example of anatomical intermediates found in the exact predicted sequence in the rock record. They are every creationist's nightmare.

No, horse evolution was not in the straight-line, gradualistic mode. But to state or imply that the horse evolution exhibit was somehow arranged to support an evolutionary story—to imply that the old museum curators deliberately misled the public by arranging the order of these horse fossils as they saw fit—is a damn lie.

The upshot here is that the fossil record of horses is now known to be many times more dense and richly diverse than in the days when that old exhibit was first mounted. Yes, there are many side branches, and stasis, rapid evolution in speciation, and turnover pulse–related phenomena (such as extinction) are as utterly typical of horse evolution as they are of all other forms of life that have left fossil records behind. If anything, we know more intermediate anatomical forms in horse evolution than we did when that fabulous old exhibit was first mounted.

Creationists hear what they want to hear because they believe what they want to believe. They obviously think that all is fair in both love and war, and they see this as a culture war. But somehow I persist in the apparently quaint belief that lying, cheating, and distortion are inherently unchristian.

In the Presence of a Lawyer: The Case of Phillip Johnson [8]

Phillip Johnson is, hands down, the most visible and successful creationist of the 1990s and early part of the new Millennium. Boalt Professor of Law at the University of California, Berkeley, early in his career Johnson clerked for Chief Justice of the United States Supreme Court Earl Warren. He is, in short, no dummy, and in the one "debate" I had with him (along with a TV interview and classroom and faculty discussion sessions—not to mention the obligatory postperformance drink)—at Calvin College in Grand Rapids, Michigan, in January 1996—I found him generally affable.

Johnson lectures widely; he also writes rather well, and I gather that his several books and many articles enjoy a wide circulation and readership. A darling of the Christian right, Johnson believes strongly that what he sees as a culture war between atheistic philosophical naturalism and what he calls theistic realism is manifested in the loss of esteem and respect for theology on university campuses. Despite directing a substantial proportion of his efforts at Christian laity, perhaps above all else Johnson seeks intellectual respectability within academe.[9] This is indeed something new in creationism, and Johnson's positions need to be examined: What, exactly, is he saying? And how much of his thinking is really new?

Johnson makes no bones about either his born-again Christian beliefs or his conservative political views, and this alone, I must say, I find refreshing after decades of combating wolf-in-sheep's-clothing scientific creationists who insisted (still do, for that matter) that theirs is actually a scientific position—rather than a religiously inspired one—and, as such, deserving a place in the science curricula of public schools. The first of Johnson's books, *Darwin on Trial* (1991), however, reveals relatively little of either Johnson's religious and philosophical background, or of what have later emerged as his main arguments. In fact, *Darwin on Trial* is really little more than a straightforward (though up-to-date) standard creationist antievolution tract—one that is curiously, yet one suspects purposively, divorced from other works of that genre.[10]

In most of his earlier public presentations, Johnson spent most of his time attacking the fossil record—the old question of gaps and intermediacy. He made many appearances with Cornell historian of science William Provine, for example, and a publicly available tape of one of their joint presentations (at Stanford University in 1994) shows Johnson performing a not overly clever attack on the lack of intermediates, as especially revealed in a museum display devoted to the Cambrian explosion. I mention this instance simply to reiterate Johnson's fundamental stripe as a fairly run-of-the-mill antievolutionist for the most part. What is different about the presentation from one given, say, by Duane Gish, is that Johnson, in the rebuttal period, finally gets down to some of the details of what really is somewhat novel about his approach: his insistence that science in general—and evolutionary biology perhaps in particular—reflects an underlying philosophical stance he calls philosophical naturalism, which inherently, by its very definition, is atheistic. On the tape, admitted atheist Provine wholeheartedly agrees—about which, more anon.

Phillip Johnson believes in a personal God—a God who is all-powerful and has, in fact, created everything we see around us. His is a decidedly proactive God, taking part in causation of things small as well as grand. Johnson has said repeatedly that, if evolution is true, then God is thereby reduced to a do-nothing, boring kind of God. Put another way, science at the very least marginalizes God: "The acceptance of naturalistic assumptions in science by Christian and secular intellectuals alike has moved God steadily into some remote never-never land ('before the big bang') or even out of reality altogether" (Johnson, 1995, p. 111). Actually, it is the "out of reality altogether" that Johnson really has in mind when he says that science *assumes* that all that exists is the material world and the forces that hold it together and cause its various elements to interact.

But, Johnson says, *if there really is a God that is shaping the Earth and creating all life, then science ought to want to know about that.* After all, as Johnson says, if science is about understanding the natural world, and if God has a direct hand in shaping that natural world, then why in the world would science choose to ignore—nay, even deny—God's very existence? In assuming that the natural, material world is all there is, scientists and their meek followers are automatically ruling out what is perhaps *the* crucial element in shaping the world! And that, in brief, is Phillip Johnson's philosophical naturalism: the assumption that the material, physical, natural world—with its bits and pieces and its characteristic modes of interaction—is really all there is out there.

Johnson's second book, *Reason in the Balance* (1995), says all this at great length, but it really doesn't try to come to grips in any detail with what "naturalism" really means until the appendix. Johnson wrote a paper prompted by "a remark by a Christian college professor who had argued that my 'creationist bias' was affecting my assessment of the scientific evidence for evolution. I include the paper here as an appendix instead of trying to fit it into the text, because the issues that fascinate persons who devote a professional interest to this subject may be overly complex for general readers who have other matters to occupy their attention. On the other hand, I want to preserve this statement as a starting point for further discussion among professional academics in particular" (p. 206).

Well, I won't try to hide my answer to Johnson's tirade against philosophical naturalism in an appendix. Here, in a nutshell, is what is wrong with Johnson's argument: his dichotomy between philosophical naturalism and theological realism. It is the answer I conceived when I accepted the offer to debate Johnson, and it is the same answer everyone else has reached.[11] Unlike Johnson, I do not see these issues as overly difficult for anyone to grasp.

Everyone—even Phillip Johnson—agrees that there is a physical, material world. Everyone also agrees that there is something called human knowledge, and that human knowledge has grown over historical time. *Science is a way of knowing about the nature—composition and behavior—of the natural, material world.* That's not nothing, but that is all science is: a set of rules and an accumulated set of ideas, some more powerfully established than others, about the nature of the material world. *By its own rules, science cannot say anything about the supernatural.* Scientists are allowed to formulate solely ideas that pertain to the material universe, and they are constrained to formulate those ideas in ways that can be testable with empirical evidence detectable by our senses.

Johnson says that restricting analysis purely to material, naturalistic terms is automatically atheistic—amounting to a de facto claim that God does not exist. But science does not—because it cannot—say that only the natural material world exists. Rather, science is restricted by the limitations of human senses and was, in any case, invented solely to explore the nature of the material universe. It does not rule out the existence of the supernatural; it merely claims that it cannot, by its very rules of evidence, study the supernatural—if, indeed, the supernatural exists.

Johnson, naturally enough, loves scientists who agree with him—scientists (and historians of science like Provine) who are all too eager to announce that science and religion are truly at loggerheads, that science implies there is no God. Once again, he uses the either-or approach: either you believe that God exists and fashioned the world we find, or you believe that the material world is all that exists and that by definition there is no God.

Johnson—like Gish and so many other creationists—intensely dislikes what the old-line creationists simply called theistic evolution, what Johnson prefers to call theistic naturalism. Theistic evolution (or theistic naturalism) is the position that God created heaven and Earth, and all manner of beast, including humans, but did so using natural laws. Johnson and other hard-line creationists find this line of argument unacceptable because it relegates God to a sort of caretaker status, more or less content to sit on the sidelines. So Johnson simply dismisses theistic naturalism, even though it has been the line of reasoning of choice of mainline Protestant denominations since the nineteenth century—one that many, many devout people (including some scientists as well as nonscientists) still profess.

Creationists are famous for their basic strategy of debunking evolution rather than proposing their own model, testable or not, on how God fashioned the diversity of life and breathed life into humanity. Johnson has been steadfast in this approach for most of his career, but he does, in *Reason in the Balance*, offer a brief characterization of his theistic realism. Johnson begins by stating, "If theologians hope to win a place in reality, however, they have to stop seeking the approval of naturalists and advance their own theory of knowledge. My intention here is to start the process, rather than finish it, but readers are entitled to expect me to provide a concrete proposal as a basis for further discussion" (1995, p. 107). After citing the Gospel of John to reveal "the essential, bedrock position of Christian theism about Creation," Johnson then concludes this brief section on theistic realism with the following statement: "If Christian theists can summon the courage to argue that preexisting intelligence really was an essential element in biological creation and to insist that the evidence be evaluated by standards that do not assume the point in dispute [Johnson means here philosophical naturalism], then they will make a great contribution to the search for truth, *whatever the outcome*" [Johnson's emphasis] (p. 110).

Well, we might ask, is there any *evidence* of God's direct participation in the formation of the Earth and the creation of all life? Johnson thinks so, and he is happy to parade the work of some of the members of his inner circle. It turns out, though, that theirs is strictly the up-to-date version of the same old creationist arguments for seeing the history of life as solely the outcome of God's direct handiwork.

Design, Chance, and Complexity

Creationist authors have devoted entire books to their interpretations of the data of biology. But, as has already become abundantly clear, apart from their convoluted arguments about fossils and basic kinds, they find relatively little in biology that they can offer as supportive of the creation model—known to Phillip Johnson as theistic realism. What little there is of substance (if it can be called such) centers on the notions of design, chance, and complexity.

As briefly mentioned in Chapter 1, one of Darwin's first and most persistent critics after *On the Origin* appeared was St. George Mivart.[12] Mivart hounded Darwin on a problem with which he was already amply troubled: how could one imagine a structure as complex and beautifully suited to perform its function as a human eye to have evolved through a series of simpler, less useful and efficient stages?

Anatomists were among the last holdouts against accepting the idea of evolution, so entranced were they with the intricate complexities of the organ systems they studied. Imagining intermediate stages between, say, the front leg of a running reptile and the perfected wing of a bird seemed to them impossible, as it still does to today's creationists. That the problem perhaps reflects more the poverty of human imagination than any real constraint on nature is an answer not congenial to the creationist line of thought. In the taped debate between Will Provine and Phillip Johnson already cited, for example, Provine lists intermediates between climbers and fliers, alleging (correctly), for example, that flying squirrels can soar like mad without relinquishing their abilities to scamper and cling to trees. Johnson, of course, never bothered to respond.

Thus the complexity argument is just a subset of the creationist claim that there are no intermediates. So naturally, and by the same token, creationists reject any evolutionary biologist's claim that, for example, there are indeed intermediate stages between simple eyes with a few cells covered by a simple lens up through more complexly configured eyes (it is noteworthy that they always say the human eye, when the human eye is configured in essentially the same way as any other mammalian eye).

The latest manifestation of the creationist argument on complexity is in the writings of one Michael Behe, a biochemist at Lehigh University. Once again, it is old wine in new bottles. In the one "debate" I had with Behe, he grudgingly acknowledged that such time-honored conundrums as the evolution of the vertebrate eye have been, in fact, effectively resolved by evolutionists. And in his book *Darwin's Black Box* (1996), Behe says that Darwin "succeeded brilliantly"—not by "try[ing] to discover a real pathway that evolution might have used to make the eye. Rather, he pointed to modern animals with different kinds of eyes (ranging from the simple to the complex) and suggested that the evolution of the eye might have involved similar organs as intermediates" (p. 16), and he goes so far as to supply a diagram of three different eyes of varying complexity.

But the real problem, according to Behe, is not so much the anatomical structure of the human eye as the problem of vision itself. The "irreducible complexity" on which he prefers to concentrate lies in the molecular (chemical) level and in general "refers to a single system composed of several well-matched, interacting parts that contribute to the basic function, wherein the removal of any one of the parts causes the system to effectively cease functioning" (p. 39). Anatomically speaking, an eye might struggle along with removal of one or more of its parts, but at the molecular level Behe swears that such is not the case, and there is no way that mutation or selection could have assembled the intricate, complex molecular pathways that underlie the physiological process of vision.[13]

Note that what Behe has done is simply push the problem back one more notch: same problem, just at a different level. There is really little reason to believe that the evolutionary pathways leading to particular molecular reactions—underlying vision or anything else—will never be completely understood. And *that* takes us to the ultimate degree, for the more intermediates paleontologists and anatomists find, the more recalcitrant creationists become: they just *won't* believe, because they already believe something else. There really is *nothing* different about Behe's argument from any other use of the argument of complexity over the past 150 years.

Interwoven with the difficulty in imagining the gradual evolution of complex organs are two separate themes: (1) the more complex a structure is, the more eloquent a silent argument it is for the conscious work of a Designer, and (2) the more complex a structure is, the more improbable it is that it arose by chance alone.

The argument that nature is so complexly organized, with each creature specially suited to the role it plays in the economy of nature, that only a Creator could have fashioned things in this way is an old one. It was the particular view of the theologian-naturalists prior to *On the Origin,* and it is still in use today in the creationist literature. Creationists usually talk of watches, though somewhat refreshingly, creationist Gary Parker (in his book *Creation: The Facts of Life*, 1980) prefers to use Boeing 747 jumbo jets as his example. The "argument" is simply that such complex machines, so admirably suited to the purposes they serve, require a watchmaker or an elaborate assembly line of airplane builders, respectively. All the parts must be premeditatedly put together by expert craftsmen. Alone, no spring or jewel can keep the time (this argument is no different from Behe's "irreducible complexity"). Only when the watchmaker cleverly arranges the parts in precisely the right way does the watch become functional. Clearly, the very existence of watches directly implies the existence of a watchmaker. So, too, creationists argue, does the existence of complex organisms imply a conscious Creator.

Now, as a scientist, I'll grant that a Boeing 747 implies a creator. I've seen pictures of the assembly line, and more to the point, I am aware that the aluminum of which the airplane is made is extracted (with great difficulty and expenditure of energy) from its complex ore—a process known only, insofar as I am aware, to human beings. I will further stipulate that, in the absence of a cogent alternative like evolution, the analogy with organisms (that they, too, bespeak a knowledgeable, conscious intelligence behind them) was a plausible argument—for the 1820s. But how compelling is the analogy today? The argument boils down simply to this: we can invoke a naturalistic process, evolution, for which there is a great deal of evidence, but which we still have some difficulties in fully comprehending. Or we can say, simply, that some Creator did it and we are, after all, only complex machines like watches. The analogy is as meaningless as that: it proves nothing. *It could even be true,* but it cannot be construed as science, it isn't biology, and in the end it amounts to nothing more than a simple assertion that naturalistic processes automatically cannot be considered as candidates for an explanation of the order and complexity that we all agree we do see in biological nature.

To bolster the argument from design, creationists jump to the other side of the complexity argument: evolution just could not, they say, produce these organic complexities, because there is no way such complex structural systems could have developed by chance alone. Just as a bunch of monkeys endlessly pounding typewriters would never duplicate the works of

Shakespeare, they argue, no mindless, materialistic process such as evolution—portrayed as acting by blind chance alone—could ever have produced the myriad wonders of the organic realm.

Evolutionary theorists are not the simpletons such statements would make them out to be. As we have seen, evolutionary biology has been very clear on just this point: mutations are random, but random only with respect to the needs of an organism. Mutations, insofar as most geneticists are concerned, do not arise because they might be useful to an organism. On the other hand, mutations are caused by real physico-chemical processes, and there is a limited number of forms that a mutation can take and still function as a viable gene. In this latter sense, mutations are not random: there are a limited number of biochemical changes that a gene can undergo.

The antichance element of evolution is, of course, natural selection. Richard Dawkins has ably described this crucial deterministic aspect of evolution in his book *The Blind Watchmaker* (1986).[14] And though biologists have with some justification referred to natural selection as the "creative" force in evolution—governing, as it patently does, the development of novel structures, behaviors, physiologies, and biochemical pathways—natural selection really is just a stolid bookkeeper, i.e., *not* a watchmaker. In a world of finite resources, on the whole it is the organisms best suited to making a living that will survive long enough to reproduce, and it is their genetically based properties that will differentially be passed along. With each generation, genetic recombination presents new packages of "variation"—the ultimate source of which is mutation—to the environment, and that is what determines—in a statistical manner—what will be passed along to the next generation. It is silly to think of natural selection as somehow the equivalent of the creationist's Creator-God. Rather—and far less grandiosely—natural selection is the natural antichance process governing the transmission of genetic information within populations from one generation to the next. In other words, natural selection is the answer to the creationist statement that the diversity of life cannot have been produced by chance alone, and natural selection should not, in any sense, be given godlike status.

So chance, design, and complexity are handled adequately, if not always stunningly, by evolutionary theory and in biological observation and experimentation—sufficiently well to be scientific on the one hand, and not to require the ad hoc intervention of a supernatural Creator on the other.

The Origin of Life

What about the origin of life? For creationists, the origin of complex, self-replicating living systems from the inorganic realm demands the action of improbable chance and implies a Creator. Pointing to the inability of biochemists to synthesize life in a test tube, creationists agree with the poet: only God can make a tree. Only a Creator could have assembled all those complex ingredients of DNA, house them in a proteinaceous sheath, and thus fashion the first primitive form of life.

Evolutionists commonly respond that complex organic molecules occur throughout the universe and many (such as amino acids, the building blocks of proteins) can be synthesized simply by passing a spark through a gaseous mixture of ammonia, methane, hydrogen, and water, as was first done by Stanley Miller in the 1950s using the ingredients thought to be the main atmospheric constituents of the primitive Earth. Creationists counter that such results are far removed from producing true life. Biologists, of course, agree, while maintaining that such experiments are both supportive and suggestive of the hypothesis that life did, indeed, arise from natural processes.

Some biologists, such as Nobel laureate Francis Crick, do stress the great difficulties involved in the origin of, say, the molecules of inheritance and protein synthesis—DNA and RNA—from simpler, and ultimately inorganic, systems. Such biologists seriously doubt the ubiquity of life throughout the universe as envisioned by some cosmologists, who argue that an improbable event becomes probable given enough tries: there are billions of stars in the universe and so, one may suppose, many planets with conditions similar to our own on which life may well have developed independently. Neither argument is particularly compelling in the absence of any hard information. But it is important to note in passing that whether or not life arose on Earth, or arose elsewhere and spread here (a view favored by Crick, for example), both sides agree that once bacteria became established on Earth, all the rest of life, as we know it, evolved from them.

It is true that DNA is complex. It is true that no one has taken primordial compounds supposedly in the Earth's primitive atmosphere and created DNA—much less a functional bacterium—in the laboratory. The creationists wish us to suppose that this situation demonstrates that life cannot have arisen by natural processes. I cannot follow their argument: in the brief history of biochemistry we have gone from laborious analysis of what proteins are (starting in the mid-nineteenth century), through the cracking of the genetic code (in the mid-twentieth century), to the heady days of genetic cloning (at the end of the twentieth century). That the origin of life, if posed as a biochemical problem, remains incompletely solved as of the year 2000 is not particularly surprising and certainly not compelling evidence that it never will be. But if we are to continue to teach our children that such problems are beyond the purview of science because "the Creator did it," we certainly will lessen our chances of ever finding out. Yet that's exactly what creationists—including Phillip Johnson and his colleagues—would have us all think.

The Last Word: A Simple Refutation of Creationism

There must be a single, hierarchically arranged pattern of resemblance interlinking all life if all life descended from a single common ancestor. This is evolution's grand prediction, and as we have seen, it has been abundantly and consistently corroborated throughout the annals of biological research.

What do creationists offer as their explanation for the manifestly hierarchical structure of the biological world? Most creationists simply affirm that it pleased the Creator to fashion life in the form in which we find it today. They maintain that the Creator was simply being efficient in using the same blueprint for the separately created basic kinds, thereby "explaining," for example, why mammals, birds, reptiles, and amphibians all have one upper and two lower leg bones (except, of course, snakes and other secondarily limbless tetrapods).

There is a simple test of the proposition that the hierarchically arranged structure of life is the product of intelligent design—of a Creator-God. It comes from the very same watchmaker analogy that creationists apply in their arguments on complexity, for if it is true that no one can devise a direct way to observe the behavior of the Creator, we certainly can do the next best thing: we can examine the history of watches—or any other product that humans have designed over time. And we ask, Does the design history of watches—or 747s, or automobiles, and so on—reveal a simple, hierarchically nested pattern of similarity, as evolution has produced in the biological realm? The answer is a resounding *no*.

By sheer coincidence, I happen to be an expert in the history of design of the cornet, the brass musical instrument that is the shorter, dumpier version of the more familiar trumpet.[15] Cornets were invented in the 1820s, and the basic configuration of modern cornets was established by the mid-1850s. For the past century and a half, a bewildering array of cornet designs has appeared—an exuberant variety that has defied all attempts at neat categorization. I tried for several years to produce a simple classification of cornets—one that resembles the classifications I have produced for trilobites and horseshoe crabs in my career as a paleontologist. And I persistently failed.

I think I know why human design systems can never yield the same sort of simple patterns that we see in the biological world. The reason is that humans are continually copying each other—and stealing each other's ideas. It was one thing for monks to copy manuscripts, which would then be copied again *in isolation* in far-flung monasteries. Copying in isolation does, as we saw in Chapter 2, produce the same simple hierarchical structure that we observe in the natural world. But out in the competitive marketplace, it is another thing altogether, and cornets of every conceivable blend of design have been produced. The result is a mélange of design that defies simple characterization and unambiguous classification. On the face of it, when we examine the only examples of intelligent design open to us, we see that the prediction that intelligent design would produce the same sort of simple hierarchically nested pattern that we observe in the biological realm fails utterly.

However, the Creator is not supposed to have had competitors in designing the biological world. The real analogy would be with the output of a single artisan or atelier. I have chronicled in detail the design history of two major cornet manufacturers, and I am thoroughly conversant with the design histories of at least a dozen others. Though there is a tendency for makers producing more than one design to keep them separate for years on end, there are plenty of examples of the blending of designs through time. And I know of only one case in which progressive modification of a design lineage in several discrete steps yields a simple, hierarchical classification scheme.

Could the single artisan, who has no one but himself from whom to steal designs, possibly be the explanation for why the Creator fashioned life in a hierarchical fashion—why, for example, reptiles, amphibians, mammals, and birds all share the same limb structure? Here, and somewhat to my surprise, I find myself agreeing with creationist Gary Parker, who says that God did not work that way at all. Denying that life really is hierarchically structured, Parker writes (alluding to patterns of similarity in different organ systems in lizards, but clearly generalizing), "The pattern is not a branching one suggesting evolutionary descent from a common ancestor; rather, it is a mosaic pattern . . . suggesting creation according to a common plan" (1980, p. 22). I would agree with Parker: if I were designing life, I probably would use the same idea over and over—but not, as Parker suggests, limiting the use of my ideas to what someone in retrospect might be tempted to identify as separate lineages. Good design ideas, in other words, should turn up here and there all over the place, wherever they prove useful, and whether or not they are stolen from others or are the product of a single fertile mind.

So, in the end, there is as little of substance in the scientific creationists' treatment of the origin and diversification of life as there is in their treatment of cosmological time. They pose no novel testable hypotheses and make no predictions or observations worthy of the name. They devote the vast bulk of their ponderous efforts to attacking orthodox science in the mistaken and utterly fallacious belief that in discrediting science (or, as they put it, evolution science or philosophical naturalism), they have thereby established the truth of their own position.

Their efforts along these particular lines are puny. Moreover, they impugn the integrity and intelligence of thousands of honest souls who have had the temerity to believe that it is both fitting and proper to try to understand the universe, the Earth, and all its life in naturalistic terms, using only the evidence of our senses to evaluate how truthful an idea might be. Yes, historical geology and evolutionary biology are sciences. They are imperfect—but self-correcting. And no, neither scientific creationism nor Johnson's theistic realism can be construed as science—not by any conceivable stretching of the term. And if it is not science, what is it? Phillip Johnson has already let the cat out of the bag: creationism, including special creationism, scientific creationism, and theistic realism, is nothing but that good, old-time religion.

Can We Afford a Culture War?

Phillip Johnson thinks that what is at stake here, in his words, is a "culture war" between the atheistic forces of naturalism on the one hand, and an essentially Christian-based (his version!) view of the origin and nature of things—with all the moral, ethical, and, yes, legal and political implications these would seem to imply to his basically conservative viewpoint—on the other. On the campus, the alternative to philosophical naturalism, Johnson fervently hopes, is to be his theistic realism, but far more is at stake in the body politic at large.

Some of my colleagues patently agree. In debate, Will Provine says that people have to "check their brains at the door" when they go to church. Others are all too willing to agree that Darwinism implies atheism—blindly rising to the bait, dismissing as "nineteenth-century fairytales" the sort of personal God espoused by Johnson (and so many others, of course), and grossly overstepping the limits of what can be said from the actual point of view of science. Scientists like Richard Dawkins seem only too willing to agree that we are indeed involved in a culture war.

I see this war, but I think it is both overstated and very risky. I do admit that there is a huge political side to it; indeed, I think that is really where the war is. Academics—Johnson and Provine alike—like to think that everything is about ideas (actually Johnson, a lawyer, knows better), where in contrast it should be fairly obvious that the essence of all this creationism fury, despite its deep-seated roots in one particular branch of religion, is not so much good old-time religion, but good old-time politics. I myself am politically left, though as a middle-class suburbanite who enjoys the niceties of life to the extent I can afford them, I am hardly a radical. I have already said that I harbor extreme doubts on the existence of such a personal God as the one in which Phillip Johnson believes (though I'll stick to my promise and say more about this in the final section of this chapter). Unlike Will Provine, though, I do not see it as my business, nor important in any intellectual sense, to attack anyone's religious beliefs—or to worry what anyone personally might think about evolution or the biblical stories of creation.

But I do think the issue of creationism in public schools is *very* important—enough so to warrant writing this book. Though intelligent-design arguments seem to be on the ascendancy as the strategy of choice when it comes to combating evolution in the public schools at the end of the twentieth century, we still are not entirely done with the older form of scientific creationism, which seeks to establish creationism as a bona fide form of science and thereby teachable in public schools in America. The real battle is still being fought at school board meetings and in public school classrooms, where local creation enthusiasts (sometimes, but not usually, in cahoots with a creationism-leaning teacher) persist in trying to inject their version of Christian theology into the public schools. Nor is Phillip Johnson alone in pretending that the tired old arguments against evolution are brand new: every year, new efforts to debunk evolution and establish the teaching of creationism—either instead, or at least alongside, of evolution—trumpet the "news" that evolution has been falsified. Creationist literature reads like the worst of the supermarket tabloids—the ones that tell you there are Martians after all, though somehow you missed the news in the *New York Times* or on CNN.

According to the National Center for Science Education—an anticreationist, pro-science organization located in Berkeley, California, that grew out of early "Committees of Correspondence" that were organized in the 1970s and early 1980s on a state-by-state basis—the teaching of evolution in the late 1990s is in as much serious trouble in the public schools of the United States as it has ever been. Alabama actually requires a disclaimer in its high school biology books that reads, "Evolution is a controversial theory some scientists present as scientific explanation for the origin of living things, such as plants, animals, and humans. No one was present when life first appeared on earth. Therefore, any statement about life's origins should be considered as theory, not fact."[1] Seven other states are said to avoid evolution as much as possible in the biology curriculum, and no fewer than 25 states have had recent difficulties fending off creationism within isolated local school districts.

So we must ask again, Why does the problem persist? And why should we care about it?

I firmly believe that the world is the way it is regardless of what anyone thinks about it—you, I, the president of the United States, the kid down the block. I am aware of the sophisticated arguments in the philosophy of science that, because any statement we make about the natural world is necessarily a mental construct, there can be no wholly objective reality—and I agree, at least to the extent that nothing we say about the material world can be counted on as absolute. On the other hand, I remain enough of a logical positivist to maintain that there is a physical reality, and we are not merely constructing it when we look critically at the stars, subatomic particles, or Devonian trilobites. It is not, in other words, a purely unobjective—subjective—statement to say that the Devonian trilobites on which I work were arthropods living in seas some 480 million years ago. On this, I'm with that other famous Johnson—Samuel (1709–1784)—who, when commenting on Bishop George Berkeley's (1685–1753) claim that the physical world is an illusion created by humans, is reported to have kicked a rock while saying, "I refute it thus." In other words, I don't think that when I walk out a door, everything in a room—the furniture, the people—cease to exist.

That is what I mean when I say that the world is the way it is regardless of what anyone says it is. Someone—say, Phillip Johnson—can swear that evolution has not happened and have absolutely no effect on the relationship between humans and chimpanzees. On the other hand, I can express my extreme doubt that the sort of personal God that Johnson knows is there is actually taking a direct hand in my affairs—or those of anyone else—and *that* should have no effect whatever on anyone else's personal construal of

God, or, for that matter, how they think the universe ticks—or who puts the bike under the Christmas tree.

All that being said, though, it very much does matter what we teach our kids at school. In the biology classroom, it simply cannot be that "my opinion is as good as yours"—not if we are to teach with integrity in the science curriculum. Anticreationists like me have for years agreed that "origin" accounts—of the Judeo-Christian tradition, but also of the Buddhist, Confucianist, Hindu, and other major religious traditions, as well as of different Native American, African, and Asian traditions, not forgetting hunter-gatherer traditions as recorded by anthropologists—are all grist for the mill of a comparative course on religious beliefs.

The scary thing about this is not that a kid might prefer to believe the creation story. After all, some 44 percent of Americans, according to one poll I saw recently, do adopt this position. The purpose of teaching science is not to indoctrinate kids on the (secular) humanist or naturalist side of the culture war in which we are supposedly engaged, but rather to teach them what science is all about. No good teacher will demand that kids "believe" evolution; kids should never be taught anything other than "this is what science thinks about this issue"—evolution, plate tectonics, quarks, and so on—and this is *why* scientists think this. In short, they should get a very clear idea about how science is done—how it *works*—and especially come to see science as a perfectly human enterprise (with all the implicit failings of anything human!). *Especially* when kids come to class espousing creationism and showing resistance to hearing anything about evolution, the teacher must work hard to make it clear that the kids' beliefs will be respected, and that they won't be asked to drop their religious beliefs and adopt a new belief in evolution.

Belief simply is not the point here; rather, a thorough grounding in science as a human endeavor is. This is important simply because we live in a technological age so heavily dependent on science—with no realistic thought or hope of turning back—that the future of this country, of the Western world generally, and undoubtedly of humanity on the planet as a whole depends very much on more and better science, especially on an informed citizenry who must continue to guide the future course of this and all other countries as wisely as possible through the ballot box. I would no sooner place our future strictly in the hands of scientists than I would see it placed in the hands of movie stars—or, for that matter, lawyers and politicians. I think the problems facing humanity at the Millennium are so great that we need the input of all segments of society to deal with them, and here I refer specifically to perhaps the greatest sector of society to which one can point: the global community of organized religion.

We will not go very far if we pretend to our kids that we cannot tell the difference between real and phony science. Yet that was the gist of all those "equal time" laws of the 1970s and 1980s: the Arkansas and Louisiana legislatures were actually telling the teachers in their public schools to pretend not to know the difference between real science—flaws and all—and outmoded or simply bad science. I cannot imagine anything more perverse, more deliberately harmful, than teaching kids that their elders cannot tell the difference between the real and the phony. Some of them, of course, cannot. But all but the relatively few creation-leaning science teachers throughout the fifty states most assuredly can, and requiring them in essence to lie to their students sends about the worst message imaginable to the younger generation. And kids, of course, can see right through that.

That's why I so fervently care about teaching evolution, and not teaching creationism, in public schools. It is not that I want kids to abandon their religious beliefs; it is that I want our kids to be able to know science for what it is, so that they can make informed choices as adults. I want people neither to follow science slavishly as if it were the only salvation—the only way of knowing—nor to condemn it outright for all the evils (real and imagined) that it has unleashed on the world. Science is a "glorious enterprise," and kids simply have to learn about it so that they may see it for what it is.

Why, then, this particular animus against evolution? Why has it persisted so long in the American political arena? Creationists attack only the part of science that they find inimical to their religious beliefs. Moreover, though the attack on evolution comes largely from the Christian right, not all political conservatives are Christians, and not all Christians, even conservative Christians, are political conservatives. Nor is it just a matter of "my story versus yours," though early opposition from Christian fundamentalists, who simply thought that anything that cast doubt on the literal truth of any part of the Bible (biblical inerrancy) cast doubt on the whole of Christian doctrine, did indeed amount to "my story against yours." And though it is also true that, when a Phillip Johnson debates a Will Provine, they still agree that it is "my story against yours" (with each insisting he has the truth, of course), it is just as obvious that something more is at stake than simply God's credibility as divined from the pages of the King James Version of the Bible versus modern biological research.

That something is morality. Perceived decline in moral values in the United States and perceptions of what might be done about it are what prompt the political right's continual war on evolution. But it is by no means just the American political right that sees a connection between evolution and what philosophically inclined biologists (and biologically inclined philosophers, such as Michael Ruse) prefer to call ethics. Starting with Herbert Spencer's social Darwinism, the tradition to develop ethical systems and, sometimes, paths of overt policy (e.g., as in the eugenics movement[2]) based on biological principles has persisted in Western culture.

In a sense, the Christian right's outright opposition to evolution is just one aspect of this hypnotic temptation to see moral or ethical implications in evolutionary biology. Phillip Johnson is glad to pounce on biologists and philosophers who have dabbled in these waters—as evidence that there is indeed a culture war taking place. I am happy to report, though, that in my lifetime few ethical ruminations derived from evolutionary biology have made it all the way to the body politic. And that is a source of some relief, for what a confusing welter of ethical systems and homilies have been drawn up in the name of evolution! I have seen very similar ethics derived from diametrically opposed evolutionary camps and, of course, very different ethics derived from essentially the same camp within the larger evolutionary circle. For example, the great geneticist Theodosius Dobzhansky, a devout and practicing Christian, derived what I can only describe as a gentle, loving worldview of, among other things, cooperation—believing deeply, as he did, that Christianity and evolution went hand in hand.

Were he alive today, I am reasonably sure that Dobzhansky would not identify with the strongest, most strident gene-competition views that underlie sociobiology. Yet natural selection is the quintessential cornerstone of all evolutionary theory in general, and surely of the genetics of both Dobzhansky and, say, Richard Dawkins. And it is notorious that the "selfish gene" underlying sociobiology has conjured up an ethical worldview to some contemporary biologists and philosophers that is very like the dog-eat-dog vision of the worst of the old social Darwinism.

Well, if evolution can prompt ethical systems of ruthless competition in some minds, and Christian-like harmony in others, what are we to conclude? Here is what I have long thought: *there is no one-to-one correlation between any principle of science and any system of human behavior. In particular, there is no necessary set of ethical implications implicit in the very idea of evolution—or emanating from any subset of evolutionary theory.* To those who say there are moral lessons and ethical systems—evil or good—implicit in the very idea of evolution, I say, A PLAGUE ON BOTH YOUR HOUSES.

There is no doubt that the creationists' tilt against what they wish was the evolutionary windmill is born in greatest part by the sincere belief that there is indeed a connection between evolution and morals—and a negative one at that. Just since I began dueling with creationists in the late 1970s, I have either experienced, or seen secondhand, a number of events that dramatize how deeply the connection between evolution and moral decay is seen by the Christian right. For example, during the "Scopes II" trial in California, Nell Segraves (the plaintiff's mother and a director of the Creation Research Center in San Diego) had the following exchange with Robert Bazell, science reporter for *NBC Nightly News:*

> Bazell: "For seventeen years since the Supreme Court banned prayer in public schools, Mrs. Segraves has been fighting to bring religion back to the schools. She believes that the teaching of evolution is the primary evil, responsible for all sorts of problems."
>
> Segraves: "What about prostitution, or the drugs, or the criminal activities, violence. It's lack of respect."
>
> Bazell: "And you think that all that can be traced to the teaching of evolution in the schools?"

Segraves: "I believe it can, and I think I can prove it."

Now it is surely an irony that the Old Testament amply documents the presence of many of the same social ills (and plenty more) plaguing Israelite society thousands of years ago, yet nothing is said of the Israelites teaching evolution to their children.

Creationist R. L. Wysong is quite explicit on the reason why evolution leads to moral decay. In his *The Creation-Evolution Controversy* (1976), Wysong argues that one's position on origins frames one's worldview, and one's worldview in turn leads to one's "approach to life." A "correct" position on origins leads to a "correct" worldview, which in turn leads to solutions to life's problems.

> A person can basically take one of two positions on origins. One is there is a creator, the other is there is not; or, evolution explains origins or it does not, Creation versus evolution, theism versus materialism or naturalism, and design versus chance, are all ways of expressing the two alternatives. (pp. 5–6)

Wysong goes on to argue that the evolutionary position influenced the thinking of such historical figures as Marx, Mussolini, Hitler, and Freud:

> but if, on the other hand, life owes its existence to a creator, a supernatural force, then life is the result of his will and purposes. Understanding these purposes would be the only way to understand life's varied questions and problems. (p. 9)

My favorite example comes from a woman in Philadelphia, who, in a letter to me written in the early 1980s, put it even more bluntly. Greatly mistaking my position (taken from a newspaper article), she wrote to thank me for my efforts in combating the notion that we humans have descended from lower forms of life, for *were we to teach that to our children, we could not expect them to conduct themselves in a moral way*. In so writing, she cut to the very heart of creationist feelings.

One need not be a materialist to note that a functioning society demands moral behavior, and that there are other, more compelling, explanations for why we are, collectively, less than perfect in our ability always to behave in the very best way. But such is the creationist belief, and the reason for their persistence is, far more than the urge for fame or the slight profit motive attributable at least to some creationists, their conviction that evolution undermines morality.

More recently, the same rhetoric has been popping up in pronouncements from right-wing political figures. Conservative columnist and erstwhile (perennial?) presidential candidate Pat Buchanan, for example, has expressed his belief that the American public has "a right to insist that Godless evolution not to be taught to their children or their children not be indoctrinated in it."[3] And, taking us right up to within a few weeks of this writing, according to a New York Times editorial, House Republican Whip Tom DeLay has also joined in:

> In the culture wars, you can credit Mr. DeLay for turning a major political axiom upside down. It used to be an article of faith for conservatives that Americans need to take more individual responsibility for their actions. But now, thanks to Mr. DeLay, we learn that violence perpetrated by gun owners is really the product of larger forces. What might those be? According to the Republican whip from Texas, nothing less than "broken homes," day care, television, video games, birth control, abortion, and, *unbelievably, the teaching of the theory of evolution* [italics mine].[4]

The most visible battles of this particular culture war are the cases that have actually found their way to the courtroom from time to time, starting with the notorious Scopes trial of 1925. Scopes was found guilty of violating the Tennessee statute known as the Butler Act, which said in part,

> It shall be unlawful for any teacher in any of the Universities, Normals and all other public schools of the State, which are supported in whole or in part by the public school funds of the State, to teach any theory that denies the story of the Divine Creation of man as taught in the Bible, and to teach instead that man has descended from a lower order of animals.

Clarence Darrow and his colleagues, including a battery of lawyers from the American Civil Liberties Union, never disputed the charge that John Scopes had indeed taught the evolution segment of the biology curriculum. (It is an amusing sidelight that, later in life, Scopes admitted he had in fact never taught evolution to his biology class—though he had covered the subject in general science.) Convicted of his "crime," Scopes was fined a hundred dollars. The Tennessee Supreme Court then threw out the conviction on the technicality that Judge Ralston had improperly levied the fine on Scopes because Tennessee law mandated that only a jury could impose fines of fifty dollars or more.

The action stymied the plans of Darrow and colleagues: their real aim was to have the law reviewed and thrown out by the U.S. Supreme Court. Their argument, of course, was to be that the law stood in violation of the Constitution, particularly the establishment clause of the First Amendment prohibiting the mixing of church and state.

The issue of creationism in the classroom finally reached the U.S. Supreme Court in 1968 in *Epperson v. Arkansas.* Mrs. Epperson, a Little Rock high school biology teacher, successfully challenged a 1929 Arkansas law forbidding the teaching of "the theory or doctrine that mankind ascended or descended from a lower order of animals." Not until the Supreme Court ruled that the Arkansas law was "an attempt to blot out a particular theory because of its supposed conflict with the Biblical account," and thus was an attempt to establish religion in the classroom, were the Tennessee and other similar statutes declared null and void.

Certainly not legally dead as a result of the Scopes trial, creationism maintained a steady though low profile through the next fifty years. I maintain my conviction that the real battleground is the classroom, and it is here that we have seen the most subtle yet profound sign that the creationists, in an important sense, actually won the day in 1925, for thereafter there was a dramatic downplay of evolution in high school biology texts from the late 1920s on. A case in point: George W. Hunter's *Civic Biology,* published in 1914—the book Scopes testified he had used in his course—originally had a brief discussion of evolution. After the trial, the publishers brought out a revised edition *(New Civic Biology)* eliminating any mention of evolution. Virtually all other texts followed suit. If Genesis had not quite made it into the classroom, the Scopes trial did at least place a tremendous damper on the teaching of evolution for the next thirty-five years or so. Only when Americans awoke one day in 1957 to see Sputnik circling the Earth—and awoke thereby to the deficiencies of science education in the United States—was anything done. The resulting massive, national effort to upgrade the quality of science education included evolution, in a sense priming the pump for the battles still under way in many of our secondary schools.

Then in the 1960s, Henry Morris and his colleagues invented scientific creationism, the wolf in sheep's clothing devised for the very purpose of circumventing the establishment clause of the First Amendment—the one that the Supreme Court invoked in 1968 when it struck down those archaic old "monkey laws." Though similar laws were pending in the legislatures of many states in the 1980s, it was Arkansas Act 590, followed soon thereafter by passage of a similar statute in Louisiana, that triggered the two famous creationism court cases of the modern era. These were "equal time" bills, which, as we saw in the case of the Arkansas statute, called for the teaching of a model of creation science alongside of evolution science. As we saw at the outset of Chapter 5, the definition of creation science in Arkansas Act 590 is virtually identical to lawyer Wendell Bird's creation science model, already encountered in Chapter 5.[5]

I was briefly involved in the preparation of the plaintiff's case against Arkansas Act 590 that was successfully argued in Judge William Overton's Little Rock courtroom in 1981. I ended up attending the trial, though, as a reporter, armed with my very own press pass. But rather than conjuring up old memories, I have chosen to reprint as Appendix 1 the "review" of the trial I wrote for my sponsoring publication, *Science 82,* a now defunct publication, aimed at the general public, of the American Association for the Advancement of Science, which publishes the very much still alive journal *Science.*[6]

What really is important, of course, is Judge Overton's opinion—widely considered to be so tightly reasoned and documented that there was little room for appeal. Overton found that Arkansas Act 590 violated all three of the by then traditional litmus tests of whether or not a statute is in violation of the establishment clause of the First Amendment to the U.S.

Constitution, pertaining to the relation of church and state. Roger Lewin's report of Overton's opinion (see note 6), provides the following citation from a 1971 opinion that established the three-pronged "Lemon test" of the establishment clause:

> For a statute to be constitutional, it must fulfill three provisions: "First, the statute must have a secular legislative purpose; second, its principal or primary purpose must be one that neither advances nor inhibits religion . . . ; finally, the statute must not foster an excessive governmental entanglement with religion."[7]

Violation of any one of these three criteria would have been sufficient to rule Act 590 unconstitutional, and Overton saw violation of all three!

The strategic mistake the Arkansas legislature made when drafting Act 590 was to include explicit definitions of evolution science and creation science. The expert witnesses especially tore through the fatuous creation science characterizations, and evidence was also adduced demonstrating the religious motivations of the bill's original sponsor.

Less clear-cut was the Louisiana case, argued in 1982: *Edwards v. Aguillard*. Here there was no explicit definition of creation science—only a much vaguer statement saying that "creation science means the scientific evidences for creation and inferences from those scientific evidences." No explicit definition, no prominent fish swimming in the barrel for expert witnesses to shoot at. But the Louisiana court, nonetheless, did find the statute unconstitutional. The case eventually made it all the way to the U.S. Supreme Court, which ruled, 7 to 2, that the statute is indeed unconstitutional on "establishment" grounds. Only Justice Antonin Scalia and Chief Justice William Rehnquist demurred, finding the Louisiana law in fact constitutional.

Though I have drawn attention to the disproportionate number of lawyers (e.g., Wendell Bird, Norman Macbeth, Phillip Johnson) who have come to the forefront among the layperson Darwin attackers and outright creationists, I must say that I took deep satisfaction, sitting in Judge Overton's courtroom all those years ago, in seeing that the argument that "creationism is really science, so we can teach it in the classroom" is as transparently preposterous to the interpreters of the law of the land as it is to anyone else who is not a creationist zealot. At least in this instance, the law proved itself *not* the "ass" that Charles Dickens's character Mr. Bumble (in *Oliver Twist)* once pronounced it to be.

Thus the legalistic charade culminating in the 1980s has—at least for the nonce—faded, and we are left with what the likes of Luther Sunderland was on record as advocating: not the conspicuous activities of legislatures and the inevitable court cases, but the much more insidious, quiet, and, sadly, effective pressuring of school boards and teachers at the grassroots level. And that is still going on. It is a shame, really, because there are some pressing problems that present a much brighter way to look at biology and religion within the larger body politic. To see this connection, we must be willing to suspend the by now hoary, wholly outmoded fight over origins, and be willing to take a fresh look at the world around us. Never mind the origins of biological diversity, including human life. Rather, we simply acknowledge that life is here, that it is in trouble, and that nonhuman life remains important to human life. When we do that, we get a whole new perspective of the connections between science and religion—*positive* connections—that help point the way to solving some of the most critical problems faced by life on this planet as we enter the new Millennium.

Ground Zero

There are some 10 million species (a conservative estimate) living right now on Earth. Of these 10 million species, we are losing roughly thirty thousand a year (again a conservative estimate).[8] Scientists so far have discovered and named just under 2 million of these species, but we know there must be many more, since random handfuls of backyard dirt reveal countless microbes and nematode worms as yet undescribed, and virtually every tree felled in the Amazon rainforest has an insect never before seen. But we *know* we are losing lots of these species as ecosystems are systematically destroyed. Humans, for example, cut down many hectares of rainforest a day, and given the known ranges of tropical species, we know that something like three species an hour are disappearing—most of them before we even have a chance to call their names. We are, in short, in the midst of an extinction crisis of proportions the Earth has not seen since the last of the five major, global mass extinctions struck the Earth some 65 million years ago.

The question becomes, Should we care? After all, human life seems to go along fine in New York, no matter how many trees are felled in the Amazon rainforest. But when we stop to consider that human beings around the planet utilize over forty thousand species of plants, animals, fungi, and microbes every day—for food, shelter, clothing, and medicine—we get an inkling of how important nonhuman life on the planet still is to human existence. We need our fisheries and forests; we need our genetic reservoirs for the production of new medicines, and for the genetic replenishment of existing agricultural stocks.

We recognize that the purely physical aspect of human existence—just being alive, breathing the air, drinking the water, converting plant and animal proteins, sugars, and starches for the energy and proteins we need to maintain, grow, and simply stay alive—depends on the availability of these precious commodities. Right now there are just over 6 billion human beings on Earth, and only roughly half of them have access to fresh water safe enough to drink. Topsoil is being stripped from the centers of the major continents at such high rates that the ever greater amounts of food we need to produce to fill the ever increasing number of human mouths is also at great risk.

It is the onslaught against ecosystems themselves that (just as in the past) accounts for species loss, but also for the degradation in air quality and water supplies, and the cycling of essential nutrients like carbon, nitrogen, and phosphorus. In short, we humans are fouling our nest at such a rapid clip that, I think it is safe to say, our own continued existence is called into question. We need to stem the tide of ecosystem destruction and species loss if we are to hope for a long and fruitful continued existence on this Earth—at least at the levels of material comfort and "high civilization" that the industrialized world currently enjoys.[9]

So much for the problem—the issue at hand. What can this possibly have to do with religion?

Everything. Over the past few years I have visited a dozen or so college campuses, discussing aspects of "science and religion" with my colleague Margaret Wertheim. I have also spoken at various "ecology and religion" symposia, and even at the United Nations (fall 1998) on this subject. What I have to say at these venues is simple: I am convinced that, to understand how humans have come to be destroying ecosystems and driving species to extinction at such prodigious rates and intensities—an understanding that is necessary to define strategies to overcome the problem—we must understand the fundamentals of the human ecological condition. And I present my scientific analysis of three distinct aspects of the human ecological condition over the past ten thousand years (i.e., within the time frame adopted by the young-Earth creationists). But I also say this: *religious traditions, especially as embodied in concepts of God, are deeply if not wholly ecological concepts as well.* And I tell my audience that there is, in effect, a resonance—not disagreement—between the modern scientific account and traditional religious accounts. Not surprisingly, people have always had a pretty shrewd grasp—not necessarily of where they came from in the first place, but of who they are and how they fit into the world around them. And they tend to reflect these deep understandings, their visions of themselves and how they fit into the world around them, in their religious accounts, including the concept of the gods, or of God.

Here, very briefly, is what I say as I compare these three parallel accounts:

Scientific Analysis I. The "state of nature" of absolutely every species that has ever lived on the planet—including, until very recently, all humans—is to be broken up into relatively small local populations living as a collective part of a local ecosystem. Each such ecosystem has a carrying capacity, a limit to the population size that is determined by the amount of food productivity, water accessibility, and other aspects of the environment, according to the behaviors and physiologies (evolutionists like me would say "adaptations") of whatever species one is considering. The role each such local population plays within its ecosystem is what is generally meant by ecologists as the ecological niche of that population.

This description of local populations of species having distinct niches within local ecosystems does not apply to the vast majority of humans now alive. However, some remnant hunter-gatherer cultures will survive into the twenty-first century—if just barely, but with their traditional cultures in all cases already radically altered. Fortunately, we have abundant documentation from anthropologists (and others, including missionaries) who studied many of these cultures in the relatively early days of Western exploration and colonization. We know that, traditionally, these peoples lived in relatively small bands and relied exclusively on the productivity of their local surroundings, meaning that they conformed exactly to the description of ecological niche occupation that is true for all other species on the planet.

Concepts of God I. Concepts of supernatural beings among hunter-gatherer peoples reveal a clear and starkly direct understanding of who they are and how they fit into the world—in effect, the universe—around them. One example I give is reported by anthropologist Colin Turnbull, who studied the Ba Mbuti people (so-called pygmies) of the Ituri forest in Africa's Congo Basin.[10] Turnbull tells of a group of Ba Mbuti—men, women, and children—venturing into the forest on a joint hunting and plant-gathering foray. As they entered the forest, they called out, "Hello Mother Forest! Hello Father Forest!" And they would tell Mother and Father Forest that they were there to take only what they needed.

The Mother and Father Forest of the Mbuti are gods—spirits of the natural world. The Mbuti are, in effect, clearing their hunting and foraging with these spirits of the forests, and by insisting that they are there only for what they need, they are acknowledging in the clearest possible terms that they see themselves as a part of the very forest ecosystem in which they live. The spirits they invoke—Mother and Father Forest—are *abstractions* of the system in which they live.

Resonance—I have no other word for it: my Western biological understanding of what constitutes an ecological niche and how species are broken up into small populations that form parts of local ecosystems—a description I claim pertains to hunter-gatherers—is mirrored precisely in the accounts the hunter-gatherers themselves provide, and it is especially clearly seen in their concepts of the supernatural.

Scientific Analysis II. Sometime around ten thousand years ago, in a variety of places around the globe—but perhaps first in the Natufian culture of the Middle East—people began actively to cultivate crops and undertake animal domestication in a systematic fashion. Though often described as an expansion of the human ecological niche, it was really far more momentous, for *with the invention of agriculture, people radically changed their position in the natural world, becoming the first species in effect to "step outside" local ecosystems.* If anything, the local ecosystem became the enemy—with all but one or two of the local plants now regarded as invasive weeds, and all but a handful of the local animals viewed more for the harm they could do to crops and livestock than as a part of the natural system.

In short, the invention of agriculture meant that *Homo sapiens* became the first species ever to exist on Earth *not* to be broken up into local populations inside of local ecosystems. In these brief ten thousand years, the human population has grown from an estimated 6 million to over 6 billion. There is no question that this surge in population (it has been logarithmic, with the big increases, of course, coming just in the last one and a half centuries), plus the unequal distribution and consumption of resources, is what underlies the conversion of ecosystems to farmlands, and later to cities and suburban settings—the prime cause, in other words, underlying the extinction crisis we now face. It is the very success of humans in taking the bold step out of ecosystems that has led to the current ecological predicament.

Concepts of God II. Did the early agriculturalists have as fine-tuned a sense of who they were and how they fit into the world around them as the Ba Mbuti? There is no doubt in my mind that they did, and I can cite no better source than my old King James Version of the Bible. I have, in the past,[11] quoted Genesis 1:26–28—the famous "dominion" passage—in which God is said to have said,

> Let us make man in our image, after our likeness: and let them have dominion over the fish of the sea, and over the fowl of the air, and over the cattle, and over all of the earth, and over every creeping thing that creepeth upon the earth.

> So God created man in his *own* image, in the image of God created he him; male and female created he them.
>
> And God blessed them, and God said unto them, Be fruitful, and multiply, and replenish the earth, and subdue it, and have dominion over the fish of the sea, and over the fowl of the air, and over every living thing that moveth upon the earth.

These words constitute the most ringing declaration of independence ever set down. They say that people, whatever their similarities with the beasts of the field, are unlike any other living species. We are entitled to the Earth, and to all its fruits. We *own* the Earth, and we must seek dominion over "every living thing that moveth on the earth."

There is no doubt in my mind that the Israelites (and presumably their agriculturally based neighbors) saw themselves as living outside—or above—the natural world surrounding them. This is an extremely accurate picture of who they in fact were, and what their actual relation to the natural world was. (I of course disagree with their account of how they got there in the first place, but we are discussing not competing versions of history, but rather functional views of the here and now, as seen in both scientific accounts and in religious traditions and concepts of God.)

I am also struck by the courage it took to make that leap—though not perhaps so much by the literal change in ecology—which was, on the whole, a logical improvement in efficiency (though some anthropologists and historians have noted how prone to famine agricultural societies through the intervening millennia have been). But there must have been a strong emotional aspect to seeing oneself as outside of nature—the local universe—that must have been deeply disturbing, perhaps even downright terrifying.

So, I see the Judeo-Christian God as an abstraction of the older gods of the Edenish ecosystems from which these early agriculturalists had so recently declared their independence. There is nothing inherently new or radical about this suggestion: theologians have long spoken of concepts of God as changing (even evolving!) and are certainly comfortable with the notion that concepts of God are essentially ideas—ideas that can and do change over time, and from culture to culture. But recognizing that concepts of God are ideas in no way jeopardizes the validity of any of those ideas: just because we can point to a correlation between a change from ecosystem spirits to a monotheistic, more abstract God correlated with actual radical changes in human ecology does not invalidate any specific notion of God.[12]

But the correlation does show, once again, deep resonance between the hyperanalytic vision of Western science (i.e., my conclusion that human beings became the first species in the history of life to leave the confines of the local ecosystem when they invented agriculture) and a statement like that in Genesis (i.e., that a Creator-God made humans *very* different from all manner of other creatures).

Scientific Analysis III. Species are, in essence, packages of genetic information—groups of organisms capable of breeding with each other but not, as the overwhelming rule, with members of other species. Entire species are not parts of ecosystems, meaning that species as a whole do not play direct economic roles in nature. *Parts* of species—local populations—do play direct economic roles in local ecosystems, but species as a whole are information repositories—nothing more. Except, once again, our own species: *Homo sapiens*.

No longer playing direct roles in local ecosystems, it turns out that, particularly with our heightened technological skills in communication, all 6 billion of us are interlocked in an extraordinary global economic network that sees the exchange of no less than a *trillion* dollars worth of goods and services every day. There are, of course, other species that have spread around the entire globe (largely through the hand of humans, like some species of rats, or fruit flies), but these species do not form an integrated economic system (the rats in Norway have no connections with those in New York or Hong Kong, except sporadically through their genes; what other rats are eating in those far-flung regions is sublimely irrelevant to rats of the same species living in London or Tokyo).

If *Homo sapiens* has emerged as the first species in the history of life on Earth to be an economic, in addition to a genetic, entity,[13] we must ask, In what larger-scale economic system is *Homo sapiens* operating? The answer is fairly clear: the sum of all the world's ecosystems is the global ecosystem (sometimes called the biosphere, or Gaia). *Homo sapiens* is exerting a direct—largely negative at the moment—economic impact on the world's ecosystems and is the culprit behind the existing—and growing—dilemma of ecosystem degradation and species loss. Only by muting our impact on the world's ecosystems—taking only what we need (like the Ba Mbuti), engaging in sustainable development and conservation practices, and becoming more efficient (including just plain taking less)—can we hope to stem the tide of the extinction event now gripping the Earth's ecosystems and species.

Concepts of God III. The emergence of the economic impact of humanity on the biosphere as a whole is so new that it is perhaps to be expected that no religious traditions independently mirroring the relatively recent scientific understanding of the problem have yet emerged. Yet, in my travels to colleges and universities across America—especially when speaking either on creationism or, more positively and interestingly, on the resonance I see between science and religion on profound ecological issues—I have learned of a growing movement in *conservative* Christian circles, a movement that can only be described as "green."

Key to this movement is—once again—the interpretation of the "dominion" passage of Genesis 1. Environmentalists for the past few decades have tended to point an accusing finger toward this very passage, saying that, in effect, the injunction to "have dominion" over the beasts of the field is really a license to plunder, rob, and rape the planet—to view everything as put there solely for our own selfish needs—and an invitation to keep taking as long as there is anything left.

But "dominion" easily yields to "stewardship"—husbanding (taking care of) all resources, biological and otherwise. This is precisely what I am hearing from many conservative Christian students—students who are not so much reformulating their concept of God, perhaps, as reinterpreting his instructions on how to treat the beasts of the field according to a sense that we are, after all, still a part of Creation—not at all something a cut above or beyond nature.

I have already remarked that not all conservative Christians are politically conservative. It is true that, in the culture wars, the Christian right—and much of the Republican Party (though there are some notable exceptions)—is genuinely hostile to espousing environmental issues, as if improved efficiency and protection of vital resources were literally inimical to big business. But the younger generation of Christian conservatives seems to have no problem whatever melding its faith with a growing sense that, if we do not address our environmental problems, including the degradation of ecosystems and consequent loss of species, perhaps not much of a Creation will remain over which to enjoy dominion.

I realize that this brief account—especially with two of its components looking strictly at the Judeo-Christian tradition—begs the question, Does this resonance also show up when we look at the religious traditions of pastoralists (generally nomadic agriculturalists)? How do the other known ancient religions associated with the early days of agriculture and the rise of cities fit in—the religions of the Egyptians, Assyrians, Phoenicians? How about the later Greeks, or the Romans? And what about the great Eastern religions?

It's about time we look at all these religions as we search for resonance—for a common understanding of the grave threats faced by the world's ecosystems and species. (Indeed, it's my intention to do so in preparation for my forthcoming book, *Who Is This Man They Call God?)* But I think I have said enough to suggest that in this, the second great arena where my chosen profession intersects matters of public interest (creationism is one, the great loss of biodiversity is the other), the shoe is on the other foot: instead of warfare, we find essential agreement.

The tired old creationism debate—mired as it so thoroughly is in the nineteenth century—simply has not prepared us for the kind of positive interaction between science and religion that I see as eminently possible as we enter the new Millennium and grapple with tough environmental issues.

Nor do I think we can afford these stupid culture wars, with people like Phillip Johnson getting upset that his version of God seems threatened because scientists have discovered that life developed over 3.5 billion years ago on the planet and feel that they can explain how that happened through purely natural causes. Nor can we afford the arrogant intolerance of the scientists who claim that their science—evolution in particular—demonstrates unequivocally that there is no God.

In 1916, sociologist James H. Leuba conducted a poll of scientists active around the nation. Leuba found that the percentage of scientists believing in a "God to whom one might pray in expectation of receiving an answer" was lower than that of the general population. He predicted that, over time, increasingly higher percentages of scientists would declare their disbelief in such a God. A few years ago, as the twentieth century began to draw to a close, Larry Witham and Edward Larson repeated Leuba's poll, contacting a thousand people listed in *American Men and Women in Science* and asking precisely the same questions that Leuba had asked. They found that the *58 percent who had expressed disbelief in such a personal God in 1914 had risen to only 60 percent by 1996*. In other words, there was virtually no change: 40 percent of the scientists polled expressed belief in such a personal God.

I was not surprised by their results. I myself may not affect such belief, but I know a number of colleagues who do. The number of religious scientists grows, of course, when one expands belief to a less proactive conception of a Christian God, or, of course, acknowledges that other religions—Judaism, Islam, Buddhism, Hinduism, and so on—are, well, actual religions, equally valid per se as the narrow-minded version of Christianity espoused by many, if not all, creationists. The intolerance for other people's views—for the genuine religious beliefs found among scientists, for the belief in theistic evolution (Johnson's "theistic naturalism," in which God is seen as having created heaven, Earth, and all of life but did so through natural law), for other religions in general—reduces this parlous little culture war down to a fight to have a purely right-wing Christian nation, where everyone speaks English, is free to tote a gun, and maybe preferably is Caucasian. This is a stupid, hurtful little political battle—this creationism stuff—having lost its last vestiges of intellectual content not long after 1859.

It's not Phillip Johnson's personal God that I'm after; it's his political agenda—specifically his desire to see science watered down in the classroom. I've said enough about concepts of God to make it clear that I think all concepts of God are valid: they are, to me, statements—largely accurate and always interesting—of how people see themselves vis-à-vis the universe in which they live, whether that universe is a local patch of forest, an early agricultural nation-state, or the enormous globe on which we live—or even the universe of modern Big Bang theory.

My wife Michelle thinks that God is gravity. I can buy that; after all, as she points out, gravity holds the universe together, and no one understands it completely either. Closer to home, if someone tells me that God is Mother Earth, that makes sense to me as well. *All* concepts of God—including the intensely personal Creator-God some people see in the Bible—have sprung from a sense of the nature of the universe and how we fit into that universe. It is high time to drop the harmful nineteenth-century stuff underlying the culture war and start the business of dealing with the very real world as we find it at Ground Zero, year 2000.

Creationism as Theater

As a flashy piece of showmanship, the creationist-evolution trial held in Little Rock a few months back did not match the famous Scopes case of 1925. The Scopes trial, after all, was deliberately staged, contrived by the local citizenry to put Dayton on the map. H. L. Mencken enjoyed a field day and found his various prejudices confirmed, William Jennings Bryan and Clarence Darrow played to the crowds, and even Judge Ralston courted reporters. And there was plenty of "color"—revival meetings, hucksters, and hawkers imparted a carnival atmosphere throughout the proceedings in Tennessee.

Little Rock, in contrast, offered little along these lines—though everyone looked for it. A man showed up in a gorilla suit, people walked around wearing banana buttons, and a crèche lay in the hotel lobby across the street. Most of the relevant symbolism, however, was overlooked. No photographer snapped the "Mon Ark" boat exhibited at the airport, probably because it was so much the obvious product of 20th century technology that its name didn't ring any bells. In 1925, it would have reminded everyone of Noah. Times have changed, and today the young man from the Moral Majority does not spout fire and brimstone but wears a three piece suit and talks quietly, if determinedly, into network microphones.

But on a more significant level, the recent trial was far better drama than Dayton could muster. Dayton gave us fire but little substance. If Little Rock was short on color, it was long on content. For one thing, it was the first such trial in which scientists played a leading role. As for story, it revolved around a carefully orchestrated, if slightly distorted, microcosm of the creationist scene today. Besides scientists, the cast of characters included creationists, prominent members of the Arkansas clergy, theologians, educators, high school science teachers, and of course, lawyers. The plot was simple: a suit brought by the American Civil Liberties Union challenging Arkansas Act 590, which tries to insert biblical literalism into the classroom by calling creationism science.

In the theater of the absurd, plays frequently present an aura of the surreal. Forcing the creationism evolution wrangle into the formalized legal mode of the courtroom evoked just such a feeling of slightly other than real. But creationists are altogether too real and their effects too manifest in the schoolrooms across America to be dismissed as mere actors in a farce. The drama in Arkansas was staged by lawyers, of course, but the effect was nonetheless illuminating: All the words were there, and science—both legitimate and ersatz—received a pretty thorough airing. In a sense, creationists, scientists, educators, and religious personages were like marionettes on strings. Naturally it was the lawyers who pulled the strings, and the sequence of testimony was all carefully geared to this or that legal point bearing on the law's constitutionality: its establishment of religion in the classroom, its abridgement of academic freedom, its vagueness.

But no one watching the events unfold daily had the slightest doubt about what was *really* going on—and here is the greatest source of the nagging feeling that we were witnessing a highly organized and well staged charade. I doubt that anyone in the courtroom really believed the Arkansas attorney general's contention that "creation-science" as defined in the act, whatever its resemblance to the *Genesis* narrative, is not religion but purely science. Certainly the fundamentalists in attendance saw the issue clearly: In their eyes, Act 590 restored God to the classroom, if not supplanting at least receiving equal time with that "atheistic" doctrine of evolution. This, of course, was what the ACLU was trying to show—but the state's defense of the act deviated far from everyone's common sense understanding of creationism and its inspiration in fundamentalist Protestantism and biblical literalism. The attorney general went so far as to produce a theologian to testify that the notion of God is not inherently religious (and this from a man who freely admitted his belief that UFOs are "fallen angels"), divorcing the proceedings from reality to impart, once again, a feeling of theater.

It is easy to understand why the defense especially feared the scientific testimony: The attorney general and his staff were simply outmanned, outgunned by the scientists' attorneys. After all, the educational backgrounds of the attorney general's lawyers at least conceivably made them conversant with many of the basic terms of history and religion—even sociology. But science? Evidently not. Like lambs to the slaughter, one by one the cross-examiners arose from their seats to try to do battle with Michael Ruse (a philosopher and historian of science at the University of Guelph, Ontario), Francisco Ayala (a geneticist at the University of California, Davis), Brent Dalrymple (chief of the western section of the United States Geological Survey and an expert on isotopic dating), Stephen Jay Gould (a Harvard paleontologist and evolutionary theorist), and Harold Morowitz (a biophysicist at Yale University). By the time we got to Dr. Morowitz, the scene had been reduced to low comedy: The fourth member of the attorney general's staff, blatantly ignorant yet doggedly determined to shake, if not break, the placid professor, was hammering away on the second law of thermodynamics. Morowitz, who had already testified in great detail on the thermodynamics of biological systems, calmly and repeatedly replied that his expertise lies in biophysics and that he could not comment on the work of astrophysicists. Undeterred, the lawyer pressed Morowitz to admit that he surely must have some opinion on "astrophysicism." Such was the strength of the attorney general's counterattack on the ACLU's science case. Such is the general strength of "creation science." Moments like this provided the dramatic high points of the trial—isolated peaks of comic buffoonery.

The basic content of science is not in itself the stuff of drama. But what scientists do in the course of their work often is—witness the shenanigans in the competitive rat race for Nobel Prizes, or the more serious issues raised when the scientific endeavor takes on some larger social significance. Creationists have spuriously convinced many citizens that huge hunks of science are antithetical to their religious beliefs—so once again "evolution scientists" have been forced into the limelight, to argue that theirs is the stuff of true science, and that "scientific creationism" is pseudoscience.

Though there will be more acts in the courtroom variety of creationist drama, Judge Overton's decision in Little Rock against statute 590 has taken a lot of wind out of creationism's legislative sails. There will be fewer eager faces in the audience when the next curtain rises—in New Orleans later this year where virtually the same bill will once again be tested in a federal court. But the more prosaic, yet more pervasive, local mini theater version of the same show enacted at school board meetings shows no signs of flagging interest.

Good drama explores and mirrors the fabric of human existence. The creationist ploy—that biblical literalism can be sold as science—is merely play-acting of the nursery school sort. It tells us little about ourselves beyond the depressing point that scientific illiteracy is pandemic—something many might have suspected, but few saw as the enormous problem it really is. Creationism fails as sustaining theater on all counts: It is bad farce and bad soap opera. And in itself it lacks the essence of true tragedy. But the real and potential effects this nonsense has on our school kids are not at all good. And that is the real tragedy.

Niles Eldredge
Science, April 1982, pp. 100-101

The National Center for Science Education

The National Center for Science Education, Inc., (NCSE) is a not for profit, membership organization that defends the teaching of evolution in the public schools. Most of its members are scientists, but many are citizens with an interest in science and education; many other members are concerned with the church and state separation issues engendered by the efforts to "balance" the teaching of evolution with the presentation of religiously based views.

And indeed, in many states and local school districts, there are ongoing efforts to eliminate or discourage the teaching of evolution, or to present religious views as science. The calls for information and assistance to NCSE steadily increase. There are now two creation science organizations funded at about $5 million per year, another major creationist organization funded at over $1 million, at least a half dozen minor ministries focusing on grassroots evangelism against evolution—and periodic antievolution assaults from television and radio evangelists listened to by millions.

Grassroots efforts require grassroots responses, and the National Center for Science Education is the only national pro-evolution organization with this grassroots focus. The NCSE recognizes that the testimony of a local science teacher or college professor at a school board meeting is more influential than a statement from a nationally-prominent scientist—and the staff of the NCSE can help that local person be effective. NCSE prefers to work behind the scenes, letting our members be the "ground troops".

NCSE provides analyses of creationist arguments, background on legal and religious aspects of the controversy, and information on science education. Unfortunately, antievolutionism will not be solved by simply throwing science at it. A clear understanding of scientific aspects of the controversy is essential, of course: if creation science is scientific, then it deserves a place in the curriculum. It is not scientific; it does not belong in the curriculum. But showing that creation science is bad science will not ensure that evolution will be taught: this requires assuaging people's fears that acceptance of evolution requires the abandonment of faith. So NCSE also must provide information beyond the scientific: connections with other interested citizens and groups—including religious denominations that accept evolution, and which do not want sectarian religion taught in the public schools—and advice on how to write effective letters to the editor and op-ed pieces, and on other media relations.

Calls for information to support the teaching of evolution and/or to counter antievolutionary approaches come from many directions, including state boards of education, state departments of education, committees charged with selecting textbooks, local boards of education, individual teachers, and citizens—a wide range of people and institutions. The NCSE has a speakers' bureau of knowledgeable scientists around the country who can help the public understand why evolution is an important scientific subject and why students should learn it. NCSE also maintains a web page with information on evolution, the creation and evolution controversy, and evolution education.

The National Center for Science Education can be reached at:

The National Center for Science Education
P.O. Box 9477
Berkeley, California 94709-0477,

1-800-290-6006
www.natcenscied.org

25 Ways to Support Evolution Education

Parents, teachers, and even scientists often ask, "What can I do to help?" Here are 25 practical, effective suggestions. Using this list is likely to inspire you, and as you work out new ideas, be sure to share them with the National Center for Science Education.

1. Donate books and videos about evolution to school and public libraries. (NCSE can help you choose appropriate materials.)

2. Encourage and support evolution education at museums, parks, and natural history centers (by positive remarks on comment forms, contributions to special exhibits, etc.).

3.Thank radio and television stations for including programming about evolution and other science topics.

4. Make sure friends, colleagues and neighbors know you support evolution education and can connect them with resources for promoting good science education.

5. Monitor local news media for news of anti-evolution efforts in your state or community, and inform NCSE—for example, by mailing newspaper clippings.

6. When there is controversy in your community, add your voice: Hold press conferences with colleagues, record public opinion announcements, and send letters or editorials supporting evolution education to local newspapers.

7. Ask organizations in your community to include questions about science education in questionnaires for school board candidates and other educational policy makers.

8. Share your views with school board members, legislators, textbook commissioners, and other educational policy makers.

9. Share NCSE publications with concerned citizens, educators, and colleagues.

10. Link your personal or organizational web-site to www.natcenscied.org

11. When you see a web site that would benefit by linking to NCSE (for example, a science education site), write to their webmaster suggesting the new link to NCSE (www.natcenscied.org).

12. Encourage professional and community organizations (like the PTA) to give public support to evolution education. Send copies of their public statements to NCSE.

13. Join the NCSE.

14. Give gift subscriptions to Reports of NCSE to friends, colleagues, and libraries.

15. Take advantage of NCSE member benefits like discounts on book purchases and car rentals.

16. PARENTS: Make sure your child's science teacher knows s/he has your support for teaching about evolution, the age of Earth, and related concepts.

17. PARENTS: Help your child's teacher arrange field trips to natural history centers and museums with appropriate exhibits.

18. PARENTS: Discuss class activities and homework with your children—this is often the way communities learn that "creation science" is being taught; or, you may learn your child's teacher is doing a commendable job of teaching evolution.

19. PROFESSIONALS: Inform your colleagues about the evolution/creation controversy and the need for their involvement: for example, by making presentations at professional society meetings, writing articles for organizational newsletters, making announcements on email listserves.

20. COLLEGE TEACHERS: Make sure that your institution has several courses that present evolution to both majors and non-majors.

21. COLLEGE TEACHERS: Create opportunities to learn about evolution outside the classroom: for example, public lectures, museum exhibits.

22. K-12 TEACHERS: Work with your colleagues to create a supportive atmosphere in your school and community.

23. K-12 TEACHERS: Work with colleagues to develop or publicize workshops and in-service units about evolution; take advantage of them yourself.

24. INFORMAL EDUCATORS: Include evolution in signage, interpretation of exhibits, docent education, and public presentations.

25. SCIENTISTS: Share your knowledge with K-12 teachers and students by visiting classrooms or speaking at teacher-information workshops (NCSE can provide tips).

Eugenie Scott
Director
The National Center for Science Education

Seven Significant Court Decisions on the Issue of Evolution versus Creationism

1. *Epperson v. Arkansas:*

   In 1968, the U.S. Supreme Court invalidated an Arkansas statute that prohibited the teaching of evolution. The Court held the statute unconstitutional on grounds that the First Amendment to the U.S. Constitution does not permit a state to require teaching and learning to be tailored to the principles or prohibitions of any particular religious sect or doctrine. (*Epperson v. Arkansas,* 393 U.S. 97; 37 U.S. Law Week 4017; 89 S. Ct. 266; 21 L. Ed 228 [1968]).

2. *Segraves v. State of California:*

   In 1981, a California Superior Court found that the California State Board of Education's Science Framework, as written and as qualified by its antidogmatism policy, gave sufficient accommodation to the views of Segraves, contrary to his contention that class discussion of evolution prohibited his and his children's free exercise of religion. The antidogmatism policy provided that class discussions of origins should emphasize that scientific explanations focus on how, not ultimate cause, and that any speculative statements concerning origins, both in texts and in classes, should be presented conditionally, not dogmatically. The court's ruling also directed the board of education to widely disseminate the policy, which in 1989 was expanded to cover all areas of science, not just those concerning issues of origins. (*Segraves v. California,* Sacramento Superior Court No. 278978 [1981]).

3. *McLean v. Arkansas Board of Education:*
   In 1982, a federal court held that a "balanced treatment" statute violated the establishment clause of the U.S. Constitution. The Arkansas statute required public schools to give balanced treatment to creation science and evolution science. In a decision that gave a detailed definition of the term "science," the court declared that creation science is not in fact a science. The court also found that the statute did not have a secular purpose, noting that the statute used language peculiar to creationist literature in emphasizing origins of life as an aspect of the theory of evolution. Although the subject of life's origins is within the province of biology, the scientific community does not consider the subject as part of evolutionary theory, which assumes the existence of life and is directed to an explanation of how life evolved after it originated. The theory of evolution does not presuppose either the absence or the presence of a creator. (*McLean v. Arkansas Board of Education,* 529 F. Supp. 1255; 50 U.S. Law Week 2412 [1982]).

4. *Edwards v. Aguillard:*
   In 1987, the U.S. Supreme Court held unconstitutional Louisiana's Creationism Act. This statute prohibited the teaching of evolution in public schools, except when it was accompanied by instruction in creation science. The Court found that, by advancing the religious belief that a supernatural being created humankind, which is embraced by the term "creation science," the act impermissibly endorses religion. In addition, the Court found that the provision of a comprehensive science education is undermined when it is forbidden to teach evolution except when creation science is also taught. (*Edwards v. Aguillard,* 482 U.S. 578 [1987]).

5. *Webster v. New Lenox School District:*
   In 1990, the Seventh Circuit Court of Appeals found that a school district may prohibit a teacher from teaching creation science, in fulfilling its responsibility to ensure that the First Amendment's establishment clause is not violated and religious beliefs are not injected into the public school curriculum. The court upheld a district court finding that the school district had not violated

Webster's free speech rights when it prohibited him from teaching creation science, since it is a form of religious advocacy. (*Webster v. New Lenox School District No. 122,* 917 F. 2d 1004 [1991]).

6. *Peloza v. Capistrano School District:*
   In 1994, the Ninth Circuit Court of Appeals upheld a district court finding that a teacher's First Amendment right to free exercise of religion is not violated by a school district's requirement that evolution be taught in biology classes. Rejecting plaintiff Peloza's definition of a "religion" of "evolutionism," the court found that the district had simply and appropriately required a science teacher to teach a scientific theory in biology class. (John E. Peloza v. Capistrano Unified School District, 917 F. 2d 1004 [1994]).

7. *Freiler v. Tangipahoa Parish Board of Education:*
   In 1997, the U.S. District Court for the Eastern District of Louisiana rejected a policy requiring teachers to read aloud a disclaimer whenever they taught about evolution, ostensibly to promote "critical thinking." The court wrote, "In mandating this disclaimer, the School Board is endorsing religion by disclaiming the teaching of evolution in such a manner as to convey the message that evolution is a religious viewpoint that runs counter to . . . other religious views." The decision is also noteworthy for recognizing that curriculum proposals for "intelligent design" are equivalent to proposals for teaching creation science. (*Freiler v. Tangipahoa Parish Board of Education,* No. 94-3577 [E.D. La. Aug. 8, 1997]). On August 13, 1999, the Fifth Circuit Court of Appeals affirmed the ruling.

National Center for Science Education

Notes

Chapter 1: In the Beginning

1. page 10
Wertheim is the author of two books and many important articles on the relation between science and religion, as well as the writer and presenter of a major PBS documentary on the subject. I have had the pleasure of sharing the podium with her on many college campuses, where we have each offered our different—yet compatible—takes on the relation between science and religion. Her thinking has deeply influenced my own and is reflected in the pages of this book.

2. page 10
I once lectured at a small, conservative Christian college in western Pennsylvania, where I was told by the dean who had invited me that some of the students at the all-campus talk I had given the previous evening probably had been looking for horns on my head—if an exaggeration, perhaps not too fanciful. I asked the dean why he had invited me, and he said to shake the kids up a bit, to let them know there were more views that could be intelligibly expressed than many of them had encountered. On that trip, I also encountered for the first time glimmers of a deep interest in environmental matters that some of the students had begun to develop—my first glimpse of the growing ecological movement within parts of the conservative Christian community.

3. page 10
In March 1984 I was invited to deliver a lecture as part of a series celebrating the hundredth anniversary of the founding of the Jewish General Hospital in Montreal, Canada. At the time, I had been busy battling creationists, and I always considered the likelihood of confronting creationist hecklers in any prospective audience (not that I ever turned down a speaking request for fear

of such hecklers, for forewarned is forearmed). I figured that a Jewish hospital in a basically Catholic city would be probably the last place on the continent I would run into creationists. Wrong! At the end of my talk, I was politely quizzed on what I thought of the correspondence between geological eras and the days of creation as outlined in the first book of the Pentateuch (i.e., Genesis). My interrogator was no Christian fundamentalist, but rather an Orthodox Jew, a doctor on the hospital staff who, for religious reasons, had trouble with the ideas of evolution and deep geological time.

4. page 20
I grew to respect—and even like—Luther Sunderland, who is since deceased. He was a worthy opponent, whom I often debated on TV shows. He was a genuinely talented engineer who built and flew his own airplanes and who was clearly no enemy of physical science or technology. On one program, during a commercial, he turned to the famous Isaac Asimov, another guest on the show, and said something to the effect of, "I don't get it; here you are probably the foremost spokesman for science in America, yet you won't fly on airplanes! Don't you believe in the laws of aerodynamics?" Creationists are right when they (some of them, at least) claim they are not antiscience per se; to which, of course, the only reply can be that to be in favor of certain fields of science (most of physics, say) but not others (evolutionary biology or historical geology) implies a set of criteria that are not themselves scientific.

Chapter 2: Telling the Difference

1. page 21
Several years after first reading reports of Reagan's remarks, I heard from Luther Sunderland (already encountered in Chapter 1) that he had managed to get through to several of Reagan's speechwriters and that he was proud to take credit for inserting these antievolution remarks into Reagan's campaign rhetoric. But I wasn't prepared to hear what he had to say next: that the scientists he had in mind—the scientists to whom Reagan was alluding in his none-too-mellifluous antievolution comments—were none other than me and Stephen Jay Gould. Sunderland was saying that our idea of punctuated equilibria (see Chapter 4) was antievolution because it seemed to be anti-Darwin.

2. page 21
Creationists, I am saddened to say, are not the only set of people who are guilty of disparagingly pronouncing evolution as "only a theory." No less a source than the editorial page of the *New York Times* (June 23, 1987, p. A30), in an

editorial marking yet another court decision on creationism, was guilty of the very same sloppy usage of the term "theory." The *Times* congratulated the U.S. Supreme Court in deciding that a Louisiana law mandating the teaching of evolution in public schools must be "balanced" by the teaching of creation science is unconstitutional. Commenting on the 7 to 2 vote, the *Times* editorial duly noted that only Justices William Rehnquist and Antonin Scalia sided with the state of Louisiana in its argument in defense of the law. But the editorial also stated, "It's true that evolution is only a theory and that some scientists, contrary to scientific method, treat it as dogma." On June 29 of that year, the Times (p. A16) published my anguished rejoinder in their Letters section:

Quantum mechanics. Special relativity. Plate tectonics. All are theories, yet no one, in my experience, ever says they are "only" theories, and that "some scientists, contrary to scientific method, occasionally treat [them] as dogma." Yet that is how you chose to characterize the scientific status of evolution in your June 23 editorial commending the recent Supreme Court decision voiding the Louisiana "equal time" statute.

Evolution is the only non-supernatural explanation of the mosaic of similarity that interconnects the vast array of otherwise so dissimilar forms of life still current in Western thought. If all organisms are descended from a single common ancestor in the remote geological past, tell-tale vestiges of their common origin should show up as traits still shared—in the macromolecules of heredity (DNA and RNA) that unite everything from bacteria to mammals.

That there is one grand pattern of similarity linking all life forms is the overwhelming conclusion of 300 years of research in systematics and paleontology. It is also the practical basis of all non-human biomedical research. Evolution is as well established as any other complex theoretical position in science.

Yes, evolution is a theory—in the sense that it is an idea that explains a tremendous amount of information about the living world. But to say "only" a theory demeans and misrepresents the very nature of the scientific enterprise. And it misses the power of evolution, which has been one of the most fruitful ideas ever introduced in Western civilization.

I explain the scientific details of this letter more fully in this chapter and examine courtroom decisions on creationism in Chapter 7 (see also appendix 3). For more on the grand pattern of relationships interconnecting all life, see Chapter 3 of my *Life in the Balance* (1998)—and if possible visit the "Wall of Life" (my informal name) in the Hall of Biodiversity (opened May 1998) at the

American Museum of Natural History in New York City. The Wall is the only place where the entire diversity of life, from bacteria through fungi, plants, and animals, can be seen in one 100-foot-long sweep in all its beauty, intricacy, and evolutionary relationships.

3. page 23
Of course, we assume the Earth has been round since not long after its inception, probably through the coalescence of smaller planetesimals and even finer bits of galactic debris. This kind of thinking is usually called induction, though when specifically applied in historical geology, it is traditionally referred to as uniformitarianism. I have discussed aspects of the scientific process in greater detail in my recent *The Pattern of Evolution* (1999), in particular examining the meanings and origins of uniformitarianism in geology and paleontology.

Chapter 3: The Fossil Record

1. page 36
Viruses are essentially strands of genetic material with a protein coat, and as such they are indeed simpler than bacteria. Yet all viruses require the presence of another organism's genetic material to reproduce, and they lack the metabolic pathways to allow them to "live" in anything other than a vegetative state when they are not reproducing. Thus viruses are not independent, free-living organisms. I agree with some biologists who see viruses as escaped snippets of the genetic material of advanced, true organisms—snippets that must reinvade a host's genetic machinery in order to reproduce. Indeed, it seems quite likely that some genes—such as the infamous cancer-causing oncogenes—are essentially viruses that have reinvaded the genomes of host species and have secondarily become permanent residents. Under this line of thinking, viruses that attack humans and other primates are more closely related to their human and other primate hosts than they are to other viruses, such as the famous tobacco mosaic virus of tobacco plants.

2. page 37
I choose the phrase "life itself" advisedly here, for none other than Nobel laureate Francis Crick (one of the codiscoverers of the structure of DNA), in a book by that title (1981), has argued that the origin of life is biochemically sufficiently difficult, hence improbable, that life may well have arisen elsewhere and spread to Earth (perhaps sent by an advanced civilization). Critics, of course, have noted that this scenario merely puts back the ultimate problem of the origin of life to another time and place. I vastly prefer the simpler idea that life is intrinsic to Earth and arose here—at least until such time as we can show otherwise.

3. page 43
See Mark McMenamin's *The Garden of Ediacara* (1998) for a good overview of the diversity of life in the Ediacaran fauna, as well as a spirited account—and defense—of his interpretation of what these fossils represent in evolutionary history.

4. page 46
See my *Life in the Balance* (1998) for a more complete rundown on the evolutionary spectrum of life, including forms of invertebrate life.

5. page 47
Just as this book was in its final stages of preparation, paleontologists announced the presence of primitive jawless fishes in Cambrian rocks from China.

6. page 47
The Burgess Shale has become familiar to modern readers through several important books, most notably Stephen Jay Gould's *Wonderful Life* (1988) and, most recently, *The Crucible of Creation* (1998) by British paleontologist Simon Conway Morris.

7. page 48
Technically speaking, a biomere is a biostratigraphic unit, meaning a sequence of sedimentary rocks recognized by its fossil content. Biomeres represent considerable spans of geological time; that is, they are also chronostratigraphic units.

8. page 48
See, for example, Brett and Baird, 1995. I have had the pleasure of collaborating on some aspects of this work. In addition, it was Carlton Brett who first told me (on a fast-food lunch break while collecting fossils in Middle Devonian rocks in upstate New York) that it was not just my trilobites that showed tremendous stability, interrupted by infrequent, but rapid, bursts of evolutionary change. The entire rich Hamilton fauna, consisting of over 300 named species of hard-shelled invertebrate organisms, showed the very same pattern. Most of the species were there at the beginning of the 6- to 7-million-year-long interval of Hamilton time, and most were still there, in recognizably the same unchanged form, at the end, when most of them abruptly became extinct, many to be replaced by similar descendant species in the next interval.

9. page 55
Paleontologist James Hopson of the Field Museum of Natural History in Chicago has been especially eloquent in expressing the fruits of his research on the evolution of mammals from mammal-like reptiles, providing one of the best antidotes to the tired old creationist claim that the fossil record reveals no transitions between "major kinds."

10. page 56
See Ian Tattersall's lucid account of human evolution in his *Becoming Human* (1998) for an entrée into the entire field of paleoanthropology.

11. page 57
The morning after I appeared in a debate with creationist Phillip Johnson at Calvin College in Grand Rapids, Michigan, I attended an informal meeting of science faculty. Though I was the evolutionist, the science faculty at this conservative Christian college (Calvin College is affiliated with the Christian Reformed Church in North America) are extremely professional: not only was I treated cordially, but many faculty members made it plain that, whatever their personal feelings about evolution may be, they know that evolution is a bona fide scientific concept—and they have great respect for science, as they themselves are professional scientists. Rather, it was Johnson with whom they had a bone or two to pick, since Johnson apparently cannot understand why, as a leading Christian conservative intellectual, he is the darling of much of fundamentalist and evangelical circles *except* science faculty at some conservative Christian schools.

In any case, as we were waiting for Johnson to show up, we talked about the program the preceding night. I'll never forget one faculty member sitting next to me (I believe he was a physicist), who said—in reference to the series of slides of fossil human skulls I had shown—"Boy, you really went for the jugular!" That's really it: if we evolutionary biologists would only stop brandishing the fossil record of human evolution as one of the very best examples of evolutionary change through time, the creationists would be deliriously happy, and all but a few diehards wouldn't give a damn what we said about trilobites, dinosaurs, or horses!

12. page 57
The ancient ecosystems of eastern Africa are well preserved in sediments that have accumulated in vast down-dropped basins. The exact same story is now emerging in South Africa—this time from a series of caves.

13. page 58
The so-called Taung child, the first discovered specimen of *Australopithecus africanus*, and thus the type specimen of the species, may have been as young as 2.3 million years old. South African lime deposits are difficult to date with precision (no suitable radiometric techniques are available), and, in any case, the limeworks at Taung have long since been quarried out completely.

14. page 59
Paleoanthropologist Ian Tattersall, my colleague at the American Museum of Natural History, makes the case that more than one early species of *Homo* was present in eastern Africa between 2.5 and 2 million years ago. For simplicity's sake, I mention here only the most familiar of these: *Homo habilis* (literally, "handy man"), first discovered and named by Louis Leakey. The most famous specimen of this species, dated at about 1.9 million years, was discovered by Leakey's son Richard. (See also Tattersall and Schwartz, 2000).

15. page 60
The dates given here for the probable time of evolution of *Homo sapiens* are derived from analysis of mitochondrial DNA diversity patterns in modern humans (the so-called Eve hypothesis). See Chapter 1 in my *Life in the Balance* (1998) for an ecological evolutionary account of human prehistory, detailing the crucial events in the physical environment that underlay so much of human evolution. How humans eventually came to declare their "independence" from local ecosystems (via the invention of agriculture beginning some ten thousand years ago) is especially germane to understanding the origins of settled existence (i.e., villages, towns, and cities) and complex social structures. It is also central to understanding how concepts of God have changed as the human ecological niche has changed, as I develop in the final chapter of this book and explore much more fully in my forthcoming book, *Who Is This Man They Call God?*

Chapter 4: What Drives Evolution?

1. page 62
Genetic cloning is simply the latest phase of human manipulation of the gene pools of plant and animal species for agricultural, biomedical, or simply experimental reasons. Artificial selection of genetic properties began with domestication of animals and plants at least ten thousand years ago, with the emergence of agriculture in a number of different areas (though archeological evidence suggests that certain species were domesticated even earlier—thou-

sands of years before the Agricultural Revolution). Genetic cloning is simply a high-tech and more direct way of manipulating the genes of organisms.

2. page 63

I once gave a talk at a meeting of the New York metropolitan chapter of the scientific "fraternity" Sigma Xi, at an IBM research center. Most of my audience consisted of physicists, chemists, mathematicians, and computer experts. I was describing some of the current debates within evolutionary biology, and in so doing I made probably the most naïve statement I have ever uttered in a public forum: I said, in effect, that the fact that evolutionary biologists tend to argue so much with one another probably sounds strange to people working in the physical sciences. That remark was met by an embarrassing gale of laughter. The audience thought it was hilarious that I would suggest that physicists, chemists, and mathematicians routinely agree on their formulas and other expressions of their scientific conclusions. This was years ago, and I was guilty of assuming, as many people routinely do, that the physical sciences are more precise, and therefore less prone to argumentative discourse and profound disagreement. Embarrassing as the episode was, it taught me an extremely valuable lesson: all areas of serious, systematic human inquiry, certainly including all areas and disciplines of science, are constantly and as a matter of course replete with disagreement—over experimental protocols, observations, and of course their interpretations. Science proceeds by matching up our perceptions of natural phenomena with our thoughts about the nature of these phenomena, and though the essential creativity underlying this work resides within the individual's mind, nonetheless the growth of knowledge (in *any* field) comes through the collective discourse of many minds—minds that often cannot agree on the nature of those phenomena, let alone their interpretations.

3. page 63

Science writer John Horgan's book *The End of Science* (1996) posits that all the major discoveries about the natural world have already been made. This conclusion, naturally, upsets many scientists, who do not like to think of themselves as merely dotting the i's and crossing the t's—i.e., relegated to a subordinated mop-up role. Of course, there is something to Horgan's thesis: nothing, for example, more fundamental in the realm of evolutionary biology than the very principle that all life has descended from a single common ancestor is, almost by definition, likely to be discovered in the future. Likewise, natural selection—so abundantly confirmed by experimentation, mathematical and other forms of theory, and observation in the wild—as the central molder and shaper of organismic adaptations, is unlikely to be supplanted or matched by another, as yet undiscovered, evolutionary process. Yet it has been my con-

..ention throughout my career that we have a long way to go toward understanding how and when natural selection acts to shape evolutionary change—what I have called the context of evolutionary stasis and change. There is still much to be learned, as this chapter endeavors to point out.

4. page 64
And differ it does. Dawkins sees evolution essentially as an active process: the direct result of competition among genes for representation in succeeding generations. Darwin's version, to my mind, is infinitely preferable: it sees natural selection as a passive recording of what worked better than what in a world of finite resources—where not every organism born within a local population can possibly expect to survive and reproduce. I have explored the significance of these differences in the fundamental meaning of "natural selection" elsewhere (Eldredge, 1995, 1999, and technical articles cited therein).

5. page 66
Philosopher David Hull has pointed out that the notion of natural selection received more criticism than any other aspect of Darwin's evolutionary ideas—up to and including the very idea of evolution itself. Thus it cannot be literally true that the concept of natural selection was the linchpin of Darwin's success. I tend to agree, since I am convinced that it was the mountain of evidence *in the form of patterns* that was primarily responsible for Darwin's immediate and lasting success. Nonetheless, because the notion of natural selection has been so completely verified and upheld through experimentation, field observation, and mathematical theory for so long—and because it remains the core aspect of our understanding, not only of the evolutionary origin and further modification of adaptations, but also of the great pattern of stasis (i.e., nonchange) itself—Darwin's development of the notion in the opening chapters of his book, added to the power of all the patterns he presented, must have created an ineluctable one-two argumentative punch that did indeed carry the day for establishing the scientific credibility of the very idea of evolution.

6. page 67
Darwin (and Alfred Russell Wallace), upon reading Thomas Malthus's *An Essay on the Principle of Population* (1798), realized that reproduction within all species (Malthus confined his gaze to human beings) is inherently geometric: if, say, every pair of sexually reproducing organisms produced two offspring, population size would grow by leaps and bounds. Darwin used slow-breeding elephants to dramatize the point—relying on a Victorian phrase still very much in use when he pointed out that the world is by no means "standing room only" in elephants, which by now it must be *unless some factor(s) were limiting the size*

of elephant populations. We now realize that it is the productivity (food and nutrients) available in local ecosystems that, along with predation, disease, and physical factors, limits sizes of local populations and thus, additively, of entire species. That the human population has exploded from an (estimated) 6 million to over 6 billion in the brief ten thousand years since the Agricultural Revolution is graphic confirmation of this very point, for it was the invention of agriculture that removed human beings from their primordial position within local ecosystems, thus removing the Malthusian limit to human population size. As we shall see in Chapter 7, in my view this radical shift in human ecology had enormous implications for the very concepts of the gods or God.

7. page 67
This is the significance of the famous cloning of the sheep Dolly in 1998: the genetic information that produced Dolly came from an udder cell—not an egg or a sperm, or indeed the nucleus of a fertilized egg mechanically removed from another sheep.

8. page 69
Occasional reports published in the scientific literature claim the experimental verification of the inheritance of an acquired character; perhaps the most discussed such instance in recent years involves the acquisition, and subsequent transmission, of immunological tolerance. Though most biologists are unwilling to go so far as to resurrect Lamarck's notions of evolutionary change, in the face of a few apparent exceptions to Weismann's doctrine (and, in any case, not all biologists accept such examples as bona fide), it is nonetheless interesting, and utterly characteristic of the process of science, that one of its most solid underpinnings—Weismann's doctrine—is still occasionally called into question.

9. page 69
Actually, the word "mutation" was first introduced to the scientific literature on evolution by the German paleontologist W. Waagen, who used the term in the 1880s to refer to discrete, stable stages that he saw in some Mesozoic ammonoid lineages he was studying.

10. page 70
For example, Henry Fairfield Osborn, paleontologist as well as President of the American Museum of Natural History, coined the term "aristogenesis" for his idea that evolution arose from innate tendencies within species to become ever better. Organisms are superior because of innate genetic propensities, or so Osborn thought. Himself a wealthy man—an American "aristocrat"—Osborn

actively supported right-wing eugenics endeavors, and some of his writing was used in support of Nazi propaganda.

11. page 71
The concept of genetic drift was introduced by Sewall Wright, who showed that, under certain circumstances, alleles (variant versions of a specific gene) could become "fixed" in a population without—or even in spite of—natural selection.

12. page 78
Indeed, the work of paleontologist Phillip Gingerich and others has recently produced convincing evidence from the Indian subcontinent of transitional mammals—intermediates between terrestrial predecessors and true whales. Simpson knew—because evolution predicts—that intermediates must always have existed. His mission, as he saw it, was to explain why it is characteristically so difficult to actually *find* intermediates in the fossil record—a situation his theory of quantum evolution was originally conceived to address.

13. page 82
For example, the English molecular biologist Gabriel Dover propounded his ideas on genetic drive, in which certain DNA sequences could alter the sequence of corresponding genes on other chromosomes; Canadian geneticist W. Ford Doolittle and his colleagues suggested the notion of selfish DNA; and Motoo Kimura and other geneticists developed the notion of neutral, or non-Darwinian, evolution—stressing the fact that many alternate genetic forms are selectively neutral (meaning equally viable). These ideas began to surface in the 1960s (neutral theory) on up through the 1980s. None are any longer seen as controversial—since the intricacies of the molecular biology of the gene and its workings offer badly needed deeper understanding of the processes of heredity—but not of phenomena at the levels of the population and higher, such as natural selection, speciation, extinction of species, and so on.

14. page 82
I say that the advent of molecular genetics prompted the emergence of this line of thought not so much because Dawkins's main emphasis concerns competition among genes for representation in succeeding generations, as because the development of molecular biology posed a challenge to more tradition-minded geneticists. This was apparent to me at a meeting on macroevolution held at Chicago's Field Museum of Natural History—where much of the discussion focused on such issues as punctuated equilibria (which I discuss later in this chapter); nonetheless, most of the attention of the population

geneticists present at the meeting focused far more on the few molecular biologists present than on those of us who were paleontologists. To put it another way, the development of molecular biology seemed to pose a threat to population geneticists back then—a threat that has dissipated because graduate students in all walks of evolutionary biology (even paleontologists) are routinely trained in the basic laboratory procedures and theoretical constructs of molecular biology.

15. page 82
Hamilton's work is often said to have been a formal extension of work done by Ronald Fisher—supposedly on an envelope in an English pub—a half century earlier.

16. page 83
See, for example, John Endler's *Natural Selection in the Wild* (1986) and John Thompson's *The Coevolutionary Process* (1994) for excellent discussions and entrée into the vast literature of modern population-level evolutionary biology.

17.page 84
See my book *The Pattern of Evolution* (1999) for a discussion of the causes of stasis and details of the idea of punctuated equilibria, including (in Chapter 1) a discussion of the genesis of the idea based on the perception of four basic patterns in these trilobite data.

18. page 87
See my book *The Pattern of Evolution,* as well as Eldredge, in press-a, for a much more detailed description of this "sloshing bucket" model of the evolutionary process.

Chapter 5: Creationists Attack: I

1. page 90
Creationism is a social rather than an intellectual (let alone *scientific)* issue, and (as we have already seen and will encounter in greater detail throughout the next several chapters) as such it has of course been prominently displayed in courtroom battles (and movies depicting such battles, such as *Inherit the Wind).* Less well known is the penchant that some lawyers have had over the years of applying their legalistic argumentative skills to debunk Darwinism, acting very much as if the debate between evolution and creationism can be handled in much the way a traditional debate—or a courtroom prosecution—is held. I am not the first to point out that lawyers arguing for one side against another in a

case are notorious for wanting to establish the truth of the matter only insofar as their side can prevail or at least reach the most favorable outcome possible. They aim to persuade a judge and jury of the rightness of their position, and the justice system presumes that, by such a process, the actual truth will emerge. At least, that is the idea.

In my professional lifetime, two such lawyers have taken up the antievolution cudgels, and in so doing they attracted not a little notoriety. The first was Norman Macbeth, who I met several times at the American Museum of Natural History and who authored *Darwin Retried* (1971)—once erroneously, if hilariously, listed in a sales catalogue as *Darwin Retired*. To my knowledge, Macbeth always denied he was a creationist, meaning someone who was opposed to evolution on religious grounds. Rather, he steadfastly maintained that his was purely an intellectual interest, and that Darwinism had many holes that could be exposed through counterscientific evidence and, perhaps especially, the cold hard stare of a dispassionate lawyer trained to get to the heart of the matter. Whatever his motivations may have been, though, Macbeth trotted out many of the same objections to evolutionary biology that creationists always do—and added none of his own.

The more recent and better-known efforts of lawyer Phillip Johnson (encountered briefly already in this book and in some greater detail in Chapter 6) are very much of the same stripe, but with a single great difference: Johnson readily admits that it is his belief in a personal Christian God, and the implications he sees (as others have before him) for a materialistic, godless universe latent in the very idea of evolution, that motivates him to wield his lawyerly legerdemain against evolutionary biology. Here I give him credit, since Johnson reflects what I see as a growing tendency through the 1990s for creationists to admit their religious convictions and hence motivations. Hiding behind a deceitful cloak of scientific creationism, as was done in the 1960s through the 1980s for the purposes of circumventing the establishment clause of the First Amendment of the U.S. Constitution—in other words, creating the pretense that creationism was motivated solely by the quest for pure scientific understanding and its communication to children in the classroom—seems no longer as fashionable as it so recently was. In rediscovering their roots and openly acknowledging their underlying religious convictions, creationists have begun to abandon their hope for ultimate legal imprimatur—the efforts of Justice Antonin Scalia of the U.S. Supreme Court to the contrary notwithstanding (see Chapter 7).

I also note that, later in this chapter, I rely not on a creation scientist but rather on yet another lawyer (Wendell R. Bird), who produced the clearest, most succinct statement of the fundamental tenets of scientific creationism—the statement that bridges the gap between openly acknowledged religiously based creationism and "scientific" creationism on the one hand, and the language defining "creation science" in Arkansas Act 590 on the other.

That being said, I reiterate my opening point: I can find nothing truly new in the antievolution rhetoric of creationists, regardless of whether it is cast in the cloak of scientific creationism or in the more recent and more open terms of a Christian lawyer merely arguing the case against evolution.

2. page 90
Phillip Johnson's attack on philosophical naturalism is an exception, since he believes that, if his version of a personal God—a God watching over everything and especially everyone, a God capable of doing everything from making mountains to creating humanity—really exists, then science, if it is to be true to its basic quest to describe the "furniture" of the universe and especially to understand its cause-and-effect workings, perforce *must* take God into account.

3. page 91
This either-or aspect of creation versus evolution was nicely displayed by an utterly coincidental (I presume) juxtaposition of two television shows aired simultaneously in the early 1980s. I used to like to watch Garner Ted Armstrong, that handsome and articulate electronic preacher, now, as far as I know, no longer in the TV business. Armstrong would occasionally devote one of his shows to evolution. The incident in question arose as I was idly cruising the TV channels and came upon Armstrong's gentle but firm rejection of evolution as a plausible explanation of nature's beauty and complexity. Up on the screen popped a film clip showing thousands of silvery grunions—small Pacific Coast fish—flopping around on the beach in Santa Barbara in the moonlight. The grunions were engaged in their annual reproductive rites. Such unusual and complex behavior!, marveled Armstrong. Only a Creator, an almighty God, could have fashioned a fish with such a remarkably intricate reproductive style.

Having gotten the message, I moved along four channels and found an episode of Jacob Bronowski's *Ascent of Man* series on the PBS network. Lo and behold, Bronowski was in the throes of his segment on evolution, and I was treated to my second view of Santa Barbara grunions within five minutes. But what a difference in the moral! How marvelous the process of evolution must be, mused Bronowski, to produce such an intricate pattern of behavior in this little fish!

The unwitting grunions had become a foil for each of the two dominant, competing explanations of how life has come to be as we see it today. Both were frank appeals to the viewer's credulity; both asked us to ask ourselves, What do I believe? I decided to skip the whole thing and watch a movie. But the coincidental Armstrong-Bronowski "debate" did show that, in the United States at least, there really are only two competing explanations for how the Earth and life came to be as we find them today.

4. page 107
Brent Dalrymple, formerly director of the western branch of the U.S. Geological Survey in Menlo Park, California, testified at the creationism trial challenging Arkansas Act 590 in late 1981. Dalrymple performed many experiments to test whether or not extremes of heat and pressure could alter isotopic decay rates and found, not surprisingly, and as atomic theory predicts, that he could *not* alter decay rates experimentally.

5. page 109
At this writing (summer 1999) some astronomers have just revised downward the estimate of the age of formation of the universe, to some 13 billion years. Science marches on, and we have heard the last word on very few issues. Still, it is reasonably certain that, whatever the final say on the exact age of the universe might be (if indeed there ever is such a "final say"), the order of magnitude will be in the range of something over 10 billion years, and a good bit less than 20 billion years, meaning that the basic dimensions of the ballpark will not change.

6. page 114
Skeptical commentators on creationism have understandably had a field day with creationists' attempts to explain modern distribution patterns of plants and animals as the outcome of dispersal from Noah's Ark on Ararat a few thousand years ago. How to get two of each of 10 million species on the ark? How to feed them? And then there is the ever popular sanitation problem: how to clean out what would have surely dwarfed the Augean stables of classical Greek mythology? And so on. Yet the ark story, so easy to poke fun at, is really no crazier than trying to explain the entire sedimentary rock record on the face of the Earth as the result of a single flooding event.

We should all recall that the "world" to the early agriculturalists of the Middle East—wellspring of the writings and religious traditions that have, in one particular extreme form, led to creationism—was limited to the immediate surroundings. Geologists have found some evidence of physical events that may be correlated with events recounted in some of these ancient writings—including, of course, the Old Testament of the Christian Bible. For example, if the geological evidence showing that the Black Sea was a freshwater lake until 5600 b.c.—when the rising level of the Mediterranean caused it to spill over into the Black Sea—is true, as geologists William Ryan and Walter Pitman (1998) report, this event indeed might be the source of the flood stories recounted in Genesis and other ancient documents. The ancients who recorded such events can be forgiven for describing the events as worldwide, for the Middle East was their entire world. What is intolerable is that modern creationists—after geologists tried and failed to make the same claim in the nineteenth century, when geology was in its infancy—still insist in the year 2000 that the Great Flood produced the entire sedimentary rock record.

Chapter 6: Creationists Attack: II

1. page 118
Biologists at this writing are still studying peppered moths, and the details of the traditional evolutionary account are under critical scrutiny. For this discussion, because *both creationists and evolutionists have agreed on the details in the past,* that the evolutionary story may well in the end be revised does not matter: at issue here is the difference in interpretation between creationists and evolutionary biologists on agreed-upon "facts."

2. page 124
At this writing (summer 1999), much is being made in the popular press of patterns of "cultural" variation between different local populations of African chimpanzees. One of my colleagues (Stephen Jay Gould, writing in the *New York Times)* elicited several indignant letters when he claimed that this pattern helps strengthen the case for continuity between chimpanzees and humans—the overall differences becoming more of degree than of kind. Though I see his point (and, as he acknowledges, such variations in behavior, including the use of simple tools, have long been recognized in other species, such as macaques, as well), I find the definition of culture here to be rather overly encompassing: repeated use of simple tools—e.g., sticks grabbed for the purpose of prizing termites from their nests—strikes me as rather a far cry from the development of learned manufacture (hence cultural traditions of copying style) of even the simplest of the hominid stone tool traditions. Even more to the point, I agree with one of the letter writers, who noted the one great gap—inherently and in principle, "bridgeable," but not in actuality so between humans and any other form of animal life known: the *consciousness* that we humans have. As the writer of the

letter pointed out, human behavior is purposive in the sense that it is consciously pursued for survival. All evidence suggests that behavior in all other extant species is instinctive. In other words, I do not think that even the wisest chimp knows, and can therefore contemplate, the fact that it will die someday.

That being said, I must remark that though we have a wonderful human fossil record that shows the continuity in anatomical terms between humans and apes—and one that, as well, preserves in outline form the development of human material culture over time—it is a real pity that, unlike the scenarios underlying Arthur Conan Doyle's *The Lost World* (1912), or the more recent movie *Quest for Fire,* we do not have still on Earth with us surviving elements of all the species of our own ancestry that have lived over the past 4 or 5 million years. Is the origin of consciousness indeed one of degrees—with elements being added as new species (with larger brains and, ultimately, more complicated behaviors, including ever more sophisticated material cultural technologies)? *Or,* did human consciousness arise relatively recently, as my friend and colleague anthropologist Ian Tattersall of the American Museum of Natural History has concluded in *Becoming Human* (1998), on the basis of cave paintings and other intricate works that began long after our own species had evolved in Africa? If the latter, then perhaps the patterns of geographic variation in simple tool use and other aspects of chimp "culture" do connect on a sliding scale with human material cultural traditions—with the further implication that consciousness itself is not a prerequisite for the development of culture or perhaps even cultural traditions, as exemplified in the toolmaking traditions of the Paleolithic.

Make no mistake: I believe as Darwin did (as opposed to his codiscoverer of natural selection, Alfred Russell Wallace), that human consciousness evolved (probably as a mechanism for survival in a social setting; inklings about what may be going on in a fellow band member's mind, after all, are not only useful but best sought by consulting one's own inner thoughts—as biologist Nicholas Humphrey was among the first to point out). But the reason why we humans have become the very first species to stop living inside local ecosystems stems from our consciousness and is, I still firmly believe, unique to us.

3. page 130
I have in mind here the then emerging, extremely valuable theoretical approach to systematics (i.e., the study of relationships among organisms and their classification) originally known as phylogenetic systematics, but much more commonly known as cladistics. Cladistics was first formulated by the German entomologist Willi Hennig, but it was actively developed and expand-

ed by a group of American and British systematists (centered largely at the American and British Museums of Natural History) beginning in the late 1960s. The aim was to sharpen the rules of analysis of relationships and bring them into line with principles of scientific testability.

One early realization was that the statement "these two species share features not seen in any other species" is a *positive* statement of evolutionary relationship that is susceptible to falsification—if, that is, other species are discovered later with the same feature, or if still other characteristics show that the species are more closely related to still other species. With ancestors, the situation is trickier because an ancestor will lack at least one of the (advanced) features of its descendant: the ancestor must in all respects be the same as, or more primitive than, its putative descendant—a harder proposition to falsify.

For the record, just because cladistics decrees that there are methodological problems concerning the positive demonstration of ancestors of course *does not mean that that there were no ancestors.* Though some cladists have been content to leave it at that—in any case having no particular, demonstrated interest in how the evolutionary process works—does not mean that some of us who adopted the principles of cladistics in our systematic work did not continue to work with the concept of ancestry and descent. I am the quintessential example: the very notion of punctuated equilibria is based on my tree that reconstructs patterns of ancestry and descent among a series of phacopid trilobites from Middle Devonian rocks in eastern and central North America. The tree was based on a cladogram that I drew up first, on the basis of cladistic principles. I then added information of geological distribution to come up with the tree, and I have always acknowledged that the cladogram on which the tree is based underlies the construction of the tree, and that the tree is therefore a step further removed from certainty than is its underlying cladogram, which of course itself remains a hypothesis subject to further testing. This, of course, is the way science works. Nothing is certain.

In an early paper written with my colleague Ian Tattersall (Eldredge and Tattersall 1976), we explored the differences among cladograms, trees, and the more elaborate scenarios (e.g., complex hypotheses on, for instance, why hominids left life in the trees to assume upright, bipedal gait for walking across the African savannas).

4. page 130
For the record, Sunderland then says, immediately after this quoted sentence, "Anyone, however, can gain access to the original typed verbatim interview

transcripts which were prepared for the New York State Education Department by going to any public library in the United States and asking for the ERIC Document Reproduction Service microfiche ED 228 056," *Darwin's Enigma: The Fossil Record.* The printed version in my possession, then, does not have the full transcripts.

5. page 130
Indeed, I must thank Wesley R. Elsberry, a student in the Department of Wildlife and Fisheries Science at Texas A&M University, who brought this matter of Sunderland and my purported statements about horse evolution to my attention.

6. page 132
I hope I wasn't literally as incoherent as this quote suggests—all of a sudden changing the discourse from horses to rhinos. But it is the case that, at least dentally, the earliest members of the rhino and horse lineages are considered very difficult to tell apart. Rather than representing variation within created kinds, the divergent horse and rhino lineages are far more different in later stages of their evolution than at the beginning. Both are members of the perissodactyl lineage of mammals.

7. page 132
This is a test: I have deliberately written this sentence with the full expectation that it will inevitably be picked up and put in creationist ravings on the Internet and in what passes for creationist "literature." I am equally certain that the following several sentences, in which I reveal what was going on with my interviews with Luther Sunderland and Sylvia Chase, will *not* appear with it.

8. page 134
I owe the title of this section to evolutionary biologist Richard Dawkins, who once remarked, "When I open a page of Darwin, I immediately sense that I have been ushered into the presence of a great mind. I have the same feeling with RA Fisher and GC Williams [two twentieth-century evolutionary biologists encountered in Chapter 4]. When I read Phillip Johnson, I feel that I have been ushered into the presence of a lawyer" (Dawkins, 1996, p. 539). Dawkins's remarks are the opening lines of a "Reply to Phillip Johnson," just one of many articles written by Johnson, some of his cohorts, and several of his critics, in a special issue of the journal *Biology and Philosophy* that I will have occasion to mention again in my treatment of the Phillip Johnson phenomenon.

9. page 134
For example, in his book *Reason in the Balance* (1995), Johnson writes, "Belief in God may persist, particularly in people who have only a shallow understanding of science, but can never have more than a tenuous standing in the world of the mind. Science can step forward at any time and employ its prestige to take control of any subject, even subjects inaccessible to empirical investigation like the ultimate beginning itself. Metaphysical statements by prominent scientists are accepted in the press and throughout public education as advances in scientific knowledge; contrary statements by theologians or religious leaders are dismissed as 'fundamentalism.' The naturalists hold the cultural power; theists in academic life have to accommodate as best they can" (p. 196).

10. page 135
Johnson does occasionally mention creationists in *Darwin on Trial* (1991). For example, at one point (p. 114), he reproduces a statement by Judge William Overton (presiding judge in the famed Arkansas trial over the Arkansas "equal time" law in 1981), who himself was citing creationist Duane Gish (according to Johnson) as reason to conclude that creationism isn't science because it invokes the supernatural. The judge quotes Gish as saying, "We do not know how God created, what processes He used, for God used processes that are not now operating anywhere in the natural universe. This is why we refer to divine creation as Special Creation. We cannot discover by scientific investigation anything about the creative processes used by God." A page later, Johnson distances himself from Gish in saying, "I am not interested in any claims that are based upon a literal reading of the Bible, nor do I understand the concept of creation as narrowly as Duane Gish does. If an omnipotent Creator exists, He might have created things instantaneously, in a single week or through gradual evolution over billions of years. He might have employed means wholly inaccessible to science, or mechanisms that are at least in part understandable through scientific investigation." Johnson elsewhere makes it plain that he is not a "young-Earth" creationist. Elsewhere in his writings, Johnson makes crystal clear his opposition to the idea that God may have used the "purposeless," "undirected" laws of random mutation and selection to create anything, whether over billions of years or not.

11. page 136
See especially philosopher Robert T. Pennock's "Naturalism, Evidence and Creationism: The Case of Phillip Johnson" (1996b)—plus Johnson's reply and Pennock's rebuttal—all in the aforementioned special issue of *Biology and Philosophy* (see note 8).

12. page 139
Ironically, later while teaching at the University of Louvain, Belgium, Mivart fell out of favor with the church for his pro-evolutionary stance and was eventually excommunicated, in 1900.

13. page 140
Behe often claims that relatively little work—even in such outlets as the *Journal of Molecular Evolution*—is actually devoted to specifying pathways of molecular evolution. Rather, much of the work is devoted to using molecular evidence to assess evolutionary relationships among groups—of mammals, say. There is some truth to the remark, but I will never forget a lecture I attended at the Smithsonian Institution in the early 1970s, at which the biochemist Emmanuel Margoliash invited his small audience to don stereovision glasses to view his slides of the reconstructed models of the intricate molecule hemoglobin—so critical to the transport of oxygen in the blood of animals. The structure of the molecule is different in different animal groups, and the DNA coding sites for the molecule have also changed in the course of animal evolution; both of these issues were ably tackled and discussed in the lecture. Biologists can and do confront the evolution of molecular pathways in their data.

14. page 142
Dawkins, like Provine and some other prominent evolutionary biologists, is proud to proclaim his atheistic proclivities. The very title of Dawkins's book—*The Blind Watchmaker*—an overt reference to natural selection as the biological equivalent of the Creator-God of the Judeo-Christian tradition, is, of course, a deliberate red flag in the face of creationists. The penchant of some scientists—especially those with a wide public following—to agree with creationists like Phillip Johnson that the naturalism of science indeed implies that the Judeo-Christian God does not exist, strikes me as crass and rather stupid. For one thing, it is almost incredibly parochial, saying, in effect, that evolution and a Johnsonesque personal God are the only alternatives in the entire earthly domain, rather than acknowledging that the entire "debate" is a peculiar and bizarrely outdated excrescence of (in its greatest part) English and (increasingly) American dated culture—as should by now be obvious to any fair-minded person who has read this far, and as I'll endeavor to characterize further in the next chapter.

15. page 145
I explore the similarities and differences between biological evolution and the history of human designed systems (specifically cornets) in Eldredge, in press-b.

Chapter 7: Can We Afford a Culture War?

1. page 150
The concept that anyone *could* have been present "when life was created" is another fine example of inane creationist writing. Note, too, the "theory, not fact" dichotomy—one that, as we saw in Chapter 2, is also meaningless. With trash like this in our textbooks, how can we hope to produce a literate society whose citizens are equipped to deal with the complex science- and technology-related issues of the day?

2. page 153
See Daniel Kevles's excellent book, In the *Name of Eugenics* (1985), for a history of the eugenics movement and the involvement of Francis Galton, Darwin's nephew, in it.

3. page 156
I take this quotation from a feature article of the *National Center for Science Education Reports* (vol. 15, no. 4, Winter 1995, p. 3) entitled "Pat Buchanan Takes on Darwin." Buchanan is a Catholic and thereby an excellent example of the marriage of right-wing political views with antievolution sentiment; the Catholic Church has, in the main, accepted evolution—formally so only very recently, but in a "render unto Caesar" sense, as it has recognized since the late nineteenth century that science and religion are essentially separate domains.

4. page 156
This quotation comes from "Mr. DeLay's Power Play," lead editorial, Sunday, June 20, 1999, p. 14, in the *New York Times, Week in Review.*

5. page 158
At this juncture, it will hardly come as a surprise that no less an important creationist figure than Henry Morris himself, also writing in *Acts and Facts* (July 1980) completed the circle, writing, "Creationism can be studied and taught in any of three basic forms, as follows: (1) Scientific creationism (no reliance on Biblical revelation, *utilizing only scientific data* to support and expound the creation model). (2) Biblical creationism (no reliance on scientific data, using *only the Bible* to expound and defend the creation model). (3) Scientific Biblical creationism (full reliance on *Biblical revelation* but *also* using *scientific data* to support and develop the creation model)" [Morris's italics]. The creation model! Morris is clearly saying that the creationist position can be interchangeably considered religion, science, or a mixture of the two—depending on the intended audience.

On another note, Judge William Overton, in his opinion striking down Arkansas Act 590, noted that Wendell Bird's article in the *Yale Law Journal* in 1978, was a "student note" with "no legal merit." Bird had tried to make the case that the religious aspect of evolution violated students' rights, thereby making it appropriate to teach creation science concurrently.

6. page 158
Science has, over the years, on the whole done a rather good job of covering the more public displays of the creationism mess in the United States. In particular, I recommend the news accounts of the Arkansas trial written by a really good and experienced reporter, Roger Lewin. I rely here particularly on Lewin's (1982) account of Judge Overton's decision, "Judge's Ruling Hits Hard at Creationism."

7. page 159
Not surprisingly, lawyer Phillip Johnson (1995) agrees with Justice Scalia of the U.S. Supreme Court that the Lemon test (i.e., the 1971 case opinion providing the three-pronged test of the establishment clause just quoted) should be voided by the Supreme Court because it has led to excessive judicial interference "with attempts by other branches of government to arrive at sensible ways of accommodating religious and secular values in public life" (p. 220).

8. page 160
The estimate of 10 million species on the planet is based in large measure on the work of ecologist Robert M. May, a professor of zoology at Oxford University, Chairman of the Board of the Natural History Museum in London, and currently science advisor to Prime Minister Tony Blair. The estimate of thirty thousand species lost per year comes from the work of biologist E. O. Wilson, acknowledged dean of biodiversity issues, recently retired from Harvard University.

9. page 161
See my *Life in the Balance* (1998) for an extended examination of the present-day biodiversity crisis, including its causes, why we should care, and what we can do to stem the tide of this Sixth Extinction. And, when in New York, once again I invite you to visit the Hall of Biodiversity at the American Museum of Natural History—our first "issues" hall, devoted to the beauties of the living world, the importance of the living world to human life, the threats that it faces, and the solutions we might find to ending the crisis.

10. page 163
See Turnbull's "Cultural Loss Can Foreshadow Human Extinctions: The Influence of Modern Civilization" (1985).

11. page 164
In my book *Dominion* (1995), p. 100.

12. page 166
Earlier in this narrative, I mentioned debating Phillip Johnson at Calvin College in Grand Rapids, Michigan. The only instance when I can say I was challenged with some degree of animus was over my remark—also in my book *Dominion* (1995)—that it seems obvious to many of us that we created God in our own image, rather than the other way around. To some, this remark is offensive. Yet there is nothing intrinsic about that remark that says that the concept of God in question—the God of the Judeo-Christian tradition—does not exist in precisely the manner Christian theology specifies (however varied that characterization may be from theologian to theologian). It does imply, however, that in acknowledging that concepts of gods are ideas, mental images of such gods are precisely that: human constructs. Nothing wrong with that, and nothing about the statement, once again, states or implies that such gods either do or do not exist.

13. page 166
The only exceptions occur when species are reduced in size to a single population within a single ecosystem, as is most likely to occur in the very earliest and very latest phases of a species' existence.

Bibliography

Behe, Michael J. 1996. *Darwin's Black Box: The Biochemical Challenge to Evolution*. New York: Free Press.

Bird, Wendell. 1978. *Acts and Facts.*

Bird, Wendell. 1991. *The Origins of Species Revisited: The Theories of Evolution and Abrupt Appearances,* 2 vols. Nashville, Tenn.: Thomas Nelson.

Brett, Carlton E., and Baird, Gordon. 1995. "Coordinated Stasis and Evolutionary Ecology of Silurian to Middle Devonian Faunas in the Appalachian Basin. In *Speciation in the Fossil Record,* R. Anstey and D. H. Erwin (eds.), pp. 285–315. New York: Columbia Unversity Press.

Bronowski, Jacob. 1973. *The Ascent of Man.* Boston: Little, Brown.

Buckland, William. 1823. *Reliquiae Diluvianae; Or, Observations on the Organic Remains Contained in Caves, Fissures, and Diluvial Gravel, and on Other Geological Phenomena, Attesting the Action of an Universal Deluge.* London: John Murray.

Crick, Francis. 1981. *Life Itself: Its Origin and Nature.* New York: Simon and Schuster.

Cuvier, Georges. 1817. *Essay on the Theory of the Earth.* Edinburgh: William Blackwood.

Dalrymple, Brent G. 1991. *The Age of the Earth.* Stanford, Calif.: Stanford University Press.

Darwin, Charles R. 1859. *On the Origin of Species by Means of Natural Selection.* London: John Murray.

Dawkins, Richard. 1976. *The Selfish Gene.* New York: Oxford University Press.

Dawkins, Richard. 1986. *The Blind Watchmaker: Why the Evidence of Evolution Reveals a Universe.* New York: W. W. Norton.

Dawkins, Richard. 1996. "Reply to Phillip Johnson." *Biology and Philosophy,* 11, 539–540.

Dobzhansky, Theodosius. 1937. *Genetics and the Origin of Species.* New York: Columbia University Press.

Doolittle, W. Ford. 1980. "Revolutionary Concepts in Cell Biology." *Trends in Biochemical Science,* 5, 146–149.

Dover, Gabriel, and Flavell, R. B. (eds.). 1982. *Genome Evolution.* London: Published for the Systematics Association by Academic Press.

Doyle, Arthur C. 1912. *The Lost World.* London: Hodder and Stoughton.

Easton, W.H. 1960. *Invertebrate Paleontology.* New York: Harper and Brothers.

Eldredge, Niles. 1971. "The Allopatric Model and Phylogeny in Paleozoic Invertebrates." *Evolution,* 25, 156–167.

Eldredge, Niles. 1981. "Creationism Isn't Science." *New Republic,* April 4, 15–17, 20.

Eldredge, Niles. 1982. *The Monkey Business: A Scientist Looks at Creationism.* New York: Washington Square Press.

Eldredge, Niles. 1989. *Fossils: The Evolution and Extinction of Species.* New York: A Peter N. Nevraumont Book, Harry N. Abrams.

Eldredge, Niles. 1995. *Dominion.* New York: Henry Holt.

Eldredge, Niles. 1998. *Life in the Balance: Humanity and the Biodiversity Crisis.* Princeton, N.J.: A Peter N. Nevraumont Book, Princeton University Press.

Eldredge, Niles. 1999. *The Pattern of Evolution.* New York: W. H. Freeman.

Eldredge, Niles. 2001. *Who Is This Man They Call God?* New York: A Peter N. Nevraumont Book, W. H. Freeman.

Eldredge, Niles. In press-a. "The Sloshing Bucket: How the Physical Realm Controls Evolution." In *Evolutionary Dynamics* (Proceedings of Santa Fe Institute Conference), J. Crutchfield and P. Schuster (eds.).

Eldredge, Niles. In press-b. "Biological and Material Cultural Evolution: Are There Any True Parallels?" *Perspectives in Ethology,* 13.

Eldredge, Niles, and Gould, Stephen. 1972. "Punctuated Equilibria: An Alternative of Phyletic Gradualism." In *Models in Paleobiolog,* T. J. Schopf (ed.), pp. 82–115. San Francisco: Freeman Cooper.

Eldredge, Niles, and Tattersall, Ian. 1976. "Fact, Theory and Fantasy in Human Paleontology." *American Scientist,* 65, 204–211.

Endler, John J.,. 1986. *Natural Selection in the Wild.* Princeton, N.J.: Princeton University Press.

Fisher, Ronald A. 1930. *The Genetical Theory of Natural Selection.* Oxford: Clarendon.

Freske, Stanley. 1981. *Creation/Evolution.*

Galton, Francis. 1867. *Hereditary Genius: An Inquiry into Its Laws and Consequences.* London: Macmillan.

Gingerich, Phillip. 1997. "The Origin and Evolution of Whales." LSA Magazine, University of Michigan, 20(2), 4–10.

Gish, Duane T. 1973. *Evolution: The Fossils Say No!* El Cajon, Calif.: Creation-Life Publishers.

Gosse, Philip. 1857. *Omphalos: An Attempt to Untie the Geological Knot.* London: John van Voorst.

Gould, Stephen J. 1977. *Ontogeny and Phylogeny.* Cambridge, Mass.: Harvard University Press.

Gould, Stephen J. 1989. *Wonderful Life: The Burgess Shale and the Nature of History.* New York: W. W. Norton.

Haeckel, Ernst. 1866. *Generelle Morphologie der Organismen.* Berlin: Georg Reimer.

Haldane, John B. S. 1931. *The Causes of Evolution.* New York: Longman, Green.

Hamilton, William D. 1963. "The Evolution of Altruistic Behavior." *American Naturalist,* 97, 31–33.

Hamilton, William D. 1964a. "The Genetical Evolution of Social Behavior, I. *Journal of Theoretical Biology,* 7, 1–16.

Hamilton, William D. 1964b. "The Genetical Evolution of Social Behavior, II. *Journal of Theoretical Biology,* 7, 17–32.

Hennig, Willi. 1966. *Phylogenetic Systematics.* Urbana: University of Illinois Press.

Hills, E.S. 1953. *Outlines of Structural Geology,* 3rd ed. London: Methuen.

Hopson, James A. 1987. "The Mammal-like Reptiles: A Study of Transitional Fossils." American Biology Teacher, 49, 16–26.

Horgan, John. 1996. *The End of Science: Facing the Limits of Knowledge in the Twilight of the Scientific Age.* Reading, Mass.: Addison-Wesley.

Hull, David. 1988. *Science as a Process: An Evolutionary Account of the Social and Conceptual Development of Science.* Chicago: University of Chicago Press.

Humphrey, Nicholas. 1992. *A History of the Mind: Evolution and the Birth of Consciousness.* New York: Simon and Schuster.

Hunter, George W. 1914. *A Civic Biology: Presented in Problems.* New York: American Book Co.

Hunter, George W. 1926. *New Civic Biology: Presented in Problems.* New York: American Book Co.

Hutton, James. 1795. *Theory of the Earth with Proofs and Illustrations,* 2 vols. Edinburgh, Scotland: William Creech.

Johnson, Phillip E. 1991. *Darwin on Trial.* Downers Grove, Ill.: InterVarsity Press.

Johnson, Phillip E. 1995. *Reason in the Balance: The Case against Naturalism in Science.* Downers Grove, Ill.: InterVarsity Press.

Johnson, Phillip E. 1996. "Response to Pennock." *Biology and Philosophy,* 11, 561–563.

Kevles, Daniel. 1985. *In the Name of Eugenics: Genetics and the Uses of Human Heredity.* New York: Knopf.

Kimura, Motoo. 1983. *The Neutral Theory of Molecular Evolution.* New York: Cambridge University Press.

Kirschvink, J. L., R. L. Ripperdan, and D. A. Evans. 1997. "Evidence for Large-Scale Reorganization of Early Cambrian Continental Masses by Inertial Interchange True Polar Wander." *Science,* 277, 541–545.

Lamarck, Jean-Bapiste. 1809. *Philosophie Zoologique.* Paris: Dentu.

Larson, Edward J. 1997. *Summer of the Gods: The Scopes Trial and America's Continuing Debate Over Science and Religion.* New York: Basic Books.

Leuba, James H. 1916. *The Belief in God and Immortality.* Boston: Sherman French.

Lewin, Roger. 1982. "Judge's Ruling Hits Hard at Creationism." *Science,* 215, 381.

Linnaeus (Carl von Linné). 1758. *Systema Naturae per Regni Tria Naturae.* Stockholm, Sweden.

Lyell, Charles. 1830–1833. *Principles of Geology: Being an Attempt to Explain the Former Changes in the Earth's Surface by Reference to Causes Now in Operation,* 3 vols. London: John Murray.

Macbeth, Norman. 1971. *Darwin Retried: An Appeal to Reason.* Boston: Gambit.

Malthus, Thomas. 1798. *An Essay on the Principle of Population, As It Effects the Future Improvement of Society.* London: J. Johnson.

Margulis, Lynn (L. Sagan). 1967. "On the Origin of Mitosing Cells." *Journal of Theoretical Biology,* 14, 225–274.

May, Robert M., and Lawton, John H. (eds.). 1995. *Extinction Rates.* New York: Oxford University Press.

Mayr, Ernst. 1942. *Systematics and the Origin of Species.* New York: Columbia University Press.

McMenamin, Mark A. S. 1998. *The Garden of Edicara: Discovering the First Complex Life.* New York: Columbia University Press.

Mendel, Gregor. 1866. "Versuche über Pflanzen-Hybriden" (Experiments on Plant Hybrids). *Verhandlungen des naturforschenden Vereins, Abhandlungen, Brünn,* 4, 3–47.

Miller, Stanley M., and Orgel, Leslie E. 1974. *The Origins of Life on the Earth*. Englewood Cliffs, N.J.: Prentice-Hall.

Mivart, St. George. 1871. *Genesis of Species*. London: Macmillan.

Morris, Henry. 1963. *The Twilight of Evolution*. Grand Rapids, Mich.: Baker Book House.

Morris, Henry M. 1977. *The Scientific Case for Creation*. El Cajon, Calif.: Creation-Life Publishers.

Morris, Henry. 1980. "The Tenets of Creationism." *Acts and Facts*, 9(7).

Morris, Henry M., and Parker, Gary E. 1982. *What Is Creation Science?* El Cajon, Calif.: Creation-Life Publishers.

Morris, Henry M., and Whitcomb, John C. 1961. *The Genesis Flood: The Biblical Record and Scientific Implications*. Grand Rapids, Mich.: Baker Book House.

Morris, Simon C. 1998. *The Crucible of Creation: The Burgess Shale and the Rise of Animals*. New York: Oxford University Press.

Murchison, Roderick. 1839. *The Silurian System*. London: John Murray.

Neufeld, B. 1975. "Dinosaur Tracks and Giant Men." *Origins*, 2(2), 64–76.

Numbers, Ronald L. 1992. *The Creationists: The Evolution of Scientific Creationism*. New York: Alfred A. Knopf.

Osborn, Henry F. 1917. *The Origin and Evolution of Life: On the Theory of Action, Reaction, and Interaction of Energy*. New York: C. Scribner's Sons.

Palmer, Allison R. (ed.). 1982. *Perspectives in Regional Geological Synthesis: Planning for the Geology of North America*. Boulder, Colo.: Geological Society of America.

Parker, Gary E. 1980. *Creation: The Facts of Life*. El Cajon, Calif.: Creation-Life Publishers.

Pennock, Robert T. 1996a. "Naturalism, Creationism and the Meaning of Life: The Case of Phillip Johnson Revisited." *Creation/Evolution*, 16(2), 10–30.

Pennock, Robert T. 1999. *Tower of Babel: The Evidence against the New Creationism*. Cambridge, Mass.: MIT Press.

Pennock, Robert T. 1996b. "Naturalism, Evidence and Creationism: The Case of Phillip Johnson." *Biology and Philosophy*, 11, 543–559.

Raup, David M. 1991. *Extinction: Bad Genes or Bad Luck?* New York: W. W. Norton.

Read, J. G. 1979. *Fossils, Strata and Evolution*. Culver City, Calif.: Scientific-Technical Presentations.

Ross, C. P., and Rezak, Richard. 1959. *The Rocks and Fossils of Glacier National Monument*. U.S. Geological Survey Professional Paper 294-K.

Rudwick, Martin. 1997. *Georges Cuvier, Fossil Bones and Geological Catastrophes: New Translations and Interpretations of the Primary Texts.* Chicago: University of Chicago Press.

Ryan, William, and Pitman, Walter C. 1998. *Noah's Flood: The New Scientific Discoveries about the Event That Changed History.* New York: Simon and Schuster.

Schindewolf, Otto. 1993. *Basic Questions in Paleontology.* Chicago: University of Chicago Press.

Schuchert, Charles. 1955. *Atlas of Paleogeographic Maps of North America.* New York: John Wiley.

Simpson, George Gaylord. 1944. *Tempo and Mode in Evolution.* New York: Columbia University Press.

Simpson, George Gaylord. 1953. *The Major Features of Evolution.* New York: Columumiba University Press.

Smith, William. 1816. *Strata Identified by Organized Fossils Containing Prints on Coloured Paper of the Most Characteristic Specimens in Each Stratum.* London.

Spencer, Herbert. 1866. *The Principles of Biology,* 2 vols. New York: D. Appleton.

Steno, Nicolaus (Niels Stensen). 1699. *De Solido intra Solidum Naturaliter Contento Dissertationis Prodromus.* Florence, Italy.

Sunderland, Luther. 1984. *Darwin's Enigma: Fossils and Other Problems.* El Cajon, California: Master Book division of CLP.

Sunderland, Luther. 1998. *Darwin's Enigma: Ebbing the Tide of Naturalism.* Santee, Calif.: Master Books.

Tattersall, Ian. 1998. *Becoming Human: Evolution and Human Uniqueness.* New York: Harcourt Brace.

Tattersall, Ian, and Schwartz, Jeffrey. 2000. *Extinct Humans.* Boulder, Colo.: A Peter N. Nevraumont Book, Westview Press.

Thompson, John J. 1994. *The Coevolutionary Process.* Cambridge, Mass.: Harvard University Press.

Turnbull, Colin. 1985. "Cultural Loss Can Foreshadow Human Extinctions: The Influence of Modern Civilization." *In Animal Extinctions: What Everyone Should Know,* R. J. Hoage, pp. 175–192. Washington, D.C.: Smithsonian Institution Press.

Vrba, Elisabeth. 1985. "Environment and Evolution: Alternative Causes of the Temporal Distribution of Evolutionary Events." *South African Journal of Science,* 8, 229–236.

Vries, Hugo de. 1910–1911. *The Mutation Theory: Experiments and Observations on the Origin of Species in the Vegetable Kingdom,* 2 vols. London: Kegan Paul.

Waagen, W. 1869. "Die Formenreihe des Ammonites subradiatus." *Beneckes Geognos t.-paläontol. Beitr.,* 2, 179–256.

Weber, Christopher. 1980. "Common Creationist Attacks on Geology." *Creation/Evolution, 2.*

Weidenreich, Franz. 1943. "The Skull of *Sinatropus pekinesis:* A Comparative Study of a Primitive Skull." (Palaeontologia Sinila New Series D, no. 10.) Pehpei, ChungKing: Geological Survey of China.

Weismann, August. 1893. *Germ Plasm: A Theory of Heredity*. London: Walter Scott.

Wertheim, Margaret. 1997. *Pythagoras' Trousers: God, Physics, and the Gender War.* New York: W. W. Norton.

Wertheim, Margaret. 1999. *The Pearly Gates of Cyberspace: A History of Space from Dante to the Internet.* New York: W. W. Norton.

Whewell, William. 1837. *History of the Inductive Sciences from the Earliest to the Present Time.* London: John W. Parker.

Willams, George C. 1966. *Adaptation and Natural Selection: A Critique of Some Current Evolutionary Thought.* Princeton, N.J.: Princeton University Press.

Wilson, Edward O. 1978. *Sociobiology*. Cambridge: Harvard University Press.

Wilson, Edward O. 1992. *The Diversity of Life.* Cambridge, Mass.: Harvard University Press.

Wright, Sewall. 1986. *Evolution: Selected Papers.* Chicago: University of Chicago Press.

Wysong, R. L. 1976. *The Creation-Evolution Controversy.* Midland, Mich.: Inquiry Press.

Acknowledgments

Production of *The Triumph of Evolution* has been truly a team effort. I thank John Michel of W. H. Freeman—who had the idea in the first place and has been stimulating and encouraging throughout; Peter N. Nevraumont, Ann Perrini, Simone Nevraumont, and Ruth Servi Zimmerman (Nevraumont Publishing Company) for their kaleidoscopically varied editorial and production skills and support; Stephanie Hiebert, world-class copyeditor, who has come to know every word of this book!; and our design team Patrick Seymour and Kevin Smith of Tsang Seymour Design, who gave the book its look, and who came up with the best cover I've ever seen!

Index